29th International Workshop on Intelligent Computing in Engineering (EG-ICE 2022)

Aarhus, Denmark
6 – 8 July 2022

Editors:

Jochen Teizer
Carl Peter Leslie Schultz

ISBN: 979-8-3313-0347-1

Printed from e-media with permission by:

Curran Associates, Inc.
57 Morehouse Lane
Red Hook, NY 12571

Some format issues inherent in the e-media version may also appear in this print version.

European Group for Intelligent Computing in Engineering (eg-ice)
Arcisstrasee 21
D-80290 Munich
Germany

Phone: +49 89 289 25117

https://eg-ice.org/

Additional copies of this publication are available from:

Curran Associates, Inc.
57 Morehouse Lane
Red Hook, NY 12571 USA
Phone: 845-758-0400
Fax: 845-758-2634
Email: curran@proceedings.com
Web: www.proceedings.com

Proceedings of the 29th EG-ICE International Workshop on Intelligent Computing in Engineering

Aarhus, Denmark, July 6-8, 2022

Jochen Teizer and Carl Peter Leslie Schultz

Editors

https://doi.org/10.7146/aul.455

The Royal Danish Library lists this book in the Danish National Bibliography; more details can be found at https://www.kb.dk/en.

1. Edition 2022

Introduction from the Workshop Chairs

This publication is the Proceedings of the 29th EG-ICE International Workshop on Intelligent Computing in Engineering from July 6-8, 2022. It is the first time this workshop was held in Denmark and at Aarhus University. The proceedings include 45 peer-reviewed papers from authors originating from 19 countries. These papers focus on new approaches, methodologies, and findings in relation to computing in engineering, including but not limited to the following application areas:

Life-cycle support
- Computer-enhanced engineering design
- Building performance analysis
- Enhancing sustainability and resilience
- Geometric and parametric modeling
- Visualization and simulations
- Design and decision support systems

Advanced computing in engineering
- Strategic aspects – opportunities and risks
- Computational design
- Data-driven design and engineering
- Machine learning
- Computer vision
- Virtual, augmented, and mixed reality
- Quantum computing
- Robust optimization

Automation and robotics
- Human-robot collaboration
- Advanced construction methods
- Proactive runtime safety, health, well-being
- Breakthrough technologies

BIM and engineering ontologies
- Building information modeling
- Semantic modeling in AEC/FM industry
- Ontology modeling and reasoning
- Spatial reasoning
- Graph algorithms
- Code compliance checking

Monitoring and control algorithms
- Sensor data interpretation
- Progress monitoring and management
- Building control systems
- Active structures

Computer-aided construction management
- Collaboration informatics
- Scheduling
- Discrete-event simulations
- Process modeling

Engineering optimization and search
- Design space exploration
- Stochastic search
- Generative design

Please note: Most EG-ICE proceedings are available at no cost here: https://www.eg-ice.org.

The workshop chairs are very grateful for the support of so many. Thank you!

Jochen Teizer, Professor, Department of Civil and Mechanical Engineering, Technical University of Denmark

Carl Peter Leslie Schultz, Associate Professor, Department of Electrical and Computer Engineering, Aarhus University

Local Organizing Committee

- Emil L. Jacobsen, Aarhus University
- Christos Chronopoulos, Aarhus University
- Karsten W. Johansen, Aarhus University
- Aparna Harichandran, Aarhus University

Technical Committee

The following individuals contributed to peer-reviews of the technical program.

- Ali Ghelmani, Concordia University
- Ali Tohidifar, University of Toronto
- Aliakbar Kamari, Aarhus University
- Amin Hammad, Concordia University
- Amir A. Ziaee, Technische Universität Wien
- Angan Mitra, Aarhus University
- Bernd Domer, University of Applied Sciences and Arts Western Switzerland
- Christian Koch, Bauhaus-Universität Weimar
- Christopher Rausch, University of Waterloo
- David Bucher, ETH Zurich
- Eduardo T. Santos, University of Sao Paulo
- Elvin Vindel, Carnegie Mellon University
- Emil Lybaek Jacobsen, Aarhus University
- Eyosias Guyo, Trimble
- Farrokh Jazizadeh, Virginia Polytechnic Institute and State University
- Frédéric Bosché, University of Edinburgh
- Georg Suter, Technische Universität Wien
- Ghang Lee, Yonsei University
- Haijiang Li, Cardiff University
- Han Liu, Tsinghua University
- Hubo Cai, Purdue University
- Ian F.C. Smith, École Polytechnique Fédérale de Lausanne
- Ian Flood, University of Florida
- Ioannis Brilakis, University of Cambridge
- Iva Kovacic, Technische Universität Wien
- Ivan Mutis, Illinois Institute of Technology
- Jakob Kirchner, Technische Universität Berlin
- Jan Martens, RWTH Aachen
- Jimmy Abualdenien, Technische Universität München
- Jinding Xing, Carnegie Mellon University
- Jonas Schlenger, Technische Universität München
- Jyrki Oraskari, RWTH Aachen
- Kay Smarsly, Technische Universität Hamburg
- Ke Chen, Huazhong University of Science and Technology
- Li Shengtao, Tsinghua University M.R. Mahendrini Fernando Ariyachandra, Kingston University
- Mathias Artus, Bauhaus-Universität Weimar
- Mathias Worm, Technische Universität Hamburg
- Mehmet Bermek, Georgia Institute of Technology
- Mehrzad Shahinmoghadam, École de technologie supérieure du Québec
- Patrick Hsieh, National Taiwan University
- Peter Hoegh Mikkelsen, Aarhus University
- Philipp Geyer, Leibniz Universität Hannover
- Pieter de Wilde, University of Strathclyde
- Pieter Pauwels, Eindhoven University of Technology
- Pingbo Tang, Carnegie Mellon University
- Rafael Sacks, Technion - Israel Institute of Technology
- Rehan Khan, DigitalTwin Technology GmbH
- Robert Amor, University of Auckland
- Sebastian Esser, Technische Universität München
- Shang-Hsien Hsieh, National Taiwan University
- Shuning Wei, Tsinghua University
- Timo Hartmann, Technische Universität Berlin
- Timson Yeung, Technion - Israel Institute of Technology
- Tomas Kulik, Aarhus University
- Volker Rodehorst, Bauhaus-Universität Weimar
- Walid Tizani, University of Nottingham
- Xia Chen, Technische Universität Berlin
- Xiaofeng Zhu, Cardiff University
- Yan Gao, Cardiff University
- Yi Wie, Stevens Institute of Technology
- Yingying Zhang, RWTH Aachen
- Yohann Schatz, Haute École du Paysage, D'ingénierie et D'architecture de Genève
- Žiga Turk, University of Ljubljana

Program and Keynotes

The image to the right outlines the organization of the workshop. Next to the 15 single-sessions that presented the authors' work, the workshop program included a reception at Aarhus University's signature building on its main campus, a gourmet gala dinner in Aarhus' yacht harbor area, several networking breaks, and a closing ceremony that announced the best paper award. Following are the details to the keynote presenters and, thereafter, the content and the technical papers.

Time (CET)	Day 0 05-Jul-22	Day 1 06-Jul-22	Day 2 07-Jul-22	Day 3 08-Jul-22
08:30-09:00	Free time	Welcome & 2021 Awardee Presentation	Session 07	Session 12
09:00-09:30				
09:30-10:00		Session 01	Session 08	Session 13
10:00-10:30				
10:30-11:00		Networking Break		
11:00-11:30		Session 02	Session 09	Session 14
11:30-12:00				
12:00-12:45		Keynote 1	Keyonte 2	Session 15
12:45-13:30		Lunch Meeting		
13:30-14:00		Session 03	Session 10	Closing and Best Paper Award Announcement
14:00-14:30				
14:30-15:00		Session 04	Session 11	Friday Afternoon Beer!*
15:00-15:30				
15:30-16:00		Networking Break		
16:00-16:30		Session 05	EG-ICE General Assembly Meeting	
16:30-17:00				
17:00-17:30		Session 06		
17:30-18:00				
18:00-18:30				
18:30-19:00	Reception	EG-ICE Committee Meeting (per invitation)	Gala Dinner	Free time
19:00-20:00				
20:00-21:00				
21:00-22:00				

* A Danish Tradition

Keynote 1: Engineering education challenges: Learning to solve real-world problems by working interdisciplinary, remotely, and with the latest technology

- Mario Wolf, Digital Engineering Chair
- Bianca Wolf, Excellent Teaching and Learning in Engineering both at Ruhr-University Bochum, Germany

As digitalization advances in all areas of life, digital and social competencies are becoming integral to the competence profile of tomorrow's engineers. Digitalization has the potential to make university teaching more efficient and effective in many aspects, in addition to conveying new and relevant knowledge in the student's chosen field. One possibility is to provide access to practical learning units when attendance at the university campus or an associated laboratory is not possible or if collaboration takes places in a concurrent course on multiple international universities. Technology further enables the type of communication and collaboration that becomes more and more relevant in, potentially, globally distributed engineering teams. In this keynote, we will briefly review the basic ideas of educational science, how to apply them in engineering education, and how to use virtual experimentation to redesign existing lectures with clearly-defined learning and practical objectives. Next, we will introduce product development and/or engineering that thrive on the interaction of people from many disciplines and backgrounds. We want to discuss what it's like to cross disciplinary boundaries and engage with the attendees to uncover synergies for future engineering (education) collaboration.

Keynote 2: How Dependable is the Digital Twin?

- John S Fitzgerald, Newcastle University, United Kingdom
- Peter Gorm Larsen, Aarhus University, Denmark

The rapid growth in interest in digital twins is fueled by advances in data gathering, machine learning and digital representation of assets. Some estimates place the size of the market in this technology as high as $100bn in the coming years. However, although the growing literature on digital twins covers applications as diverse as transport, energy, and built environment, it is limited on the principles underpinning their successful design and construction. Combining real-world data with design information and learned models, a digital twin can support analyses that inform interventions in a physical system, updating the digital twin in turn. As we come to rely on such twins, we must consider how dependable they are as a basis for decision making. Can we rely on a twin that is a heterogeneous multi-disciplinary compound of models owned by different stakeholders that constantly evolves with its physical counterpart? Drawing on experience in several domains, we will begin to chart a course towards a discipline of Dependable Digital Twin Engineering including foundations, methods, and tools to engineer digital twins that so that reliance can justifiably be placed on their correct operation.

Contents

Development of an ontology for the representation of firefighters' data requirements during building fire emergencies

Guyo E.[1, 2], Hartmann T.[1]
1. Technische Universität Berlin, Germany, 2. Trimble Solutions Oy, Finland
eyosias.guyo@trimble.com

Abstract. Firefighters require accurate and timely information regarding a building and its environment to perform their duty safely and effectively during a fire emergency. However, due to the chaotic nature of building fires, firefighters often receive erroneous, conflicting, or delayed information that can affect the outcome of a hazard. In this paper, we propose a solution in the form of an ontology that defines building and environmental data needed by firefighters during a building fire emergency. The ontology can be a basis for developing intelligent tools and systems that collect building and environmental data from different data sources and provide comprehensive information to firefighters. It can also facilitate the data exchange process between the different personnel involved in emergency response. The ontology was developed by following the METHONTOLOGY method, and it was implemented using the web ontology language (OWL) in Protégé 5.5.0.

1. Introduction

Firefighters employ different strategies to safeguard occupants, reduce property damage, and protect themselves during building fires. They devise their strategy based on the best available information they have at any given time (OSHA, 2015). Hence, the availability and quality of information play a vital role in the outcome of an emergency. Additionally, Firefighters should be made aware of any hazards or obstacles they may come across outside or inside the affected building ahead of time. At the same time, overloading firefighters with excess information should be avoided since it can cause difficulty and confusion in data collection and interpretation (Li et al., 2014). The success of a firefighting strategy relies on providing the correct information and resources to the right people at the right time (Xu and Zlatanova, 2007).

However, acquiring and communicating accurate and timely information during a fire emergency is challenging. Occupational safety and health administration (OSHA, 2015) provides insight into the difficulties firefighters face when acquiring information at an incident site. According to OSHA (2015), firefighters have a frequently changing workplace which is an emergency site. Hence, it is unlikely for them to know their next workplace ahead of time. Furthermore, they operate in a mentally stressful environment while performing physically exhausting work that makes collecting, interpreting, and communicating information challenging. Moreover, they may need to operate during the night or in harsh weather conditions. These conditions, possibly combined with smoke from the fire, will reduce visibility. In such conditions, firefighters find it difficult to fully comprehend their environment and gather information from different signs that are used to communicate valuable information to the firefighters. The challenges are further magnified in complex building structures such as high-rise buildings and underground structures. Any delay caused by these issues might adversely affect the subsequent operation and the overall outcome of the incident. Mishaps such as poorly located fire hydrants, unclear fire alarm information, or inaccessible equipment can result in a delay during which the fire likely grows and becomes more hazardous to occupants' and firefighters' lives (OSHA, 2015).

https://doi.org/10.7146/aul.455.c190

Solution for the problems discussed in the previous paragraph can be provided through intelligent tools and systems that collect required data about an affected building and its surrounding from different data sources and provide comprehensive information to firefighters. Such intelligent tools and systems can assist firefighters in conducting their tasks with the utmost safety and effectiveness (Balding, 2020). However, before designing such systems, we need to have a well-defined understanding of firefighters' data requirements. Ontologies can be used to establish such understanding. They enable us to develop machine-understandable definitions of different concepts in a given domain along with their relationships (Noy and McGuinness, 2001). Through ontologies, a shared understanding of a domain between people and systems can be established (Neto et al., 2021).

In this research paper, we present an ontology that models firefighters' data requirements. The ontology will represent the data firefighters require regarding different elements and features inside an affected building and its surrounding. The ontology can then be used to design systems that gather and integrate data from different data sources and provide comprehensive information to firefighters during building fires. Having a well-defined data requirement will also facilitate the data exchange process through various mediums between the different personnel involved in the emergency response (Jones et al., 2005). Understanding how first responders interact with building features can also assist building designers in designing structures that ensure firefighters' safety and provide necessary firefighting features (OSHA, 2015). The paper is structured as follows. Section 2 discusses existing ontologies related to building fire emergencies. Section 3 presents the method we employed to develop our ontology. Section 4 provides a detailed discussion of the firefighters' data requirement ontology we developed. Discussions and conclusions are provided in Sections 5 and 6, respectively.

2. Related Works

A study conducted by Li et al. (2014) has shown first responder's heavy reliance on peoples' experience, memory, and observation to gather information during fire emergencies. This reliance could bring negative consequences. A fire emergency site may become chaotic and confusing (Li et al., 2014). Under such circumstances, firefighters may find it hard to describe and communicate information accurately. Additionally, memory and experience differ from personnel to personnel. Moreover, as noted by Li et al. (2014), human memory might introduce human errors. Hence, Li et al. (2014) concluded that advanced tools and technologies that assist first responders in overcoming these limitations are necessary.

Adapting new tools and technologies for firefighting should be done with great care since firefighting is a potentially dangerous work (Balding, 2020). Therefore, having a well-defined understanding of firefighters' data requirements is essential to developing tools that ensure safety and effectiveness. Ontologies are one method of creating such understanding. Ontologies can establish a shared understanding of a domain between people and systems (Neto et al., 2021). We can define a set of data and their structure through ontologies, which can then be used by different problem-solving tools, applications, and systems (Noy and McGuinness, 2001).

Some ontologies we identified, such as the *DoRES* ontology (Burel et al., 2017), focused on the general representation of concepts related to wide-ranging crisis events. Other ontologies, such as *SEMA4A* ontology (Malizia et al., 2010), focused on communicating information to affected people during emergencies. In some ontologies, the focus was put on the emergency providers, including firefighters. However, in these ontologies, the emergency was not mainly focused on building fires. Fan and Zlatanova (2011) proposed an ontology that relates the different organizational units involved in emergency response with the data they require and the processes they take part in. spatial data was the focus of the ontology. Their proposal requires emergency responders, including fire brigades, to have their own ontology representing their geospatial data requirement. Saad et al. (2018) developed and implemented an ontology that established a common vocabulary between team members (human and robots) during urban search and rescue efforts. Gang Liu et al. (2011) developed an ontology that focused on community-based fire management. However, it only represents high-level concepts that are aimed towards the affected community rather than firefighters.

We have also identified a group of ontologies that are explicitly focused on emergency scenarios in buildings. Nuo et al. (2016) developed an ontology to generate a semantic graph of a building in times of fire emergency. The graph could then be used to obtain smoke spread information and escape routes. The ontology aimed to support rescuers and victims during the rescue process. Bitencourt et al. (2018) developed the *EmergencyFire* ontology to support standardization and sharing of building fire response protocols. The ontology models the procedures and actions taken during a fire emergency, and it provides terms that can help describe the emergency. It also captures knowledge regarding the involved organizations, the resources they can deploy, and the form of communication they use. However, a detailed representation of knowledge regarding building features and building surroundings that are important for firefighters' operation was absent since it was outside the scope of the ontology. Neto et al. (2021) presented an ontology to assist the information exchange between the different parties involved in the building evacuation process during fire emergencies. The authors believe the ontology helps to understand the building evacuation domain and contributes to the development of applications and systems that can be used during building evacuation. Finally, we have the *Smart Building Evacuation Ontology (SBEO)* that represents knowledge regarding buildings and their occupants that can be useful for the safe evacuation of people during emergencies (Khalid, 2021).

Overall, several ontologies with concepts that can apply to building fire have been developed in the past. Some provided only a general representation by focusing on top-level disaster management. Other ontologies explicitly made their focus on building fire emergencies. They described concepts related to hazard description, firefighters' actions, and building evacuation. However, the representation of data needed by firefighters regarding building features and the building's surroundings were minimal and outside the scope of those ontologies. Therefore, we propose an ontology that can fill the gap. The ontology we present in this paper provides a detailed and comprehensive representation of the data firefighters need about several features and components of an affected building and its surroundings. Based on this new ontology, intelligent systems and technologies that collect and provide essential data to firefighters can be developed. The ontology can also be used to facilitate the data exchange between the different personnel involved in building fire emergency response.

3. Research Approach

To develop our ontology, we followed the METHONTOLOGY method proposed by Fernandez et al. (1997). METHONTOLOGY is a well-structured method to develop ontologies from scratch. The consecutive phases of the method we followed are specification, conceptualization, and Implementation. While going through the three development phases, knowledge acquisition was also conducted simultaneously. METHONTOLOGY includes two additional phases, which are integration and evaluation. These phases are outside of the scope of this paper.

Knowledge Acquisition: The knowledge captured in the ontology was gathered from the analysis of scientific papers, a manual, and two international codes. The scientific papers include a study conducted by Li et al. (2014) with 29 first responder participants to evaluate firefighters' information need during a building fire emergency response; A study by Isikdag et al. (2008) where data requirements for a successful fire response management operation were identified; a workshop conducted by the National Institute of Standards and Technology (NIST) with 25 participants on the information need of first responders (Jones et al., 2005) and multiple studies regarding environmental factors that influence the spread of fire (Ghodrat et al., 2021)(Santarpia et al., 2019)(Heron et al., 2003). A manual published by OSHA that provided detailed information regarding firefighters' typical interaction with building features and fire protection systems during fires hazards was another source of knowledge (OSHA, 2015). The international building code (International Code Council (ICC), 2018a) and the international fire code (ICC, 2018b) were also used.

Specification: In this phase of the ontology development, a specification document is prepared. The document specified the purpose and scope of the ontology and its intended use (see Table 1). A glossary of terms that should be included in the ontology was also prepared. This action continued with the subsequent phases as more knowledge was acquired. The glossary of terms allowed tracking of terms that needed to be modelled and ensured they were not missed (Fernandez, Gómez-Pérez and Juristo, 1997). It was also helpful to filter out synonyms or irrelevant terms.

Table 1: Ontology specification document.

Requirements	Descriptions
Domain	Building fire emergency
Purpose	Building an ontology to represent data regarding several features and components of a building and its surroundings that firefighters need when responding to building fires.
Scope	The focus is on data about an affected building, its different components, and its surrounding.
Intended use	The ontology can be a basis for developing tools and systems that gather essential data about a building and its surroundings and provide the collected data to firefighters in an integrated form. It can also facilitate the data exchange process between different personnel involved in emergency response.
knowledge source	Scientific papers: (Li et al., 2014), (Isikdag, Underwood and Aouad, 2008), (Jones et al., 2005), (Ghodrat et al., 2021), (Santarpia et al., 2019), and (Heron et al., 2003). Manual: (OSHA, 2015). International codes: (ICC, 2018a), and (ICC, 2018b).

Conceptualization: In this phase of ontology development, knowledge is structured in a conceptual model (Fernandez, Gómez-Pérez and Juristo, 1997). First, the glossary of terms that were created in the specification phase was completed. These terms represented different concepts and their properties acquired through knowledge acquisition. A middle-out approach was used to identify the terms. As pointed out by Fernandez et al. (1997), this approach first identifies primary concepts that need to be represented in the ontology. Then, based on necessity, the concepts could be specialized or generalized. International codes were used whenever possible to generate concise and consistent terms that others can reuse in the future (see Table 1). The terms in the glossary were grouped into classes, properties, and instances. Finally, relationships were established between the terms.

Implementation: The next phase in the ontology development was implementing the ontology in a formal language. The web ontology language (OWL) was used to implement the ontology. OWL can represent the meaning of terms and the relationship between terms in a machine-interpretable language. Protégé 5.5.0, an open-source application, was used as the development environment to create the OWL file. The following section will describe the ontological model that we named *Firefighters' Data Requirement Ontology*.

4. Firefighters' Data Requirement Ontology

The firefighters' data Requirement ontology represents concepts regarding the data firefighters need about an affected building, the building's features, and the building's surroundings. In protégé, several classes were created to represent different concepts. OWL provides the *ObjectProperty* feature to represent the relationship between two classes and the *DatatypeProperty* feature to represent the relationship from a class to a data value (McGuinness and van Harmelen, 2004). We have used both features extensively in the ontology.

In this section, the ontology is described with the help of figures (Figure 1 – 3). In the first two figures, the following convention is used. The red box emphasizes a class, and the yellow boxes represent all other classes related to the class in the red box. Different lines are used to represent different relationships. Solid lines with a black 'is a' text indicate subclass relationship. Solid lines with a blue text indicate *ObjectProperty* relationship between classes, and broken lines with a green text indicate *DatatypeProperty* relationship from a class to a data value. Lastly, the deep purple blocks indicate instances of a class. Sometimes a thick black arrow is extended from a class to indicate the existence of more information that is not shown in the figure. And a yellow box with three dots is used to indicate the existence of more subclasses.

The ontology uses *IncidentSite* class to represent the site where the building with fire hazard is located. This class is shown in a red box in Figure 1. The class is related to *IncidentBuilding, SurroundingTerrain, SurroundingStructure,,* *FireCommandCenter* and *WeatherCondition* classes. The *IncidentBuilding* class represents the building where the fire hazard occurred. The classes *SurroundingTerrain* and *SurroundingStructure* represent the terrain and structures surrounding the incident building, respectively. A fire command center is a dedicated location where the status of fire protection systems, alarms, and other emergency systems can be monitored and controlled (ICC, 2018b). The *FireCommandCenter* class is related to the *ControlPanel* class, which represents the different control panels firefighters would want to locate and use to control several building systems and utilities. The *IncidentSite* class is also related to the *WeatherCondition* class, which represents weather-related information firefighters may want to know, such as wind speed, temperature, and precipitation. The *IncidentSite* class is also related to the *Address* class, which captures several types of addresses required during a building emergency.

The *SurroundingStructure* class represents all artificial and natural structures surrounding the incident building. The subclass of *SurroundingStructure* represents powerlines, pipelines, hazardous materials, and obstructions such as fences. Information about these environmental elements is essential because they could obstruct firefighting operations or even cause severe injuries to the firefighters (OSHA, 2015). Fire can spread from the incident building to its surrounding through vegetation. Hence, vegetation surrounding an incident building is represented using the *Vegetation* class. A fire lane is an access road designated for the passage of fire apparatus (ICC, 2018b). This class is also a subclass of the *Road* class. In addition to the fire lane, the *Road* class represents the road that leads to the incident site (*RoadToIncident*).

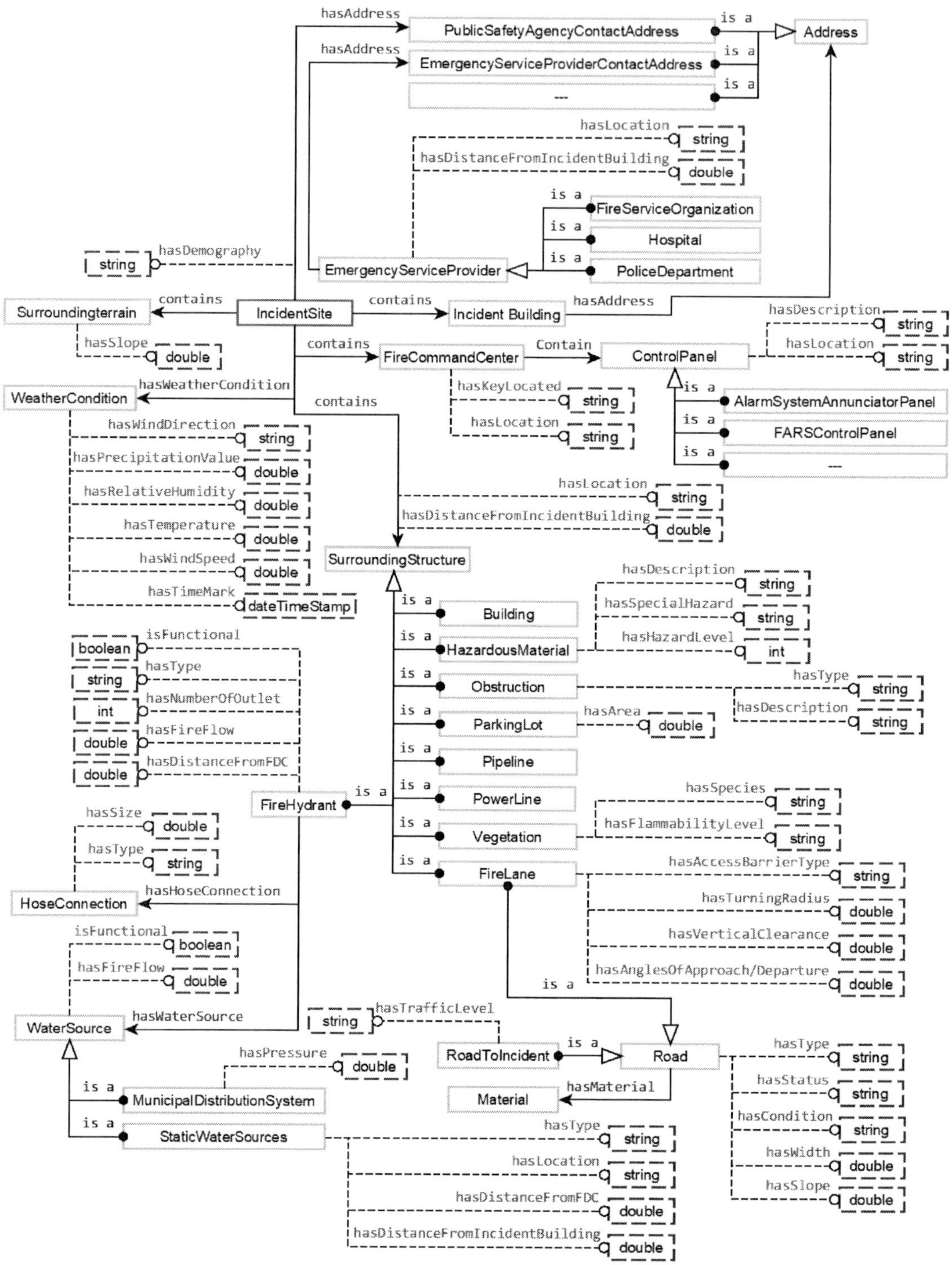

Figure 1: The *IncidentSite* class, its properties, and its relationship with other classes.

Fire hydrants are essential for most fire suppression operations since they provide access to a water supply system. We modelled information that should be provided to firefighters in advance to locate and connect to a fire hydrant rapidly. The *FireHydrant* class is related to two classes representing water sources and hose connections. An adequate water supply is essential for firefighting since most fire suppression systems and operations are water-based (OSHA, 2015). Accurate information about hose connection type and size should be provided to firefighters because incompatible hose connections can create severe problems during firefighting operations (OSHA, 2015). We also connected all other concepts in our ontology related to some form of hose connection to *HoseConnection* class.

Several information requirements about the incident building are modelled as properties of the *IncidentBuilding* class. A complete list of the requirements can be seen in Figure 2. The figure also shows the relationship between *IncidentBuilding* and other classes. These classes include the *BuildingOccupancy* class, which represents a building's occupancy based on the international building code (ICC, 2018a), the *BuildingComponent* class, which represents information about the different components of the building, and the *constructiontype* class with its five possible alternatives (ICC, 2018a).

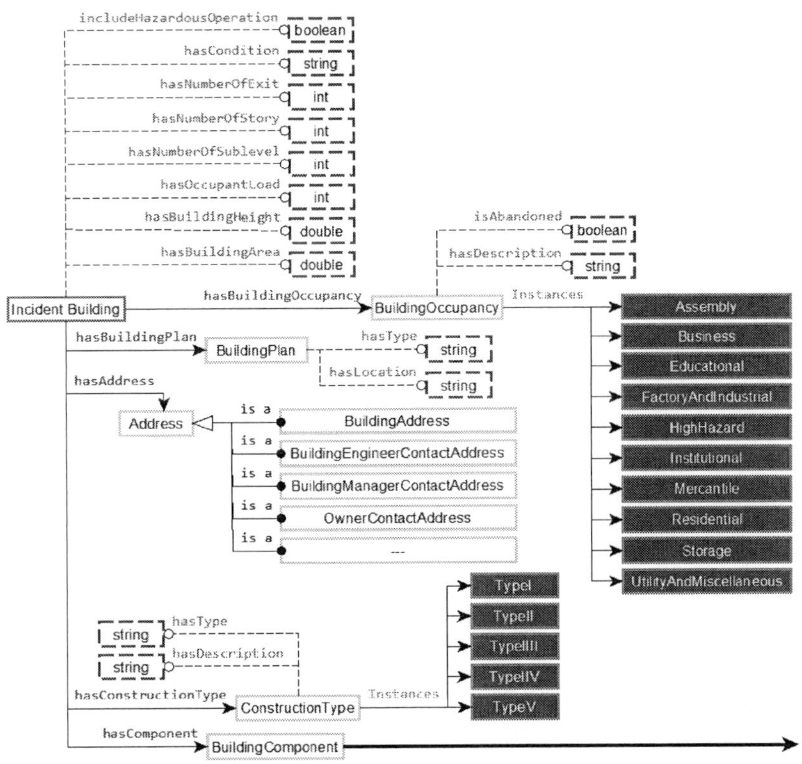

Figure 2: The *IncidentBuilding* class, its properties, and its relationship with other classes.

The *BuildingComponent* class has several subclasses representing different building elements and systems firefighters interact with during their operations (see Figure 3(A)). *BuildingSafetySystem* is the largest subclass of *BuildingComponent.* Several subclasses are defined for *BuildingSafetySystem* that capture information about the different fire safety systems found inside buildings. The complete list is shown in Figure 3(B). An automatic fire extinguishing system refers to sprinkler systems or another automatic fire extinguisher system installed in a building. In most buildings, a sprinkler system is separated into coverage zones

(OSHA, 2015). This information is valuable to firefighters because the fire can be located based on the active sprinkler zone. The Fire alarm system and other sensors and detectors are also divided into different zones. A standpipe system is a system of pipes in a building that provides water for manual firefighting and, in some cases, to sprinkler systems (OSHA, 2015). A fire department connection (FDC) is an inlet through which firefighters feed water into the standpipe system. In contrast, fire hose connections (FHC) are outlets of the standpipe system inside the building where firefighters can connect their fire hoses (OSHA, 2015).

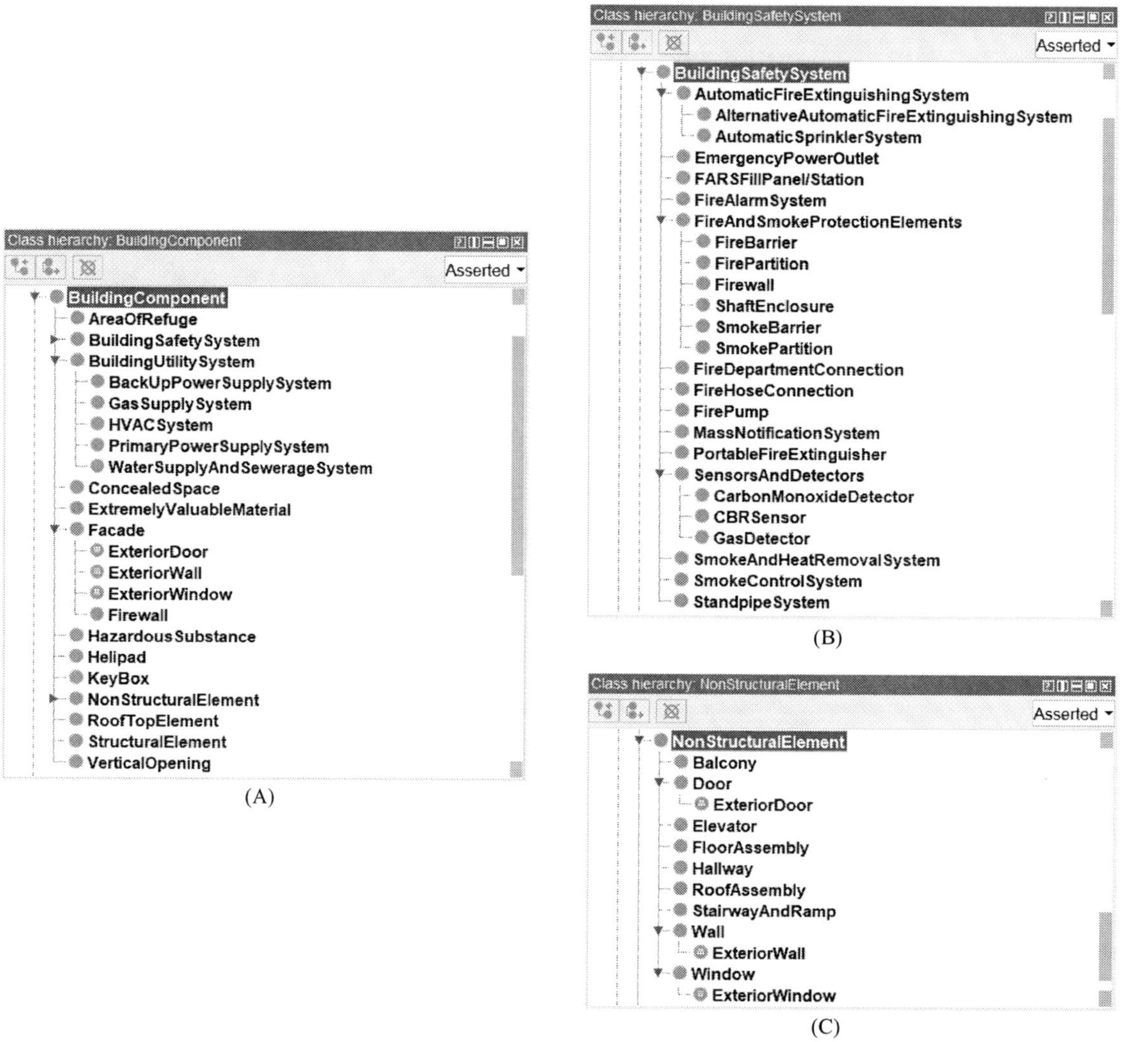

Figure 3: Subclasses of (A) *BuildingComponent* class, (B) *BuildingSafetySystem* class, and (C) *NonStructuralElement* class.

In addition to safety systems, other building components firefighters may interact with are also captured in the ontology. This includes several building utilities that usually need to be shut down or at least controlled during fire emergencies (OSHA, 2015). Firefighters should also be informed of the location and type of any hazardous material they may come across in the building. Information regarding the façade of an incident building is essential for firefighters. It could be used to predict the spread of fire to the surrounding buildings or other structures. Some rooftop elements could be helpful in some firefighting operations, but they can also cause hazards. For instance, skylights can be used to ventilate a building, but they can also cause firefighters to fall through (OSHA, 2015).

Limited information about structural and nonstructural building elements is modelled in the ontology to not overload firefighters with excess information. OSHA (2015) describes how building elements could assist firefighters or sometimes cause a hazard. Doors, hallways, stairways, and in some cases, elevators are essential during egress. Meanwhile, floor and roof assemblies made with lightweight construction members could collapse and injure firefighters. The complete list of the nonstructural elements (subclasses of *NonStructuralElement*) is given in Figure 3(C).

5. Discussion and Future Activities

The last two phases of the METHONTOLOGY method are evaluation and documentation. The documentation phase refers to documenting each step of the development process, which we have done so far. According to Fernandez et al. (1997), evaluation covers verification and validation of the ontology. The authors defined *verification* as the technical process that confirms the correctness of an ontology. Then, they defined *validation* as the process that confirms whether an ontology corresponds to the concepts it was modelled to represent. We plan to conduct verification and validation in our future work. For that purpose, we plan to reach out to fire departments, firefighter associations, and other related organizations to find firefighters. Then, by consulting with the firefighters, we will validate the ontology. We plan to develop a prototype based on the ontology to facilitate the discussion with the firefighters. The prototype will use the concepts established in the ontology to provide a platform that provides essential information to firefighters.

After verifying and validating our ontology, we will explore possible data sources that can provide the data identified by our ontology. Examples of possible data sources include Building information models (BIM), city models and asset management systems. We will study these and other possible data sources and how they can provide necessary data that can assist firefighters in conducting their life-saving activity safely and successfully.

6. Conclusion

In this research work, we introduced the firefighters' data requirement ontology. The ontology models relevant data regarding a building, its features, and its surroundings that is essential for firefighters' operation during building fires. The ontology was built using the METHONTOLOGY method of ontology development. The ontology can be the basis for developing systems that collect building and environmental data from various data sources and provide comprehensive information to firefighters. Such systems can support firefighters during building fire emergencies to make decisions that safeguard occupants, protect the firefighters themselves and reduce property damage. The ontology can also facilitate the data exchange process between the different personnel involved in emergency response. Our future objective is to verify and validate the ontology through discussion with experts and to develop a prototype tool based on the ontology. Additionally, we will explore potential data sources that can meet firefighters' data requirements established in the ontology.

Acknowledgement

This project is receiving funding from the European Union's Horizon 2020 research and innovation programme under the Marie Skłodowska-Curie grant agreement No 860555.

References

Balding, D. (2020). Embracing technology - Fire Fighting in Canada. Available at: https://www.firefightingincanada.com/embracing-technology/, accessed 2 August 2021.

Bitencourt, K., Araújo Durão, F., Mendonça, M. and Laique Bomfim de Souza Santana, L. (2018). An ontological model for fire emergency situations. In: IEICE Transactions on Information and Systems. Institute of Electronics, Information and Communication, Engineers, IEICE, pp. 108–115. doi:10.1587/transinf.2017SWP0003

Burel, G., Piccolo, L.S.G., Meesters, K. and Alani, H. (2017). DoRES-A three-tier ontology for modelling crises in the digital age. In: Proceedings of the International ISCRAM Conference, pp. 834–845

Fan, Z. and Zlatanova, S. (2011). Exploring ontologies for semantic interoperability of data in emergency response. Applied Geomatics, 3(2), pp. 109–122. doi:10.1007/s12518-011-0048-y

Fernandez, M., Gómez-Pérez, A. and Juristo, N. (1997). Methontology: from ontological art towards ontological engineering. In: Proceedings of the AAAI97 Spring Symposium Series on Ontological Engineering. Facultad de Informática (UPM), pp. 33–40. Available at: http://speech.inesc.pt/~joana/prc/artigos/06c METHONTOLOGY from Ontological Art towards Ontological Engineering - Fernandez, Perez, Juristo - AAAI - 1997.pdf, accessed 16 August 2021.

Gang Liu, Boshi Xu, Qiang Tu, Yongzhong Sha and Zijun Xu (2011). Towards building ontology for community-based fire management. In: Proceedings 2011 International Conference on Transportation, Mechanical, and Electrical Engineering (TMEE). IEEE, pp. 1366–1369. doi:10.1109/TMEE.2011.6199460

Ghodrat, M., Shakeriaski, F., Nelson, D.J. and Simeoni, A. (2021). Existing Improvements in Simulation of Fire–Wind Interaction and Its Effects on Structures. Fire, 4(27). doi:10.3390/fire4020027

Heron, D., Thomas, G., Cousins, J., Lukovic, B. and Schmid, R. (2003). Modelling Fire-Spread In and Around Urban Centres. New Zealand Fire Service Commission Research Report Number 44

International Code Council (ICC) (2018a). 2018 International Building Code. International Code Council, Inc.

International Code Council (ICC) (2018b). 2018 International Fire Code. International Code Council, Inc.

Isikdag, U., Underwood, J. and Aouad, G. (2008). An investigation into the applicability of building information models in geospatial environment in support of site selection and fire response management processes. Advanced Engineering Informatics, 22(4), pp. 504–519. doi:10.1016/j.aei.2008.06.001

Jones, W.W., Holmberg, D.G., Davis, W.D., Evans, D.D., Bushby, S.T. and Reed, K. a (2005). Workshop to define information needed by emergency responders during building emergencies. National Institute of Standards and Technology. Gaithersburg, MD. doi:10.6028/NIST.IR.7193

Khalid, Q. (2021). SBEO: Smart Building Evacuation Ontology. version: 0.2. Available at: https://qasimkhalid.github.io/SBEO/, accessed 13 August 2021.

Li, N., Yang, Z., Ghahramani, A., Becerik-Gerber, B. and Soibelman, L. (2014). Situational awareness for supporting building fire emergency response: Information needs, information sources, and implementation requirements. Fire Safety Journal, 63, pp. 17–28. doi:10.1016/j.firesaf.2013.11.010

Malizia, A., Onorati, T., Diaz, P., Aedo, I. and Astorga-Paliza, F. (2010). SEMA4A: An ontology for emergency notification systems accessibility. Expert Systems with Applications, 37(4), pp. 3380–3391. doi:10.1016/j.eswa.2009.10.010

McGuinness, D.L. and van Harmelen, F. (2004). OWL Web Ontology Language Overview. W3C recommendation. Edited by D.L. McGuinness and F. Van Harmelen. W3C. Available at: http://www.w3.org/TR/owl-features/,

Neto, J., Morais, A.J.D.N., Gonçalves, R. and Coelho, A. (2021). An Ontology for Fire Building Evacuation. In: ICICT 2021 - 6th International Congress on Information & Communication Technology

Noy, N.F. and McGuinness, D.L. (2001). Ontology Development 101: A Guide to Creating Your First Ontology. Stanford Knowledge Systems Laboratory. doi:10.1016/j.artmed.2004.01.014

Nuo, N., Tay, W., Ubota, N.K. and Botzheim, J. (2016). Building Ontology for Fire Emergency Planning and Support. E-Journal of Advanced Maintenance, 8(2), pp. 13–22

Occupational Safety and Health Administration (OSHA) (2015). Fire Service Features of Buildings and Fire Protection Systems

Saad, E., Hindriks, K. V. and Neerincx, M.A. (2018). Ontology Design for Task Allocation and Management in Urban Search and Rescue Missions. In: Proceedings of the 10th International Conference on Agents and Artificial Intelligence. SCITEPRESS - Science and Technology Publications, pp. 622–629. doi:10.5220/0006661106220629

Santarpia, L., Bologna, S., Ciancio, V., Golasi, I. and Salata, F. (2019). Fire Temperature Based on the Time and Resistance of Buildings—Predicting the Adoption of Fire Safety Measures. Fire, 2(2), p. 19. doi:10.3390/fire2020019

Xu, W. and Zlatanova, S. (2007). Ontologies for Disaster Management Response. In: Li, J. Zlatanova, Sisi; and Fabbri, A.G. (eds). Geomatics Solutions for Disaster Management. Berlin, Heidelberg: Springer Berlin Heidelberg, pp. 185–200. doi:10.1007/978-3-540-72108-6_13

MVDLite: a Fast Validation Algorithm for Model View Definition Rules

Liu H.[1], Gao G.[1,2,*], Zhang H.[1,2], Liu Y.[1,2], Song Y.[3], Gu M.[1,2]
[1] Tsinghua University, China. [2] Beijing National Research Center for Information Science and Technology (BNRist), China. [3] Digital Horizon Technology Co., Ltd., China.
gaoge@tsinghua.edu.cn

Abstract. Model View Definition (MVD) is the standard methodology to define the data exchange requirements and rule constraints for Building Information Models (BIMs). In this paper, the MVDLite algorithm is proposed for the fast validation of MVD rules. A "rule chain" structure is introduced to combine the data templates, constraint statements, and logical interconnections in an input mvdXML ruleset, which leads to fast filtering of data nodes through the rule chain. By establishing the correspondence of each prefix of the rule chain with a string, the deep-caching strategy further improves efficiency. The outperforming experimental results show that our algorithm significantly reduces the running time of MVD validation on large real-world BIMs.

1. Introduction

Model View Definition (MVD) is the standard methodology to define the data exchange requirements and rule constraints for Building Information Models (BIMs). MVD defines the subsets of a specific Industry Foundation Classes (IFC) schema, with constraints on entities, attributes, geometry representations and so on.

The mvdXML is the formal representation format for MVDs recommended by buildingSMART. The mvdXML rules can be parsed by computers, which can be used for supporting software implementation in IFC-based data exchange, and for automatically validating whether IFC models conform to the MVD rules. Compared with the semantic rule-checking methods for BIMs (Pauwels, et al., 2011;2015; Beach, et al., 2015; Zhang, et al., 2019) with enriched geometry calculation and semantic inferencing, the MVD checking focuses on fast validation of data structures and values in the IFC raw data, which is recommended in the Information Delivery Manual (IDM) standard (buildingSMART, 2010).

The rules in mvdXML are represented in two separated parts: the data structures and the rule statements. The data structures are defined in the header part as nested XML tags, which represent the subgraph structures in IFC data, indicating the paths to find related data nodes starting from a root entity nodeset. The rule statements are written in "mvdXML Rule Grammar" with value constraints and logical interconnections for checking the subgraphs matched with a data template.

At present, there have been several implementations of MVD validation algorithms. In accordance with the separation of templates and rule statements in mvdXML, the current validation algorithms usually follow the two-step "matching-checking" process: first matching the template to find the subgraphs, and then checking the rule statements on each found subgraph. Different caching strategies have been applied by the algorithms, however, the efficiency of MVD validation of large rulesets on real-world size models is still a challenge.

In this paper, the MVDLite algorithm is proposed for the fast validation of MVD rules. A "rule chain" structure is introduced to combine and reorganize the data structures, value constraints and logical interconnections from an input mvdXML rule, which leads to faster searching and filtering of data nodes through the rule chain.

https://doi.org/10.7146/aul.455.c192

2. Related Work

2.1 The mvdXML Ruleset

MVD is the technical solution of the IDM in the IFC data, which intends to support meaningful IFC implementations for software developers. IDM defines data delivery process, exchange requirements and domain concepts for BIM data exchange, then MVD binds the domain concepts to IFC entities, and represents the constraints about required information for geometry, attributes and relationships in rule statements.

The mvdXML is based on several early studies about MVD rule representation. The Extended Process to Product Modeling (xPPM) (Lee, et al., 2013) is about the formal definition of IDM, and provides a tool for mapping the IDM functional parts to MVD. The Semantic Exchange Modules framework (SEM) (Venugopal, et al., 2012) is about the object-oriented definition of domain concepts in ontologies. SEM provides a mapping between the domain entity concepts and the data structure concepts in specific data forms. The Generalised Model Subset Definition (GMSD) (Weise, et al., 2003) is about the specification of rules for selecting a subset of entities from the IFC model.

Based on the previous studies about MVD, an integrated IDM-MVD process for IFC data exchange is proposed and recommended by buildingSMART (See, et al., 2012), which combines the strengths of the previous studies. The mvdXML format (Chipman, et al., 2016) is used for this integrated IDM-MVD process, which involves abundant information about exchange requirements, domain concepts, and rule constraints. An example ruleset in mvdXML is shown in Figure 1.

```xml
<?xml version="1.0"?>
<mvdXML xmlns:xsi="http://www.w3.org/2001/XMLSchema-instance" xmlns:xsd="http://www.w3.org/2001/XMLSchema"
uuid="ca533756-fc05-4f56-b091-04b953e362ed" status="sample" xsi:schemaLocation="http://www.buildingsmart-
tech.org/mvd/XML/1.1 http://www.buildingsmart-tech.org/mvd/XML/1.1/mvdXML_V1.1_add1.xsd"
xmlns="http://buildingsmart-tech.org/mvd/XML/1.1">
  <Templates>
    <ConceptTemplate uuid="d22c5deb-95d9-4686-800b-a23d292062c9" status="sample" applicableSchema="IFC4"
        applicableEntity="IfcWall">
      <Rules>
        <AttributeRule RuleID="IsTypedBy_0" AttributeName="IsTypedBy">
          <EntityRules>
            <EntityRule EntityName="IfcRelDefinesByType">
              <AttributeRules>
                <AttributeRule RuleID="RelatingType_1" AttributeName="RelatingType">
                  <EntityRules>
                    <EntityRule EntityName="IfcTypeObject">
                      <AttributeRules>
                        <AttributeRule RuleID="HasPropertySets_2" AttributeName="HasPropertySets">
                          <EntityRules>
                            <EntityRule EntityName="IfcPropertySet">
                              <AttributeRules>
                                <AttributeRule RuleID="Name_3" AttributeName="Name">
                                  <EntityRules>
                                    <EntityRule EntityName="IfcLabel" />
                                  </EntityRules>
                                </AttributeRule>
                                <AttributeRule RuleID="HasProperties_4" AttributeName="HasProperties">
                                  <EntityRules>
                                    <EntityRule EntityName="IfcPropertySingleValue">
                                      <AttributeRules>
                                        <AttributeRule RuleID="Name_5" AttributeName="Name">
                                          <EntityRules>
                                            <EntityRule EntityName="IfcIdentifier" />
                                          </EntityRules>
                                        </AttributeRule>
                                        <AttributeRule RuleID="NominalValue_6" AttributeName="NominalValue">
                                          <EntityRules>
                                            <EntityRule EntityName="IfcValue" />
                                          </EntityRules>
      ......

  </Templates>
  <Views>
    <ModelView uuid="d305b4eb-b668-437a-a9ef-a9ce0d55aa2b" status="sample">
      <Roots>
        <ConceptRoot uuid="9ebbc41e-b172-474a-a45e-b862ddd423b8" name="IfcWall" status="sample"
            applicableRootEntity="IfcWall">
          <Concepts>
            <Concept uuid="309fe979-2673-414a-a85b-b34b3b22fd03" name="Rule 1" status="draft" override="true">
              <Template ref="d22c5deb-95d9-4686-800b-a23d292062c9" />
              <TemplateRules operator="and">
                <TemplateRule Parameters="Name_3[Value]='Pset_WallCommon' AND Name_5[Value]='IsExternal' AND
                NominalValue_6[Type]='IfcBoolean'"/>
              </TemplateRules>
      ......

  </Views>
</mvdXML>
```

Templates about subgraph structures

Rule statements

Figure 1: An example mvdXML ruleset.

The mvdXML format involves natural language information for human-read purposes (including concept definitions and exchange requirements) as well as computer-usable rules for supporting software implementations. The computer-usable rules are in two separated parts: the data structure templates in "ConceptTemplate" tags in the header part, and the rule statements in "TemplateRules" tags in the body part. The "ConceptTemplate" part is about the subgraph structures in IFC data, indicating the paths to find related attributes and target entities starting from a certain root entity type, which is represented in nested "AttributeRule" and "EntityRule" tags. The "TemplateRules" part is about the value constraints in "mvdXML Rule Grammar" for checking the matched subgraphs, and also the applicability conditions and logical interconnections. Each attribute defined in "ConceptTemplate" is assigned with a "RuleID", so that the attribute can be referred to in the rule statements in "TemplateRules".

2.2 Automated MVD Validation

Automated MVD validation is a type of application to check the conformity of an IFC model with an MVD ruleset. Several studies are about modularized MVD validation (Eastman, et al., 2009; Zhang, et al., 2014; Solihin, et al., 2015; Lee, et al., 2016; 2018; Simplebim, 2022), which supports only several commonly-used MVD rule types (such as the value of attributes or the existence of relationships), and implement different program modules for different MVD validation tasks. Generalized MVD validation (Weise, et al., 2016; xBimTeam, 2016; Oraskari, et al., 2021) performs subgraph template matching and rule constraint checking directly based on the mvdXML rule, and can support arbitrary mvdXML rulesets.

Since the templates and statements are separated in mvdXML, the current MVD validation algorithms usually follow the two-step "matching-checking" process. First, for each root entity, find the subgraphs and required attributes which matches a template. Second, the rule statements (including logical combinations) are checked on each matched subgraph. The conformance result for each root entity is obtained from the existence of a subgraph that satisfies the rule statements.

For a single root entity, there are usually multiple subgraphs that can match the same template. For example, if one root entity has multiple properties and each property is an "IfcProperty" node, then for this single root entity, there are the same numbers of subgraphs that can match the template for this rule. Typically, in checking a rule on a root nodeset with n entities, the total number of matched subgraphs for all the root entities is nm (i.e. each root entity can match m subgraphs in average), and each subgraph has p attributes, then the algorithm complexity is $O(nmp)$.

Different caching strategies have been applied by the algorithms, in order that the found subgraphs can be reused in checking multiple rules. For example, one implementation in xBIM (xBimTeam, 2016) caches the found subgraphs for each root entity set in a DataTable with size $nm \times p$, and another implementation in BIMserver (Oraskari, et al., 2021) caches the edges in found subgraphs for each root entity in a HashMap with size $n \times m \times p$.

However, since the IFC model of a real-world project usually exceeds millions of nodes, with hundreds of megabytes of data, the efficiency of MVD validation of large rulesets on real-world size models is still a challenge.

3. The MVDLite Algorithm

The motivation of the MVDLite algorithm is based on the following two observations. First, there are usually common nodes in multiple subgraphs with different root entities. For example, if multiple instances are assigned with the same type node, then this type node (as well as properties of this type node) would be shared in the subgraphs of all instances. Second, if the constraints in rule statements are considered in subgraph matching, many false branches can be pruned at early stages in searching.

In this section, the MVDLite algorithm is proposed for the fast validation of MVD rules. First, the "rule chain" structure with several types of "rule segments" is introduced. Second, the algorithm for parsing the mvdXML rule statements and performing fast round-trip search is introduced. Then, the complexity analysis of the MVDLite algorithm is provided. Finally, the deep-caching strategy is introduced to further speed up the checking tasks.

3.1 The Rule Chain Structure

A rule segment is the representation of a rule as a mapping from source nodeset to target nodeset. There are three types of rule segments (attribute segment, metric segment, and compound segment). A rule chain is a sequence of rule segments starting with a root nodeset, in which the target nodeset of the former rule segment is the source nodeset of the latter rule segment.

There are three types of rule segments: attribute segment, metric segment and compound segment.

An attribute segment is a mapping defined by an attribute in the IFC data. Each attribute segment has an attribute name and a target node type, corresponding to the "AttributeRule" and "EntityRule" tags in mvdXML. Figure 2(a) shows an example attribute segment.
A metric segment is a mapping from the source nodeset to itself, which works as a filter for the source nodes. Each metric segment is with a metric (`[Type]`, `[Value]`, `[Size]`, `[Exists]`, `[Unique]`), an operator (`=`, `>`, `<`, `>=`, `<=`, `!=`) and a value constraint (string, boolean, or numeric value), corresponding to the components in the mvdXML Rule Grammar. Among the metric segments, the `[Type]` and `[Value]` metrics are "single metric segments", which can be evaluated by every single node in the nodeset, and act as filters for the nodeset itself. Figure 2(b) shows an example single metric segment. The `[Exists]`, `[Size]` and `[Unique]` are "collection metric segments", which can only be evaluated by a collection of nodes, and act as filters for the parent nodeset. Figure 2(c) shows an example collection metric segment.

A compound segment encapsulates one or more rule chains into brackets, and acts as a single rule segment. There are two different types of compound segments: compound attribute segment and compound metric segment. A compound attribute segment encapsulates the paths between the source nodeset and the target nodeset, and acts as a single attribute segment, as

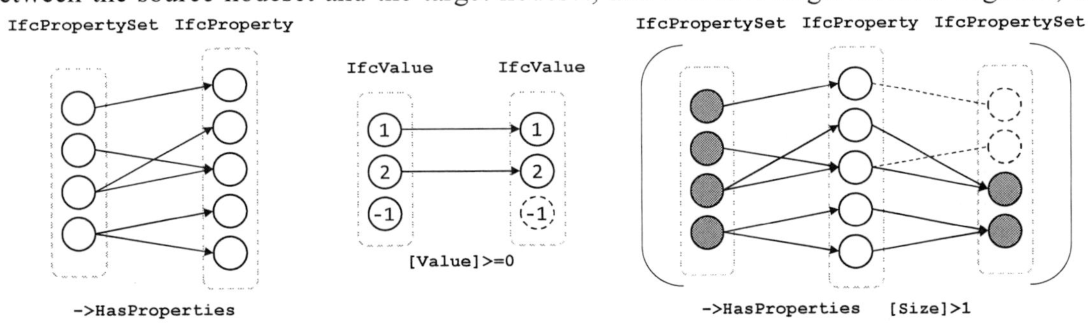

(a) Attribute segment. (b) Single metric segment. (c) Collection metric segment.

Figure 2: Examples of attribute segment and metric segments.

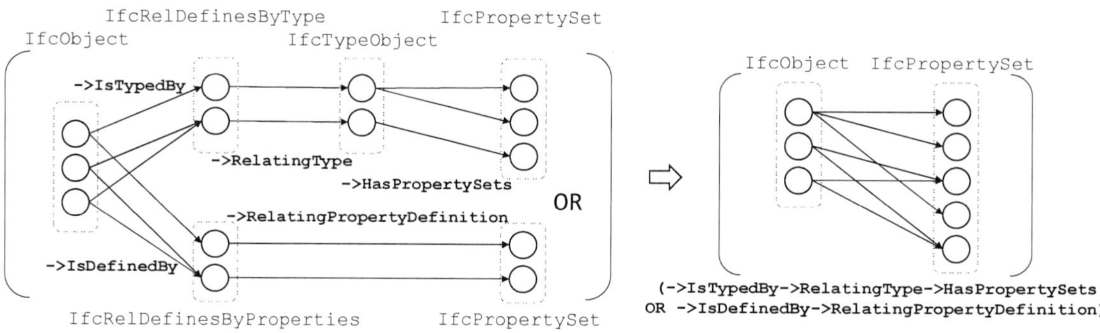

(a) Compound attribute segment.

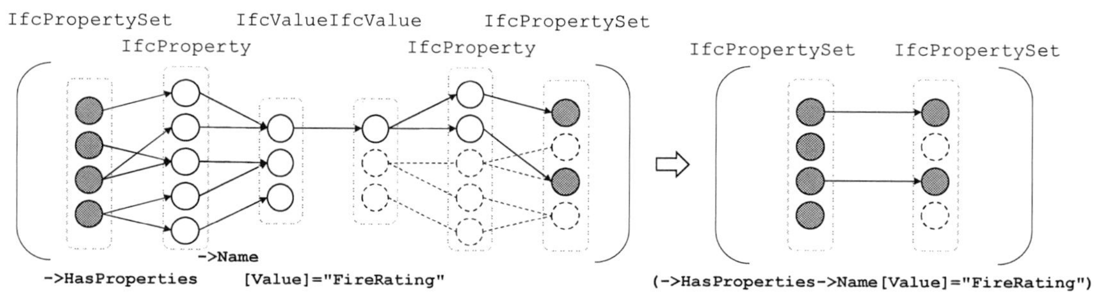

(b) Compound metric segment.

Figure 3: Examples of compound segments.

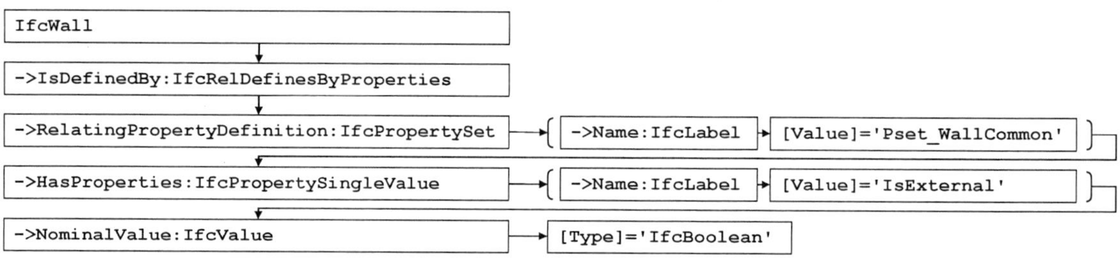

Figure 4: An example rule chain structure.

shown in Figure 3(a). A compound metric segment encapsulates the filter result of the source nodeset, and acts as a single metric segment, as shown in Figure 3(b). Each sub-chain in a compound metric segment must end with a metric segment, and each sub-chain in a compound attribute segment must end with an attribute segment. A compound segment can also be nested inside another compound segment and act as a corresponding attribute segment or metric segment.

Inside a compound segment, several sub-chains can be combined with logical interconnections (`AND`, `OR`, `NOT`), which corresponds to the intersection, union and complement operations of the target nodesets. Specifically, since each metric segment can be viewed as a filter of its source nodeset, the `AND` operation of metric segments can also be represented as the series connection of metric segments.

Each rule segment is named with a string, so that each rule chain can be uniquely identified by linking the strings of all segments. An attribute segment is named with "`->`" followed by the attribute name, and the optional entity type rule can be linked afterward with a "`:`", such as "`->Name:IfcLabel`". A metric rule is named with the metric name, an operator and a value

Algorithm 1 GeneratingRuleChain

Input: template **T**, rule statement **R**.
rule chain **c** = NULL
for (interconnection u, RuleID v, value constraint w) in **R** :
    c' = GetAttributeSegChain (v, **T**)
    c' += GetMetricSeg (w)
    if c == NULL :
        c = **c'**
    else :
        x = GetLowestCommonAncestor (**c**, **c'**)
        c = MergeRuleChains(**c**, **c'**, x, u)
Output: c

Algorithm 2 SearchingOnRuleChain

Input: root nodeset $\mathbf{n}_1$, rule chain **c**, data graph **G**
for segment $\mathbf{s}_i$ in **c** :
    if $\mathbf{s}_i$ is attribute segment :
        $\mathbf{n}_{i+1}$ = FindSucceedingNodes($\mathbf{n}_i$, $\mathbf{s}_i$)
    else if $\mathbf{s}_i$ is metric segment :
        $\mathbf{n}_{i+1}$ = FilterNodes($\mathbf{n}_i$, $\mathbf{s}_i$)
    else if $\mathbf{s}_i$ is compound segment :
        $\mathbf{n}_{i+1}$ = EmptyNodeset()
        for (interconnection u, branch $\hat{\mathbf{c}}$) in $\mathbf{s}_i$:
            $\hat{\mathbf{n}}$ = SearchingOnRuleChain($\mathbf{n}_i$, $\hat{\mathbf{c}}$, **G**)
            $\mathbf{n}_{i+1}$ = CombineNodeset($\mathbf{n}_{i+1}$, $\hat{\mathbf{n}}$, u)
$\mathbf{n}_{out}$ = Backtrack($\mathbf{n}_{last}$, $\mathbf{n}_1$)
Output: $\mathbf{n}_{out}$

constraint in order, such as "`[Value]=TRUE`". A compound segment is named with exterior brackets, inside which are the strings of the interior rule chains and logical interconnections.

Figure 4 shows a rule chain structure generated from an mvdXML rule statement. The meaning of this rule is that if a property "IsExternal" in property set "Pset_WallCommon" is assigned to an "IfcWall" instance, then the value type should be "IfcBoolean".

3.2 Performing Validation on the Rule Chain

The MVDLite algorithm uses mvdXML as input ruleset. The pseudo-code of the MVDLite algorithm is provided.

First, in Algorithm 1, each rule statement in an mvdXML ruleset is parsed into a rule chain structure. An mvdXML rule statement is composed of multiple sub-clauses, each with a logical interconnection, a RuleID, and a value constraint. The RuleID indicates a path from the root entity nodeset to a target nodeset, which can be parsed into a branch of the rule chain with multiple attribute segments. The value constraint can be parsed into a metric segment appended to the branch. Several branches are merged into one chain at the lowest-common-ancestor attribute. The merged chain has a shared prefix, and the suffix branches with interconnections are wrapped into compound segments.

Then, in Algorithm 2, a round-trip search is performed based on the rule chain to get the validation results. A rule chain is a series of instructions in finding and filtering the nodes. Starting from the root entity set, a round-trip search is performed: first go forward through the chain to find the existence of the paths which can pass all the rule segments, and then trace back to find the root entity nodeset where these paths started. For compound segments, each inner branch is a sub-chain starting from the current nodeset, so Algorithm 2 is performed for each branch, and the combined result acts as a single segment in the host chain.

Figure 5 compares the round-trip search algorithm on the rule chain with the "matching-checking" process in mvdXML rule validation. Rather than traversal subgraph-by-subgraph according to the template matching result, the MVDLite algorithm is able to find the results of all subgraphs through one single turn of round-trip search starting from the root nodeset.

3.3 The Complexity of MVDLite Algorithm

The complexity of MVD validation is mainly due to the node searching process. The complexity of the MVDLite algorithm is $O(e)$, in which e is the number of visited edges in the

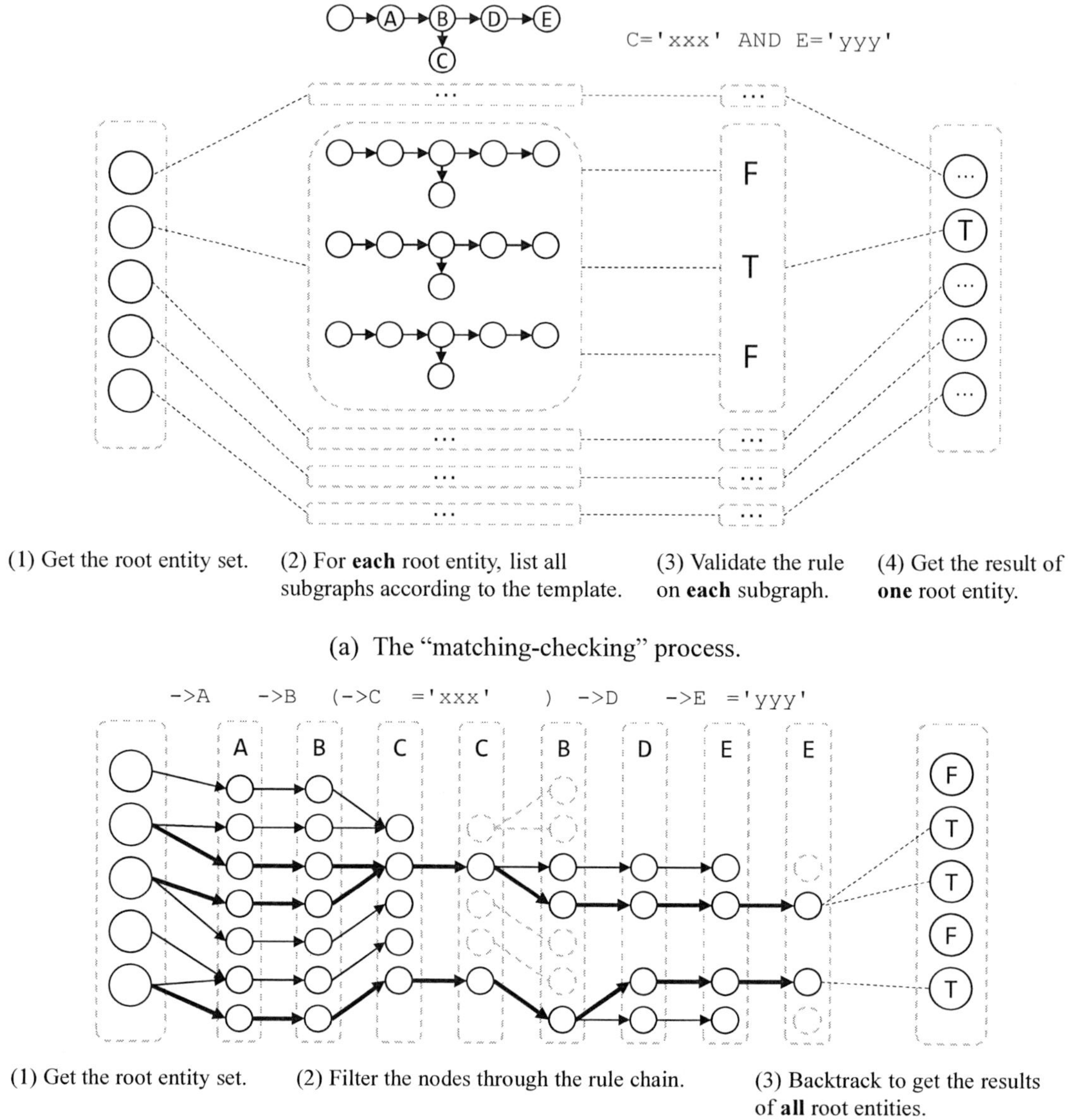

(a) The "matching-checking" process.

(b) The round-trip search on the rule chain in the MVDLite algorithm.

Figure 5: The comparison of two types of MVD rule validation algorithms.

searching, and each edge is visited at least once and at most twice (forward and backward in a round-trip). In comparison, the complexity of "matching-checking" method is *O(nmp)*.

Before comparing the complexity of the two algorithms, the formal representation of subgraph matching process in the "matching-checking" method is shown as follows.

Since the template is a directed acyclic graph, the attributes can be sorted with topological sorting, so that all prefixes of any attribute are ranked before itself. For a template with p attributes (regarding the root entity set as the first attribute), let $\mathrm{f}(i)$ be the index of the direct prefix of the *i*-th attribute, $1 \leq \mathrm{f}(i) < i \leq p$. The subgraph matching process searches the nodes by each attribute, and records all matched (including partial-matched) subgraphs.

Let $\mathbf{K}^{(i)}$ be the record DataTable after scanning the *i*-th attribute, which is a matrix with the size $k_i \times i$, and k_i is the number of matched subgraph prefixes. In particular, $\mathbf{K}^{(p)}$ is with size

$nm \times p$, and $k_p = nm$ is the total number of subgraphs. Let $\mathbf{n}^{(i)}$ be the non-repeated nodeset of the i-th attribute. Specifically, the size of the root nodeset $|\mathbf{n}^{(1)}| = n$. Let $\mathbf{q}^{(i)}$ be the number of succeeding edges in scanning the i-th attribute for each node in $\mathbf{n}^{(\mathrm{f}(i))}$, with $|\mathbf{q}^{(i)}| = |\mathbf{n}^{(\mathrm{f}(i))}|$.

Theorem 1. $e \leq nmp$.

Proof. In the "matching-checking" method, let $\mathbf{k}^{(i,j)}$ be the j-th column of $\mathbf{K}^{(i)}$, in which each item is from $\mathbf{n}^{(j)}$ and may repeat several times. Let $\mathbf{r}^{(i,j)}$ be the array of repeating times for the nodes in $\mathbf{k}^{(i,j)}$, and the size $|\mathbf{r}^{(i,j)}| = |\mathbf{n}^{(j)}|$. In scanning the i-th attribute, for each node in $\mathbf{k}^{(i-1,\mathrm{f}(i))}$, every succeeding edge corresponds to a new matched subgraph prefix, so

$$k_i = \mathbf{r}^{(i-1,\mathrm{f}(i))} \cdot \mathbf{q}^{(i)} . \tag{1}$$

If some subgraph prefixes do not have succeeding edges, they are kept in the DataTable as partial-matched subgraphs by appending a null node, which keeps $k_i \geq k_{i-1}$.

In the MVDLite algorithm, since the value constraints are evaluated during the searching, some of the nodes are excluded before scanning the next attribute. Let $\mathbf{h}^{(i)}$ be a mask array for $\mathbf{n}^{(i)}$, in which kept nodes are marked with 1 and excluded nodes are marked with 0. In scanning the i-th attribute, the number of visited edges e_i is

$$e_i = \mathbf{h}^{(\mathrm{f}(i))} \cdot \mathbf{q}^{(i)} . \tag{2}$$

Specifically, $e_1 = k_1 = n$. Since every item in $\mathbf{r}^{(i-1,\mathrm{f}(i))}$ is not less than 1, and every item in $\mathbf{h}^{(\mathrm{f}(i))}$ is not greater than 1, then $e_i \leq k_i$. As a result,

$$e = \sum_{i=1}^{p} e_i \leq \sum_{i=1}^{p} k_i \leq \sum_{i=1}^{p} k_p = nmp . \tag{3}$$

□

Theorem 1 indicates that the complexity of the MVDLite algorithm is not greater than the "matching-checking" method. The first "≤" sign gets equal only when every item in $\mathbf{r}^{(i-1,\mathrm{f}(i))}$ and $\mathbf{h}^{(\mathrm{f}(i))}$ equals 1, i.e. no repeated nodes in any subgraph prefix, and no excluded nodes by any value constraint. The second "≤" sign gets equal only when every $k_i = k_p = n$, i.e. each root entity matches only one subgraph. In real-world MVD validation tasks, the two "≤" signs usually make significant differences, which remarkably speeds up the calculation.

3.4 The Deep-Caching Strategy

For the checking task on a large ruleset with multiple rules, the efficiency of the MVDLite algorithm can be further improved by applying the "deep-caching" strategy. Based on the correspondence between the rule chain structure and a prefix string, the checking results can be reused across multiple rules.

By naming each rule segment with a string, the whole rule chain can be named with a string by linking the strings of all segments, and then each prefix of a rule chain has a corresponding prefix string, as shown in Figure 4. The deep-caching strategy records the correspondence so that a previously visited nodeset can be re-found according to the prefix string of a rule chain.

As a result, rather than starting from the root nodeset every time, the algorithm can start from a visited nodeset with the longest common prefix. In a large ruleset, there are usually multiple rules with a common prefix. For example, all rules for checking the type properties of an "IfcWall" instance should have the common prefix "`IfcWall->IsTypedBy: IfcRelDefinesByType->RelatingType:IfcTypeObject->HasPropertieS ets:IfcPropertySet`", so the nodeset of the corresponding "IfcPropertySet" nodes can be reused across the rules. In our experiments, the deep-caching strategy is effective in speeding-up without significantly increase memory usage.

4. Experiments

4.1 Experiment Setup

The performance of the proposed MVDLite algorithm is compared with several "matching-checking" tools on models and rulesets in different sizes. The effect of the deep-caching strategy is also compared.

Tools. The MVDLite tool is implemented in C# based on an IFC tool named "STEParser". The compared tools include the xBIM MVD plugin (xBimTeam, 2016) with DataTable caching, and the tool based on BIMserver and IfcOpenShell (Oraskari, et al., 2021) with HashMap caching. For a fair comparison, our own "matching-checking" implementation with HashMap caching on the same STEParser tool is also tested.

Rulesets. Three mvdXML rulesets based on IFC4 are used, including **UnitTest.mvdxml** with 58 statements (xBimTeam, 2016), **RV.mvdxml** with 1,770 statements and **DTV.mvdxml** with 1,791 statements (buildingSMART, 2018).

Models. The IFC4 models used are shown in Figure 6, including two sample models from NIBS (2012) (**Duplex.ifc** with 52 MB and **Office.ifc** with 193 MB, both converted to IFC4 and merged parts in multiple disciplines), and a real-world model **B01.ifc** with 841 MB.

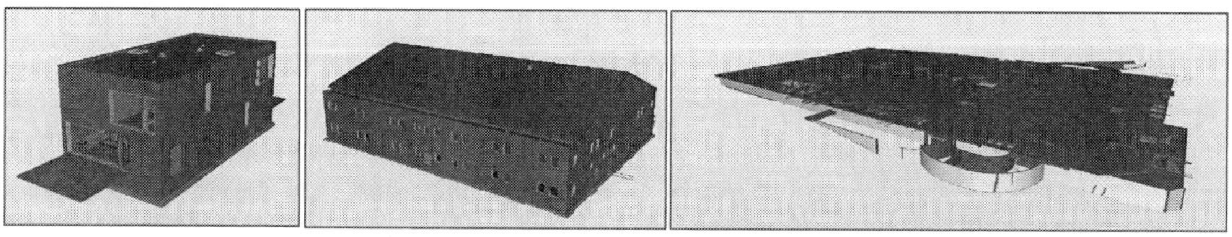

(a) Duplex.ifc (b) Office.ifc (c) B01.ifc

Figure 6: The models used in the experiments.

Table 1: Time usage in MVD validation tasks (in seconds).

Models	Rulesets	Tools				
		MVDLite	MVDLite (no deep-caching)	STEParser matching-checking	(Oraskari, et al., 2021)	(xBimTeam, 2016)
Duplex.ifc	UnitTest.mvdxml	**0.4**	0.5	1.3	2.5	2.4
	RV.mvdxml	**1.3**	2.0	11.2	21.1	7.1
	DTV.mvdxml	**1.4**	2.0	11.5	21.6	6.0
Office.ifc	UnitTest.mvdxml	**0.8**	1.5	5.8	8.6	177.3
	RV.mvdxml	**6.0**	9.7	88.5	97.0	185.7
	DTV.mvdxml	**6.0**	10.3	84.5	107.9	178.3
B01.ifc	UnitTest.mvdxml	**5.0**	13.1	49.8	55.8	10745.1
	RV.mvdxml	**73.2**	126.7	388.9	480.6	8722.8
	DTV.mvdxml	**68.6**	123.9	393.5	613.7	8707.5

4.2 Experimental Results

The time usage of the tools in MVD validation tasks are listed in Table 1 (in which the time usage for loading and parsing IFC data are excluded), with minimum values in bold. All the experiments are performed on a PC with a 3.60 GHz processor and 32GB of physical memory.

The experimental results show that the MVDLite algorithm is significantly faster than the "matching-checking" tools in all tasks. The results also show that the deep-caching strategy can improve the performance of MVD validation in checking multiple rules.

5. Conclusion and Future Work

The proposed MVDLite algorithm remarkably speeds up MVD validation. In a typical task, the time usage may reduce from minutes to seconds, which is beneficial in promoting IDM-MVD applications in the industry.

With the fast MVD validation algorithm, the future work will focus on the usage of MVD technology in more flexible scenarios, such as querying the IFC dataset using MVD, and extracting the partial model according to an MVD ruleset for a certain exchange requirement.

Acknowledgements

This work was supported by the National Key Research and Development Program of China (2021YFB1600303) and the 2019 MIIT Industrial Internet Innovation and Development Project "BIM Software Industry Standardization and Public Service Platform".

References

Pauwels, P., Van Deursen, D., Verstraeten, R., De Roo, J., De Meyer, R., Van de Walle, R., Van Campenhout, J. (2011). A semantic rule checking environment for building performance checking. Automation in Construction, 20(5), pp. 506–518.

Pauwels, P., Zhang, S. (2015). Semantic rule-checking for regulation compliance checking: an overview of strategies and approaches. In: 32rd international CIB W78 conference, 2015, Eindhoven, Netherlands.

Beach, T.H., Rezgui, Y., Li, H., Kasim, T. (2015). A rule-based semantic approach for automated regulatory compliance in the construction sector. Expert Systems with Applications, 42(12), pp. 5219–5231.

Zhang, H., Zhao, W., Zhang, R., Liu, H., Gu, M. (2019). Semantic web based rule checking of real-world scale BIM models: a pragmatic method. In: International Congress and Conferences on Computational Design and Engineering (i3CDE), 2019, Penang, Malaysia.

buildingSMART. (2010). Information Delivery Manual Guide to Components and Development Methods. https://standards.buildingsmart.org/documents/IDM/IDM_guide-CompsAndDevMethods-IDMC_004-v1_2.pdf, accessed January 2022.

Lee, G., Park, Y.H., Ham, S. (2013). Extended Process to Product Modeling (xPPM) for integrated and seamless IDM and MVD development. Advanced Engineering Informatics, 27(4), pp. 636–651.

Venugopal, M., Eastman, C.M., Sacks, R. (2012) Configurable model exchanges for the precast/pre-stressed concrete industry using semantic exchange modules (SEM). In: International Conference on Computing in Civil Engineering, 2012, Clearwater Beach, United States.

Weise, M., Katranuschkov, P., Scherer, R.J. (2003). Generalised model subset definition schema. In: CIB W78's 20th International Conference on Construction IT, 2003, Waiheke Island, New Zealand.

See, R., Karlshoej, J., Davis, D. (2012). An Integrated Process for Delivering IFC Based Data Exchange. https://standards.buildingsmart.org/documents/IDM/IDM_guide-IntegratedProcess-2012_09.pdf, accessed January 2022.

Chipman, T., Liebich, T., Weise, M. (2016). mvdXML: Specification of a standardized format to define and exchange Model View Definitions with Exchange Requirements and Validation Rules. https://standards.buildingsmart.org/MVD/RELEASE/mvdXML/v1-1/mvdXML_V1-1-Final.pdf, accessed January 2022.

Eastman, C.M., Lee, J.M., Jeong, Y.S., Lee, J.K. (2009). Automatic rule-based checking of building designs. Automation in Construction, 18(8), pp. 1011–1033.

Zhang, C., Beetz, J., Weise, M. (2014). Model view checking: automated validation for IFC building models. In: eWork and eBusiness in Architecture, Engineering and Construction: ECPPM, 2014, Vienna, Austria.

Solihin, W., Eastman, C., Lee, Y.C. (2015). Toward robust and quantifiable automated IFC quality validation. Advanced Engineering Informatics, 29(3), pp. 739–756.

Lee, Y.C., and Eastman, C.M. and Solihin, W., See, R. (2016). Modularized rule-based validation of a BIM model pertaining to model views. Automation in Construction, 63, pp. 1–11.

Lee, Y.C., Eastman, C.M., Solihin, W. (2018). Logic for ensuring the data exchange integrity of building information models. Automation in Construction, 85, pp. 249–262.

Simplebim. (2022). Support site for Simplebim users - mvdXML. https://www.simplebim.com/support/addon-mvdxml.html, accessed January 2022.

Weise, M., Liebich, T., Nisbet, N., Benghi, C. (2016). IFC model checking based on mvdXML 1.1, In: eWork and eBusiness in Architecture, Engineering and Construction: ECPPM, 2016 Limassol, Cyprus.

xBimTeam. (2016). XbimMvdXML. https://github.com/xBimTeam/XbimMvdXML, accessed January 2022.

Oraskari, J., Zhang, C. (2021). mvdXML Checker. https://github.com/jyrkioraskari/mvdXMLChecker, accessed January 2022.

buildingSMART. (2018). IfcKit - exchanges. https://github.com/buildingSMART/IfcDoc/tree/master/IfcKit/exchanges, accessed January 2022.

NIBS. (2012). Common Building Information Model Files And Tools. https://www.wbdg.org/bim/cobie/common-bim-files, accessed January 2022.

Modeling and Validating Temporal Rules with Semantic Petri-Net for Digital Twins

Liu H.[1], Song X.[2], Gao G.[1,3,*], Zhang H.[1,3], Liu Y.[1,3], Gu M.[1,3]
[1] Tsinghua University, China. [2] Portland State University, United States. [3] Beijing National Research Center for Information Science and Technology (BNRist), China.
gaoge@tsinghua.edu.cn

Abstract. Semantic rule checking on RDFS/OWL data has been widely used in the construction industry. At present, semantic rule checking is mainly performed on static models. There are still challenges in integrating temporal models and semantic models for combined rule checking. In this paper, Semantic Petri-Net (SPN) is proposed as a novel temporal modeling and validating method, which implements the states and transitions of the Colored Petri-Net directly based on RDFS and SPARQL, and realizes two-way sharing of knowledge between domain semantic webs and temporal models in the runtime. Several cases are provided to demonstrate the possible applications in digital twins with concurrent state changes and dependencies.

1. Introduction

The digital twin technology integrates spatio-temporal data with domain semantic models, which enables tracking and simulating the change of building components, users and environment over time. There have been various applications of digital twins in construction and asset management stages in the construction industry.

Semantic rule checking on RDFS/OWL data have been widely used in the construction industry (Pauwels, et al., 2015; Beach, et al., 2015; Zhang, et al., 2019). At present, semantic rule checking is mainly performed on static models, in which the properties and relationships do not change in time. There have been researches about spatio-temporal rule checking, such as extending SPARQL for querying geometries (Battle and Kolas, 2011; Zhang, et al., 2018) and time periods (Koubarakis and Kyzirakos, 2010). However, digital twin applications usually have more complicated temporal states than just time periods, and also rule constraints to decide whether a state change is allowed. Such rules are closely related to semantic properties and relationships, so there is a requirement in integrated semantic and temporal rule checking.

Temporal modeling methods such as Finite State Machines (FSM) (Mealy, 1955; Moore, 1956), Colored Petri-Nets (CPN) (Jensen, 1987) and Business Process Modeling Notation (BPMN) (Decker, et al., 2010) are used in modeling the temporal states and rules. Related researches have focused on the interaction between temporal models and semantic webs. However, there are still challenges in two-way sharing of knowledge in the runtime for supporting integrated semantic and temporal rule checking.

In this paper, based on the CPN method, the Semantic Petri-Net (SPN) is proposed as a novel temporal modeling method. The temporal states and transitions are defined in RDFS, and the temporal transition rules are represented in SPARQL statements. As a result, SPN can run on semantic engines like Apache Jena and dotNetRDF, which enables direct usage of the vast semantic information in the domain semantic web such as ifcOWL (Beetz, et al., 2009) in the runtime of the temporal model. Experiments are performed to show the SPN application cases in modeling concurrent state change with dependencies and implementing automatic agents in the process maps.

https://doi.org/10.7146/aul.455.c193

2. Related Work

2.1 Temporal Modeling Methods

FSM is a popular method for modeling temporal states in the information industry. FSM represents a temporal model with a finite set of states, an input alphabet, and a global transition function defining the next state on each input. FSM is suitable for modeling systems in response to various signals or events, so that analysis tools such as temporal logic checking can be performed on the system.

BPMN is commonly used in engineering and project management, which represents events, activities and gateways in process maps. BPMN is suitable for modeling concurrent systems with multiple participants, such as a streamlined workflow. In the construction industry, BPMN is introduced in the Information Delivery Manual (IDM) (buildingSMART, 2010) method for representing the process maps of BIM data exchange.

Petri-Net and its variant methods are also widely used in modeling concurrent systems, among which the CPN is a method with both formality and ease of use. A Petri-Net is a graph with "places" to store tokens, "transitions" to consume and generate tokens, and "arcs" as the connection between places and transitions. CPN is a type of high-level Petri-Net with rules on places, transitions and arcs. Each token in a CPN can have an attached data value named a "color", which must be defined in a finite "colorset". A CPN can be equivalently unfolded to low-level Petri-Nets without colors, which enables mathematic tools (such as state space analysis and place invariant analysis) for applying temporal logic computation on the concurrent systems (Jensen and Kristensen, 2009).

CPN is powerful in modeling and analyzing both sequential and concurrent systems, and both FSM and BPMN can be implemented using CPN. It is also known that the extended CPN with an infinite colorset is Turing-complete (Peterson, 1980). In this paper, the Semantic Petri-Net is proposed based on the CPN, with the purpose to extend the ability in accessing the knowledge in semantic webs, and meanwhile to keep the downward compatibility to the mathematic tools for Petri-Nets.

2.2 Interaction between Temporal Models and Semantic Webs

Related researches have focused on the interaction between temporal models and semantic webs. The researches can be classified into the following topics.

Describing the static structure of a temporal model using an ontology. The contents of the ontologies are mainly about the temporal models themselves, but not much domain knowledge is included. The described temporal models include FSM (Belgueliel, et al., 2014), BPMN (Natschläger, 2011; Rospocher, et al., 2014; Annane, et al., 2019) and Petri-Nets (Gašević, 2004; Ma and Xu, 2009; Zhang, et al., 2011).

Knowledge-based generation of temporal models. Based on the knowledge graph of a certain domain, a temporal model is generated to perform as a runnable agent, for implementing a certain task such as a classifier (Yim, et al., 2011) or a workflow simulator (Wang, et al., 2007; Arena and Kiritsis, 2017). In such researches, domain knowledge is introduced in initializing the temporal models, but is no longer be referred to in the runtime.

Knowledge sharing in the runtime of temporal models. Such researches try to transfer information in the runtime either from the semantic web to the temporal model or in the opposite way. The Petri-Nets over Ontological Graphs (PNOG) (Szkoła and Pancerz, 2017) uses knowledge from the semantic web in the runtime of a Petri-Net, in which the tokens are with hierarchical classification, and the synonyms and hyponyms rules are supported. Knowledge-driven FSM (Moctezuma, et al., 2015) and DARPA Agent Markup Language (DAML) (Hendler, 2001) write the structure and the current state of an FSM into the semantic web, so that the current state and next states can be queried through a SPARQL endpoint.

Compared with the previous researches, the idea in this paper is to implement a runnable Petri-Net based on a semantic engine, for realizing the two-way sharing of knowledge between domain semantic webs and temporal models in the runtime, so that the SPARQL statements can be used inside the temporal model as transition rules concerning domain knowledge, and also outside the temporal model as domain queries concerning current temporal states.

A more detailed literature review of researches on knowledge sharing between temporal models and semantic models can be found in reference (Cheng and Ma, 2016).

3. Semantic Petri-Net

The definition of SPN is provided in section 3.1. The representation of SPN structure in RDFS is shown in section 3.2. The implementation of SPN rules in SPARQL is shown in section 3.3. The downward compatibility of SPN is discussed in section 3.4.

3.1 The Definition of SPN

For a semantic web **W**, let **Σ** be its vocabulary, which is a finite set of terms (including literals and URIs) that are allowed in the semantic web. Using **Σ** as the colorset, the definition of SPN inherits from CPN, which is a tuple

$$\mathrm{SPN} = \langle \mathbf{\Sigma}, \mathbf{P}, \mathbf{T}, \mathbf{A}, \mathbf{N}, \mathbf{C}, \mathbf{G}, \mathbf{E}, \mathbf{I}\,; \mathbf{W} \rangle \tag{1}$$

P, **T**, **A**, **N** are about the structure of an SPN, and **C**, **G**, **E**, **I** are about the rules in the SPN. **P** is the set of places, **T** is the set of transitions, **A** is the set of arcs, and **N** is the assignment of each arc to link one place and one transition. **C** is the assignment of a subset of allowed colors to each place. **G** is the set of guard rules, which assigns each transition with a rule that returns a boolean value, deciding whether this transition is enabled. **E** is the set of arc expressions, which assigns each arc with an expression that returns a multiset of tokens, deciding which tokens to consume (place-to-transition arcs) or to generate (transition-to-place arcs). **I** is the assignment of an initial multiset of tokens to each place. Usually, the places are drawn as circles, the transitions are drawn as boxes, the arcs are drawn as directed arrows, and the tokens are drawn as little dots contained in the places.

The unit of the behavior of CPN is a "binding". A transition has a set of arguments, which is shared in the guard rules and the arc rules. A binding is an assignment of values to each argument, and a transition is enabled when the guard rule returns `true`, and there are enough tokens to consume in each input place according to the returned values of the corresponding arc expressions. SPN inherits the binding behavior of CPN, which is implemented by evaluating SPARQL queries and handling the tokens in the RDF graph.

3.2 SPN Structure Representation in RDFS

The RDFS classes and properties for representing SPN structures are with the namespace "`spn:`". The classes and properties for representing SPN structures are listed in Table 1.

Transitions. A transition is of the class `spn:Transition`, which may have a guard rule related with `spn:guardRule`. The arguments used in the guard rule and all related arcs are related with `spn:hasArg`. If the guard rule is not assigned, by default the transition is always enabled as long as enough input arguments are provided in a binding.

Places. Based on the Linked Data Platform (LDP) standard (W3C, 2015), the `spn:Place` is defined as a subclass of `ldp:Container`, in which the contained tokens are linked with `ldp:contains`. By implementing SPN place based on LDP container, the SPN place can be used in maintaining dynamic relationships in RDF, and the HTTP requests defined in the LDP standard can be adopted in manipulating the contained tokens in the SPN place. The `spn:colorRule` defines the allowed colors for the place, which can return a boolean value deciding whether a token is allowed. The `spn:initRule` defines the rule to get the initial tokens for the place.

Arcs. The `spn:Arc` is the abstract superclass for arcs, which must relate one place with `spn:relPlace` and one transition with `spn:relTransition`. The `spn:Arc` has two subclasses: `spn:ArcT2P` is for arcs pointing from a transition to a place, and `spn:ArcP2T` is for arcs pointing from a place to a transition. An arc must have at least one argument with `spn:hasArg`, and all arguments must also be assigned to the related transition. An arc expression can be related with `spn:arcExpr` to calculate the tokens to be consumed or generated. When there is only one argument, the arc expression can be null and the argument is directly consumed or generated.

Table 1: SPN structure components in RDFS.

Class	Property	Range	Cardinality	Description
spn:Transition	spn:guardRule	spn:Rule	0:1	A boolean rule deciding whether the transition is enabled.
	spn:hasArg	spn:ArgDef	1:?	Definition of arguments used in guard rules and arc rules.
spn:Place	ldp:contains	rdfs:Resource	0:?	Contained tokens.
	spn:colorRule	spn:Rule	0:1	A boolean rule deciding whether a token is allowed in the place.
	spn:initRule	spn:Rule	0:1	A rule assigning initial tokens.
spn:Arc	spn:relPlace	spn:Place	1:1	Related place.
	spn:relTransition	spn:Transition	1:1	Related transition.
	spn:arcExpr	spn:Rule	0:1	An arc expression deciding which tokens to consume or to generate.
	spn:hasArg	spn:ArgDef	1:?	Definition of arguments, must be a subset of the arguments of the related transition.

3.3 SPN Rule Implementation in SPARQL

The SPN rules are formed as a tree structure in RDFS, in which each leaf node has a SPARQL statement. The classes and properties for representing SPN rules are listed in Table 2.

The `spn:Rule` is the abstract superclass of all SPN rule nodes, which has the following subclasses:

- The `spn:SPARQLRule` contains a SPARQL statement.
- The `spn:ConstantRule` contains a constant which can be any URI or literal value.
- The `spn:CompoundRule` contains multiple sub-rules connected by a logical operator

(AND, OR, XOR, or NOT), and each sub-rule returns a boolean value. Specifically, there can be only one sub-rule with a NOT operator.

- The `spn:ConditionRule` contains an "if" sub-rule returns a boolean value, and with the `true` and `false` conditions returned by the "if" sub-rule, the "then" and "else" sub-rules are checked respectively.

The rule nodes compose a rule tree structure, in which each leaf node should be an `spn:SPARQLRule` or an `spn:ConstantRule`. The SPARQL statements can be ASK queries returning a boolean value, or SELECT queries returning the queried tokens from the semantic web.

The `spn:ArgDef` is the class for defining the name and allowed types of an argument, which can be assigned to the transitions and arcs. The name of the argument is used as the input variable in SPARQL statements.

Table 2: SPN rule components in RDFS.

Class	Property	Range	Cardinality	Description
spn:SPARQLRule	spn:hasSPARQL	xsd:string	1:1	The SPARQL statement of the rule
spn:ConstantRule	spn:hasValue	rdfs:Resource	1:1	The constant value of the rule
spn:CompoundRule	spn:operator	xsd:string	1:1	The logical operator. The allowed values are AND, OR, XOR, and NOT.
	spn:subRule	spn:Rule	1:?	The sub-rules connected by operator.
spn:ConditionRule	spn:if	spn:Rule	1:1	The "if" condition rule, which must return a boolean value.
	spn:then	spn:Rule	1:1	The "then" condition rule when "if" condition returns true.
	spn:else	spn:Rule	1:1	The "else" condition rule when "if" condition returns false.
spn:ArgDef	spn:argName	xsd:string	1:1	The argument name.
	spn:argType	rdfs:Class	0:?	Allowed argument types in a binding.

3.4 Downward Compatibility of SPN

In CPN, the tokens are unrelated and the rules are static, so that the actions in a far-away transition do not change the behavior of a local transition, which is essential for the analysis of concurrent systems. While in SPN, the latent connections between tokens are introduced from domain semantic webs, so the local behavior may change due to a far-away transition. The benefit is that the structure of the Petri-Net can be simplified without explicitly representing the coupled states. However, the downward compatibility of SPN is necessary to ensure that the concurrency analysis methods for CPN are still applicable for SPN.

The conversion of the SPN to an equivalent CPN can be inspired by the "unfolding" of a CPN to lower-level Petri-Nets. Figure 1(a) shows an example unfolding of a CPN. A colored place is represented as multiple non-colored places corresponding to each allowed color of this place. A transition with conditions can be represented as multiple sub-transitions dealing with each condition, which can always be established by listing all possible bindings due to the "finite colorset".

In this section, a three-step unfolding process for SPN is proposed for obtaining an equivalent CPN, as shown in Figure 1(b).

Step 1: putting all variables of the domain semantic web inside the SPN. This ensures a "static domain semantic web" condition, in which the latent connections in the domain semantic web are not changeable by external editing operations. This can be done by representing all variable items in the domain semantic web as LDP containers, and representing the editing operations as transitions connected to the containers, since the LDP method is recommended for maintaining variable members and relationships in a semantic web.

Step 2: splitting latent semantic connections into explicit arcs. The SPARQL rules in SPN may concern latent connected remote tokens. In the "static domain semantic web" condition, for each SPARQL rule, a finite set of concerned remote tokens can be listed, and then a finite set of concerned remote places which may contain such tokens can be listed. As a result, the latent semantic connections can be split into explicit arcs. For each remote place, a pair of arcs are added for fetching the remote tokens and sending them back to keep the remote place unchanged.

Step 3: implementing SPARQL rules in CPN. Similar to the unfolding of CPN, due to the "finite vocabulary", the SPARQL rules can always be equivalently implemented in CPN, at least by listing all possible conditions of the bindings. There are also related researches about simplified unfolding methods (Liu, et al., 2012) rather than listing the bindings, which is out of the scope of this paper.

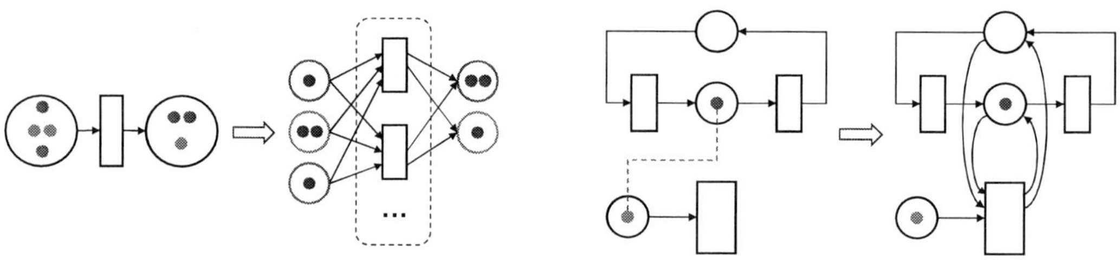

(a) unfolding a CPN to non-colored Petri-Net. (b) unfolding an SPN with latent connections to CPN.

Figure 1: Examples of unfolding CPN and SPN.

4. Application Cases

In this section, two cases are provided to demonstrate the applications of SPN in modeling state changes with dependency in the construction industry: dependency checking in the construction process, and automatic agent for building information delivery. The system is developed based on the dotNetRDF as a SPARQL query engine. The experiments are performed on a PC with a 3.60GHz processor and 16GB of physical memory.

4.1 Case 1: Dependency Checking in Construction Process

The digital twin for modeling the construction process of an asset can be represented as a spatio-temporal model in which each building object changes the state from "unbuilt" to "built". There are various dependency rules for deciding whether a state change is allowed, such as the amount of material and tools, the time period constraint, the state of host objects, or some permission files. In this section, an SPN use case is provided for modeling the construction process and checking the state change dependencies. A sample model of an office building (NIBS, 2012) is used in the experiment, as shown in Figure 2(a). The input data is a schedule of the starting and ending times for the construction phases of the levels, in which each phase corresponds to a discipline, including structure (ST), architecture (AR) and mechanical-electrical-plumbing (MEP), as shown in Figure 2(b).

(a) The sample model.

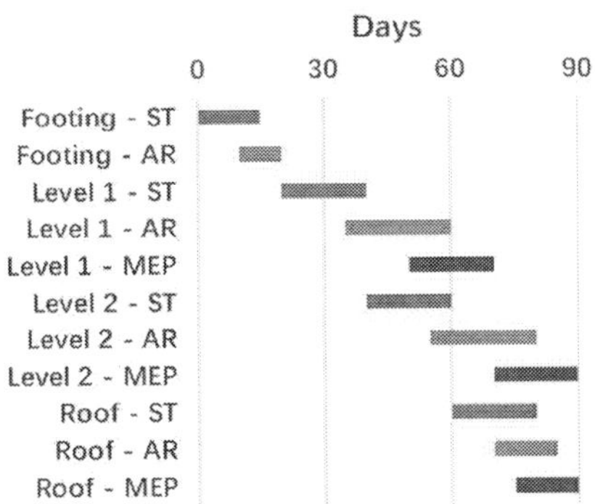

(b) The input schedule data for 4 levels.

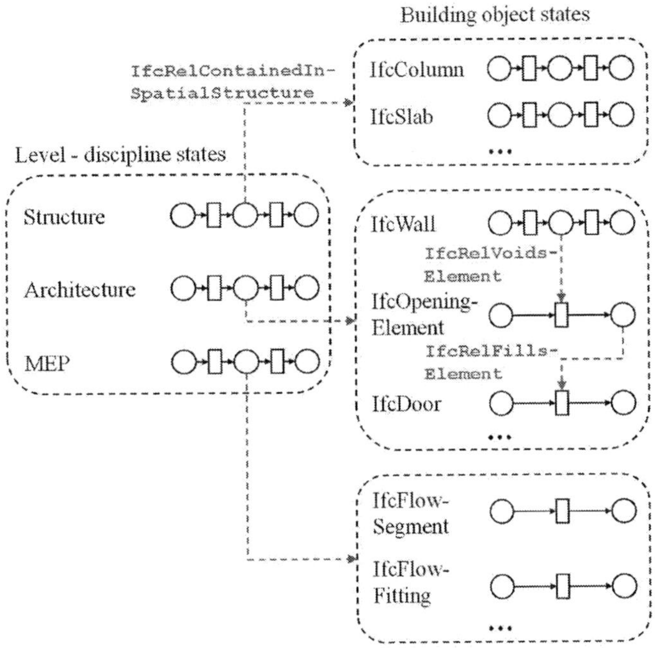

(c) The SPN structure and dependency relationships.

```
proj:T_Level_End_Struct  a                        spn:Transition;
                         bimspn:disciplineTag     "STRUCT";
                         spn:guardRule            proj:cprule_0;
                         spn:hasArg               "?TOKEN".

proj:cprule_0  a             spn:CompoundRule;
               spn:operator  "NOT";
               spn:subRule   proj:sprule_1.

proj:sprule_1  a             spn:SPARQLRule;
               spn:hasSPARQL  "ASK {
                         ?place a spn:Place.
                         ?place bimspn:disciplineTag ?dTag1.
                         ?SELF  bimspn:disciplineTag ?dTag2.
                         ?place bimspn:stateTag ?sTag.
                         FILTER (?dTag1 = ?dTag2 && ?sTag != 'END')
                         ?TOKEN ifc4:containsElements/ifc4:RelatedElements ?elem.
                         ?place ldp:contains ?elem. }".
```

(d) The RDF representation of an example transition and its guard rule nodes.

Figure 2: A use case of SPN in dependency checking in the construction process.

For each type of building objects, the states are represented as a series of places, and the dependencies are represented as the guard rules of the transitions. Small building components have two states (uninstalled and installed), and large components like walls and slabs have three states (not-started, in-processing and finished). The generated SPN structure is with 70 places and 43 transitions, as shown in Figure 2(c), with latent semantic connections as dashed arrows.

The states of the levels are concerned in the guard rules of other building objects with the "`IfcRelContainedInSpatialStructure`" relationships. The relationships between building objects are also included. For example, the openings must be installed during the construction of the host walls, and the installation of windows and doors must be after the finish of the host openings and walls. Other constraints added into the guard rules include maximum allowed tokens in each place, maximum triggering count allowed in one day for each transition, and minimum time span since the last state change for each token. In our experiment, there are in total 135 rules added to the SPN. Figure 2(d) shows the RDF representation of an example transition that ends the structure construction phase of levels, in which the guard rule requires that for each level (the "?TOKEN"), all structural objects contained in the level must be at the end place before the level is allowed to end the phase.

On initializing the model, the 4 levels and 7140 building objects from the IFC model are dispatched to the starting places as tokens. In our experiment, a clock ticks to simulate the days going by, and the guard rules are checked on each day to trigger the enabled transitions. The result shows whether the schedule is reasonable, or some sub-processes would stop with objects unfinished. In the experiment, the 90-days simulation finishes in 712 seconds with rules checked 441162 times and transitions triggered 8200 times in total.

Considering a real digital twin application, the transitions can be triggered manually or by sensors, and the guard rules are checked to ensure that the state changes are allowed, and to provide next-day recommendations according to a current state.

4.2 Case 2: Automatic Agent for Information Delivery Process

IDM is a standard method defining the process maps, use cases and information requirements in the delivery of BIM data between multiple parties. The SPN can be used to represent the process map, so that the states of the process can be queried through SPARQL. If automatic agents are included in the process map, the agent workflow can also be implemented in SPN.

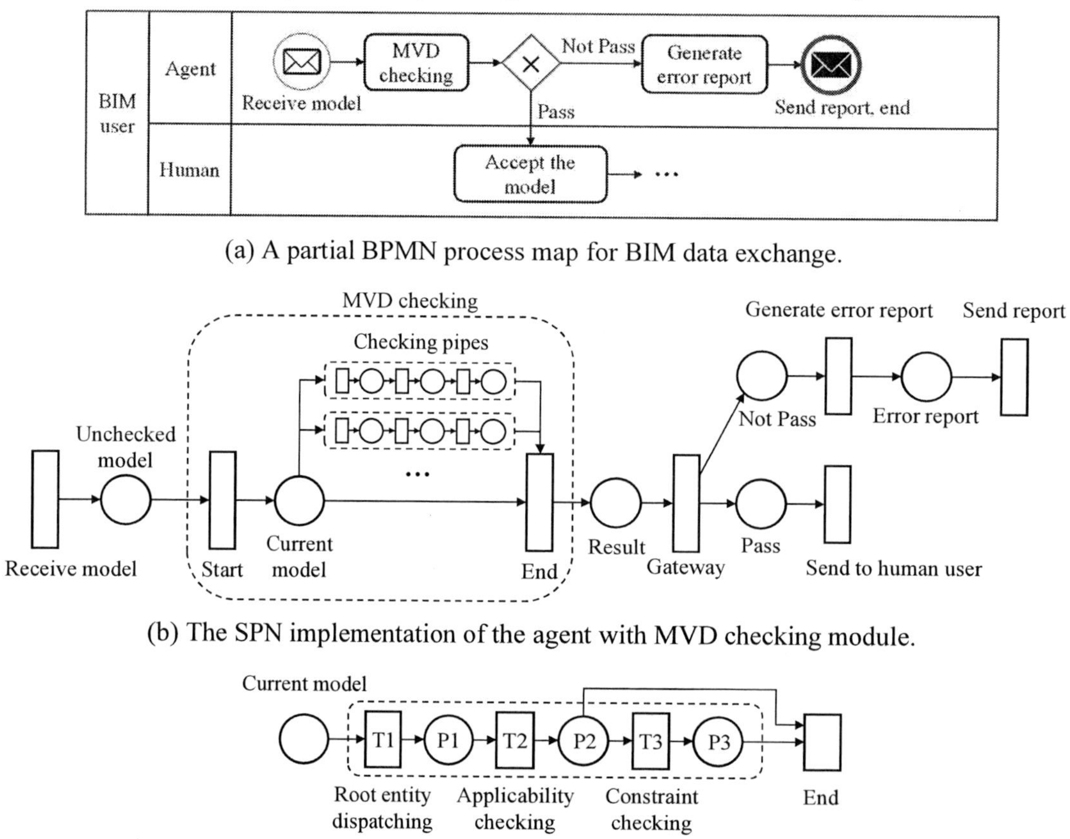

(a) A partial BPMN process map for BIM data exchange.

(b) The SPN implementation of the agent with MVD checking module.

(c) The structure of an MVD checking pipe.

Figure 3: A use case of SPN in modeling the information delivery process.

The IDM method uses Model View Definition (MVD) for checking the compliance of data with information requirements. The MVD checking can be triggered by an automatic agent. Figure 3(a) shows a partial process map of BIM data exchange, in which an agent performs MVD checking on receiving the model to decide whether accept it. Figure 3(b) is the representation of the process map in SPN. Specifically, if the data is in RDF, the MVD checker can also be implemented with SPN. Figure 3(c) is the structure of a "checking pipe" for implementing the MVD checking process. An MVD rule is composed of an applicability rule and a constraint rule for a certain type of root entities. In running a checking pipe, first, the root entities are fetched from the model into place P1; next, the applicability rule is performed to filter the applicable entities into place P2; then, the constraint rule is performed for filtering the passed entities into place P3, and leaving unpassed entities in place P2.

In our experiment, the property existence rules from IFC4 Reference View MVD (buildingSMART, 2018) are used. An SPN is generated with 119 checking pipes and 1865 rule nodes. Using the same model in Figure 2(a) as input, the checking pipes are performed concurrently and the checking task finishes in 253 seconds.

5. Conclusion and Future Work

In this paper, the SPN is proposed as a novel temporal modeling and validating method directly based on RDFS and SPARQL, which realizes two-way sharing of knowledge between domain semantic webs and temporal models in the runtime. Compared with the current semantic model checking methods for BIM data, the SPN method explores a new scenario where the rule constraints are not only about the entities and relationships, but also about the process. Several cases demonstrate the ability of SPN in integrated rule checking involving both semantic information and temporal states, which shows the possible usage in digital twins with concurrent state changes and dependencies.

One topic for future work is to improve the usability of the current method. A more user-friendly way to compose the state model and define the constraints is needed for spreading the application in real projects. Another interesting topic is applying various concurrency analyses (such as state space analysis and place invariant analysis), and also involving logical quantifiers, especially those for temporal logic (such as Linear Temporal Logic and Computation Tree Logic) in SPN models, which can be helpful in complicated digital twin applications such as resource allocation and optimization.

Acknowledgements

This work was supported by the 2019 MIIT Industrial Internet Innovation and Development Project "BIM Software Industry Standardization and Public Service Platform".

References

Pauwels, P., Zhang, S. (2015). Semantic rule-checking for regulation compliance checking: an overview of strategies and approaches. In: CIB W78, 2015, Eindhoven, Netherlands.

Beach, T.H., Rezgui, Y., Li, H., Kasim, T. (2015). A rule-based semantic approach for automated regulatory compliance in the construction sector. Expert Systems with Applications, 42(12), pp. 5219–5231.

Zhang, H., Zhao, W., Zhang, R., Liu, H., Gu, M. (2019). Semantic web based rule checking of real-world scale BIM models: a pragmatic method. In: i3CDE, 2019, Penang, Malaysia.

Battle, R., Kolas, D. (2011). Geosparql: enabling a geospatial semantic web. Semantic Web Journal, 3(4), pp. 355–370.

Zhang, C., Beetz, J., de Vries, B. (2018). BimSPARQL: Domain-specific functional SPARQL extensions for querying RDF building data. Semantic Web Journal, 9(6), pp. 829-855.

Koubarakis, M., Kyzirakos, K. (2010). Modeling and querying metadata in the semantic sensor web: the model stRDF and the query language stSPARQL. In: ESWC, 2010, Heraklion, Greece.

Mealy G.H. (1955). A method for synthesizing sequential circuits. The Bell System Technical Journal, 34(5), pp. 1045-1079.

Moore E.F. (1956). Gedanken-experiments on sequential machines. Automata Studies, 34, pp. 129-154.

Jensen K. (1987). Coloured petri nets. Petri nets: central models and their properties.

Decker, G., Dijkman, R., Dumas, M., García-Bañuelos, L. (2010). The Business Process Modeling Notation. Modern Business Process Automation, pp. 347-368.

Jensen K., Kristensen L.M. (2009). Coloured Petri nets: modelling and validation of concurrent systems.

Peterson J.L. (1980). A note on colored Petri nets. Information Processing Letters, 11(1), pp. 40-43.

Beetz, J., Van Leeuwen, J., De Vries, B. (2009). IfcOWL: A case of transforming EXPRESS schemas into ontologies. A. I. for Engineering Design, Analysis and Manufacturing, 23(1), pp. 89-101.

buildingSMART. (2010). Information Delivery Manual Guide to Components and Development Methods. https://standards.buildingsmart.org/documents/IDM/IDM_guide-CompsAndDevMethods-IDMC_004-v1_2.pdf, accessed January 2022.

Belgueliel, Y., Bourahla, M., Brik, M. (2014). Towards an ontology for UML state machines. Lecture Notes on Software Engineering, 2(1), pp. 116-120.

Natschläger, C. (2011). Towards a BPMN 2.0 ontology. In: International Workshop on Business Process Modeling Notation, 2011, Lucerne, Switzerland.

Rospocher, M., Ghidini, C., Serafini, L. (2014). An Ontology for the Business Process Modelling Notation. Formal Ontology in Information Systems, 2014, pp. 133-146.

Annane, A., Aussenac-Gilles, N., Kamel, M. (2019). BBO: BPMN 2.0 Based Ontology for Business Process Representation. In: ECKM, 2019, Lisbon, Portugal.

Gašević, D. (2004). Petri nets on the semantic web guidelines and infrastructure. Computer Science and Information Systems, 1(2), pp. 127-151.

Ma, B., Xu, Y. (2009). Integrating PNML with OWL for Petri nets. In: ICCSIT, 2009, Beijing, China.

Zhang, F., Ma, Z.M., Ribarić, S. (2011). Representation of Petri net with OWL DL ontology. In: FSKD, 2011, Shanghai, China.

Yim, J., Joo, J., Lee, G. (2011). Petri Net Representation of Ontologies for Indoor Location-Based Services. In: International Conference on Grid and Distributed Computing, 2011, Jeju Island, Korea.

Wang, Y., Bai, X., Li, J., Huang, R. (2007). Ontology-based test case generation for testing web services. In: ISADS, 2007, Sedona, United States.

Arena, D., Kiritsis, D. (2017). A methodological framework for ontology-driven instantiation of petri net manufacturing process models. In: PLM, 2017, Seville, Spain.

Szkoła, J., Pancerz, K. (2017). Petri Nets over Ontological Graphs: Conception and Application for Modelling Tasks of Robots. In: International Joint Conference on Rough Sets, 2017, Olsztyn, Poland.

Moctezuma, L.E.G., Ferrer, B.R., Xu, X., Lobov, A., Lastra, J.L.M. (2015). Knowledge-driven finite-state machines. Study case in monitoring industrial equipment. In: IEEE International Conference on Industrial Informatics, 2015, Cambridge, United Kingdom.

Hendler, J. (2001). Agents and the semantic web. IEEE Intelligent systems, 16(2), pp. 30-37.

Cheng, H., Ma, Z. (2016). A literature overview of knowledge sharing between Petri nets and ontologies. The Knowledge Engineering Review, 31(3), pp. 239-260.

W3C. (2015). Linked Data Platform 1.0. https://www.w3.org/TR/ldp/, accessed January 2022.

Liu, F., Heiner, M., Yang, M. (2012). An efficient method for unfolding colored Petri nets. In: Winter Simulation Conference (WSC), 2012, Berlin, Germany.

NIBS. (2012). Common Building Information Model Files and Tools. https://www.wbdg.org/bim/cobie/common-bim-files, accessed January 2022.

buildingSMART. (2018). ReferenceView_V1-1. https://github.com/buildingSMART/IfcDoc/blob/master/IfcKit/exchanges/reference/ReferenceView_V1-1.mvdxml, accessed January 2022.

A Comprehensive Data Schema for Digital Twin Construction

Schlenger J.[1] , Yeung T.[2] , Vilgertshofer S.[1] , Martinez J.[2] , Sacks R.[2] , Borrmann A.[1]
[1]Technical University of Munich, Germany, [2]Israel Institute of Technology, Israel
jonas.schlenger@tum.de

Abstract. Lean construction, originating from lean management, aims to proactively improve the overall efficiency of construction processes. This requires continuous assessment of performance to identify key problems, which allows continuous improvement of construction processes. Novel digital twin approaches form an excellent technological foundation for performance assessment through regular updates with product and process information directly from the construction site. While some publications favour a schema-less approach to digital twins, we argue that well-defined data structures are required to represent complex information reliably and transparently. Existing process and product models are inadequate with respect to the requirements of a digital twin of the construction phase. As a result, we introduce a new process-oriented model that provides an improved basis for advanced process evaluation in the digital twin environment. This data schema, which is the main outcome of this paper, is presented in UML format together with a first approach to transfer it to an ontology usable in the Semantic Web context.

1. Introduction

In the last few decades, digital twins have become a rapidly growing field of interest in industry and academia in several domains. Just recently, they found their way to the construction sector. Here, a digital twin is understood as the digital replica of a real-world physical construction asset, updated at regular intervals to reflect any changes to the asset (Bolton et al. 2018). Many existing approaches focus on either the design phase, where BIM tools are applied to create digital prototypes, or the operational phase, where sensor data available on IoT platforms is evaluated to monitor parameters relevant to building operations (Jones et al., 2020). The construction phase, however, was missing a digital twin that gives a comprehensive overview of the entire project. Sacks et al. (2020) were among the first researchers to approach this topic holistically. They envision a digital twin of the whole construction project to gain situational awareness during the complete construction phase and thus, to support a full-cycle lean model of planning and control.

Although monitoring construction products is essential in building situational awareness, capturing the construction processes is at least as critical, and perhaps more so. Due to the dynamic nature and dependence of production activities on multiple input flows (e.g., components and materials, information, equipment, and availability of space), their execution in practice is often far from optimal. Accurate situational awareness is crucial for good production planning and control that can manage the input flows reliably (Koskela, 2000).

While some publications favour a schema-less approach to digital twins (El-Diraby, 2021; Miloslavskaya and Tolstoy, 2016), we argue that well-defined data structures are required to represent complex information in a reliable and transparent manner. This is indispensable for construction performance evaluation and assessment of the execution of construction processes. Currently, there is no standard data model established in the context of digital twins in construction (Akanmu, Anumba and Ogunseiju, 2021). Existing product and process model data schemata (buildingSMART International, 2021; Rasmussen et al., 2020; Bonduel, 2021; Zheng, Törmä and Seppänen, 2021) lack completeness with respect to the requirements of a digital twin of the construction phase.

https://doi.org/10.7146/aul.455.c194

The overall aim of this study is to introduce a model schema that allows easy comparison of the intent and status of a digital twin of a construction site, which sets the basis for calculating performance-related indicators like cycle times, work in progress, throughput, and others (Sacks, 2016). In contrast to existing models, the differences between project intent and status should be carefully addressed. The process model schema does not purport to give a complete view of the construction project but instead proposes a set of core classes that can be used for a wide range of digital twin use cases. In this way, it shall be used as a foundation to be further extended by partial models for domain-specific use cases. With the help of real-world monitoring data organized in this model, one can detect or even anticipate patterns of activities and thus work proactively to initiate timely countermeasures. The scope of the developed schema is limited to building projects. Linear infrastructure projects differ significantly in their process workflows and related data schema requirements. For this reason, they are outside the scope of this paper.

The theoretical background of the paper is set with an introduction to the use of Semantic Web Technologies in the civil engineering domain and the state of the art of process and product models in Section 2. Subsequently, the methodology applied to develop a process-oriented data schema is described in Section 3. This schema is presented in close detail in Section 4, comprising both the planned project intent and the project status of the actual execution, including the first steps on how to transfer the process-oriented model to Semantic Web Technologies. The paper closes off with a discussion on the model's limitations in Section 5 and a conclusion containing a summary and future works in Section 6.

2. Theoretical Background

2.1 Semantic Web in the Realm of Civil Engineering

The Digital Twin Construction, which refers to a mode of construction management supported by digital twins, defined by Sacks et al. (2020) adopts a holistic approach to the digital twin concept. This entails capturing data from multiple sources that vary highly in their nature and the way they are captured. Useful information about project status is obtained by fusing and interpreting several data streams simultaneously. In such a multi-data environment, interconnecting these various types of data in a meaningful way is challenging. Interoperability, in general, is a well-known issue in the civil engineering domain. The great number of stakeholders in a singular construction project presents a significant challenge in communication and data exchange and makes interoperability an essential factor in further optimization and improvement of the whole construction workflow. As a possible solution for data connection and interoperability, Semantic Web Technologies (SWT) comprising Linked Data are an active area of research in the construction sector (Pauwels et al., 2017).

Tim Berners-Lee (2009) introduced the Semantic Web concept with Linked Data as a subpart in the early 2000's. His idea lies in overcoming the disadvantages of the decentralized structure of storing data on the web by linking and sharing it. This is done using structured, directed graphs. Since its invention, the Semantic Web has established a set of standards and functionalities. Included are, e.g., OWL, SHACL, and SPARQL that allow knowledge inference, reasoning, rule checking, and data querying. Furthermore, RDF provides the basis to store, interlink, and exchange data in graph form. All of these standards are not only useful in the web context but can also be applied to use cases that require another form of interlinking data belonging to different sources (W3C, 2019).

In their literature review, Pauwels et al. (2017) discussed how the Semantic Web concept is applied in the AEC industry. Here, linking data across domains is identified as one of the three main advantages that justify SWT usage. The Semantic Web standards could provide a good foundation for interoperability in the digital twin environment that requires interconnected data. With the use of ontologies, data becomes machine-readable and machine-interpretable, which is a great advantage when working with big data.

2.2 Existing Process and Product Data Models

There are various already existing product and process data models tailored for the civil engineering domain. The most suited ones are introduced briefly and compared against the requirements for application in the process-oriented digital twin context.

The Industry Foundation Classes (IFC) developed by buildingSMART International (2021) are a well-known and internationally used standard for data exchange of construction-related information. It supports multiple serializations, with the most common one being the EXPRESS format for the definition of the IFC schema and STEP files for instantiation. Among others, a mapping to IfcOWL was developed, replicating the EXPRESS schema in an OWL ontology (Pauwels and Terkaj, 2016). One of the characteristics of IFC is the rich variety of geometry representations ranging from boundary representations to procedural descriptions including CSG and sweeping operations. The representation chosen for a concrete exchange depends on the purpose of the data handover: explicit representations are used for pure checking and analysis tasks, while procedural representations allow modifications on the receiving side.

The large number of possibilities to represent geometries make the IFC format a powerful, but extensive schema and increases its complexity significantly. Its complex structure and lack of modularity are some of the most criticized aspects (van Berlo et al., 2021). Regarding semantic information, IFC contains classes for comparatively fine-grained categorizations. A minimal set of classes is provided for process information, e.g., the *IfcTask*, which can be understood as any kind of construction process. Such a task can be connected to a respective building element, a set of other tasks in a specific order, or *IfcResources* representing the required resources of the construction task. According to the authors' experience, the process part of the IFC format is, however, barely used in practice. Furthermore, the IFC format exclusively considers information about the planning phase, so to say as-designed and as-planned data. There is no straightforward way to include as-built and as-performed data, which is essential for the digital twin context. Although simple processes can be represented in an ordered sequence, the construction digital twin environment demands representation of dynamic schedule changes, where task prerequisites play an essential role in rescheduling (Dori, 2015). In the current version of IFC, such task dependencies cannot be modeled appropriately. As the building element subpart of IfcOWL with some minor extensions, the Building Element Ontology (BEO) allows more flexible use but is still limited to product information (Pauwels, 2018).

Getuli (2019) developed an extension for IFC to support the scheduling construction processes better. His work is based on IfcOWL, which he extended with four new sub-ontologies for construction time, construction workspace, buildings, and construction scheduling. Even though they significantly improve the modeling of construction processes, the fundamental IFC issues - its complexity and focus on the as-planned side - persist. Additionally, the IfcOWL extension is not available online, making the reuse of the defined classes challenging.

In contrast to IFC, the Building Topology Ontology (BOT) by Rasmussen (2020) is a minimal ontology, exclusively focusing on the building elements and their subcomponents and the ways in which they relate to one another. With fewer than 25 classes and properties, it is meant to be combined with domain-specific data models. Its most important classes are the zones to define spatial areas, like buildings, spaces, and stories, the building elements contained in them, and the interfaces between them. It is not specifically designed for either as-designed or as-built construction, but can be used in both contexts. For Digital Twin Construction, it is clearly missing the process-related portion and further requires additional distinctions between as-designed and as-built information. Nevertheless, it provides high-level classes that can be the basis for a wide range of use cases.

Both BOT and IFC are stand-alone models, whereas Bonduel (2021) introduces an extensive ontology network. His framework builds a common foundation for combining data from different stakeholders belonging to build heritage use cases. He combines various existing ontologies with newly created ontologies to cover many aspects of built heritage-related information. Contrary to the IFC model, the focus lies on representing the as-built context and its decay over time. For building elements and zones, the BOT ontology is coupled with ontologies that allow to add geometric information to the building elements. Additionally, national and international taxonomies for furniture, building elements, and MEP elements are used for further specification. The Construction Tasks Ontology (CTO) is used for modeling processes, defining five types of tasks (maintenance, repair, inspection, removal, and installation). These classes are designed for maintenance tasks during the operational phase but are not well suited for the construction phase. The absence of definitions of construction resources and task prerequisites further affirms this statement. To differentiate between project intent and status, the context class is provided to group entities accordingly. However, it is highly questionable if the same set of classes can adequately describe both intent and status.

Finally, the Digital Construction Ontologies (DiCon) (Zheng 2021) are an ontology looking at construction and renovation tasks, with a focus on construction planning during the complete building lifecycle from construction to demolition. It considers the different types of flows that are relevant for construction processes. These are the labor performed by agents, construction equipment, workspace, construction components like building elements, information entities, external conditions, and prerequisite tasks. Overall, this enables a detailed description of process input and output. It also uses the context concept to represent as-planned and as-performed indirectly. On the other hand, the processes themselves are represented only in a generic way with so-called object activities, which can be any activity related to any type of entity. For more detailed process types, DiCon refers to OmniClass, Uniformat, and Talo2000. Nevertheless, this does not allow structuring of construction processes hierarchically. Like the built heritage BIM framework, the context class allows grouping object instances to either the as-planned or the as-performed side of the construction data.

To summarize, there are various already existing data models specific to the civil engineering domain. While the majority of them focus on construction products, some also represent construction management and processes. Although there are possibilities to assign data to a specific context (e.g., as-planned and as-performed context), they fail to address differences that do exist between data from the design and the construction phase. Currently, there is no data model that represents construction processes considering digital twin use cases and copes with varying requirements for project intent and status.

3. Schema Development

A schema development approach similar to Zheng, Törmä and Seppänen (2021) has been applied as a research methodology. It includes four steps for developing a data model: specification, knowledge acquisition, implementation, and validation. Although this approach is tailored to developing ontologies, it also suits data modelling purposes. First, the overall goals and requirements of the process model were specified. There are already product models in various complexities specific to the civil engineering domain like the Building Topology Ontology (BOT) and IFC, which is not the case for process models. Currently, no existing schema covers the core classes required for construction performance evaluation, including the construction intent as well as the construction status. Therefore, the goal was to fill this gap with a lightweight schema that is meant to be extended with domain-specific classes.

Furthermore, the authors decided to organize the overall data in three layers, according to Ackoff (1989). These three layers: data, information, and knowledge, can be seen as horizontal layers of a pyramid where the end-user value and conciseness of the data increase from bottom to top. For a digital twin in construction, the data layer will include point clouds, sensor data, pictures from the construction site, and other raw data, as it is generated by various devices. Information is then gained mainly through the statistical and arithmetical analysis of data, e.g., by extracting the as-built geometry of a building element from a large point cloud. Through further evaluation and interpretation, one acquires knowledge like key performance indicators (KPIs), delays in the construction schedule, and prominent issues that help construction managers to get a condensed overview of the project. The model presented below concerns the middle layer, the information layer. For the raw data layer, simple data structures already suffice. For this purpose, existing ontologies like SOSA and SSN can be reused to define monitoring devices together with the data they capture and additional metadata (Janowicz et al., 2019). The knowledge layer, however, requires global reasoning on the lower-level information, which first requires an adequate representation of the information layer.

With the overall goal set, a literature review was conducted to identify existing process and product models in the realm of civil engineering, as described in Section 2.3. Furthermore, the schema development was heavily based on the results from the online questionnaires and expert interviews executed by Torres et al. (2021). They identified an optimal construction workflow enabled by digital twin construction by interviewing a wide range of personnel involved in construction projects. The questions targeted the main inefficiencies of construction processes, possible ways to counteract these, and the data required from construction sites to monitor the status of construction processes in real-time. Their results were further used by Mediavilla et al. (2021) to derive main semantic concepts (with their relationships) in a top-down approach. We developed the digital twin construction data schema introduced in Section 4 in a bottom-up approach based on these two reports. During the development, close attention was put on identifying overlaps and differences with existing process and product models to align the new model with the current state-of-the-art.

4. Digital Twin Process Model as a Basis for Advanced Performance Evaluation

The data model for Digital Twin Construction is divided into two parts. On the one hand side, there are the classes related to the as-planned information (Figure 1). These describe the intent, which can be understood as the future state of the construction project formulated in plans and schedules. On the other hand, there are the classes relevant for the as-performed status of the project (Figure 2). Here, only the information about the present status of the executed processes are considered. Where as-planned and as-performed refer to processes, equivalent terms exist for product information. In this case, as-designed represents the product intent and as-built the product status. Since products result from the corresponding processes, they form a subpart of the respective as-planned or as-performed model side (Sacks, 2020).

Some classes are used on both sides of the model since they do not differ in their attributes, but only in the attribute values of the class instances. Others are represented through separate distinctly named classes because status and intent require differing attributes. Furthermore, additional classes only exist on one side of the model, e.g. defects of building elements are only part of the project status since they are not planned upfront. For this reason, the two sides of the model should be understood as two information containers that partially share classes.

Although the model is presented in two parts, there are clear connections between them that are omitted in Figures 1 and 2 for clarity. The classes *site*, *building*, *storey* and *space* form a bridge between as-planned and as-performed because they are not expected to be influenced by the process execution on-site but hold true for project status and intent. Furthermore, *resource* and *zone* form common parent classes for the context-specific subclasses. Moreover, every class from the as-planned side directly connects to its equivalent class on the as-performed side. Any deviation between the two would be stored in the knowledge layer because global reasoning could be required to assess the difference between an as-planned product and its corresponding as-performed process.

4.1 Core Data Model Classes

All in all, the model classes can be grouped into four main categories. First, there are the classes that represent the construction processes. Second, the resources that are used by the processes. Third, the products that are the end result of the processes, and fourth, the working zones where the processes are executed. This again shows the strong orientation for processes of the developed model. The following section explains the four groups of classes in more detail and discusses their differences between the as-planned and the as-performed model sides.

Processes: The processes are the central part of the model and can be found in the middle part of Figures 1 and 2. They are organized on three levels, starting on the left side with the most general level up until the most low-level information on the right-hand side. On the most general level, there is the *work package*. It holds information about the used construction method and can be seen as an aggregation of more detailed processes. On the level below, there is the *activity*. Every *work package* consists of multiple *activities,* where the *activity* describes one construction step to build one or a group of objects, like placing formwork or pouring concrete. Each *activity* is further dissected into *tasks*, where each *task* represents an *activity* related to a singular *building element* or *building element part*. *Preconditions* can be connected to *activities* and *tasks* that describe the requirements of a process to support the proactive make-ready steps of lean construction. There are various types of *preconditions*, e.g., a *zone* that needs to be available or another process that needs to be finished beforehand. All types of preconditions can be found in Figure 1 directly to the right of the process classes. Where the as-planned processes hold details about long-term averaged performance factors dependent on the construction company, the construction method, and the project's particularities (Hofstadler, 2007), the as-performed processes (*construction*, *operation*, and *action*) need to support short-term performance evaluation. Fine-grained insight into performance variation and process disruption allows the development of timely countermeasures to improve the overall construction performance.

Products: In terms of products, the model contains *building elements* and *building element parts* (see lower right corner of Figures 1 and 2). This possibility of decomposition should be highly oriented towards the corresponding processes, e.g. a wall with multiple layers that are constructed in separated steps should have its layers represented as *building element parts*. On the contrary, a window that might consist of various parts but is entirely installed by a single *task* should be represented by a single *building element* without multiple parts. However, the level of granularity of the just mentioned decomposition is one of the main modeling challenges and needs to be carefully chosen according to the present use case. The same applies to the granularity of the construction processes. The *building elements* are logically organized according to the overall spatial structure of the building with the classes in the lower left corner of both figures. Here the project is broken down into the *site*, one or multiple *buildings*, their *storeys*, and their *spaces*. Depending on its type, a *building element* is either associated to a *space*, e.g., a specific room or to a complete *storey*. None of these classes hold geometric information but only indicate the general building breakdown. There are no significant differences between the as-designed and as-built sides regarding required attributes. Therefore, the same classes are used for both sides of the model. To tell the class instances apart nevertheless, the Boolean attribute *IsAsDesigned* is introduced.

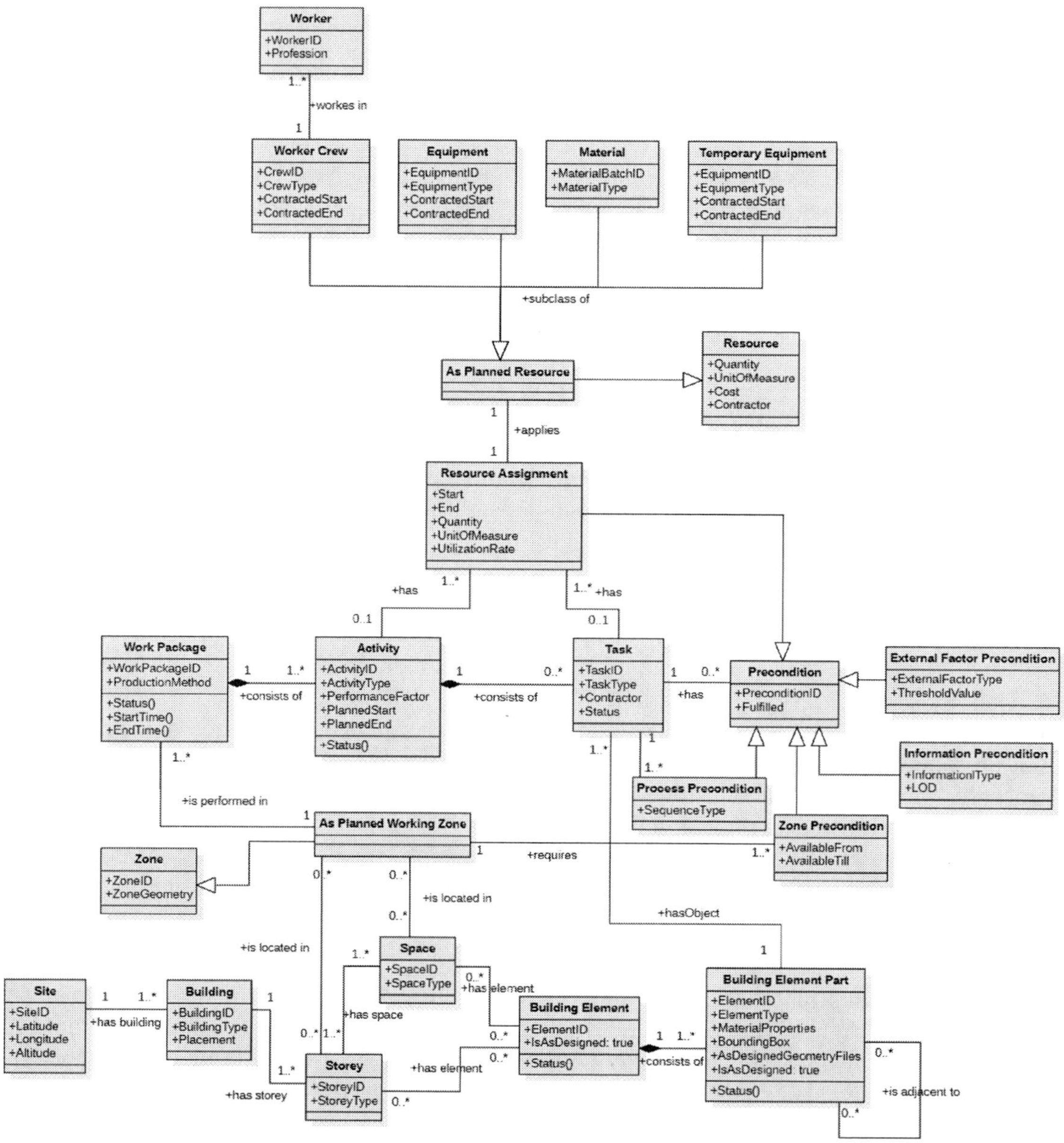

Figure 1: UML model of the project intent information (as-designed and as-planned).

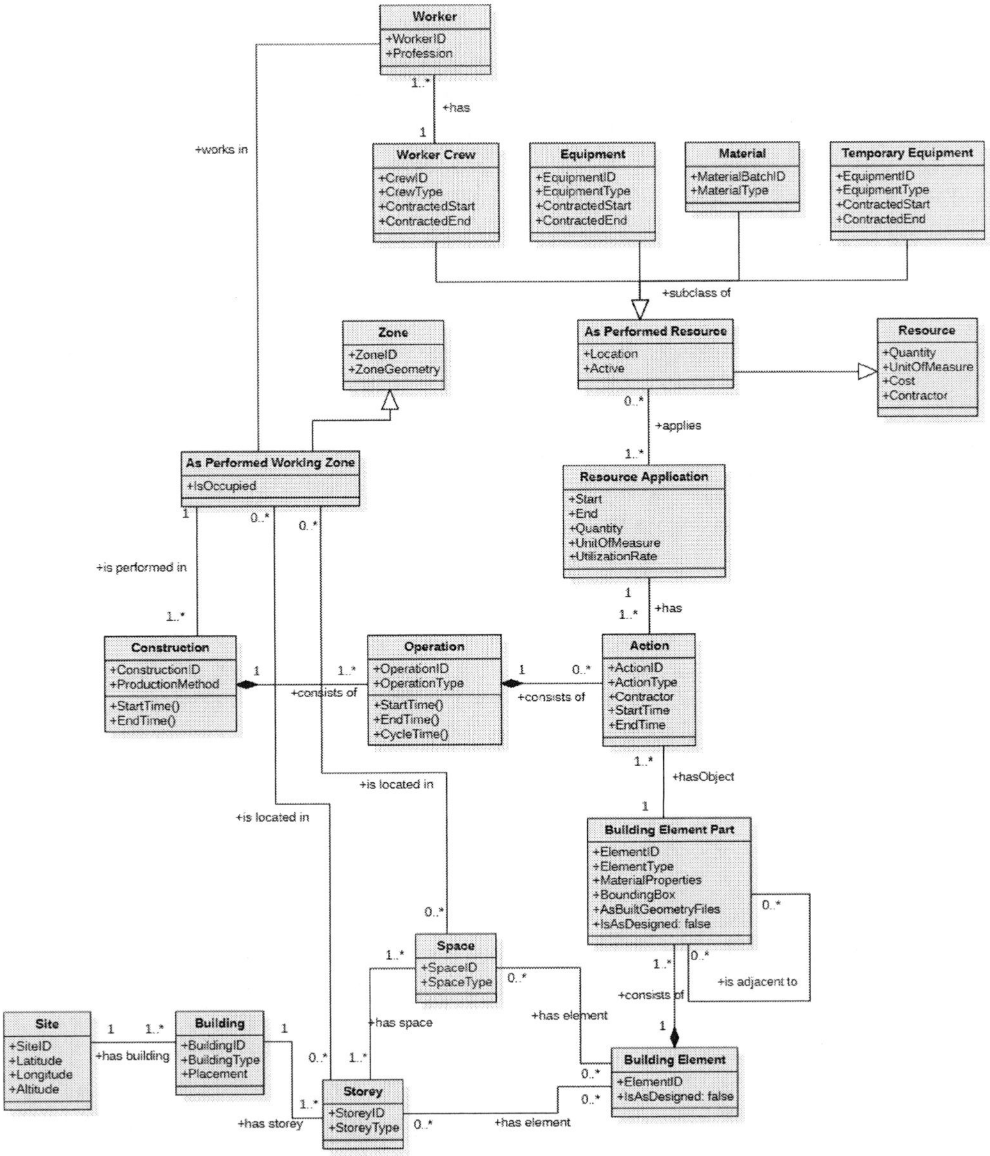

Figure 2: UML model of the project status information (as-built and as-performed).

Resources: In the presented model, the *resources* are all persons or physical things that are required during a process to build a specific *building element.* They are grouped into four classes. These are the labor force in the form of *worker crews*, *equipment* like heavy machinery and small tools, *materials*, and *temporary equipment* like formwork and guardrails. All resource classes, together with their parent classes, are located in the top section of Figures 1 and 2. It is essential to note the difference between the *resource assignment* and the *resources*. The *resource assignment* represents the *resources* required by a specific process, whereas the *resource* classes are used to model the amount of resources existing on the construction site (planned or performed). In this way, a *resource* instance can be connected to multiple *resource assignments.* The *resource assignment* is replaced with the *resource application* on the as-performed side of the model. The *resources* also differ between as-planned and as-performed because, during execution, exact location and current activity/ inactivity are available, which are not planned in this detail ahead of time.

Zones: Finally, the *zones* enable modeling of the location breakdown structure of the construction project. Every *zone* represents a spatial area where construction is executed. For this reason, the *zone* is directly connected to the processes. Unlike the *space* and *storey*, the *zones* do have geometric information. In some cases, a *zone* might be equivalent to a *storey*, or a *space*, but a direct relationship is not always given. Overall, the *zones* are an essential indicator of the construction flow because flow can be judged on the occupation rate of worker crew and flow of materials but also on the occupancy of working locations (Sacks, 2016).

4.2 BIM2TWIN Core Ontology

As discussed in Section 2.1, the Linked Data concept is suited well for the digital twin context, which requires uniting data from various sources. In addition, when sharing data across digital twins, the interoperability provided by the Semantic Web Technologies gains even greater importance. For this reason, the first steps for converting the presented data model into an ontology that can be used in the Linked Data context are provided. Reusing existing ontologies is a central idea in the Semantic Web. Therefore, one should evaluate thoroughly which classes can be reused from existing ontologies and which should be created newly.

The BIM2TWIN Core Ontology was developed completely based on the UML diagrams presented in Section 4.1. All classes, relationships, and class attributes were translated into the corresponding ontology classes, object properties, and data properties. Only domains and ranges of object and data properties were defined to allow other researchers and practitioners to reuse the B2T Core Ontology without restricting them too much in the application. The cardinalities were not integrated into the ontology to broaden the application range.

Within the B2T Core Ontology, several existing ontologies are reused. Most importantly, the lightweight BOT ontology, which closely resembles the structure of building elements organized in spaces, storeys, and buildings, is completely integrated into B2T Core. However, the process classes did not coincide with the definitions in existing ontologies and were modelled with entirely new classes. Finally, the resources required a mixed approach, with some classes reused from DiCon and others added newly. In terms of object and data properties, several other ontologies could be reused: Basis Geo WGS84 for spatial referencing, QUDT for representing units of literals, and OWL Time for all time-related attributes. While the first preliminary version of the B2T Core ontology is finished, further refinement regarding alignment with existing ontologies is required before the ontology can be published. Publishing the ontology in a well-documented form is the next goal, which will be part of future work.

5. Discussion

Even though a data model that serves as a basis for advanced performance evaluation was presented, this forms only the first step in reaching the goal of facilitating process assessment. The actual data structure to organize performance indicators is part of the knowledge layer of Ackoff's data pyramid, which the present paper has not touched. However, a solid foundation has been set in presenting a set of core classes that represent the essential parts of the information layer in the required level of detail. A data model alone, without any data, is useless. Since the data model breaks down processes in a fine-grained process network, it will be a significant challenge to collect sufficiently detailed process-related data from construction projects. Doing this in a mainly automated way without interrupting the ongoing construction process is still a great challenge that is not yet resolved in the current state-of-the-art.

Furthermore, finding the right granularity of processes and products is a task that the model leaves to the data modeler. Regarding the proposed ontology, an initial concept was introduced. To be used properly, it still needs further refinement and thorough documentation. According to adhere to Semantic Web principles only once this is done, can the ontology be published online.

6. Conclusion

Digital twin concepts together with lean construction principles are promising approaches to raise a project's efficiency and lift the design and operation phases but also the execution phase to the next level. Tackling the execution phase of building projects in a holistic approach will require clear data structures to be able to extract meaningful information and knowledge. Existing data models lack relevant aspects of the process analysis with a digital twin of construction. A thorough process description with input and output flows and process prerequisites is required for dynamic rescheduling. Also, the distinction between as-planned and as-performed processes is an essential part of it.

The present paper introduced a novel process model tailored to building projects that serves as a foundation for advanced construction performance evaluation, fulfilling all of the mentioned requirements. It defines a core set of classes that can be accompanied by domain-specific extensions. Moreover, a concept was developed to translate the process-oriented model into an ontology that can be used in the semantic web context. However, the data model has not been applied yet in a real-world digital twin scenario. Therefore, it will be the highest priority to carry out a test study that thoroughly evaluates the model's performance and compares it to other alternatives. Additionally, the model is limited exclusively to the execution phase. During the operational phase, a similar performance evaluation can be conducted. Extending the model by classes specific to the operational phase and allowing a smooth transition from the execution to the operation phase could also be interesting for future work. Further extension and adaption of the model should also be dedicated to linear infrastructure projects like rails, roads, and tunnels whose process workflows vastly differ from conventional high-rise buildings and are currently not covered. Finally, the first concepts to apply the data model to the semantic web context were executed. Still, they will require further work to result in a publicly available ontology that complies with linked data standards.

7. Acknowledgement

The research described in this paper has received funding from the European Union's Horizon 2020 research and innovation programme under grant agreement no. 958398, "BIM2TWIN: Optimal Construction Management & Production Control". The authors thankfully acknowledge the support of the European Commission in funding this project.

References

Ackoff, R. (1989). From data to wisdom - Presidential address to ISGSR, June 1988. *Journal of Applied Systems Analysis*, Vol. 16, pp. 3–9.

Akanmu, A.A., Anumba, C.J. and Ogunseiju, O.O. (2021). Towards next generation cyber-physical systems and digital twins for construction. *J. Inf. Technol. Constr.*, Vol. 26, pp. 505–525.

Berners-Lee, T. (2009). Linked Data - Design Issues. Available at: https://www.w3.org/DesignIssues /LinkedData.html (Accessed Jan. 05, 2022).

Bolton, A., Butler, L., Dabson, I., Enzer, M., Evans, M., Fenemore, T., Harradence, F., Keaney, E., Kemp, A., Luck, A., Pawsey, N., Saville, S., Schooling, J., Sharp, M., Smith, T., Tennison, J., Whyte, J., Wilson, A. and Makri, C. (2018). Gemini Principles. Apollo – University of Cambridge Repository, Cambridge, UK, https://doi.org/10.17863/CAM.32260.

Bonduel, M. (2021). A Framework for a Linked Data-based Heritage BIM. PhD thesis, Katholieke Universiteit Leuven – Faculty of Engineering Technology, Leuven, Belgium.

buildingSMART International (2021). IFC Schema Specifications Database Website, https://technical.buildingsmart.org/standards/ifc/ifc-schema-specifications/, accessed November 2021.

Dori, G. (2015). Simulation-based methods for float time determination and schedule optimization for construction projects. PhD thesis, Technical University of Munich – Chair of Computational Modeling and Simulation, Munich, Germany.

El-Diraby, T. (2021). Can IFC (mentality) be the basis of digital twins? No. *Keynote talk at the 38th Int. Conference of CIB W78 2021.*

Getuli, V. and Capone, P. (2019). Ontology-based modeling for construction site planning: Towards an ifcOWL semantic enrichment. *36th Int. Conference of CIB W78*, pp. 701–713.

Hofstadler, C. (2007), Bauablaufplanung und Logistik im Baubetrieb. Springer-Verlag Berlin Heidelberg, 2007.

Janowicz, K., Haller, A., Cox, S., Le Phuoc, D. and Lefrançois, M. (2019) SOSA: A lightweight ontology for sensors, observations, samples, and actuators. *J. Web Semant.*, Vol. 56, pp. 1-10.

Jones, D., Snider, C., Nassehi, A., Yon, J. and Hicks, B. (2021). Characterising the Digital Twin: A systematic literature review. *CIRP J. Manuf. Sci. Technol.*, Vol. 29, pp. 36-52.

Koskela, L. (2000). An exploration towards a production theory and its application to construction. PhD thesis, Helsinki University of Technology, Espoo, Finland.

Mediavilla, A., San Mateos, R. and Torres, J. (2021). Definition of the digital workflows for the construction process (Deliverable 1.2). EU Horizon 2020 BIM2TWIN.

Miloslavskaya, N. and Tolstoy, A. (2016). Big Data, Fast Data and Data Lake Concepts. *7th Annual Int. Conference on Biologically Inspired Cognitive Architectures*, vol. 88, pp. 300–305.

Pauwels, P. and Terkaj, W. (2016). EXPRESS to OWL for construction industry: Towards a recommendable and usable ifcOWL ontology. *Automation in Construction*, vol. 63, pp. 100–133.

Pauwels, P. (2018). Building Element Ontology. Available at: https://pi.pauwel.be/voc/buildingelement/index-en.html (Accessed Feb. 02, 2022).

Pauwels, P., Zhang, S. and Lee, Y.C. (2017). Semantic web technologies in AEC industry: A literature overview. *Automation in Construction*, Vol. 73, pp. 145–165, doi: 10.1016/j.autcon.2016.10.003.

Rasmussen, M.H., Lefrançois, M., Schneider, G.F. and Pauwels, P. (2020) BOT: The building topology ontology of the W3C linked building data group. *Semantic Web*, Vol. 12(1), pp. 143-161.

Sacks, R. (2016). What constitutes good production flow in construction? *Construction Management and Economics*, Vol. 34(9), pp. 641-656.

Sacks, R., Brilakis, I., Pikas, E., Xie, H.S. and Girolami, M. (2020). Construction with digital twin information systems. *Data-Centric Engineering*, Vol. 1(e14), pp. 1-26.

Torres, J., San Mateos, R., Lasarte, N., Gonzalo Pinto, H., Noiray, F., Alhava, O., Tual, M. and Velasquez, S. (2021). D1.1 - As-is analysis and end-user requirements. EU Horizon 2020 BIM2TWIN.

Van Berlo, L., Krijnen, T., Tauscher, H., Liebich, T., van Kranenburg, A. and Paasiala, P. (2021). Future of the Industry Foundation Classes: towards IFC 5. *38th Int. Conference of CIB W78*, pp. 123-137.

W3C (2019). Semantic Web Wiki. Available at: https://www.w3.org/2001/sw/wiki/Main_Page (Accessed Jan. 05, 2022).

Zheng, Y., Törmä, S. and Seppänen, O. (2021). A shared ontology suite for digital construction workflow. *Automation in Construction*, Vol. 132, pp. 1-23.

Requirements for event-driven architectures in open BIM collaboration

Esser, S., Abualdenien, J., Vilgertshofer, S., Borrmann, A.
Technical University of Munich, Germany
sebastian.esser@tum.de

Abstract. Current practice of BIM-based collaboration relies on the exchange of entire domain models, which are managed and shared using Common Data Environments. Such platforms are well standardized in terms of states, roles, and participants. However, the coordination of changes by exchanging entire models requires manual identification of any added, modified, or deleted information from one shared version to another. This paper proposes the application of an event-driven system architecture, which is in widespread use in modern communication systems. Combining the publish-subscribe design pattern, patch-based update mechanisms for BIM models, and the established concept of asynchronous, decentralized collaboration in BIM projects can significantly ease the process of understanding design changes and reduce the overall overhead of information already shared in previous versions among project members.

1. Introduction

A major advantage of the Building Information Modeling (BIM) methodology is to facilitate collaboration and coordination among the various domain experts in designing and constructing built assets. In today's practice, reflected in ISO 19650, data management in BIM projects is realized through Common Data Environments (CDE). While the standard does not define the technical implementation, a typical CDE is a web application with centralized file storage for sharing model files and associated documents. Domain experts involved in a project can upload and download files from and to the CDE. It is important to note that current BIM practice relies on the notion of federated domain models (such as architectural, structural, and electrical models) as specified in ISO 19650 (CEN, 2018). Accordingly, no overall model is collaboratively edited, but each domain creates individual models and coordinates them with other parties in discrete time intervals. Currently, this federation concept is realized by uploading information containers comprising entire domain models (typically in an open BIM format) to a CDE. However, today's practice entails significant limitations, as modifications cannot be tracked for individual objects, forcing all collaborators to perform global checks for potential coordination with their domain models.

Numerous studies over the past decades have highlighted the advantages of vendor-neutral data exchange over closed-BIM solutions (Shafiq et al., 2012; Solihin et al., 2016; Zhang et al., 2015). Design processes are often multi-disciplinary and iterative, demanding the use and integration of various design and simulation tools. Thus, novel methods for distributing design changes are highly required to support decisions and project management. Currently available open-BIM solutions can only facilitate exchanging complete BIM files rather than specific changes on object level, which impedes a seamless integration and evaluation of the exchanged updates.

To overcome this deficiency, a patch-based update mechanism can be used to track model modifications on object level representing them as graph-based transformations (Esser et al., 2021). A core requirement of realizing such a decentralized object synchronization system lies in a suitable network architecture and adequate communication protocols. Advanced techniques of distributed computing systems appear promising as various protocols support bidirectional

https://doi.org/10.7146/aul.455.c195

and asynchronous communication, particularly relevant for the fragmented construction industry with highly specialized domains.

This paper proposes an event-based mechanism to transfer update patches among project stakeholders and highlights different protocols that support bidirectional communication in a distributed, asynchronous environment. The approach enhances the information value of BIM-based exchange workflows because it provides direct access to the modifications, which helps to assess the impact on other domain models. Nevertheless, it is essential to state that each domain will continue authoring individual domain models, which other parties should use for reference purposes. The benefits of the proposed approach are twofold: First, clear authorship for each dataset shared within a project remains existing. Second, the proposed system reduces the overall data exchange and simplifies the evaluation of shared modifications as each party can register itself for events relevant to its design and simulation tasks. Furthermore, the subscription to specific change events assists in raising alerts to the user in case of critical updates that affect interdisciplinary dependencies.

2. Existing approaches in the context of BIM-based collaboration systems

The design and planning of civil and building assets are typically iterative processes as the achieved results must fit various boundary conditions, such as environmental and economic aspects. Finding consensus across the involved parties typically involves consistency and clash detection checks, performed on coordinated models that assemble all partial domain models (Preidel & Borrmann, 2015). Studies have shown that decentralized federation-based collaboration using independent domain models and merging them regularly into coordination models shows higher performance than jointly working on a single centralized BIM model (Counsell, 2012). Shafiq et al. (2013) have researched user requirements against CDEs and how existing platforms supply suitable functions accordingly. Even though the results achieved back then are not directly comparable to today's market situation, some key findings are still valid. Mainly deviating naming conventions and considering proprietary formats produced by desktop products hinder an unbiased comparison of various processes. From a technical perspective, current CDE systems require sharing BIM models as monolithic files and uploading them manually to the project platform.

Contrary to this practice, Sattler et al. (2020) proposed a query-based approach to consume information from federated models. The extracted information assists in interdisciplinary problems as their framework can handle heterogeneous data sets. However, project-wide coordination of all delivered models remains not possible with their approach.

Chen & Hou (2014) have presented a hybrid approach consisting of peer2peer and Client-Server connections for model-based collaboration workflows. Each domain connects to the centralized project hub, enabling project-wide management and coordination of interdisciplinary tasks. Additionally, all members of a specific domain can jointly collaborate within their domain system to synchronize their achievements in real-time. However, a downside of their approach is the strong focus on aspects related to the architectural and MEP domain. Following the vision of extending the decentralized nature of design processes with the ability to share updated information in an event-driven style, a flexible system architecture is required to respect existing paradigms and enhance the information flow among experts and disciplines participating in a project.

Recently, multiple researchers have investigated leveraging cloud capabilities and linked data techniques to foster the delivery and exchange of project files, including BIM models, drawings, images, and others. Senthilvel et al. developed a micro-service approach for delivering project files following the information containers ISO standard 21597 (Senthilvel et al., 2021). Additionally, Karlapudi et al. (2021) have analyzed the capabilities of ISO°21597 and presented a case study evaluating SPARQL queries in information containers. Schulz & Beetz (2021) proposed the use of the BIM collaboration format (BCF) on a centralized web server to document existing buildings.

3. Distributed architectures and technologies

The concept of distributed computing has been researched and applied in various research and industry applications. This section highlights best-practice approaches to event-oriented programming, network architectures, and related communication protocols.

3.1 Design patterns for event-driven programming

Design patterns assist in defining standard implementation recipes on how a specific feature should handle data in a best-practice manner. Two prominent patterns must be considered when discussing the application of event-driven architectures for BIM-based collaboration workflows.

Observer pattern: Consider a set of objects that must be notified about the change applied to object A. Then, object A maintains a list of observers. Every time the state of this object changes (e.g., a new value is set to a particular object property), the object instance reports to all observers about the change. Each observer, in turn, can then perform actions to react to this event. Even though the object knows its observers, there is no vice-versa interaction between an observer and the object itself, like notifying the entity about the observers' state. Nevertheless, one can implement a second observer to enable a bidirectional communication structure between both objects.

Publish-Subscribe pattern: Contrary to the principle of having a single consumer for each message, the publish-subscribe pattern features the distribution of an incoming message to many receivers. Clients can specify a topic or channel within their message, which is then used in the middleware to distinguish to whom the message should be delivered. Clients can subscribe to topics relevant to their business and will automatically receive incoming messages from the middleware if they contain the subscribed topic.

In addition to the observer and pub-sub approach, the Point-To-Point pattern distributes occurring events to other parts of the system. Each connected object can formulate a message and send it to a centralized middleware. The middleware uses a message queue following the First-In-First-Out approach to store all incoming messages. Then, it forwards the message to (exactly) one receiver with free capacities. Usually, each message is delivered to only one receiver and exactly once. As an advantage of this restriction, the receivers do not need to coordinate after receiving a message but can perform the necessary tasks. Such an implementation is often applied for load-balancing use cases (Curry, 2004).

3.2 Event-driven architectures in distributed network systems

The outlined design patterns typically act on a single computer or even within a single application. However, these concepts are also extensively used for distributed systems consisting of multiple devices connected to each other or through a central server. In the latter case, the server exposes interfaces and enables several clients to connect simultaneously and to exchange information using standardized communication protocols. A client can emit a message and receive data other clients (or the server itself) has published to the system. In addition to client-server architectures, peer2peer systems support non-hierarchical network layouts, in which each computer can communicate with others in a direct manner.

In all types of network architectures, standard web-based communication protocols, such as Hypertext Transfer Protocol (HTTP) and Transmission Control Protocol (TCP), can realize the information transfer. Accordingly, REpresentational State Transfer (REST) is a popular means for creating Web APIs (Fielding, 2000). RESTful web APIs are typically based on HTTP methods to access resources (API functions) via URL-encoded parameters and the use of JSON or XML to transmit data. Each HTTP method is executed as a request to a server that responds with content and a status code (indicating whether the request was successful or not). REST is well suited for various applications that involve manipulating and maintaining the status of data at the client-side while requiring efficient communication with a server. However, the server is typically stateless when using REST, i.e., no session information is retained by the server. As a result, information about the requesting clients (e.g., their IP addresses) is not stored. Hence, achieving an event-driven communication requires the client to periodically send requests to the server, check whether an event has occurred, and then retrieve the data. Hence, the stateful WebSocket communication protocol is more suitable for the envisioned application in the field of BIM-based collaboration as it can provide (using its built-in capabilities) a full-duplex communication between clients and servers. Communication using WebSockets ensures a real-time notification of clients by the server when a particular event occurs as the clients' connection address and state is maintained at the server. From a systematic perspective on the network architecture, servers implementing event-driven mechanisms are often named *Message-oriented middleware* (MOM). The server itself manages incoming messages and distributes them to all connected clients. Curry (2004) compares this architecture to the idea of a classical postal service. Messages are delivered to a post office; then, the postal service is responsible for providing the item to the correct receiver.

Looking into systems featuring the Internet-of-Things (IoT), prominent MoM examples are the MQTT and the CoAP protocols, which are often used in machine-to-machine (M2M) communication. The MQTT protocol facilitates topic-based communication where each client can publish payloads under hierarchically structured topic lists. In turn, clients can listen to any level of the topic hierarchy and receive a notification in case of a new message. The MQTT protocol uses a TCP-based communication based on IP routing (Light, 2017). In contrast to MQTT, the CoAP protocol specifies events by *Universal Resource Identifiers* (URIs) instead of topics. Thus, receivers subscribe to a particular resource rather than a topic (Bormann et al., 2012). Both protocols focus on situations where collecting, storing, sending, and receiving data with a minimum of overhead to protect the available power and network resources. Therefore, a key objective of MQTT and CoAP is a data transfer with almost no data overhead.

3.3 Serverless approaches

The latest advancements in cloud computing have reduced the burden of configuring, securing, and deploying servers. A new paradigm that is recently gaining popularity is the serverless architecture, supported by leading cloud providers like Amazon Web Services, Google Cloud Platform, and Microsoft Azure. "Serverless" means that a developer does not need to manage an entire server infrastructure but uses the existing infrastructure (managed by the cloud provider) and mounts single scripts and partial implementations into the provided system. These features can be triggered by a series of events like uploading a new file into a storage system or by any other system interaction. A significant benefit of serverless approaches is the extreme flexibility in scaling system resources to demand.

3.4 Summary

The concepts and protocols presented in the previous paragraphs provide a sound technical base to realize an open system that is applicable to any kind of information exchanged within a project. Architecting an open BIM cloud-based collaboration platform requires deep knowledge about both, capabilities of communication techniques as well as domain use cases and needs. Some methods and techniques are better suited for exchanging large files (when comparing REST and Sockets vs. MQTT) or establishing a bidirectional communication channel (Sockets vs. REST). The realization of these approaches would combine diverse design patterns, fulfilling the underlaying use case and purpose. Given the architectures and patterns presented in the previous paragraphs, it appears promising to combine the advantages of event-driven approaches, transferring only updates applied to models instead of entire monolithic data items.

4. Proposed concept

We describe an exemplary situation of two interacting domains to motivate the proposed concept, as depicted in Figure 1. The architect creates a design model and hands it over to the structural engineer. The structural engineer subsequently develops a structural model using the information delivered by the architect. Later, the architect modifies the architectural model by inserting a new balcony. This operation leads to a change of the slab geometry and a new door and railing insertion into the architectural model. As the update affects load-bearing elements, the structural engineer should get notified about the applied change because the structural application referenced it. To this end, the structural engineer needs to consider the impact of the applied architectural change on the structural model (e.g., the extended area for vertical loads on the balcony and horizontal loads on the railing). After modifying the structural model and re-running subsequent simulations, the structural engineer may send the results back to the project platform reporting the corresponding changes in the structural model.

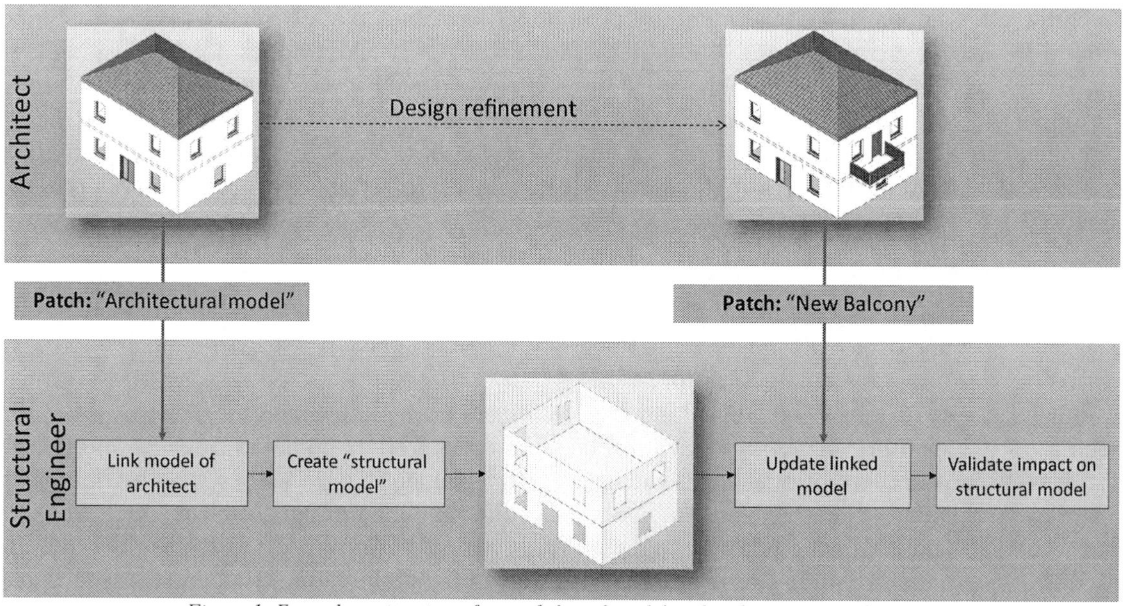

Figure 1: Exemplary situation of a patch-based model update between two domains.

4.1 Requirements resulting from cross-domain collaboration

Inspired by the current practice of BIM-based collaboration, its supplementary standards, and the outlined scenario, an event-driven CDE should meet the following set of criteria:

- Each domain continues to work in specialized authoring and simulation tools suited to fulfill assigned tasks. Accordingly, each domain publishes resulting model updates using update patches and remains full ownership over their respective domain models.
- New parties can join the project at any time and may subscribe to events that are particularly interesting for their tasks. Depending on the role and project setup, the project platform should provide appropriate access control and other business-related mechanisms.
- A copy of all discipline models is maintained on a centralized server, enabling the system to provide access to the latest state of each discipline model on-demand without the need to re-interpret the entire chain of change events. Additionally, the whole history of all changes communicated within the project is stored on the server to enable switching between several versions of BIM models.

4.2 Proposed solution

Combining the shortcomings of current CDE platforms and already existing techniques for distributed computing, the following architecture is proposed:
The publish-subscribe approach is applied to consider the distributed, asynchronous nature of design processes in the AEC industry while expressing necessary dependencies among various domains. Additionally, each involved party in the project can emit updates and subscribe to events relevant to its specific design and simulation tasks. A central server acts as a message broker, managing access rights, storing clients' subscriptions, and forwarding events according to their specified subscriptions. The server maintains a history of all raised modification events and supplies the latest model versions using HTTP-based interfaces. The data transfer between

each client and the server is realized through WebSocket connections offering bidirectional communication.

Each event consists of a topic and the patch content transferring the actual modification applied to a particular model. As design information produced and distributed during AEC projects varies in complexity and representations, the topic hierarchy must be agreed upon individually. Like other project-specific agreements, the concept of Employer's information requirements (EIR) and BIM execution plans (BEPs) are reasonable mechanisms to state these project-wide definitions. The topic of each event is then chosen according to this topic hierarchy and helps the server forward each event to the correct clients without analyzing the individual patch content. Figure 2 depicts an exemplary situation for a design project of a building.

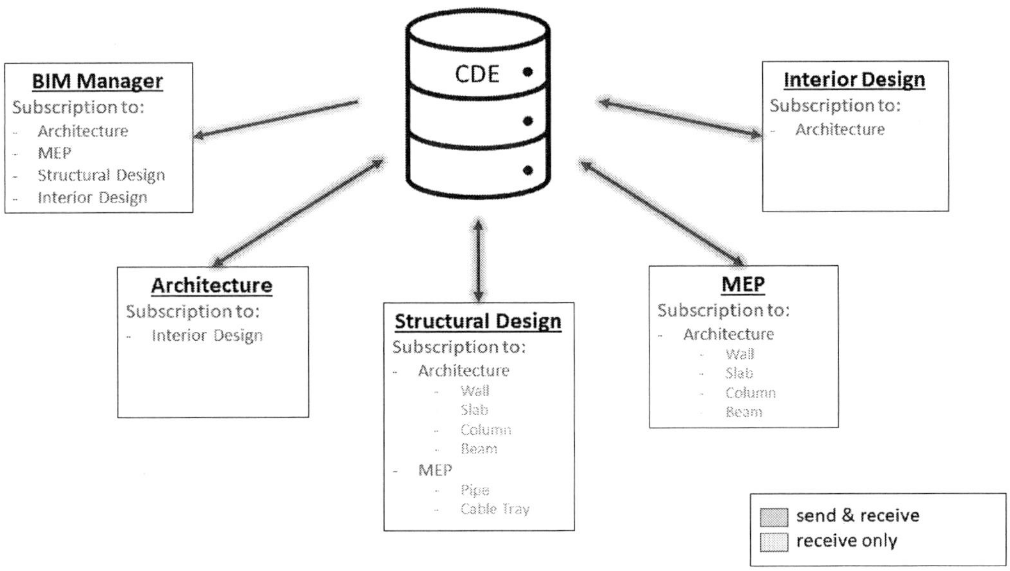

Figure 2: Topic subscription model for a building project consisting of various parties and diverse topic subscriptions

The subscription of a client happens either *implicitly* or *explicitly*. The implicit subscription method is envisioned as an automatic process if a domain requests a copy of a foreign discipline model for reference purposes. If an update affects these models, the collaboration system forwards the event to the subscribers. The update is applied to their local machines without further notice ("silent" integration). This way, it is ensured to keep all copies of a shared discipline model up to date at any storage location.

Contrary to implicit subscriptions, clients can express their explicit interest in specific object types or all objects within a logical container (e.g., building, building storey, system, etc.). Spatial and geometrical relationships within a BIM model could facilitate advanced subscription topics (e.g., all objects of any domain within a volume/box). For such cases, approaches like BIMQL and GraphQL may be employed to formally describe interests in a computer-readable manner (Daum & Borrmann, 2014). If a client receives an update of explicit interest, an alert is triggered, pointing the user to evaluate the event's impact on his domain tasks and models.

Additionally, explicit subscriptions help express interdisciplinary dependencies even though the essential principle of asynchronous project management is retained. Given the example in Figure 1, the structural engineer may subscribe to model changes affecting specific building elements such as walls, beams, columns, and slabs because of their load-bearing capacities. If the architect adds the balcony and thus edits the geometric shape of the slab, the structural engineer receives a notification about the corresponding changes in the referenced architectural model. Subsequently, the engineer evaluates this modification in the architectural model and updates the structural model accordingly. After emitting another change event by the structural engineer transferring the changes applied to the structural model, all copies of any discipline model are synchronized again and reflect the latest state of the design.

5. Analysis of advantages and disadvantages of the proposed system

The proposed system features event-driven communication between clients and a centralized server. Synchronization on any desired time interval can be achieved. Intervals range from weekly synchronization of all models to an almost real-time collaboration if modification events are emitted immediately after applying changes in the authoring system. Letting the user choose the synchronization frequency according to specific needs enables a flexible yet controlled collaboration environment that supports agile and proactive project management.

Similar to the definition of suitable topic classifications, the choice of an appropriate synchronization interval depends on the individual project characteristics and is therefore difficult to define in a standardized manner. Furthermore, the transfer of changes on object-level instead of federating entire models demands dedicated checks to ensure the correct receipt of patches and their proper integration on all receivers. Besides integration verification, accompanying mechanisms are essential to indicate a specific version of foreign models as an engineer bases domain tasks on one state. Indeed, the proposed architecture drastically reduces the risk of making decisions on superseded models if a frequent information exchange is implemented in the project. However, it is of considerable benefit for conflict and clash resolution if tracing back design decisions and associated versions is possible. Therefore, the benefits of the proposed system outweigh the disadvantages, especially if all model replicas are synchronized frequently and users take design changes of foreign disciplines into account in their planning.

6. Summary and Outlook

Implementing event-driven exchange mechanisms can foster an intelligent and smooth BIM-based collaboration. It enables a quicker exchange of modifications applied to shared discipline models. Furthermore, it supports the understanding of whether and to what extent an update in foreign models impacts design tasks of a specific domain. Clients can register their interest in particular update scenarios by subscribing to events from similar or different domains. Each domain keeps the author's rights on its models and publishes patches that comprise the modification logic to a specific model. Thus, the established and well-adopted principle of asynchronous design environments in federated systems and the coordination of all domain models in regular time intervals remains unchanged. Nevertheless, the proposed approach reduces the amount of information a client must evaluate and provides notification mechanisms to highlight updates relevant to an individual client.

The authors will report on experiences and results after validating the proposed system in real-world projects.

References

Bormann, C., Castellani, A. P., & Shelby, Z. (2012). CoAP: An application protocol for billions of tiny internet nodes. IEEE Internet Computing, 16(2), 62–67. https://doi.org/10.1109/MIC.2012.29

CEN. (2018). DIN EN ISO 19650-2:2018 Organization and digitization of information about buildings and civil engineering works, including building information modelling (BIM) — Information management using building information modelling — Part 2: Delivery phase of the assets.

Chen, H. M., & Hou, C. C. (2014). Asynchronous online collaboration in BIM generation using hybrid client-server and P2P network. Automation in Construction, 45, 72–85. https://doi.org/10.1016/j.autcon.2014.05.007

Counsell, J. (2012). Beyond level 2 BIM, web portals and collaboration tools. Proceedings of the International Conference on Information Visualisation, 510–515. https://doi.org/10.1109/IV.2012.88

Curry, E. (2004). Message-Oriented Middleware. Middleware for Communications, 1–28.

Daum, S., & Borrmann, A. (2014). Processing of topological BIM queries using boundary representation based methods. Advanced Engineering Informatics, 28(4), 272–286. https://doi.org/10.1016/j.aei.2014.06.001

Esser, S., Vilgertshofer, S., & Borrmann, A. (2021). Graph-based version control for asynchronous BIM level 3 collaboration. EG-ICE 2021 Workshop on Intelligent Computing in Engineering, 98–107. https://doi.org/10.14279/depositonce-12021

Fielding R. (2000). Architectural styles and the design of network-based software architectures. https://www.ics.uci.edu/~fielding/pubs/dissertation

Karlapudi, J., Valluru, P., & Menzel, K. (2021). An explanatory use case for the implementation of Information Container for linked Document Delivery in Common Data Environments. EG-ICE 2021 Workshop on Intelligent Computing in Engineering, 76–86.

Light, R. A. (2017). Mosquitto: server and client implementation of the MQTT protocol. The Journal of Open Source Software, 2(13), 265. https://doi.org/10.21105/joss.00265

Preidel, C., & Borrmann, A. (2015). Automated Code Compliance Checking Based on a Visual Language and Building Information Modeling. ISARC. Proceedings of the International Symposium on Automation and Robotics in Construction, 1–8.

Sattler, L., Lamouri, S., Pellerin, R., Fortineau, V., Larabi, M., & Maigne, T. (2020). A query-based framework to improve BIM multi-domain collaboration. Enterprise Information Systems, 00(00), 1–23. https://doi.org/10.1080/17517575.2020.1845810

Schulz, O., & Beetz, J. (2021). Image-documentation of existing buildings using a serverbased bim collaboration format workflow. EG-ICE 2021 Workshop on Intelligent Computing in Engineering, 108–117.

Senthilvel, M., Oraskari, J., & Beetz, J. (2021). Implementing Information Container for linked Document Delivery (ICDD) as a micro-service. EG-ICE 2021 Workshop on Intelligent Computing in Engineering, 66–73.

Shafiq, M. T., Matthews, J., & Lockley, S. (2012). Requirements for model server enabled collaborating on building information models. First UK Academic Conference on BIM, 5 -7 September 2012, Northumbria University, Newcastle upon Tyne, UK, 23–35. https://doi.org/10.1108/17410391111097438

Shafiq, M. T., Matthews, J., & Lockley, S. R. (2013). A Study of BIM Collaboration Requirements and Available Features in Existing Model Collaboration Systems. Journal of Information Technology in Construction (ITcon), 18(18), 148–161. http://www.itcon.org/2013/8

Solihin, W., Eastman, C., & Lee, Y. C. (2016). A framework for fully integrated building information models in a federated environment. Advanced Engineering Informatics, 30(2), 168–189. https://doi.org/10.1016/j.aei.2016.02.007

Zhang, C., Beetz, J., & Weise, M. (2015). Interoperable validation for IFC building models using open standards. Journal of Information Technology in Construction (ITcon), 20 (Special issue ECPPM 2014-10th European Conference on Product and Process Modelling), 24–39. https://doi.org/10.18154/RWTH-CONV-213541

Uncertainty and Sensitivity Analysis of Building Integrated Photovoltaics

Chen, L.[1], Tian, W. [1*], de Wilde, P.[2], Zhang, H.[1]
[1]College of Mechanical Engineering, Tianjin University for Science and Technology, China
[2]Department of Architecture, University of Strathclyde, United Kingdom
weitian@tust.edu.cn

Abstract. The performance of building-integrated photovoltaics (BIPV) shows high variations due to several factors, including design model uncertainty, installation mode, dirt/soil effects, aging factors, and manufacturing issues. This paper explores the uncertainty of BIPV outputs from the perspectives of both model uncertainty and parameter uncertainty using the EnergyPlus program. The sampling-based Monte Carlo method is implemented to conduct the uncertainty analysis of BIPV outputs. The meta-model global sensitivity analysis (Bayesian adaptive spline surfaces) is used to obtain important factors affecting BIPV outputs due to its high computational efficiency. The results indicate that both model and parameter uncertainty has significant influences on PV outputs. The combined remaining effect, power rating, and model uncertainty are three important factors influencing PV electricity. Therefore, these factors should be carefully chosen or adjusted to provide a reliable estimation of PV outputs.

1. Introduction

BIPV (building-integrated photovoltaics) has been widely considered a promising method to provide sustainable energy for buildings (Sun et al, 2021). There are different types of integration methods in buildings, including walls, roofs, windows, and skylights. Chen et al. (2021) investigate the energy performance of BIPV windows in street canyons. They found that energy savings due to BIPV window increase in north-south orientated open canyons. Pabasara et al. (2022) investigate the design options of building-integrated photovoltaics using multi-objective optimization in terms of life-cycle cost and energy performance. The method proposed includes four steps: data inputs, performance simulation, optimizer, and optimized results. The results show that there are seven optimum roof BIPV design solutions and fourteen skylight BIPV design options. Rounis et al. (2021) explore the design, development, and experiments of BIPV/T (building-integrated photovoltaics/thermal) in an indoor solar simulator. Their study provides a design standardization of air-based BIPV/T design and emphasizes the importance of convective heat transfer in this BIPV/T system. Most previous studies concentrate on the electricity and thermal performance of BIPV systems. There are studies to explore the uncertainty of PV systems. Liu et al. (2018) apply a two-stage procedure to predict both the point and interval estimation of short-term PV outputs. The first step is to create neural network models and the second step is to apply the kernel non-parameter density estimation to estimate the associated prediction intervals. Thenevard et al. (2013) discuss the long-term uncertainty of PV outputs. They found that the standard deviation of PV outputs is approximately 8.7% for the first year of operation and 7.9% for the other years over the PV lifetime. However, a few studies focus on both uncertainty and sensitivity analysis of building-integrated photovoltaics. The variations of energy performance in BIPV due to uncertain inputs are not fully explored yet.

Therefore, this research investigates the uncertain results of BIPV outputs and identifies the key factors affecting PV electricity. Both the model and parameter uncertainty in a BIPV system would be explored in this research. The meta-modeling sensitivity analysis is used to

https://doi.org/10.7146/aul.455.c196

obtain the sensitivity index influencing BIPV outputs. Moreover, the convergence of both uncertainty and sensitivity results for the BIPV system is evaluated to obtain robust results.

2. Method

The procedures of uncertainty and sensitivity analysis of building-integrated photovoltaics can be divided into six steps as illustrated in Figure 1. The first step is to determine the distributions of input parameters from previous studies. The second step is to obtain the sampling results using the Latin hypercube method. The third step is to compute the PV models with the EnergyPlus program in the R environment. The fourth step is to collect the PV electricity from the EnergyPlus models. The fifth step is to display the uncertain results of PV systems. The sixth step is to conduct the sensitivity analysis based on the meta-model global sensitivity analysis. The BP Solar BP275 PV panels are used in this case study. The area of a PV panel is 0.63 m^2 with 36 solar cells. The short-circuit current is 4.75 A and the open-circuit voltage is 21.4 V. More detailed information on these PV panels is available in the EnergyPlus example file (DOE, 2021).

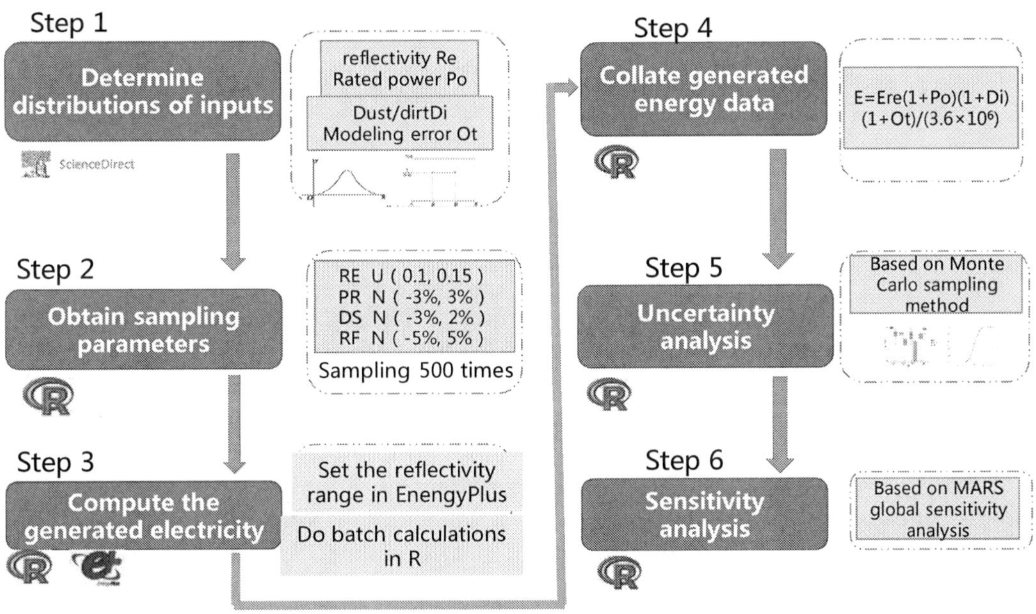

Figure 1: Flow chart of uncertainty and sensitivity analysis of building-integrated photovoltaics.

2.1 Uncertainty analysis

Two types of uncertainty will be considered in this study: model and parameter (Tian et al., 2018), as listed in Table 1. Model uncertainty refers to various PV models to estimate the electricity of PV systems, whereas parameter uncertainty refers to the parameters influencing PV outputs. Three types of PV models are considered: simple, TRNSYS, and Sandia (DOE, 2021). The simple PV model is used to compute the electricity output by the incident solar radiation multiplying the constant PV efficiency. The TRNSYS model is a four-parameter empirical equivalent circuit model to estimate the PV output (Duffie and Beckman, 2013). The Sandia model is developed by David King from the Sandia National Lab using empirical relationships (King et al., 2003). The uncertain parameters include installation modes, Albedo, power rating, dirt/soil, and other variables. Two types of installation modes are considered: stand-alone (decoupled) and natural ventilation, which can be regarded as a uniform categorical variable. For standalone PV, the cell temperature of modules in the array is obtained from the energy balance relative to NOCT (Nominal operating cell temperature) conditions. The NOCT temperature is the operating temperature of the module with a wind speed of 1 m/s, no electrical load, and a certain specified insolation (800 W/m2) and 20oC ambient temperature (Beckman and Duffie, 2013). For the natural ventilation BIPV, the PV temperature is obtained from the exterior baffle temperature in the naturally ventilated exterior cavity model. The albedo is taken as a uniform distribution between 0.1 and 0.15. The change of PV power rating is regarded as a normal distribution of mean -3% and standard deviation of 3%. The influence of soil and dirt is represented as a normal distribution of mean -3% and a standard deviation of 2%. The remaining variables including spectral effects, aging effects, etc. (named as other variables) are considered as a normal distribution of a mean of -5% and a standard deviation of 5% (Thevenard and Pelland, 2013).

Table 1: Uncertainty parameters for uncertainty and sensitivity analysis of PV system.

Uncertainty type	**Factor**	**Short names**	**Values/Distributions**
Model uncertainty	PV computation method	PM	Simple (SP), TRNSYS (TS), Sandia (SN)
Parameter uncertainty	Installation mode	IM	Stand-alone (DE), natural ventilation (VN)
	Albedo	RE	U(0.1, 0.15)
	Power rating	PR	N(-3%, 3%)
	Dirt soil	DS	N(-3%, 2%)
	Remaining factors	RF	N(-5%, 5%)

The PV panel is assumed to be installed in Tianjin, China, and the typical year data in Tianjin is used to obtain PV electricity. Figure 2 shows the variations of daily solar radiation in different months. There are more variations of daily solar radiation in summer than those in winter. The simulation is conducted using the EnergyPlus V9.6 program (DOE, 2021). There are three types of PV models and two types of installation modes. Hence, there are 6 cases in this study. The PV models are run 1000 times using the Sobol sampling method to obtain reliable results of PV outputs for every case. The Sobol sequence is a low discrepancy quasirandom sequence with a good convergence performance (Sun, 2021). The convergence test of uncertainty and sensitivity analysis would be discussed in section 3.1 and section 3.2, respectively.

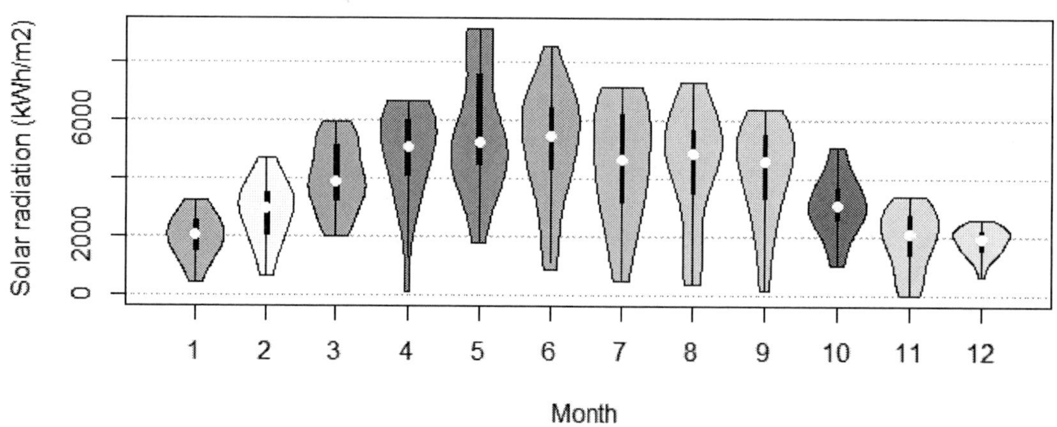

Figure 2: Violin plots for daily horizontal solar radiation by month in Tianjin.

2.2 Sensitivity analysis

The meta-modeling Sobol sensitivity analysis is conducted to obtain the importance rankings of the factors above influencing PV output (Tian, 2013). The meta-model used in this method (Bayesian adaptive spline surfaces) is one of the polynomial spline models in which the integrals can be computed analytically without the Monte Carlo simulation (Francom and Sanso, 2020). Hence, the computational efficiency would increase significantly compared to the conventional meta-model variance-based global sensitivity analysis. The Bayesian adaptive spline surface models are firstly created using the 1000 samples from the uncertainty analysis. Then the sensitivity index is derived based on the definition of the main and total effects of global sensitivity analysis. The main effects and total effects can be obtained at the same time from this meta-model sensitivity analysis. The main effects refer to the influences of a single factor without considering the effects of other factors, whereas the total effects include the main effects of one specific factor and interaction effects with the other factors. The interaction effects can be two-way or higher-order effects for a complex engineering system. R Bass package is used for sensitivity analysis (Francom and Sanso, 2020).

3. Results and discussion

3.1 Results from uncertainty analysis

This section would firstly discuss the convergence of uncertainty analysis of PV electricity to make sure the results are stable. Then the total uncertainty results would be described to compare the results in three PV computation methods and two installation modes. Finally, the uncertainty results would be illustrated due to separate factors.

Convergence of results from uncertainty analysis

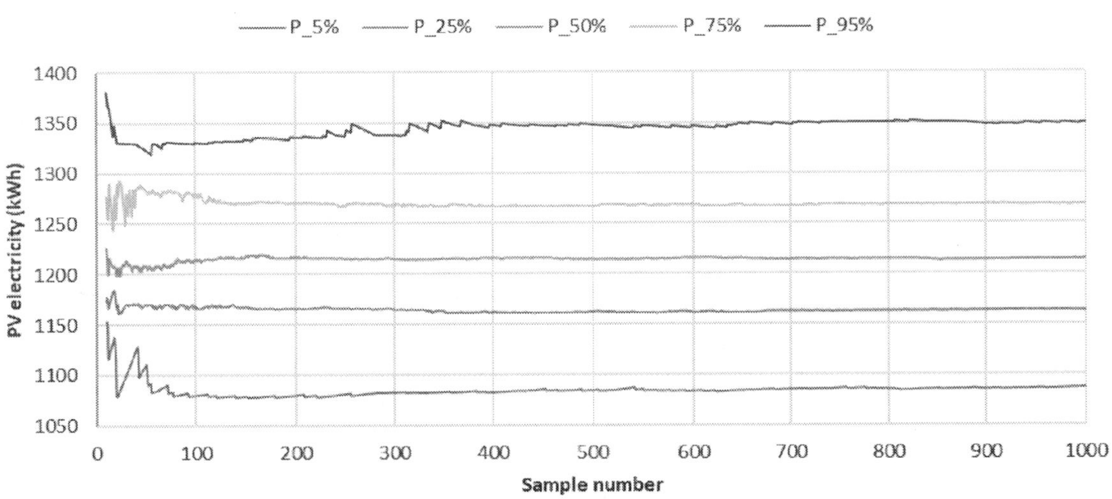

Figure 3: Stability of percentiles of electricity generated by PV systems with the sample number for the ventilation mode using the TRNSYS model.

It is necessary to check the convergence of uncertainty results using sampling-based methods. Figure 3 shows the change of various percentiles of PV electricity with the ventilation mode using the TRNSYS model. These percentiles tend to be stable after 400 simulation runs using the Sobol sequence sampling method. The 95th percentile of PV electricity has more variations in this case study as might be expected. This is because more extreme values require more sampling runs. The 50th percentile (median) of PV electricity has slight variations after 200 simulation runs. The 1000 sample runs are chosen in this research for the stable results of both uncertainty and sensitivity analysis. The convergence of sensitivity results would be discussed in section 3.2.

Results from total uncertainty analysis Figure 2 and Figure 3 show the cumulative density function and box plots of annual electricity in six cases, respectively. The model uncertainty has a marked influence on the results of PV electricity. The results from the simple model (SP) are almost the same for two installation modes (stand-alone and natural ventilation), whereas the results from the stand-alone are around 12% higher than those from the natural ventilation using the Sandia model and TRNSYS model. This is because the influences of change in PV temperature can be properly considered in the more detailed PV models, including Sandia and TRNSYS models. Hence, it is necessary to implement suitable PV models in estimating PV outputs when integrating with buildings. As also can be seen from Figure 3, the differences in mean values from the Sandia and TRNSYS models are less than 2%. As a result, the PV electricity using both the Sandia and TRNSYS is reliable to provide an accurate estimation of PV outputs.

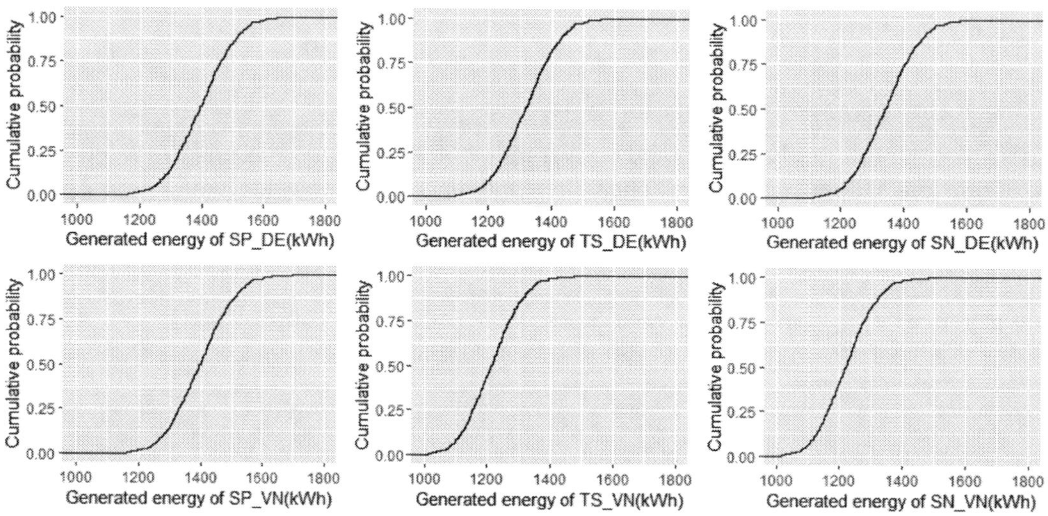

Figure 4: Electricity generated by PV systems in two installation modes (DE, decoupled; VN, ventilation) and three PV models (SP, simple; TS, TRNSYS; SN: Sandia National Laboratories).

The IQR (inter-quartile range) values of PV electricity are 132 kWh when using the simple PV model. These IQR values would be decreased to 124 kWh in the case of stand-alone PV installation mode using the TRNSYS and Sandia models. The IQR values would further slightly be reduced in the case of natural ventilation BIPV. Hence, the uncertainty of PV electricity would change with the variations of PV models and PV installation modes although the change of uncertainty is not significant. It is also found that the coefficients of variation for PV outputs in all six cases are around 6.44% in this research. This suggests that the relative variations of PV electricity normalized to the mean values for three PV computation methods and two installation modes are almost the same in this case study. As also can be seen from Figure 5, the ranges of PV outputs in every case study are larger than the difference between the three PV computation methods. Hence, the variations of PV electricity due to the parameter uncertainty are larger than those from the model uncertainty.

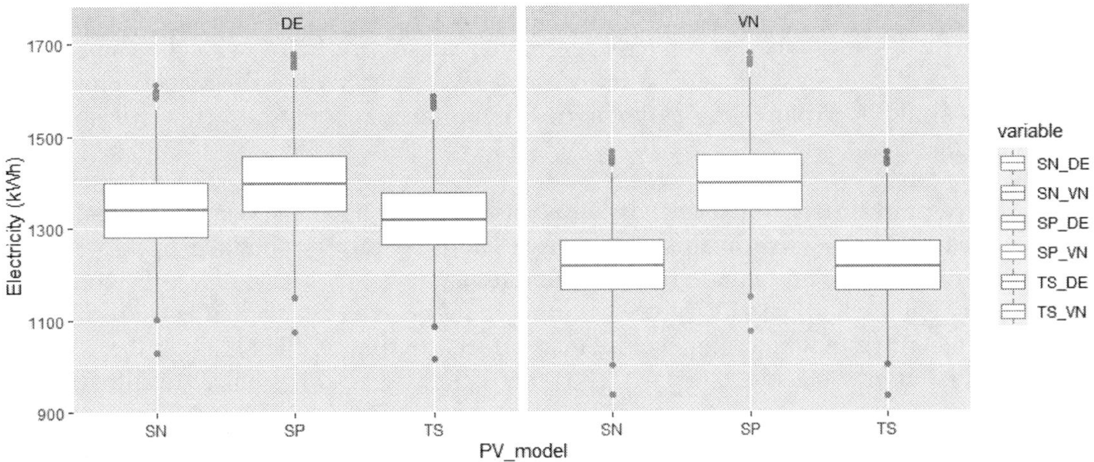

Figure 5: Box plots of electricity generated by PV systems in two installation modes (DE, decoupled; VN, ventilation) and three PV models (SP, simple; TS, TRNSYS; SN: Sandia National Laboratories).

Results from uncertainty analysis from four separate factors It is also interesting to explore the density plots for separate factors in a specific PV computation method and a specific installation mode. The PV electricity with the ventilation mode and TRNSYS method would be investigated because this PV calculation method can present more reliable results as discussed in this section. Figure 6 illustrates the kernel density plots of PV electricity due to four factors: Albedo (RE), power rating (PR), dirt/soil (DS), and other variables (RF). The largest variation of PV electricity is due to the RF (other variables, including aging and spectral effects) in which the interquartile is 92 kWh. The next factor is PR (power rating) with the interquartile of 55 kWh. The third-largest variation of PV electricity is because of dirt on the PV surface and its variation only accounts for around one-third of variations due to RF factors. There are almost no variations of PV electricity due to RE (Albedo) in this case study.

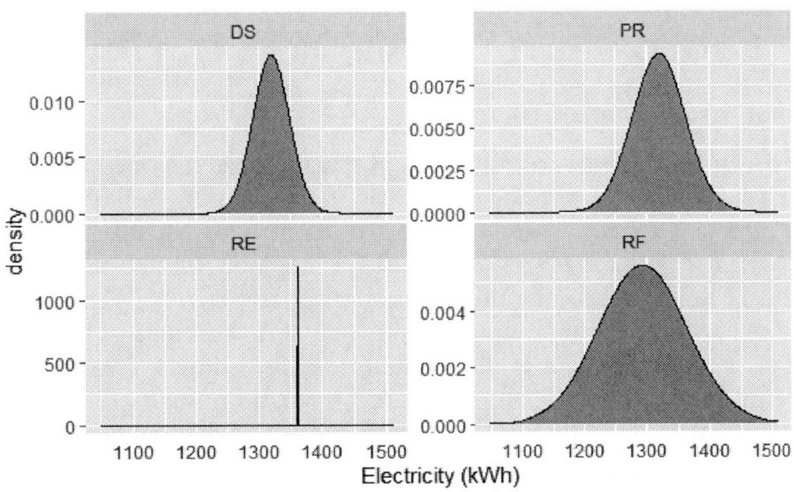

Figure 6: Density plots of PV electricity using the TRNSYS model in the ventilation mode due to four factors (DS, dirt soil; PR, power rating; RE: reflectivity; RF, remaining factors).

3.2 Results from sensitivity analysis

This section firstly presents the convergence of the sensitivity index with the sample size. Then the main effects and interactions influencing PV electricity are illustrated. Finally, the total effects would be explored to obtain the final importance rankings affecting PV outputs in this case study.

Convergence of results from sensitivity analysis Figure 6 shows the change of total effects as a function of sample size in this case study. The total effects obtained from sensitivity analysis would be very unstable before the 300 simulation runs. The ranking results for PM (PC computation method) and PR (power rating) would be even changed after 100 simulation runs. After the 500 simulation models, the total effects become stable although there exists a slight change after 900 model runs. The simulation runs for stables results between uncertainty and sensitivity analysis are different by comparing Figure 4 and Figure 6. In this case study, more simulation runs are required for sensitivity analysis than those for uncertainty analysis.

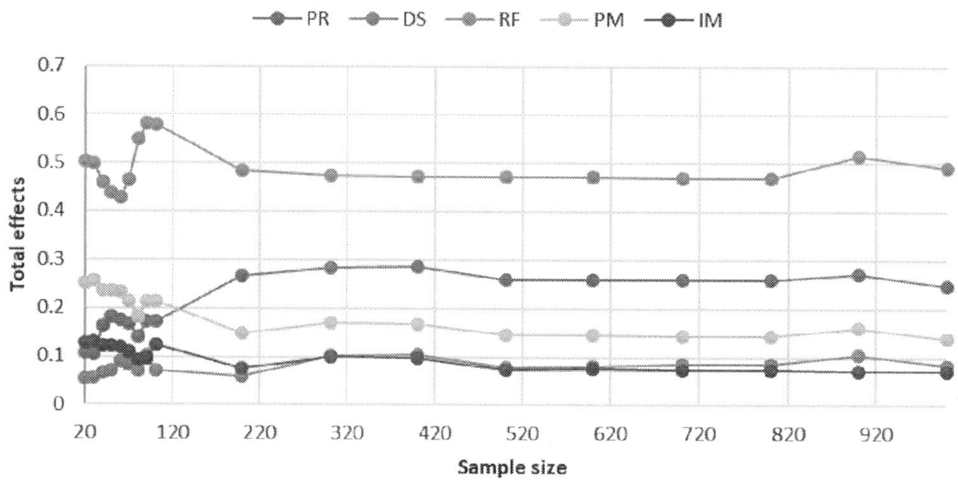

Figure 6: Stability of total effects with the sample number for the PV systems.

Main effects and two-way interactions

Figure 7 shows the sensitivity results of input parameters using the meta-model global sensitivity analysis. The most important factor is the remaining variables, including spectral effects, aging effects, etc., which account for around 58% of variations of PV outputs. The next two important factors are the PV power rating and model uncertainty, which are responsible for 17% and 11% of output variations, respectively. The sum of these three important factors accounts for approximately 86% of total variations of PV outputs. The other factors have only slight influences on the variations of PV outputs. Hence, these three factors should be carefully considered in computing PV outputs to properly evaluate the uncertainty of electricity generated from the BIPV system. As also can be seen from Figure 4, the interactions of the PV model and installation modes also have influenced the variations of PV outputs. This can be explained from Figure 3 that the PV results would be changed in two installation modes using the Sandia or TRNSYS models, while the PV outputs would almost be the same in two different installation modes using the simple PV model.

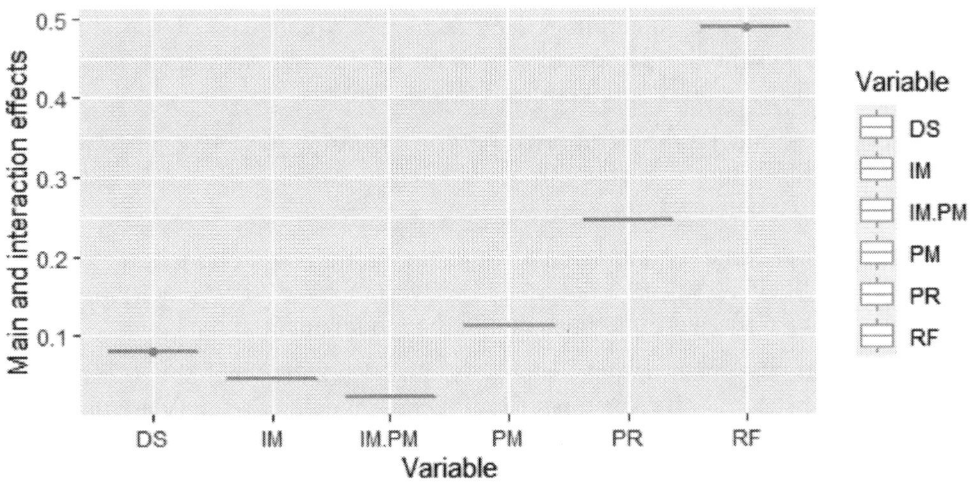

Figure 7: Main and interaction effects of input parameters influencing PV electricity.

Total effects

Figure 8 shows the total effects of factors influencing PV electricity. A similar conclusion can be obtained as discussed in Figure 7. The total effects are almost the same as the main effects for three factors, including RF, PR, and DS, since there are almost no interactions between these three factors. The total effects for both IM and PM would be increased by around 0.0234 due to the interactions of these two factors as shown in Figure 7. Therefore, the total sensitivity index for all the factors would be above one due to the interactions. It can be also observed that the variations of total effects are very small in this case. Therefore, the rankings results influencing PV electricity would be very robust since there are no overlapping total effects. The albedo effects have almost no influence on PV outputs in this case study, which are not shown in Figure 8. The RF (including aging, spectral, and other variables) has a large influence on the PV outputs. More detailed research is required to decompose this combined factor into specific variables, which could provide more guidance on how to reduce the uncertainty of PV estimation.

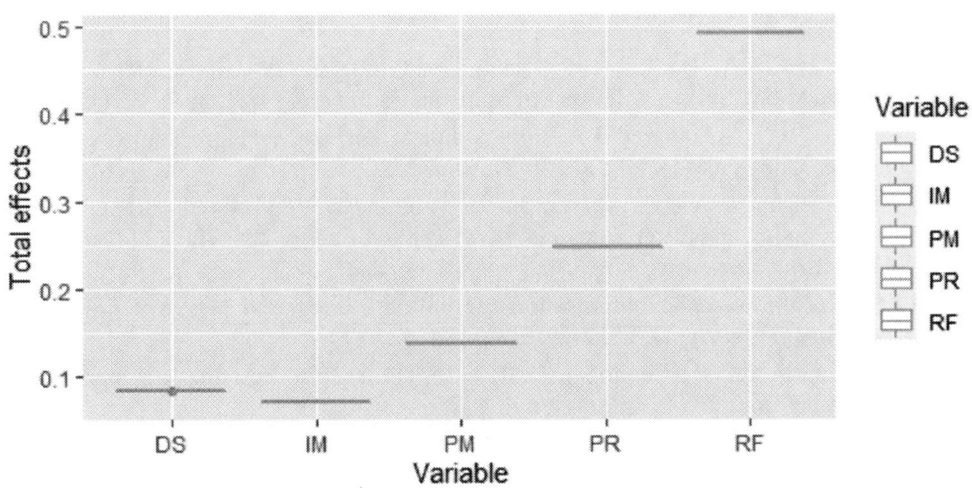

Figure 8: Total effects of input parameters influencing PV electricity.

4. Conclusion

This paper investigates the uncertainty and sensitivity analysis of building-integrated photovoltaics (BIPV) from the perspective of both model and parameter uncertainty. The following conclusions have been obtained from this research:

(1) The convergence of uncertainty and sensitivity in exploring the BIPV performance should be properly evaluated. In this case study, more simulation runs for the sensitivity analysis are required compared to the uncertainty analysis.

(2) The results from uncertainty analysis indicates that both model and parameter uncertainty have significant influences on PV outputs. The variations of PV electricity due to the parameter uncertainty are larger than those due to the model uncertainty.

(3) The results from the meta-model sensitivity analysis show that the remaining effects (including aging and spectral effects), power rating, and model uncertainty are three important factors influencing PV electricity. Therefore, these factors should be carefully chosen or adjusted to provide a reliable estimation of PV outputs.

Further research is be required to understand the effects of uncertain factors for different types of BIPV, such as PV windows, and PV/T systems.

Acknowledgments

This research was supported by the National Natural Science Foundation of China (No. 51778416) and the Key Projects of Philosophy and Social Sciences Research, Ministry of Education (China) “Research on Green Design in Sustainable Development” (contract No. 16JZDH014).

References

Chen L., Zheng X., Yang JC., Yoon JH., (2021) Impact of BIPV windows on building energy consumption in street canyons: Model development and validation, Energy and Buildings, 249, 111207

DOE (2021) EnergyPlus V9.6 September 2021, Department of Energy, USA.

Duffie, John A., and William A. Beckman. 2013. Solar Engineering of Thermal Processes. New York: John Wiley & Son

Francom, D., Sanso, B. (2020). BASS: An R Package for Fitting and Performing Sensitivity Analysis of Bayesian Adaptive Spline Surfaces. Journal of Statistical Software, **94**(8), pp. 1–36.

King, D.L., Boyson, W.E., Kratochvil J.A. 2003. Photovoltaic Array Performance Model. Sandia National Laboratories, Albuquerque, NM 87185, November 2003.

Liu, L., Y. Zhao, D. Chang, J. Xie, Z. Ma, Q. Sun, H. Yin and R. Wennersten (2018). "Prediction of short-term PV power output and uncertainty analysis." Applied Energy 228: 700-711.

Pabasara Upalakshi Wijeratne, W.M. Tharushi Imalka Samarasinghalage, Rebecca Jing Yang, Ron Wakefield, (2022). Multi-objective optimisation for building integrated photovoltaics (BIPV) roof projects in early design phase, Applied Energy, 309,118476.

Rounis, E.D., Athienitis, K. A., Stathopoulos T., (2021). BIPV/T curtain wall systems: Design, development and testing, Journal of Building Engineering, 42,103019.

Sun, H., Heng, C.K., Tay S.E.R, Chen T., Reindl T., (2021). Comprehensive feasibility assessment of building integrated photovoltaics (BIPV) on building surfaces in high-density urban environments, Solar Energy, 225, pp. 734-746.

Sun, X., B. Croke, S. Roberts, A. J. R. E. Jakeman and S. Safety (2021). "Comparing methods of randomizing Sobol′ sequences for improving uncertainty of metrics in variance-based global sensitivity estimation." 210: 107499.

Thevenard, D., Pelland, S. (2013). Estimating the uncertainty in long-term photovoltaic yield predictions,

Solar Energy, 91, pp. 432-455.

Tian, W., Heo, Y., de Wilde, P., Li, ZY, Yan, D., Park C.S., Feng, XH, Augenbroe, G. (2018) A review of uncertainty analysis in building energy assessment. Renewable and Sustainable Energy Reviews, 93, 285-301.

Tian, W. A review of sensitivity analysis methods in building energy analysis, Renewable and Sustainable Energy Reviews, 2013, 20, 411-419.

Semantic Segmentation of building point clouds based on Point Transformer and IFC

Wei S.[1], Gao G.[1,2,*], Ke Z.[1], Fan G.[1], Liu Y. [1], Gu M. [1,2]
[1]School of Software, Tsinghua University, Beijing, China, [2]Beijing National Research Center for Information Science and Technology(BNRist), Tsinghua University, Beijing, China
gaoge@tsinghua.edu.cn

Abstract. In the process of building construction, the semantic understanding of building point clouds provides potential solutions for efficient building quality supervision, progress monitoring, and sub-system deviation analysis. However, the lack of suitable public labeled datasets, the low degree of color discrimination and the particularity of multi-system coexistence in construction scenes have brought certain challenges to semantic segmentation of point clouds. But rich semantic information in related Industry Foundation Classes(IFC) can be used to synthesize effective labeled data. Our main contributions are as follows:1) We propose a synthetic conversion method from BIM model to point cloud, and construct a synthetic dataset for construction scenes based on IFC. 2) We segment the colorless point cloud of the construction scene into five types (IfcSlab, IfcBeam, IfcWall, IfcColumn, IfcDistributionFlowElement) with Point Transformer and use focal loss to improve the segmentation accuracy of small-area components with synthetic data for data enhancement.

1. Introduction

In the building life cycle, the construction phase is a key part to control the quality of the entire building, but the traditional way of building supervision relies more on manual inspection. The development of 3D laser scanning technology has enabled us to collect and understand buildings more conveniently and quickly. Recently, there have been many related studies to achieve great progress on point cloud semantic recognition, but they either focus on the indoor scenes which contain too many components that are not applicable in the construction scene (such as furniture) or only focus on the segmentation of building structural systems (walls, beams, slabs, columns) without considering the piping system. In the existing building datasets, there are few public datasets only for construction scenes with rich semantic information annotations, and also meet the standard for the classification of component types in IFC. At the same time, the low degree of color discrimination and the special types of components included in the construction scene bring challenges to the point cloud segmentation in the construction scene. We found that many IFC models corresponding to construction scenes have not been used. If the rich semantic information in IFC can be used to synthesize effective labeled data, the problem of data shortage in real construction scenes can be solved.

Not only for the analysis of deviations between components within a single system, but also for subsystem component division, especially when MEP systems and structural systems coexist, to meet the regulatory requirements of different systems, we propose an IFC-based point cloud semantic segmentation system for building electromechanical coexistence construction scenarios.

The main contributions are as follows: 1) We propose a synthetic conversion method from BIM model to point cloud, and construct a synthetic dataset for construction scenes based on the

https://doi.org/10.7146/aul.455.c197

classification of component types in IFC. 2) We segment the colorless point cloud of the construction scene into five types (IfcSlab, IfcBeam, IfcWall, IfcColumn, IfcDistributionFlowElement) with Point Transformer and use focal loss to improve the segmentation accuracy of small-area components with synthetic data for data enhancement.

2. Related Work

Quality supervision, progress monitoring, and deviation analysis of buildings in the past relied more on manual inspection and has not yet formed a perfect automated process. With the development of 3D scanning technology, point clouds have gradually become a format for fast scanning and fully expressing building. Point cloud data of buildings under construction can be obtained directly or indirectly through laser scanners and RGB-D cameras. Without the limitations of image resolution and multi-perspective image processing, the point cloud data obtained by laser scanning is more accurate and suitable for the acquisition of construction data of large construction scenes, which is also the way we use in our method.

In order to propose a more automated and efficient solution in quality supervision, progress monitoring, and deviation analysis of buildings, many methods have been proposed to compare as-built and as-planned buildings. There are two main categories: one is Scan-vs-BIM (Bosché et al., 2014; Rebolj et al., 2017; Tran et al., 2019) and the other is Scan-to-BIM (Murali et al., 2017; Avetisyan et al., 2020; Bosché et al., 2015). The former does not require complete modeling of the building, focusing on the comparison of the corresponding structures; the latter requires a complete modeling of the building and further analysis based on the modeling results. But in both approaches, understanding the semantic information of architectural point clouds is crucial. Traditional point cloud segmentation methods are widely used such as methods based on area growth which are over-reliance on the selection of seed points and require trade-offs between accuracy and efficiency, and methods based on model fitting such as k-means clustering algorithms which still need to manually determine K values.

Compared with traditional segmentation methods, methods based on deep learning can extract high-dimensional features from training data better and cluster better. TangentConv (Tatarchenko et al., 2018) projects the 3D point cloud onto the 2D plane, which will lose information and not make full use of the spatial features such as the sparseness of the point cloud. At the same time, the selection of the projection plane may also seriously affect the recognition accuracy. OCTNET (Riegler et al., 2017) converts irregular point cloud data into the expression of point cloud voxels and uses coefficient-based convolution to reduce computation and memory consumption. Despite this, the loss of geometric information due to point-to-voxel conversion is still unavoidable. The Pointnet series of deep learning networks that can directly input 3D point cloud output segmentation results is a point-level segmentation method which completely retains the geometric information of point clouds. Pointnet (Qi et al., 2017a)extracts global features for all point cloud data, Pointnet++ (Qi et al., 2017b) can extract local features at different scales, through multi-scale combination and multi-resolution combination which ensure better feature extraction. However, it's still not sufficient to learn local features of points, so other methods such as graph convolution are proposed. DGCNN (Phan et al., 2018)introduced a new module Edgeconv to extract the local features of point clouds, and learn the semantic information of point sets by dynamically updating the graph structure. But the direction information between points is ignored.

These methods have been applied to building elements(such as walls, floors). Based on Stanford Large-Scale 3D Indoor Spaces(S3DIS) dataset, Collins (2020) uses DGCNN network to divide 4 classes (pipe system, wall, slab, stair), without taking into account the distinction between walls and columns, which are common and important structures in construction scenarios. Kim et al(2020) automatic pipe and elbow recognition from three-dimensional point cloud model of industrial plant piping system using the convolutional neural network without considering the segmentation of large-area structural components except for the specific subdivision of the pipe categories in the MEP system. Correspondingly, Kim et al. (2021) uses DGCNN network to divide five types(wall, beam, ceiling, floor and column), without considering the pipe system at all. However, in the construction scene, the structure and the pipe system are often integrated, and because the distribution of pipe is generally close to the wall or near the beam, it will have a certain impact on the division of the two systems. Therefore, how to accurately distinguish between two systems and multiple categories within the system also has certain challenges. At the same time, the classification criteria in these articles are not unified with the IFC standards, which are important in the field of architecture.

Furthermore, the above deep learning-based methods require a large number of point cloud datasets similar to the application scenario, but the existing datasets including S3DIS, Scannet,etc contain a large number of interior furniture and the scene color is diverse, which are quite different from the construction scene. Due to the high cost of the manual labeling point cloud, there are very few point cloud datasets only for construction scenarios that are public and meet IFC standards. Considering many IFC files including rich semantic information of the building itself in the design stage have not been used, IFC-based method of synthesizing data is a good choice. Ma, Czerniawski and Leite (2020) proposes a method of synthesizing data, from Revit to point cloud. But it still doesn't shed its reliance on the S3DIS dataset. Therefore, we propose a synthesis method for construction scenarios closely integrated with IFC, and use the synthesis dataset for data enhancement.

With the significant improvement achieved by the transformer and self-attention models in the image domain, the introduction of self-attention mechanisms on point clouds has been motivated. Point transformer (Engel et al., 2021) introduces a local-global attention mechanism to combine global and local features which are used to obtain the relationship and shape information between points. Point transformer has achieved state of the art in classification and segmentation tasks.

Therefore, to provide a better solution for multi-system and multi-component semantic understanding of construction scenes, we propose a method of synthesizing point cloud datasets to solve the problem of lack of labeled construction buildings dataset; On the basis of data enhancement of synthetic datasets, we use Point transformer to divide construction point clouds into five categories (IfcSlab, IfcBeam, IfcWall, IfcColumn, IfcDistributionFlowElement) to solve the problem of semantic understanding when multiple systems coexist in the construction scene; and focal loss is introduced to solve the problem of unbalanced component samples in the construction scene.

3. Methodology

The method is mainly divided into two parts: Synthetic dataset based on IFC and Semantic segmentation of building point clouds based on Point transformer.

3.1 Constructive Conversion Method from BIM to Point Cloud

Nowadays, more and more related products in the construction industry provide data exchange interfaces based on the IFC standard. Especially in construction scenarios. Synthetic point cloud data based on IFC files can effectively make up for the lack of data in construction scenarios.

The flow chart of the entire BIM to point cloud conversion is as follows:

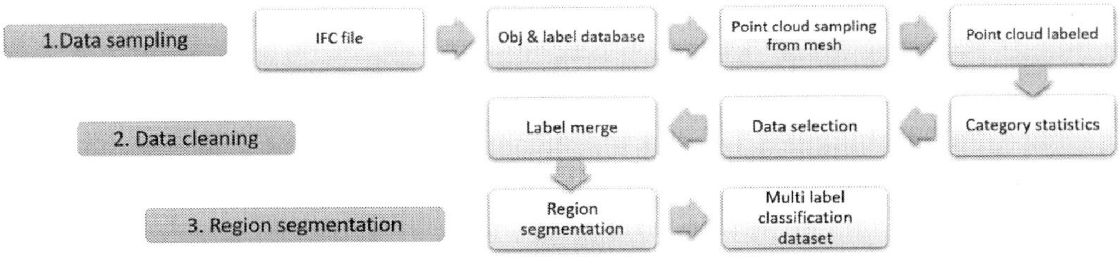

Figure 1: The flow chart of the entire BIM to point cloud conversion.

Synthesize Point Clouds from IFC. The first step is to construct building foundation components datasets automatically. We start from the IFC file of the actual building and generate a synthetic data set for training. In the first step, we convert the files from the industry foundation class format (.ifc) to obj format files (.obj) for each object based on CBIMS software platform. Second, we performed point cloud sampling and labeling from the mesh of the obj files for each foundation components class (such as wall, column, pipe, door, window, etc) through open3D. The sampling method is not random sampling but uniform sampling according to the size of the area. At the same time, the unit of length and area in IFC is unified into meters.

Label Classification and Data Cleaning Based on IFC Standards. There are more than 20 common types of IFC in construction scenarios according to statistics, but the main data types are IfcSlab, IfcBeam, IfcWall, IfcWallStandardCase, IfcColumn, IfcDoor, IfcWindow, IfcFlowFitting...These are also the main component in the construction process. According to the business needs of component identification in the construction scene, the IFC type is merged and finally focused on the following five types: IfcSlab, IfcBeam, IfcWall, IfcColumn, IfcDistributionFlowElement. IfcWall is a mixed representation of IfcWallStandardCase, and IfcDistributionFlowElement is a mixed representation of all categories related to IfcFlow. IfcBuildingElementProxy is deleted because of not a key category during construction, IfcGrid is deleted due to the existence only in IFC and not in actual buildings, and the remaining types are included in the other category.

Extract Different Small Blocks from Point Clouds. Since the point clouds extracted from the multi-story building are too large, which is not conducive to segmentation, we divide the point cloud data obtained in the previous step into blocks. Different from the point cloud voxelization operation, we only convert a large-scale point cloud into a small-scale point cloud according to certain rules, and there is no change for base objects.IfcSpace and floor elements are two kinds of available information. IfcSpace-based separation methods have certain limitations due to the lack of IFC files containing complete IfcSpace information, as well as inaccuracies at the edges of the room. Therefore, we first cut multi-story buildings into single-story buildings, then randomly cut on the XY plane of single-story buildings. Finally, the optimal division results are obtained after testing different block sizes through experiments.

3.2 Semantic Segmentation Based on Point transformer and Focal Loss

Semantic Segmentation Network. Point transformer is the classification and segmentation network for point clouds proposed by Oxford University et al, which has been verified to perform well on many point clouds datasets like S3DIS. And the most important design layer is Point transformer layer. This layer is invariant to arrangement and cardinality, so it is essentially suitable for point cloud processing. Besides, U-net structure is used in semantic segmentation, including 5 encoders and 5 decoders. The encoder uses Transition Down and Point transformer Block to down-sampling and extracts features, and the decoder uses Transition Up and Point transformer Block to up-sampling and mapping feature. Figure 3 shows the structure of Point transformer.

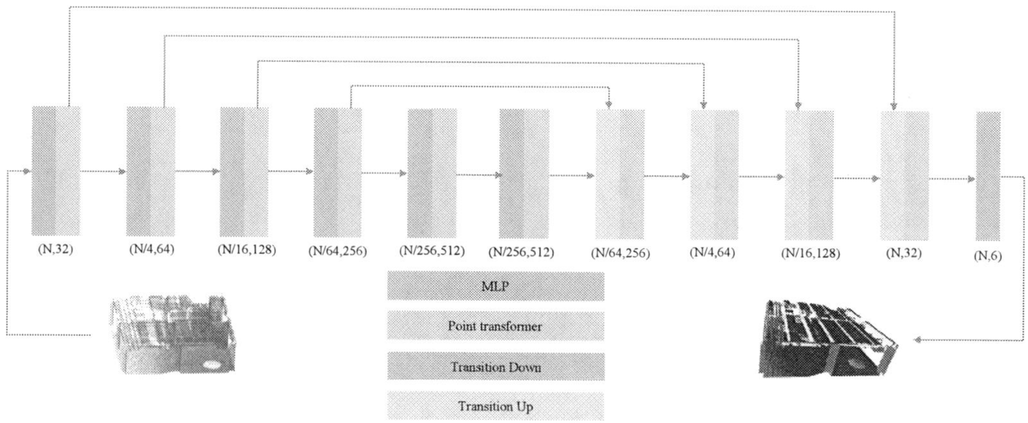

Figure 4 : The structure of Point transformer.

Based on Point transformer, we segment the construction scene point cloud into the above five types of components with the synthetic point cloud dataset obtained in the previous step as data enhancement and compared the effects of different ways of division on semantic segmentation through experiments.

Focal Loss Replaces Cross-entropy Loss. In the construction scene, the number and area of slabs and walls are large, and the relative sample number of columns, beams, and pipes is relatively small, which leads to the problem of multi-class sample imbalance. Therefore, we replace the cross-entropy loss function with the focal loss function, and give different weights to different categories according to the number of sample points and the difficulty of segmentation, so as to improve the segmentation effect.

$$Loss_{cross\ entropy} = -\frac{1}{N}\sum_{i}\sum_{c=1}^{M} y_{ic}\log(p_{ic}) \tag{1}$$

$$Loss_{focal} = -\frac{1}{N}\sum_{i}\sum_{c=1}^{M} y_{ic} * \alpha_c(1-p_{ic})^{\gamma}\, log(p_{ic}) \tag{2}$$

Equations (1) and (2) represent the loss calculation formulas of cross-entropy loss and focal loss in multi-classification where M is the number of label, y_{ic} (symbolic function)is 1 if ground truth is c, else 0, p_{ic} is predicted probability that the observed sample i belongs to the class c, a_c is the weight of class c and γ is the hyperarameter adjusted according to experiments. In the experiment, we set $\gamma = 0.2$, and α is adjusted according to the number of samples.

4. Experiments

4.1 Point Cloud Collection on Real Construction Scenes

The Trimble x7 laser scanner was used in the point cloud collection process with a scanning accuracy of 2mm. There are two types of scanned construction scene buildings. The first collection scene is on the tenth floor of a residential building under construction, covering an area of about 490 square meters. Most of the scenes are wall, beam, and slab structures, without electromechanical pipelines and column components; the second scene is a square in a square. On the first floor of the basement, the actual scanned model area is about 8,000 square meters. In addition to the basic wall, beam, and slab structures, it includes a large number of column structures and electromechanical pipe structures.

Due to the large amount of data collected on-site results in the high memory usage, the point cloud data was down-sampled under the premise of meeting the accuracy requirements, and the minimum point distance of the final point cloud was 0.03m. The region is also divided to eight sub-scenarios.

4.2 Synthetic Dataset for Construction Scenes

According to the synthetic conversion method from BIM to point cloud proposed in Section 3, the design model(IFC) of the construction building is converted to a synthetic point cloud dataset on the construction site. Each scene is a single-story building, not containing decorations such as furniture, and the basic components such as beams, columns, and walls occupy the majority. Figure 4 shows one of these synthetic data scenarios.

Figure 4: One Sysnthetic Scene.

We optimized the size of the block and slide into the Point transformer on synthetic datasets. Considering whether the column can be included in a block facade, we set the minimum block size to 1m, and test the segmentation accuracy on the synthetic dataset under different parameter configurations(see Table 1). In the experiment, block=2.5m and slide=1m achieved the highest accuracy.

Table 1: The effect of different blocks and slides on the segmentation accuracy of synthetic datasets.

Block size	**Slide**	**Accuracy**
5	2.5	0.74
2.5	1	0.88
1	0.5	0.62

4.3 Semantic Segmentation Results

Through comparison of different block divisions, we choose the optimal parameter (block = 2.5m, slide size = 1m) to generate the segmentation dataset, and then segment on the synthetic data and the real dataset scanned in Section 4.1.

Table 2: Compare results using S3DIS for enhancement and synthetic data for enhancement.

Class	**Acc(S3DIS+real)**	**Acc(synthetic+real)**
IfcSlab	0.990	0.990
IfcBeam	0.758	0.783
IfcWall	0.960	0.966
IfcColumn	**0.559**	**0.905**

Table 2 shows the results of comparative experiments using S3DIS for enhancement and synthetic data for enhancement. Since there is no pipe in S3DIS, we only chose four real sub-scenarios including only four types (IfcSlab, IfcBeam, IfcWall, IfcColumn), to compare the experimental results obtained by using S3DIS for enhancement and synthetic data for enhancement. It shows that indoor datasets like S3DIS that contain a large number of furniture, stairs, and other irrelevant components and have high color discrimination are not suitable for construction scenarios. However, when the synthetic dataset proposed in this paper is used for data enhancement, the segmentation accuracy on beams and columns is improved to a certain extent.

Table 3: Compare segmentation accuracy of five types under cross-entropy loss and focal loss.

Class	**Acc(cross entropy loss)**	**Acc(focal loss)**
IfcSlab	0.960	0.951
IfcBeam	**0.679**	**0.794**
IfcWall	0.915	0.837
IfcColumn	**0.122**	**0.422**
IfcDistributionFlowElement	**0.695**	**0.746**

In order to better distinguish pipe in the MEP system and important structural components, we added four construction sub-scenarios containing pipe and structural categories. At the same time, in order to improve the segmentation effect of beams and columns, we use focal loss function. We compared the segmentation accuracy of five types under cross entropy loss and focal loss(see Table 3). We compared IOU of five types under cross-entropy loss and focal loss(see Table 4).

Table 4: Compare IOU of five types under cross entropy loss and focal loss .

Class	IOU(no focal loss)	IOU(focal loss)
IfcSlab	0.905	0.913
IfcBeam	0.470	0.431
IfcWall	0.677	0.640
IfcColumn	**0.106**	**0.248**
IfcDistributionFlowElement	**0.612**	**0.655**

Table 4 shows that after replacing the loss function with our segmentation network, the segmentation accuracy of beams, columns, and pipes is improved, especially for columns, while the segmentation accuracy of beams and walls remains unchanged. Figure 5 shows three real sub-scene segmentation results, the left column is ground truth, and the right column is the segmentation result.

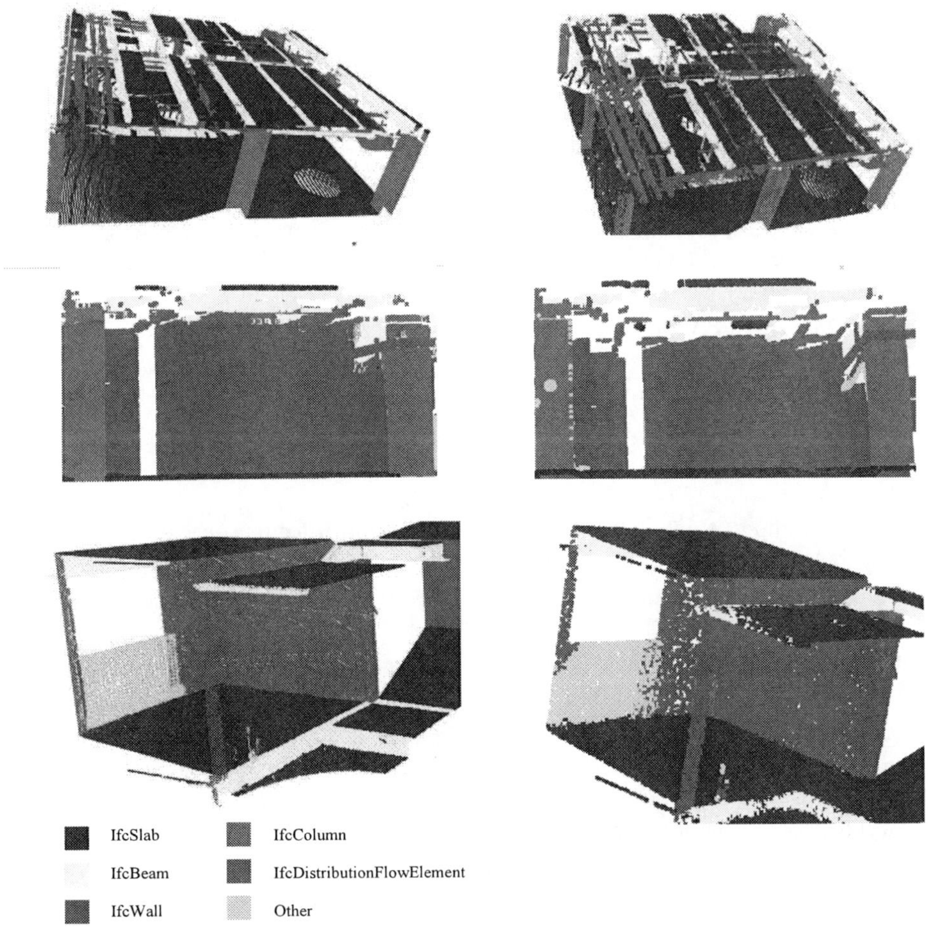

Figure 5: Three real sub-scene segmentation results, the left column is ground truth, and the right column is the segmentation result.

5. Conclusion & Outlook

In this paper, a more efficient solution is proposed for multi-system multi-component semantic understanding, from generating data, to proposing methods and solving special difficulties in construction. In view of the lack of synthetic data of construction buildings, we propose a method for generating synthetic point cloud datasets from IFC, which automatically generates annotated synthetic point cloud datasets. Aiming at the problem of non-uniform component classification standards, we use IFC as a reference to determine the category of segmentation objects to ensure the unification of upstream and downstream tasks. Aiming at the inaccurate segmentation of multi-category components in multiple systems, we use synthetic datasets for data enhancement, segment the construction point cloud into five categories(IfcSlab, IfcBeam, IfcWall, IfcColumn, IfcDistributionFlowElement) with a better segmentation network Point transformer, and introduce focal loss to solve the problem of unbalanced component samples in construction scenes. We hope that more good methods can be proposed in the future to solve the problem of semantic information understanding in more subdivided categories for construction scenarios.

Acknowledgement

This work was supported by the 2019 MIIT Industrial Internet Innovation and Development Project " BIM Software Industry Standardization and Public Service Platform".

References

Avetisyan, A., Khanova, T., Choy, C., Dash, D., Dai, A., and Nießner, M. (2020, August). Scenecad: Predicting object alignments and layouts in rgb-d scans. In European Conference on Computer Vision. Springer, Cham., pp. 596-612.

Bosché, F., Ahmed, M., Turkan, Y., Haas, C. T., and Haas, R. (2015). The value of integrating Scan-to-BIM and Scan-vs-BIM techniques for construction monitoring using laser scanning and BIM: The case of cylindrical MEP components. Automation in Construction, 49, pp.201-213.

Bosché, F., Guillemet, A., Turkan, Y., Haas, C. T., and Haas, R. (2014). Tracking the built status of MEP works: Assessing the value of a Scan-vs-BIM system. Journal of computing in civil engineering, 28(4), 05014004.

Collins, F. (2020). Encoding of geometric shapes from Building Information Modeling (BIM) using graph neural networks.

Engel, N., Belagiannis, V. and Dietmayer, K. (2021). Point transformer. IEEE Access, 9, pp.134826-134840.

Kim, H., and Kim, C. (2021). 3D as-built modeling from incomplete point clouds using connectivity relations. Automation in Construction, 130, p.103855.

Kim, Y., Nguyen, C. H. P., and Choi, Y. (2020). Automatic pipe and elbow recognition from three-dimensional point cloud model of industrial plant piping system using convolutional neural network-based primitive classification. Automation in Construction, 116, p.103236.

Ma, J., Czerniawski, T. and Leite, F. (2020). Semantic segmentation of point clouds of building interiors with deep learning: Augmenting training datasets with synthetic BIM-based point clouds. Automation in Construction, 113, p.103144.

Murali, S., Speciale, P., Oswald, M. R., and Pollefeys, M. (2017, September). Indoor Scan2BIM: Building information models of house interiors. In 2017 IEEE/RSJ International Conference on Intelligent Robots and Systems (IROS)., pp. 6126-6133.

Phan, A.V., Le Nguyen, M., Nguyen, Y.L.H. and Bui, L.T. (2018). Dgcnn: A convolutional neural network over large-scale labeled graphs. Neural Networks, 108, pp.533-543.

Qi, C.R., Su, H., Mo, K. and Guibas, L.J. (2017). Pointnet: Deep learning on point sets for 3d classification and segmentation. In Proceedings of the IEEE conference on computer vision and pattern recognition.,pp. 652-660.

Qi, C.R., Yi, L., Su, H. and Guibas, L.J. (2017). Pointnet++: Deep hierarchical feature learning on point sets in a metric space. Advances in neural information processing systems, 30.

Rebolj, D., Pučko, Z., Babič, N. Č., Bizjak, M., and Mongus, D. (2017). Point cloud quality requirements for Scan-vs-BIM based automated construction progress monitoring. Automation in Construction, 84, pp.323-334.

Riegler, G., Osman Ulusoy, A. and Geiger, A.(2017). Octnet: Learning deep 3d representations at high resolutions. In Proceedings of the IEEE conference on computer vision and pattern recognition.,pp. 3577-3586.

Tatarchenko, M., Park, J., Koltun, V. and Zhou, Q.Y. (2018). Tangent convolutions for dense prediction in 3d. In Proceedings of the IEEE Conference on Computer Vision and Pattern Recognition.,pp.3887-3896.

Tran, H., and Khoshelham, K. (2019). Building change detection through comparison of a lidar scan with a building information model. The International Archives of Photogrammetry, Remote Sensing and Spatial Information Sciences, 42, pp.889-893.

A Redundancy-free IFC Storage Platform For Multi-model Scenarios based on Block Hash

Li S.[1], Gao G.[1,2,*], Wang W.[3], Liu H.[1], Zhu S.[1], Gu M.[1,2]
[1]School of Software, Tsinghua University, Beijing, China, [2]Beijing National Research Center for Information Science and Technology(BNRist), Tsinghua University, Beijing, China, [3]State Key Laboratory of Rail Transit Engineering Informatization (FSDI), China
gaoge@tsinghua.edu.cn

Abstract. This paper proposes a block hash (BH) method for efficiently storing multiple Industry Foundation Classes (IFC) models in the database. We find that there are lots of duplications when we store different models or different versions of a model into the database because of the temporal-spatial correlation of data between these models. The main idea of our approach is to divide these model files into appropriate blocks and to calculate the hash values of these blocks to reuse the them in different models. These blocks should not be too small in case too many nodes need to be compared, nor should they be too large in case it is difficult to find identical blocks to share between different models. So the BH method is proposed to efficiently make the database redundancy-free. For the experiments we use multi-versions of multiple models of a same project to validate this method. The experimental results show that our method is practicable and efficient.

1. Introduction

Building Information Modeling (BIM) technology has been widely applied in the construction industry. Since every stage of a facility will involves multiple institutions, data resource sharing becomes significant and urgent. BuildingSMART proposed Industry Foundation Classes (IFC), a standardized, digital description of the build asset industry. It provides an international standard for many different applications and promotes the exchange and sharing of data. As a way to exchange a BIM file between different software, IFC is designed to be non-redundant and concise in a monolithic file. However, with the application of BIM becoming more and more collaborative, and the model size becoming increasingly larger, non-file based BIM sharing platform is becoming necessary. These platforms, such as CDE (Common Data Environment), FM (Facility Management platform) and Archiving, etc., usually provide storing, querying, managing and viewing functions for multiple BIM models supported by database.

Typically, many of these models may be different parts of a same project, or different versions of a same design, or generated by the same team, so the data in these models may have temporal or spatial correlation. The well-designed inner structure of the IFC file cannot prevent the large amount of duplicate data across these models.

So many people try to extract IFC model information and store it in different types of databases. Nevertheless, the existing approaches seem inefficient for some multi-model task scenarios.

In this work, we proposed the block hash (BH) method to merge the duplicate nodes in IFC files. This method takes advantage of the structure of IFC. It not only reduces the space cost of the storage, but also reduces the upload time required for the storage. Based on this method, we have established a redundancy-free IFC storage platform. In the platform we provide the interfaces for saving and querying information from multiple models. we adopt MongoDB for the underlying database of the platform for its good applicability and great read performance in the case of high load. Moreover, the block hash method may also be used for storage based on other databases. The current experimental results show that BH method is very effective in handling with multi-model tasks. And it also has good scalability for subsequent research.

https://doi.org/10.7146/aul.455.c198

2. Related Works

2.1 Model Storage in BIM

IFC has many expression formats like the SPF (STEP Physical File) format, XML, JSON and so on. The SPF format includes HEADER and DATA two parts. HEADER is used to record some meta data such as IFC Schema version, model name and description etc. DATA is for the real model data which is organized according to the IFC specification.

Krijnen and Beetz (Krijnen and Beetz, 2016) put forward the method of using HDF5 to store IFC models, which greatly reduces the querying time of some components such as obtaining the largest window in the model. This method is more advantageous than the traditional formats in many aspects. But there are still difficulties in data sharing and updating.

These file-based methods mentioned above are still unstructured or semi-structured. This makes it difficult to realize the data features urgently needed by BIM, such as data management, sharing and updating. Therefore, more people are exploring other storage methods like using databases or blockchain to store BIM model to solve these problems.

BuildingSMART is carrying out the experiment of using SQLite to store IFC model. The purpose is to provide a standard format of SQLite to store IFC data. In the aspect of relational database, Li et al. stored IFC model into ORACLE database in order to verify the feasibility of IFC database storage idea (Li et al., 2016). The experiment proved the feasibility of lossless storage of IFC data by database, but the actual speeds were not satisfactory. Beetz et al. proposed BIM Server of BerkeleyDB which is a key-value database (Beetz et al., 2010). The architecture realized the conversion from IFC file to database by building a service layer and the KeyValueStore Interface was provided to connect to different databases. But so far, only the open source BerkeleyDB Java Edition database is realized (opensourceBIM, 2021). Yuan et al. also adopted the column-oriented database HBase to store IFC model (Yuan and Shihua, 2017). Jiang and Wu put forward the method of storing IFC by using Elastic Search framework and the graph database Neo4j. However only the spatial data of IFC model was stored (Jiang and Wu, 2018). In 2019, Gao et al. proposed to use knowledge base and graph database to store IFC model data. This method was mainly used to improve the efficiency of automatic model checking (Gao et al., 2019).

Apart from the methods mentioned above, there are some storage systems such as the BIM-server (Singh, Gu and Wang, 2011). These achievements indicate that structured storage of BIM data is promising. The purpose of this research is to provide a general hashing method to effectively compare the differences between different models or versions. It is helpful to reduce the duplicate data and get the difference easily.

2.2 Model Compression in BIM

IFC has excellent structural design, which can reuse data to reduce storage space. However due to the different IFC export algorithms adopted by different applications, there will be some duplicate nodes in one model. Especially some fundament types like IfcCartesianPoint and IfcPropertySingleValue will have some duplicate instances. There are some compression algorithms to remove these like the IFCCompressor which compresses the IFC files by line by line (Sun et al., 2015) and ACC4IFC which takes the default value into consideration (Du et al., 2020). The basic ideas of these algorithms are very concise. They want to remove the duplicate nodes and reuse the left one to make the model as small as possible. And the facts have proved that these methods can effectively compress IFC models. These algorithms mainly focus on the compression of single model. But the more important problem that this research intends to solve is the duplicate data between different models especially different versions of the same model like Figure 1. Although we can still use similar methods to compress these models but there will be some problems and we will discuss in the methodology and experiment section.

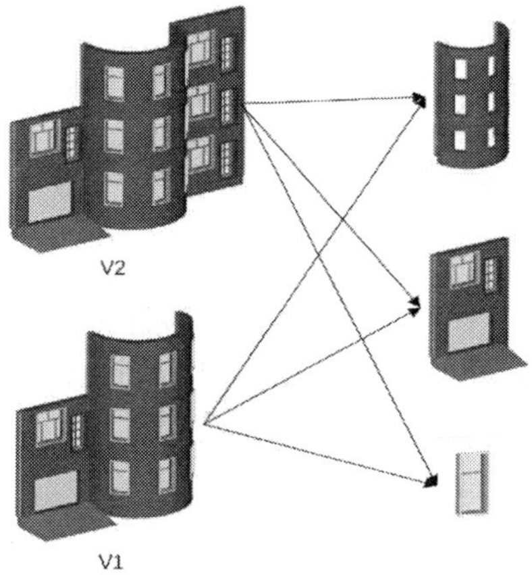

Figure 1: The elements shared in different model versions.

In addition to the content-based compression methods, there are also some other compression algorithms like the mesh simplification (Algorri et al., 1996; Cignoni et al., 1998) and so on. Most of these methods simplify the geometric information of the model and will lose some fine geometric information. In this study we want to keep all the information in the origin model and we will not use these lossy compression methods.

3. Research Methodology

In this section, we mainly present the methodology how we implement hashing algorithm and the way we build our platform based on BH.

Every release of the IFC specifications has strict regulations on every node type. The inheritance diagram (or specification) of IfcRoot in IFC2X3 is presented below.

```
ENTITY IfcRoot
    ABSTRACT SUPERTYPE OF (ONEOF (IfcPropertyDefinition, IfcRelationship, IfcObjectDefinition));
        GlobalId          :    IfcGloballyUniqueId;
        OwnerHistory      :    IfcOwnerHistory;
        Name              :    OPTIONAL IfcLabel;
        Description       :    OPTIONAL IfcText;
    UNIQUE
        UR1               :    GlobalId;
END_ENTITY;
```

It's clear to figure out every parameter in this basic type. There are some reference parameters like the OwnerHistory. According to the specification we can define one IfcOwnerHistory node here or reference another node whose type is IfcOwnerHistory.

The size of one node is determined by these parameters. Assuming that the average size of one certain type is s and the file size is S, we can get that:

$$S = \sum_{t \in types} s_t \times c_t \quad (1)$$

where the c_t means the number of the node whose type is t.

It can be seen from Equation (1) that in order to reduce the storage space of IFC models, we can reduce the size of a single node or the number of nodes. It is obvious that we can use one algorithm similar to the content-based compression algorithms to compare these models as one to remove the duplicate nodes. However, the number of nodes is too large to deal with and the different content makes it hard to compare these nodes one by one. The hash algorithm is used to convert an arbitrary node into an encrypted output of a fixed length and it helps to decrease the complexity of comparison. Our platform adopts MD5 (Rivest and Dusse, 1992) as the hash algorithm, so each hash is 16bytes long. The number of nodes in a 200MB IFC file is about 3000000, which means that about 45.78MB of hash data needs to be saved.

If we get rid of the hash method, although we don't need to save these hashes, the comparison between different lengths of content will become more difficult. Each new model uploading will need to load all the models which is impossible for the current hardware. So, it is necessary to reduce the number of hashes, that is, the number of nodes, in order to speed up the calculation. For the above reasons it's important to merge some nodes as one whole part to participate in the procession.

3.1 Calculate one block from IFC model

Because of the reference relationship in IFC structure, the algorithm can start from one node that is not referenced by other nodes, and recursively find all the referenced nodes to form a data block. However, this will cause a lot of duplicate nodes. For example, there is usually only one IfcOwnerHistory node in one IFC model and all other nodes that inherit from IfcRoot reference to this one. And the above blocking strategy will cause this node to be repeated tens of thousands of times, resulting in a sharp increase in storage space. So, in this circumstance, the nodes with many references should also be partitioned and the equation of S becomes:

$$S = s_t + \sum_{t' \in refs} B_{s_{t'}} \times Q_{t'} \tag{2}$$

$$S \approx \sum_{t' \in types} B_{s_t} \times c_t \times (1 - Q_t) \tag{3}$$

where B_{s_t} means the block starts with the node whose type is t, s_t means the average size of node whose type is t, refs means other node types referenced by type t, and Q_t represents whether the node is the head node, which can be expressed as Equation (4).

$$Q_t = \begin{cases} 0, & t \text{ is the head type} \\ 1, & t \text{ is not head type} \end{cases} \tag{4}$$

If every type is the head type, the Equation (3) degenerates to Equation (1) which means calculating hash for each line.

According to the above analysis, it can be concluded that in order to reduce the data expansion, the key is to define the head type. Therefore, the following BH method is proposed.

1. Considering that the header nodes are easy to create index, all types with GlobalId need to be used as header type.
2. Count the quantities of nodes corresponding to each type of all IFC models in this project and save them.
3. Start from the nodes with GlobalId to find the referenced nodes recursively. The number of referenced nodes corresponding to each type in the recursion process is counted and saved.

4. Divide the referenced number of this type by the number of nodes, and set a threshold. When the result is greater than this threshold, the Q value of this type is set to 0.

The change of the threshold will result in the following results: If the threshold value is too high, most types will not be partitioned. It will result in excessive data redundancy. If the threshold value is too low, it will lead to a large number of types. In extreme cases, it will degenerate into Equation (1). Therefore, the factors to be considered when setting the threshold include the configuration of the server for storage, the total model size of the project, the network situation for uploading and the general configuration of the computer hardware for uploading IFC files, etc.

Since the project models may be constantly increasing from the beginning of the project, the threshold cannot be accurately calculated. Considering the various factors that affect the storage space, querying efficiency and processing speed, we can finally roughly estimate a threshold range according to the required hash quantity and storage space. If the total number of nodes is in the order of tens of millions, it is hoped that the number of hashes can be reduced to the previous 1/4. In this algorithm, the threshold can be selected in the range of 4-6.

3.2 Calculate hash for each block.

After we get the blocks of the model, we require removing the duplicate blocks. Calculating the hash for each block is necessary. For there is only one header in each block, we can replace the reference with the node itself in this header. In this way we can get one node that combines all nodes in this block like the nodes #13 and #14 in Figure 2 which replace the reference in #7 and # 12. And the final block is only related to the existing blocks like #14. It should be noted that the existing blocks not only refer to the blocks in this model, but also include the blocks in the other uploaded models. Therefore, the line number cannot be duplicated and must be incremented even in different models. Then we will calculate hash for #13 and #14 using the text. Although the hashing algorithms are sensitive to changes like adding or removing just one whitespace. We will pay attention to the IFC models derived from other applications like Revit for it's hard to modify the IFC model itself currently. So, the format of IFC is fixed and we can ignore some small changes.

```
DATA;
#1= IFCPERSON($,'\X2\672A5B9A4E49\X0\',$,$,$,$,$,$);
#3= IFCORGANIZATION($,'\X2\672A5B9A4E49\X0\',$,$,$);
#7= IFCPERSONANDORGANIZATION(#1,#3,$);
#10= IFCORGANIZATION('GS','GRAPHISOFT','GRAPHISOFT',$,$);
#11= IFCAPPLICATION(#10,'22.0.0','ARCHICAD-64','IFC add-on version: 4005 CHI FULL');
#12= IFCOWNERHISTORY(#7,#11,$,.ADDED.,$,$,$,1557220048);

#13= IFCPERSONANDORGANIZATION(IFCPERSON($,'\X2\672A5B9A4E49\X0\',$,$,$,$,$,$),IFCORGANIZATION($,'\X2\672A5B9A4E49\X0\',$,$,$),$);
#14= IFCOWNERHISTORY(#13, IFCAPPLICATION(IFCORGANIZATION('GS','GRAPHISOFT','GRAPHISOFT',$,$);
                    ,'22.0.0','ARCHICAD-64','IFC add-on version: 4005 CHI FULL');,$,.ADDED.,$,$,$,1557220048);
```

Figure 2: Example to Calculate BH.

3.3 Hash comparison based on the node block

The way to store and query all hash data has a strong impact on the upload time. Here we use the Redis and bloomfilter (Bloom, 1970) to store and query hash data. To accelerate this process, we also add the local cache to save the known results. When querying whether this value exists, first we need to look for it in local hash cache, next the local bloomfilter and finally the Redis until we get the precious consequence. The process can be shown as Figure 3.
The bloomfilter essentially holds an array of bits of length m. K ($k<m$) positions of each data are calculated by k hash functions, and the corresponding position is set to 1 in the array. The

structure can be shown as Figure 4. When querying, the data is also calculated by these k hash functions to get the corresponding positions. If the corresponding positions are all 1, it is proved that the data may exist. If one of them is 0, the data must not exist. It is originally a plug-in in Redis. We will load these data into one local self-developed bloomfilter before the upload starts to reduce the impact of network delay.

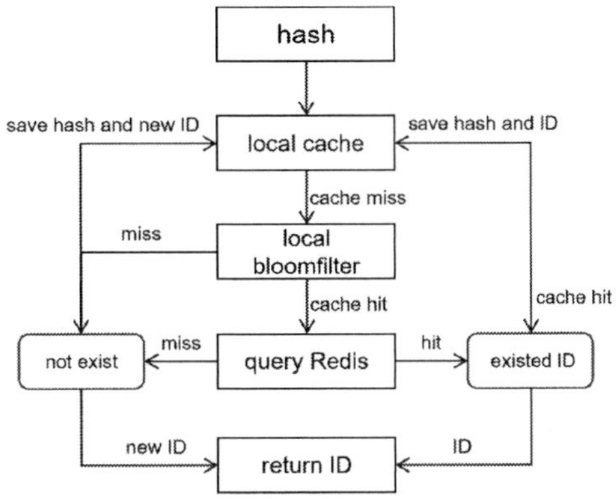

Figure 3: Hash Querying Process.

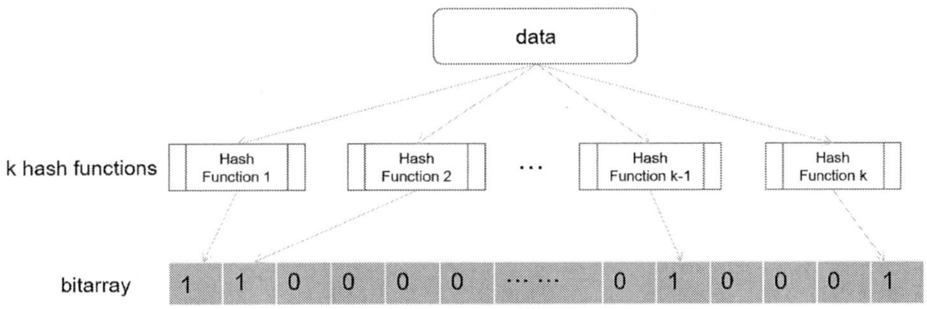

Figure 4: Bloomfilter Structure.

3.4 Creating block index in the database

After the model is uploaded, the index that indicates the reference between different nodes and some other indexes will be constructed, which will also include composite index. All subsequent query processes are based on these indexes. These indexes include the GlobalId index, the model index, the reference blocks index etc. According to the document of MongoDB, for a compound multikey index, each indexed document can have at most one indexed field whose value is an array. So here we can create as more as possible compound indexes apart from those who have two fields whose value is an array to help the data querying.

4. Experiments and Results

4.1 Test environment and models

First of all, we need to set up our platform. It includes MongoDB and Redis two databases. To reduce network delay, we recommend to deploy them on one server or two servers located in the same high-speed LAN (1GbE we used in our experiments). We chose the latter in order to present the experimental results better. The following experiments were performed on two laptop computers both equipped with an Intel Core i7-10700F CPU (2.9 GHz), 32GB RAM and 128G hard disk.

For the experimental models we selected three models from different floors of the same building. We removed parts of these models and got another three models that we called the second version (V2). Figure 5 presents the first version (V1) and V2 of these models. There are so many similar elements like pipelines, walls between different models or different versions. All the evaluations were performed on the six models. The sizes of the six models are 353MB, 360MB, 261MB, 196MB, 11.4MB and 10.8MB from a to f in Figure 5. We used three methods to upload the models, namely BH, line hash (LH) which means calculating hash line by line and no hash (NH) which means just storing every line of the IFC models. Two experiments were carried out for each method and tested removal of the spatial and temporal redundancy respectively. Because we will not change the BH strategy in the whole experiment, so the results are independent of the order of upload, which represents the addition or deletion of some parts. As for the modification, we can regard it as deletion and then addition. So, these experiments are enough to cover the common operations in the real-world version.

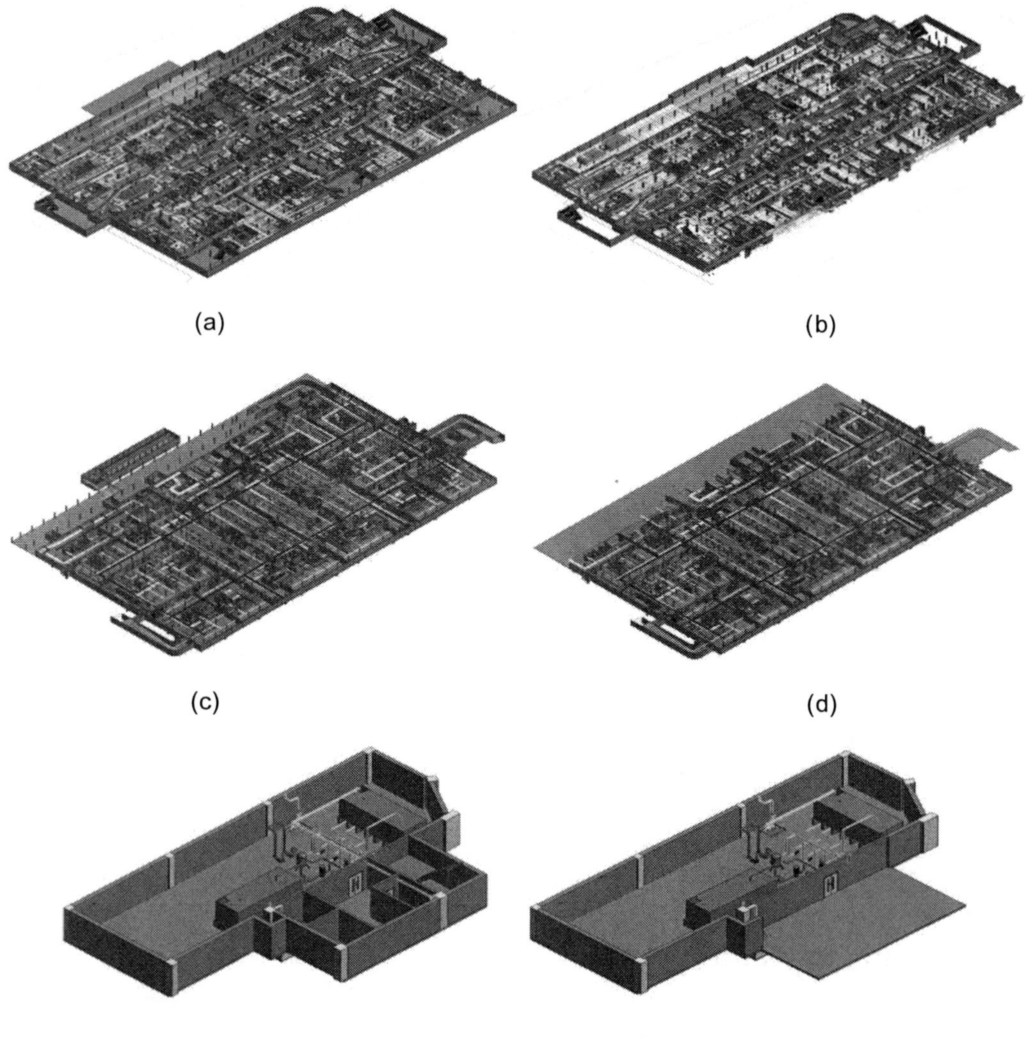

Figure 5: Test models. These models are from the basements of the same building. (a), (c), (e) are V1 models and (b), (d), (f) are V2 models.

4.2 Evaluation of removing structural redundancy.

We uploaded all the V1 models to test these methods and the Table 1 shows the upload results.

Table 1: Upload V1 models results.

Upload method	Time (m)	MongoDB space (MB)	No. of Block or Line	Redis Mem (MB)	Mem (GB)
BH	20	788.7 + 400.6	2899510	220.72	5.1
LH	132	653.6 + 682.2	6577498	489.17	5.3
NH	120	993.5+ 940.4	10578153	0	9.3

The occupied MongoDB space is divided into two parts because we need to build some index for querying. In order to be more intuitive, we show this part of data separately. The first part is the model data and the second is the index data. The index space is positively correlated with the number of hashes because we need to build index for every node.

Comparing the results of LH and NH, we can find that there are so many duplicate data between different models. The method LH can effectively remove these duplicate data but because of too many hashes, the speed, occupied Redis memory and index space are not satisfactory. By BH, we reduced the number of hashes to 27% of NH and 44% of LH. Although the space occupied by model data of BH is bigger than LH, the index takes up much less space than the other two methods. Due to less hashes, BH is six times faster than the other two methods and Redis takes less memory. Too many nodes will cause frequent reading and writing of a small amount of data for MongoDB and Redis, which will greatly affect the upload speed. The maximum memory occupied by the program during running is also reduced.

4.3 Evaluation of removing version redundancy.

We uploaded the V2 models on the basis of experiment 4.2 and get the final results which are show in Table 2. Except for the time and memory, all the remaining records are the sum of two experiments.

Table 2: Upload V2 models results.

Upload method	Time (m)	MongoDB space (MB)	No. of Block or Line	Redis Mem (MB)	Mem (GB)
BH-V1	20	788.7 + 400.6	2899510	220.72	5.1
BH-V2	15	1.0 GB + 696	3772968	286.05	4.8
LH-V1	132	653.6 + 682.2	6577498	489.17	5.3
LH-V2	98	826.1 +1.2GB	7455914	566.72	3.2
NH-V1	120	993.5+ 940.4	10578153	0	9.3
NH-V2	102	1.9GB+1.78GB	20090161	0	9.1

According to the NH results, the line number of V2 is almost the same as V1. In this experiment the method LH removed more nodes and the proportion of remaining nodes in the total decreased from 62% to 37%. In the method BH, the number of blocks is just about 1.3 times of V1. All these indicate that these two methods can remove lots of redundant data between model versions. It is still the number of nodes that causes the other two methods to be slow. Although there is no hash in NH means we don't need to calculate, save and query the hash, too many nodes will still cause slow writing to MongoDB and large memory consumption. At the same time the index space is also a factor that cannot be ignored. There are so many nodes we will never query or get. It's a waste to build index for these nodes. If we take the index space into consideration, BH's space occupation will become the lowest. The other advantages of BH are the same as experiment 4.2.

5. Conclusion

In this work, we have implemented the redundancy-free IFC storage platform which is based on the BH method. Compared with the other method like the traditional storage ways or the other hash methods, this approach has the following advantages:

- There is a lot of redundancy between different models or different versions. BH can help to remove these duplicate data and save space.
- Compared with other method, BH can greatly improve efficiency by reducing the number of hashes. This method can reduce the reading and writing times of the database, and organize IFC data more efficiently.
- The memory required for BH operation and Redis is lower which makes it better used in practical application.

By BH and other improvements we built the redundancy-free IFC storage platform. The advantages of this platform largely match the current BIM development trend-fast data sharing and exchange. However, due to the huge amount of data, storage based on database cannot completely replace file-based storage at present. In this study, MongoDB, a non-relational database is used to store IFC model data, and some algorithms such as BH and hash querying acceleration are proposed by using the structural characteristics of IFC, which greatly improves the usability of BIM database.

This proposed method has been successfully approved that BH is effective. But there are still some problems to be solved, such as how to reach the optimality, build more efficient indexes or make the database support more IFC data. The future research may explore how to modify the current database technology and make it more suitable for the massive, rapid-changing BIM data.

Acknowledgement

This work was supported by the State Key Laboratory of Rail Transit Engineering Informatization (FSDI) "Research on the framework of Enterprise Railway BIM collaborative platform" and the 2019 MIIT Industrial Internet Innovation and Development Project "BIM Software Industry Standardization and Public Service Platform". The conclusions herein are those of the authors and do not necessarily reflect the views of the sponsoring agency.

References

Algorri, M.E. and Schmitt, F. (1996, August). Mesh simplification. In Computer Graphics Forum (Vol. 15, No. 3, pp. 77-86). Edinburgh, UK: Blackwell Science Ltd.

Beetz, J., van Berlo, L., de Laat, R., & van den Helm, P. (2010, November). BIMserver. org– An open source IFC model server. In Proceedings of the CIP W78 conference (p. 8).

Bloom, B.H., (1970). Space/time trade-offs in hash coding with allowable errors. Communications of the ACM, 13(7), pp.422-426.

Cignoni, P., Montani, C. and Scopigno, R. (1998). A comparison of mesh simplification algorithms. Computers & Graphics, 22(1), pp.37-54.

Du, X., Gu, Y., Yang, N., & Yang, F. (2020). IFC File Content Compression Based on Reference Relationships. Journal of Computing in Civil Engineering, 34(3), 04020012.

Jiang, S., Wu, Z. (2018). Research on Cloud Storage and Retrieval Method of BIM Spatial Relational Data. Journal of Graphics, 39(5), p.835.

Gao, G., Zhang, Y., Liu, H., Li, Z., Gu, M. (2019). Research on IFC Model Checking Method Based on Knowledge Base. Journal of Graphics, 40(6), p.1099.

Krijnen, T., & Beetz, J. (2016). Efficient binary serialization of IFC models using HDF5. In Proceedings of the 16th International Conference on Computing in Civil and Building Engineering (ICCCBE2016) Osaka, Japan.

Li, H., Liu, H., Liu, Y., & Wang, Y. (2016). AN OBJECT-RELATIONAL IFC STORAGE MODEL BASED ON ORACLE DATABASE. International Archives of the Photogrammetry, Remote Sensing & Spatial Information Sciences, 41.

opensourceBIM, (2021). Database Versioning · opensouceBIM/BIMserver Wiki · Github, https://github.com/opensourceBIM/BIMserver/wiki/Database---Versioning, accessed January 2022.

Rivest, R. and Dusse, S., (1992). The MD5 message-digest algorithm.

Singh, V., Gu, N., & Wang, X. (2011). A theoretical framework of a BIM-based multi-disciplinary collaboration platform. Automation in construction, 20(2), 134-144.

Sun, J., Liu, Y. S., Gao, G., & Han, X. G. (2015). IFCCompressor: A content-based compression algorithm for optimizing Industry Foundation Classes files. Automation in Construction, 50, 1-15.

Yuan, C., & Shihua, Y. (2017). Research on HBase-based BIM Model Storage Technology. Journal of Information Technologyin Civil Engineering and Architecture, 9(4), 74-81.

Real-Time Noise Sensing at Construction Sites based on Spatial Interpolation for Effective Reduction Measures

Lee G.[1], Moon S.[2], Hwang J.[1], Chi S.[1], Rim D.[3]
[1] Department of Civil and Environmental Engineering, Seoul National University, South Korea, [2] Institute of Construction and Environmental Engineering, Seoul National University, South Korea, [3] Department of Architectural Engineering, Pennsylvania State University, United States
lgt0427@snu.ac.kr

Abstract. Construction site noise needs to be properly managed because it affects the health and safety of workers and nearby residents. Therefore, the authors attempted to develop a real-time noise information mapping system for construction sites that can support the establishment of noise reduction measures by practitioners using spatial interpolation. Field constraints were identified to ensure that the noise-estimation model has high accuracy without disturbing workers. Spatial interpolation was utilized to develop the noise-estimation model, and the performance was evaluated by installing sensors in an experimental environment according to the field constraints. The model showed optimal performance, with maximum and minimum accuracies of 97.5% and 92.4%, respectively, when using eight sensing points as inputs. The research results were visualized through the Unity 3D Engine for the convenience of field workers. Through the results of this study, practitioners will be able to easily understand information on high-noise areas that need to be managed, thereby minimizing the cost and time required for on-site noise management.

1. Introduction

Proper noise monitoring at construction sites is crucial because noise pollution causes numerous health and safety issues and civil complaints (Ballesteros et al., 2010; Eom and Paek, 2009; Hughes et al., 2015; Jung et al., 2020; Kang et al., 2021). In practice, the field manager installs sound-level meters on the site fences to measure the noise, which does not help to understand the noise propagation mechanism of the site. Accordingly, it is difficult for the contractors to prepare appropriate countermeasures when civil complaints arise due to site noise, which hinders the construction process (Choi et al., 2021; Hong et al., 2021a; Kwon et al., 2016).

This disparity has led to many studies being conducted focusing on simulating noise using noise propagation models rather than collecting and analyzing noise through sensors. (Cai et al., 2015; Gulliver et al., 2015; Hong et al., 2021b; Lee et al., 2008). The results of these approaches are suitable for one-off environmental impact assessments; however, there are technical limitations to applying the results to monitoring noise that is constantly generated during the construction stage. Estimating field noise pattern with a noise propagation model requires the real-time directivity and location of the on-site noise source. However, it is challenging to accurately collect such information in real time given the changing field environment over time. For instance, since field noise sources perform their tasks while moving, it is impossible to collect directivity by placing sensors at the same distance from the noise source according to the regulations.

To overcome the application limitations of the previous approaches using the noise propagation model, in the construction stage, the research team aims to develop a method to sense real-time noise of the overall construction site using spatial interpolation. The spatial interpolation can estimate the noise levels of the desired area if only the noise levels at some points and the distances between the sensors are known, enabling it to be applied at the construction stage more accurately and efficiently compared to the noise propagation model.

https://doi.org/10.7146/aul.455.c199

2. Literature Review

Most of the research on estimating the noise patterns of construction sites is conducted based on noise propagation models specified in international standards such as ISO 9613-1 and 2 (Di et al., 2018; Gilchrist et al., 2003; Hong et al., 2015; Liu et al., 2021). The researchers have mainly analyzed how construction site noise spreads to the outside to respond to civil complaints that may occur during construction (Cai et al., 2015; Gannoruwa and Ruwanpura, 2007; Gulliver et al., 2015; Hong et al., 2021b; Lee et al., 2008; Santos de Oliveira et al., 2019). The propagation model calculates noise information at each point, considering the directivity of the noise source, the noise level for each octave band, as well as the surrounding terrain, temperature, and humidity. If the model has specific input data available, the noise level near the site can be estimated with good performance; as such, it can be used to estimate the damage caused by the field noise based on the equipment specification at the design phase. However, the detailed information about the input data is tricky to collect during the actual construction phase due to the constantly changing field environments. Thus, applying the propagation model to real-time monitoring of construction sites that continually change and have high levels of uncertainty is limited in practice.

Some researchers eventually decided that sensors should be utilized to obtain noise information reflecting irregularly changing field characteristics. Therefore, their research focused on developing a wireless sensor network that can be used more efficiently in construction sites by solving the inconvenience of installation and data transmission of conventional measurement systems. (Hong et al., 2022; Hughes et al., 2015; Kang et al., 2021). However, it is difficult to provide information to help practitioners manage noise by simply measuring the noise level at specific points like in practice.

It is true that existing studies have solved various problems that can occur due to construction noise, but attempts to derive meaningful information by analyzing the noise patterns generated during the construction stage were insufficient. Field managers still have a hard time checking which construction factors are the main cause when construction noise causes problems. If the problem cannot be responded to promptly, the construction must be stopped according to regulations, which inflicts significant financial damage on the contractors. For the purpose of bridging this research gap, the authors developed a method to sense and visualize the noise of the overall construction site in real time based on spatial interpolation.

3. Research Process

The process of this study consists of three steps. The first step involves identifying field constraints to be considered when placing sensors to ensure the performance and field applicability of the proposed system. Second, a low-computational yet accurate noise estimation model is developed to achieve real-time noise levels at every spot of the site. Lastly, in order to map the noise information at the grid level, the maximum noise value is extracted in units of 10m x 10m, and it is visualized in three dimensions (3D) by setting a representative value for each grid. The processing and analysis of the research data were implemented using Python version 3.7.10, and Unity 3D Engine version 2020.3.23f1 was utilized for visualization.

3.1 Identifying Field Constraints

There are various noise sources and factors that can affect noise propagation on construction sites. In addition, it may not be possible to install sensors at some points due to safety and productivity issues and space constraints. Accordingly, the authors identified field constraints that must be considered to minimize the number of sensor placements while maximizing the spatial interpolation performance without compromising safety and productivity. Based on 18 site experiments performed at different times, it was confirmed that to achieve satisfactory performance, the noise-estimation results must reflect the local extremum. This is because the spatial interpolation method estimates the noise level of the non-sensed points based on the measurement values of the surrounding sensors. In terms of noise, the local extremum points are located at the noise sources or around obstacles blocking the propagation path. Following the consultation of field workers, the authors found that noise-emission equipment, site fences (i.e., outer boundaries), steep slopes, and sound barriers were the points where sensors should be installed to detect noticeable noise changes.

On the other hand, the work areas and equipment traveling paths cannot be approached within a certain distance for various reasons. According to the safety management manual, the access restriction distance is determined differently depending on the type of work (MOLIT, 2014). In the case of earthworks covered in this study, 15m was defined as the access restriction distance. Therefore, this value was adopted as the minimum distance required when installing sensors near work areas and equipment traveling paths.

3.2 Developing Noise-Estimation Model

The authors developed a noise-estimation model based on spatial interpolation to obtain real-time noise levels at every spot of the site. Inverse Distance Weighted (IDW) interpolation, which gives greater weight to measurements near the estimated point, was utilized as the basis for the noise-estimation model. IDW is suitable for real-time estimation because it has the smallest amount of computation among the various interpolation methods. In addition, users can customize the equation in an uncomplicated way to achieve the desired results. The estimated noise level is calculated as shown in Equations 1 and 2 by the proposed model, where x^*, x_i, w_i, n, and d_i indicate the estimated noise level, actual value from the sensing data, weight, the number of measurement points, and distance between measured and estimated points, respectively. Since noise attenuation is largest at a location closest to the noise source (i.e., where the noise level is relatively high in the construction site), the weight of IDW was customized for this study by dividing it by the actual noise value. In this way, relatively low weights can be given to the points with high noise values to increase the attenuation effect for the points close to the noise source.

$$x^* = \sum_{i=1}^{n} \frac{x_i \cdot w_i}{w_i} \tag{1}$$

$$w_i = \frac{1}{(d_i \cdot x_i)^2} \tag{2}$$

The model's performance was verified through an experiment in a similar environment to the earthworks. In the experiment, noise sources were built to simulate construction site noise, and the system consisted of a passive speaker, an amplifier, and a mixer. The researchers selected the system components, considering whether they could generate loud noises like heavy equipment (i.e., more than 120dB). The excavator noise data acquired at the earthworks site were used as a sound source. The Tnsmars 103 sensor was selected, which complies with the international standard for sound level meter manufacturing. The error range of the sensor is decent at 1.5dB, while the cost is low at US$145, which is suitable for applying a large number of sensors for the experiment. The scale of the area was set to 200m x 50m by targeting the road construction site. The sensors were placed at intervals of 10m, and two noise sources were positioned. According to the field constraints, the experiment assumed that the sensor must be located more than 15m away from each noise source. The data collected from the placed sensors were stored in MongoDB, a NoSQL-based database system. The data contained time, latitude, longitude, and noise level information, as shown in Figure 1, and were sorted in ascending order by time. By randomly changing the input data, the interpolation model estimated the value from the remaining sensors. For instance, if noise data were collected by ten sensors installed at random positions among the 111 placement points, the interpolation model estimated the noise levels of the 101 non-sensed points. The performance of the model was evaluated as the difference between the actual ground truths and the estimated values.

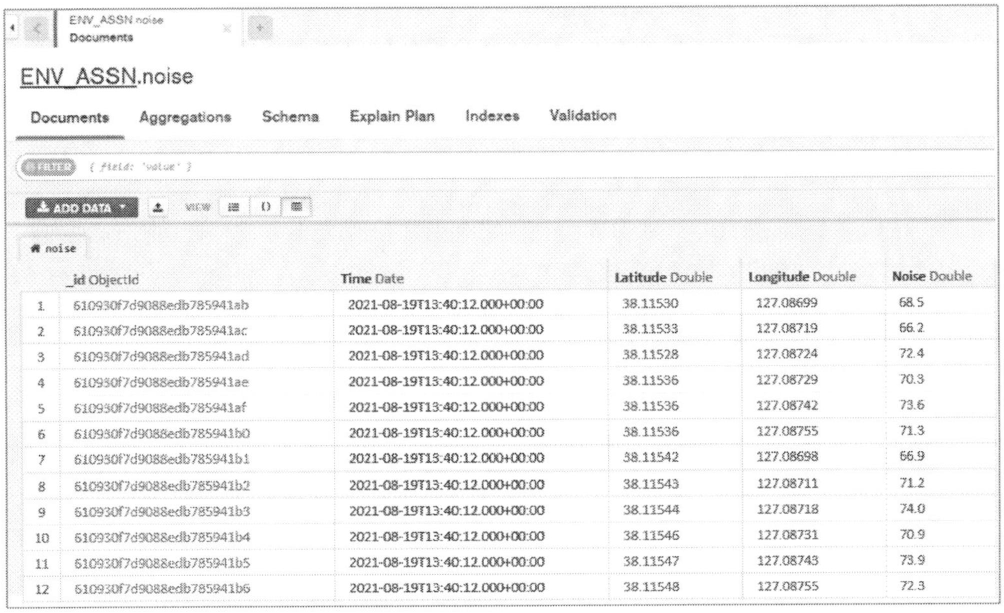

	_id ObjectId	Time Date	Latitude Double	Longitude Double	Noise Double
1	610930f7d9088edb785941ab	2021-08-19T13:40:12.000+00:00	38.11530	127.08699	68.5
2	610930f7d9088edb785941ac	2021-08-19T13:40:12.000+00:00	38.11533	127.08719	66.2
3	610930f7d9088edb785941ad	2021-08-19T13:40:12.000+00:00	38.11528	127.08724	72.4
4	610930f7d9088edb785941ae	2021-08-19T13:40:12.000+00:00	38.11536	127.08729	70.3
5	610930f7d9088edb785941af	2021-08-19T13:40:12.000+00:00	38.11536	127.08742	73.6
6	610930f7d9088edb785941b0	2021-08-19T13:40:12.000+00:00	38.11536	127.08755	71.3
7	610930f7d9088edb785941b1	2021-08-19T13:40:12.000+00:00	38.11542	127.08698	66.9
8	610930f7d9088edb785941b2	2021-08-19T13:40:12.000+00:00	38.11543	127.08711	71.2
9	610930f7d9088edb785941b3	2021-08-19T13:40:12.000+00:00	38.11544	127.08718	74.0
10	610930f7d9088edb785941b4	2021-08-19T13:40:12.000+00:00	38.11546	127.08731	70.9
11	610930f7d9088edb785941b5	2021-08-19T13:40:12.000+00:00	38.11547	127.08743	73.9
12	610930f7d9088edb785941b6	2021-08-19T13:40:12.000+00:00	38.11548	127.08755	72.3

Figure 1: Example of the Data Collected from the Placed Sensors.

3.3 Noise Information Visualization

Finally, the noise information of the entire site derived by the noise-estimation model was mapped by 10m grids. The authors visualized in 3D by setting the representative value of each grid as the maximum noise value. In order to obtain 3D data of the experimental site, overlapping images were acquired with a drone, and the collected image data were converted into a point cloud through pix4d (commercially available software). In the case of a geographic coordinate system, it is difficult to visualize in a 3D space because the coordinate units are mixed (i.e., latitude and longitude: degrees, altitude: meters). Therefore, the latitude and longitude coordinates of the collected noise data were converted into the UTM coordinate system in meters, which is the same as the point cloud. Unconverted values were also utilized when presenting information onto the visualizer since the geographic coordinates displayed on the digital map are easier for users to understand. The Unity 3D Engine used to develop the visualizer in this study is a game-based development tool with strengths in rendering, lighting, terrain generation, and special effects. In addition, the user interface (UI) can be designed and implemented with less effort compared to existing Python or JavaScript-based visualization tools, and input data can be updated in real time by linking with the database.

4. Experimental Results

4.1 Noise-Estimation Results

Table 1 shows the results of evaluating the performance of the proposed noise-estimation model by changing the number of input points. The performance was evaluated by calculating the accuracy at each non-sensed point and averaging them. The average accuracy is calculated as in Equation 3, where x_i, x^*, n, and A indicate the actual value from the sensing data, estimated noise level, the number of non-sensed points, and average accuracy, respectively. The input data was set from six to 12 with the condition that the sensors are placed in zones that comply with the field constraints. The maximum and minimum accuracy were evaluated by random sampling of 1,000 sensor placement combinations in each case.

$$A = \frac{100}{n}\left(\sum_{i=1}^{n}\left(1 - \left|\frac{x_i - x^*}{x_i}\right|\right)\right) \tag{3}$$

As a result, the noise-estimation model obtained decent performance for the cost when using eight sensing points as inputs and the remaining 103 points as outputs; the maximum and minimum accuracies were 97.5% and 92.4%, respectively. The maximum accuracy was slightly improved to less than 0.1% per additional sensor as the number of input points increased more than eight, so the authors judged that the efficiency became less important from that number when considering the sensor cost. It was confirmed that the necessary conditions for deriving high performance were to place the sensor at the points of outskirts, noise source, and the region where the directivity and interference effect of the two noise sources existed, as shown in Figure 2. These points showed specific patterns for sensor installation to explain on-site noise distribution and ensure performance.

Table 1: Performance Evaluation Result of the Noise Estimation.

Number of input points	Number of remaining (estimated) points	Maximum accuracy (%)	Minimum accuracy (%)
6	104	95.36	95.36
7	103	96.71	93.73
8	102	97.50	92.42
9	101	97.56	92.15
10	100	97.49	92.13
11	99	97.70	91.90
12	98	97.64	91.92

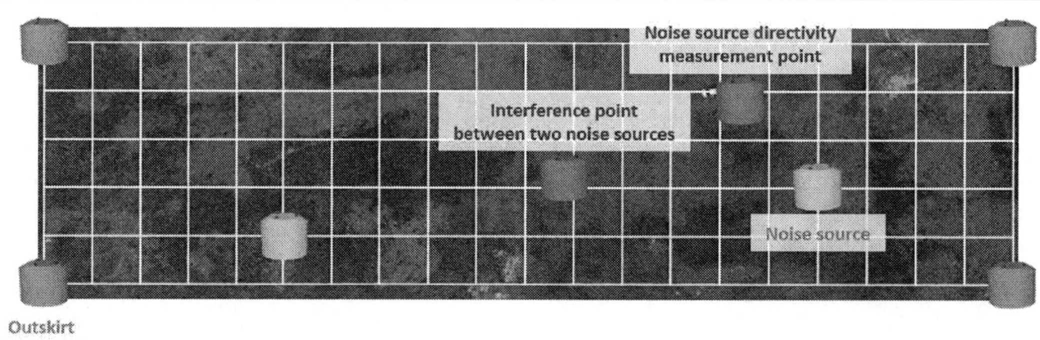

Figure 2: Sensor Placement Combination with the Best Performance for the Noise-Estimation Model.

4.2 Noise Information Visualization Results

The noise information estimated based on the sensing data was mapped to the point cloud. The proposed Unity-based visualizer updated the information by calculating each grid's maximum, minimum, and average noise levels every hour. The GPS and noise information of the grid can be displayed by clicking the desired grid in the visualizer (Figure 3(a)). The GPS coordinates were plotted as the center point of the grids. The user could use the Ctrl key to check the grids generating more than 88dB noise, significantly affecting workers' hearing loss (Figure 3(b)). In addition, the Shift key functions to highlight the grids that generate noise of more than 65dB to identify areas where noise regulations are violated (Figure 3(c)).

Using the research results, practitioners can easily identify areas that workers should not enter for long periods for health reasons and check how the noise changes in real time depending on the type of work. The authors plan to upgrade the UI to access various field data stored in the database so that such data can be displayed by selecting the target site, date, time, and type of information to be mapped.

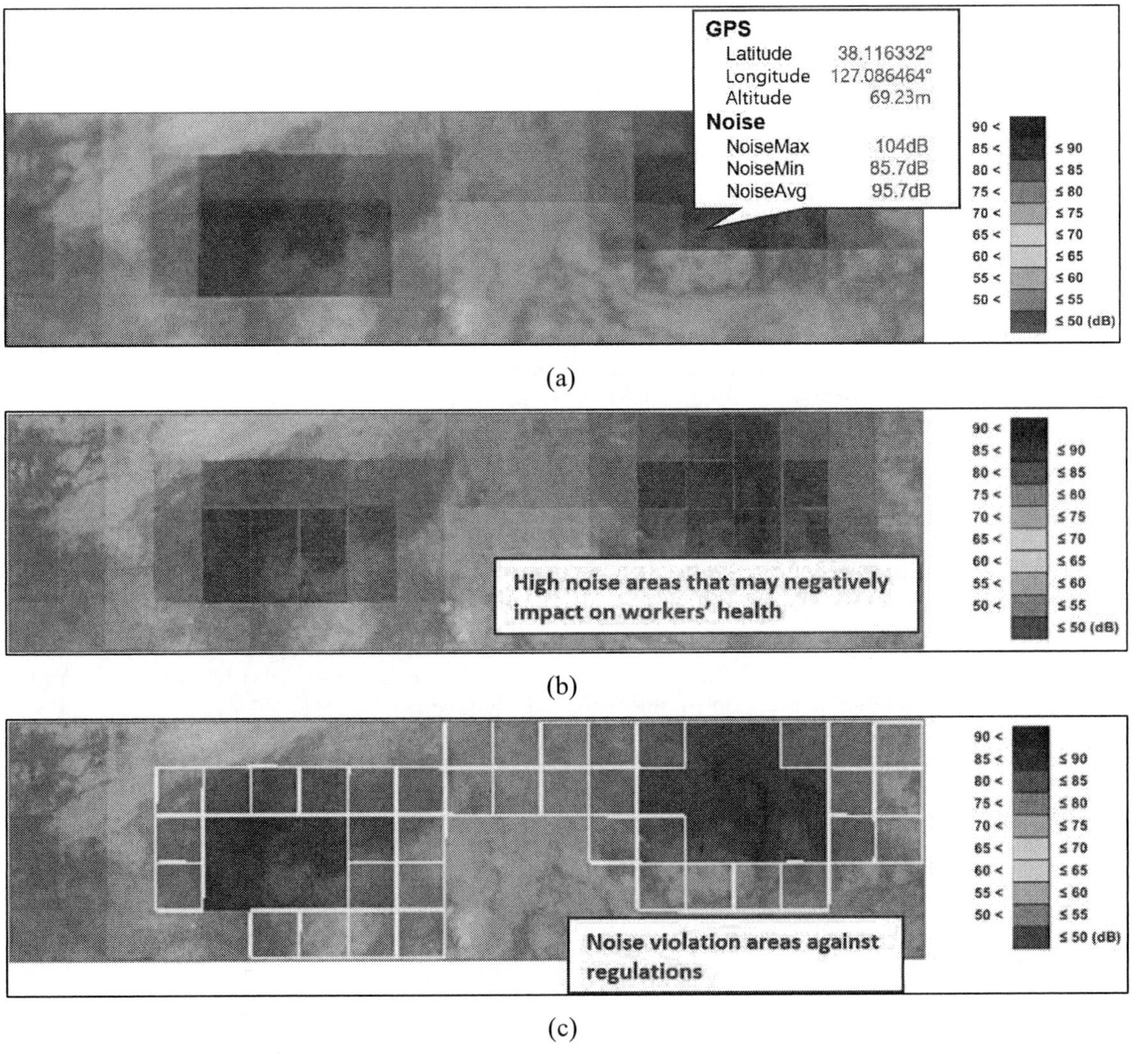

Figure 3: Example of Noise Information Visualization: (a) grid information display, (b) highlighted high-noise areas, (c) highlighted noise regulation violation areas

5. Conclusion

This study proposed a system that can monitor real-time noise information based on a spatial interpolation model. The authors experimented in a designed outdoor environment similar to that of a construction site to evaluate the performance of the developed system and obtained satisfactory performance. Since this study is the first study to estimate noise information based on sensing data at a construction site, it was targeted to a road construction site that can have simple acoustic behavior without being significantly disturbed. This study can facilitate noise management in the construction stage by accurately estimating and showing real-time noise information for every spot on the site. In addition, the in-depth on-site noise data derived from the results of this study will be used as an input for noise simulation of construction activities, providing an opportunity for future research to estimate the spread of noise to the outside of the site in real time. The applicability of the model developed in this study will be evaluated in practice through actual field demonstrations.

Acknowledgments

This research was conducted with the support of the "National R&D Project for Smart Construction Technology (No.22SMIP-A158708-03)" funded by the Korea Agency for Infrastructure Technology Advancement under the Ministry of Land, Infrastructure, and Transport. This research was also supported by the Seoul National University research grant in 2021.

References

Ballesteros, M. J., Fernández, M. D., Quintana, S., Ballesteros, J. A. and González, I. (2010). Noise emission evolution on construction sites. Measurement for controlling and assessing its impact on the people and on the environment. Building and Environment, 45(3), 711-717.

Cai, M., Zou, J., Xie, J. and Ma, X. (2015). Road traffic noise mapping in Guangzhou using GIS and GPS. Applied Acoustics, 87, 94-102.

Choi, J., Kang, H., Hong, T., Baek, H. and Lee, D. E. (2021). Automated noise exposure assessment model for the health of construction workers. Automation in Construction, 126, 103657.

Di, H., Liu, X., Zhang, J., Tong, Z., Ji, M., Li, F., Feng, T. and Ma, Q. (2018). Estimation of the quality of an urban acoustic environment based on traffic noise evaluation models. Applied Acoustics, 141, 115-124.

Eom, C. S. and Paek, J. H. (2009). Risk index model for minimizing environmental disputes in construction. Journal of Construction Engineering and Management, 135(1), 34-41.

Gannoruwa, A. and Ruwanpura, J. Y. (2007). Construction noise prediction and barrier optimization using special purpose simulation. In 2007 Winter Simulation Conference, Washington D.C, United States.

Gilchrist, A., Allouche, E. N. and Cowan, D. (2003). Prediction and mitigation of construction noise in an urban environment. Canadian Journal of Civil Engineering, 30(4), 659-672.

Gulliver, J., Morley, D., Vienneau, D., Fabbri, F., Bell, M., Goodman, P., Beevers, S., Dajnak, D., Kelly, F. J. and Fecht, D. (2015). Development of an open-source road traffic noise model for exposure assessment. Environmental Modelling & Software, 74, 183-193.

Hong, J., Kang, H., Hong, T., Park, H. S. and Lee, D. E. (2021a). Construction noise rating based on legal and health impacts. Automation in Construction, 104053.

Hong, J., Kang, H., Hong, T., Park, H. S. and Lee, D. E. (2021b). Development of a prediction model for the proportion of buildings exposed to construction noise in excess of the construction noise regulation at urban construction sites. Automation in Construction, 125, 103656.

Hong, T., Ji, C., Park, J., Leigh, S. B. and Seo, D. Y. (2015). Prediction of environmental costs of construction noise and vibration at the preconstruction phase. Journal of Management in Engineering, 31(5), 04014079.

Hong, T., Sung, S., Kang, H., Hong, J., Kim, H. and Lee, D. E. (2022). Advanced real-time pollutant monitoring systems for automatic environmental management of construction projects focusing on field applicability. Journal of Management in Engineering, 38(1), 04021075.

Hughes, J., Yan, J. and Soga, K. (2015). Development of wireless sensor network using bluetooth low energy (BLE) for construction noise monitoring. International Journal of Smart Sensing and Intelligent Systems, 8(2), 1379-1405.

Jung, S., Kang, H., Choi, J., Hong, T., Park, H. S. and Lee, D. E. (2020). Quantitative health impact assessment of construction noise exposure on the nearby region for noise barrier optimization. Building and Environment, 176, 106869.

Kang, H., Sung, S., Hong, J., Jung, S., Hong, T., Park, H. S. and Lee, D. E. (2021). Development of a real-time automated monitoring system for managing the hazardous environmental pollutants at the construction site. Journal of Hazardous Materials, 402, 123483.

Kwon, N., Park, M., Lee, H. S., Ahn, J. and Shin, M. (2016). Construction noise management using active noise control techniques. Journal of Construction Engineering and Management, 142(7), 04016014.

Lee, S. W., Chang, S. I. and Park, Y. M. (2008). Utilizing noise mapping for environmental impact assessment in a downtown redevelopment area of Seoul, Korea. Applied Acoustics, 69(8), 704-714.

Liu, Y., Oiamo, T., Rainham, D., Chen, H., Hatzopoulou, M., Brook, J. R., Davies, H., Goudreau, S. and Smargiassi, A. (2021). Integrating random forests and propagation models for high-resolution noise mapping. Environmental Research, 195, 110905.

MOLIT (2014). Safety Management Manual for Construction Work. Korea: Ministry of Land, Infrastructure and Transport.

Santos de Oliveira, R., Mendes da Cruz, F., Zlatar, T., Arezes, P., Barkokébas Junior, B., & Gorga Lago, E. M. (2019). Case study: Analysis of the propagation of noise generated by construction equipment. Noise Control Engineering Journal, 67(6), 447-455.

Enabling Federated Interoperable Issue Management in a Building and Construction Sector

Oraskari J. [1], Schulz O. [1], Werbrouck J.[1,2], Beetz J.[1]
[1] Chair of Design Computation, RWTH Aachen, Germany, [2] Department of Architecture and Urban Planning, Ghent University, Belgium
jyrki.oraskari@dc.rwth-aachen.de, schulz@dc.rwth-aachen.de, jeroen.werbrouck@ugent.be

Abstract. A Common Data Environment (CDE) is an agreed-upon source of information on building-related projects to collect, manage, and exchange data between stakeholders. The approach in the AEC domain is to use buildingSMART's BIM Collaboration Format (BCF) as the digital issue communication part of CDEs. Contrasting with the federated nature of the AEC industry, CDEs are typically organised in a centralised fashion. This work proposes a potential transition of BCF into a distributed environment that serves as an example for further developments in the distribution of CDEs and CDE-independent data management. We show how a single source of truth over the project data and the advantages of the central approach can be realised in a distributed setup using a Solid architecture environment, enabling decentralised authentication and stakeholders' ability to control their data.

1. Introduction

In recent years, multiple international standards and specifications have been agreed upon to facilitate the information exchange in the Architecture, Engineering and Construction (AEC) industry. According to ISO 19650, a Common Data Environment (CDE) is defined as an agreed-upon source of information for a building-related project (ISO 19650-1, 2018). It should serve as a single source of truth and is therefore helping to structure the information and data exchange process in the course of a project between the different stakeholders.

Figure 1: Abstraction of buildingSMART's OpenCDE APIs, originally presented by Yoram Kulbak and Pasi Paasiala in October 2019[1]. The BCF API is part of buildingSMARTs OpenCDE APIs.

The German standard DIN SPEC 91391-1 (2019) extends on the ideas of ISO 19650 and emphasises that a CDE for a building can change during the different phases of its life. Hence, there is a need for the different CDEs to communicate. The specification's authors suggest that standardised RESTful interfaces should be used to ensure the exchange of information containers between different CDEs at the BIM maturity stage 2.

A standardised approach for digital issue communication in AEC projects is the BIM Collaboration Format (BCF), which is commonly used in combination with CDEs (Preidel et al., 2018). BCF exists in two flavours: a file-based version and a centrally organised, server-based approach (van Berlo and Krijnen, 2014), allowing project managers and clients to study the entire body of issue descriptions via APIs to infer insights into the design team's work.

https://doi.org/10.7146/aul.455.c200

BuildingSMART International regards this server-based approach as part of the OpenCDE APIs[1] (Figure 1). Using BCF enables the user to communicate problems on a component-by-component basis, making BCF an integral part of the planning process. It supplements conventional e-mail communication about issues and can be seen as a central interface for communicating changes in the model. Hence, we focus on this format for this work.

Even though the standards mentioned above describe the exchange of information in detail, implementation remains scarce regarding container-based information exchange or the interconnection of CDEs. While streamlining information exchange is beneficial to the industry as a whole, it is not for commercial CDE providers. As in many sectors, the construction industry has followed the general trend toward Big Data and built data-driven ecosystems that centralise as much data as possible on their central servers. There are many challenges in this model. Data access is regulated via vendor-specific APIs, which often limit query parameters. Duplicated data in the silos can lead to a situation where the users do not have a single source of truth, making it harder to get insights into the project's status. Also, the legal aspects and the responsibilities of the data content, like the General Data Protection Regulation (GDPR) in the European Union, are harder to control if the data is not at the hands of their producers. The Solid initiative (Mansour et al., 2016) aims to change the overall course into a model where individual players control the data produced by them and about them. These players need a decentralised authentication mechanism included in the Solid specification for this to work.

This work proposes a potential transition of BCF into a distributed environment that can serve as an example for further developments in the distribution of CDEs and CDE-independent data management. We show how a single source of truth over the project data and the advantages of the central approach can be realised in a distributed environment, which enables decentralised authentication, lower risk of system failure, and stakeholders' ability to control their data.

The paper is structured as follows: the next section introduces the technologies and related works regarded for this paper. Section 3 describes the proposed way to express the federated structure of BCF data on the Solid platform. The paper concludes with a discussion on the proposed framework, including prospects on this topic.

2. Background

This section describes the background technologies on which the proposed framework will be based and related research projects. Although this paper bases heavily upon Semantic Web technologies, an elaborate discussion on these topics is outside the scope of this work. For a deeper understanding of technologies such as the Resource Description Framework (RDF) and the SPARQL Protocol, and RDF Query Language (SPARQL), the reader is referred to (Hendler et al., 2020).

2.1 BIM Collaboration Format and Common Data Environments

In the context of the ongoing establishment of open BIM processes, the need for a communication interface arose in order to be able to transmit information and issues within the models in a software-independent manner. Therefore, the BIM Collaboration Format (BCF) – a buildingSMART standard - was developed to provide a software- and vendor-neutral

[1] OpenCDE-API Documentation: https://github.com/buildingSMART/OpenCDE-API/tree/master/Documentation (Accessed 20.02.2022)

exchange format for model-based issue communication[2]. Three main parts - *Topics*, *Comments* and *Viewpoints* - together form the main structure behind BCF and are all connected to a *Project* concept:

1) The *Topic* carries general information about an issue. It uses properties like a current status, a definition of the type of *Topic*, the person who created it and who is responsible for fixing it.
2) *Viewpoints* are used to connect the format to BIM by providing a virtual camera located inside the model that looks at the scene that is part of a current discussion. They can also provide links to specific building elements by stating their GUID in a list.
3) A *Comment* concept provides the textual information and an author in a discussion. It is linked to the *Topic* and can reference a *Viewpoint* as well.

The BCF data can either be exchanged in a file-based format using BCF XML[3] or by using a server (van Berlo and Krijnen, 2014) via a REST API (called BCF API[4]) that returns its information in a JSON format. Even though the data can be serialised in two different ways, the overall concept behind both formats is the same, and the structures of BCF API and BCF XML differ only slightly. For example, BCF Servers - using the BCF API - often allow archiving and downloading of the *Project* and its issues as a file in the BCF XML format.

Since the communication in an open BIM process is usually an integral part of many workflows, it is often integrated directly into a Common Data Environment (CDE) (Preidel et al., 2018), which serves as a single source of truth throughout the planning and construction phase. Research regarding the decentralisation of these CDEs can also be observed. In Werbrouck et al. (2019), the authors suggest a decentralised CDE based on Solid principles, whereas Tao et al. (2021) describe a CDE distributed via a blockchain. The latter example also combines the principles of a CDE with BCF by distributing them as BCF XML over the blockchain.

2.2 bcfOWL

Since the current BCF serialisations lack the general contextual information and shared metamodels that RDF solutions have, the bcfOWL ontology (Schulz et al., 2021) was created to bring together the worlds of issue communication and Linked Data. In the proposed linked data model, BCF issues are stored as RDF triples and can be queried using SPARQL. Additionally, the different concepts for the *Topics* – defined in the BCF *Extensions* – can be enriched with further semantics. Therefore, the *Extensions* in bcfOWL can be used as a gateway to other ontologies in the context of Linked Building Data (LBD).

The ontology is not introducing new concepts to BCF and has semantic interoperability with BCF XML and BCF API. A converter can be created to serialise bcfOWL data into the standard BCF JSON and XML formats. Thus the ontology can serve as a shared foundation for both formats. By using SPARQL to query the data stored as bcfOWL, it is also possible to overcome the accessibility limitations of BCF caused by its hierarchical structure, as described in (Schulz and Beetz, 2021).

[2] BIM Collaboration Format (BCF) - An Introduction https://technical.buildingsmart.org/standards/bcf/ accessed 28.02.2022
[3] BCF XML: https://github.com/BuildingSMART/BCF-XML accessed 24.01.2022
[4] BCF API: https://github.com/buildingSMART/BCF-API accessed 24.01.2022

2.3 Authenticated Data Federation on the Web

Using the Linked Data Platform (LDP) specification[5], the Web of data can be accessed and managed using the read-write operations of the Hypertext Transfer Protocol (HTTP) standard version 1.1, the basis of data communication for the World Wide Web.

LDP incorporates the Linked Data principles (Bizer et al., 2009) of Tim Berners-Lee into a data container architecture. LDP relies on containerisation, where an ldp:Container refers to a specific, dereferenceable RDF graph listing its resources (ldp:contains). By dereferencing the container URL, it is easy to discover and, in turn, dereference its content (RDF or non-RDF) in a chain of HTTP requests. As container URIs are also RDF resources themselves, nesting containers is possible, resulting in a data organisation system that resembles file storage on a computer – yet now file paths are URLs.

While LDP on its own is well-suited for serving *open* data on the Web, it does not specify access-control mechanisms for protected datasets. Where a centralised data store often relies upon local storage of credentials, this is no viable option in a decentral environment. Since a client may combine hundreds of web resources to find what it needs, it is not feasible to maintain an account for these sources separately.

Established technologies like OpenID Connect (OIDC)[2] allow outsourcing this part of identity management to specialised identity providers (IDPs) that act as a service in the middle, e.g., Facebook, Google, or GitHub. The Solid initiative (Mansour et al., 2016; Sambra et al., 2016) eliminates the need for a third party: it provides the specifications to create an online identity based on a personal URL (a "WebID"[6]) on a domain chosen by the user. An office can thus become its own IDP and maintain its credentials for authenticating against decentralised construction management services (Werbrouck et al., 2019). A WebID is associated with a Personal Online Data storage ("Pod"): a data vault based on the LDP specification but now enabling fine-grained access control to containers and resources defined using the Web Access Control (WAC) [7] ontology. The resources that govern access control in Solid, ACL (Access Control List) resources use the WAC ontology to link specific access rights to specific WebIDs, agent groups *(vcard:Group*) or (un)authenticated agents (*acl:Agent* or *acl:AuthenticatedAgent*). This way, it can be easily verified by a Solid Pod provider whether an actor can interact with a resource in a specific way: read, append, write or control, i.e., modifying the ACL document itself.

Apart from the ACL resources that govern access rights, the Solid specifications define '.meta' resources: RDF resources that contain metadata statements related to an ldp:Container instance. A .meta resource is served upon dereferencing a container URL. The details of .meta resources are yet to be agreed upon within the Solid community, but by default, they include the LDP containment triples and modification dates. Attaching a custom, persistent .meta resource to a Solid container with domain-specific metadata is possible.

2.4 LBDserver

A related initiative that uses Solid to store AEC data in a decentral way is the ongoing LBDserver project (Werbrouck et al., 2021). This project proposes data structures to discover project resources, metadata storage and cross-document linking of heterogeneous datasets using

---

[5] Linked Data Platform: https://www.w3.org/TR/ldp/ accessed 28.01.2022

[6] WebID 1.0: https://www.w3.org/2005/Incubator/webid/spec/identity/ accessed 31.01.2022

[7] Web Access Control, https://solid.github.io/web-access-control-spec/, accessed 31.01.2022

the LBDserver vocabulary[8]. Throughout this paper, we will re-use certain patterns proposed in the LBDserver ecosystem (Section 3). However, where the LBDserver proposes a very generic way for data organisation, the BCF specification has a distinct way of structuring BCF-related datasets. As this is standardised within the AEC industry, we will maintain this way of data organisation in this work.

3. Federated BCF projects

In this section, we sketch the outline for the setup of federated BCF projects. Therefore, we combine domain-agnostic Web specifications from the Solid ecosystem with domain-specific concepts proposed in the bcfOWL and LBDserver initiatives. Section 3.1 describes an organisational structure for discovering and managing federated BCF data. The project becomes a federated graph in such a setup: the union of contributions stakeholders make on their own "office server", shared using WebIDs. Similarities with the existing BCF API and BCF XML will be drawn where relevant. Based on Solid's existing Web Access Control specifications, an access-control layer is devised upon this organisational structure.

3.1 Project Discovery

To make federated BCF projects easily discoverable, we base upon the aggregation structures proposed in the LBDserver. This means that an office can maintain its projects in a root *ldp:Container* on its Pod, i.e., the Project Repository. The URL of this registry is referenced in the office's WebID (*lbds:hasProjectRegistry).* A project registry has sub-containers for each

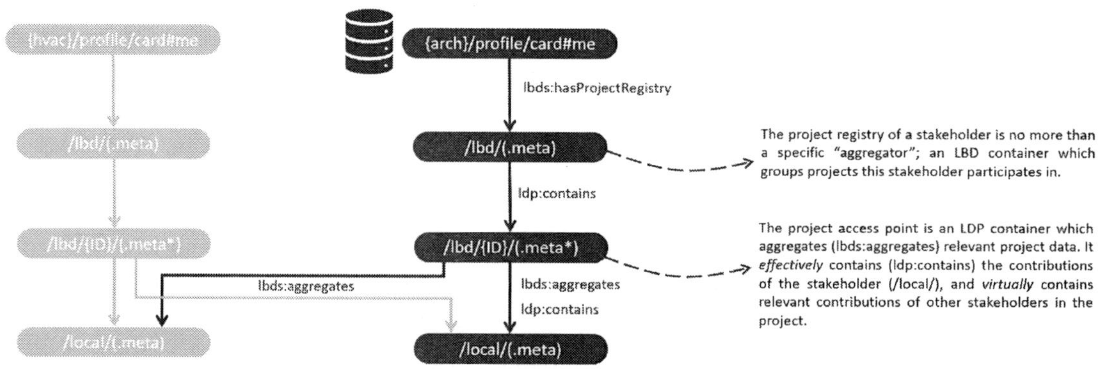

Figure 2: LBDserver patterns for project discovery. The project access point allows finding contributions in the federated project network.

project the Pod owner participates in ('project access points'). These sub-containers, in turn, have pointers to the contributions ('partial projects') of each stakeholder, including the contribution of the owner of the Pod, which we identify by a </local/> sub-container (Werbrouck et al., 2022). The first type is "virtually contained", and the second type is effectively hosted by this container on the Solid Pod. Thus, by dereferencing the project access point, a client discovers a list of federated partial projects.

---

[8] The LBDserver vocabulary, https://w3id.org/lbdserver#, accessed 08/02/2022

This paper focuses on arranging the BCF data (i.e. *Projects*, *Topics*, *Viewpoints* and *Comments*) inside a Pod, leaving the storage of auxiliary resources (e.g. PDF documents, IFC models) out of scope. In this regard, we suggest a tree-like structure that mimics the routes in the BCF API

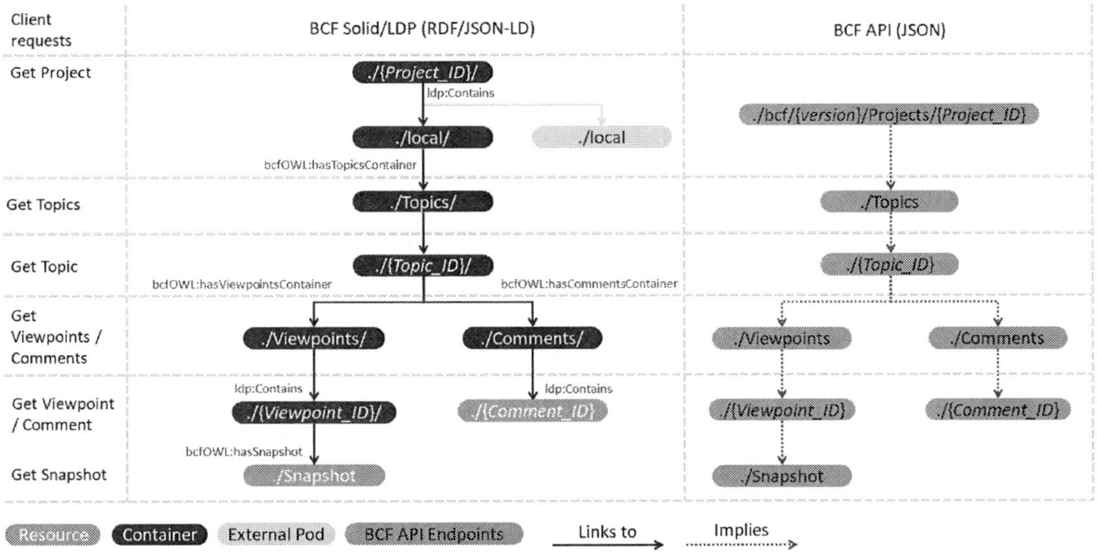

Figure 3: Comparison between the structure of the container-based BCF Solid approach and the BCF API (buildingSMART). The structure of the BCF API is not discoverable by the client without previous knowledge of the standard (it is implied). The BCF Solid approach implements a machine-readable discovery pattern (RDF graph) by linking to its sub-containers.

and the folder structure in BCF XML (Figure 3), in contrast to the flattened approach in the LBDServer.

The metadata resource corresponding with the </local/> folder (i.e. at the top level) contains general information about the *Project*, such as its name, what BCF *Extensions* it contains and how they are defined. Furthermore, it links to one or many sub-containers that contain information about the *Topics* belonging to the *Project*, using dedicated sub-properties of "*ldp:contains*". These properties are described in detail in the following section.

3.2 Project organisation

Sub-containers containing BCF *Topics* are identified with the RDF predicate "*bcfOWL:hasTopicsContainer*". Each *Topic* is itself located in a sub-container in this container, described with a metafile that contains the *Topics* information in bcfOWL and links to its *Viewpoints* and *Comments* by using the predicates "*bcfOWL:hasViewpointsContainer*" and "*bcfOWL:hasCommentsContainer*". These sub-containers correspond in their structure to the *Topics* route defined in the BCF API by including *Viewpoints* and *Comments*. Each *Viewpoint* is a container in itself. The *Comment* is represented as a resource (Figure 3). The *Viewpoint*, in turn, contains more concepts, such as a *Snapshot* (e.g. .png or .jpeg) or a *Perspective Camera*.

If we take a closer look at this hierarchy (Figure 3), we can see that there are many similarities to the server routes of the BCF API. Whereas in BCF XML, each issue is located in its folder (identified by the GUID of the *Topic*). The *Topic* is summarised together with the *Comments* in a Markup file. The BCF API provides all this information as hierarchically organised REST API URI patterns that are accessed sequentially. The BCI APIs sequence is mainly preserved in our proposed structure and allows finding data using standardised endpoints. Apart from the fact that every partial project acts as a "partial BCF server" on its own, which means they need to be queried using multiple HTTP requests, a client will not experience a difference between a Solid-based *Topics* container and a centralised one. A single Pod can be used as a complete BCF server without referencing external partial projects. However, the same infrastructure can be used to federate the project's information.

However, some benefits arise with the RDF-based organisational approach compared with the mere implementation of standardised API routes. Although in an LDP (Solid) environment, similar endpoint patterns to the BCF API are used, these endpoints are also semantically described using the metadata files. Instead of just receiving BCF JSON responses from the server, the server describes what each container entails and what its metafiles depict. The information is easily discoverable in these containers on the Pod. Because resources are stored as files but served in a REST API, it combines the file-based BCF XML and the service-oriented BCF API approaches.

Furthermore, the links to the sub-containers do not have to be restricted to local resources and can point to any number of other Pods from other stakeholders. Thus, a distributed communication of issues is achieved, in which each participant can store remarks and additions in their Pod.

Lastly, this approach allows the dynamic discovery of data. Although the proposed tree structure mimics the BCF API and the BCF XML structure, it is not the only possible configuration. The property-based discovery of containers and sub-containers allows a client to discover how a project is organised. However, this resource could have been stored in a completely different location. An external service may then present this data "as if" it is compliant with a specific standard such as BCF.

3.3 Access Control and Groups

In a decentral project, each office may maintain access control to the resources they contribute. The WAC ontology supports *acl:AgentGroup*-s, which point to a *vcard:Group* instance, referencing its members (*vcard:hasMember*) via their WebID. For each project, an office can publish one or more groups containing the employees' WebIDs (e.g., 'localEmployees.ttl'). The ACL that governs the resources in the local project folder can then grant these groups specific access rights. For instance, the responsible project manager in the office gets *acl:Control* rights and the *acl:Read* and *acl:Write* rights of the other employees working on this project. Agent groups defined by other project stakeholders (i.e., hosted in their project container) are granted only acl:Read permissions. Although the above describes a project-specific approach, this works similarly for resource-specific access rights.

3.4 Project interaction

This paper does not yet tackle the challenges of a complete workflow, where people create, comment, and update new and existing Issues. When we take the update of an issue as an example, the question must be asked, where this update will be stored in the distributed system. A possible option is that the person who creates the update is storing the new issue - or just the updated content – on their Pod and notifies the original Pod of the issue of its existence. Thereby, when the issue gets queried, it returns a reference to its new version. This option allows tracing the complete history of the *Topic* without ever really deleting or changing existing data. However, it also creates much redundancy that could, in the long run, influence the performance of the queries. Another option that is more in line with the current implementation of the BCF API is to implement a logging system that keeps track of the changes by the users. This topic is further discussed in Oraskari et al. (2022).

4. Proof of Concept

A proof of concept was created to demonstrate the feasibility of the proposed framework for federated management of BCF data. This includes using the Solid Community Server[9], an open-source implementation of the Solid specifications. The data used in this demonstration is based on the BIM models of the DC chair at RWTH Aachen University[10].

To emulate the federated environment, three Pods were set up, containing a total of six issues:

- The Pod owned by the project architect office contains four topics
- The Pod owned by the HVAC engineer contains one topic
- The Pod owned by the structural engineer contains one topic

In this demonstrative scenario, Oliver, working at the engineering office, wants an overview of the current issues registered for the DC chair project. He is registered at the Architect Office's Pod in the list of employees assigned to this project (Listing 1).

Listing 1: the employee group (http://pod.myoffice.org/Projects/8b71315b-7db2-4b35-a1e9-fcddaf8556f5/groups#committed)

```
<#committed> a vcard:Group ;
    dc:created "2022-02-22T22:22:22Z"^^xsd:dateTime ;
    dc:modified "2022-02-22T22:22:22Z"^^xsd:dateTime ;
    vcard:hasMember <http://localhost:3000/oliver/profile/card#me> ,
            <https://localhost:3000/jeroen/profile/card#me> .
```

Every stakeholder's </local/> partial projects contain an .acl file that references this group and assigns to acl:Read rights to its members (Listing 2). Of course, editing rights (acl:Write, acl:Append) can be granted in the partial project provided by the architect's office itself.

Listing 2: access rights for employee group in Listing 1

```
<#us>
    a acl:Authorization;
      acl:agentGroup  <http://localhost:3000/office/Projects/8b71315b-7db2-4b35-a1e9-
fcddaf8556f5/groups#commited> ;
    acl:accessTo <./>;
    acl:default <./>;
    acl:mode acl:Read, acl:Write, acl:Append .
```

First, the available partial projects need to be discovered. The SPARQL query covers this:

```
SELECT ?partial WHERE {<> lbds:aggregates ?partial}
```

As indicated in Figure 3, the organisation of partial projects corresponds with the BCF API specification data patterns. Because these are standardised routes, further discovery is not necessary, and the Web client can send the following (authenticated) requests to each of the partial projects:

```
GET {partial project}/topics
```

This will yield an LDP container with pointers to the contained *Topics*, which can now be easily retrieved and presented in a GUI. This series of HTTP requests is not identical to those required to access the BCF API. However, they can be easily implemented under the hood by a BCF server to expose federated information to conform to the standard. In that case, the server acts as a middleware to regulate access to information on the stakeholder Pods.

---

[9] Solid Community Server, https://github.com/solid/community-server, accessed 28.01.2022
[10] Demo dataset: https://github.com/Design-Computation-RWTH/EG-ICE_2022_BCFdemo accessed 28.02.2022

5. Discussion and Conclusion

The translation of BCF into a Solid environment introduces its main concepts in a federated setup, using the Solid specifications and the Linked Data Platform. This way, issue communication can be spread over multiple Pods that belong to different stakeholders. *Project* stakeholders are no longer solely identified by their e-mail addresses, as implied by the BCF user concept. Instead, the use of semantically rich WebIDs for offices and employees allows the dynamic creation of user groups (e.g. defined by role or participation) and the re-use of credentials in multiple federated *Projects*. A project team from an architectural stakeholder can define its members in their Pod and manage who has access to the *Project* data and who does not. The resulting group (vcard:Group) is then linked to BCF *Project* data to control access. Hence, it becomes possible to define more granular access rights for the different roles on the *Project* pod. This corresponds to the structures in the federated construction industry.

The decentral authentication mechanism, as defined in the Solid specifications, does not require the server to store the login credentials for every user. The service is just responsible for verifying if the access rights associated with a given WebID allow a user to interact with a specific resource in a specific way. The need for the user to create an account for every service is thereby removed by using WebIDs.

Future developments in this area include investigating the guaranteed availability of the federated data to prevent the loss of project information (either accidentally or intentionally). Furthermore, a notification system between Pods in the network will enable automated synchronisation (e.g. when someone updates a Topic or creates a new Comment). In this paper, we proposed a tree-like structure that combines the traits of BCF XML and the BCF API. The URL routes of the BCF API thereby serve as a means to access the individual containers. Information in these containers is stored in a .meta file, and the different containers holding the BCF data are linked via bcfOWLs properties. We have shown that BCF projects information can be queried using a one-stop access point implemented using distributed Solid architecture and offered as a single source of truth. In the platform, authentication can be self-hosted, and the stakeholders can manage their data using a tree-like structure that mimics the hierarchical pattern of the BCF API endpoints. It was also shown that the data authorisation enforcement can be set using the container architecture of the Solid specification.

Since BCF is a member of the OpenCDE API family, we hope this research can serve as a template for further research on aligning AEC standards with future-proof concepts for federation on the Web.

Acknowledgements

This research is funded by the Research Foundation Flanders (FWO) as a Strategic Basic Research grant (grant no. 1S99020N) and by the EU through the H2020 project BIM4REN grant (grant no. 820773).

References

Bizer, C., Heath, T., Berners-Lee, T., 2009. Linked Data - The Story So Far. Int. J. Semantic Web Inf. Syst. 5, 1–22. https://doi.org/10.4018/jswis.2009081901

DIN SPEC 91391-1 Common Data Environments (CDE) for BIM projects - Function sets and open data exchange between platforms of different vendors - Part 1: Components and function sets of a CDE; with digital attachment, 2019.

Hendler, J., Gandon, F., Allemang, D., 2020. Semantic Web for the Working Ontologist: Effective Modeling for Linked Data, RDFS, and OWL. Morgan & Claypool.

ISO 19650-1 Organization and digitization of information about buildings and civil engineering works, including building information modelling (BIM) - Information management using building information modelling - Part 1: Concepts and principles, 2018.

Mansour, E., Sambra, A.V., Hawke, S., Zereba, M., Capadisli, S., Ghanem, A., Aboulnaga, A., Berners-Lee, T., 2016. A Demonstration of the Solid Platform for Social Web Applications, in: Proceedings of the 25th International Conference Companion on World Wide Web, WWW '16 Companion. International World Wide Web Conferences Steering Committee, Republic and Canton of Geneva, CHE, pp. 223–226. https://doi.org/10.1145/2872518.2890529

Oraskari, J., Schulz, O., Beetz, J., 2022. (in press) Towards describing version history of BCF data in the Semantic Web, in: Proceedings of the 10th Linked Data in Architecture and Construction Workshop.

Preidel, C., Borrmann, A., Mattern, H., König, M., Schapke, S.-E., 2018. Common Data Environment, in: Borrmann, A., König, M., Koch, C., Beetz, J. (Eds.), Building Information Modeling: Technology Foundations and Industry Practice. Springer International Publishing, Cham, pp. 279–291. https://doi.org/10.1007/978-3-319-92862-3_15

Sambra, A., Mansour, E., Hawke, S., Zereba, M., Greco, N., Ghanem, A., Zagidulin, D., Aboulnaga, A., Berners-Lee, T., 2016. Solid : A Platform for Decentralized Social Applications Based on Linked Data.

Schulz, O., Beetz, J., 2021. Image-documentation of existing buildings using a server-based BIM Collaboration Format workflow., in: EG-ICE 2021 Workshop on Intelligent Computing in Engineering. Presented at the EG-ICE, Berlin.

Schulz, O., Oraskari, J., Beetz, J., 2021. bcfOWL: A BIM collaboration ontology, in: Proceedings of the 9th Linked Data in Architecture and Construction Workshop. Presented at the LDAC2021, Luxembourg.

Tao, X., Das, M., Liu, Y., Cheng, J.C.P., 2021. Distributed common data environment using blockchain and Interplanetary File System for secure BIM-based collaborative design. Autom. Constr. 130, 103851. https://doi.org/10.1016/j.autcon.2021.103851

van Berlo, L., Krijnen, T., 2014. Using the BIM Collaboration Format in a Server Based Workflow. Procedia Environ. Sci., 12th International Conference on Design and Decision Support Systems in Architecture and Urban Planning, DDSS 2014 22, 325–332. https://doi.org/10.1016/j.proenv.2014.11.031

Werbrouck, J., Pauwels, P., Beetz, J., Mannens, E., 2021. Data Patterns for the Organisation of Federated Linked Building Data, in: Proceedings of the 9th Linked Data in Architecture and Construction Workshop. Presented at the LDAC2021, Luxembourg.

Werbrouck, J., Pauwels, P., Beetz, J., van Berlo, L., 2019. Towards a Decentralised Common Data Environment using Linked Building Data and the Solid Ecosystem.

Werbrouck, J., Pauwels, P., Beetz, J., Mannens, E., 2022. LBDserver - a Federated Ecosystem for Heterogeneous Linked Building Data. (Under review).

IM2DR: Incentive Based Multi-tier and Multi-agent Approach for Demand Response in Electricity Market with Reinforcement Learning

Abbasloo A., Valenzuela G., Gebhardt G.H.W., Tomar R., Piesk J.
Nuromedia GmbH, Germany
gabriel.valenzuela@nuromedia.com

Abstract. Imbalance between consumption and supply in grids causes a challenge to electricity utilities, leads to grid instability and results in failures of the grid. Traditionally, the demand for power is satisfied by increasing supply which is costly and against environmental regulations. Instead, demand response strategy harmonises the demand at the customer side e.g the utilities offer rates to customers to reduce their consumption at specific times of the day. While most research focuses on finding a strategy on just one side in this work, we approach it with an end-to-end reinforcement learning based methodology such that optimal strategies for parties are achieved with training on historical records. Agents are trained for individual customers and the electricity utilities for finding the optimal policies for the consumption, hence manifesting a multi-agents and multi-tiers approach. The new method achieves the full potential of a proactive framework for implementing the demand response strategy.

1. Introduction

Residential districts in 2019 represented 26% of final energy consumption in the EU[1] and compensating on the electrical grid seems to be possible by new innovations in renewable energy. As well, energy storages can help align peaks of renewable energy generation with peaks of consumption. However, their integration and adoption into the grid infrastructure takes time and requires extensive investigations regarding the reliability and usability. Demand response (DR) strategy aims to create stability by making the demand side flexible and shifts peak demand by providing customers with economical offers. But forcing customers to delay the usage of home appliances, undesired temperature set-points and the effort needed for acquiring information about prices and the consumption patterns create discomfort and dissatisfaction. Reinforcement learning (RL) has been successfully adopted in energy resource management such as electric vehicles, heating ventilation and air conditioning (HVAC) systems and storage management. The challenge in front of DR strategy is about its ability to minimise customer discomfort and integrate their feedback. Model-free RL seems to be the potential methodology very adaptable to its environment and can directly integrate human feedback into the decision making with least user intervention. Most of the research studies that considered human comfort focus on single-agent systems with demand-independent prices Vazquez and Nagy (2019). Moreover, modelling the electricity prices as demand-dependent variables might lead to the risk of shifting the consumption peak instead of shaving it.

We propose IM2DR, a system based on RL to coordinate multi-agent systems participating in the DR program with demand-dependent prices. As discussion concerning implementing a DR program in the EU begins, data shows that the peak reduction from DR programs in the US was only 6.6% of the peak demand in 2015. Vazquez and Nagy (2019) argued that the reason is that electricity is a commodity whose value is way higher than its price for the customers. Electricity customers generally will not give up their comfort for a lower bill.

[1] eurostat: Statistics Explained

https://doi.org/10.7146/aul.455.c201

Therefore, the implementation of DR strategy depends on offering more convenient economical savings than discomfort of customers. Moreover, the framework is required to be both automated and able to minimise user discomfort as much as possible. As Vazquez and Nagy (2019) also provided an overview of different scenarios for implementing the DR strategy with RL, districts connected to a grid require some sort of dynamic coordination. IM2DR introduces an end-to-end solution, where the regulatory-tier (Service Providers agent) coordinates the automation-tier (CUstomer multi-agents). Assuming that the market is elastic, customers receive their hourly rate from the regulatory-tier and the automation-tier schedule the appliances. As a consequence, the demand curves are flattened and the consumption peaks are shaped during high demand time of the day. The CityLearn simulation environment, empowered by EnergyPlus, provided a framework to implement the method and train the agents on historical records. We achieved the optimal policies for the individual agents by decoupling the training procedure and using the Soft Actor Critic algorithm Haarnoja (2018). To our knowledge this is the first study that models the supply and demand together.

2. Literature Review

Vazquez and Nagy (2019) discussed that a group of districts where the consumption independently is controlled under demand-independent prices is not a multi-agent approach. Moreover, they explained that if considering demand-dependent prices, the actions of any district has impacts on the price of electricity, and as the decisions taken by others. Vazquez and Detjeen (2019) demonstrated a multi-agent RL schema for load shaping in a model-free and decentralised manner where the price of electricity increases linearly with the total electricity demand of all the districts. The multi-agent framework was improved by introducing MARLISA that uses a reward with individual and collective goals, and the agents predict their own future consumption and share this with each other following a leader-follower framework Vazquez and Henze (2020). It is also unclear how RL can control a multitude of energy systems in a scalable coordinated way. Hence, Park (2019) presented LightLearn, an automating system for district lighting and HVACLearn for HVAC system Park (2020). GridLearn considers grid into the account Pigott (2021).

Lu (2019) proposes a novel incentive based demand response algorithm for smart grid systems with RL, aiming to help the electricity utilities to purchase energy resources from its customers to balance energy fluctuations. Game theoretic methods and simulations based on RL are used to analyse electricity market equilibrium as well. Liang (2020) adopts a deep deterministic policy gradient algorithm to model the bidding strategies of utilities companies. However all of these studies just modelled the electricity market and none of them took optimization over demand (finding an optimal strategy for scheduling the appliances) into consideration.

CityLearn is an open source OpenAI Gym environment for testing RL for energy optimization Vazquez and Dey (2020). Its objective is to standardise the evaluation of RL agents such that algorithms can be easily compared. CityLearn allows the easy implementation of agents to change their demand aggregation by controlling storages of energy. Currently, CityLearn allows controlling the storage of domestic hot water, and chilled water, for sensible cooling and dehumidification. CityLearn also has models of air-to-water heat pumps, electric heaters, solar photovoltaic arrays, and the pre-computed energy loads of the districts from EnergyPlus simulations Crawley (2000) which include space cooling, dehumidification, appliances, domestic hot water, and solar generation. Refer to the CityLearn challenge Nagy (2021) for further information.

3. Problem Formulation

Modelling of the DR strategy and automating the customers electricity consumption requires understanding how different players interact in the market. Figure 1 shows an overview of the electricity market. Such, the service provider works as a middleman in the wholesale market with grid operators and in the retail market with customers. Therefore, the role of service provider can be represented as an agent, namely the SP agent which regulates the consumption of automation-tier, where CU multi-agents operate. CU multi-agents automate the energy consumption of individual districts by scheduling the appliances and storages.

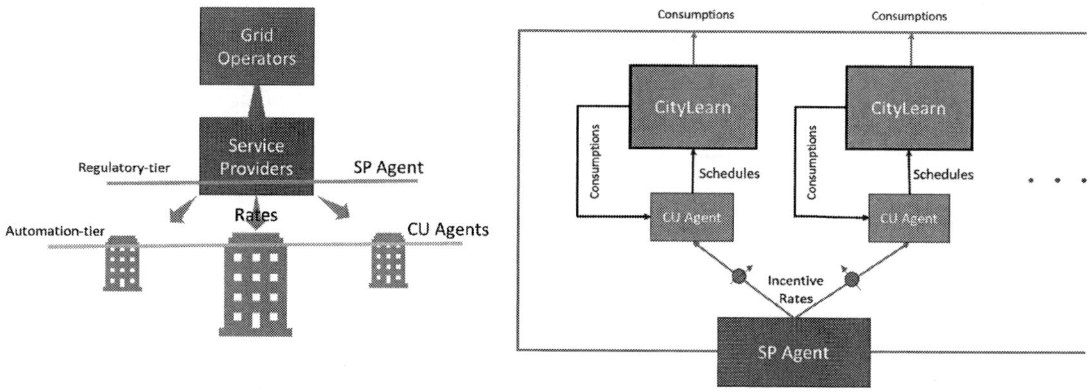

Figure 1: Left, the schematic of the electricity market. Right, demonstration of the system methodology.

DR strategy is an optimal policy in which the SP agent proactively coordinates the consumption of districts by offering some type of discounts in the form of incentive rates for convincing them to reduce the consumption and CU multi-agents schedule the entire appliances in order to satisfy the residents comfort and assuring the overall consumption is optimised using storages and domestic power generation. Lu (2019) introduced an RL based method for modelling the retail market and we will follow a similar approach in this paper. The parameters for modelling the retail market and implementing the incentive-based DR strategy is listed in Table 1. CU multi-agents are modelled in CityLearn as it is described in Vazquez and Dey (2020). The parameters for the simulation have been chosen in such a way that each district has a different attitude in the DR program.

3.1 Service Provider Model

The SP agent offer $\lambda_{n,h}$ such that the costumer n at time h needs to drop the curtailable consumption by $\Delta E_{n,h}^{curt}$ therefore the goal of the SP agent is to maximise its gain by:

$$max \sum_{n=1}^{N} \sum_{h=1}^{H} (p_h \cdot \Delta E_{n,h}^{curt} - \lambda_{n,h} \cdot \Delta E_{n,h}^{curt}) \text{ s.t. } \lambda_{min} < \lambda_{n,h} < \lambda_{max}$$

3.2 Customer's Regulatory-tier Model

The customers aim to maximise their outcome from the trade with the SP agent by finding a good balance between the gain from the incentive package and discomfort $\varphi_{n,h}$ by:

$$max \sum_{h=1}^{H} (\rho . \lambda_{n,h} . \Delta E_{n,h}^{curt} - (1 - \rho). \varphi_{n,h}(\Delta E_{n,h}^{curt}))$$

where $\varphi_{n,h}(\Delta E_{n,h}^{curt}) = \mu_n/2(\Delta E_{n,h}^{curt})^2 + \omega_n \Delta E_{n,h}^{curt}$.

The consumption drops are calculated as follows defined with a set of parameters characterising the customers and the market.

$$\Delta E_{n,h}^{curt} = E_{n,h}^{curt} . \xi_h . \frac{\lambda_{n,h} - \lambda_{min}}{\lambda_{min}} \text{ s.t. } K_{min} < \Delta E_{n,h}^{curt} < K_{max}$$

3.3 Objective Function for Regulatory-tier

The SP agent needs to find an optimal policy such that it maximises the gains of both sides of the trade by:

$$max \sum_{n=1}^{N} \sum_{h=1}^{H} (p_h . \Delta E_{n,h}^{curt} - \lambda_{n,h} . \Delta E_{n,h}^{curt} + \rho . \lambda_{n,h} . \Delta E_{n,h}^{curt} - (1 - \rho). \varphi_{n,h}(\Delta E_{n,h}^{curt}))$$

3.4 Objective Function for Multi-agents Automation-tier

CU multi-agents minimise the consumption but this time integrating the SP agent contributions by introducing $\Delta E_{n,h}^{curt}$ and $\Phi(\lambda_{n,h}, \Delta E_{n,h}^{curt})$ that may reflect, e.g., the customer's discomfort in the objective:

$$min \sum_{h=1}^{H} (p_h . (E_{n,h} - \Delta E_{n,h}^{curt}) + \Phi(\lambda_{n,h}, E_{n,h}^{curt}))$$

While CU single-agents schedule the home appliances by minimising the very first term. The action and state space are defined in CityLearn with the simulation episode of a year.

4. Reinforcement Learning for Achieving the Optimal Policy

Showing that each tier's contribution in the electricity market is a Markov Decision Process (MDP) and therefore can be modelled by RL methodology has been discussed by Lu (2019) and Vazquez and Dey (2020) in detail. Therefore, the optimal policy for the market consists of a policy for the regulatory-tier (SP agent) which implements the DR strategy as well as individual optimal policies of the CU agents that minimise the consumption and are trained against the SP agent's policy. Because of the decoupled nature of the problem, we can obtain the policies for the SP agent and the CU agents independently by training on the historical records using an off-policy algorithm like Soft Actor Critic (SAC). SAC optimises a stochastic policy to maximise a trade-off between expected return and entropy, a measure of randomness in the policy Haarnoja (2018).

4.1 Multi-tier Training Procedure

In order to train the agents from different tiers, we take advantage of the decoupled nature of the problem such that the SP agent is trained with an episode of a month (the SP agent is aware of which month it is) on the historical consumption records from the districts in which CU single-agents schedule the consumption. Training single-agents is carried out in the CityLearn environment as well. CU multi-agents are later trained by integrating already-trained SP agent in the training loop such that any district participating in the DR program needs to be aligned with the policy of the SP agent as depicted in Figure 1. We remark that the entire training and integration of the SP agent is carried on curtailable consumption.

Table 1: List of parameters for modelling the SP agent.

Parameters	Definition
p_h, $\lambda_{n,h}$, λ_{min} and λ_{max}	Electricity price, incentive rate for customer n at time h and its bounds
$E_{n,h}$, $E^{curt}_{n,h}$, $\Delta E^{curt}_{n,h}$, K_{min} and K_{max}	(curtailable) Consumption for customer n at time h, its drop and bounds
N, H, ρ and ξ_h	Number of districts, simulation length, trade-off and elasticity at time h
$\varphi_{n,h}$, μ_n and ω_n	Discomfort of customer n at time h with the flexibility and the attitude parameters

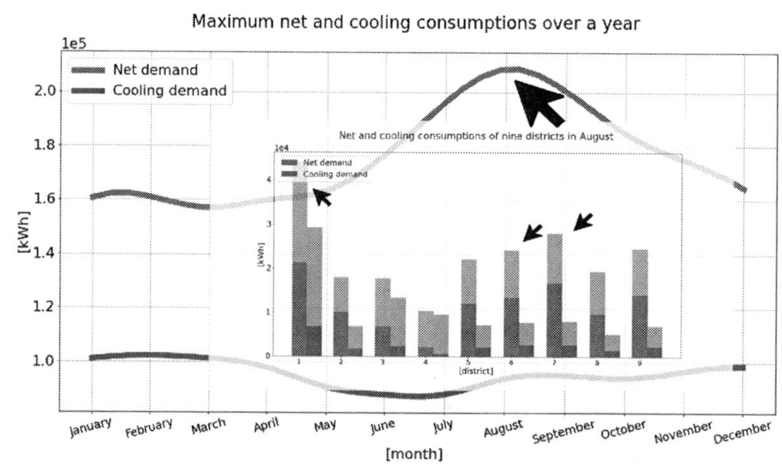

Figure 2: Consumption of all districts over a year. Bar chart shows consumption ranges over samples in August.

5. Simulation and Result

The SP agent is modelled in OpenAI Gym and later integrated in the CityLearn environment for training CU multi-agents. The CityLearn environment provides nine different districts with different architecture, thermal behaviour and occupancies. Several climate zones exist as well. The thermal behaviour is modelled in EnergyPlus and is given as input to CityLearn. We run the algorithm of each stage five times to evaluate the statistical properties of the agents. In the following sections, we provided plots of medians, minimums or maximums of the generated samples at time h to explain the different expected outcomes of the DR program compared with single-agents performance.

5.1 Configuration and Scenarios

Figure 2 shows the maximum net consumption of nine districts over a year. To evaluate the DR program, we want to see if we can flatten the consumption peak in August. Moreover, for the purpose, we choose climate zone five where the curtailable consumption is the cooling demand such that the DR program requests participants drop the cooling consumption. Imitating the customers dropping their cooling consumption is implemented by subtracting the amount from the cooling demands calculated by EnergyPlus. As Figure 2 depicts the consumption range in August, we choose district one, six and seven with high consumption participating in the DR program in July, August and September. The rest will join the first and second half of the year according to Table 2 to evaluate the RL inherent bias towards maximising short term rewards Vazquez and Henze (2020).

Table 2: Participation in the DR program for simulations.

Districts	Participation program
One, six and seven	July, August and September
Two, three and four	The first half of the year
Five, eight and nine	The second half of the year

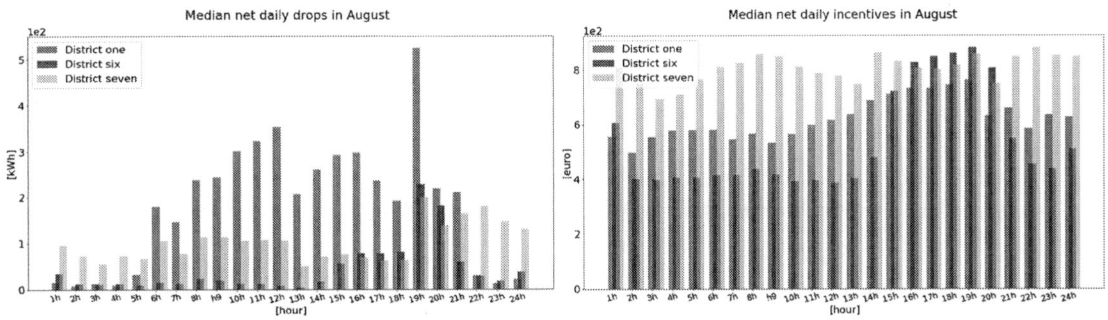

Figure 3: Daily drops and incentives statistics over several free rollouts of the SP agent.

5.2 Training and Evaluating of the SP Agent

In order to show the statistics of the optimal policy of the SP agent, we plotted the hourly net incentives and drops over several rollouts from the SP agent in Figure 3. Plots show the nontrivial statistics of the policy which has different behaviors for districts reflecting the impact of parameters characterise districts in DR programs e.g. district one has tendency to drop more for receiving less rates.

5.3 Integration of the SP Agent and Performance of CU Multi-gents

The SP agent impacts the multi-agents environment by introducing consumption drop $\Delta E^{curt}_{n,h}$ and $\Phi(\lambda_{n,h}, \Delta E^{curt}_{n,h})$ which is assumed to zero for simplicity. The SP agent takes action at time n as a form of offering incentives and will be informed about the realised drops at time n which are the state of the environment under the corresponding action. The realised drops are calculated based on the difference between the actual and expected curtailable consumption. The expected curtailable consumption needs to be predicted in the best scenario but here for simplicity, we calculated it by creating a template by taking maximum over generated samples obtained from repeating single-agents training. Figure 4 gives a good comparison of the consumption of nine districts in August and the metrics introduced in CityLearn e.g. see the arrows for changes of the range over samples. Moreover, the daily and monthly drops for district one, six and seven over a year and in August. The plots illustrate the maximums over the samples interpreted as the worst outcome.

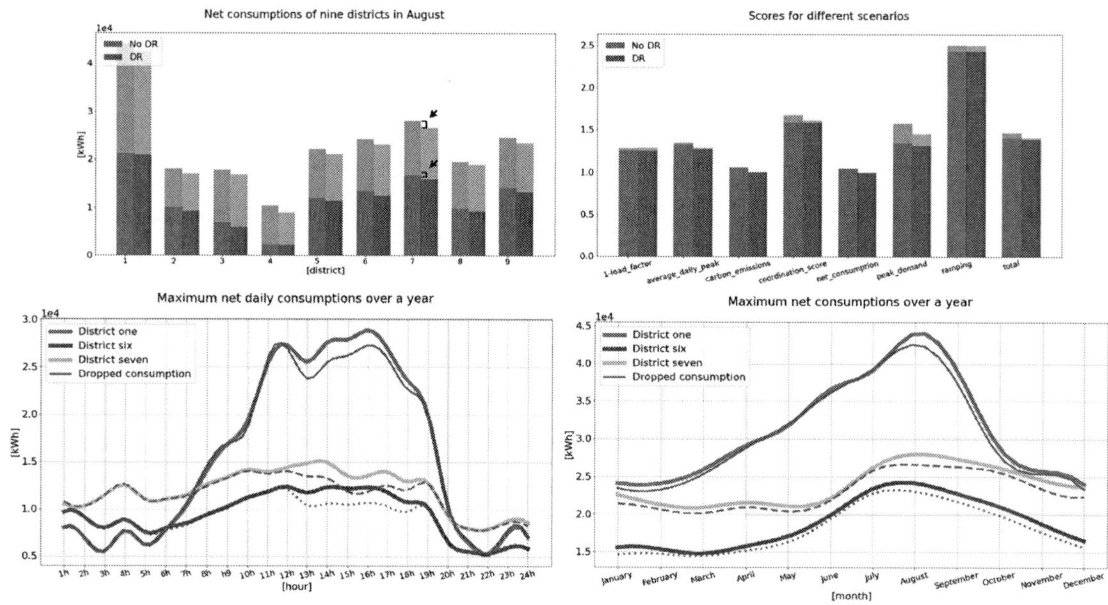

Figure 4: CU multi-agents performance compared to single-agents. Top, depicts some indicator's ranges. Bottom, presenting the consumption in different time frames.

5.4 Statistics and Insights

To have more insights about the SP agent, we calculated the histogram of free rollouts drawn from the SP agent. We also calculated the same free rollouts statistic when the states for all districts are forced to zero except district one (shown by arrow in Figure 5). Comparing them shows that the policy for each district proactively changes based on the contributions of the others. Figure 5 also shows those statistics when the SP agent is integrated with CU multi-agents. The statistics completely changed and the minimums over the samples tended to cover the whole range meaning the SP agent adapted to the task. We evaluate CU multi-agents by comparing the unrealised and realised daily drops presented in Figure 5. The unrealised drops are obtained by the free rollout of the SP agent and the consumption scheduled by CU single-agents. We can interpret it as such that CU multi-agents' policies seem to integrate well with the SP agent's policy after going through a round of training.

Figure 6 shows that the districts in the second half of the year program are able to maintain the consumption reduction despite pressures from previous months therefore, IM2DR seems not to be inherently biased towards consuming less energy now at the expense of consuming more later. For those in the first half of the year program, the reduction propagates to the entire year supporting the same claim as well. Even though the consumption are characterised to be less elastic in the middle of the day the net daily consumption over the year show a significant reduction during this time across all participants showing that the IM2DR tends to flatten the high peak hours, daily plots in Figure 4 and 6.

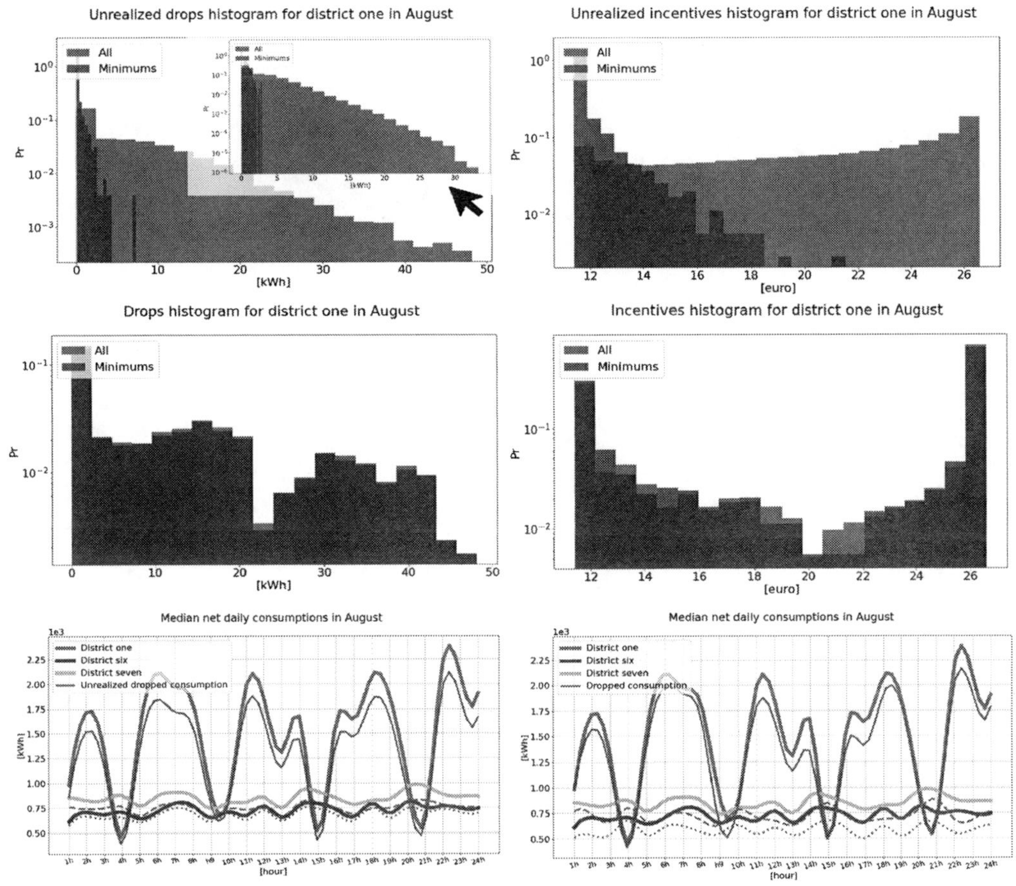

Figure 5: Top, histograms of drops and incentives for the SP agent in different scenarios. Bottom, consumption with CU single and multi-agents.

6. Guideline for Real Life System Implementation

We proceed now to the real life implementation of IM2DR. As depicted in Figure 7, the service provider collects the consumption records of all districts over time and (re)trains the SP agent. At the beginning of the year, each customer receives a deal concerning the offers via the system as a message shown in the UI. Individuals can see the possible options of the consumption reductions in the UI e.g. shifting the cooling setpoints with two degrees can fulfil the deal. After agreeing partially on the offer, the service provider receives them. Then CU multi-agents will go through (re)training with considering the agreement, and schedule the appliances for the year.

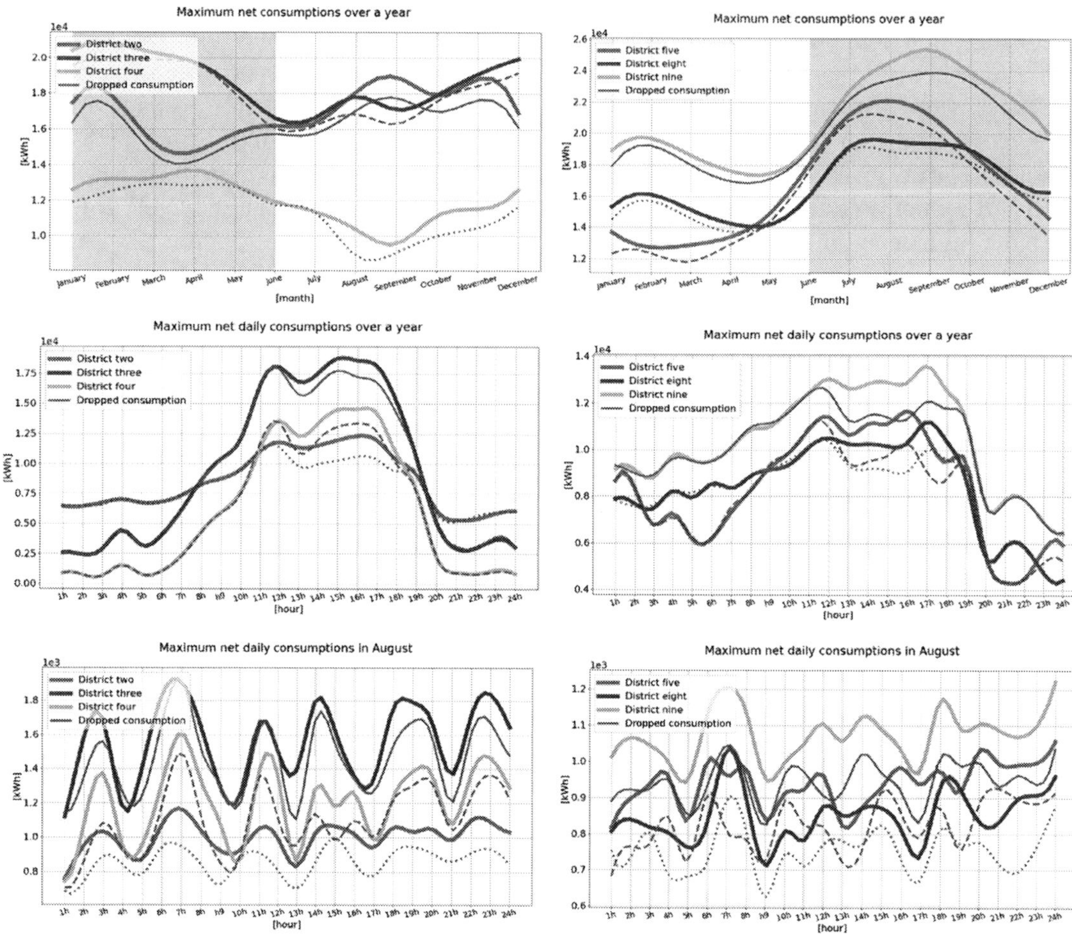

Figure 6: Consumption comparison of districts participating in the half of the year DR program.

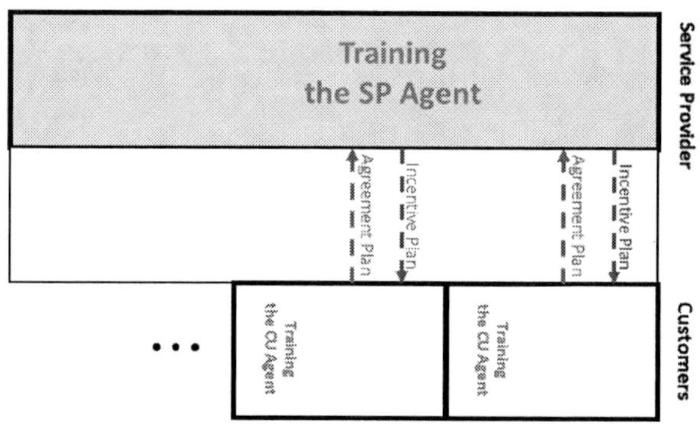

Figure 7: Real life implementation of the system.

Meanwhile the service provider needs to do some maths over the deals for estimating the expectations. It becomes challenging when dealing with agents with stochastic policies. If you collect a good amount of run sessions, by looking at consumption range over all samples at a specific time, following the procedure in Figure 8, one gets a rough estimate of the consumption expectation bounds e.g. see the arrows for August. In this way, a baseline can be estimated for the DR program.

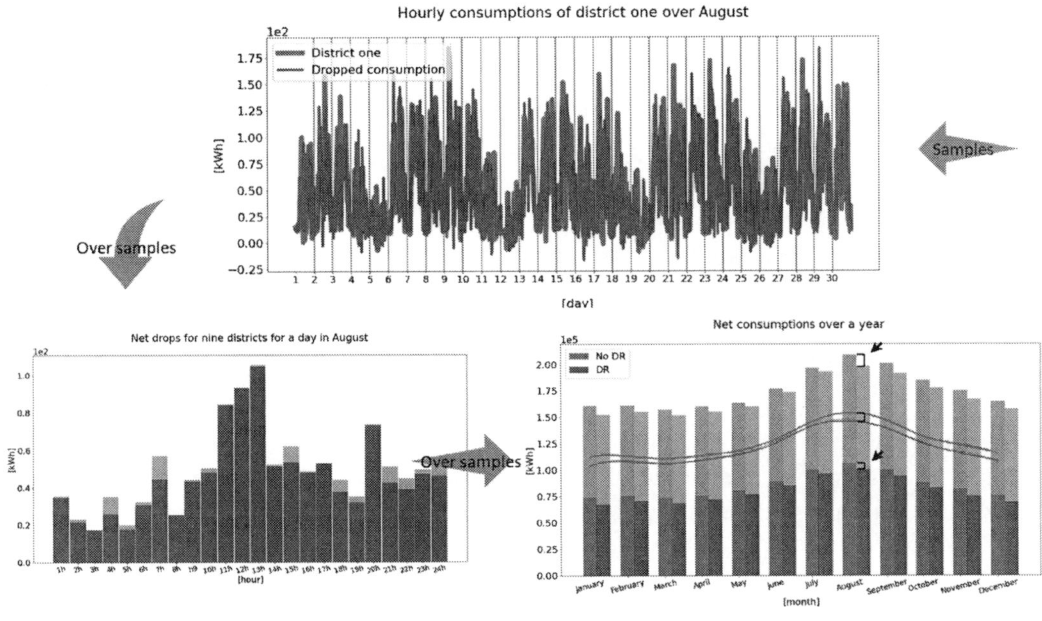

Figure 8: Calculating DR program expectation's outcomes for the service provider.

7. Conclusion and Future Work

We have introduced an end-to-end system for implementing DR strategy that lets the customer's automation agents schedule the appliances while the service provider agent harmonises the market by creating balance between demand and response. On the other hand we obtained a set of optimal policies with which the service provider proactively coordinates the consumption and customers in the program schedule their appliances. The customers are modelled by a set of parameters in the DR program therefore, for future work, it is the very first step to investigate the external realisation of those parameters related to the comfort of the residents in terms of heating, cooling and air conditioning. Overall such an automated decision making is more sensible if customers also receive the offers during the year in form of monthly, weekly or daily offers. This leads to retraining CU multi-agents for the rest of the year achieving a policy that is suboptimal for the entire year but is an optimal policy for the rest of the year. And integrating different SP agents optimised with different time scales e.g. one for daily and one for weekly offers. Moreover, looking into alternative rewards can show more insights since the incentive and reductions contain the MDP states of the other agents so it helps the agents to reach a better policy during training.

Acknowledgement

This research has been financially supported by PRECEPT, an EU Horizon 2020 project registered with the topic: LC-EEB-07-2020, the type of action: IA and the proposal number: 958284. The first author would like to thank the ML team in Nuromedia GmbH and other industrial partners in the project for their collaboration.

References

Vázquez-Canteli, J.R. and Nagy, Z. (2019). Reinforcement learning for demand response: A review of algorithms and modelling techniques. Applied energy, 235, pp. 1072-1089.

Park, J.Y., Dougherty, T., Fritz, H. and Nagy, Z. (2019). LightLearn: An adaptive and occupant centred controller for lighting based on reinforcement learning. Building and Environment, 147, pp. 397-414.

Park, J.Y. and Nagy, Z. (2020). HVACLearn: A reinforcement learning based occupant-centric control for thermostat set-points. In Proceedings of the Eleventh ACM International Conference on Future Energy Systems, pp. 434-437.

Vazquez-Canteli, J., Detjeen, T., Henze, G., Kämpf, J. and Nagy, Z. (2019). Multi-agent reinforcement learning for adaptive demand response in smart cities. In Journal of Physics: Conference Series, Vol. 1343, No. 1, p. 012058. IOP Publishing.

Vazquez-Canteli, J.R., Henze, G. and Nagy, Z. (2020). MARLISA: Multi-agent reinforcement learning with iterative sequential action selection for load shaping of grid-interactive connected buildings. In Proceedings of the 7th ACM International Conference on Systems for Energy-Efficient Buildings, Cities, and Transportation, pp. 170-179.

Pigott, A., Crozier, C., Baker, K. and Nagy, Z. (2021). GridLearn: Multiagent Reinforcement Learning for Grid-Aware Building Energy Management. arXiv:2110.06396 [cs.MA].

Vázquez-Canteli, J.R., Dey, S., Henze, G. and Nagy, Z. (2020). CityLearn: Standardising Research in Multi-Agent Reinforcement Learning for Demand Response and Urban Energy Management. arXiv:2012.10504 [cs.LG].

Nagy, Z., Vázquez-Canteli, J.R., Dey, S. and Henze, G. (2021). The citylearn challenge 2021. In Proceedings of the 8th ACM International Conference on Systems for Energy-Efficient Buildings, Cities, and Transportation, pp. 218-219.

Wang, J., Guo, C., Yu, C. and Liang, Y. (2022). Virtual power plant containing electric vehicles scheduling strategies based on deep reinforcement learning. Electric Power Systems Research, 205, p.107714.

Lu, R. and Hong, S.H. (2019). Incentive-based demand response for smart grid with reinforcement learning and deep neural network. Applied Energy, 236, pp. 937-949.

Haarnoja, T., Zhou, A., Hartikainen, K., Tucker, G., Ha, S., Tan, J., Kumar, V., Zhu, H., Gupta, A., Abbeel, P. and Levine, S. (2018). Soft Actor-Critic Algorithms and Applications. arXiv:1812.05905 [cs.LG].

Crawley, D.B., Lawrie, L.K., Pedersen, C.O. and Winkelmann, F.C. (2000). EnergyPlus: Energy simulation program. ASHRAE Journal, 42(4), pp. 49-56.

Integrated data-driven and knowledge-based performance evaluation for machine assistance in building design decision support

Chen X. [1], Saluz U. [1], Staudt J. [2], Margesin M. [2], Lang W. [2], Geyer P. [1, 3]
[1] Technische Universität Berlin, Germany, [2] Technische Universität München, Germany, [3] Leibniz University Hannover, Germany
xia.chen@tu-berlin.de

Abstract. The building design process requires architects to consider interdisciplinary knowledge and data support based on the vision of sustainable development. In this context, we develop a process-integrated, dynamic machine assistance to support the decision-making process for building designers in the early design phases. In this paper, we present 1. a framework for integrating data-driven models with knowledge-based methods that provide multi-objective assistance considering energy performance and embodied environmental impact; 2. the alignment of the methods in the design process and respective decision situations to disclose the potential situated design space including its uncertainty ranges as well as detailed strategy suggestions. A case of real-world building data serves to illustrate and validate the approach. The research presented in this paper is part of research aiming at assistance by augmented intelligence for sustainable building design decision support.

1. Introduction

The vision of sustainable development already demands consideration in the early building design phases. To address this challenge, various design support tools have been developed to provide information in different aspects: building performance simulation (BPS) tools such as EnergyPlus, Sefaira (Østergård, Jensen & Maagaard, 2016), and data-driven machine learning methods (Seyedzadeh, Rahimian, Glesk & Roper, 2018) for energy performance evaluation, etc. Embodied emissions are accounted for by BIM-based life cycle assessment (LCA) tools, such as (CAALA, 2019) and (One Click LCA® software, 2022). While in fact, these tools are implemented based on different principles, requiring building designers to access interdisciplinary knowledge and data to estimate building performance. This creates the design space in the early design phases (Østergård, Jensen & Maagaard, 2017) and involves intertangled interdependencies and complexity, which surpasses the capacity of conventional design methods. Although the digitalization trend supports the integration of different methodologies, both data-driven and domain knowledge-based, up to now, the synergy of both methodologies is not integrated into design processes at different development levels.

For building energy performance, energy consumption information is relatively easily accessible via smart meter measurements with a particular set of building characteristics representation, such as building geometric features, activity behavior, material properties, etc. (Hensen & Lamberts, 2019). A diverse dataset is available via large-scale records in the real world from existing buildings or generated by validated simulation under first-principles methods. Such a dataset is suitable for data-driven approaches, or more specifically, machine learning approaches for supervised learning to capture the implicit relationship between inputs and outputs. The trained model (after learning from the dataset) is fit for a certain range of interpolation or extrapolation for new cases, which brings the model the advantage of flexibility. The effectiveness and accuracy are well-proved in many domains (Bélisle, Huang, Le Digabel & Aimen E. Gheribi, 2015; Thessen, 2016; Jia & Ma, 2017). Comprehensive reviews report the wide acceptance of data-driven approaches in our domain in the aspect of

https://doi.org/10.7146/aul.455.c202

energy performance (heating, cooling, lighting, etc.) and consumption prediction (Westermann & Evins, 2019; Amasyali & El-Gohary, 2018).

Knowledge-based methods required in this study for LCA, are involved in the sustainable building design process (Schneider-Marin & Lang, 2020; Hollberg, Tschetwertak, Schneider & Habert, 2018). They widely exist in the general engineering process for solving specific problems. Related first-principles tools require detailed information input that is typically not accessible at early design phases or suggests a level of precision that might obscure the potential outcomes of various construction types. The shared characteristics of these problems are: The data acquisition is relatively implicit; The calculation or assessment process requires induction, reasoning, and referring to other background knowledge with limited information. In this context, knowledge representations from experts are inevitably more effective and interpretable, which conducts the gap between knowledge-based and data-driven approaches in the general engineering domain and raises the research need for method integration. In most current design processes embodied emissions are evaluated at a later phase when most construction and material decisions have already been made. The prediction of embodied emissions in early design phases is subject to significant uncertainties due to a lack of detailed information (Schneider-Marin, Harter, Tkachuk & Lang, 2020; Harter, Singh, Schneider-Marin, Lang & Geyer, 2020). Bridging the gap between the lack of information in early design phases and the LCA methodology to predict embodied emissions has been identified as a significant research gap (Theißen, Höper, Wimmer, Zibell, Meins-Becker, Rössig, Goitowski & Lambertz, 2020).

In this study, we propose a general framework to integrate both data-driven and knowledge-based approaches. We intend to investigate the path of integration toward multi-objective support applied to the sustainable building design domain. In this case, both energy performance and embodied environmental impact are selected as objectives. The novelty of this framework is as follows:

- We propose an integrative modelling approach: By introducing decomposition knowledge from design, LCA and BPS simultaneously into the data generation process for data-driven model training, while both approaches share the same representation of building modelling.
- The approach combines the advantages of the flexibility and interpretability from both approaches with the shared information for supporting well-informed decision-making.
- The combined information of building environmental impact and energy performance evaluation makes trade-off analysis in the design space as an assistance for the early design phase accessible.

The remaining sections of the paper are organized as follows: Section 2 introduces example methodologies implemented in the framework in this study; Section 3 sets up a real-world case study in the early design phase scenario; Section 4 discusses the results, and Section 5 concludes the paper.

2. Methodologies for LCA and energy performance evaluation integration

The general illustration of the integrative evaluation process is presented schematically in Figure 1. In this process, buildings are represented by a digital model exhibiting parametric features based on indicators. We exclusively focus on two indicators: energy performance (heating load / total energy consumption) and embodied environmental impact (global warming potentials, GWP). By integrating approaches including data-driven (Chen & Geyer, 2022) and knowledge-based methods (Schneider-Marin, Tanja Stocker, Oliver Abele, Johannes Staudt, Manuel Margesin & Werner Lang) for prediction, uncertainty evaluation, and model interpretation, we create a shared feature list for implementing both approaches simultaneously to align with the design scenario. Eventually, indicators, uncertainties information, and model explanations are integrated to provide valuable insights for designers to conduct answers for "what-if" questions. This process of providing users with possible "assumptions" with regard to defined features as a potential design space with intervention consequences is called machine assistance (Chen & Geyer, 2022).

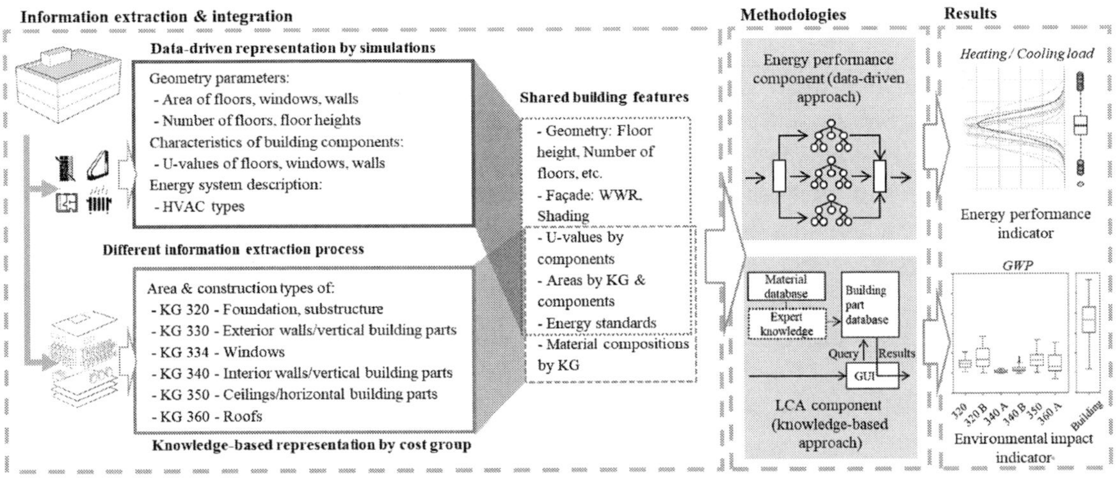

Figure 1: Performance evaluation: different approaches under the machine assistance framework

2.1 Data-driven modelling for operational energy

For the energy performance, we used a synthetic dataset generated by parametric BPS to train machine learning models to capture relationships between building features and heating load/ total energy consumption. Since we applied the framework to the building early design phase scenario, one characteristic should be necessarily included: the evaluation of information uncertainties. To represent this process, a probabilistic, tree-based surrogate model – NGBoost (Duan, Avati, Ding, Thai, Basu, Ng & Schuler, 2020) is chosen to fulfill the requirements mentioned above: Instead of generating output as a point prediction, the design of the algorithm involves the uncertainties quantification process, which provides insights into the output range within the set of feature input descriptions.

Furthermore, we consider the model explainability of the data-driven model for informed decision support. An interpretation method: SHAP (Lundberg & Lee, 2017), is integrated to analyze the feature importance and assumption consequences. Eventually, the combination improves the reusability of data-driven models by generalization and trustworthiness by explainability (Geyer, Singh & Chen, 2021). The result with the training process explanation is shown in section 3.3. For further parametric fine-tune detail and extension material, we refer to (Duan et al., 2020; Chen & Geyer, 2022).

2.2 Knowledge-based LCA evaluation methods integration

For the embodied emissions (GWP), we rely on a knowledge-based method where a database of material properties is enriched via expert input and knowledge regarding construction types and physical properties, such as thermal properties, is added to calculate results based on simple geometric models (Schneider-Marin, Tanja Stocker, Oliver Abele, Johannes Staudt, Manuel Margesin & Werner Lang). The database is fed with a multitude of options possible at an early design stage resulting in a range of outcomes. Additional modules can be integrated for cost, maintenance, repair, replacement, end-of-life, and environmental costs. This method enables users without LCA expertise to make decisions in early design phases based on reliable primary data collected in a knowledge-based decomposed LCA database ("Knowledge Database" on the basis of the publicly available database Ökobaudat (Bundesministerium des Innern, für Bau und Heimat, 2022)). This material database is enriched with expert knowledge regarding different construction types, including material composition and quantities of typical building components. Their quantities are determined by external requirements, such as energy standards or structural properties.

In this paper, we investigate different isolation standard properties as one part of material functionality in the case study. Materials are then classified according to their applicability based on the location of material and the functionality it fulfills. To organize the building elements according to their respective locations, we refer to the cost groups (Kostengruppen, KG) based on the German standard DIN 276 (Siemon, Speckhals & Siemon, 2021). In this study, we only consider KG 300 (building structure and finishes). The resulting building part properties are combined with geometric data extracted from digital models available as IFC files to predict the embodied emissions for a complete building.

3. Case study

3.1. Design scenarios

To test the described method, we used a case study of a real-world building design of a mixed-use building. The described project is called the Building.Lab on a tech campus in Regensburg, Germany (see Figure 2). The function of this 2308 sqm building is office and seminar use as well as housing. It consists of 4 above-ground stories and one underground level with a concrete skeleton structure. As we are studying an early design phase, the precise façade composition has not been determined yet. The housing areas are located in the south, and their balconies also function as passive solar protection. The larger seminar rooms are oriented to the north and can therefore be well illuminated by a high percentage of window area while avoiding overheating. The building is arranged in a U-shape around an atrium that extends across all stories.

Figure 2: Building.Lab conceptual & BIM model illustration; Source: Lang Hugger Rampp GmbH / Bayerischer Bauindustrieverband e.V.

The case study examines the building design for three different window-to-wall ratios (WWR = 0.2, 0.4, 0.6), three different isolation standards (base, medium, high), and two shading options (External-Shading, Low-HGC-Value). Table 1 shows areas of the various building components for the real-world variant with a WWR of 0.4.

Table 1: Areas of building components (window-to-wall ratio = 0.4)

Cost group	Subdivision	Description	Area
KG_320	-	Foundation	966 m²
KG_330	-		
	KG_330 A	Exterior wall underground	416 m²
	KG_330 B/C	Exterior wall above ground (load bearing & non-load bearing)	901 m²
KG_334	-	Windows	600 m²
KG_340	-		
	KG_340 A	Internal wall (load bearing)	1088 m²
	KG_340 B	Internal wall (non-load bearing)	1478 m²
KG_350	-	Ceilings/Floors	1945 m²
KG_360	-	Roof (Building)	583 m²
		Roof (Garage)	369 m²

3.2. Data description

To generate data that allow well-generalizing models, we created a dataset based on the target scenario for the data-driven and knowledge-based performance evaluation. A parametric model for a generic H-shape office building has been developed that covers a wide configuration variety of building components and zones. The number of floors was set to four with an additional basement. Besides the basement, all floors have the same floor plan scheme. The modelling platform was Grasshopper (Robert McNeel & Associates, 2022). A high-level simulation interface for EnergyPlus, Honeybee (*Ladybug Tools | Honeybee)* was chosen. Figure 3 presents an illustrative sample.

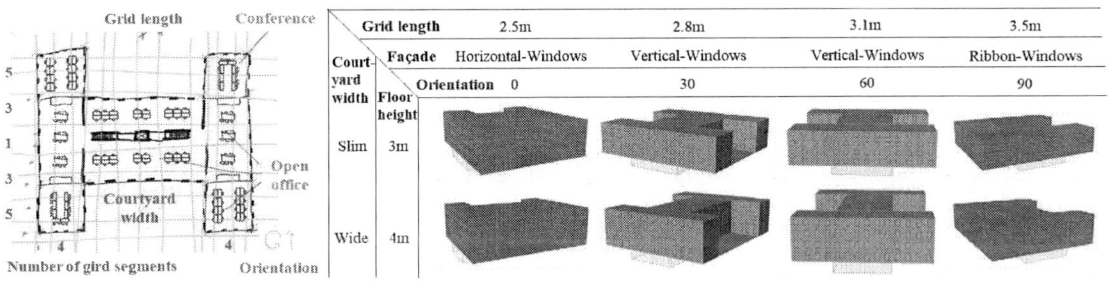

Figure 3: Floor plan scheme of generic H-shape office building and samples

For the dataset generation, the varied parameter list is shown in Table 2.

Table 2: List of input features

Parameters	Description
Standard of U-Values	Base, Medium, High
Façade	Horizontal-Windows (WWR: 0.19-0.30), Vertical-Windows (WWR: 0.20-0.46), Ribbon-Windows (WWR: 0.55-0.68)[1]
Shading	External-Shading, Low-HGC-Value
Courtyard width	Narrow – 7, Wide – 13 [number of raster segments] (17.5, 20, 22, 24.5, 30, 34, 38, 42) [m]
Floor height	3.4 [m]
Orientation	0, 30, 60, 90 [°]
Grid length	2.5, 2.8, 3.1, 3.5 [m] (Floor areas: 1150, 1400, 1800, 2250, 2700) [m²]

[1] *window-to-wall ratio*

Besides these parameters, every combination, i.e., the full factorial, has been simulated, which resulted in 1152 simulated samples. Construction and HVAC system were kept constant. For the construction, an external thermal insulation composite system (ETICS) was modelled with a massive generic material with a heat capacity of 1100 J/kg·K and 900 J/kg·K for the slabs. Furthermore, we defined three sets of u-values which would scale the thickness of the thermal layer accordingly. In this context, we selected three well-accepted energy standards in Germany and referred to u-values requirements as three isolation categories (base, medium, and high), as shown in Table 3.

Table 3: U-value requirements under different isolation standards [W/m²K.]

Standard of U-Values	Base: GEG (2020 German Energy Act for Buildings)	Medium: NZEB (Net Zero Energy Building)	High: Passive House
- Base plate	0.2625	0.206	0.15
- Roof	0.15	0.135	0.12
- Exterior wall, bearing, above ground	0.21	0.18	0.15
- Exterior wall, bearing, under ground	0.2625	0.206	0.15
- Window	0.975	0.888	0.8

The HVAC system is modelled with an ideal load air system template from EnergyPlus as it provides good comparability of loads at an early stage of the design. For zone programs, the open office area was modelled with 0.057 people/m² and conference areas with 0.053 people/m². As for shading mechanism, either windows with a solar-heat-gain-coefficient (SHGC) of 0.5 and an additional shading layer with the reflectance of 0.5, and transmission of 0.4 will be activated as soon as zone temperatures rise above 25°C or windows with a low SHGC of 0.3 have been modelled.

3.3. Model training

The surrogate model (NGBoost) consists of a set of Classification and Regression Trees (CART), which requires the input features in the form of integer or float (Loh, 2011). Only semantic features in the dataset require label-encoding by transferring descriptions into numerical categories. In this context, three features require feature engineering: *IsolationStandard*, *Façade*, and *Shading.*

The training process randomly splits the dataset into training (80%) and test (20%) sets. We set input features as in Table 2 with the prediction target of building heating load and total energy consumption. Since the dataset is relatively simple, models are trained by the default setting of hyperparameters (Schuler, 2020).

For the performance evaluation, we selected the most typical metrics in the BPS domain (Vogt, Remmen, Lauster, Fuchs & Müller, 2018) as well as in machine learning regression prediction tasks: Root Mean Square Error (RMSE), Mean Absolute Percentage Error (MAPE), Normalized Root Mean Square Error (NRMSE) and R-squared (R2). Table 4 presents the model performance based on the test set.

Table 4: Accuracy metrics of model result

	RMSE	MAPE	NRMSE	R2
Heating Load	0.3246	0.2529%	0.8137	0.9986
Total Energy Consumption	0.4450	0.2091%	1.0868	0.9971

The result shows a decent performance for the data-driven approach, the average errors of both models are lower than 1%. More specifically, we see that the performance of the heating load model is better than the total energy consumption prediction. The reason behind it is intuitive:

total energy consumption depends on more implicit factors, e.g., cooling, equipment, and lighting load. To sum up, the surrogate model based on feature representation in Table 2 is capable to capture the building energy performance accurately.

Additionally, NGBoost as the surrogate model provides the output as a set of Gaussian distribution parameters: *loc* and *scale,* which stands for mean (point prediction) and standard deviation (uncertainty range), respectively. Figure 4 and Figure 5 illustrate how different input features impact point output and uncertainty range in the task of heating load and total energy consumption prediction.

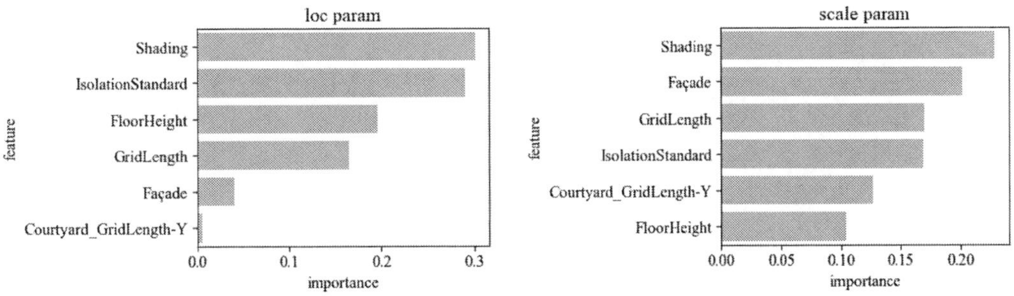

Figure 4: Feature importance for heating load prediction

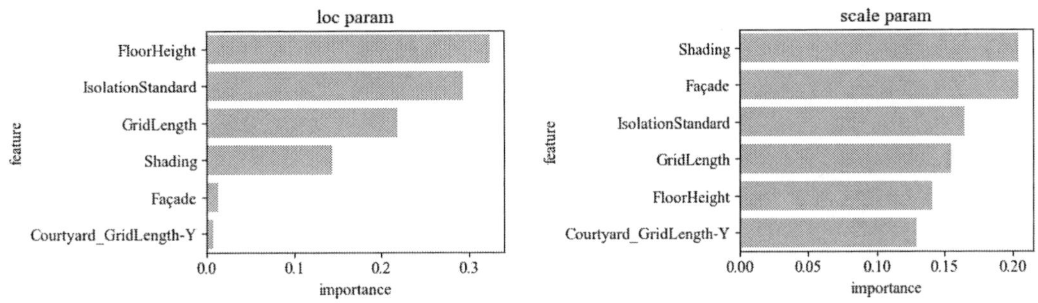

Figure 5: Feature importance for total energy consumption prediction

For heating load prediction, Figure 4 shows that the design of shading, isolation standard choices, and floor height affects the point prediction (mean value of the output) the most, followed by building geometry, especially the internal wall area. For output uncertainties, options of shading, façade, and grid length have the most effects in the uncertainty range (standard deviation of the output). Similar feature importance is also observed for the task of total energy consumption prediction (Figure 5) with regard to the question, of which shading option and building façade features should gain the most attention in consideration of building energy performance.

3.4. Results

For the building operational energy, the prediction presents regular patterns aligned with isolation standard and WWR iterations, as shown in Figure 6: The heating load varies between 80 and 115 kWh/m^2 per year, which increases with higher WWRs and decreases with higher isolation standards. The same patterns are observed in total energy consumption as well. The consumption increases with higher WWR with the option of low-HGC-value strengthening this trend. Compared with heating load, it contains more factors: Intuitively, we observed that with the higher isolation standard, external shading, and lower WWR, the total energy consumption drops accordingly.

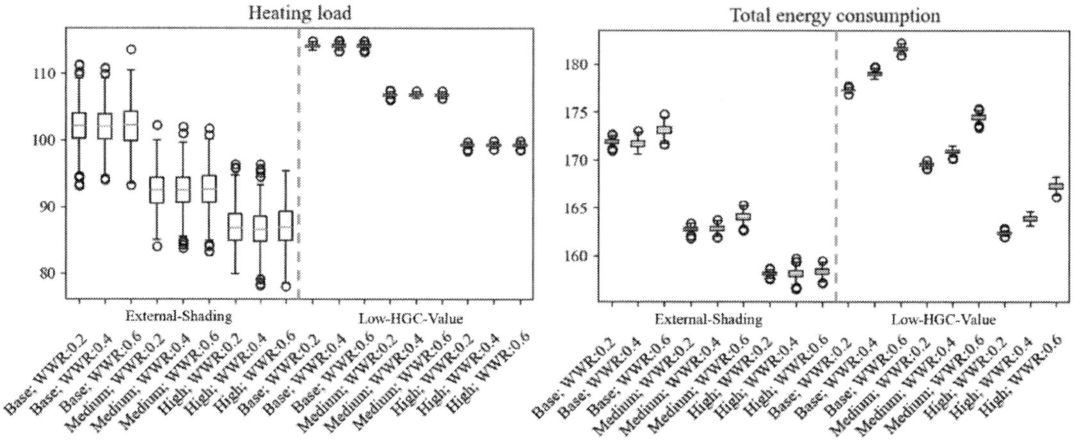

Figure 6: Heating load and total energy consumption prediction under different isolation standard, window-to-wall ratio (WWR), and shading combinations

Some interesting quantitative insights are worth mentioning from Figure 6: In heating load prediction, the range of energy consumption is partially overlapped between adjacent insulation standards. Compared to the isolation standard difference, the impact of different WWRs is relatively small. The reason is the assumption of state-of-the-art glazing and shading that allows windows to level out higher heat transfer losses by solar gains without overheating in summer. Such information provides designers with valuable benchmarks and alternative scenarios, enabling them to involve other factors (cost, CO2 emissions, etc.) for further decision support.

For the embodied emissions, the predictions show that the GWP increases for higher isolation standards as shown in Figure 7. The increase in GWP related to improved isolation standards is relatively small compared to the overall embodied emissions. For the given concrete construction type, the predictions for three WWRs show that the GWP decreases with the increasing ratio of windows with the option of low-HGC-value.

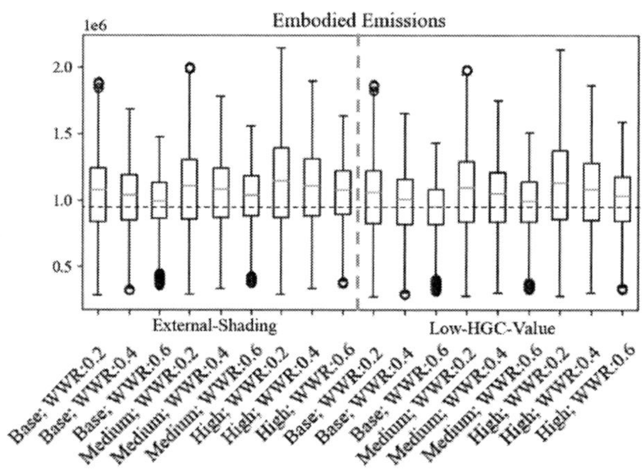

Figure 7: Embodied emissions (GWP) prediction under different isolation standard, window-to-wall ratio (WWR), and shading combinations

The simultaneous presentation of operational energy and embodied emissions predictions allows designers to evaluate parameters such as isolation standards, WWR, and shading options at early stages and adjust their design accordingly for further development and trade-off analysis. Based on these predictions, we recognized that the increase of embodied emissions for a higher isolation standard is comparatively small compared to the impact of emissions resulting from operational energy.

3. Discussion

In this paper, we explored the integration path of data-driven methods and knowledge-based methods for building design machine assistance. The key pillar of the integration depends on the connection between the available data description (features) and the knowledge-based methods' representation.

From the result of the case study, we generated alternative design scenarios in different isolation standards & window-to-wall ratio (WWR) combinations with shading options and evaluated energy performance and embodied impact. This combined information and required data are accessible in the early design phase. Both approaches contain the potential to further enhance the ability of general assistance scenarios in future research: For data-driven methods, involving, e.g., a component-based modelling process (Geyer et al. 2018) or hybrid-model approach (Chen, Guo & Geyer, 2021) would provide further insight into the energy performance at the building component level with better modelling flexibility and interpretability. For knowledge-based methods, based on the trade-off analysis, indicators to represent building cost factors would enhance the machine assistance practicability.

To explore the path of data-driven method integration into domain knowledge-based approach in general scenarios, it is vital to invest efforts in aligning representations to bridge exposed features from digital models and knowledge. For example, to provide designers with useable feedback regarding the overall life cycle impact of the design decisions taken, the operational energy results would have to be converted to GWP based on realistic primary energy scenarios. In this context, the integration between data-driven methods and knowledge-based methods is not only necessary in the feature representation process, but also vital for output interpretations.

Finally, although we particularly checked the availability of data during the early design phase to ensure practicality, the evaluation of information utility has not been addressed, especially when generated suggestions are inter-disciplinary. From this perspective, the investigation of the designers' feedback based on the integrated decision support is, in our opinion, worth further research. A related study on user effect has been carried out for the component-based prediction of operational energy planned to be repeated, including the new methods (Singh, Deb & Geyer, 2022).

4. Conclusion

This study presents a step toward a machine assistance framework for the building design process that achieves multi-objective decision support. This framework serves as augmented intelligence to accelerate the digitalization process of user decision-making assistance in domains that require not only data-driven support but also knowledge-based analysis, such as early building design. The structure organized by components and modules allows for the generalization of data-driven models aligned to domain knowledge. Moreover, this approach forms a basis for data and knowledge integration from which the design process will immensely benefit. The integration allows for involving operational energy and embodied environmental impact at an early design phase and raises the reconsideration of the design process toward the objective of sustainable development in our domain.

Acknowledgement

We gratefully acknowledge the support of the German Research Foundation (DFG) for funding the project under grant GE 1652/3-2 in the Researcher Unit FOR 2363. We would like to thank Lang Hugger Rampp GmbH / Bayerischer Bauindustrieverband e.V. for data resources support.

References

Amasyali, Kadir, & El-Gohary, Nora M. (2018). A review of data-driven building energy consumption prediction studies, *Renewable and Sustainable Energy Reviews,* vol. 81, pp. 1192–1205

Bélisle, Eve, Huang, Zi, Le Digabel, Sébastien, & Aimen E. Gheribi. (2015). Evaluation of machine learning interpolation techniques for prediction of physical properties, *Computational Materials Science,* vol. 98, pp. 170–177

Bundesministerium des Innern, für Bau und Heimat. (2022). ÖKOBAUDAT, Available online: https://www.oekobaudat.de/en.html [Accessed 2 February 2022]

CAALA. (2019). Die CAALA Software ist ein umfassendes Werkzeug zur energetischen Vordimensionierung und Ökobilanzierung - CAALA, Available online: https://caala.de/features [Accessed 15 November 2021]

Chen, Xia, & Geyer, Philipp. (2022). Machine assistance in energy-efficient building design: A predictive framework toward dynamic interaction with human decision-making under uncertainty, *Applied Energy,* vol. 307, p. 118240

Chen, Xia, Guo, Tong, & Geyer, Philipp. (2021). A hybrid-model time-series forecasting approach for reducing the building energy performance gap, EG-ICE 2021 Workshop on Intelligent Computing in Engineering

Duan, Tony, Avati, Anand, Ding, Daisy Y., Thai, Khanh K., Basu, Sanjay, Ng, Andrew Y., & Schuler, Alejandro. (2020). NGBoost: Natural Gradient Boosting for Probabilistic Prediction, Available online: http://arxiv.org/pdf/1910.03225v4

Geyer, Philipp, Singh, Manav M., & Chen, Xia. (2021). Explainable AI for engineering design: A unified approach of systems engineering and component-based deep learning, *ArXiv Preprint ArXiv:2108.13836*

Harter, Hannes, Singh, Manav M., Schneider-Marin, Patricia, Lang, Werner, & Geyer, Philipp. (2020). Uncertainty analysis of life cycle energy assessment in early stages of design, *Energy and Buildings,* vol. 208, p. 109635

Hensen, Jan L., & Lamberts, Roberto. (2019). Building Performance Simulation for Design and Operation, Available online: https://research.tue.nl/en/publications/building-performance-simulation-for-design-and-operation-expanded

Hollberg, Alexander, Tschetwertak, Julia, Schneider, Sven, & Habert, Guillaume. (2018). Design-integrated LCA using early BIM, in *Designing Sustainable Technologies, Products and Policies*, Springer, Cham, pp. 269–279

Jia, Yongna, & Ma, Jianwei. (2017). What can machine learning do for seismic data processing? An interpolation application, *Geophysics,* vol. 82, no. 3, V163-V177

Ladybug Tools | Honeybee, Available online: https://www.ladybug.tools/honeybee.html [Accessed 3 February 2022]

Loh, Wei-Yin. (2011). Classification and regression trees, *Wiley Interdisciplinary Reviews: Data Mining and Knowledge Discovery,* vol. 1, no. 1, pp. 14–23

Lundberg, Scott M., & Lee, Su-In. (2017). A Unified Approach to Interpreting Model Predictions, Advances in Neural Information Processing Systems, Available online: https://proceedings.neurips.cc/paper/2017/file/8a20a8621978632d76c43dfd28b67767-Paper.pdf

One Click LCA® software. (2022). Automate Building Life Cycle Assessment with One Click LCA, Available online: https://www.oneclicklca.com/construction/life-cycle-assessment-software/ [Accessed 2 February 2022]

Østergård, Torben, Jensen, Rasmus L., & Maagaard, Steffen E. (2016). Building simulations supporting decision making in early design – A review, *Renewable and Sustainable Energy Reviews,* vol. 61, pp. 187–201

Østergård, Torben, Jensen, Rasmus L., & Maagaard, Steffen E. (2017). Early Building Design: Informed decision-making by exploring multidimensional design space using sensitivity analysis, *0378-7788,* vol. 142, pp. 8–22, Available online: https://www.sciencedirect.com/science/article/pii/S0378778817306916 [Accessed 23 February 2022]

Robert McNeel, & Associates. (2022). Grasshopper - New in Rhino 6, Available online: https://www.rhino3d.com/en/6/new/grasshopper/ [Accessed 3 February 2022]

Schneider-Marin, Tanja Stocker, Oliver Abele, Johannes Staudt, Manuel Margesin, & Werner Lang. Re-structuring of eco-data to include functional criteria: using data enhanced with knowledge in early phases of design, (unpubl.)

Schneider-Marin, Patricia, Harter, Hannes, Tkachuk, Konstantin, & Lang, Werner. (2020). Uncertainty analysis of embedded energy and greenhouse gas emissions using BIM in early design stages, *Sustainability,* vol. 12, no. 7, p. 2633

Schneider-Marin, Patricia, & Lang, Werner. (2020). Environmental costs of buildings: monetary valuation of ecological indicators for the building industry, *The International Journal of Life Cycle Assessment,* vol. 25, no. 9, pp. 1637–1659

Schuler, Alejandro. (2020). NGBoost User Guide, Data 100 at UC Berkeley, 26 October, Available online: https://stanfordmlgroup.github.io/ngboost/1-useage.html [Accessed 28 February 2022]

Seyedzadeh, Saleh, Rahimian, Farzad P., Glesk, Ivan, & Roper, Marc. (2018). Machine learning for estimation of building energy consumption and performance: a review, *Visualization in Engineering,* vol. 6, no. 1, pp. 1–20

Siemon, Klaus D., Speckhals, Raphael, & Siemon, Anna. (2021). Kostengruppen nach DIN 276/2018, in Klaus D. Siemon, Raphael Speckhals & Anna Siemon (eds), *Baukostenplanung und -steuerung,* Wiesbaden: Springer Fachmedien Wiesbaden, pp. 219–240

Singh, Manav M., Deb, Chirag, & Geyer, Philipp. (2022). Early-stage design support combining machine learning and building information modelling, *Automation in Construction,* vol. 136, p. 104147

Theißen, S., Höper, J., Wimmer, R., Zibell, M., Meins-Becker, A., Rössig, S., Goitowski, S., & Lambertz, M. (2020). BIM integrated automation of whole building life cycle assessment using German LCA data base ÖKOBAUDAT and Industry Foundation Classes, IOP Conference Series: Earth and Environmental Science

Thessen, Anne. (2016). Adoption of machine learning techniques in ecology and earth science, *One Ecosystem,* vol. 1, e8621

Vogt, Marcus, Remmen, Peter, Lauster, Moritz, Fuchs, Marcus, & Müller, Dirk. (2018). Selecting statistical indices for calibrating building energy models, *Building and Environment,* vol. 144, pp. 94–107

Westermann, Paul, & Evins, Ralph. (2019). Surrogate modelling for sustainable building design – A review, *Energy and Buildings,* vol. 198, pp. 170–186

Analyzing Operation Logs of Nuclear Power Plants for Safety and Efficiency Diagnosis of Real-Time Operations

Xing J. [1], Liu P. [1], Tang P. [1], Yilmaz A. [2], Boring R. [3], Gibson Jr G. [4]

[1] Carnegie Mellon University, the United States; [2] The Ohio State University, the United States; [3] Idaho National Laboratory, the United States; [4] Arizona State University, the United States

ptang@andrew.cmu.edu

Abstract. Operators' lack of understanding of the plant's operation state significantly contributes to human errors in Nuclear Power Plant (NPP) control room operations. The state of an NPP at a particular time is represented by values of analog (e.g., measurements of flow properties) and switch parameters (e.g., the status of a valve). Previous studies focused on analyzing analog parameters rarely considered the switch parameters. Estimating the plant state without considering the timings of switches can be inaccurate. This paper utilizes analog parameters to infer the timing of switches. Two main challenges of establishing a reliable prediction model are 1) high dimensional analog parameters and 2) an imbalanced switch parameter dataset with few control actions. This paper uses PCA to reduce the dimensions and SMOTE to generate more samples capturing the impacts of various control actions. Then the pre-processed data was used to train variants of KNN classifiers. Testing results show that the KNN with SMOTE oversampling but without PCA best predicts switches' timing.

1. Introduction

Human error is a significant contributor to the efficiency and safety issues in Nuclear Power Plant (NPP) operations (Preischl & Hellmic, 2016). Industry reports show that more than 60% of the reported events are related to human errors, among which nearly 30% of events are attributed to operation errors (IAEA, 2020). Human errors in NPP control room operations include pushing the wrong button, operating too late, controlling deviation reduced too slowly, etc. (Preischl et al., 2013). These human errors can make operators miss control goals and targets, thus leading to uncontrolled release of energy or hazardous substances. Hence, it is essential to reduce human error in NPP control room operations.

Operators' lack of understanding of the plant's real-time state and their inaccurate predictions about future plant states are the primary causes of human errors in control room operations (NRC Web, 2011). As shown in Figure 1, the operating state of NPP at a particular time is represented by two types of parameters – 1) switch parameter, which reflects the NPP component state (e.g., Valve A, valve B), and 2) analog parameter, which shows the value of process variables captured by sensor measurements (Wang et al., 2022). The analog and switch parameters within a plant have complex physical and functional interactions. Nevertheless, NPP consists of thousands of components and instruments. The large size of the plant and the many relationships within NPP systems control make it challenging for operators to maintain a holistic understanding of the plant's state and correctly predict the future states.

Many studies utilized NPP operation data to provide faster and more accurate plant behavior predictions, thus reducing human errors in control room operations. These studies used machine learning algorithms such as artificial neural networks to predict NPP behavior under different transients, monitor NPP parameter trends, and detect anomalies (Chen et al., 2018; El-Sefy et

https://doi.org/10.7146/aul.455.c203

al., 2021). However, many studies only considered analog parameters. Discrete switch parameters containing information about plant components' states are rarely considered.

Recently, Wang et al. (2022) proposed a method to fill missing operation data of an NPP by searching the similar system operation states in control histories. In this study, the operation state of NPP is represented by a combination of analog and switch parameters. Nevertheless, few studies explored the relationship between analog and switch parameters. Joint consideration of analog and switch parameters for monitoring NPP operation is critical. Different combinations of switch parameter values can share the same analog parameter values. Relying on analog parameters alone can hardly distinguish if an anomaly is caused by the failure of process variable sensors or process fault. Thus, analog parameter-based diagnostic systems require extra human efforts to investigate the root causes of anomalies. Therefore, relying solely on analog parameters can provide human operators limited or even unreliable operation support.

This paper presents a model that maps the relationship between analog and switch parameters. The proposed model can mimic the human decision-making process in NPP control room operations. The model takes time series of analog parameter values as inputs, and operation decisions, such as whether to manipulate a component or not, at what times, as outputs (Figure 1). The key contributions are: 1) revealing the necessity of understanding the interwoven relationship between analog and switch parameters. Such understanding can lay a foundation for developing intelligent operation support tools that imitate human operators to generate control decisions. 2) proposing a modeling framework based on k Nearest Neighbours that predict the switch parameters using time series of analog parameters as inputs. We tested and validated the proposed framework through pseudo-operators' control histories collected in a human-in-the-loop NPP operation experiment.

2. Problem Formulation

The problem tackled in this paper is to map a set of analog parameter values to control actions based on control histories. The data structure of control histories and the problem formulation are introduced below.

All NPP operators must follow strict technical standards (Medema et al., 2012). These technical standards, also known as NPP operation procedures, provide step-by-step directions on observing real-time NPP sensors alarms and manipulating NPP control objects (e.g., turn-on valves). Stepwise instructions define the operational processes and control actions. However, the task guidance provided by these procedures is static. Operators must rely on their experiences and knowledge to estimate the "waiting" time between different steps to avoid missing the control targets.

Control actions defined in the procedures trigger changes in switch parameters. This paper uses switch parameters to infer the control action and the corresponding wait time before performing that control action. Eq. (1) illustrates if a component's state c_t at time t is different from its state at time $t-1$ indicates the occurrence of a control action $CtrlA_t$. For example, Figure 1 shows three plant components' states. Valve A and valve B have discrete states, and Rod has a continuous state. According to Eq. (1), when $t=1$, the operator did not perform any control action; therefore, the algorithm will label the work status as $\{\text{wait}\}$, the operator turned on valve A at time 2s and then manipulated Rod 1 at time 3s.

$$CtrlA_t = \begin{cases} 0, & c_t = c_{(t-1)} \\ 1 & c_t \neq c_{(t-1)} \end{cases} \quad (1)$$

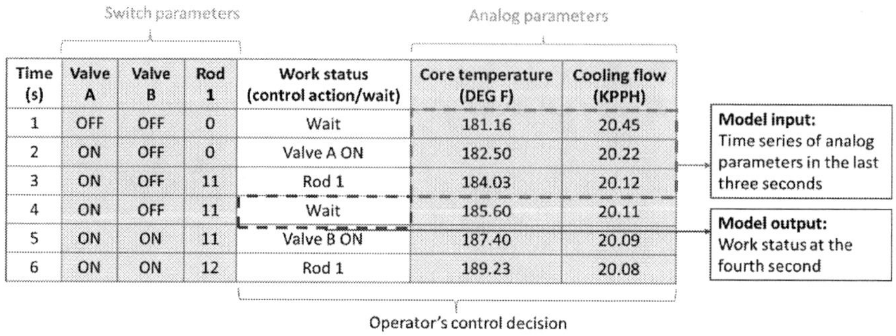

Figure 1: The operating state of NPP at a specific time is represented by a set of analog parameters and switch parameters (Wang et al., 2022). The changes in switch parameters reflect the operator's control decision.

A combination of plant analog and switch parameters can describe the operational state of the NPP. Similarly, the analog parameters and control action represent the operator's control decision at a particular time. Each control action corresponds to a specific range of analog parameter values (also called "operation context"). In other words, when one or multiple analog parameter values reach a certain degree, the operator in charge should manipulate the corresponding control object to ensure plant safety. NPP control room operators need to observe tens of analog parameters, indicators, and alarms to monitor plant operation. In the monitoring process, operators need to closely follow the trending of analog parameters to avoid missing the optimal contextual timing for performing each control action. Thus, the operators spent most of the time monitoring the analog parameters and little time performing control actions in an operation task. Therefore, two main challenges associated with NPP operations are: 1) the high dimension analog parameters make it challenging for operators to gain a comprehensive understanding of analog parameters' trends; 2) the control histories are imbalanced datasets because of the less frequent work status of control actions compared to {wait} class. As a result, operators are likely to miss the optimal operation context.

3. The Proposed Methodology

This paper aims to develop models to predict the most likely control actions based on control histories while overcoming the two challenges mentioned above: 1) high dimensional data and 2) imbalanced data samples for control actions and waiting times. The proposed framework consists of three steps (Figure 2): data pre-processing, model training, and model testing. The data pre-processing step employed dimension reduction and oversampling techniques to resolve the challenges brought by high dimensional analog parameters and imbalanced control histories. The model training step carefully selected the hyperparameters of the k Nearest Neighbour (KNN) classifiers. The testing step assessed the performance of the variant of KNN classifiers for predicting the control actions based on similar contextual analog parameters' values.

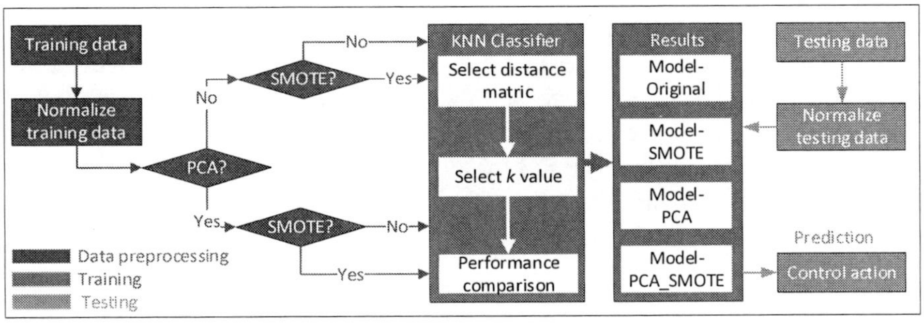

Figure 2: The framework of the proposed method for predicting switch parameters.

3.1 Principal Component Analysis (PCA)

Principal component analysis (PCA) has been proven very powerful in extracting critical information within process data, and it is widely applied for data-driven process monitoring (Shi et al., 2018). In PCA, let $X \in R^{m \times N}$ denote a set of normalized data with m process variables and N samples. The principal component of the data is determined by performing singular value decomposition on the covariance matrix Σ of X derives:

$$\Sigma = \frac{1}{N-1} X X^T = P \Lambda P^T \quad (2)$$

Where $\Lambda = \mathrm{diag}(\lambda_1, \cdots, \lambda_m)$ and $\lambda_1 \geq \lambda_2 \geq \cdots \geq \lambda_m \geq 0$. In PCA, the load matrix $P \in \mathbb{R}^{m \times m}$ is divided as $P = [P_{pc}, P_{res}]$ and Λ is divided as $\Lambda = \begin{bmatrix} \Lambda_{pc} & 0 \\ 0 & \Lambda_{res} \end{bmatrix}$.

3.2 Synthetic Minority Oversampling Technique (SMOTE)

Oversampling techniques in the pre-processing step are necessary for enabling the proposed model to learn patterns from the minority class, namely control actions. This paper use SMOTE to oversample the minority class (control actions). Figure 1 shows, at time 1s, the label of the work status is {wait}. "Wait" means that the operator didn't perform any control action. NPP control histories are imbalanced since the frequency of control actions is considerably fewer than the number of {wait} status. This paper proposes SMOTE to augment the operating history. SMOTE creates synthetic samples for over-sampling the minority classes. SMOTE firstly selects several neighbors specified by the over-sampling rate. Synthetic operation states (set of analog parameters and switch parameters) are created somewhere between the original operating context and its neighbors. SMOTE is easy to implement and avoids overfitting because the synthetic samples are randomly created and prevent information loss (de Andrade Lopes et al., 2021).

3.3 K-nearest-neighbours (KNN)

KNN classifier is one of the most widely applied classifiers in process control research. KNN is performed by 'searching' for the nearest distance and selecting the class with the majority number among the k training data as the resulting class. In KNN, the k indicates the number of nearest neighbors to be considered in decision-making. The distance between the data is calculated by applying the distance metric. This paper adopts KNN to identify a similar operation context for performing each control action.

The classification performance of KNN is affected by the choice of distance metric and the value of k. Appropriate selection of the distance metric and value of k is important for ensuring good model performance. The pre-processed data were trained using several distance metrics and k values to select the suitable distance metric and k value. In this paper, the minimum k is set as 0, and the maximum k is determined by the minimum count of the control action classes. The paper adopted different distance metrics for the KNN classifiers and used five-fold cross-validation to evaluate and compare the performance of these classifiers.

Table 1: Distance metrics applied in KNN.

Distance metrics	Definition	Distance function
Euclidean distance	The Euclidean distance is the length of a line segment between two points.	$\sqrt[2]{\sum (X-Y)^2}$
Manhattan distance	The Manhattan distance between two vectors (city blocks) equals the one-norm of the distance between the vectors (Szabo, 2015).	$\sum \lvert X-Y \rvert$
Chebyshev distance	The Chebyshev distance between two vectors is the greatest of their differences along any coordinate dimension (Abello et al., 2013).	$\text{Max}\lvert X-Y \rvert$

4. Case Study

The authors used a gamified microworld to collect NPP control histories for testing the proposed framework of mapping time series of analog parameters to control actions. The gamified microworld reactor-Rancor was developed by Idaho National Laboratory (Ulrich et al., 2017). The Rancor simulator models five typical NPP systems: the cooling system, the reactor core, the steam generator, the feedwater system, and the turbine. As shown in Figure 3 (a), Rancor's user interface allows the experiment participants to experience NPP operation via interacting with these simulated systems of an NPP. The following introduces the experiment setup and model performance evaluations.

4.1 Experiment Setup

This paper selected the reactor start-up procedure as the operation task. The reactor start-up procedure is a typical NPP operation process involving various actions requiring NPP operators' attention to ensure power supplies (Boring et al., 2018). Figure 3 (b) shows the operation steps included in the start-up procedure.

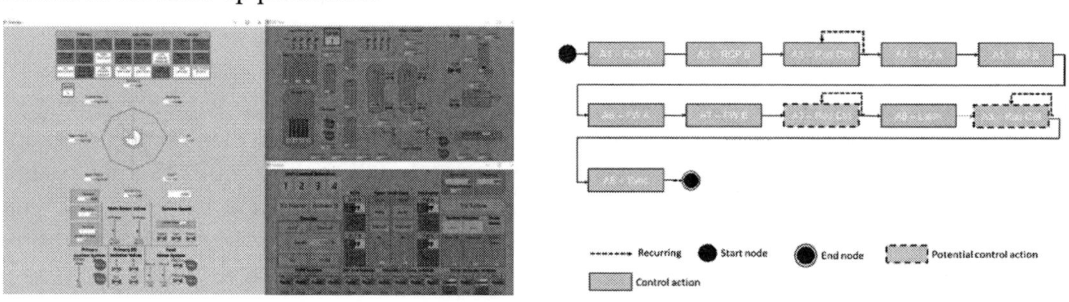

Figure 3: (a) Rancor Reactor simulator user interface; (b) Operation step in the start-up procedure.

The reactor start-up tasks involve 15 analog parameters and 10 switch parameters. The Rancor simulator updates the plant operation state each second. This paper assumes that each control action occurs at different times and that there are no concurrent control actions. The authors recruited ten student operators to perform the reactor start-up task on the Rancor simulator. Experiment participants were asked to follow the start-up procedure to start the reactor two times, and twenty control histories were collected. The experiment collected twenty control logs. As shown in Table 2, this paper used 12 logs for training and 8 logs for testing. The model input is time series of analog parameter values in the last three seconds. The model output is the work status at the fourth second. In each control log, {wait} class occupies most of the count. The training and testing set's control action ratios are 0.197 and 0.172, respectively.

Table 2: Statistics of the training set and testing set.

	NO. of logs	Analog parameter and switch parameter pairs	Control action ratios
Training set	12	1143	0.197
Testing set	8	964	0.172

4.2 Performance Metrics

The goal of the model is to predict control action using time series of analog parameters as input. Whether the proposed model has good prediction accuracy on the {wait} class is not the focus of this paper. This paper only considered the model's prediction accuracy on control actions. To ensure the proposed model is robust against the minority class ({wait} class) and focus on the prediction performance of the control action, this paper uses the minority classes to evaluate the model performance (Table 3).

Table 3: Confusion matrix used for calculation of performance metrics.

Predicted	Actual	
	Target control action (P)	**Other control actions (N)**
Target control action (PP)	True Positive (TP)	False Positive (FP)
Other control actions and wait (PN)	False Negative (FN)	True Negative (TN)

Precision, recall, F1 score, and the area under the precision-recall curve (AUC-PR) are popular performance evaluation metrics, particularly for imbalanced datasets. This paper calculated the F1 score, AUC-PR, using the confusion matrix presented in Table 3. The accuracy rate represents the percentage of correctly classified control actions and is calculated through the following equation:

$$Accuracy = \frac{number\ of\ correctly\ predicted\ control\ actions}{P + N} \quad (3)$$

5. Results and Discussions

5.1 KNN Parameter Selection

KNN algorithm has two essential parameters: the distance function and the number of K. The optimal parameters of the KNN models are decided by the best results on the training set via five-fold cross-validation. This paper use KNN to predict the correct control action by calculating the distance between the input analog parameter values and all the analog parameter values sets in the training data. Figure 4 shows the effect of the distance function and value of k. The optimal parameters k value and distance function for each model suggested in Figure 4 are shown in Table 4.

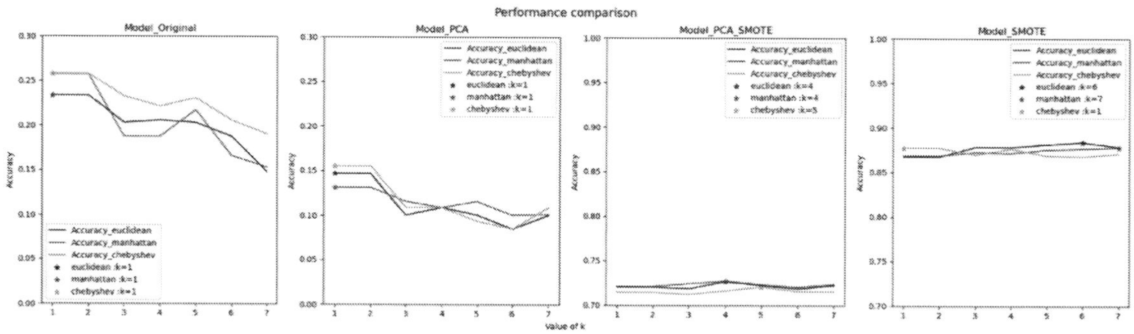

Figure 4: KNN parameter selection. Models with SMOTE oversampling have better prediction performance compared to models without oversampling.

Table 4: Parameter selection results on the four models.

Model	Distance function	K-value	Highest Accuracy
Model-Original	Chebyshev distance	1	0.258
Model-PCA	Chebyshev distance	1	0.155
Model-PCA_SMOTE	Manhattan distance	4	0.727
Model-SMOTE	Euclidean distance	6	0.883

5.2 Model Performance Evaluation

This section aims to compare the performance of models with different pre-processing methods. Such comparison can help identify which model can provide a more reliable mapping from the operation context to control actions. Table 5 shows the classification results of different models. The best classification results are indicated in bold. Model-SMOTE significantly outperforms the rest of the models. There are two possible reasons. Firstly, a distance-based classifier such as KNN for imbalanced datasets is always biased towards the majority classes because of its large number of samples (Prusty et al., 2017). SMOTE technique arbitrarily interpolates new minority samples in between several samples of a minority group can help counteract the imbalanced dataset problem. Secondly, PCA projects the high dimensional analog parameters to a new subspace to get a low-dimension representation of the original dataset by retaining some variance, causing information loss. Even though many studies showed PCA does not involve significant information loss, in the experiment, Model-PCA and Model-PCA_SMOTE have lower f1 scores compared to the model without PCA.

Table 5: Compare classification results of different pre-processing approaches.

	Accuracy	Precision	Recall	F1 score
Model-Original	0.247	0.29	0.369	0.263
Model-PCA	0	0.075	0.091	0.082
Model-PCA_SMOTE	0.084	0.082	0.087	0.084
Model-SMOTE	**0.223**	**0.316**	**0.441**	**0.323**

The count of control action is significantly less than the {wait} class. This paper use precision-recall curves (PR curve) to further compare the performance of Model-Original and Model-Smote. Figure 5 displays the PR curves of the two model variants. The Area Under Curve (AUC) for different control actions varies significantly. Notably, some PR curves have extremely low AUC (below 0.1), indicating that the classifiers perform even worse than random classifiers. One reason for the low AUC is the small testing sample size. Although the total number of testing samples is high, the control action ratio in the testing sample is low (0.172). The other reason is due to the nature of NPP operations. An accurate prediction in the proposed model indicates that the occurrence timing of the predicted control action is the same as the testing data. However, different operators rarely perform the same control action exactly at the same value set of analog parameters in practice. Instead, it's more reasonable to perform each control action in a set of analog parameters with similar values.

The confusion matrix shows the potential of this classifier. In Figure 6, all the diagonal elements denote correctly classified control actions. The off diagonals of the confusion matrix display the misclassified outcomes. Hence, the higher the values in the diagonal, the better the classifier. Model-SMOTE shows decent performance in predicting the majority of the control actions. Rod control action can repeat multiple times under different operation contexts. Thus, the KNN algorithm can hardly find a similar pattern for the operational contexts of rod control action. Therefore, the Rod control action has the lowest prediction accuracy.

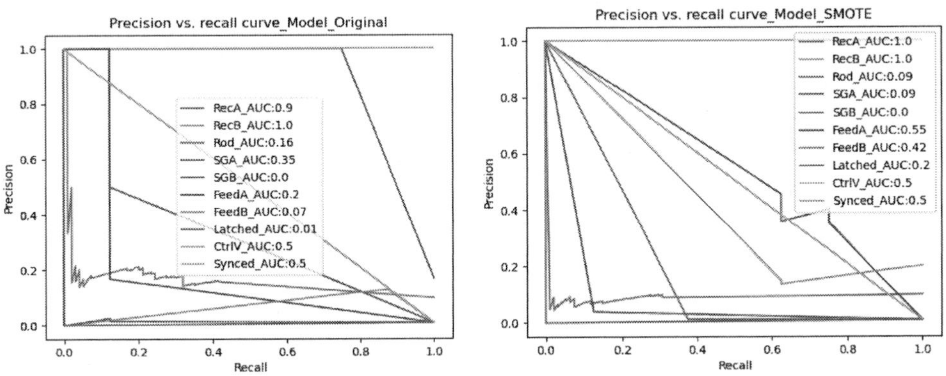

Figure 5: Precision-Recall curves.

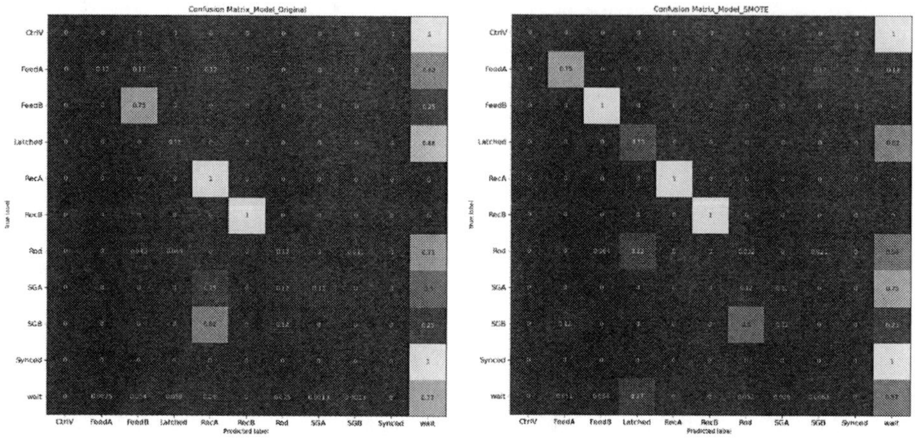

Figure 6: Confusion matrix of Model-Original and Model-SMOTE.

6. Conclusion

This paper proposed a variant of models based on KNN classifiers that uses analog parameters to infer the timing of the most suitable control actions. The proposed model employed PCA to compress the analog parameters to lower dimensions and SMOTE to help augment the less frequent control actions in the collected control histories. Additionally, hyperparameters of the KNN classifiers are carefully selected using 5-fold cross-validation. The authors also designed a human-in-the-loop experiment of reactor start-up to collect NPP control histories for validating the proposed control action prediction framework. The testing results indicate that the model with SMOTE data augmentation has better prediction performance than the models without SMOTE. Models with PCA have lower prediction accuracy compared to models without PCA.

Two limitations of this paper are the small data size and model performance evaluation metrics. The KNN classifier is an instance-based learning method that can make a prediction for new observations based on a few data samples. This paper used 20 logs, and the number of control actions in these logs is relatively small. In addition, an accurate prediction in the proposed model indicates that the occurrence timing of the predicted control action is the same as the testing data. In practice, the occurrence timing of control action is more likely to concentrate in operational contexts with similar analog parameter values rather than the same analog parameter values. The authors will improve the model performance evaluation method by defining a suitable time window for each control action in future work. Specifically, the authors will estimate the distribution of individual control actions in the operation process by considering analog parameter values and time.

Acknowledgment

This material is based on work supported by the Nuclear Engineering University Program (NEUP) of the U.S. Department of Energy (DOE) under Award No. DE-NE0008864. The support is gratefully acknowledged.

Reference

Abello, J., Pardalos, P. M., & Resende, M. G. (Eds.). (2013). Handbook of massive data sets (Vol. 4). Springer.

Boring, R. L., Ulrich, T. A., and Lew, R. (2018). "Findings From an Operator-In-The-Loop Study on System Overview Displays in a Modernized Nuclear Power Plant." Proceedings of the Human Factors and Ergonomics Society Annual Meeting, SAGE Publications Sage CA: Los Angeles, CA, 1658–1662.

Chen, X. L., Wang, P. H., Hao, Y. S., & Zhao, M. (2018). Evidential KNN-based condition monitoring and early warning method with applications in power plant. Neurocomputing, 315, 18-32.

de Carvalho, P. V. R., dos Santos, I. L., Gomes, J. O., da Silva Borges, M. R., & Huber, G. J. (2006, November). The role of nuclear power plant operators' communications in providing resilience and stability in system operation. In 2nd Symp. on Resilience Engineering, Juan-les Pins, France.

El-Sefy, M., Yosri, A., El-Dakhakhni, W., Nagasaki, S., & Wiebe, L. (2021). Artificial neural network for predicting nuclear power plant dynamic behaviors. Nuclear Engineering and Technology, 53(10), 3275-3285.

IAEA, (2020). Nuclear Power Plant Operating Experience, IAEA, Vienna.

Medema, H. D., & Farris, R. K. (2012). Guidance for Deployment of Mobile Technologies for Nuclear Power Plant Field Workers (No. INL/EXT-12-27094). Idaho National Laboratory (INL).

NRC Web. (2011). Standard Technical Specifications – General Electric Plants (BWR/6): Bases (NUREG-1434, Revision 4,. [online] Available at: https://www.nrc.gov/reading-rm/doc-collections/nuregs/staff/sr1434/r4/v2/index.html, accessed on 1 Oct. 2021.

Preischl, W., & Hellmich, M. (2013). Human error probabilities from operational experience of German nuclear power plants. Reliability Engineering & System Safety, 109, 150-159.

Preischl, W. and Hellmich, M., 2016. Human error probabilities from operational experience of German nuclear power plants, Part II. Reliability Engineering & System Safety, 148, pp.44-56.

Prusty, M. R., Jayanthi, T., & Velusamy, K. (2017). Weighted-SMOTE: A modification to SMOTE for event classification in sodium cooled fast reactors. Progress in nuclear energy, 100, 355-364.

Szabo, F. (2015). The linear algebra survival guide: illustrated with Mathematica. Academic Press.

Shi, X., Nie, F., Lai, Z., & Guo, Z. (2018). Robust principal component analysis via optimal mean by joint ℓ2, 1 and Schatten p-norms minimization. Neurocomputing, 283, 205-213.

Ulrich, T. A., Lew, R., Werner, S., and Boring, R. L. (2017). "Rancor: a gamified microworld nuclear power plant simulation for engineering psychology research and process control applications." Proceedings of the Human Factors and Ergonomics Society Annual Meeting, SAGE Publications Sage CA: Los Angeles, CA, 398–402.

Wang, T., Yu, R., & Peng, Q. (2022). Study on Missing Data Filling Algorithm of Nuclear Power Plant Operation Parameters. Science and Technology of Nuclear Installations, 2022, 1–14. https://doi.org/10.1155/2022/4172622

Reinforcement Learning for Active Monitoring of Moving Equipment in 360-Degree Videos

Nath N.D., Cheng C., Behzadan A.H.
Texas A&M University, USA
abehzadan@tamu.edu

Abstract. Computer vision techniques have been introduced recently to assist with visual surveillance of jobsite activities. However, multiple reality capture devices are needed to guarantee uninterrupted view of key objects. We propose to use deep learning with reinforcement learning (RL) to create a self-navigating active vision camera. The trained RL camera gains sufficient spatiotemporal knowledge to fix its gaze on an object by dynamically adjusting its position and view angle. We use a deep Q-learning network (DQN) to decide whether to move or rotate the camera to monitor moving forklifts in a 360-degree video. Results show that the RL camera can find a new position and angle with better view of the forklift in 73% of cases, and in the remaining 27% of cases, the visibility of the forklift remains unchanged. This indicates the effectiveness of the RL agent in locating the object of interest in complex and dynamic real-world settings.

1. Introduction

In recent years, the number of photos and videos collected daily by various digital capture devices has exponentially increased. In 2020 alone, 1.43 trillion digital images were captured with more than 91% taken on mobile phones (Canning, 2020). This growth in the volume of visual data can be in part attributed to the ubiquity of mobile devices (e.g., smartphones, tablets), digital cameras, and unmanned aerial vehicles (UAVs) also known as drones with onboard cameras. Visual data is also widely utilized to record construction fieldwork and commonly used to document progress reports, complement requests for information (RFIs), prepare safety training materials, and litigate claims. Moreover, continuous and unobtrusive monitoring of jobsite activities is key to work progress measurement and monitoring safety compliance on construction sites. Advancements in computer vision (CV) and artificial intelligence (AI) have created new solutions to automate visual surveillance tasks. For example, Nath and Behzadan (2020a) applied deep learning (DL) to detect common construction objects (e.g., building, equipment, worker) in real-time under diverse visual conditions. Nath et al. (2020b) and Fang et al. (2018) proposed DL techniques to monitor workers' compliance with regulations pertaining to the use of personal protective equipment (PPE) (i.e., hard hat, safety vest).

While the uptake of AI integration into construction practices is expected to continue, the next-generation construction and manufacturing systems will enable humans and AI to collaborate in more meaningful ways (NSF, 2020, Autodesk, 2020), as evident by the success of similar efforts in other domains such as medicine (McCoy et al., 2020, Tschandl et al., 2020), data science (Wang et al., 2019), and business management (Sowa et al., 2021). A key prerequisite to the successful completion of complex machine-operated tasks with vision-based AI is the ability of the machine to understand the content and context of its surroundings. In a nutshell, it is critical for an AI-enabled machine to not only know what objects are located in its proximity, but also infer the spatiotemporal relationships between those objects. This crucial ability, however, may be hindered for several reasons. In a constantly evolving workspace such as a construction site, for example, objects are often on the move and frequently occlude one another. In fact, occlusion is a major impediment to the performance of CV algorithms (Hoiem

https://doi.org/10.7146/aul.455.c204

et al., 2011). A previous study, for instance, has found a significant drop in the performance of facial recognition systems when the face is partially occluded (Ekenel and Stiefelhagen, 2009). Similarly, when an AI algorithm is used by a fixed-viewpoint camera to monitor the workspace for safety compliance or progress evaluation, the visual recognition task may yield low accuracy because of workers and equipment not being fully visible due to displacement or occlusion. A rhetorical solution to this problem is to move the camera (i.e., adjust the viewpoint) or install multiple cameras so that objects of interest always appear sufficiently visible. However, due to the constantly evolving nature of construction sites and cluttered workspaces, and the need for continuous calibration and installation, this approach will translate into a daunting task, consuming a significant amount of project resources.

To address the abovementioned challenge, this study proposes to design an active vision camera capable of navigating in the scene and operating autonomously while searching for the optimal viewpoint from which occlusion-free scenes can be captured for a given task. To validate the performance of the designed methods, an AI-enabled drone camera (with 2 degrees of freedom) is trained with reinforcement learning (RL) and tested in an active work environment.

2. Literature review

DL is a subset of machine learning (ML) and is characterized as a neural network with more than three layers (Chollet, 2021). Deep learning models have been successfully trained to perform tasks in various fields including but not limited to visual recognition (Krizhevsky et al., 2017), natural language processing (Deng and Liu, 2018), and self-driving vehicles (Rao and Frtunikj, 2018). RL, on the other hand, expands the traditional boundaries of ML by dynamically training a function to take optimal actions given the environment states based on continuous feedback to maximize its cumulative reward. RL was first tossed in the early 1980s in psychology, to describe a trial-and-error methodology where animals learn and change specific behaviors based on their perceived experiences (Busoniu et al., 2010). Similarly, modern RL algorithms rely on trial-and-error to train computational agents to make decisions. In the late 1990s, the use of RL was expanded to other domains including robotics (Kormushev et al., 2013), game playing (Szita, 2012), and industrial process control (Nian et al., 2020).

In an RL problem, the learner is referred to as agent, and everything in the surrounding, that the agent can interact with, is called the environment (Chollet, 2021; Géron, 2019; Sutton and Barto, 2018; Szepesvári, 2010). At any given time, the part of the environment that is accessible to the agent can be described in a mathematical form that is called the state of the environment. The RL agent can perform an action to transition from the current state to the next state of the environment. When an agent performs an action, it also receives feedback from the environment indicative of the merit of the action in meeting the ultimate learning goal of the problem. This feedback is described in a numerical form and referred to as reward (Chollet, 2021; Géron, 2019; Sutton and Barto, 2018; Szepesvári, 2010).

With advancements in processing speed and computing power, conventional RL algorithms and neural network architectures have been combined to form new Deep RL paradigms (Henderson et al., 2018). For example, the AlphaGo algorithm, trained with RL and deep neural networks, can win a game against a human player almost 100% of the time (Silver et al., 2016; Silver et al., 2017). Other important Deep RL applications include autonomous driving, industry automation, and natural language processing (NLP) (Zhang et al., 2018; Nguyen et al., 2020). In the civil engineering domain, RL and Deep RL have been primarily leveraged in transportation applications including traffic signal control (Lin et al., 2018; Muresan et al., 2019; Tan et al., 2019; Rasheed et al., 2020; Xu et al., 2020) and speed limit control (Wu et al.,

2018). For example, Wu et al. (2018) proposed a Deep RL-based model for dynamic control of posted speed limits in response to prevailing traffic. They defined variable speed limit (VSL) controllers as RL agents and trained them with the deep deterministic policy gradient (DDPG) algorithm. For this particular application, the state variables of the RL environment were the occupancy rate (reported by loop detectors) of each merge, upstream, and on-ramp lane, while the reward function was based on total travel time, crash probability, and vehicular emission. Compared to a baseline scenario where no speed control was used, trained agents were able to dynamically change vehicle speed limits in each traffic lane based on the traffic flow. Results indicated a reduced average travel time (ATT), by nearly 40 seconds, and fewer vehicle emergency braking by approximately 6%.

In another study, Muresan et al. (2019) trained and validated a Deep Q-learning Network (DQN) to control the duration of traffic lights. In a nutshell, DQN refers to the use of Q-learning algorithm for Deep RL model training (Li, 2017). Since such networks can leverage the advantages of deep convolutional neural networks (CNN), they are widely used in CV applications (Li, 2017, Jang et al., 2019). Using a simulated intersection with psycho-physical cars, Muresan et al. (2019) proceeded to represent the state space by a bit-level matrix that described the queue length, signal state, and time of the day. In each second, the RL agent took one of the two actions, namely continuing the current phase or commencing the next phase. Subsequently, the agent was rewarded or penalized based on the traffic discharge and waiting times of the vehicles. The DQN model, trained with 61 days of simulated data, reduced the average delay by 32% compared to an actuated controller, and by 37% compared to the fixed time control of traffic lights. Mullapudi et al. (2020) explored the use of DQN to enable a stormwater system to dynamically adapt its response to a storm by controlling distributed assets including valves, gates, and pumps. In a simulated storm environment, the state was described by water level and flow sensor readings. At any given time, considering the state, an RL agent took the action of opening a valve or turning on a pump. The agent was trained with three different reward functions. In the first function, the agent received a positive reward for maintaining the outflow below a specific threshold and a negative reward otherwise. In the second function, the agent was rewarded for reaching flows that were close to the desired flow threshold. Finally, in the third function, the agent received the highest reward for keeping the basin empty. It was found that the trained RL agent could immediately observe the impact of its control actions and make adjustments in a 4 km^2 simulated stormwater network. Yao et al. (2020) applied DQN to long-term pavement maintenance planning by representing the state of the environment using 42 features that described pavement condition. The action space was composed of three features, namely maintenance types, maintenance materials, and distress treatment, which considering different combinations, formed a total of 38 actions (i.e., types of treatment) including “do nothing”. Furthermore, the reward function was defined as the increase or decrease in cost effectiveness after taking each action. Using two case studies, the researchers demonstrated the ability of the RL agent to reduce maintenance cost and length of the pavement segment that had to be maintained, ultimately leading to better maintenance strategies that maximized the long-term cost effectiveness in a 15-years period. Lastly, dos Santos et al. (2013) proposed an RL-based method to control and transport structural components to designated locations and assemble truss-like 3D structures in a real-world constrained but dynamic environment. The state of the environment in this case was composed of the status of the components as well as the location of the robot. The RL agent was rewarded based on the assembly sequence and the selection of structural elements for each assembly point, with an error in assembly leading to a negative reward (i.e., penalty). The developed approach reduced the tedious task of developing an assembly plan by allowing robots to efficiently assemble and construct multiple 3D structures.

Despite past efforts in designing RL or Deep RL algorithms in civil engineering applications, successful use cases of these methods in the construction domain are yet to be documented. While the majority of previous work has devised simulated environments with controlled parameters, the efficacy of DL or Deep RL agents in real-world settings where environment parameters are subject to change remain largely unknown and needs to be investigated and benchmarked. In particular, jobsite safety and accident prevention is an active area of research with real implications (OSHA, 2019). Therefore, the goal of the research presented in this paper is to make new strides in enabling the application of Deep RL for safety monitoring in real-world settings. Particularly, an RL agent with active vision capability is trained to locate and monitor forklifts in a dynamic workspace with the ultimate goal of alerting workers of imminent contact collisions (e.g., due to the worker and forklift moving too close to each other, or the worker moving into the blind spot of the forklift). In addition to safety applications, uninterrupted monitoring of equipment can be of value to supply chain management, asset management, resource allocation, and productivity assessment.

3. Methodology

The environment. In this study, the environment is generated from a warehouse operation 360°-video (obtained from YouTube under Creative Commons license), which is hereinafter referred to as Pictor-360 video. As shown in Figure 1, each frame of this video encompasses a 360° panoramic view of the warehouse. The resolution of each frame is 5120×1080 from which a 420×420 window is cropped to mimic the camera view of an autonomous drone. At each time step, the drone can rotate 11.25° to left or right (i.e., rotation along the yaw axis) and 5° upward or downward (i.e., rotation along the pitch axis). These actions result in translating the 420×420 window by 160 pixels along the horizontal direction or by 60 pixels along the vertical direction, as shown in Figure 1. In total, there are 32 horizontal positions and 12 vertical positions for each of the 699 frames of the video, resulting in 32×12×699=268,416 discrete states of the RL environment.

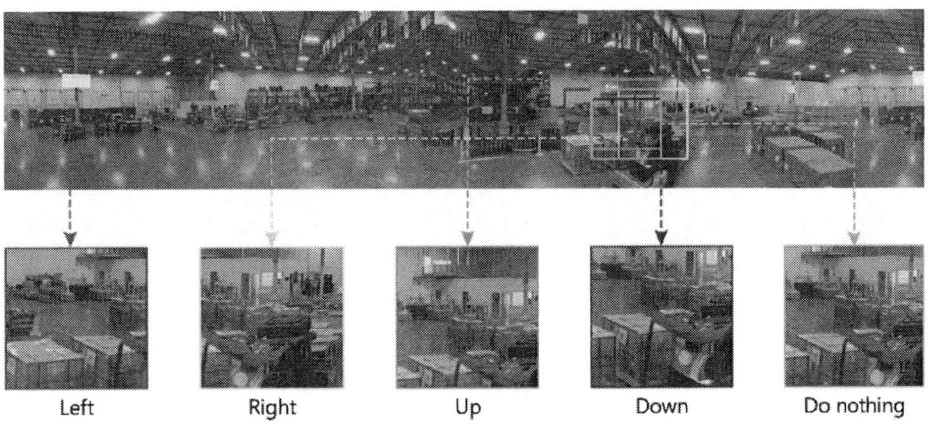

Figure 1: A sample frame of the Pictor-360 video and extracted camera views by taking different actions (source video courtesy of Direct Relief under CC BY license).

Q-learning. In each state, the RL agent can take one of the five actions of moving "up", "down", "left", "right", or "do nothing". The RL agent would take the action that will ultimately lead to the maximum reward. The value of the action in each state is called *action value* or *Q-value* (Géron, 2019, Szepesvári, 2010, Sutton and Barto, 2018), and mathematically denoted as

$\boldsymbol{Q(S_t, a)}$, where $\boldsymbol{S_t}$ is the state at time $\boldsymbol{t}$ and $\boldsymbol{a}$ is the action. Therefore, the agent learns to take the action with the maximum Q-value, i.e., $\mathbf{argmax}_a \boldsymbol{Q(S_t, a)}$. The term *Q-learning* refers to the algorithm for learning Q-values through iteration (Sutton and Barto, 2018). Equation (1) expresses the mathematical formulation for Q-learning, where $\boldsymbol{\alpha}$ is the learning rate, $\boldsymbol{r_t}$ is the reward received at time $\boldsymbol{t}$, and $\boldsymbol{\gamma}$ is the discount factor. Through this Equation, the model updates the Q-value for an action $\boldsymbol{a}$ at state $\boldsymbol{S_t}$, from $\boldsymbol{Q^{old}(S_t, a)}$ to $\boldsymbol{Q^{new}(S_t, a)}$. The value of reward $\boldsymbol{r_t}$ is defined based on the intersection over frame (IoF), which is defined as the percentage of the bounding box area of the forklift that intersects with the viewing frame of the RL camera.

$$Q^{new}(S_t, a) = Q^{old}(S_t, a) + \alpha[r_t + \gamma \max_{a'} Q(S_{t+1}, a') - Q^{old}(S_t, a)] \quad (1)$$

3.1 Model Architecture

In this experiment, we propose to use a DQN model to predict the Q-values corresponding to the five actions named above (i.e., "up", "down", "left", "right", "do nothing"). For this purpose, the 420×420 RGB image viewed by the RL camera, is resized to a 224×224 resolution using bicubic interpolation (Shan et al., 2008). As shown in Figure 2, a VGG-16-based model is utilized to extract features. The choice of VGG-16 is due to its high performance in classifying numerous real-world objects (Simonyan and Zisserman, 2014). The VGG-16 network is amended with three convolution blocks, each consisting of a convolution with exponential linear unit (ELU) activation function, followed by a max-pooling layer. Features are then flattened and connected with a dense layer with 64 nodes. The final output layer consists of 5 nodes to output individual Q-values corresponding to the five actions.

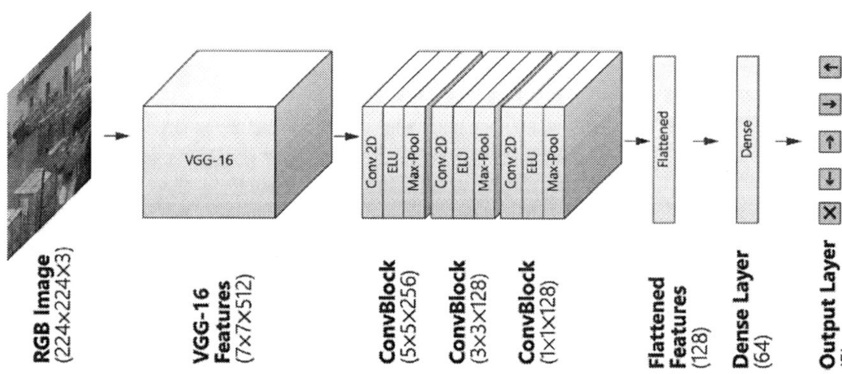

Figure 2: The architecture of the DQN model adopted for the Pictor-360 experiment.

3.2 Model Training

A well-known dilemma in training an RL agent is the *exploration vs. exploitation* problem. The goal of exploration is to allow the RL agent to take random actions to visit new states that were not previously traversed. However, exploitation describes a learning process where the RL agent takes the best action (a.k.a., greedy action) based on current knowledge to reinforce its learning (Géron, 2019, Sutton and Barto, 2018). In this paper, we adopt *ε-greedy policy* where at each state, the RL agent will explore a randomly selected action with probability ε ($0 \leq \varepsilon \leq 1$), and exploit this greedy action with probability $1 - \varepsilon$ (Géron, 2019; Sutton and Barto, 2018). Particularly, we start with a high ε ($\varepsilon_{\max} = 1.0$) to encourage the agent to explore. However, as the agent becomes mature through training, we linearly decay the value of ε to reach a minimum value ($\varepsilon_{\min} = 0.1$) so to focus the attention of the agent on exploiting its previously learned knowledge. The training stops at that minimum value to avoid overfitting.

In any given time step, the *experience* of the RL agent is composed of the following elements: current state, action taken, reward received, next state, and a Boolean value (i.e., true or false) indicating if the next state is the terminal state. To expedite training, in any one iteration, the agent is trained on multiple experiences (a.k.a., batch of experience) simultaneously rather than on a single experience (Schaul et al., 2015; Géron, 2019; Sutton and Barto, 2018). To train the model more effectively, we adopt a scheme called *experience replay* (Schaul et al., 2015; Géron, 2019; Sutton and Barto, 2018) where a fixed number of past experiences are stored in the RL agent's memory. In each iteration, several sample experiences are randomly drawn from the stored experiences and a sample batch of experience will be generated to train the RL agent. Particularly, we use a batch of size 200 and a deque data structure of 400,000 capacity to store the experiences. Also, we do not train the model during the first 2,000 iterations (a.k.a., *warm-up period*) and use these iterations only to gather enough experiences to fill up the deque memory. A complete list of the training hypermeters is presented in Table 1.

Table 1: Hyperparameters for the Pictor-360 experiment.

Category	Hyperparameter	Value
Environment	Number of states	268,416
	Number of actions	5
	Image resolution	420×420
	# Time steps in each episode	100
Reward	Step reward	IoF
	Discount factor, γ	0.995
Policy	$\varepsilon_{\mathrm{max}}$	1
	$\varepsilon_{\mathrm{min}}$	0.1
	$n_{\mathrm{iteration}}$	10,000,000
Experience	Deque memory size	400,000
	Batch size	200
Training	Number of iterations	10,000,000
	Warm-up period	2,000 steps
	Target model update interval	2,000 steps
	Optimizer	Adam
	Learning rate	0.00001

4. Results and Discussion

Figure 3 shows the average reward received by the RL agent in 1,000-episode intervals. It can be seen that the model achieves higher rewards over time. During the test episode, the RL agent starts from 1,024 randomly selected positions to find better visibility of the forklift. The IoF at the very first frame is called initial IoF (I_o) while the maximum IoF achieved during one test episode is called maximum IoF (I_m). Figure 4(a) displays the I_o versus I_m. In this Figure, the 45° equality line represents the positions where $I_m = I_o$, i.e., the IoF of the forklift remains unchanged. In this experiment, all (100%) of the points are on or above the equality line (i.e., $I_m \geq I_o$), and 73% of the points are above the equality line (i.e., $I_m > I_o$). This finding implies that in 73% of the times the RL agent has found a position from where the forklift was more visible, indicating the effectiveness of the RL agent in successfully locating the object of interest in complex and dynamic real-world settings. It is worth noting that in the remaining 27% of cases, the visibility of the forklift was preserved at the same level, and in no cases, the movement of the RL agent resulted in lower visibility. Figure 4(b) exhibits the percentage of times that the RL agent was able to find a better position from different initial IoFs. The Figure shows that when the initial IoF is low (e.g., 0.0-0.1), the RL agent can improve visibility in 65% of the times. However, if the initial IoF is higher (e.g., > 0.1), the RL agent performs better in improving visibility (i.e., 80% of the times or more).

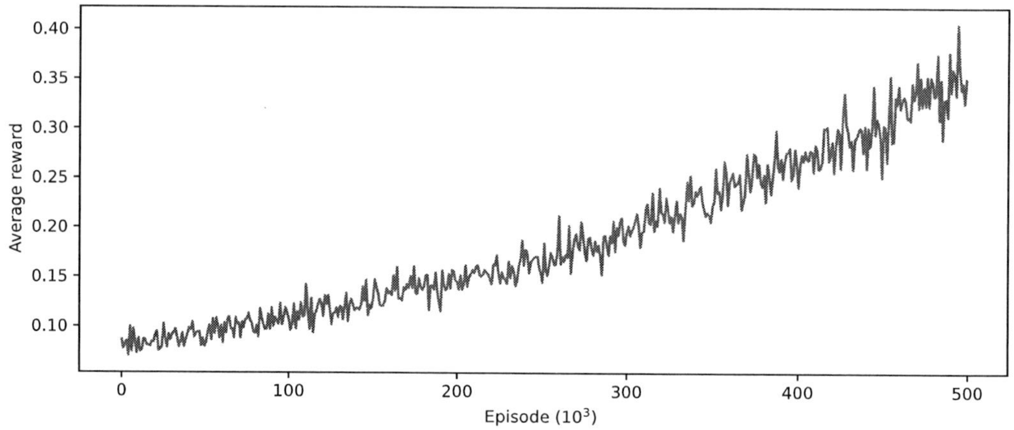

Figure 3: Average reward received in 1,000-episode intervals during training.

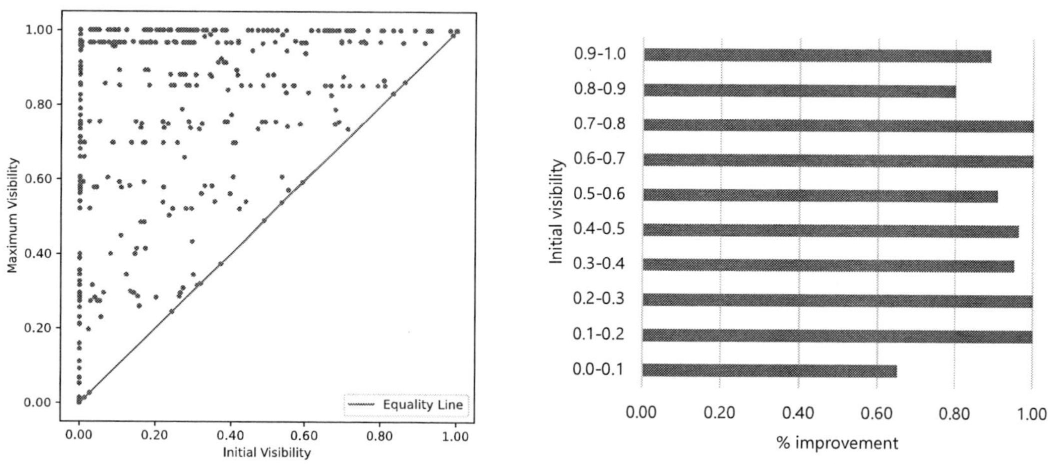

(a) (b)

Figure 4: Improvement in visibility for finding forklifts in the warehouse, for various initial positions of the camera – (a) initial vs. maximum visibility, and (b) % improvement for various initial visibilities.

5. Summary and Conclusion

Continuous and unobtrusive monitoring of jobsite activities is critical for safety monitoring, supply chain management, asset management, resource allocation, and productivity assessment. In this paper, we introduced a self-navigating camera capable of finding a moving object of interest (i.e., forklift) by autonomously browsing a real-world warehouse environment. We trained a DQN with RL to provide situational awareness to the camera. Particularly, the RL agent was trained to take one of the five actions of moving "up", "down", "left", "right", or "do nothing" to navigate through the environment. The value of reward was determined based on the IoF between the bounding box of the forklift and the viewing window of the RL camera. The model was validated with a 360-degree video of a real-world warehouse operation. Results indicated that starting from a random initial position, the RL agent was able to successfully find a moving forklift by autonomously browsing the warehouse environment, and in 73% of the times, improve the visibility of the tracked object. This, for example, exceeds the 71% true positive rate in detecting objects in still images, as reported by Caicedo and Lazebnik (2015).

One of the major challenges in conducting RL experiments in real-world settings is to evaluate the models thoroughly and safely without compromising the safety of human participants or causing unwanted damage to physical assets. Therefore, a potential direction of future work will be to conduct experiments in controlled real-world environments as a first step toward improving the performance of RL models in a wide variety of applications such as construction safety, warehouse operations, smart spatiotemporal surveillance, and post-disaster search and rescue operations. Another potential implementation challenge is the inference time which can undermine the usefulness of the developed RL models for real-time decision-making. A potential way to reduce inference time is to perform neural network pruning by reducing redundant layers (Pi et al., 2021).

References

Autodesk (2020). Future of Work, Autodesk website, https://www.autodesk.com/future-of-work, accessed April 2022.

Busoniu, L., Babuska, R., De Schutter, B., Ernst, D. (2010). Reinforcement learning and dynamic programming using function approximators. CRC press.

Caicedo, J. C., Lazebnik, S. (2015). Active object localization with deep reinforcement learning. In: IEEE International Conference on Computer Vision (ICCV), 2015, Santiago, Chile.

Canning, J. (2020). 1.43 trillion photos were taken in 2020 but how many of them were captured on our mobile phones?, Buymobile website, https://www.buymobiles.net/blog/1-43-trillion-photos-were-taken-in-2020-but-how-many-of-them-were-captured-on-our-mobile-phones, accessed April 2022.

Chollet, F. (2021). Deep Learning with Python. Simon and Schuster.

Deng, L., Liu, Y. (2018). Deep learning in natural language processing. Springer.

Dos Santos, S. R. B., Givigi, S. N., Nascimento, C. L. (2013). Autonomous construction of structures in a dynamic environment using reinforcement learning, In: IEEE International Systems Conference (SysCon), 2013, Orlando, FL.

Ekenel, H. K., Stiefelhagen, R. (2009). Why is facial occlusion a challenging problem?, In: Third International Conference on Advances in Biometrics, 2009, Alghero, Italy.

Fang, Q., Li, H., Luo, X., Ding, L., Luo, H., Rose, T. M., An, W. (2018). Detecting non-hardhat-use by a deep learning method from far-field surveillance videos, J. Automation in Construction. 85, pp. 1–9.

Géron, A. (2019). Hands-on machine learning with Scikit-Learn, Keras, and TensorFlow: Concepts, tools, and techniques to build intelligent systems. Sebastopol, CA, O'Reilly Media.

Henderson, P., Islam, R., Bachman, P., Pineau, J., Precup, D., Meger, D. (2018). Deep reinforcement learning that matters, In: AAAI Conference on Artificial Intelligence, 2018, New Orleans, LA.

Hoiem, D., Efros, A. A., Hebert, M. (2011). Recovering occlusion boundaries from an image, International J. Computer Vision. 91(3), pp. 328–346.

Jang, B., Kim, M., Harerimana, G., Kim, J. W. (2019). Q-learning algorithms: A comprehensive classification and applications. IEEE Access 7:133653-133667.

Krizhevsky, A., Sutskever, I., Hinton, G. E. (2017). ImageNet classification with deep convolutional neural networks. Communications of the ACM. 60(6), pp. 84–90

Kormushev, P., Calinon, S., Caldwell, D. G. (2013). Reinforcement learning in robotics: Applications and real-world challenges, J. Robotics. 2(3), pp. 122–148.

Li, Y. (2017). Deep reinforcement learning: An overview. arXiv preprint arXiv:1701.07274.

Lin, Y., Dai, X., Li, L., Wang, F.-Y. (2018). An efficient deep reinforcement learning model for urban traffic control. arXiv preprint arXiv:1808.01876.

Mccoy, L. G., Nagaraj, S., Morgado, F., Harish, V., Das, S., Celi, L. A. (2020). What do medical students actually need to know about artificial intelligence?, J. Digital Medicine. 3(1), pp. 1–3.

Mullapudi, A., Lewis, M. J., Gruden, C. L., Kerkez, B. (2020). Deep reinforcement learning for the real time control of stormwater systems, J. Advances in Water Resources. 140, pp. 103600.

Muresan, M., Fu, L., Pan, G. (2019). Adaptive traffic signal control with deep reinforcement learning an exploratory investigation. arXiv preprint arXiv:1901.00960.

Nath, N. D., Behzadan, A. H. (2020a). Deep convolutional networks for construction object detection under different visual conditions, J. Frontiers in Built Environment. 6(97), pp. 1–22.

Nath, N. D., Behzadan, A. H. (2020b). Deep generative adversarial network to enhance image quality for fast object detection in construction sites. In: IEEE Winter Simulation Conference (WSC), 2020, Orlando, FL.

Nath, N. D., Behzadan, A. H., Paal, S. G. (2020). Deep learning for site safety: Real-time detection of personal protective equipment, J. Automation in Construction. 112, pp. 103085.

Nguyen, T. T., Nguyen, N. D., Nahavandi, S. (2020). Deep reinforcement learning for multiagent systems: A review of challenges, solutions, and applications, IEEE Transactions on Cybernetics. 50(9), pp. 3826–3839.

Nian, R., Liu, J., Huang, B. (2020). A review on reinforcement learning: Introduction and applications in industrial process control, Computers and Chemical Engineering. 139, pp. 106886.

NSF (2020). Future of Work at the Human-Technology Frontier, United States National Science Foundation website, https://www.nsf.gov/news/special_reports/big_ideas/human_tech.jsp, accessed April 2022.

OSHA (2019). Commonly Used Statistics, Unite States Department of Labor website, https://www.osha.gov/oshstats/commonstats.html, accessed April 2022.

Pi, Y., Nath, N. D., Sampathkumar, S., Behzadan, A. H. (2021). Deep learning for visual analytics of the spread of COVID-19 infection in crowded urban environments, J. Natural Hazards Review. 22(3), pp. 04021019.

Rao, Q., Frtunikj, J. (2018). Deep learning for self-driving cars: Chances and challenges. In: 1st International Workshop on Software Engineering for AI in Autonomous Systems, 2018, Gothenburg, Sweden.

Rasheed, F., Yau, K.-L. A., Low, Y.-C. (2020). Deep reinforcement learning for traffic signal control under disturbances: A case study on Sunway City, Malaysia, J. Future Generation Computer Systems. 109, pp. 431–445.

Schaul, T., Quan, J., Antonoglou, I., Silver, D. (2015). Prioritized experience replay. arXiv preprint arXiv:1511.05952.

Shan, Q., Li, Z., Jia, J., Tang, C.-K. (2008). Fast image/video upsampling, ACM Transactions on Graphics (TOG). 27(5), pp. 1–7.

Silver, D., Huang, A., Maddison, C. J., Guez, A., Sifre, L., Van Den Driessche, G., Schrittwieser, J., Antonoglou, I., Panneershelvam, V., Lanctot, M. J. N. (2016). Mastering the game of Go with deep neural networks and tree search, J. Nature. 529(7587), pp. 484–489.

Silver, D., Schrittwieser, J., Simonyan, K., Antonoglou, I., Huang, A., Guez, A., Hubert, T., Baker, L., Lai, M., Bolton, A. J. N. (2017). Mastering the game of go without human knowledge, J. Nature. 550(7676), pp. 354 –359.

Simonyan, K., Zisserman, A. (2014). Very deep convolutional networks for large-scale image recognition. arXiv preprint arXiv:1409.1556.

Sowa, K., Przegalinska, A., Ciechanowski, L. (2021). Cobots in knowledge work: Human-AI collaboration in managerial professions, J. Business Research. 125, pp. 135–142.

Sutton, R. S., Barto, A. G. (2018). Reinforcement learning: An introduction. MIT press.

Szepesvári, C. (2010). Algorithms for reinforcement learning. San Rafael, CA, Morgan & Claypool Publishers.

Szita, I. (2012). Reinforcement learning in games. Reinforcement learning. Springer, pp. 539–577.

Tan, K. L., Poddar, S., Sarkar, S., Sharma, A. (2019). Deep reinforcement learning for adaptive traffic signal control. In: ASME Dynamic Systems and Control Conference. 59162, V003T18A006.

Tschandl, P., Rinner, C., Apalla, Z., Argenziano, G., Codella, N., Halpern, A., Janda, M., Lallas, A., Longo, C., Malvehy, J. (2020). Human-computer collaboration for skin cancer recognition, J. Nature Medicine. 26(8), pp. 1229–1234.

Wang, D., Weisz, J. D., Muller, M., Ram, P., Geyer, W., Dugan, C., Tausczik, Y., Samulowitz, H., Gray, A. (2019). Human-AI collaboration in data science: Exploring data scientists' perceptions of automated AI. Proceedings of the ACM on Human-Computer Interaction, 3, pp. 1–24.

Wu, Y., Tan, H., Ran, B. (2018). Differential variable speed limits control for freeway recurrent bottlenecks via deep reinforcement learning, arXiv preprint arXiv:1810.10952.

Xu, M., Wu, J., Huang, L., Zhou, R., Wang, T., Hu, D. (2020). Network-wide traffic signal control based on the discovery of critical nodes and deep reinforcement learning, J. Intelligent Transportation Systems. 24(1), pp. 1–10.

Yao, L., Dong, Q., Jiang, J., Ni, F. (2020). Deep reinforcement learning for long-term pavement maintenance planning, J. Computer-Aided Civil Infrastructure Engineering. 35(11), pp. 1230–1245.

Zhang, D., Han, X., Deng, C. (2018). Review on the research and practice of deep learning and reinforcement learning in smart grids, CSEE J. Power Energy Systems. 4(3), pp. 362–370.

A digital twin-driven deformation monitoring system for deep foundation pit excavation

Chen K.[a], Liu Y.[a], Hu R.[a], Fang W.[b]
[a] Huazhong University of Science and Technology, China; [b] Technical University of Berlin, Germany
flabour@hust.edu.cn

Abstract. Deformation happening in deep foundation pit excavation is a growing concern to underground construction, threatening not only the construction safety but also the adjacent environment. Traditional deformation monitoring is conducted once a day through the method of manual measurement. Such monitoring strategy has been blamed for inefficiency and error-prone, and also the monitoring results cannot be timely received by on-site managers for safety management. Therefore, the study proposes a digital twin-driven deformation monitoring system to support accurate risk-preventing decisions. The proposed system comprises four interconnected components for data acquisition, data processing, result visualization, and risk warning, respectively. A real-life tunnelling construction project – Lianghu tunnelling construction in Wuhan, China – is used to illustrate the functionality of the proposed system. Findings show that the system will be a valuable step for implementing digital twin to deep foundation pit excavation from concept to practice.

1. Introduction

Deep foundation pit excavation in underground construction is characterized by a long duration of construction, substantial uncertainties, and serious effects on the surrounding environment. One of the most dangerous issues is the failure of a retaining structure during excavation. Therefore, deformation monitoring of a deep foundation pit has a pivotal role in construction safety management. However, traditional manual monitoring is often conducted once a day by using measurement tool to collect the deformation data at each of the measurement points, and in the next few days, the measurement data is processed into various types of charts and 2D drawings recorded in paper-based reports. During this process, several problems cannot be omitted: (1) Human error in measurement; (2) delayed information response to safety management decisions, especially for dewatering and surging in a deep foundation pit and other circumstances that easily occur local deformation in short term; (3) dazzling result presentation in a layout plan that cannot comprehensively reflect the actual deep foundation pit in 3D.

Advanced digital technologies, such as wireless sensors and monitors, have been used to overcome the limitations of manual deformation monitoring (Zhu et al., 2019; Wu et al., 2021), but a comprehensive solution is still required which can automatically collect deformation data and facilitate accurate data processing and visualization for effective safety management. Recently, digital twin (DT) is considered to be an enabler for such a comprehensive solution. A DT system commonly comprises real-time monitoring, diagnostics, forecasting, and visualization through artificial intelligence, data analysis, and machine learning algorithms. Jiang et al. (2021) reviewed the applications of DT in the civil engineering sector characterized by (1) using virtual representations to express the physical counterpart, (2) requiring data transfer from the physical object to the virtual part, (3) the virtual part can control the physical counterpart, and (4) the DT must provide a specific service. Liu et al. (2021) clarified the connotation of construction digital twin and noted that the applications of DT were still limited in the construction sector.

https://doi.org/10.7146/aul.455.c205

This study attempts to propose a digital twin-driven deformation monitoring system (DTDMS) to solve delayed monitoring information and ineffective analysis of the overall safety situation of a deep foundation pit. The DTDMS makes use of the Internet of Things (IoT) and Building Information Modeling (BIM) technologies, and can provide a real-time, accurate, and visualized approach for rapid deformation monitoring and safety evaluation of deep foundation pit. A real-life underground construction project is used to illustrate the feasibility of the DTDMS.

The remainder of this paper was structured as follows. The next section briefly reviews published literature with a focus on how DT has been used in the construction sector. The third section shows the system framework of the DTDMS. The fourth section demonstrates the applications of the DTDMS through a case study, and the last section concludes this study.

2. Related work

As the construction sector is gradually entering the digital age, digital technologies have been widely used in all stages of a construction project (Chen et al., 2015; Turner et al., 2020). Facing the serious problems of deformation monitoring during deep foundation pit excavation, Liu et al. (2018) applied laser image recognition technology to monitor the horizontal displacement of deep foundation pit. Wu et al. (2021) used unmanned aerial vehicle (UVA) images to monitor and reflect the safety situation of deep foundation pit. However, the safety management of deep foundation pit excavation is much more than assessing a single type of displacement, but need to deal with a huge amount of monitoring data and complex data types. Challenges remain in the data analysis, and improvements in safety situation visualization and decision making are still required (Dong et al., 2020). At present, the most popular digital technologies used in this area include BIM (Wang et al., 2021), IoT (Chuang et al., 2021), and artificial intelligence (AI) (Tian et al., 2021).

The application of advanced digital technologies can solve some problems in deep foundation pit monitoring, but there are still limitations if only applied one of them. For example, the conventional 3D BIM – a static BIM – has many limitations that constrain its benefits to safety management because using BIM alone lacks two-way information exchange between virtual objects and their physical counterparts and cannot give real-time feedback on the actual safety situation. To make the digital model accurately reflect the physical project, DT in construction means a set of virtual information constructs that fully describes a potential or actual physical construction entities from the micro atomic level to the macro geometrical level, including physical components, virtual components, and the data that connects them (Grieves and Vickers, 2017). Compared with BIM that concentrates on a semantic rich representation of construction objects, DT conveys a more holistic process-oriented characterization (Sacks, et al., 2020).

In terms of a building life cycle, the operation and maintenance stage has received much attention for DT applications, followed by the construction stage (Jiang et al., 2021). Xie et al. (2020) established a dynamic DT platform in the Institute for Manufacturing building of the University of Cambridge, which can detect environmental anomalies and support operation and maintenance. Greif et al. (2020) developed a digital twin of silos to optimize in-situ logistics. Zhang et al. (2020) created the DT model of construction equipment to enable action recognition. However, the application of DT in deformation monitoring of deep foundation pit excavation is immature and still has some limitations. For example, Dong et al. (2020) proposed a safety monitoring platform for deep foundation pit excavation that can visualize data information, but the input of monitoring data is still done manually, which might cause high human error rates in measurement. Likewise, Fan et al. (2021) established a safety management system to achieve automatic early warning, but failed to identify false alarms from various sensor faults and false measurements. Furthermore, Tian et al. (2021) proposed an intelligent early warning system, whose data sources come from both the monitoring system and manual monitoring, but the information presented by the system is insufficient to support decision-making. Thus, this study aims to propose an accurate and timely digital twin-driven deformation monitoring of deep foundation pit excavation in order to support effective risk-preventing decisions.

3. System framework

To alleviate risks to the construction workers and losses to the adjacent environment when a severe deep foundation pit collapse occurs in underground engineering, a deformation monitoring system is preferably provided for the on-site safety management decisions. Figure. 1 illustrates the overall framework of the DTDMS, which includes five key components. The curved arrows in the diagram denote the direction of information flow and interaction between two components.

1) Engineering entity, presenting the main structures of a deep foundation pit that will be constructed during excavation.

2) Sensor network, which could measure the deformation continuously during deep foundation pit excavation. The sensors should be installed before the commencement of excavation in order to collect the on-site deformation data as much as possible.

3) Data collection component, which transmits real-time data from the physical sensor network to the cloud data server.

4) Cloud data server and process component, which reads the data remotely transferred from the sensor network and stores the data in a standard format. This component will use a series of AI algorithms to generate decision-support information by mining the collected data.

5) Visual decision aid component, which could fetch the output of the AI algorithms and display the nearly real-time deformation level to on-site managers in a user-friendly mode.

The remaining section will explain each component further.

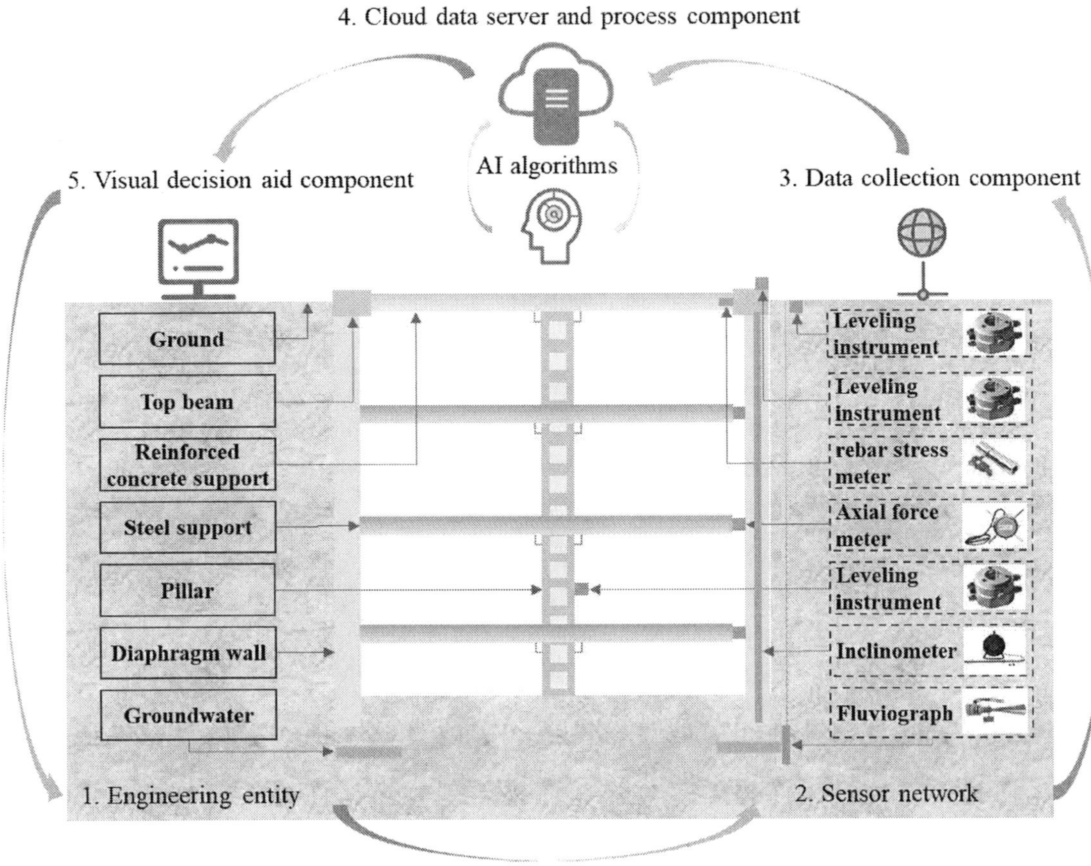

Figure 1: Overall Framework of the DTDMS.

3.1 Engineering entity

The DTDMS contains bidirectional data flow between the physical and digital parts. The engineering entity, or the physical part, for constructing a deep foundation pit mainly involves envelope structures and bracing systems. The envelope structures are commonly composed of diaphragm walls and top beams, and the bracing systems generally contain reinforced concrete struts, steel struts, and pillars. In addition, surrounding soil and groundwater, which have a significant impact on the structure stability, are often considered as the integration of deep foundation pit engineering. Deformations of the aforementioned elements during excavation might cause significant safety accidents.

3.2 Sensor network

As presented in Figure 1, a deep foundation pit perceiving network has five types of sensing devices: levelling instruments, rebar stress meters, axial force meters, inclinometers, and fluviographs. These sensing devices can automatically collect data associated with deformation and thus replace the error-prone manual measurement. A levelling instrument is used to monitor the vertical displacement of the surrounding ground, top beams, and pillars. A rebar stress meter is used to observe the stress fluctuation of reinforced concrete struts, while an axial force meter can monitor the stress corrosion of steel struts. The horizontal displacement of diaphragm walls is measured by inclinometers in order to identify the lateral pressure of the soil on the deep foundation pit. Meanwhile, considering the risk of groundwater surge, a fluviograph is also required to measure the groundwater level in a real-time manner.

All the sensors should be installed at the appropriate locations of the monitored object to ensure that they are not interfered by construction activities. The optimal distance between sensors should be determined according to existing standards and construction plans.

3.3 Data collection component

The DTDMS relies on the data collection component to transfer the monitoring data from the physical deep foundation pit excavation to the cloud data server for further data process. Both cables or wireless communication networks have been used for data collection in construction, but excessive wiring network might interrupt the construction activities. Therefore, a wireless connection becomes a preferable choice. The selection of public wireless networks (i.e., GPRS, 3G, 4G) or private WiFi depends on many external and internal factors such as the signal strength on the construction site. With the fast development of communication technologies, the 5G network will become available to better respond in almost real-time to dynamic changes in local deformation of deep foundation pit excavation and connect an extensive number of sensors. In addition, note that deploying a large number of sensors would make it tricky to uphold the system, and the service life of sensors would be significantly reduced if the data collection frequency is set unnecessarily high. Thus, the data collection frequency in a magnitude of one hour is adopted by the DTDMS.

3.4 Cloud data server and process component

The collected data is stored in a cloud data server for remote access. The cloud data server can be managed by an off-site safety office, and the data in the database is organized by Database Management System like MySQL in multiple tables connecting each other according to their relationships. Due to the lack of data standards related to various sensor information, a clear database structure is required before filling data in. The DTDMS creates a major database containing three tables: a measurement table to store deformation data measured by each sensor in each column; a processing table to be filled with processed data output from AI algorithms; a cyber scene table to store the 3D models and relevant elements of a deep foundation pit in practice. A Python program with an application programming interface (API), is installed on the server to connect, query, and write to the database.

Affected by strong vibrations caused by heavy equipment and other interferences from surrounding construction activities, the deformation monitoring data from sensors would change with large fluctuations and cause false alarms during deep foundation pit excavation. In order to reduce the time delay and workload of manually eliminating outliers, an important feature of this layer is to use the extended isolated forest (EIF) algorithms to automatically check abnormal values of monitoring data. Compared with other traditional outlier detection methods, the results of EIF are more reliable and robust anomaly scores, and more accurate detection can be achieved without sacrificing computational efficiency (Hariri et al., 2021). Such a data process strategy can ultimately reduce false alarms to a large extent.

3.5 Visual decision aid component

As highlighted by Brilakis et al. (2019), BIM provides a suitable basis for holding various types of data along with the construction progress, closing the information loop as demanded by the digital twin concept. Therefore, in the visual decision aid component, BIM is used to visualize structural deformations containing vertical and horizontal displacement and generate warnings for safety management. Specifically, the component adopts the colour display of monitoring points in the BIM model, and the monitoring point family links the monitoring data curve in that model. At the same time, through the 4D function of the BIM technology, dramatic changes in deformation data of a deep foundation pit can be automatically identified. With the help of the DTDMS, on-site managers can intuitively understand the dynamic deformation situation and safety status of the deep foundation pit, and corresponding measures can be taken in order to avoid any potential collapse.

4. Case Study

4.1 General description of the project

The Lianghu tunnelling construction located in Wuhan, China is currently one of the largest urban underwater double-layer road tunnels in the world. Its length is about 19 kilometres, passing through the East Lake, the South Lake, and many existing subway lines, viaducts, and buildings. This study selects a 160 m (length) × 28.3 m (width) × (22-28.76) m (depth) cuboid-like deep foundation pit as the case to demonstrate the functionality of the DTDMS (see Figure 2). The retaining structure consists of a cast in situ diaphragm wall with a thickness of 1.2 m. The depth of the diaphragm wall is 20.65 m. During the excavation to a depth of 17.2 m, the retaining walls are supported at the top by beams and in depth by four levels of temporary reinforced concrete struts and steel struts. This deep foundation pit is surrounded on the east side by residential buildings, on the west side by the Hubei Museum, and on the south side by the East Lake Scenic Area of Wuhan. The complexity of the surrounding environment emphasizes the demand for improved deformation monitoring and safety evaluation.

Figure 2: The Selected Deep Foundation Pit for Case Study.

4.2 Data monitoring and analysis

In this case study, the top beam settlement is one of the most important indicators to evaluate the vertical deformation of the deep foundation pit. Sensing devices were installed on the outside of top beams, as presented in Figure 3a. Figure 3b shows a solar-powered data integrator colleting the monitoring data of all sensors. Figure 3c presents a data transmitting device to transfer the monitoring data to the cloud data server.

(a) Sensors (b) Data integrator (c) Data transmitter

Figure 3: Data Monitoring Devices Installed on the Construction Site.

After receiving the monitoring data, the cloud data server applies the EIF algorithms, mentioned in Section 3.4, to conduct anomaly detection in order to prevent false alarms. Take the dataset collected in December 2021 as an example, Figure 4 shows the anomaly detecting results output. Figure 4a depicts a scatter plot of the original dataset and Figure 4b presents the anomaly score map obtained using the EIF. We sample points uniformly within the range of the plot and assign scores to those points based on the trees created for the forest. Then, it can be clearly seen that the points in the centre get the lowest anomaly score, and the score values increase as moving radially outward. Figure 3c presents the 9 anomalies coloured in black in 237 data, of which 3 anomalies raised false alarms.

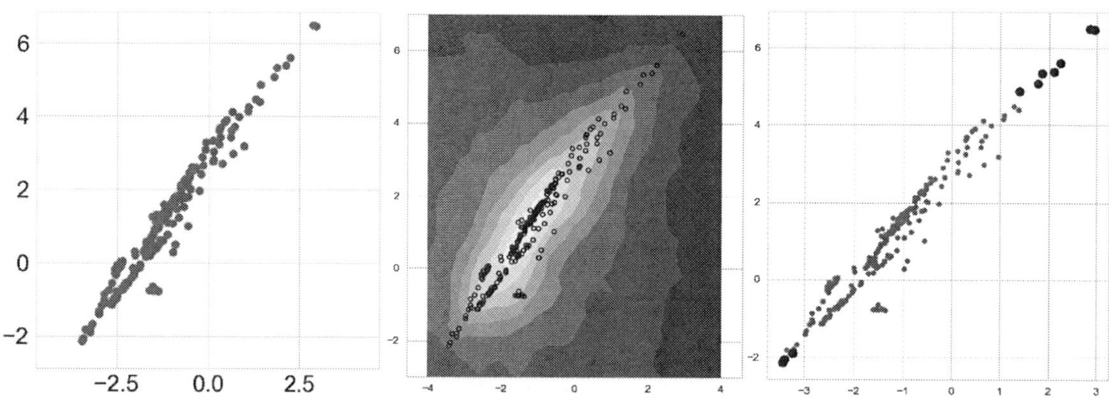

(a) Sample dataset (b) Anomaly score map (c) Anomalies labelling

Figure 4: Anomaly Detection by EIF Algorithms.

4.3 3D interactive model

The visual user interface for decision support is shown in Figure 5. The BIM model of the presented deep foundation pit was developed in Autodesk Revit, and digital representations of the deformation sensors were also integrated into the model. Once the BIM model acquires a monitoring value from the cloud data server, it will compare the value with the alarm thresholds and display hierarchical colours at the corresponding monitoring location of the structural elements. For example, the red colour represents a Class I hazardous area, indicating that there is an obvious deformation and thus a high probability of a collapse accident. Additionally, a plan view of all real-time data monitoring points of the deep foundation pit is presented underneath the BIM model. The historical information and statistical analysis of a certain monitoring point will be shown in the user interface after clicking individual points. Based on this 3D interactive model, the on-site managers can be informed regarding the real-time monitored conditions, and then will establish a feasible safety management plan for the deep foundation pit.

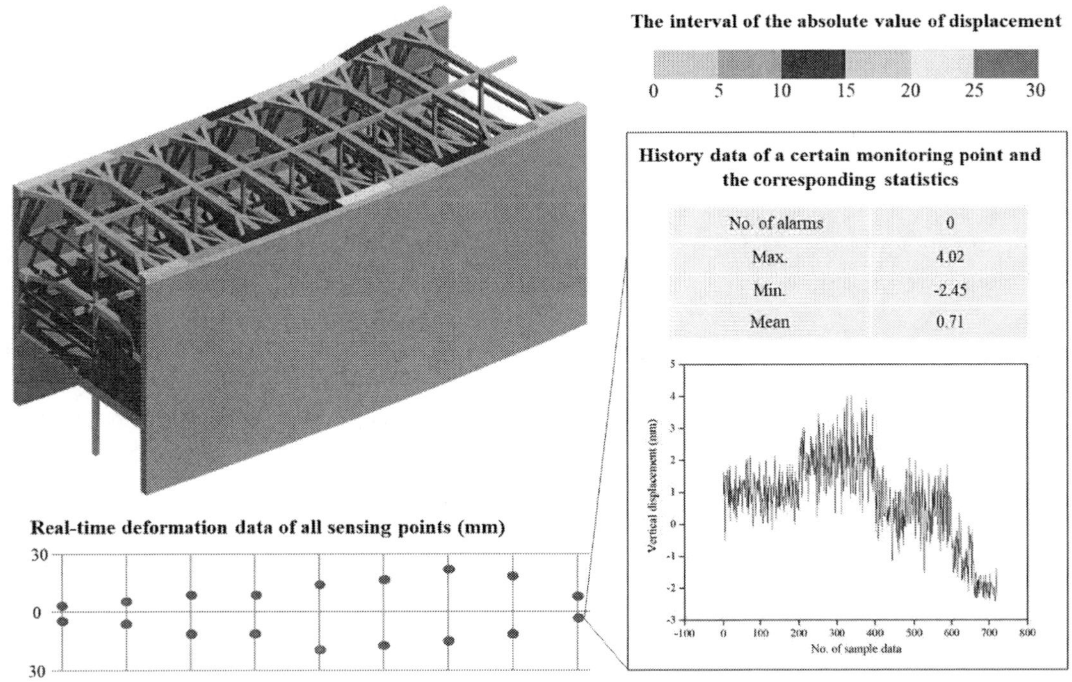

Figure 5: Visual User Interface for Decision Support.

5. Conclusion

This paper introduced the application of DT to support deformation monitoring during deep foundation pit excavation. A DT-driven deformation monitoring system with five interconnected components was designed. The DTDMS takes advantage of BIM, IoT, and AI technologies, and can integrate multiple data resources under a unified data structure and provide more confident safety warning. The DTDMS was applied to a deep foundation pit of Lianghu tunnelling construction to demonstrate its feasibility. The key benefits of the DTDMS were found to be: real-time and efficient query of relevant data, integrated capabilities of data processing and interpretation, user-friendly interface for safety warning of deep foundation pit excavation.

Future work will be conducted to further expand the capabilities of the DTDMS by integrating various types of simulation and prediction models into the system. This will help to understand the deformation trend in advance. In addition, a quantitative assessment of the efficiency and robustness of the DTDMS involved with experienced construction engineers should be made in order to ensure that the DTDMS suits in other deep foundation pit excavation scenarios.

Acknowledgement

This study is supported by National Natural Science Foundation of China (U21A20151, 72101093) and the Major Scientific and Technological Innovation Project in Hubei Province (2020ACA006).

References

Boje, C., Guerriero, A., Kubicki, S. and Rezgui, Y. (2020). Towards a semantic Construction Digital Twin: Directions for future research, Automation in Construction, 114, pp. 103179.

Brilakis, I., Pan, Y., Borrmann, A., Mayer, H. G., Rhein, F., Vos, C., Pettinato, E. and Wagner, S. (2019). Built Environment Digital Twining, International Workshop on Built Environment Digital Twinning presented by TUM Institute for Advanced Study and Siemens AG.

Chen, K., Lu, W., Peng, Y., Rowlinson, S. and Huang, G. Q. (2015). Bridging BIM and building: From a literature review to an integrated conceptual framework, International Journal of Project Management, 33(6), pp. 1405-1416.

Chuang, G., Yiqun, C., Zhongmou, C. and Peng, L. (2021). Research on Foundation Pit Monitoring and Management System Based on BIM+ GIS+ IOT, IOP Conference Series: Earth and Environmental Science, 791(1), pp. 012005.

Dong, W.P., Qin, M.X., Fang, X.F. and Wang, Y.X. (2020). Safety monitoring platform for deep excavation based on BIM and big data technology, 2020 International Conference on Robots & Intelligent System (ICRIS), IEEE, 2020, pp. 537-540.

Fan, W., Zhou, J., Zhou, J., Liu, D., Shen, W. and Gao, J. (2021). Safety management system prototype/framework of deep foundation pit based on BIM and IoT, Advances in Civil Engineering, 2021, pp. 5539796.

Greif, T., Stein, N. and Flath, C. M. (2020). Peeking into the void: Digital twins for construction site logistics, Computers in Industry, 121, pp. 103264.

Grieves, M. and Vickers, J. (2017). Digital twin: Mitigating unpredictable, undesirable emergent behavior in complex systems, In Transdisciplinary perspectives on complex systems, Springer, Cham, 2017, pp. 85-113.

Hariri, S., Kind, M. C., and Brunner, R. J. (2021). Extended Isolation Forest, IEEE Transactions on Knowledge and Data Engineering, 33(4), pp. 1479–1489.

Jiang, F., Ma, L., Broyd, T., Chen, K. (2021). Digital twin and its implementations in the civil engineering sector, Automation in Construction, 130, pp. 103838.

Liu, P., Xie, S., Zhou, G., Zhang, L., Zhang, G. and Zhao, X. (2018). Horizontal displacement monitoring method of deep foundation pit based on laser image recognition technology, Review of Scientific Instruments, 89(12), pp. 125006.

Liu, Y., Chen, K., Ma, L., Tang, S. and Tan, T. (2021). Transforming data into decision making: A spotlight review of construction digital twin, In Proceedings of International Conference on Construction and Real Estate Management 2021.

Sacks, R., Brilakis, I., Pikas, E., Xie, H. S. and Girolami, M. (2020). Construction with digital twin information systems, Data-Centric Engineering, 1, pp. e14.

Tian, W., Meng, J., Zhong, X. J. and Tan, X. (2021). Intelligent early warning system for construction safety of excavations adjacent to existing metro tunnels, Advances in Civil Engineering, 2021, pp. 8833473.

Turner, C. J., Oyekan, J., Stergioulas, L. and Griffin, D. (2020). Utilizing industry 4.0 on the construction site: Challenges and opportunities, IEEE Transactions on Industrial Informatics, 17(2), pp. 746-756.

Wang, Y., Fang, X., Fei, W., Dong, W. and Qin, M. (2021). Development and application of BIM-based foundation pit construction simulation system, IOP Conference Series: Earth and Environmental Science,714(2), pp. 022062.
Wu, J., Peng, L., Li, J., Zhou, X., Zhong, J., Wang, C. and Sun, J. (2021). Rapid safety monitoring and analysis of foundation pit construction using unmanned aerial vehicle images, Automation in Construction, 128, pp. 103706.
Xie, X., Lu, Q., Rodenas-Herraiz, D., Parlikad, A.K., and Schooling, J. M. (2020). Visualised inspection system for monitoring environmental anomalies during daily operation and maintenance, Engineering, Construction and Architectural Management, 27(8), pp. 1835-1852.
Zhang, J., Zi, L., Hou, Y., Wang, M., Jiang, W. and Deng, D. (2020). A deep learning-based approach to enable action recognition for construction equipment, Advances in Civil Engineering, 2020, pp. 8812928.
Zhu, C., Yan, Z., Lin, Y., Xiong, F. and Tao, Z. (2019). Design and application of a monitoring system for a deep railway foundation pit project, IEEE Access, 7, pp. 107591-107601.

Design and validation of a mobile structural health monitoring system based on legged robots

Smarsly K., Worm M., and Dragos K.
Hamburg University of Technology, Germany
kay.smarsly@tuhh.de

Abstract. Structural health monitoring (SHM) has been witnessing the transition from cable-based systems to wireless systems, owing to the reduced installation costs and efforts of wireless sensor nodes. However, reliable information on civil infrastructure requires dense arrays of wireless sensor nodes, which may nullify the merits of wireless SHM. This paper proposes a mobile SHM system, comprising maneuverable quadruped robots equipped with sensors for collecting, processing, and analyzing structural response data. The mobile SHM system is validated through field tests on a pedestrian bridge, proving that a minimum deployment of quadruped robots yields the same structural information as an array of wireless sensor nodes. Furthermore, the tests results are compared to results obtained from a benchmark SHM system, showcasing the accuracy of the mobile SHM system. The proposed mobile SHM system marks an advance towards employing fully autonomous robotic fleets for SHM in lieu of stationary wireless sensor nodes.

1. Introduction

In the wake of climate change, discussions on the exposure of critical infrastructure have been growing vivid around the globe, especially following catastrophic incidents of structural failures, such as the collapse of Morandi Bridge in Genoa, Italy (Rania et al., 2019). The importance of timely structural maintenance has been brought to the forefront, considering the large investments made in infrastructure (Zachariadis, 2018). In recent years, timely interventions in repairing and retrofitting aging and degrading infrastructure have been significantly aided by structural health monitoring (SHM), which traditionally has been applied via cable-based sensor networks for collecting and analyzing structural response data (Farrar and Worden, 2007). Moreover, in the last two decades, the developments in wireless communication technologies have been driving the transition from traditional cable-based SHM systems to wireless SHM systems (Lynch and Loh, 2006). Tethered sensor nodes have been replaced by wireless sensor nodes, which are easy to install and cost-efficient (typically employing low-cost sensors). In addition, the elimination of cables significantly adds to the cost-efficiency as well as to the scalability of wireless sensor networks, while offering convenient alternatives to cable-based SHM systems in case of aesthetic constraints when instrumenting structures (Smarsly and Petryna, 2014).

Notwithstanding the benefits of wireless SHM, extracting reliable information on critical infrastructure usually requires spatially dense arrays of wireless sensor nodes, thus entailing the risk of nullifying the cost-efficiency merits of wireless sensor nodes. Alternatives suggesting SHM approaches with mobile wireless sensor nodes have been introduced (Zhu et al., 2010), albeit having received scarce attention. Mobile wireless sensor nodes essentially behave as miniature robots capable of navigating and scanning large areas of civil infrastructure for collecting structural response data of high spatial density (Rubio et al., 2019). Furthermore, utilizing wireless communication, mobile wireless sensor nodes form ad-hoc wireless networks for exchanging information to collaboratively analyze structural conditions. As a result, mobile SHM systems exhibit the potential to overcome limitations of wireless SHM systems with stationary wireless sensor nodes (Smarsly, et al., 2022). In this direction, this paper introduces a mobile SHM system comprising legged robots. Representing a step towards enhancing

https://doi.org/10.7146/aul.455.c206

previously proposed mobile SHM systems based on wheeled robots, the mobile SHM system presented herein leverages the agility of legged robots, which are capable of maneuvering and traversing locations with impediments, such as stiffener beams and secondary structures, frequently seen in civil infrastructure (Biswal and Mohanty, 2021). Specifically, a mobile SHM approach based on quadruped robots is proposed, which, compared to other types of legged robots, are ideal in terms of stability and efficiency. Maintaining levels of intelligence similar to stationary wireless SHM systems, the quadruped robots of the mobile SHM system are equipped with (i) peripherals, i.e. cameras for navigation and accelerometers for collecting acceleration response data and (ii) microcontrollers for embedding algorithms to analyze the acceleration response data. The idea behind the proposed mobile SHM system is to extract the same level of information on the structural condition with a minimal deployment of quadruped robots as with a dense array of wireless sensor nodes.

The remainder of the paper is organized as follows: Section 2 describes the design and implementation of the mobile SHM system in terms of hardware and software, followed by validation tests conducted at a pedestrian overpass bridge in Thessaloniki, Greece, which are presented in Section 3. The paper ends with a summary and conclusions as well as with a brief outlook on potential future research directions.

2. Design and implementation of a mobile SHM system based on quadruped robots

System identification strategies in traditional cable-based SHM typically have been limited by instrumentation sparsity. In particular, due to the cost of sensors and cabling as well as to the physical labor of installation, structural response data, from which information on structural conditions is extracted, has been collected from only a few locations. Instrumentation sparsity in system identification has been challenging to engineering practitioners, who have traditionally been accustomed to elaborate numerical representations of structures, used in structural design, which are able to capture detailed structural responses. System identification represents an inverse problem to structural design, and instrumentation sparsity renders this problem ill-posed.

While wireless SHM has been serving as an attractive solution in terms of cost and installation, the spatial density of wireless sensor nodes required for overcoming instrumentation sparsity may still be prohibitive from a budgetary perspective. As a result, wireless SHM stands to benefit from the proposed mobile SHM system, which integrates robotics into SHM strategies. Specifically, a minimal deployment of quadruped robots, substituting dense arrays of stationary wireless sensor nodes, could efficiently scan large areas of civil infrastructure, thus fulfilling the need for spatial density of structural response data. Moreover, the maneuverability capabilities of quadruped robots allow navigating areas that may be hard to reach physically or via wheeled robots. Finally, as will be shown in this paper, the mobile SHM system is capable of yielding information on structural conditions comparable to information obtained from a SHM system with cable-based sensors.

Drawing from the state of the art in SHM, system identification builds upon statistical processing of structural response data performed in a fully data-driven manner. System identification usually takes the form of operational modal analysis (OMA), in which vibration mode shapes are estimated from correlations between acceleration response data collected from different locations. In other words, an output-only method for extracting the mode shapes is applied in this study, which does not require to generate mechanical impulses or other strategies to induce vibration, which would fall into the category of experimental modal analysis. Consequently, conducting an OMA-based SHM strategy with the proposed mobile SHM system requires a minimal deployment of two quadruped robots equipped with accelerometers for collecting acceleration response data simultaneously. Furthermore, the quadruped robots form an intrinsically distributed SHM system, in which the processing power of the robots is leveraged to embed most tasks of the OMA-based SHM strategy, including (i) navigating across large areas of monitored structures, (ii) communicating wirelessly for exchanging information with other robots and with computer systems, and (iii) collecting, processing, and analyzing acceleration response data. The hardware and software implementation of the mobile SHM system are described below.

2.1 Hardware design and implementation

The quadruped robots used for the mobile SHM system are of type "mini intelligent documentation gadgets" (mIDOGs). The mIDOGs offer advanced maneuverability capabilities with multi-degree-of-freedom locomotion, as well as on-board intelligence, allowing attaching sensors for collecting acceleration response data and embedding algorithms for performing SHM tasks. The hardware implemented for operating the mIDOGs within the framework of the OMA-based SHM strategy is built around a Petoi Bittle system (Petoi, Inc., 2021) and encompasses:

(i) The ***robot component***, which enables the multi-degree-of-freedom locomotion,

(ii) The dual-board ***processing component***, which includes an Arduino board dedicated to locomotion in cooperation with the robot component as well as a Raspberry Pi board that allows embedding algorithms for controlling sensors and analyzing acceleration response data, and

(iii) The ***sensing component***, which allows attaching sensors as peripherals; in this paper, an Analog Devices ADXL355 accelerometer and a Raspberry Pi v1.3 camera with an OmniVision OV5647 image sensor are attached to the sensing component (Analog Devices, 2010; Raspberry Pi Trading Ltd., 2021; OmniVision Technologies, Inc., 2009).

As mentioned previously, the OMA-based SHM strategy is designed around three SHM tasks, (i) navigation, (ii) communication, and (iii) data processing and analysis, which are allocated to the hardware components of a group of mIDOGs. The allocation of the SHM tasks is depicted in Figure 1.

As can be seen from Figure 1, *navigation* requires the cooperation of all hardware components of the mIDOGs. In particular, the robot component manages the motion of the mIDOG across all measurement points, the sensing component allows the mIDOG to identify measurement points (pinpointed with markers) via image recognition, and the processing component confirms that a measurement point has been reached using position data obtained from the sensing component. Once all mIDOGs have reached measurement points, *communication* is established among the mIDOGs, via the processing component, for confirming the status of the mIDOGs and for synchronizing internal clocks. Following the status confirmation, the mIDOGs use the robot components to assume measuring postures. Finally, the mIDOGs perform *data processing and analysis*, which is a task that also involves all three hardware components. Specifically, upon reaching a measurement point and assuming measuring posture, each mIDOG uses the robot component to attach the accelerometer to the surface of the monitored structure. For the execution of the SHM tasks, dedicated software modules are developed and embedded into the microcontrollers of the mIDOGs, which are described in the next subsection.

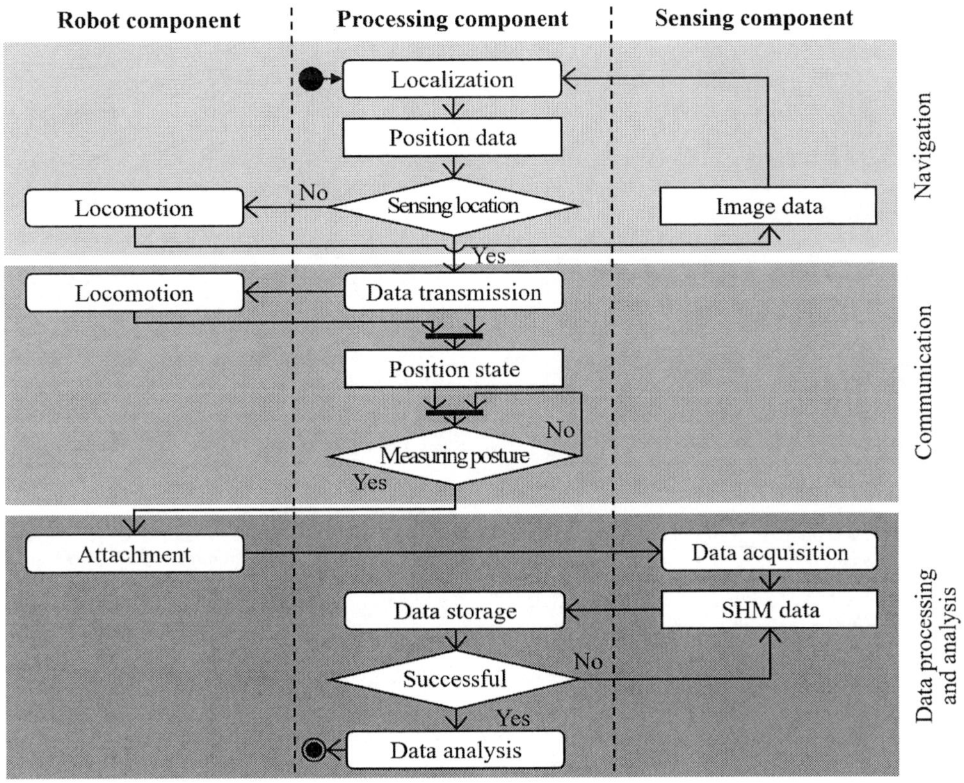

Figure 1: Flow diagram of the SHM tasks executed by the mIDOGs, divided into navigation, communication, and data processing and analysis.

2.2 Software design and implementation

The following discussion provides an overview of the embedded software modules designed and implemented in the mobile SHM system. The design rationale of the software modules follows the task allocation of the OMA-based SHM strategy to the hardware components. In this context, each SHM task is executed by a dedicated software module, i.e. the navigation module, the communication module and the data processing and analysis module, whose main classes and interfaces are shown in Figure 2. As an exception, a sensing module, which manages the accelerometer and the camera, is used as a standalone software module.

Navigation is managed by the *navigation module*. A single class, termed `Navigation-Processor`, defines motion parameters and inflicts motion on the robot component using processes encapsulated into two interfaces, designated as `Locomotor` and `Locator`. The encapsulation allows for modularity in the selection of classes for path detection. The classes used herein for path detection, implementing the `Locomotor` and `Locator` interfaces, are the `PathDetectionLocomotor` class and the `PathDetectionLocator` class, respectively. For retrieving position data with respect to the longitudinal axis of the mIDOG, which is used as reference, the `PathDetectionLocator` class uses images collected by the sensing component to follow a path using embedded image recognition. Based on the position data, the `PathDetectionLocomotor` class determines the motion parameters to reach the target, i.e. a measurement point. The motion parameters are forwarded to the `ProcessManager` class, which is also part of the navigation module, and, subsequently, to the `CommunicatonManager` class (of the communication module), which eventually passes the motion parameters to the `Arduino` class, interfaced with the Arduino microcontroller and the robot component.

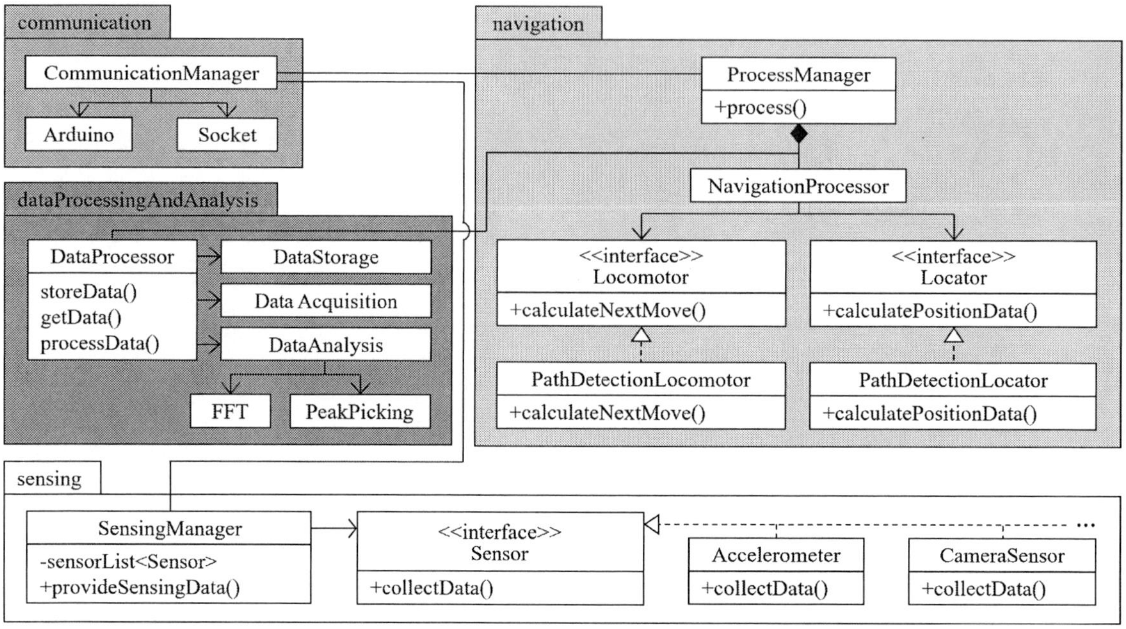

Figure 2: Embedded software modules, designed for the mobile SHM approach.

The communication task is executed by the *communication module.* The module is implemented based on sockets using the Transmission Control Protocol (TCP), which is reliable, as it ensures, through its acknowledgment mechanism, that no data gets lost and that all data received will be identical and in the same order as the data being sent. The module consists of three main classes, the `Socket` class, the `CommunicationManager` class, and the `Arduino` class. The `Socket` class is used for initializing wireless communication channels among mIDOGs, following the machine-to-machine communication paradigm. The majority of communication activities is managed by the `CommunicationManager` class, including utilization of wireless communication channels created by the `Socket` class for establishing ad-hoc wireless networks between mIDOGs and forwarding motion parameters to the `Arduino` class. The versatility of the ad-hoc wireless networks is ensured by the `CommunicationManager` class, which allows each mIDOG to establish a wireless network as a server and enable other mIDOGs to connect to its network as clients. In other words, the `CommunicationManager` class of each mIDOG is capable of recognizing if an instance of the `CommunicationManager` class of another mIDOG exists and functions as server, so as to connect as a client to the respective wireless network. The `Arduino` class, as mentioned previously, leverages the locomotion module of the Arduino microcontroller, which is used to inflict motion on the mIDOG via the robot component. Last, but not least, the `CommunicationManager` class is devised to manage the internal communication between distinct modules, such as the sensing module and the navigation module.

The last task of the OMA-based SHM strategy is executed by the data processing and analysis module. The `DataProcessor` class is responsible for retrieving the acceleration response data collected by the accelerometer through the `ProcessManager` class of the navigation module. The acceleration response data is forwarded from the `SensingManager` class of the sensing module to the `CommunicationManager` class and, finally, to the `ProcessManager` class. The `DataStorage` class performs persistent storage of the acceleration response data and offers access to the data, and the `DataAcquisition` class manages data acquisition. Finally, OMA-related activities are managed by the `DataAnalysis` class, which is responsible for frequency-domain operations on the acceleration response data. More specifically, fast Fourier transform (FFT) is performed on the acceleration response data by the `FFT` class and peak picking is applied to the FFT by the `PeakPicking` class. The mobile SHM system described in this section is validated through field tests, which are presented in the next section.

3. Field validation tests at a pedestrian bridge

The mobile SHM system is validated through field tests conducted on a pedestrian bridge, as shown in Figure 3. The validation tests serve to proof the capabilities of the mobile SHM system (i) to provide spatially dense acceleration response data with a minimal deployment of quadruped robots and (ii) to extract information on the structural condition of the same level as a benchmark SHM system with cable-based sensors of higher precision than the accelerometers attached to the mIDOGs. In what follows, the pedestrian bridge and the benchmark SHM system are briefly described, the validation tests are presented, and the results are discussed.

3.1 Description of the pedestrian bridge and the benchmark SHM system

The pedestrian bridge is an overpass bridge located at Evosmos, Thessaloniki, Greece, servicing pedestrian traffic over the Inner Ring Road of Thessaloniki. The bridge was built in 2016 and its deck has a single span with a total length of 40.80 m and width of 5.35 m. The deck is made of a steel trough filled with concrete and rests on two steel girders of square hollow sections along its longitudinal edges. The girders are suspended from two skewed steel arches of the same cross section as the girders via twisted strand steel cables and are supported on each end of the bridge by cylindrical reinforced concrete columns. The girder-to-column connection is achieved through bearings allowing partial fixity. In the transversal bending direction, the deck is supported by 20 equidistant steel beams. Lateral support is provided by 10 x-braces, which are fixed to the steel beams.

Figure 3. View of the pedestrian bridge in Evosmos, Thessaloniki, Greece.

Specifically for the field validation tests conducted in this study, the bridge is instrumented with a benchmark SHM system consisting of 7 uniaxial accelerometers, placed along the middle line of the deck, as shown in Figure 4, to enable capturing translational vibration mode shapes. The accelerometers measure in the vertical (z) direction and are connected to a single data acquisition unit. The accelerometers of the benchmark SHM system are of type Syscom MS2002+, measuring at a range of ±2 g with a sensitivity of 1 V/g and at a sampling frequency of 400 Hz (Syscom, 2015).

3.2 Validation tests and results

The purpose of the validation tests is to showcase the efficiency of the mobile SHM system in obtaining the same level of information on the structural condition, in the form of vibration mode shapes, as compared to the benchmark SHM system. To this end, a minimal deployment of mIDOGs is selected to scan all measurement points of the benchmark SHM system. In particular, the mIDOGs are assigned the following tasks:

(i) Navigating the bridge deck by using its image recognition capabilities to cover all measurement points,

(ii) Collecting acceleration response data from all measurement points,

(iii) Analyzing the acceleration response data to obtain Fourier values at modal peaks for computing mode shapes.

Although the mIDOGs are capable of yielding acceleration response data of acceptable spatial density through progressively navigating the measurement points, extracting mode shapes requires synchronicity between acceleration response data from different locations. As a result, at least two mIDOGs are required to collect acceleration response data simultaneously at different measurement points. Furthermore, to extract mode shapes of the same level as the benchmark SHM system, it is necessary to scan all measurement points in overlapping pairs, the outcomes of which will be synthesized into global mode shapes. The comparison between the mode shapes extracted by the mIDOGs to the respective mode shapes of the benchmark SHM system will serve as a proof of accuracy of the proposed mobile SHM system.

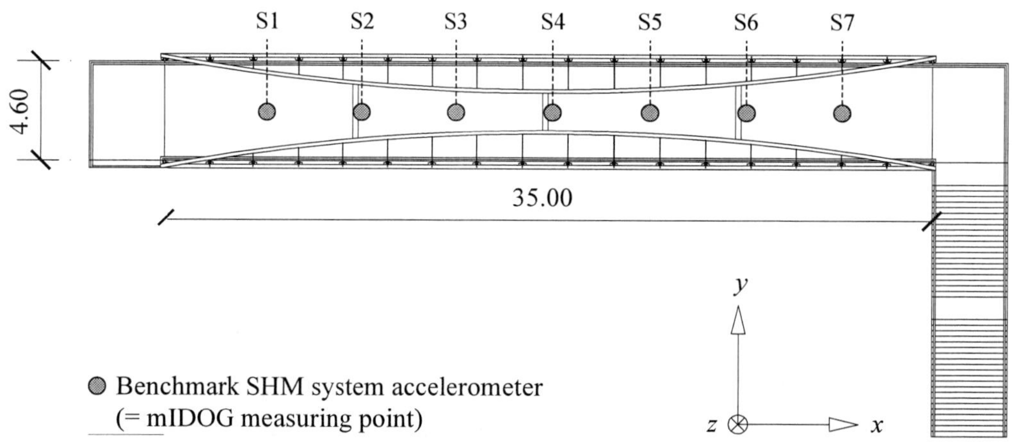

Figure 4. Benchmark SHM system installed on the pedestrian bridge and mIDOG measuring points.

At the beginning of the validation tests, the two mIDOGs are placed at one end of the bridge, serving as "deployment point". The mIDOGs are tasked to navigate the bridge deck along a black line, leveraging image data collected by the camera and identifying measuring points, which are pinpointed by markers. The initial localization is given by the starting location and direction on the line to be followed. Upon reaching the first pair of measurement points, the mIDOGs use the communication modules to establish a wireless network with the first mIDOG functioning as a server and the second mIDOG as a client. The server and the client exchange messages to confirm the status and to synchronize the internal clocks. Synchronization is achieved using traditional concepts in wireless sensor networks, i.e. through the exchange of time-stamped messages. Next, the mIDOGs switch to a measuring posture and attach the accelerometer to the surface of the deck, using the robot component. Figure 5 shows the walking posture and the measuring posture of a mIDOG. Thereupon, each mIDOG uses its sensing component to collect acceleration response data. Once both mIDOGs have completed the acquisition of acceleration response data, the server and the client exchange messages to confirm completion of data acquisition and proceed with data processing and analysis to store and analyze the acceleration response data.

For each pair of measuring points, the acceleration response data is transformed from the time domain into the frequency domain via FFT, and the peaks corresponding to vibration modes are selected. The Fourier values of the peaks (i.e. not all Fourier values) are wirelessly transmitted to a centralized server, where local mode shapes are computed offline for the pair of measurement points by applying the frequency domain decomposition method (Brincker and Zhang, 2009). If the Fourier values at the peaks would not be sent to a centralized server, one of the dogs would have to undertake this task, but it would function itself as a centralized "hub", which would entail unnecessary over-burdening of its processing unit. Then, the mIDOGs proceed to the next pair of measurement points. After having navigated all measuring points, the mIDOGs use the local mode shapes to synthesize the global mode shape with all measuring points. The pairs of measurement points are listed in Table 1. The duration of data acquisition for each pair is set equal to t = 60 s and the sampling frequency is set equal to f_s = 125 Hz.

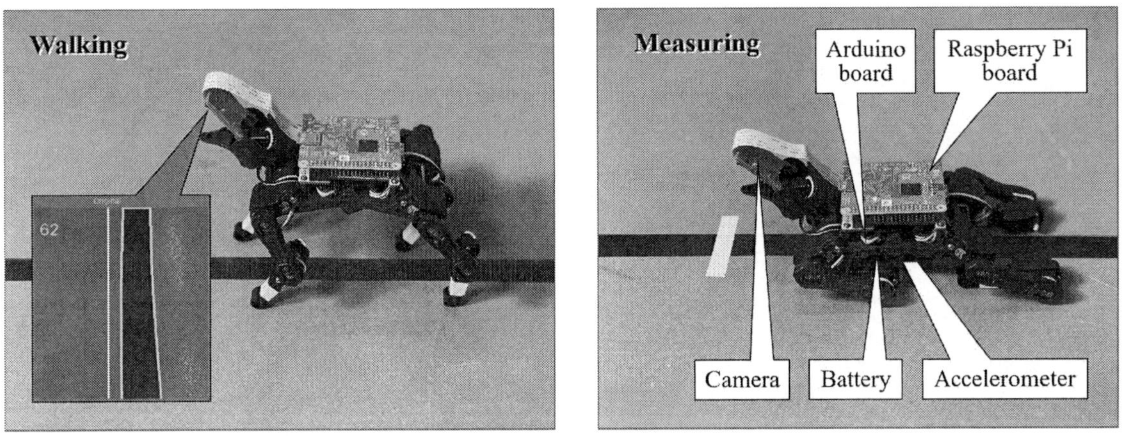

Figure 5: Field of view, walking posture, and measuring posture of a mIDOG.

Table 1: Overview of the pairs of measurement points.

Setup	mIDOG 1			mIDOG 2		
	Measurement position	f_s **(Hz)**	t **(s)**	**Measurement position**	f_s **(Hz)**	t **(s)**
1	S1	125	60	S2	125	60
2	S2	125	60	S3	125	60
3	S3	125	60	S4	125	60
4	S4	125	60	S5	125	60
5	S5	125	60	S6	125	60
7	S6	125	60	S7	125	60

Six mode shapes are synthesized from the outcomes of the mobile SHM system and are plotted in Figure 6, next to the mode shapes computed from the benchmark SHM system for comparison purposes. To quantify the similarity between the mode shapes, the modal assurance criterion (MAC) is employed, which is a well-established measure of similarity between vectors

(Allemang, 2003). Indicated by MAC values shown in Figure 7, it is evident that the majority of mode shapes extracted with the mobile SHM system and the mode shapes computed with the benchmark SHM system exhibit high similarity. The similarity serves as proof that the mobile SHM system proposed in this paper is capable of yielding information on the structural condition with accuracy comparable to a traditional cable-based SHM system. Moreover, the minimal deployment of quadruped robots has not compromised the spatial density of the SHM outcomes. Rather, the agility of the quadruped robots has enabled efficient scanning of all measuring points, thus eliminating the labor and cost of extensive installations. The results of this study clearly demonstrate that quadruped robots can be efficiently used for SHM in lieu of traditional cable-based SHM systems as well as of stationary wireless SHM systems.

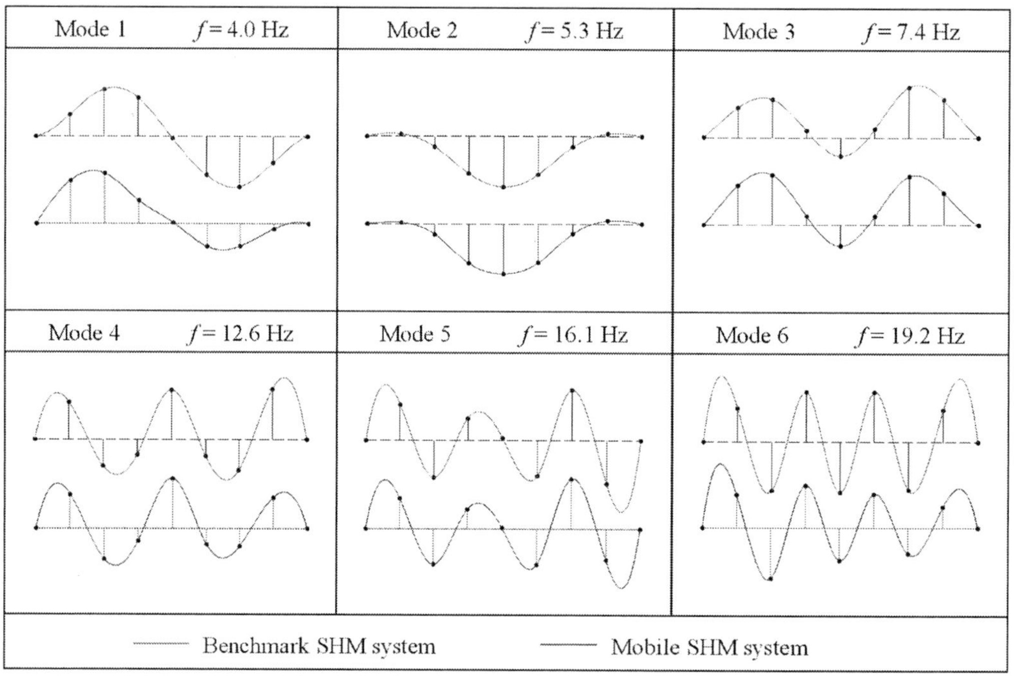

Figure 6: Mode shapes from the mobile SHM system (L) and from the benchmark SHM system (R).

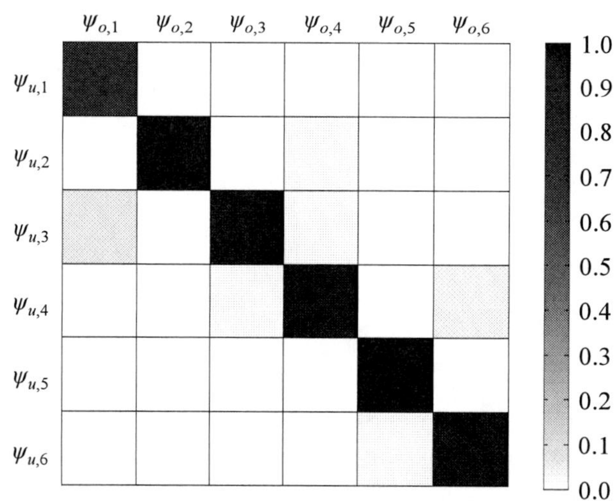

Figure 7: MAC matrix computed from the results of the validation tests.

4. Summary and conclusions

Wireless sensor networks offer promising opportunities towards enhanced flexibility and scalability, as compared to cable-based SHM systems. However, wireless sensor nodes are installed at fixed locations and, causing high installation costs, need to be employed at high density to reliably monitor large infrastructure. This study has proposed legged robots for wireless SHM of civil infrastructure, leveraging advantages regarding cost-efficiency and maneuverability. The legged robots implemented herein are equipped with sensors to collect acceleration data relevant to SHM of civil infrastructure, with cameras for navigation, and with embedded algorithms, facilitating autonomous data processing, analysis, and communication. The accuracy of the legged robots has been validated on a pedestrian bridge by comparing the outcomes of an operational modal analysis SHM strategy (conducted by the robots) with the respective outcomes achieved from a dense array of cable-based sensors (implemented as a benchmark SHM system). The results confirm that the legged robots, as compared to stationary wireless sensor nodes, require a smaller number of nodes to achieve the same information on the structural condition, entailing more cost-efficient SHM. As compared to wheeled robots, the legged robots offer better maneuverability, as critical parts of civil infrastructure may be hard to reach by wheeled robots. Future work may include further steps towards fully autonomous SHM based on robotic fleets, which requires autonomous capabilities regarding localization and communication, representing upcoming research endeavors.

Acknowledgments

The authors would like to gratefully acknowledge the support offered by the German Research Foundation (DFG) under grant SM 281/20-1. Our sincere thanks go as well to the dedicated staff of the Laboratory of Strength of Materials at Aristotle University of Thessaloniki for offering support in conducting the field validation tests. Any opinions, findings, conclusions, or recommendations expressed in this paper are those of the authors and do not necessarily reflect the views of the DFG.

References

Allemang, R.J. (2003). The modal assurance criterion – Twenty years of use and abuse. Journal of Sound and Vibration, 37(8), pp. 14-23.

Analog Devices (2010). ADXL335 Datasheet (Rev. B). Norwoord, MA, USA: Analog Devices, Inc.

Brincker, R. and Zhang, L. (2009). Frequency domain decomposition revisited. In: Proceedings of the 3rd International Operational Modal Analysis Conference, Portonovo, Italy, 04/05/2009.

Farrar, C.R. and Worden, K. (2007). An introduction to structural health monitoring. Philosophical Transactions of the Royal Society A, 365(1851), pp. 303-315.

Lynch, J.P. and Loh, K.J. (2006). A summary review of wireless sensors and sensor networks for structural health monitoring. Shock and Vibration Digest, 38(2), pp. 91-130.

OmniVision Technologies, Inc. (2009). OV5647 Datasheet: Preliminary specification. Santa Clara, CA, USA: OmniVision Technologies, Inc.

Petoi, LLC (2021). Petoi Bittle: Overview. Available at https://www.petoi.com/pages/bittle-open-source-bionic-robot-dog. Accessed on November 11, 2021.

Rania, N., Coppola, I., Martorana, F. and Migliorini, L. (2019). The collapse of the Morandi Bridge in Genoa on 14 August 2018: A collective traumatic event and its emotional impact linked to the place and loss of a symbol. Sustainability, 11(23), 6822.

Raspberry Pi Trading, Ltd (2021). Raspberry Pi Camera Algorithm and Tuning Guide, Cambridge, UK: Raspberry Pi Trading, Ltd.

Smarsly, K. and Petryna, Y. (2014). A Decentralized Approach towards Autonomous Fault Detection in Wireless Structural Health Monitoring Systems. In: Proceedings of the 7th European Workshop on Structural Health Monitoring (EWSHM) 2014. Nantes, France, 07/08/2014.

Syscom (2015). MS2002+ acceleration sensor. Sainte-Croix, Switzerland: Syscom Instruments SA.

Zachariadis, I. (2018). Investment in infrastructure in the EU. Briefing to the European Union. Available at https://www.iberglobal.com/files/2018-2/infrastructure_eu.pdf. Accessed November 29, 2021.

Zhu, D., Yi, X., Wang, Y., Lee, K.-M., and Guo, J. (2010). A mobile sensing system for structural health monitoring: Design and validation. Smart Materials and Structures, 19(5), pp. 55011-55021.

Biswal, P. and Mohanty, P.K. (2021). Development of quadruped walking robots: A review. Ain Shams Engineering Journal, 12(2), pp. 2017-2031.

Rubio, F., Valero, F. and Llopis-Albert, C. (2019). A review of mobile robots: Concepts, methods, theoretical framework, and applications. International Journal of Advanced Robotic Systems, 16(2), DOI: 10.1177/1729881419839596.

Smarsly, K., Worm, M., Dragos, K., Peralta, J., Wenner, M. and Hahn, O. (2022). Mobile structural health monitoring using quadruped robots. In: Proceedings of the SPIE Smart Structures/NDE Conference: Health Monitoring of Structural and Biological Systems. Long Beach, CA, USA, 03/06/2022.

An Efficient and Resilient Digital-twin Communication Framework for Smart Bridge Structural Survey and Maintenance

Gao Y., Li H.*, Xiong G.
Cardiff University, UK
lih@cardiff.ac.uk

Abstract. A bridge digital twin (DT) is expected to be updated in near real time during inspection and monitoring but is usually subject to massive heterogeneous data and communication constraints. This work proposes an efficient framework for a bridge DT with decreased communication complexity to achieve updates synchronously and provide feedback to the physical bridge in time. The integrated edge computing and non-cellular long-distance wireless communication enable DT resilience when cloud servers become unresponsive due to the loss of internet connection. This framework is validated by different scenarios for DTs in support of bridge inspection and monitoring. It is demonstrated that the framework can enable dynamic interaction between on-site inspection and online bridge DT during the survey as well as knowledge transfer among different sectors in time. It can also support local decision-making on a single bridge as well as regional dynamic coordination for multiple bridges without cloud-server involvement.

1. Introduction

Bridges serve a critical role in transport systems, and their failure will result in traffic disruption, economic loss, and even severe casualties. According to the ASCE report in 2021, 6154 or 7.5% of the nation's bridges are considered structurally deficient in the US, and unfortunately 178 million trips are taken across these bridges every day (ASCE, 2021). Therefore, regular inspections and effective monitoring of bridges are mandatory in many countries. A bridge digital twin (DT) is a promising tool for bridge management and predictive maintenance (PdM), which is expected to be updated in near real time as new data is collected, as well as provide feedback to the physical bridge for assessment and prediction in time (Ye *et al.*, 2019). For example, bridge DTs can release early warnings (load restriction, closure, etc.) for bridge capability based on real-time simulation, can provide dynamic responses based on monitoring and prediction with real-time data, and can enhance the efficiency of collaboration among different stakeholders. However, data transmission in real time (or near real time) has not been well addressed under situations with massive heterogeneous data and various communication constraints (low data rates, small payload size, limited duty cycle, etc.), especially for the bridges in remote areas without a stable cellular network. Moreover, the cloud-based DT services will become unavailable when the cloud server is unresponsive, e.g., the internet connection is lost. This brings in potential risks for both physical bridges and people on the site when an emergency has been predicted to take place.

This paper aims to propose an efficient and resilient framework for a bridge DT via edge computing and non-cellular long-distance wireless communication to tackle the issues stated above. In this framework, massive heterogeneous data generated from drone inspection and real-time structural health monitoring (SHM) are interpreted into the information required for relevant DT services (e.g., visualization, structural analysis, prediction) in reduced forms (e.g., semantic information, geometric coordinates, binary profiles), thus decreasing communication complexity and cloud-processing burden significantly and achieving DT updates in near real time. Then by fusing the transmitted information with multi-source data, information and knowledge (e.g., life-cycle information, inventory, traffic, weather), the DT can provide holistic feedback (e.g., early warnings, inspection advice, optimized maintenance planning) to the

https://doi.org/10.7146/aul.455.c207

physical bridge in time based on AI and big-data analysis. Hence, this framework can enable dynamic interaction between on-site inspection and online bridge DT services, information exchange across different stakeholders, as well as knowledge transfer among different sectors, e.g., the knowledge gap between local inspectors and remote structural specialists (or drone inspection suppliers and bridge maintenance contractors). In terms of resilience, this framework can support local decision-making on a single bridge based on SHM, e.g., load restriction, as well as regional dynamic coordination for multiple bridges through non-cellular long-distance wireless communication without cloud-server involvement, e.g., decentralized dynamic evacuation.

This framework is validated with different scenarios for DTs in support of bridge inspection and monitoring. It is demonstrated that the framework can enable effective updating and feedback between a physical bridge and its DT in near real time. The framework is suitable for long-distance wireless communication with low data rates (e.g., LoRa), and exhibits fault tolerance by operating autonomously at a local and regional level when the cloud server is unresponsive due to the loss of internet connection.

2. Related Work

2.1 Bridge Digital Twin

A bridge DT is defined as a virtual representation of a physical bridge, which updates in near real time as new data is collected, provides feedback to the physical bridge and performs 'what-if' scenarios for assessing asset risks and predicting asset performance (Ye *et al.*, 2019). Bridge DT models can be created by building information modelling (BIM), physics-based approach (finite element modelling), data-driven approach (statistical modelling) and data-centric engineering approach (hybrid modelling), with the key features, including digital replica (geometry and others); data composition; bidirectional connection (update and feedback) in near real time; the life-cycle span of a physical bridge; common data environment (CDE); visualization; simulation; learning from real measurement data (Ye *et al.*, 2019). Dang and Shim et al (Dang *et al.*, 2018) developed a bridge maintenance system based on digital-twin models, including 3D geometry models and structural analysis models. The structural monitoring data (strain, displacement, loading, etc.) and the environmental data (temperature, wind, etc.) during operation are collected to provide essential information for bridge condition assessment and prediction. Structure deterioration is linked to the elements of the bridge, changing the structural parameters for analysis. Then, the bridge DT can be updated with each inspection and online monitoring to support decision-making for bridge maintenance. Dang et al. (Dang, Tatipamula and Nguyen, 2021) proposed a cloud-based DT framework (cDTSHM) for real-time SHM and proactive maintenance of bridges, which was demonstrated via both model and real bridges using deep learning for damage detection with high accuracy, but it requires advanced communication such as 5G, which brings in high service costs (infrastructure building, data charges, etc.) and is not suitable for bridges in remote areas without stable cellular networks. Meanwhile, when cloud servers are unresponsive, e.g., the internet connection breaks down, the cloud-based DT services such as early warnings will become unavailable. Moreover, from the practitioners' view in the UK, a major gap between academic research and industrial practice towards applications of the digital twin supporting bridge O&M is the difficulty to keep the bridge DT updated in routine practice (Ye *et al.*, 2021).

2.2 IoT Wireless Communication

Although wired networks are generally faster than wireless, the latter enables monitoring of remote bridges which used to be inaccessible by cables. The capability of different IoT wireless communication technologies is indicated in Figure 1 (Mekki *et al.*, 2019; Foubert and Mitton, 2020). Short-range wireless communication (e.g., WIFI, Zigbee) is suitable for data acquisition on site. Commercial cellular networks work at a medium range with higher service costs such as data charges. Meanwhile, with the rise of frequency bands, bandwidth and data rates increase, while ratio wavelength and coverage range decrease, i.e., distance 3G > 4G > 5G. For long-range wireless communication, NB-IoT and LTE-M rely on existing cellular networks, while the others are non-cellular networks working on unlicensed ISM bands, which are suitable for remote areas where cellular communication is not available. However, long-range wireless communication technologies usually have limited data rates, e.g., NB-IoT (up to 158.5kbps), LoRa (sub-GHz, up to 50kbps), as well as limited payload size and a constrained duty cycle, e.g., LoRa has up to 250-byte payload size and 1% duty cycle. This results in the difficulty to update the bridge DT synchronously with massive heterogeneous data through long-range wireless communication.

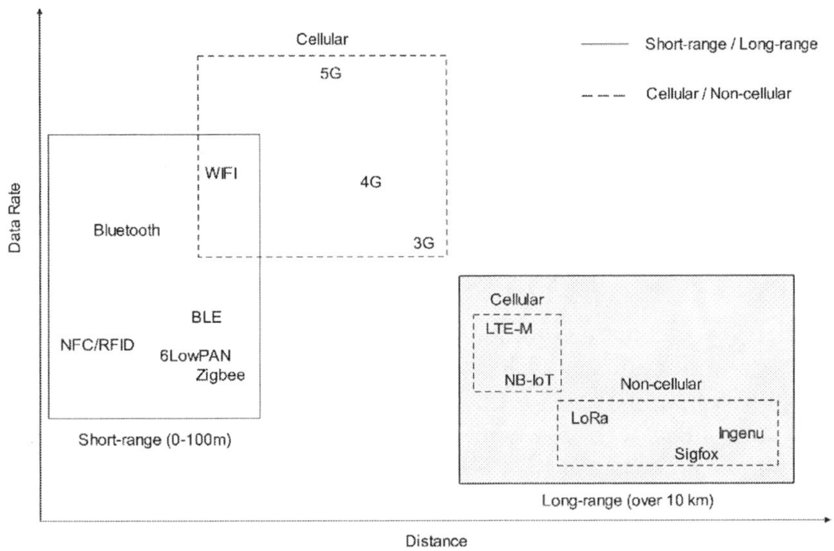

Figure 1: Capability of IoT wireless communication technologies (data rate vs distance).

2.3 Bridge Inspection and Monitoring

Drones are taken as a game-changer in bridge inspection, which can get less limited access as well as better angles to the areas difficult or dangerous for people to reach. Drone inspection for bridges is taken by payloads with fast data collection, e.g., thousands of points per hour for photogrammetry, and millions of points per hour for Lidar. Many approaches have been developed for drone inspection to detect surface deficiency automatically (e.g., cracking). Xu et al. proposed an end-to-end crack detection model for bridges based on a convolutional neural network (CNN), achieving a detection accuracy of 96.37% without pre-training (Xu *et al.*, 2019); Dorafshan et al. proposed an automatic crack identification and segmentation on a concrete surface with Otsu's thresholding and morphological operations (Dorafshan and Qi, 2016). Furthermore, Kim et al. developed a system for crack identification and measurement, equipped with a pre-calibrated camera and an ultrasonic distance sensor to obtain crack images and the distance from the camera to the target surface, achieving successful measurement for the cracks (thicker than 0.1mm) with the maximum length estimation error of 7.3% (Kim *et al.*,

2017). Moreover, drones can be located with geo-coordinates (latitude, longitude and height) through differential positioning at centimetre-level accuracy (Bisnath, 2020), e.g., real-time kinematic (RTK), post-processing kinematic (PPK).

Bridge SHM uses a sensor network attached to the bridge to acquire measurements in real time, including structural response (acceleration, strain, displacement, inclination, etc.) and ambient parameters (loading, temperature, wind, flood, etc.), and then employ data-driven approaches to assess bridge structural integrity, e.g., damage detection, remaining-useful-life prediction. The approaches can be indicator-based (e.g., natural frequencies, mode shapes) or direct use of data in the time and/or frequency domain. Kim et al. proposed a damage indicator with the vehicle-induced vibration from a set of multivariate autoregressive models in the case study of the ADA bridge with different artificial damages (Kim *et al.*, 2021). Neves et al. employed an artificial neural network (ANN) with the train-induced acceleration data to identify the structure health conditions of the KW51 railway bridge (Neves, González and Karoumi, 2021). Sajedi and Liang proposed a framework for structural damage diagnosis based on a fully convolutional encoder-decoder architecture using the vibration signals from a grid sensor network, which can localize damages and distinguish multiple damage mechanisms with reliable generalization capacities (Sajedi and Liang, 2020).

3. Methodology

Drone inspection and real-time SHM have been accepted as effective approaches to indicate structural defects before maintenance. Current drone inspection for bridges is usually project-based and updated asynchronously, which heavily depends on the expertise of inspectors in situ. Meanwhile, the huge amount of data from real-time SHM is also arduous for transmission, especially when wireless networks are required. Although pre-processing (e.g., downsampling, feature extraction) can decrease communication complexity to a degree, it will result in a loss of high-frequency information, and local services will become unavailable when the cloud server is unresponsive. Moreover, it is difficult to employ the approaches with direct use of data on the cloud, e.g., deep learning, which requires massive data transferred to the cloud. Advanced communication such as 5G/6G is supposed to solve these problems, but it also brings in high infrastructure investment and service costs. Therefore, as communication time is calculated with equation 1, instead of increasing transmission capability, if the massive heterogeneous data can be interpreted into critical information in reduced forms via edge computing, it can decrease communication complexity and cloud-processing burden significantly. The derived transmittable information depends on domain knowledge and DT services, e.g., damage mechanism, location and extent for structural assessment and prediction. Many technologies can play a significant role in this procedure, e.g., machine learning, knowledge representation, computer vision and SLAM (simultaneous localization and mapping). Meanwhile, the information in transmission should be as precise as possible, such as the damage profile, which means the loss before and during transmission should be minimized, e.g., the compression loss. Then the derived information can be updated in the bridge DT in near real time, and fused with multi-source data and information, e.g., life-cycle information, inventory, traffic, as well as domain-specialist knowledge, such as maintenance knowledge from similar bridges, to provide holistic feedback to the physical bridge in time.

$$Communication\ Time = Complexity/Bandwidth + Latency \quad (1)$$

This strategy becomes available with the development of edge devices, e.g., MCU (microcontroller unit), SBC (single-board computer), FPGA (field-programmable gate array), as well as AI and deep learning development at the edge, such as edge AI and tinyML. The edge-based processing in the strategy does not only generate the required transmittable information with low complexity but also supports decision-making locally and triggers autonomous responses on the bridge site via the control system such as actuators. The bidirectional data flow is shown in Figure 2. Furthermore, with non-cellular long-distance wireless communication such as LoRa, the strategy can enable regional dynamic coordination for multiple bridges (as well as other infrastructures such as tunnels) without cloud-server involvement via data transmission between adjacent edge devices such as sensor nodes and gateways. This is suitable for decentralized dynamic evacuation.

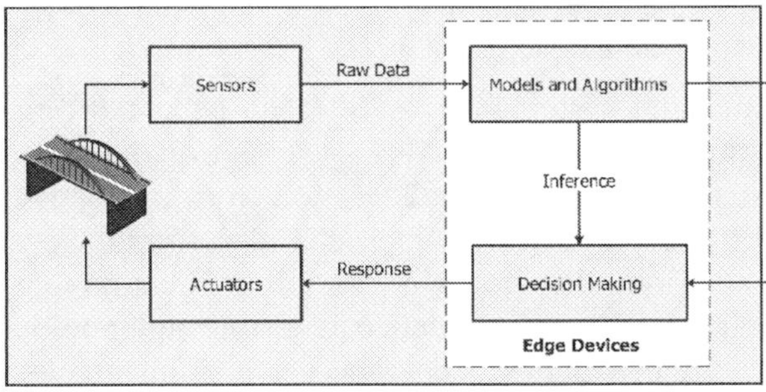

Figure 2: Proposed strategy and data flow for a bridge DT.

4. Framework Development

The framework is developed for a bridge DT in support of both drone-enabled inspection and real-time SHM. It aims to use the derived information with low communication complexity from edge computing to overcome communication constraints in bandwidth, achieving synchronous updates in the bridge DT, as well as provide feedback to the physical bridge based on DT services in near real time. In the drone inspection, defect detection, localization and quantification can be taken on board or a control station and then transmitted in reduced forms to gateways via long-distance communication. The detection of defects (e.g., cracking) can be carried out by object detection such as YOLO. Defect quantification including dimensions, areas, etc., can be taken based on semantic segmentation by image processing or deep learning (e.g., DeepLab). An approach based on PPK is developed to provide defect localization in the bridge coordinate system, as indicated in Figure 3 and equation 2. The coordinates can be further linked to bridge elements based on geometric information. The crack direction (such as latitudinal or longitudinal) can be determined by drone position and camera angle. Given situations without stable GNSS signals, e.g., underneath a bridge, SLAM based on IMUs (inertial measurement units), and cameras (or laser scanners) can help to improve accuracy.

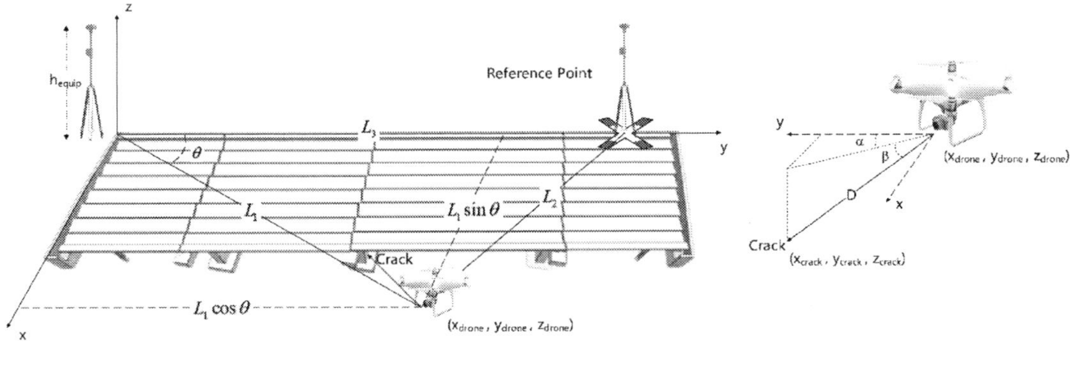

Figure 3: Defect localisation in the bridge coordinate system.

$$
\begin{aligned}
L_1 &= R\sqrt{(\phi_2-\phi_1)^2+(\lambda_2-\lambda_1)^2} \\
x_{crack} &= L_1 \sin\theta - D\cos\beta\cos\alpha \\
y_{crack} &= L_1 \cos\theta - D\cos\beta\sin\alpha \\
z_{crack} &= H_{drone} - H_{base} + h_{equip} - D\sin\beta
\end{aligned} \tag{2}
$$

Note: φ_1, φ_2 – base and drone latitude; λ_1, λ_2 – base and drone longitude; R is earth's radius; H_{drone} – drone height; H_{base} – top receiver height; h_{equip} – equipment height.

In the real-time SHM, data collection to embedded systems on the site can be wired (e.g., fieldbus) or wireless (e.g., WIFI). Data transmission from embedded systems to gateways is based on a long-distance wireless network such as NB-IoT or LoRa. The algorithms and AI models are deployed on embedded systems in the framework, which can also support local decision-making. In addition, there is non-cellular long-distance wireless communication (e.g., LoRa) between adjacent gateways (or embedded systems), which can enable autonomous coordination for multiple bridges. This non-cellular network is designed as a supplementary approach to cloud-based communication, starting to work when the cloud server becomes unavailable, e.g., the internet connection is lost. Then the interpreted information required for DT services from both scenarios with low complexity can be transmitted via the internet to the cloud server (MQTT broker) and published to the DT applications (MQTT client) through the MQTT protocol, while the feedback based on DT services can be published to the broker and transmitted to the physical bridge and local inspectors in time, as shown in Figure 4.

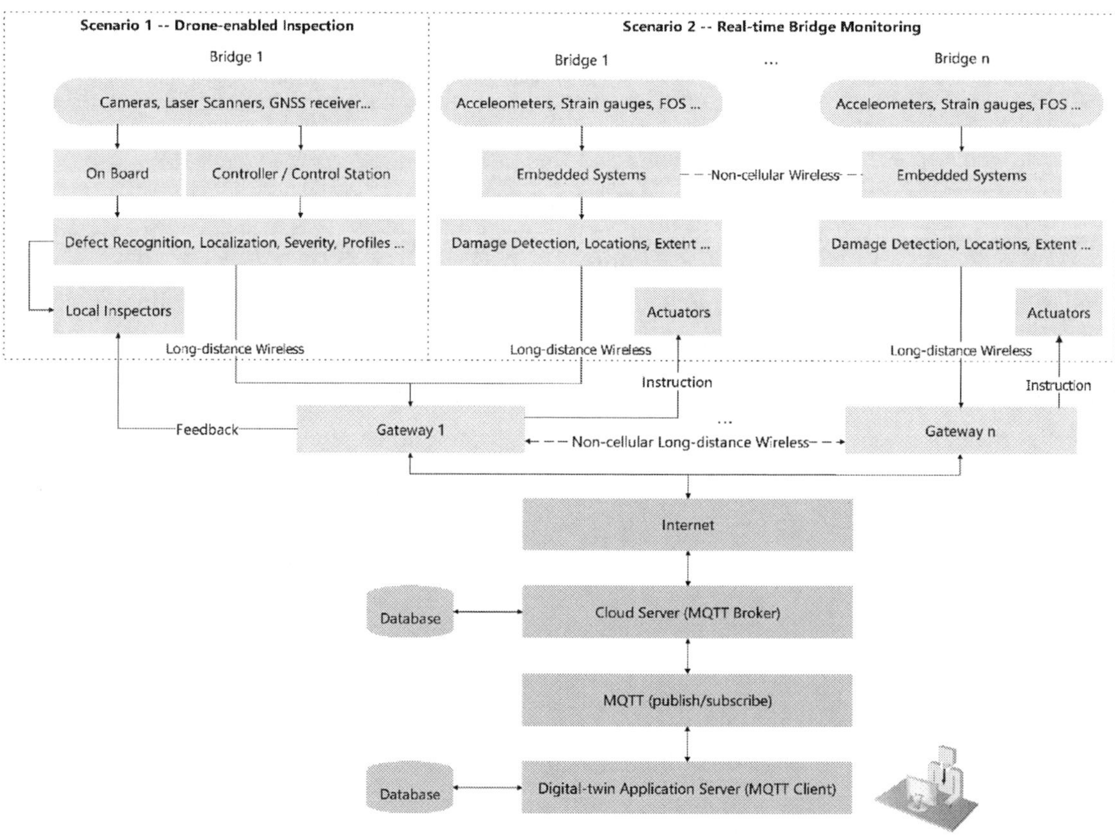

Figure 4: Proposed data transmission framework for a bridge DT.

5. Framework Validation

Three scenarios for DTs in support of bridge inspection and monitoring are adopted for framework validation: 1) drone-enabled crack inspection; 2) vibration-based damage detection; 3) decentralized dynamic evacuation. A LoRa module (embedded in Arduino MKR WAN 1310) is used for data transmitting (TX) and receiving (RX). The Things Network (TTN) is used as the LoRaWAN network server and MQTT broker. The MQTT clients are created with Eclipse Paho to publish/subscribe messages.

5.1 Scenario 1 – Drone-enabled Crack Inspection

During drone inspection, the images of potential deficiency areas of a bridge are taken by the onboard camera. Here, the images are from the dataset created for automatic bridge crack detection (Xu *et al.*, 2019). A laptop is taken as the control station. Firstly, the crack image is identified with a pre-trained CNN model with an accuracy of 96.05%. Then crack images are segmented with Otsu's thresholding and morphological operations. Moreover, the dimensions (width and length) can be obtained with the spanned pixel number and pixel length (predetermined before the inspection by distances from the camera to a target surface). The crack location and direction can be determined by drone position, camera angle, and the distance from the camera to the surface with the developed approach (as indicated in Figure 3 and equation 2). The crack coordinates can be linked to the bridge element based on geometric information. Moreover, the extracted binary profile is suitable for lossless compression (e.g., PNG) with the run-length encoding (RLE) to minimize image bytes, as shown in Figure 5. Compared to previous image transmission through LoRa (Pham, 2018), this method has less communication complexity with a lossless profile for cracking.

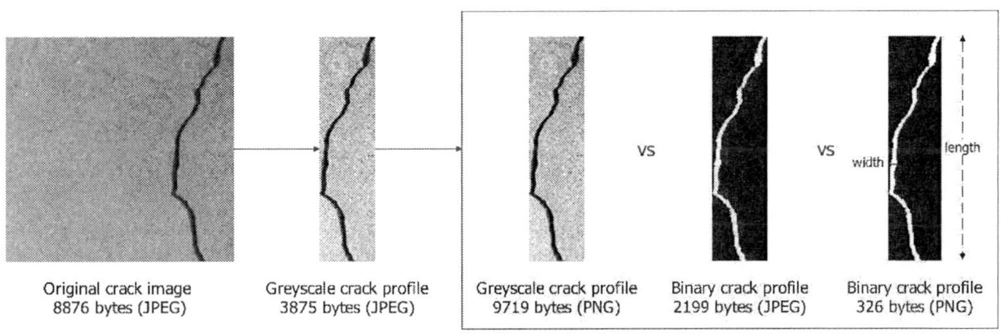

Figure 5: Crack profile segmentation and compression.

The derived defect information can be transmitted through LoRa and MQTT to a web-based bridge DT application. Then the DT can provide feedback based on domain knowledge to local inspectors in time, e.g., more in-depth inspection or even closure, as shown in Figure 6.

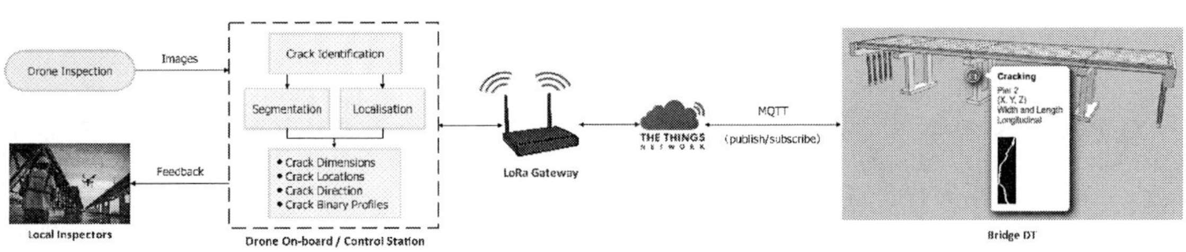

Figure 6: Bridge DT in support of drone inspection with the proposed framework.

5.2 Scenario 2 – Vibration-based Bridge Monitoring

The real-time vibration signals are collected in an embedded system on the bridge. Here, the acceleration data is from a VBM project of the KM51 bridge (Maes and Lombaert, 2021) generated by 6 uniaxial accelerometers before and after maintenance (damaged and healthy conditions respectively). Raspberry Pi 4 (Model B, 8G RAM) is taken as the SBC of the embedded system. The SVM models with statistical features (root mean square, shape factor, kurtosis, skewness, peak, impulse factor, crest factor, clearance factor) and wavelet-packet energy (at level-3 decomposition with sym4 wavelet) respectively are trained on the SBC for pattern recognition, achieving the accuracy of 91.45% and 96.58%. A 1D-CNN with input data (50176×6) from 6 accelerometers is trained on the Google Codelabs with the accuracy of 95.73% and deployed on the SBC. Therefore, both SVM with feature extraction and CNN with direct use of data can make the inference for damage detection based on the embedded system, thus supporting decision-making (such as load restriction) on the bridge site without cloud-server intervention. Then the derived structural health information (e.g., healthy or damaged) is transmitted to a web-based bridge DT application through LoRa and MQTT in near real time (as shown in Figure 7). Moreover, with a grid sensor network and specific algorithms for semantic damage segmentation (Sajedi and Liang, 2020), the derived information including damage mechanisms, locations, extent, etc., can also be transferred to the bridge DT in the same way. Finally, the feedback based on DT services (e.g., structural assessment and prediction) can be provided to the physical bridge reversely in near real time.

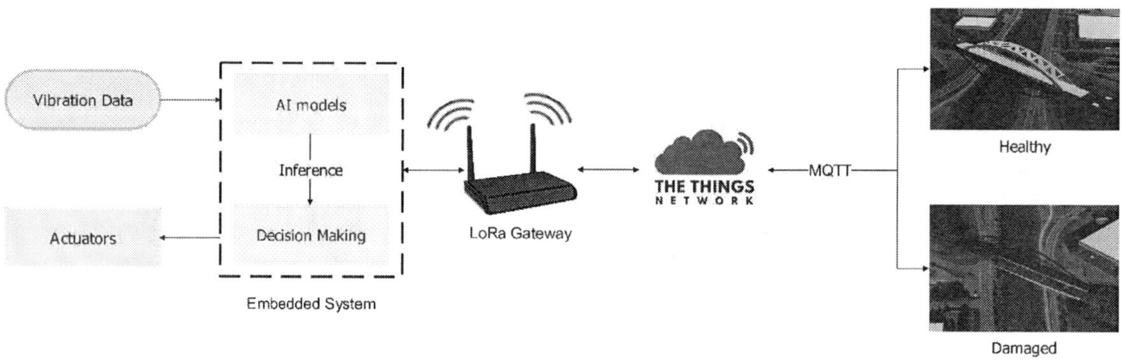

Figure 7: Bridge DT in support of VBM through the proposed framework.

5.3 Scenario 3 – Decentralized Dynamic Evacuation

When the cloud server becomes unresponsive, e.g., the internet connection is lost, the framework will start autonomous coordination for multiple bridges based on a non-cellular long-distance network in response to emergencies, e.g., dynamic evacuation. Here in assumption, an area with 6 bridges is under the threat of flooding and the internet connection is lost. The LoRa sensor node for flood monitoring on each bridge is supposed to be Class B or C and activated by its adjacent LoRa gateway, which is built on a Raspberry Pi. Both gateways have multiple channels, allowing sufficient opportunities to uplink and downlink messages, and can also transmit data between each other through LoRa. The communication topology (left) and bridge network (right) are shown in Figure 8. The dash lines represent the LoRa network; the stars represent the gateways; the squares stand for the bridges; the full lines and the weights are for roads and distances between bridges. People need to transfer from the flooding area (left side of the dashed line) to the safety area (right side).

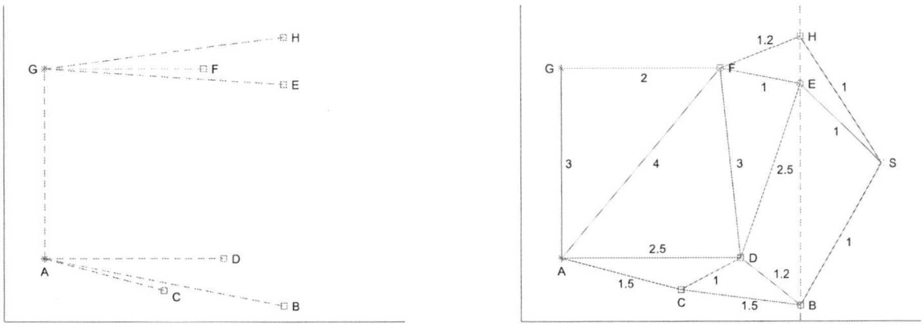

Figure 7: Communication topology (left) and bridge network (right) diagrams for simulation

An open-source LoRa emulator (Al Homssi *et al.*, 2021) is adopted here simulating TX and RX. To simplify the simulation, there are only two bridge conditions (Y – open, N – closed). The evacuation route is only updated as a gateway receives a message that a bridge becomes unavailable (closed), and the affected weights become infinitely great. Therefore, when a bridge is closed, the evacuation routes will be updated via edge computing on the gateways using the Floyd algorithm without cloud-server involvement, and then the results (as shown in Table 1) are downlinked to each node through LoRa.

Table 1: Evacuation routes updated for each node

Nodes	**Status / Shrotest Route and Distance**	**Status / Shrotest Route and Distance**
A	Initial / A C B S and 4	BN and EN / A F H S and 6.2
B	Initial / B S and 1	BN and EN / B D F H S and 6.4
C	Initial / C B S and 2.5	BN and EN / C D F H S and 6.2
D	Initial / D B S and 2.2	BN and EN / D F H S and 5.2
E	Initial / E S and 1	BN and EN / E F H S and 3.2
F	Initial / F E S and 2	BN and EN / F H S and 2.2
G	Initial / G F E S and 4	BN and EN / G F H S and 4.2
H	Initial / H S and 1	BN and EN / H S and 1

6. Discussion and Conclusion

This work proposed an efficient and resilient digital-twin communication framework to support smart bridge survey and maintenance. Thanks to decreased communication complexity, the framework can update the bridge DT synchronously during drone inspection and real-time SHM, as well as provide feedback based on DT services to the physical bridge in time. It enables dynamic interaction between on-site inspection and online bridge DT, as well as knowledge transfer among different sectors during the survey. The framework can support decision-making locally for a single bridge as well as dynamic coordination for multiple bridges via a non-cellular long-distance wireless network without cloud-server involvement. It has the potential for automated drone-enabled bridge inspection in remote areas, which can be taken as an alternative to in-person regular inspection. Furthermore, ultra-low-power MCUs (e.g., Arduinos, STM32 microcontrollers) with limited memory and optimised algorithms for tinyML are expected to be applied in this framework to provide bridge DTs with long-term performance based on batteries under the situation without cable-based power supply.

Acknowledgement

This research is funded by the Cardiff University – China Scholarship Council joint programme.

Reference

ASCE (2021) Structurally Deficient Bridges | Bridge Infrastructure | ASCE's 2021 Infrastructure Report Card. Available at: https://infrastructurereportcard.org/cat-item/bridges/.

Bisnath, S. (2020) Relative Positioning and Real-Time Kinematic (RTK), Position, Navigation, and Timing Technologies in the 21st Century, 1, pp. 481–502. doi:10.1002/9781119458449.ch19.

Dang, H.V., Tatipamula, M. and Nguyen, H.X. (2021) Cloud-based Digital Twinning for Structural Health Monitoring Using Deep Learning, IEEE Transactions on Industrial Informatics, 18(6), pp. 3820–3830. doi:10.1109/TII.2021.3115119.

Dang, N., Kang, H., Lon, S. and Shim, C. (2018) 3D digital twin models for bridge maintenance, in Proceedings of 10th International Conference on Short and Medium Span Bridges, Quebec city, Quebec, Canada.

Dorafshan, S. and Qi, X. (2016) Automatic Surface Crack Detection in Concrete Structures Using OTSU Thresholding and Morphological Operations, (August). doi:10.13140/RG.2.2.34024.47363.

Foubert, B. and Mitton, N. (2020) Long-range wireless radio technologies: A survey, Future Internet, 12(1). doi:10.3390/fi12010013.

Al Homssi, B., Dakic, K., Maselli, S., Wolf, H., Kandeepan, S. and Al-Hourani, A. (2021) IoT Network Design Using Open-Source LoRa Coverage Emulator, IEEE Access, 9, pp. 53636–53646. doi:10.1109/ACCESS.2021.3070976.

Kim, C.-W., Zhang, F.-L., Chang, K.-C., McGetrick, P.J. and Goi, Y. (2021) Ambient and Vehicle-Induced Vibration Data of a Steel Truss Bridge Subject to Artificial Damage, Journal of Bridge Engineering, 26(7), pp. 1–9. doi:10.1061/(asce)be.1943-5592.0001730.

Kim, H., Lee, J., Ahn, E., Cho, S., Shin, M. and Sim, S.H. (2017) Concrete crack identification using a UAV incorporating hybrid image processing, Sensors (Switzerland), 17(9), pp. 1–14. doi:10.3390/s17092052.

Maes, K. and Lombaert, G. (2021) Monitoring Railway Bridge KW51 Before, During, and After Retrofitting, Journal of Bridge Engineering, 26(3), p. 04721001. doi:10.1061/(asce)be.1943-5592.0001668.

Mekki, K., Bajic, E., Chaxel, F. and Meyer, F. (2019) A comparative study of LPWAN technologies for large-scale IoT deployment, ICT Express, 5(1), pp. 1–7. doi:10.1016/j.icte.2017.12.005.

Neves, A.C., González, I. and Karoumi, R. (2021) A combined model-free Artificial Neural Network-based method with clustering for novelty detection: The case study of the KW51 railway bridge, in IABSE Conference, Seoul 2020: Risk Intelligence of Infrastructures - Report, pp. 181–188. doi:10.2749/seoul.2020.181.

Pham, C. (2018) Robust CSMA for long-range LoRa transmissions with image sensing devices, IFIP Wireless Days, 2018-April, pp. 116–122. doi:10.1109/WD.2018.8361706.

Sajedi, S.O. and Liang, X. (2020) Vibration-based semantic damage segmentation for large-scale structural health monitoring, Computer-Aided Civil and Infrastructure Engineering, 35(6), pp. 579–596. doi:10.1111/mice.12523.

Xu, H., Su, X., Wang, Y., Cai, H., Cui, K. and Chen, X. (2019) Automatic bridge crack detection using a convolutional neural network, Applied Sciences (Switzerland), 9(14). doi:10.3390/app9142867.

Ye, C., Butler, L., Calka, B., Iangurazov, M., Lu, Q., Gregory, A., Girolami, M. and Middleton, C.

(2019) A digital twin of bridges for structural health monitoring, in Structural Health Monitoring 2019: Enabling Intelligent Life-Cycle Health Management for Industry Internet of Things (IIOT) - Proceedings of the 12th International Workshop on Structural Health Monitoring, pp. 1619–1626. doi:10.12783/shm2019/32287.

Ye, C., Kuok, S.C., Butler, L.J. and Middleton, C.R. (2021) Implementing bridge model updating for operation and maintenance purposes: examination based on UK practitioners' views, Structure and Infrastructure Engineering, 0(0), pp. 1–20. doi:10.1080/15732479.2021.1914115.

Optimizing IFC-structured Data Graph for Code Compliance Checking

Schatz Y., Domer B.
University of Applied Sciences and Arts Western Switzerland, Switzerland
yohann.schatz@hesge.ch

Abstract. Construction code compliance checking requires applying specific computer-interpretable rules on datasets. A proposed solution is to represent IFC data as an RDF graph and perform rule-checking using a rule engine. However, the generated graph has a complicated structure since it follows the IFC data model. Consequently, the definition of compliance rules can be challenging, and rules are sensitive to variations of input graphs structure. A methodology is proposed to optimize graphs by giving them a predefined or "standardized" structure. A case study shows that optimization allows the formulation of more straightforward and easier-to-write compliance rules, applicable to all standardized graphs regardless of the initially used BIM authoring tool. In addition, graph size is significantly reduced.

1. Introduction

Automated rule checking is the process by which software evaluates objects and properties of a digital model against predefined rules (Eastman et al., 2009). In the context of automated code compliance checking, formal computer-interpretable rules are used to validate that the design meets the requirements of a construction standard (e.g., verify if a curved road segment has a sufficient radius considering vehicle speed).

Such a process replaces the long and error-prone manual plan review (Eastman et al., 2009) and optimizes projects in terms of construction time, quality and cost. The task can be handled by a BIM authoring tool or dedicated software (Eastman et al., 2009).

Existing rule-based programs, such as Solibri Model Checker (Solibri, 2021), allow validating models from various sources when data is communicated via an interoperable format. In the AEC domain, the neutral model representation is conveyed by the Industry Foundation Classes (IFC) (buildingSMART, 2021).

The downside of most commercial tools is that they hide checking routines from the user (Burggräf et al., 2021). In addition, the development of custom rules may be limited (Beach et al., 2015; Preidel and Borrmann, 2015). Since code compliance checking requires the system to support multiple different and highly specific rulesets, more flexible solutions are needed.

A promising approach (Pauwels et al., 2011) is based on semantic web technologies. First, IFC data is transformed into a knowledge graph. Second, rulesets are applied to it. In such a data model, also called "RDF graph" (Resource Description Framework) (W3C, 2014), IFC entities, as well as their properties and relationships (i.e., the business data) are expressed as statements called "triples".

IFC-to-RDF (Pauwels, 2017) generates an RDF graph from an IFC-STEP Physical File (SPF). As the service maps every entity to an IfcOWL class and every attribute to an IfcOWL property (Pauwels and Van Deursen, 2012), the RDF graph follows the main structure of IFC (Pauwels and Roxin, 2016).

However, IFC exports are heterogeneous, depending on the software used (Belsky et al., 2016). As a consequence, no unique graph structure for a given model exists. This requires providing software-specific compliance rulesets.

https://doi.org/10.7146/aul.455.c208

In addition, output graphs carry information that is not needed for code compliance checking. This applies particularly to some *IfcResource* elements and instances of *IfcPropertyDefinition* and *IfcRelationship* that do not provide any semantic richness and even complicate access to other relevant data (e.g., a single typed value). Inversely, the limitations of IFC exporters may cause a loss of information required for checking, since they do not integrate program-specific object properties.

Graph optimization, i.e., cleaning (removing unnecessary data) and simplifying its structure to transfer it into a targeted shape (standardized graph), will lead to an easier compliance rule formulation, a better handling of differences in IFC exports, and finally, a maintainable code checking system.

Solutions for graph simplification, such as selective information removal (Fahad et al., 2018; Pauwels and Roxin, 2016) and the addition of straightforward constructs between data (Beach et al., 2015; Bouzidi et al., 2012; de Farias et al., 2015; Pauwels et al., 2017, 2011; Zhang et al., 2018) have been proposed.

This paper aims to develop and complete these principles and integrate them into a coherent workflow, in the context of code compliance checking of IFC models based on a graph representation of data.

2. Methodology

The methodology (Figure 1) has been developed in the context of code compliance checking applied to road infrastructure projects. It combines a set of linked processes, identified by a color code:

- : construction code analysis, leading to a structured representation of construction and regulation vocabularies (ontology).
- : data graph analysis, where information to be added or removed is identified.
- : definition of rulesets to optimize/standardize the data graph.
- : definition of rulesets to check data compliance with construction codes.

Applying the methodology involves four distinct competencies, represented in Figure 1:

1. BIM modeling and data flow management: create the model, configure the IFC export to correspond to information requirements, initiate the IFC-STEP file conversion to RDF graph, run the graph optimization process (based on optimization rules) and launch the rule-checking process (based on compliance rules).
2. Domain knowledge: expertise in construction codes, design and execution of construction. Ability to build a structured representation of domain-specific concepts and formulate compliance rules in natural language.
3. Data science: proficiency in knowledge graph processing using semantic web technologies and automated reasoning systems.
4. IFC: strong knowledge of the IFC schema (including the latest IFC 4.3 version) and related MVDs.

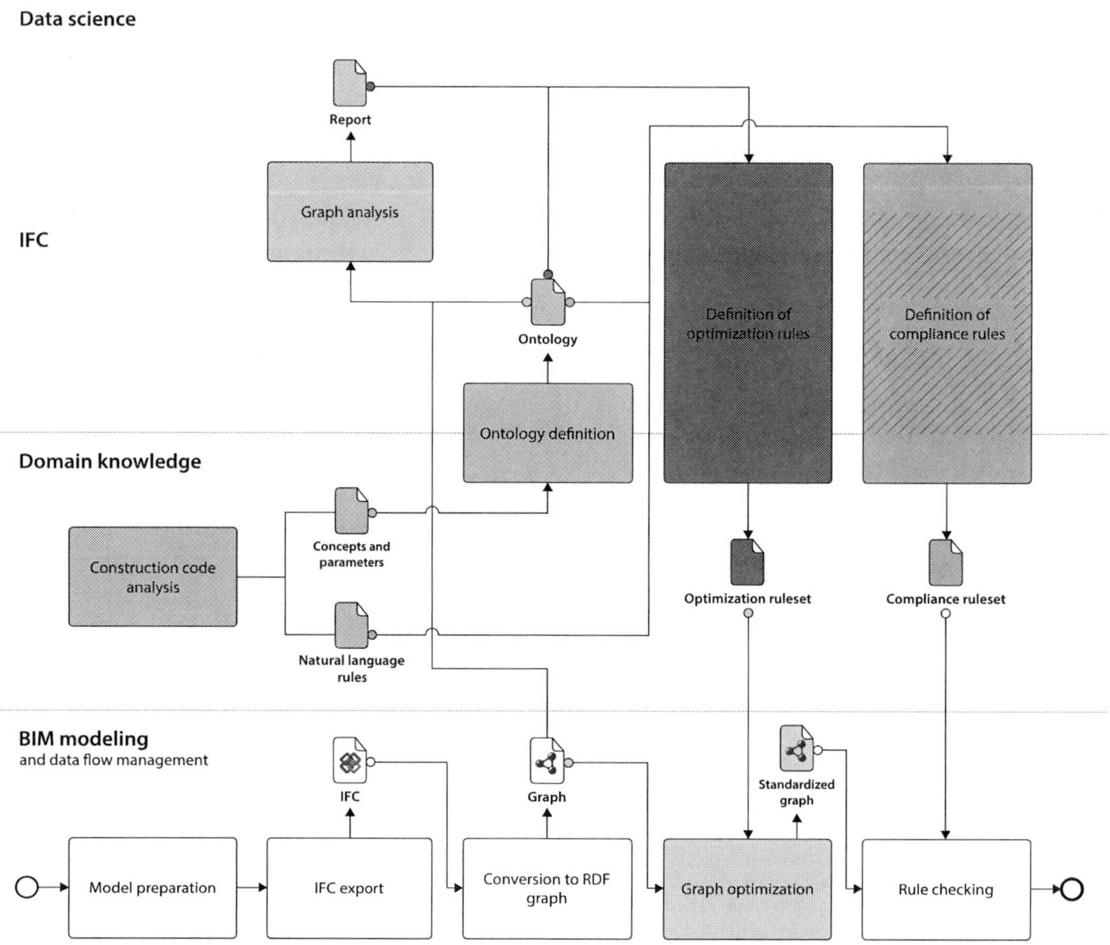

Figure 1: Methodology for optimizing IFC-RDF graphs.

Combining the above-mentioned competencies allows to optimize the graph generated from the initial BIM model. This results in a standardized graph specifically designed for compliance rule checking (represented in pink in Figure 1).

2.1 Blue - Ontology definition

An ontology is a representation of concepts from a given domain, linked by relationships (Martin et al., 2021). Construction code analysis aims to define a single ontology combining domain and regulation concepts. An excerpt of such an ontology for road infrastructure projects is shown in Figure 2.

Classes correspond to physical and virtual components of the building or infrastructure to be modeled (e.g., road, road segment, carriageway, island, etc.). Data literals correspond to single typed values (e.g., a string, an integer, a boolean, etc.). Object properties relate to object-to-object relationships, while datatype properties assign data values to objects (W3C, 2012).

In this context, datatype properties relate to parameters with values constrained by construction codes.

For example, in the sentence "If the road is of type "A", then the design speed is 100 km/h.", *road type* and *design speed* are implicit parameters related to a *road* concept.

All parameters concerned by code compliance checking are added to the ontology as datatype properties, and the associated concepts are integrated as classes (Figure 2).

Classes and properties are labeled with an IRI (Internationalized Resource Identifier), which is a unique sequence of characters. An IRI comprises a namespace prefix (e.g., "*ont*") and the resource name, separated by a colon.

It is assumed that:

- A class IRI has the form *ont:ClassName.*
- An object property IRI has the form *ont:objectPropertyName.*
- A datatype property IRI has the form *ont:datatypePropertyName.*

As the ontology describes the desired structure of data after the optimization process, it is strongly recommended to ensure that information present in IFC data can be mapped to defined domain classes and properties. Ideally, defining the ontology is a joint effort of domain and IFC experts (Figure 1).

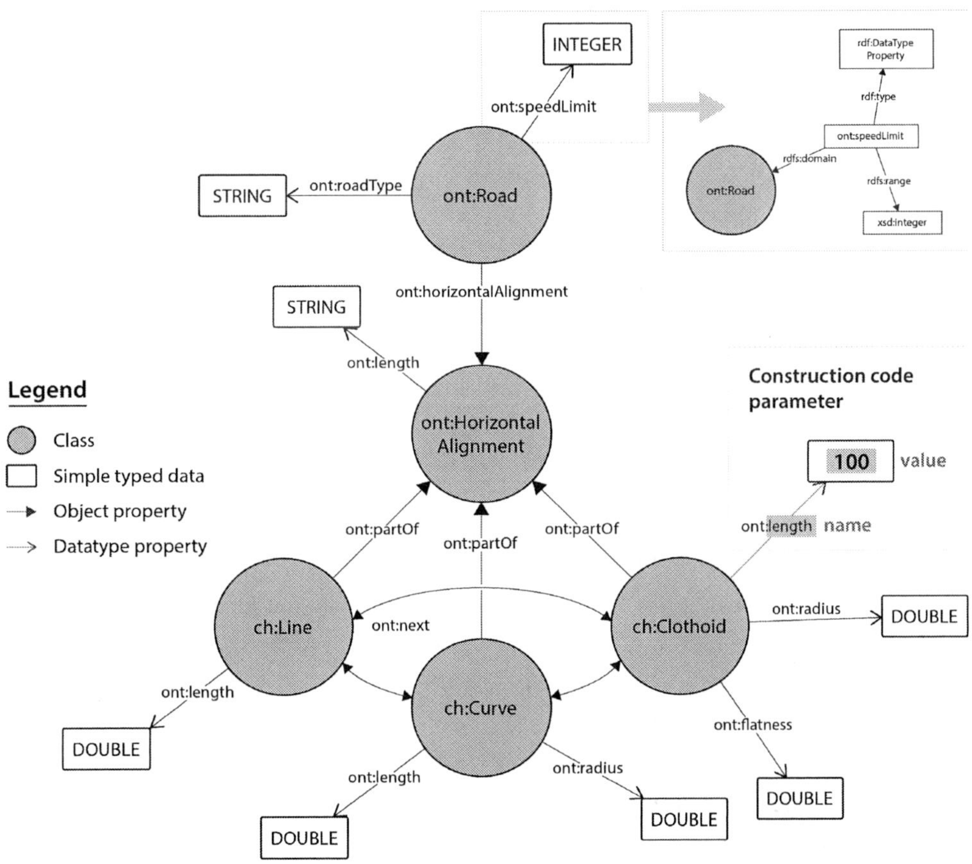

Figure 2: Excerpt of an ontology for road design.

2.2 Orange - Graph analysis, identification of relevant and missing data

The RDF graph is generated from the IFC-SPF file (using IFC-to-RDF). Then, its structure and content are analyzed.

The analysis aims to answer the following questions:

- Which instances (nodes) and relationships (edges), often leading to cumbersome constructs, should be removed from the graph to keep only what is needed for code compliance checking? In other words, what information is outside the scope of the ontology?
- Conversely, which required information is missing and should be provided by other means (e.g., deduced from data)?
- Which constructs should be added so that the graph has the desired structure?
- Finally, which approach to be employed?

Pauwels and Zhang (Pauwels and Zhang, 2015) presented SPARQL query engines and rule engines with dedicated rule languages as solutions for code compliance checking. These technologies are also suitable for graph optimization.

SPARQL (W3C, 2013) is a protocol and a language to query RDF data. SPARQL queries can have different purposes: retrieving information, adding/removing statements, or constructing a new graph. It supports conjunction, disjunction, negation, and aggregation through dedicated functions.

A rule engine (or inference engine) is a tool that produces new information from facts (in this case, all triple statements) and rules (conditional instructions). There are many different rule engines and rule languages (Rattanasawad et al., 2013), which can be selected according to:

- The inference method of the rule engine (iterative, forward chaining, backward chaining, hybrid, etc.).
- The expressiveness, extensibility, and functionality of the rule language.
- The flexibility and openness of the related framework/environment.

2.3 Red - Optimization ruleset definition

Standardizing graph data implies six steps, each one applying different rules:

1. Map IFC instances to ontology classes (Figure 3, a).
2. Create direct constructs (links, object properties from the ontology) between instances (Figure 3, b).
3. Create direct constructs (datatype properties from the ontology) between instances and data typed literals (Figure 3, c).
4. Compute missing parameter values (e.g., the total length of the road) and integrate them (as literals) into the graph with dedicated constructs (Figure 3, d) (optional).
5. Infer missing instances with their corresponding constructs (Figure 3, e) (optional).
6. Delete all undesired information (Figure 3, f) (optional).

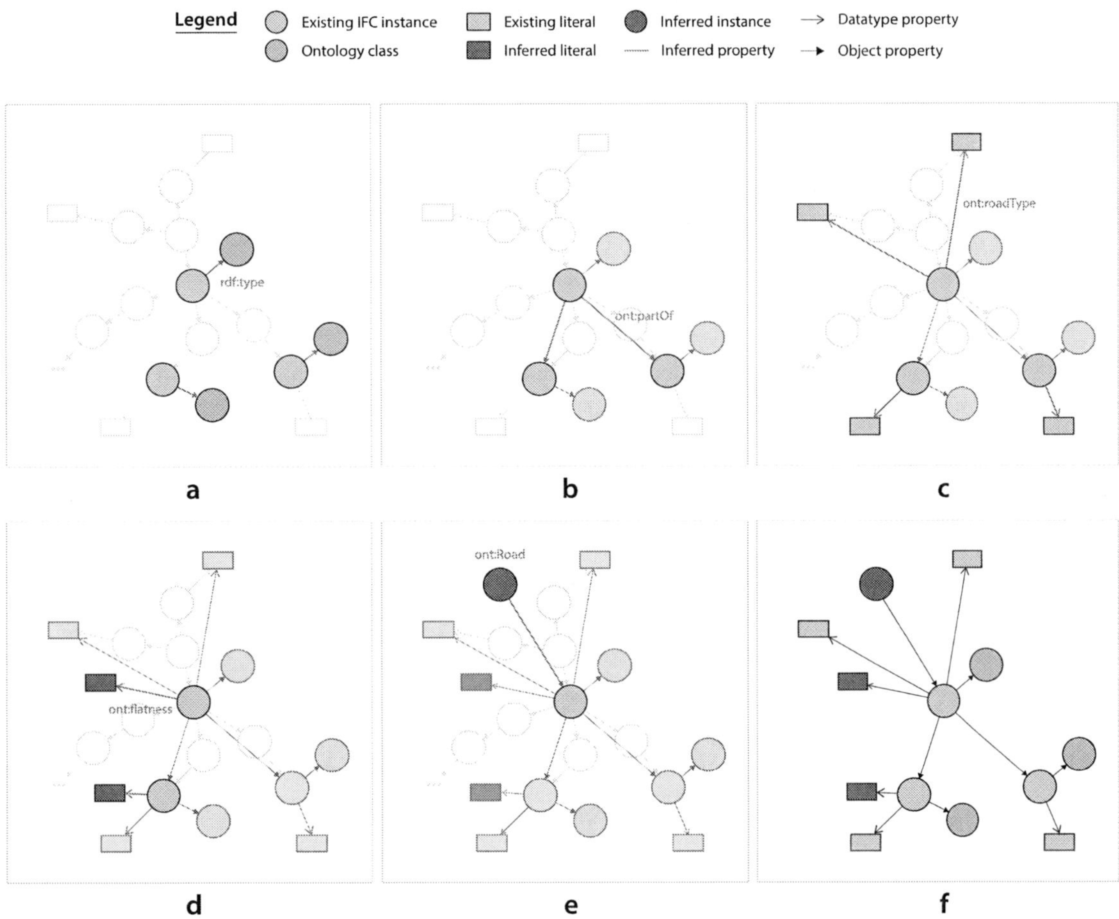

Figure 3: Operations to optimize and standardize IFC-RDF graphs.

Identification of correspondence between graph instances and ontology classes (Figure 3, a) is based on:

- The IFC class of the instance: *if O is an instance of Ifc(...), then O is an instance of C, where C is a class from the ontology* (e.g., IfcRoad → ch:Road).
- The type, property set, or classification associated with the instance (e.g., *IfcRoadPart* instance has type "Road section" → ch:RoadSection).

Note that computing parameter values (Figure 3, d) may require specific functions that are not supported by all rule languages. The solution for data processing must therefore be carefully chosen.

3. Case study

The procedure presented in Figure 1 is applied to check the compliance of a road infrastructure model with the construction code extract given in Figure 4. The data graph will be standardized beforehand, following the methodology described in Section 2. Figure 2 shows the desired data structure.

For roads of type RGD and RP, a curve preceded by a straight section shall have a minimum radius as defined in **Table 16**.

Straight section length (m)	Minimum radius (m)
≤ 100	100
100 < L ≤ 500	200
> 500	300

Table 16. Minimum curve radius

Figure 4: Excerpt of a road design standard.

Concepts related to the excerpt above are "road", "straight section", and "curved section". "Road" corresponds to *ont:Road* class (Figure 2). "Straight section" and "curved section" each describe a geometrical component of the road's horizontal alignment and will be mapped to *ont:Line* and *ont:Curve* classes, respectively. Required properties for the checking are "road type" (*ont:roadType*), "straight section length" (*ont:length*), and "radius" (*ont:radius*) (Figure 2).

A road section, composed of straight segments and curves, is modeled in Autodesk Civil 3D. The IFC model provides required geometric information such as segments length and radius. Road type values are defined in custom property sets.

The model is exported in IFC 4.1 (since Civil 3D does not yet support release 4.3) and converted with IFC-to-RDF. At this stage, the graph has about 690,000 triples (file size: 50.3 MB, Turtle syntax).

Apache Jena is used to perform both tasks: optimization and compliance checking. Jena is an "all-in-one" framework for processing RDF graphs, including a SPARQL query engine (Jena ARQ) and a general-purpose rule engine with a dedicated rule language (The Apache Software Foundation, 2021). Additional functions are implemented in the Jena rule language to enhance its expressivity and make it more functional.

Graph analysis leads to the following conclusions:

- Only instances of the *IfcAlignment* class, combined with their associated property sets and geometric information, contain data indicated as relevant by the ontology and have to be preserved.
- Objectified relationships and other undesired information such as *IfcPropertyDefinition* concepts, instances without semantics (*IfcBuildingElementProxy*), and unnecessary resources can be removed from the graph. This is not mandatory but recommended when the graph is used exclusively for code compliance checking to improve its readability and reduce data quantity.
- Direct constructs must be created, according to the ontology.
- Properties such as "flatness", which may be required for another checking, are missing and should be computed from existing data.

Then, optimization rules (Jena rules and SPARQL CONSTRUCT queries) are formulated:

```
# Step 1: Class mapping (Jena rules)

[optimization_01: (?i rdf:type ifc:IfcAlignment2DHorizontal) -> (?i rdf:type
ont:HorizontalAlignment) ]

...
```

```
# Step 6: Undesired information removal (SPARQL CONSTRUCT query)
CONSTRUCT {?i ?j ?k} WHERE
{
        SELECT ?i ?j ?k WHERE {
                ?i rdf:type ?type
                FILTER (
                        ?type = ont:Road ||
                        ?type = ont:HorizontalAlignment ||
                        ...
                                )
                ?i ?j ?k
        }
        GROUP BY ?i ?j ?k
}
```

Once the rules were applied, the graph size dropped to about 4000 triples (file size: 0.3 MB). Data representation has been modified to comply with the ontology. Compliance rules are shorter and more intelligible since they are only composed of meaningful and straightforward triple statements based on ontology's vocabulary:

```
# Checking compliance with Figure 4 (Jena rule)
[compliance_with_Figure_4: (?line rdf:type ont:Line), (?curve rdf:typeont:Curve), (
?alg rdf:type ont:HorizontalAlignment), (?road rdf:type ont:Road),(?line ont:partOf
?alg), (?line ont:next ?curve), (?road ont:horizontalAlignment ?alg), (?line ont:le
ngth ?length), (?curve ont:radius ?radius),(?road ont:roadType ?type), filter(?type
= RGD|RP), check((?length<=100&radius>100)|?length=]100;500]&radius>200)|?length>50
0&radius>300), ?result) -> print(?result) ]
--> PASS
```

Without optimization, the same rule (compliance_with_Figure_4) would have had a far more complex and lengthy content and could not have been applied without a prior inference rule:

```
[prior_inference: (?algh ifc:segments_IfcAlignment2DHorizontal ?list1), (?list1 lis
t:hasNext ?list2) -> (?algh ifc:segments_IfcAlignment2DHorizontal ?list2) ]
# Checking compliance with Figure 4 (Jena rule)
[compliance_with_Figure_4: (?line rdf:type ifc:IfcLineSegment2D), (?hseg1 ifc:curve
Geometry_IfcAlignment2DHorizontalSegment ?line), (?list1 list:hasContents ?hseg1),
(?list1 list:hasNext ?list2), (?list2 list:hasContents ?hs2), (?hseg2 ifc:curveGeom
etry_IfcAlignment2DHorizontalSegment ?curve), (?curve rdf:type ifc:IfcCircularArcSe
gment2D), (?algh ifc:segments_IfcAlignment2DHorizontal ?list1), (?algh ifc:segments
_IfcAlignment2DHorizontal ?list2), (?algc ifc:horizontal_IfcAlignmentCurve ?algh),
(?alg ifc:axis_IfcLinearPositioningElement ?algc), (?alg rdf:type ifc:IfcAlignment)
, (?rdbp ifc:relatedObjects_IfcRelDefinesByProperties ?alg), (?rdbp ifc:relatingPro
pertyDefinition_IfcRelDefinesByProperties ?pset), (?pset ifc:name_IfcRoot ?label1),
(?label1 express:hasString ?psetname), filter(psetname="Pset_Road"), (?pset ifc:has
Properties_IfcPropertySet ?prop), (?prop ifc:name_IfcProperty ?label2), (?label2 ex
press:hasString ?propname), filter(propname="roadType"), (?prop ifc:nominalValue_If
cPropertySingleValue ?label3), (?label3 express:hasString ?roadType), filter(roadTy
pe=RGD||RP), (?line ifc:segmentLength_IfcCurveSegment2D ?pos1), (?pos1 express:hasD
ouble ?length), (?curve ifc:radius_IfcCircularArcSegment2D ?pos2), (?pos2 express:h
asDouble ?radius), check((?length<=100&radius>100)|?length=]100;500]&radius>200)|?l
ength>500&radius>300), ?result) -> print(?result) ]
--> PASS
```

4. Conclusion and future work

Code compliance checking based on graphs is a promising approach since graph data structures can easily be transformed to represent information in the desired way. It is proposed to optimize (standardize) IFC-RDF graphs before using them in a checking system. Standardization leads to a manageable formulation of rules.

Results of a case study showed that the graph size is considerably reduced in addition to simplifying and clarifying the content of formal compliance rules. In case the resulting standardized graph has to be stored (for example, in a triplestore) for further compliance checking, this allows significant storage space savings.

Moreover, the advantage of giving the data graph a predefined structure is that compliance rules become independent of the initially employed software and can be reused for all previously standardized graphs. Consequently, maintenance efforts are equally distributed among domain and software experts.

Without standardization, compliance rules must be modified when building codes or input data structure change. With standardization, compliance rules are adjusted only when regulations change. As indicated, formulating optimization rules requires multiple competencies, implicitly a collaboration between several experts.

The next stage is to enhance and further automate the process of graph simplification and standardization by using graph theory and advanced techniques such as machine learning. In the same way, generating compliance rules directly from paper documents, using methods such as NLP (Natural Language Processing), is a subject of interest.

Acknowledgment

This research is supported by Innosuisse in the framework of the Innovation project 34406.1 IP-ENG: Digital method for efficient analysis and benchmarking of road infrastructure projects "digiMABS".

References

Beach, T.H., Rezgui, Y., Li, H., Kasim, T. (2015). A rule-based semantic approach for automated regulatory compliance in the construction sector. Expert Syst. Appl. 42, pp. 5219–5231. DOI: https://doi.org/10.1016/j.eswa.2015.02.029

Belsky, M., Sacks, R., Brilakis, I. (2016). Semantic Enrichment for Building Information Modeling. Comput.-Aided Civ. Infrastruct. Eng. 31, pp. 261–274. DOI: https://doi.org/10.1111/mice.12128

Bouzidi, K.R., Fies, B., Faron-Zucker, C., Zarli, A., Thanh, N.L. (2012). Semantic Web Approach to Ease Regulation Compliance Checking in Construction Industry. Future Internet 4, pp. 830–851. DOI: https://doi.org/10.3390/fi4030830

buildingSMART (2021). IFC Formats - buildingSMART Technical. Available at: https://technical.buildingsmart.org/standards/ifc/ifc-formats/, accessed December 2021.

Burggräf, P., Dannapfel, M., Ebade-Esfahani, M., Scheidler, F. (2021). Creation of an expert system for design validation in BIM-based factory design through automatic checking of semantic information. Procedia CIRP 99, pp. 3–8. DOI: https://doi.org/10.1016/j.procir.2021.03.012

de Farias, T.M., Roxin, A., Nicolle, C. (2015). IfcWoD, Semantically Adapting IFC Model Relations into OWL Properties. DOI: https://doi.org/10.48550/ARXIV.1511.03897

Eastman, C., Lee, Jae-min, Jeong, Y., Lee, Jin-kook (2009). Automatic rule-based checking of building designs. Autom. Constr. 18, pp. 1011–1033. DOI: https://doi.org/10.1016/j.autcon.2009.07.002

Fahad, M., Bus, N., Fies, B. (2018). Semantic topological querying for compliance checking, in: Karlshøj, J., Scherer, R. (Eds.), EWork and EBusiness in Architecture, Engineering and Construction. CRC Press.

Martin, S., Szekely, B., Allemand, D. (2021). The Rise of the Knowledge Graph. O'Reilly Media Inc.

Pauwels, P. (2017). GitHub page of IFCtoRDF. GitHub. Available at: https://github.com/pipauwel/IFCtoRDF, accessed November 2021.

Pauwels, P., de Farias, T.M., Zhang, C., Roxin, A., Beetz, J., De Roo, J., Nicolle, C. (2017). A performance benchmark over semantic rule checking approaches in construction industry. Adv. Eng. Inform. 33, pp. 68–88. DOI: https://doi.org/10.1016/j.aei.2017.05.001

Pauwels, P., Roxin, A. (2016). SimpleBIM : from full ifcOWL graphs to simplified building graphs. Ework Ebusiness Archit. Eng. Constr. pp. 11–18.

Pauwels, P., Van Deursen, D. (2012). IFC/RDF: Adaptation, Aggregation and Enrichment.

Pauwels, P., Van Deursen, D., Verstraeten, R., De Roo, J., De Meyer, R., Van de Walle, R., Van Campenhout, J. (2011). A semantic rule checking environment for building performance checking. Autom. Constr. 20, pp. 506–518. DOI: https://doi.org/10.1016/j.autcon.2010.11.017

Pauwels, P., Zhang, S. (2015). Semantic Rule-checking for Regulation Compliance Checking: An Overview of Strategies and Approaches.

Preidel, C., Borrmann, A. (2015). Automated Code Compliance Checking Based on a Visual Language and Building Information Modeling. Presented at the 32nd International Symposium on Automation and Robotics in Construction, Oulu, Finland. DOI: https://doi.org/10.22260/ISARC2015/0033

Rattanasawad, T., Saikaew, K.R., Buranarach, M., Supnithi, T. (2013). A review and comparison of rule languages and rule-based inference engines for the Semantic Web, in: 2013 International Computer Science and Engineering Conference (ICSEC). Presented at the 2013 International Computer Science and Engineering Conference (ICSEC), IEEE, Nakorn Pathom, Thailand, pp. pp. 1–6. DOI: https://doi.org/10.1109/ICSEC.2013.6694743

Solibri (2021). Webpage of Solibri. Available at: https://www.solibri.com/, accessed November 2021.

The Apache Software Foundation (2021). Webpage of Jena inference support. Available at: https://jena.apache.org/documentation/inference/#extensions, accessed November 2021.

W3C (2014). RDF 1.1 Primer. Available at: https://www.w3.org/TR/2014/NOTE-rdf11-primer-20140624/, accessed October 2021.

W3C (2013). SPARQL 1.1 Overview. Available at: https://www.w3.org/TR/sparql11-overview/, accessed October 2021.

W3C (2012). OWL 2 Web Ontology Language Primer (Second Edition). Available at: https://www.w3.org/TR/2012/REC-owl2-primer-20121211/, accessed October 2021.

Zhang, C., Beetz, J., de Vries, B. (2018). BimSPARQL: Domain-specific functional SPARQL extensions for querying RDF building data. Semantic Web 9, pp. 829–855. DOI: https://doi.org/10.3233/SW-180297

Cross Domain Matching for Semantic Point Cloud Segmentation based on Convolutional Neural Networks

Martens J., Blut T., Blankenbach J.
Geodesic Institute and Chair for Computing in Civil Engineering & Geo Information Systems, RWTH Aachen University, Germany
jan.martens@gia.rwth-aachen.de

Abstract. Together with roads, rails and tunnels, bridges represent ubiquitous infrastructure objects holding an essential role in transportation. Nevertheless, due to the elevated age of many bridges, structural deficiencies are becoming more common. Digital Twins in conjunction with Building Information Modelling (BIM) may significantly support asset management but are only now garnering more attention for infrastructure objects. To ease the transition towards creating digital twins for existing constructions, this work presents a method for automated segmentation of bridge point clouds based on images using convolutional neural networks. For this purpose, semantic segmentation is used for labelling the photographs captured during laser scanning. The classifications masks of this image-based approach are then projected back into 3D, resulting in a labelled point cloud ready for further processing and building component reconstruction.

1. Introduction

The shift towards digitization has led to a notable transformation in the architecture, engineering and construction (AECO) industry. Since its introduction, Building Information Modelling (BIM) is being adopted in civil engineering for digital design and construction and is also seen in the life cycle and asset management due to apparent benefits for data handling and exchange (Blankenbach 2018). While the IFC data model has matured for real estate objects over the past years (Borrmann et al. 2018), an extension of it tailored towards infrastructure objects is only recently being pushed forward (Borrmann et al. 2019). This development makes sense, as infrastructure objects are commonly encountered in everyday life. It also emphasizes the role of BIM, which serves as the origin for the concept of the term "digital twin" in construction and describes data-driven systems for the monitoring, maintenance and management of objects throughout their life cycle (Sacks et al. 2020; Errandonea, Beltran and Arrizabalaga 2020).

However, the creation of semantic-rich 3D models representing the actual (as-is) state of the construction as important basis for digital twins is a notable challenge, as up-to-date plans are rarely present or incomplete as repairs and restructuring may have taken place over the life span of the construction. In consequence, reality capture techniques such as laser scanning or photogrammetry must be used for as-is data acquisition, followed by elaborative manual modeling based on the collected data. This step requires specialized modelling software, trained staff and time. Automated as-is modelling is therefore a hot topic in both, research and the industry, as it cuts down on modelling time and costs. Typically, this process can be broken down into four stages as illustrated in Figure 1.

Capturing and surveying represent the first of these stages and have improved notably over the past years due to unmanned data capturing platforms (drones), laser scanning systems and capturing methods in general having evolved towards high accuracy, low-cost, ease-of-use and fast capturing (Blankenbach 2018). Because of some capturing methods suffering from reduced accuracy, preprocessing aims to rectify the impact of sensor noise and artefacts to clean up the point cloud data and guarantee optimal conditions for semantic segmentation and

https://doi.org/10.7146/aul.455.c209

modelling. Segmentation is typically achieved using geometric algorithms; however methods based on machine learning are becoming an increasingly more popular option. While segmentation can be performed to extract specific regions of interest and planar patches, it can also be used to find and label specific objects and structures. Finally, these are then used to create suitable building components and construct the final 3D model. Depending on whether or not additional information has been gathered during the segmentation step, it may be added to the model alongside semantic attributes. This means that segmentation and modelling are closely intertwined, as the model quality will strongly depend on the segmentation quality.

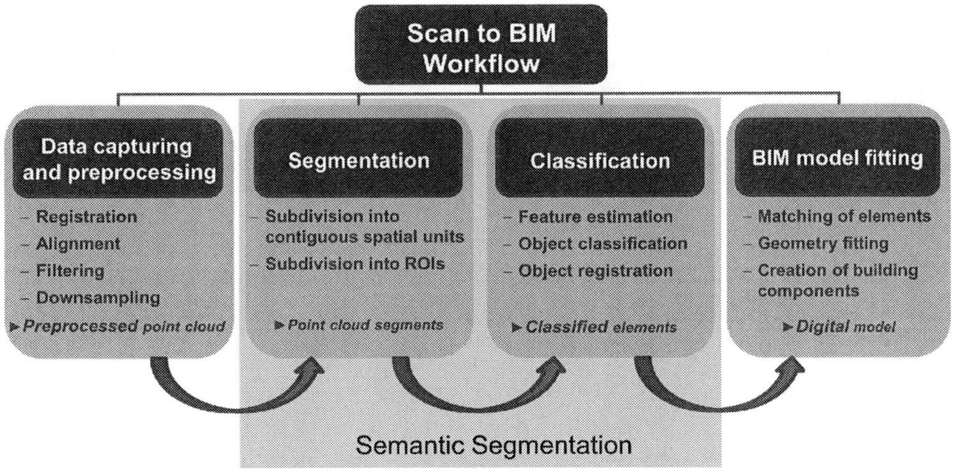

Figure 1: Stages of the Scan-to-BIM process. The presented approach covers the segmentation and classification stages.

Both, segmentation and classification may also be combined into one single step commonly referred to as semantic segmentation. Supervised machine learning methods are already increasingly being used for this purpose, with Deep Learning (DL) in particular holding much potential. However, (supervised) DL requires a large amount of training data with high variability and annotated point clouds are rare or even not available for many construction types like bridges. As part of a larger research project with the overarching goal of automatically deriving digital bridge models from survey data, we try to tackle this problem by a multi-stage semantic segmentation workflow.

Arising from the lack of point cloud training data, this contribution presents an image-based classification approach where 2D semantic segmentation results are transferred to 3D point clouds (cross-domain matching) in order to achieve point cloud segments which can afterwards be refined using prior knowledge. The approach is driven by the fact that photos are usually taken in addition to a point cloud as part of the surveying. The approach is depicted in Figure 2 and shows a neural network performing an initial instance-based pre-segmentation on photos. Segmentation masks then being projected as a coarse segmentation into the point cloud, in order to then carry out a fine segmentation. The advantage of this approach is that on one hand, training data (photos of infrastructure objects) is publicly available (e.g. on the internet) and can also be produced quite easily and quickly. On the other hand, due to neural networks being famous for their performance in image classification tasks, the point cloud data required for training within the fine segmentation step being rather scarce. Although the approach still holds potential for improvement, the presented results prove that it already delivers solid results when combined with suitable post-processing techniques, making it a promising tool for the integration into modelling workflows.

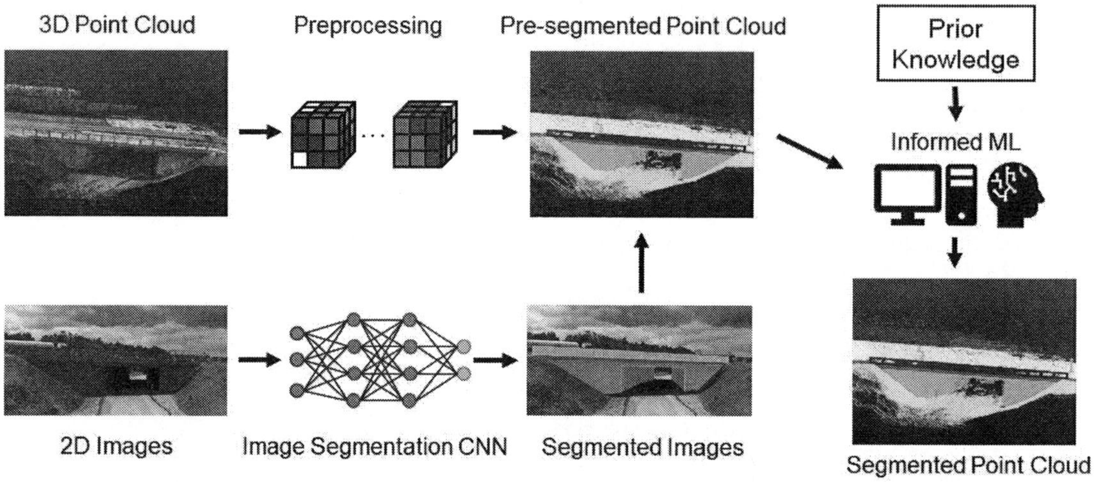

Figure 2: Overall workflow for infrastructure point cloud semantic segmentation. This work deals with the image segmentation part and generation of a pre-segmented point cloud.

2. Related Works

For years, machine learning methods for point clouds have been an ongoing research topic in the field of robotics with most early approaches using the then widely-used Support Vector Machines (SVM) alongside hand-crafted features (Brodu and Lague 2012). At roughly the same time, neural networks and deep learning have gained more traction in object recognition, as their requirements for large training data sets and computational power were starting to get satisfied. Since the massive success of neural networks for image classification and the subsequent improvements of their architecture in the following years (Krizhevsky, Sutskever and Hinton 2017), early experiments in voxel-based approaches such as VoxNet (Maturana and Scherer 2015). In the face of their limitations, native 3D-based neural networks such as PointNet (Qi et al. 2016) have been developed. Interestingly, hybrid approaches which combine information from the point cloud and image domains have been presented as well (Sindagi, Zhou, and Tuzel 2019).

In an effort of exploiting the high accuracy of image-based neural networks, a handful approaches have already been developed to act as indoor object classifiers (Su et al. 2015, Stojanovic et al. 2019). These methods classify isolated objects or pre-segmented point clouds by rendering them from different viewports and classifying the resulting images. Adaptations for use with automated driving have been made as well (Wolf et al. 2019), proving that this approach can not only be applied to outdoor environments, but even has a better chance of classifying objects in their spatial context than most native 3D approaches.

When it comes to capturing training data, MLS has become widely used for capturing large infrastructure objects, as it benefits from high mobility and capturing speeds (Ma et al. 2018). Due to the application of machine learning in the field of automated driving being pushed into focus recently, urban point cloud data sets captured with MLS such as KITTI (Fritsch, Kuehnl and Geiger 2013) and Paris-Lille-3D (Roynard, Deschaud and Goulette 2018) have become popular benchmarks for the detection of cars, pedestrians and road elements. The crux however lies in the fact that these datasets are not concerned with infrastructure objects such as bridges. Consequently, 3D training data specifically for bridges is highly-limited, rendering 3D-based neural networks unsuitable for bridge component classification.

Given this context, image-based classification approaches like the one employed in this work represent the best option for 3D classification tasks where training is either sparse or non-existent. Image datasets are rather ubiquitous, with the COCO dataset (Lin et al. 2014) being one well-known example and even datasets with bridge data (albeit with labels for cracks and damages rather than components) are available (Bianchi and Hebdon 2021).

This accessibility of existing data makes image-based semantic segmentation a valuable tool for the underlying point cloud classification problem. Due to these techniques being part of the digital twin reconstruction process, their role in capturing the bridge's state and updating the digital model accordingly aligns well with the goal of maintenance and damage tracking of the Industry 4.0 movement (Shim et al. 2019).

3. Methodology

The presented image-based workflow for point clouds can be subdivided into four incremental stages: neural network training, image-based semantic classification, 3D projection and post-processing.

3.1 Neural Network Training

As discussed earlier, the problem of obtaining specific training data for bridges poses a problem due to the lack of labelled bridge images. However, transfer learning represents a solution to this problem (Zhu et al. 2021, Kora et al. 2022). Neural networks for image classification typically consist of a feature detection body where distinct features are recognized and a classification head which associates these features with one of the output classes. Transfer learning describes the process of modifying a pre-trained network such that the features learned in the body are kept, while the classification head is being re-trained and adapted for a new set of object classes. Thus, training is drastically reduced and as an added benefit, the time-consuming and tedious hyper parameter tuning process is omitted.

3.2 Image-based Semantic Segmentation

For the classification of the captured images, Mask R-CNN network (He et al. 2017), an extension of Faster R-CNN was used. Mask R-CNN relies on a feature detection backbone such as ResNet, ResNeXt or SpinNet for feature detection and uses RoIAlign for proposing Regions of Interest (RoI). These regions are subsequently classified by one network branch, while a second branch predicts an object mask for each RoI. Due to Mask R-CNN generating not only object bounding boxes and annotations, but also pixel-accurate classification masks, the resulting regions of interest are well-suited for projection into 3D point clouds, given the camera's extrinsic and intrinsic parameters.

3.3 3D Projection and Postprocessing

Extrinsic camera parameters represent spatial camera parameters in 3D space and encompass location and orientation parameters. They can be captured directly through GNSS/IMU data and tracking of scan positions when using ~~drones, TLS~~ and MLS systems or, if camera systems without GNSS/IMU are used, can additionally be reconstructed through image matching methods. Intrinsic parameters on the other hand represent the focal length, coordinates of the principal point and distortion parameters of the camera and are therefore needed to describe mathematically and physically how captured images are projected onto the image plane. Typically, a camera calibration process is used to estimate intrinsic parameters and the type of distortion present in the images. Using the extrinsic and intrinsic camera parameters, it is possible to project the 3D point cloud into the camera's image plane.

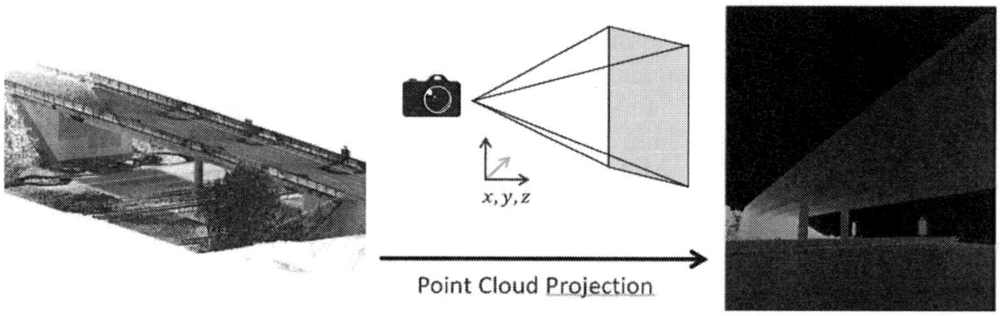

Figure 3: Point cloud projection for the solving occlusion problem through depth map generation. This process requires intrinsic and extrinsic camera parameters to render out each point's distance from a given camera position.

As apparent from their lack of 3D information, a naive projection of 2D images into point clouds will run into the problem of labelling points occluded by the ones in front of them, leading to many points being labelled incorrectly. Regular photographs are missing the required depth information, but through use of the extrinsic and intrinsic camera parameters, point clouds can be aligned with the images, thus bringing them into the camera's view frustum. In a process inspired by computer graphics, this allows for the calculation of each point's distance to the camera. By rendering out these distances into a depth map (also referred to as z buffer or depth map), it is possible to solve the depth occlusion problem. As shown in Figure 3, the depth map is created by constructing a view matrix from the extrinsic parameters and projection matrix from the intrinsic parameters and multiplying all visible points with it. In the case of multiple points falling into the same pixel of the depth map, only the one with the smallest distance to the camera is kept for labelling, due to it occluding the ones behind it.

Once the projection process is complete, candidate labels for each point are post-processed using majority voting. Most points are typically visible from multiple views, which can lead to contradicting labels due to classification masks potentially overlapping, being imprecise or in some cases belonging to the wrong class. The majority voting allows for these problems to be resolved in a simple yet effective way, but shows potential for improvements due to its ignorance towards geometric structures.

4. Experiments

For training, a variety of images ranging UAS (Unmanned Aerial System) survey data taken by the TU Munich to images taken from Internet search engines as well as selfrecorded images and those from bridge inspections were used. Validation was performed on survey data of two different bridges. The first survey was done using a camera-equipped UAS. Based on the captured video footage, a point cloud was reconstructed, meaning that image data and a point cloud suffering from quality degradations characteristic of image reconstruction techniques were available. A second survey was performed using a geodetic terrestrial ~~laser scanner~~ (TLS) equipped with a NIKON D800 camera a~~nd based on~~ 20 scan positions 140 pictures and a high-quality point cloud were obtained. In both cases, intrinsic and extrinsic camera parameters were known.

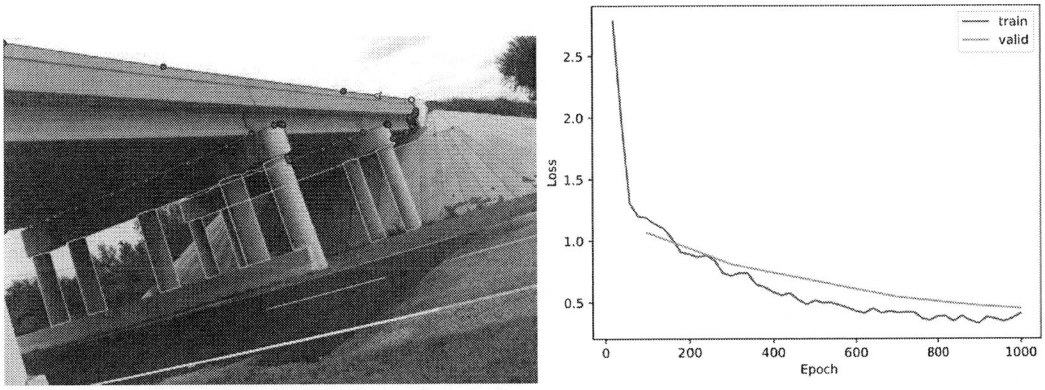

Figure 4: Left: Sample image of the provided training data set. Right: Training and validation loss for Mask R-CNN on the given training dataset.

For the classification of the captured images, a Mask R-CNN network with a backbone network consisting of a ResNet with 50 layers which has been pre-trained on the COCO dataset (Lin et al. 2014). To improve classification accuracy, transfer learning was applied, where the original network was modified and retrained on a hand-annotated bridge dataset to detect and classify bridge abutment, railing and deck components. The corresponding data set for retraining was created from around 600 hand-annotated images (a sample image is depicted in Figure 4, left) and expanded using typical data augmentation operations such as cropping, rescaling and mirroring to make the resulting classifier more robust. Training and validation loss dropped sharply during the first 600 iterations, before slowly converging as indicated by Figure 4 (right).

As shown in Figure 5, results for classification show that the trained network performs favourably for most images and can reliably detect the three object classes (abutment, railing and deck) within the images regardless of camera distance and angle to the object. Detection masks, however, have a tendency towards displaying a jagged rather than smooth border, making these regions somewhat unreliable. Masks for the railing class are occasionally slightly imprecise, which may be a result of their fine structure which allows for objects behind them to still be visible. Projections of the classification masks into the point cloud result in a decent segmentation of the bridge components alongside some unpleasant artefacts (see Figure 5, right column). While the majority voting algorithm and depth occlusion are capable of resolving glaring issues, additional post-processing would improve result quality even further.

Despite different camera parameters, TLS survey data was processed analogously to the UAS ~~data.~~ Results for this dataset are similar in terms of robustness but also present different challenges. Unlike the UA~~S survey~~ data, where the bridge is always in frame, it also contains images in which the bridge not visible. One should note that as a form of negative control, the resulting classification masks of these images are empty and thus do not contribute to the overall point cloud classification process. Additionally, some scans were acquired underneath the bridge and show components which are typically occluded from view when looking at it from an outside perspective and were not included in the training data set. Reliability of classifications masks in these regions is therefore lower, such that components are occasionally correctly recognized despite the lack of training data but also oftentimes incorrectly labelled or not recognized. This issue can be resolved through retraining with the appropriate images though.

Figure 5: Results of image-based segmentation for two different bridges. Top left: Image captured by a UAS ~~with~~ superimposed segmentation masks. Top right: Point cloud with labels from multiple viewpoints projected onto it. Bottom left: Image captured during TLS survey with superimposed classification masks. Bottom right: TLS point clouds with labels from multiple viewpoints projected onto it.

Another challenge occurs for images where the bridge is visible from an oblique angle (shown in Figure 5, bottom left) and where the perspective results in a severely reduced resolution of the deck and railing components. Classification masks have a tendency to be less accurate in both cases, as the lower resolution of these areas makes it harder to make out defining features, such that deck and railing components are more likely to be confused for one another as apparent in Figure 5 (bottom right). A projection of these masks into the point cloud labels the abutment consistently correctly, but segmentation of deck and railing can suffer from degraded quality in aforementioned cases. While the method already works admirably well in most cases, this factor proves that retraining and further post-processing e.g. using spatial and geometric reasoning is required to achieve a more consistent result quality.

5. Discussion and Outlook

As shown by the early results, the presented approach provides a viable way of semantic segmentation for point clouds using supervised machine learning and is capable of bypassing the current scarcity of point cloud training data. Semantic segmentation is used to generate object masks, which are projected onto the point cloud. Occlusions specific to camera perspectives are being simulated by rendering out a depth map using the underlying camera parameters. Afterwards, a post-processing cleans up point labels to improve result quality by means of a majority voting for point with multiple overlapping regions. Among the observed challenges are inaccurate region borders, misclassifications of low-resolution regions and occasional outliers. Further investigations into the performance of image classification are currently being carried out, involving commonly-used metric such as Intersection over Union (IoU), precision and recall. An investigation of the same metrics for the labelled point clouds are of major interest as well.

Aside from the image segmentation quality which can be improved by adding more data to the training process, the most apparent way of dealing with inaccurate results and improving segmentation quality lies in the post-processing step. The success of earlier works in image classification, where post-processing has led to improvements of the overall results, points towards the same conclusion (Tivive and Bouzerdoum 2006). In its current state, the overall process does not take the spatial context into account and is thus limited when it comes to dealing with wrong or incomplete labels. Methods such as 3D-nearest neighbour labelling for unlabelled points are obvious methods to include, but more sophisticated methods which pre-segment the 3D point cloud and then propagate labels inside these segments are more promising. In a similar vein, the use of spatial reasoning for correcting labels based on object height, surface structure and orientation should yield improved results and will help clean up undesirable classification artefacts. This sort of prior knowledge can also be integrated into the machine learning process itself to further lessen the impact of limited training data (von Rueden et al. 2021) and improve results further, as indicated in Figure 2.

Extensions for post-processing and an introduction of new classes for a more granular segmentation will be another issue worth investigating, as bridges consist of more components than the ones represented in this work. Especially automated reconstruction will benefit from this factor, as the presented image-based segmentation can help inform the choice of reconstruction algorithm for each individual building component. After all, with the current scarcity in labelled point cloud data for infrastructure objects, the presented approach thus represents a key element automated reconstruction workflows.

Acknowledgements

This work has been supported and funded by the German Ministry of Transportation (BMDV) as part of the "TwinGen" research project. The authors thank their project partners from the Chair of Computational Modelling and Simulation at the Technical University of Munich, Computing in Engineering at Ruhr University Bochum, Design Computation at RWTH Aachen University and ZPP Ingenieure AG.

References

He, K., Gkioxari, G., Dollár, P., Girshick, R. (2018). Mask R-CNN. 2017 IEEE International Conference on Computer Vision (ICCV), pp. 2980-2988.

Qi, C.R., Su, H., Mo, K., Guibas, L.J. (2016). PointNet: Deep Learning on Point Sets for 3D Classification and Segmentation. arXiv preprint arXiv: 1612.00593.

Maturana, D., Scherer, S., (2015). VoxNet: A 3D Convolutional Neural Network for real-time object recognition, 2015 IEEE/RSJ International Conference on Intelligent Robots and Systems (IROS), 2015, pp. 922-928, doi: 10.1109/IROS.2015.7353481.

Sindagi, V.A., Zhou, Y., Tuzel, O. (2019). MVX-Net: Multimodal VoxelNet for 3D Object Detection, 2019 International Conference on Robotics and Automation (ICRA), 2019, pp. 7276-7282, doi: 10.1109/ICRA.2019.8794195.

Wolf, J., Richter, R., Discher, S., Döllner, J. (2019). Applicability of Neural Networks for Image Classification on Object Detection in Mobile Mapping 3D Point Clouds. The International Archives of the Photogrammetry, Remote Sensing and Spatial Information Sciences. XLII-4/W15. 111-115. 10.5194/isprs-archives-XLII-4-W15-111-2019.

Stojanovic, V., Trapp, M., Richter, R., Döllner, J. (2019). Classification of Indoor Point Clouds Using Multiviews. In The 24th International Conference on 3D Web Technology (Web3D '19). Association for Computing Machinery, New York, NY, USA, 1–9. DOI:https://doi.org/10.1145/3329714.3338129

Su, H., Maji, S., Kalogerakis, E., Learned-Miller, E. (2015). Multi-view Convolutional Neural Networks for 3D Shape Recognition, 2015 IEEE International Conference on Computer Vision (ICCV), pp. 945-953, doi: 10.1109/ICCV.2015.114.

Brodu, N., Lague, D. (2012). 3D terrestrial lidar data classification of complex natural scenes using a multi-scale dimensionality criterion: Applications in geomorphology, ISPRS Journal of Photogrammetry and Remote Sensing, Volume 68, 2012, pp. 121-134, ISSN 0924-2716 doi: https://doi.org/10.1016/j.isprsjprs.2012.01.006

Krizhevsky, A., Sutskever, I., Hinton, G., E. (2017). ImageNet classification with deep convolutional neural networks. Commun. ACM 60, 6 (June 2017), 84–90. doi: https://doi.org/10.1145/3065386

Lin, T.Y., Maire, M. Belongie, S., Hays, J., Perona, P., Ramanan, D., Dollar, P., Zitnick, C.L. (2014). Microsoft COCO: Common Objects in Context. Processings of Computer Vision ECCV 2014, Springer International Publishing. pp. 740-755, ISBN: 978-3-319-10602-1

Fritsch, J., Kuehnl, T., Geiger, A. (2013). A New Performance Measure and Evaluation Benchmark for Road Detection Algorithms. In: International Conference on Intelligent Transportation Systems (ITSC), 2013.

Roynard, X., Deschaud, J., Goulette, F. (2018). Paris-Lille-3D: A Point Cloud Dataset for Urban Scene Segmentation and Classification, 2018 IEEE/CVF Conference on Computer Vision and Pattern Recognition Workshops (CVPRW), pp. 2108-21083, doi: 10.1109/CVPRW.2018.00272.

Bianchi, E., Hebdon, M. (2021). COCO-Bridge 2021+ Dataset. doi: 10.7294/16624495.v1, https://data.lib.vt.edu/articles/dataset/COCO-Bridge_2021_Dataset/16624495

Borrmann A., Beetz J., Koch C., Liebich T., Muhic S. (2018) Industry Foundation Classes: A Standardized Data Model for the Vendor-Neutral Exchange of Digital Building Models. In: Borrmann A., König M., Koch C., Beetz J. (eds) Building Information Modeling. Springer, Cham. https://doi.org/10.1007/978-3-319-92862-3_5

Blankenbach J. (2018). Building Surveying for As-Built Modeling. In: Borrmann A., König M., Koch C., Beetz J. (eds) Building Information Modeling. Springer, Cham. https://doi.org/10.1007/978-3-319-92862-3_24

Borrmann, A., Muhic, S., Hyvarinen, J., Chipman, T., Jaud, S., Castaing, C., Dumoulin, C., Liebich, T., Mol, L. (2019). The IFC-Bridge Project – Extending the IFC standard to enable high-quality exchange of bridge information models. In: Proceedings of the 2019 European Conference on Computing in Construction, pp. 377-386, ISBN: 978-1-910963-37-3

Tivive, F. H. C., Bouzerdoum, A., (2006). Texture Classification using Convolutional Neural Networks. TENCON 2006 - 2006 IEEE Region 10 Conference, 2006, pp. 1-4, doi: 10.1109/TENCON.2006.343944.

Zhu, W., Braun, B., Chiang, L.H., Romagnoli, J.A. (2021). Investigation of transfer learning for image classification and impact on training sample size, Chemometrics and Intelligent Laboratory Systems, Volume 211, 2021, ISSN 0169-7439, doi: https://doi.org/10.1016/j.chemolab.2021.104269.

Kora, P., Ooi, C.P., Faust, O., Raghavendra, U., Gudigar, A., Chan, W.Y., Meenakshi, K., Swaraja, K., Plawiak, P., Rajendra Acharya, U. (2022). Transfer learning techniques for medical image analysis: A review, Biocybernetics and Biomedical Engineering, Volume 42, Issue 1, 2022, pp. 79-107, ISSN 0208-5216, doi: https://doi.org/10.1016/j.bbe.2021.11.004.

Ma L, Li Y, Li J, Wang C, Wang R, Chapman MA. Mobile Laser Scanned Point-Clouds for Road Object Detection and Extraction: A Review. *Remote Sensing*. 2018; 10(10):1531. https://doi.org/10.3390/rs10101531

Sacks, R., Brilakis, I., Pikas, E., Xie, H., & Girolami, M. (2020). Construction with digital twin information systems. Data-Centric Engineering, 1, E14. doi:10.1017/dce.2020.16

Shim, C.-S., Dang, N.-S., Lon, S., Jeon, C.-H. (2019) Development of a bridge maintenance system for prestressed concrete bridges using 3D digital twin model, Structure and Infrastructure Engineering, 15:10, 1319-1332, doi: 10.1080/15732479.2019.1620789

Errandonea, I., Beltran, S., Arrizabalaga, S. (2020). Digital Twin for maintenance: A literature review, Computers in Industry, Volume 123, 2020, ISSN 0166-3615, https://doi.org/10.1016/j.compind.2020.103316.

von Rueden, L., Mayer, S., Beckh, K., Georgiev, B., Giesselbach, S., Heese, R., Kirsch, B., Walczak, M., Pfrommer, J., Pick, A., Ramanmurthy, R., Garcke, J., Bauckhage, C., Schuecker, J. (2021). Informed Machine Learning - A Taxonomy and Survey of Integrating Prior Knowledge into Learning Systems, in IEEE Transactions on Knowledge and Data Engineering, May 2021, doi: 10.1109/TKDE.2021.3079836.

End-to-end GRU model for construction crew management

Song, Z. [1], Florez-Perez, L [2]
[1]University of Cambridge, UK, [2]University College London, UK,
l.florez@ucl.ac.uk

Abstract. Crew management is critical towards improving construction task productivity. Traditional methods for crew management on-site are heavily dependent on the experience of site managers. This paper proposes an end-to-end Gated Recurrent Units (GRU) based framework which provides site managers a more reliable and robust method for managing crews and improving productivity. The proposed framework predicts task productivity of all possible crew combinations, within a given size, from the pool of available workers using an advanced GRU model. The model has been trained with an existing database of masonry work and was found to outperform other machine learning models. The results of the framework suggest which crew combinations have the highest predicted productivity and can be used by superintendents and project managers to improve construction task productivity and better plan future projects.

Introduction

Productivity is the main indicator of the performance in the construction industry. Performance on-site is measured through task productivity. In the field, site managers are faced with multiple factors such as external conditions, site conditions, and workers characteristics that influence task productivity of construction crews. Choosing the most productive crew is one of the most critical factors to improve construction task productivity in this labour-intensive industry. For this, site managers need to consider the factors' effect to form crews and strategically assign crews to tasks to achieve high productivity rates. Site managers however typically manage crews based on experience, which is often unreliable and time consuming. Additionally, there are multiple factors and interrelationships between factors that affect the productivity of crews (external conditions, site conditions, and workers characteristics). This complexity poses a challenge for site managers to fully understand the factors effects. Reliable and robust methods are needed to process large amounts of data to determine optimal crew formations.

Machine learning (ML) is an application of artificial intelligence (AI) that provides systems the ability to automatically learn and improve from experience without being explicitly programmed (Expert.ai Team, 2020). In recent years, ML is starting to gain its significance with the potential to transform the construction industry with the use of data-based solutions to improve the way construction projects are delivered. ML techniques have been successfully applied to model and predict construction productivity (Reich, 1997; Al-Zwainy, Rasheed and Ibraheem, 2012; Mahfouz, 2012; Akinosho., 2020; Song., 2020; Cheng, Cao and Jaya Mendrofa, 2021; Florez-Perez, Song and Cortissoz, 2022). Challenges however remain. Firstly, the existing work mainly relies on the review of literature, surveys, and expert interviews (El-Gohary and Aziz, 2014; Ebrahimi, Fayek and Sumati, 2021) to identify the factors that affect productivity, with limited considerations of the complexity due to non-linearity of underlying factors, interrelationships between the factors, and temporal information and interdependencies of the data (Reich, 1997; Ebrahimi, Fayek and Sumati, 2021), Secondly, the data collected does not provide sufficient information regarding the conditions and complexity of construction sites as well as the tacit knowledge of on-site personnel. (Xu, 2021). This lack of integration of site realities and industry experts' knowledge hinders the ability to model processes in a comprehensive way (Bilal and Oyedele, 2020).

https://doi.org/10.7146/aul.455.c210

Our previous work proposes a combined ML approach that offers a solution for classifying and predicting task productivity with experimental data of masonry tasks (Florez-Perez, Song and Cortissoz, 2022). "Compatibility" a measure of "how the masons get along" is a factor used by superintendents to form crews. This subjective characteristic (associated with the workforce) is a novel consideration for building more robust ML models to forecast construction productivity. In this work we used compatibility of personality, together with external and site conditions, and workers' characteristics (age and years of experience) to predict task productivity. K-nearest neighbour (KNN) (Batista and Monard, 2002; Delany, 2021), deep neural network (DNN) (Canziani, Paszke and Culurciello, 2016), logistic regression (Field, 2009), support vector machine (SVM) (Noble, 2006), and Residual Neural Network (ResNet18) (He, 2016; Wu, Shen and van den Hengel, 2019) alongside rigorous statistical analyses were employed to interpret data and investigate the pattern mapping between input factors and productivity class labels. Results suggest that: 1) small crews have relatively higher productivity than large crews, 2) compatibility among the masons has more significant impact on the productivity in easy but not in difficult tasks; and 3) the relevance of experience to task productivity may depend on the difficulty of the task.

Two shortcomings about our work can be stated. The data was collected in 5-minute intervals, that is, temporal sequential data. The ML models chosen however lack the capability to capture the temporal dependence in the sequential data, which leads to the loss in information and affects the performance of the ML model. Furthermore, our previous work only interprets the input data and predicts productivity with no indications of crew formation. Therefore, it is worth investigating the performance of advanced deep learning models which can solve problems with sequential input data to identify data correlations and patterns through time-series. The data at hand can be used to provide indications for superintendents to choose and assemble crews on-site.

In this article, an end-to-end GRU framework for construction project crew management is proposed to classify and predict construction task productivity from the temporal-sequential data of the existing database (external site conditions, masons' characteristics, and compatibilities). The result of the framework provides superintendents with the crew combination with the highest predicted productivity for the given task. To capture the temporal-dependency of the sequential data, variants of Recurrent Neural Network (RNN) models including Long Short-Term Memory (LSTM) and Gated Recurrent Unit (GRU) are employed to predict construction task productivity. The performance of the LSTM and GRU models are compared with the baseline models including DNN, KNN, SVM and ResNet18. The advanced deep learning models (RNN, LSTM and GRU) have achieved state-of-the-art performance. Furthermore, to help superintendents assemble the most productive crews, the end-to-end framework automatically calculates the predicted productivity of all possible crew combinations (from the available masons) and identifies the combinations with the highest predicted productivity (Bai, 2019; Hegde, 2020; Kraft, 2020). These combinations will serve as suggestions for superintendents on site, to improve productivity of construction tasks with more productive crew combinations.

Literature Review

Researchers in the construction industry have made several remarkable attempts to keep up with the pace of applying ML techniques (Akinosho, 2020). Supervised learning uses a training set to teach models to yield the desired output (Caruana and Niculescu-Mizil, 2006). Supervised learning algorithms have been extensively applied in construction including SVM, logistic regression, random forest, and KNN for supporting decision making (Wong, 2004; Akinosho,

2020), forecasting occupational accidents (Kang and Ryu, 2019), and evaluating projects (Erzaij, 2020). Unsupervised learning on the other hand uses machine learning algorithms to analyse and cluster unlabelled datasets (Marsland, 2020). Given the presence of large amounts of unlabelled data in the construction field, unsupervised machine learning algorithms such as K-means clustering and principle component analysis serve as effective tools in competitive positioning (Horta and Camanho, 2014) and sustainability evaluation (Li, 2012).

Deep learning (DL) is a subfield of ML which is based on artificial neural networks with representation learning. DL methods aim at learning feature hierarchies with features at higher levels of the hierarchy formed by the composition of lower-level features. DL has been employed to tackle construction challenges such as construction site safety (Yu, 2019), building occupancy modelling (Chen and Jiang, 2018) and energy demand prediction (Rahman, Srikumar and Smith, 2018). For the specific case of productivity, studies have benefited from the application of DL because these techniques provide an effective approach to determine the relationship between the influencing factors and productivity rates and the complexity of the combined effects between factors (Courville, 2016; Li, 2021). A noteworthy point is that many proposed approaches have been dealing with the problem of predicting productivity while ignoring the spatial-temporal dependencies of the collected dataset. In addition, many approaches generate predictions and analyse results, but do not go beyond to provide project managers and superintendents with practical tools for crew management that can support productivity improvement in real construction sites.

Construction Task Productivity

Productivity refers to the measure of the full utilization of inputs to achieve an expected output (Durdyev and Mbachu, 2011). In the field, productivity is measured at the task level, for practical considerations. Since masonry is one of the most labour-intensive trades in construction, the task-level model will be used in this study as single-factor productivity, which is expressed as the unit of work per labour hour (Shehata and El-Gohary, 2011). To detail the factors three sections, namely, external conditions, site conditions, and workers characteristics describe typical attributes of masonry jobsites. The reader is referred to Florez-Perez, Song and Cortissoz (2022) for an extended description of the factors.

1) External conditions: the external conditions refer to the temperature regarding the building the crews were working at the specific time the data were collected. The temperature, both low and high temperature, was recorded for the day at the time the data were collected. 2) Conditions in masonry sites: extensive site observations and interviews with masonry practitioners (Florez, 2017) were used to collect information of typical site conditions related to walls. The masonry tasks were classified as three different levels, namely Easy (difficulty = 1), Normal (difficulty = 2), and Difficult (difficulty = 3). 3) Workers' characteristics: masons have different ages and length of experience in the field, which could have an impact on their productivity together with other external factors and conditions in construction sites. The size of crews was annotated as it happened on site, which is typically determined by site managers in accordance with the workload. Compatibility between masons, defined as a measure of the capability of a group to interact and work well together to attain higher productivity, was collected during the extensive site visits and interviews with the site manager.

Dataset

In our previous work, a dataset of masonry work was used to analyse the factors that affect task productivity and to predict task productivity. In this study, using the same dataset, we will analyse the temporal dependency of the factors and provide site managers with indications of optimal crew formations. The dataset had 1977 data samples, each of which includes the following features: low temperature of the day; high temperature of the day; level of difficulty of the masonry task; number of masons; compatibility of mason 1; compatibility (mason 1 & mason 2); compatibility (mason 1 & mason 3); compatibility (mason 2 & mason 3); age (mason 1,2&3); experience (mason 1,2&3). Productivity was measured by the number of blocks built in 5-minute time intervals, thus makes the dataset temporal-sequential. Therefore, LSTM and GRU models are applied to capture the temporal dependencies in the time series dataset to forecast task productivity.

Methodology

DL is a subfield of ML concerned with algorithms inspired by the structure and function of the brain called artificial neural networks. RNN is a type of artificial neural network which uses sequential data or time series data. The variants of RNN models including LSTM and GRU (Chung, 2014; Greff, 2017) were used to predict the level of productivity of construction tasks using the information from the dataset. Then, an end-to-end framework was developed to predict productivity of all possible crew combinations, from the masons available, and provide superintendents with the crew combinations with the highest predicted productivity.

Data Processing

The dataset contains 1977 data samples with 14 dimensions for training and prediction. The dataset was divided into training and testing data sets and input data labelled by their corresponding productivity, which is measured by the number of blocks built per minute per mason. In the experiments, the level of productivity was classified as low (< 0.2), medium low ($(0.2,0.4]$), medium high ($(0.4,0.6]$), and high (≥ 0.6), considering that the average productivity of the whole data set is 0.433 and the standard deviation is 0.182. To ensure the input data was internally consistent, standardisation was implemented using Scikit-learn to pre-process the data using the formula below:

$$X_{standardisation} = \frac{X - \bar{X}}{\sigma X} \quad (1)$$

where $\bar{X}$ and σX are the mean and standard deviation of the input dataset.

The dataset was balanced so that each class had approximately the same amount of data samples. To prevent the trained model from overfitting on certain classes while underfitting on other classes, a sufficient amount of duplication of the data in the minority classes were added to the dataset. Then, the dataset was shuffled and divided into training, validation and testing sets in the ratio 2400:700:711. Further details of data processing can be found in Florez-Perez, Song and Cortissoz (2022).

Experiments

A RNN (Zaremba, Sutskever and Vinyals, 2014) is a class of artificial neural network, where connections between nodes form a directed or undirected graph along a temporal sequence. This allows the network to have memory for the earlier data points in the sequential data, to gain context and identify correlations and patterns to improve the prediction. Since our data was collected in 5-minute time intervals, the temporal dependences in this sequential dataset can be captured with the RNN networks to predict construction productivity. The original RNN model however suffers from short-term memory due to the vanishing gradient problem during back propagation (Zaremba, Sutskever and Vinyals, 2014). For this reason, LSTM and GRU can be proposed by implementation of gates, which is a memory cell to store the activation value of previous data in the long sequences. Gates are capable of learning which inputs in the sequence are important and storing their information in the memory unit. They can pass the information in long sequences and use them to make predictions. The LSTM and GRU networks differ in their structure. GRU has two gates (reset and update), while LSTM has three gates (input, output, forget). Hence, GRU is simpler than LSTM because it has a smaller number of gates. Experiments were performed with both LSTM and GRU networks, and compared with the baseline models including DNN, KNN, SVM and ResNet18 with the evaluation matrices of classification accuracy and F1 score.

For the LSTM network, a batch size of 64 was chosen which is a hyperparameter of gradient descent that controls the number of training samples to work through before the model's internal parameters are updated. Three hidden layers, with a hidden size of 32, were chosen as the structure of the LSTM model with Adam as the optimizer (Kingma and Ba, 2015) and learning rate of 0.01. To train the neural network, cross-entropy loss was selected as the loss function, which is a commonly used loss function for multi-class classification problems. The LSTM model was trained for 80 epochs until there was no significant change in the plots of training and validation loss. The best performing epoch in terms of validation loss was saved for testing the model on the testing dataset. A classification accuracy of 71.9% and an F1 score of 0.703 were achieved. The confusion matrix of the LSTM network on the testing set is shown in Figure 1. Columns represent the ground truth of the classification and rows stand for the predicted classification results.

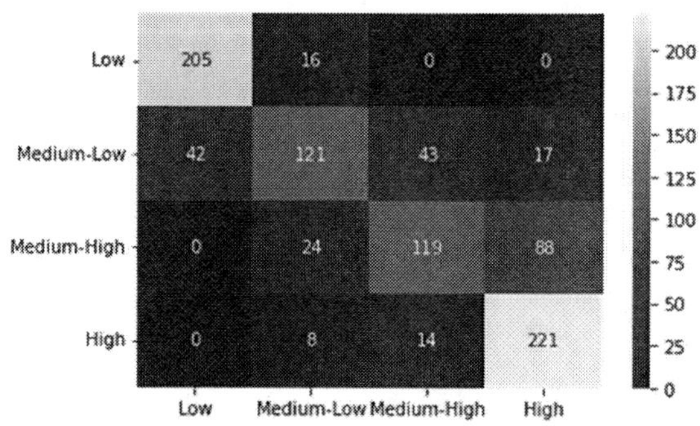

Figure 1: Confusion matrix for the LSTM network

For the GRU model, a network with three hidden layers with a size of 24 was built. A batch size of 32 was chosen together with Adam optimizer and learning rate of 0.01. The cross-entropy loss was employed as the loss function to train the GRU model for 80 epochs and the model from the epoch with lowest validation loss was saved for testing. The GRU network achieved a classification accuracy of 74.5% and an F1 score of 0.729. The confusion matrix of the GRU model on the testing dataset is shown in Figure 2.

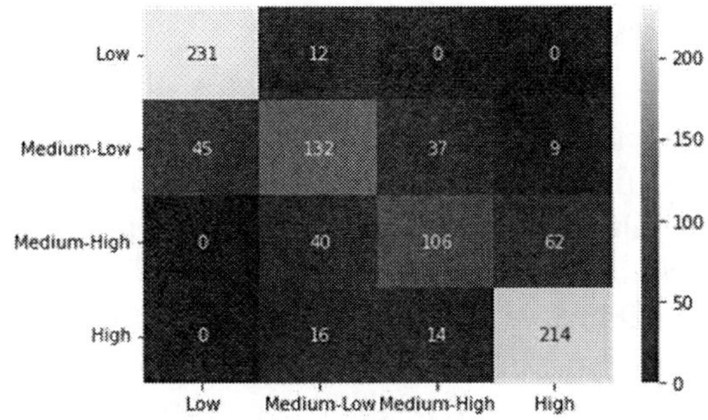

Figure 2: Confusion matrix for the GRU network

Performance Comparison

The experimental results of the LSTM and GRU models are compared with the baseline machine learning models in Florez-Perez, Song and Cortissoz (2022), which include KNN, SVM, logistic regression, DNN, and ResNet18. The comparison was made using evaluation matrices for classification accuracy and F1 scores, calculated using equations (2) and (3) below:

$$Classification\ Accuracy = \frac{TP + TN}{TP + FP + TN + FN} \quad (2)$$

$$F1 = \frac{TP}{TP + \frac{1}{2}(FP + FN)} \quad (3)$$

where TP, TN, FP, and FN refer to true positive, true negative, false positive and false negative, respectively. The results of the proposed methods and the baseline models on the testing dataset are shown in Table 1. Note that the highest classification accuracy and F1 scores are for the GRU model.

Table 1: Performance comparison using classification accuracy and F1 scores

Machine Learning model	Classification Accuracy	F1 Score
KNN	70.7%	0.711
Sigmoid SVM	73.7%	0.728
Logistic Regression	61.3%	0.604
DNN	67.9%	0.576
ResNet18	72.9%	0.711
LSTM	71.9%	0.703
GRU	74.5%	0.729

As shown in Table 1, the GRU model achieves the best performance in terms of both classification accuracy and F1 score, indicating that the GRU model provides the best prediction for task productivity among all experimented models.

End-to-end Framework for Crew Management

To provide superintendents with indications to assemble the most productive crews and thus maximise construction task productivity, an end-to-end framework was developed using the trained GRU network. The proposed framework can automatically calculate the predicted productivity of all possible crew combinations, with a given size from the pool of available masons and suggest superintendents which combinations which have the highest predicted productivity. The proposed framework is illustrated in Figure 3 and includes three stages, namely data collection, crew generation, and productivity prediction and ranking. In the first stage, assuming that there are n masons available to form a crew of k masons, information including external conditions, conditions in masonry sites and the workers' characteristics, including every pairwise compatibility among the masons, will need to be collected by the site manager as explained in Section 0. The compatibility of each pairwise of masons needs to be calculated. Then, for a task that requires a crew of k masons, the second stage generates all possible combinations of masons for that crew from a total number of N crews, calculated using equation (4):

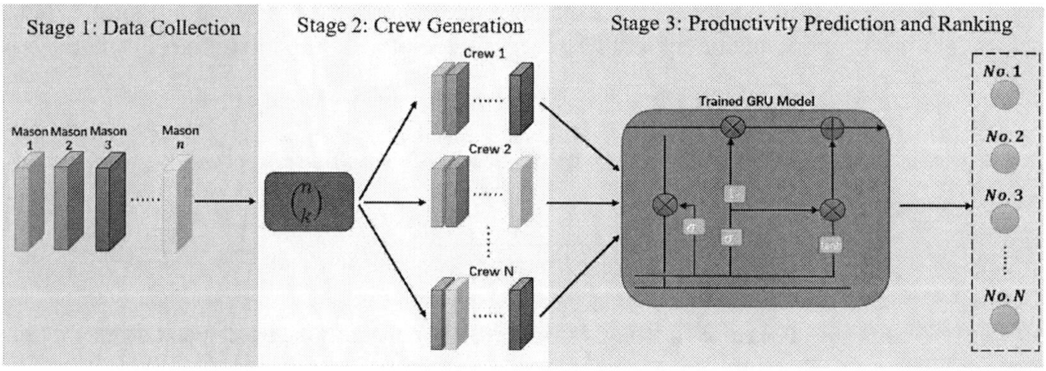

Figure 3: Pipeline of the proposed end-to-end GRU-RNN model for construction project resource management

$$N = \binom{n}{k} = \frac{n!}{k!\,(n-k)!} \tag{4}$$

Next, the information data of each possible crew is fed into the trained GRU model (discussed in Section 0), since the GRU model outperformed the baseline machine learning models and LSTM network both in terms of classification accuracy and F1 score. Given the external conditions, conditions in masonry sites and the workers' characteristics as the input data, the GRU model can be used to predict for the class of the productivity of each crew combination option and then rank the results as the output of the framework. This output provides superintendents with a simple and straightforward indication to choose the crew that maximises the productivity of the construction project.

Compared to the traditional experience-based method of choosing crews, this proposed end-to-end framework provides site managers a more reliable and robust method to improve construction productivity, as site managers may focus more on certain variables, however our model will consider all the variables affecting the productivity, making it more robust to predict the productivity. Also, this proposed framework ensures that crew management at the construction site does not only rely on the experience of superintendents, but on an autonomous system that reduces time and supports the decision-making process of crew formation.

Conclusions

This paper proposes an end-to-end GRU based method for construction crew management. The GRU is an advanced DL model, able to capture the temporal dependencies in the sequential data, to provide an accurate prediction on the class of the productivity of construction tasks. An existing real-world database of masonry work which includes external conditions, site conditions and workers' characteristics, was used to train the GRU model. This proposed GRU based framework provides a reliable and robust platform for project and site managers to efficiently select crews for different construction tasks.

Acknowledgements

This research has been partly funded by University College London's Bartlett Research Grants Scheme 2020-2021.

References

Akinosho, T. D., Oyedele, L. O., Bilal, M., Ajayi, A. O., Delgado, M. D., Akinade, O. O. and Ahmed, A. A. (2020). Deep learning in the construction industry: A review of present status and future innovations, *Journal of Building Engineering*, 32, p. 101827. doi: 10.1016/j.jobe.2020.101827.

Al-Zwainy, F. M. S., Rasheed, H. A. and Ibraheem, H. F. (2012). Development of the construction productivity estimation model using artificial neural network for finishing works for floors with marble, *ARPN Journal of Engineering and Applied Sciences*, 7(6), pp. 714–722.

Bai, S., Li, M., Kong, R., Han, S., Li, H. and Qin, L. (2019). Data mining approach to construction productivity prediction for cutter suction dredgers, *Automation in Construction*, 105, p. 102833. doi: 10.1016/j.autcon.2019.102833.

Batista, G. E. A. P. A. and Monard, M. C. (2002). A study of k-nearest neighbour as an imputation method, *Frontiers in Artificial Intelligence and Applications*, 87, pp. 251–260.

Bilal, M. and Oyedele, L. O. (2020). Guidelines for applied machine learning in construction industry—A case of profit margins estimation, *Advanced Engineering Informatics*, 43, p. 101013. doi: 10.1016/j.aei.2019.101013.

Canziani, A., Paszke, A. and Culurciello, E. (2016). An Analysis of Deep Neural Network Models for Practical Applications, pp. 1–7. Available at: http://arxiv.org/abs/1605.07678.

Caruana, R. and Niculescu-Mizil, A. (2006). An empirical comparison of supervised learning algorithms, *ACM International Conference Proceeding Series*, 148, pp. 161–168. doi: 10.1145/1143844.1143865.

Chen, Z. and Jiang, C. (2018). Building occupancy modeling using generative adversarial network, *Energy and Buildings*, 174, pp. 372–379. doi: 10.1016/j.enbuild.2018.06.029.

Cheng, M. Y., Cao, M. T. and Jaya Mendrofa, A. Y. (2021). Dynamic feature selection for accurately predicting construction productivity using symbiotic organisms search-optimized least square support vector machine, *Journal of Building Engineering*, 35, p. 101973. doi: 10.1016/j.jobe.2020.101973.

Chung, J., Gulcehre, C., Cho, K and Bengio, Y (2014). Empirical Evaluation of Gated Recurrent Neural Networks on Sequence Modeling, pp. 1–9. Available at: http://arxiv.org/abs/1412.3555.

Courville, I. G. and Y. B. and A. (2016). Deep learning Deep Learning', *Nature*, 29(7553), pp. 1–73.

Delany, S. J. (2021). k-Nearest Neighbour Classifiers - A Tutorial, 54(6).

Durdyev, S. and Mbachu, J. (2011) 'On-site labour productivity of New Zealand construction industry: Key constraints and improvement measures', *Australasian Journal of Construction Economics and Building*, 11(3), pp. 18–33. doi: 10.5130/ajceb.v11i3.2120.

Ebrahimi, S., Fayek, A. R. and Sumati, V. (2021). Hybrid artificial intelligence hfs-rf-pso model for construction labor productivity prediction and optimization, *Algorithms*, 14(7). doi: 10.3390/a14070214.

El-Gohary, K. M. and Aziz, R. F. (2014). Factors Influencing Construction Labor Productivity in Egypt, *Journal of Management in Engineering*, 30(1), pp. 1–9. doi: 10.1061/(asce)me.1943-5479.0000168.

Erzaij, K. R., Rashid, H. A., Naji, H. I., and Ali, R. H. (2020). Projects evaluation in construction industry, *Periodicals of Engineering and Natural Sciences*, 8(3), pp. 1808–1816. doi: 10.21533/pen.v8i3.1593.

Expert.ai Team (2020). *No Title, What is Machine Learning? A Definition.* Available at: https://www.expert.ai/blog/machine-learning-definition/.

Field, A. (2009). Aims and Objectives Logistic Regression When and Why do we Use Logistic With One Predictor P (Y) = The Wald Statistic Exp (b) Methods of Regression An Example Logistic Regression on SPSS Methods Residuals, *Options*, pp. 1–4.

Florez-Perez, L., Song, Z. and Cortissoz, J. C. (2022). Using machine learning to analyze and predict construction task productivity, *Computer-Aided Civil and Infrastructure Engineering*, pp. 1–15. doi: 10.1111/mice.12806.

Florez, L. (2017). Crew Allocation System for the Masonry Industry, *Computer-Aided Civil and Infrastructure Engineering*, 32(10), pp. 874–889. doi: 10.1111/mice.12301.

Greff, K., Srivastava, R. K., Koutn´ık, J., Steunebrink, B. R. and Schmidhuber, J. (2017) LSTM: A Search Space Odyssey, *IEEE Transactions on Neural Networks and Learning Systems*, 28(10), pp. 2222–2232. doi: 10.1109/TNNLS.2016.2582924.

He, K., Zhang, X., Ren, S. and Sun, J. (2016). Deep residual learning for image recognition', *Proceedings of the IEEE Computer Society Conference on Computer Vision and Pattern Recognition*, pp. 770–778. doi: 10.1109/CVPR.2016.90.

Hegde, C., Pyrcz, M,. Millwater, H., Daigle, H. and Gray, K. (2020). Fully coupled end-to-end drilling optimization model using machine learning, *Journal of Petroleum Science and Engineering*, 186, p. 106681. doi: 10.1016/j.petrol.2019.106681.

Horta, I. M. and Camanho, A. S. (2014). Competitive positioning and performance assessment in the construction industry, *Expert Systems with Applications*, 41(4 PART 1), pp. 974–983. doi: 10.1016/j.eswa.2013.06.064.

Kang, K. and Ryu, H. (2019). Predicting types of occupational accidents at construction sites in Korea using random forest model, *Safety Science*, 120, pp. 226–236. doi: 10.1016/j.ssci.2019.06.034.

Kingma, D. P. and Ba, J. L. (2015). Adam: A method for stochastic optimization', *3rd International Conference on Learning Representations, ICLR 2015 - Conference Track Proceedings*, pp. 1–15.

Kraft, P., Kang, D., Narayanan, D., Palkar, S., Bailis, P. and Zaharia,. M. (2020). Willump: A Statistically-Aware End-to-End Optimizer, *MLSys*, (113), pp. 13–21. Available at: http://arxiv.org/abs/1906.01974.

Li, S., Shi, W., Wang, J. and Zhou, H. (2021). A Deep Learning-Based Approach to Constructing a Domain Sentiment Lexicon: a Case Study in Financial Distress Prediction, *Information Processing and Management*, 58(5), p. 102673. doi: 10.1016/j.ipm.2021.102673.

Li, T., Zhang, H., Yuan, C., Liu, Z. and Fan, C. (2012). A PCA-based method for construction of composite sustainability indicators, *International Journal of Life Cycle Assessment*, 17(5), pp. 593–603. doi: 10.1007/s11367-012-0394-y.

Mahfouz, T. (2012). A Productivity Decision Support System for Construction Projects Through Machine Learning (ML), *Proceedings of the CIB W78 2012: 29th International Conference*, (ML), pp. 1–10.

Marsland, S. (2020). Unsupervised Learning, *Machine Learning*, pp. 211–236. doi: 10.1201/9781420067194-13.

Noble, W. S. (2006). What is a support vector machine?, *Nature Biotechnology*, 24(12), pp. 1565–1567. doi: 10.1038/nbt1206-1565.

Rahman, A., Srikumar, V. and Smith, A. D. (2018). Predicting electricity consumption for commercial and residential buildings using deep recurrent neural networks, *Applied Energy*, 212(December 2017), pp. 372–385. doi: 10.1016/j.apenergy.2017.12.051.

Reich, Y. (1997). Machine learning techniques for civil engineering problems, *Computer-Aided Civil and Infrastructure Engineering*, 12(4), pp. 295–310. doi: 10.1111/0885-9507.00065.

Shehata, M. E. and El-Gohary, K. M. (2011). Towards improving construction labor productivity and projects' performance, *Alexandria Engineering Journal*, 50(4), pp. 321–330. doi: 10.1016/j.aej.2012.02.001.

Song, W., Song, Z., Vincent, J., Wang, H. and Wang, Z. (2020). Quantification of extra virgin olive oil adulteration using smartphone videos, *Talanta*, 216(March), p. 120920. doi: 10.1016/j.talanta.2020.120920.

Wong, C. H. (2004). Contractor Performance Prediction Model for the United Kingdom Construction Contractor: Study of Logistic Regression Approach, *Journal of Construction Engineering and Management*, 130(5), pp. 691–698. doi: 10.1061/(asce)0733-9364(2004)130:5(691).

Wu, Z., Shen, C. and van den Hengel, A. (2019). Wider or Deeper: Revisiting the ResNet Model for Visual Recognition, *Pattern Recognition*, 90, pp. 119–133. doi: 10.1016/j.patcog.2019.01.006.

Xu, Y., Zhou, Y., Sekula, P. and Ding, L. (2021). Machine learning in construction: From shallow to deep learning, *Developments in the Built Environment*, 6(February), p. 100045. doi: 10.1016/j.dibe.2021.100045.

Yu, Y., Li, H., Yang, X., Kong, L., Luo, X., Wong and A. Y.L.(2019). An automatic and non-invasive physical fatigue assessment method for construction workers, *Automation in Construction*, 103(March), pp. 1–12. doi: 10.1016/j.autcon.2019.02.020.

Zaremba, W., Sutskever, I. and Vinyals, O. (2014). Recurrent Neural Network Regularization, (2013), pp. 1–8. Available at: http://arxiv.org/abs/1409.2329.

Computation of Ranges in Interval-based Constraint-Geometry of Building Models

Kirchner, J.
Fachgebiet Bauinformatik, TU Berlin, Germany
jakob.kirchner@tu-berlin.de

Abstract. Determining the optimal design of geometry in building models is an essential task for architects and engineers. Although many constraints are considered, only a small part is currently integrated into digital models as design knowledge. Current software products do not support the declarative approach of creating constraints and permissible ranges to parameter values. The reason is the algorithmic complexity in analyzation and evaluation of such a constraint model. In this paper the problem is summarized and a solution for the computation of possible ranges is presented. It makes use of existing algorithms. This research is part of the so-called geometric constraint satisfaction problem (GSCP). Although former approaches exist, they weren't applicable to the general case. The success of this approach is shown for a selected example. Future steps are discussed. These would be required for a modelling software benefitting from this approach.

1. Introduction

The state of the art in the creation of digital building models including 3D geometry requires an iterative process. This includes the placement of building objects and checking whether the current model meets certain requirements. These requirements comprise rules from standards and laws, but also originate from project contracts, architectural design intent, feasibility of building processes or valid geometric consistency. The paradigm of parametric modeling is common for adjusting a model to certain requirements, creating variants or reducing the time needed for subsequent modifications. Therefore, input parameters and computation rules are used to create a computational system. This can be used for an efficient recomputiation of a solution whenever a parameter value gets changed. One approach is the modeling of dependencies between the parameters as a computational plan. This concept distinguishes between input and output parameters and can be represented as a directed acyclic graph with edges describing the computational direction. A different approach is the use of so-called constraints which includes dependencies between parameters with no predefined computational direction. The approach is declarative and usually requires a solver with sophisticated algorithms to obtain solutions. That's because, a computational plan has to be identified or an equation system has to be solved. In complex models including many dependencies the computational plan and the feasible values for the parameters cannot be obtained easily because of the structural properties of the modeled problem.

Current modeling software like Autodesk Revit 2022, AutoCAD 2022, ArchiCAD 25 by Graphisoft is based on the principle of parametric design, but does only support single values for each parameter value. The basic principle - although not explicitly mentioned by the companies and not every piece of information is presented to the user – is apparently history-based design and its variants (Shah, 2001). History-based design requires a strict modeling direction. Although variational design by constraints (Shah, 2001) is also supported in these software products, it is limited to 2-dimensional sketches as parts of the construction history tree. In practice these limits prevent a massive use of constraints regarding the optimization of design. Nevertheless, there exist practical approaches for optimizing the design, e.g. generative methods or machine learning. As a limitation, these approaches allow only as many constraints

https://doi.org/10.7146/aul.455.c211

as needed for ensuring a single solution can be computed. Additional constraints cannot be considered or have to be validated iteratively. Alternative visions describe a software environment which can be used to control the number of variants by adding, removing or modifying requirements. Variants would be ready for examination and for adjusting the limits (Bettig et al. 2005, p. 8). Valdes et al. (2016) expect such approaches to increase the consistence of a model and the reduction of errors.

Another limit in current CAD and modeling software is the support for exactly one existing value for each parameter or coordinates. This principle known as *point-based design* leads to the situation where the possible ranges of parameter values are not clearly evident. In contrast to that, the idea of set-based design was introduced by the Japanese automobile company Toyota (Sobek et al. 1999) and has the goal of representing all sections of the design space. The design is refined by narrowing and cutting the remaining design space until the project converges to a point-based state (Liker et al. 1996, p. 167). Applying the idea of set-based design to digital models was already proposed for building projects (Gil et al. 2008). Yannou et al. (2013) developed a small model of interval values for parameters and computed possible values using interval arithmetic. Assuming a working software product supporting set-based design there are different workflows which are of interest for engineers and architects. They accumulate in questions like:

- What are the possible values for a parameter considering all other parameters and their dependencies?
- How can a solution be found which fulfills different criteria and how can these criteria be formulated as a query?
- How can the available solution space be visualized?

Currently there exists no known CAD (computer-aided design) or modeling software which supports set-based design using intervals for the ranges of parameters and constraints for describing the dependencies in geometry. The idea of developing such kind of tools has not yet been realized, but Bettig et al. (2005) state, the benefits would be significant especially in planning processes of the building industry.

The implementation of algorithms to answer the raised questions requires a large effort, but is highly useful for engineering or architectural design tasks. This paper focuses on algorithms needed to compute efficiently the available range of parameters for geometry considering all modeled constraints. As the underlaying problem is the computation of solutions of linear equations – therefore also nonlinear equations – with interval values is NP-hard (Kreinovich and Lakeyev, 1996), this research has the goal of combining existing algorithms which are highly efficient in computing these ranges. The presented solution combines existing algorithms especially from the field of interval computation. It is capable of solving arbitrary systems, can be applied to any constraint graph and is independent of structural properties of the problem in the sense of completeness. This includes systems that are weak or strongly under-constraint as well as well-constraint systems. Linear and non-linear equations are supported. The direction of dependency between parameters has not to be determined as there has no difference to be made between input and output parameters. The presented example is intentionally small, because the complexity of constraint systems usually increases sharply with the number of objects. Relating thereto, it is difficult to describe and to explain plainly the structure of a constraint system. Research in presenting structures of constraint systems is beyond the scope of this paper. This paper has a focus on the computational aspect. It also introduces the idea of set-based design, the geometric constraint satisfaction problem and interval computation which aren’t widespread, especially their combination.

2. Methodology

2.1 Geometric Constraint Satisfaction Problem

Geometric constraint systems - a special case of constraint systems - include geometric objects like points, lines, circles, etc. and geometric constraints like *orthogonal lines*, *parallel lines*, *coincident points*. Geometric constraints describe the relations of geometric objects in a semantical way. This is different to numeric constraints which can be regarded as linear or nonlinear equations. Nevertheless, it's possible to describe geometric constraints as numerical constraints using one or more equations. The description of a constraint system is declarative which means the problem itself is described instead of the so-called imperative approach which prescribes the steps to solve the problem. Because of missing information about the way of solving, this is regarded as the geometric constraint satisfaction problem (GCSP) as a part of the field of constraint satisfaction problems (CSP).

According to Hoffmann and Joan-Arinyo (2005), Joan-Arinyo (2009), Bettig and Hoffmann (2011) and Sitharam et al. (2019) there exist different approaches of solving GCSP: An algebraic approach by solving equation systems; theorem proving by analyzing axioms linked to theorems; a logic-based approach by assumptions and axioms which get solved with a rule-based reasoner rewriting the constraint system to generate procedural solving steps and graph-based by dividing the constraint graph into subproblems and using known solution strategies for the subproblems

Solving algorithms heavily depend on the properties of the constraint system. Various algorithms only solve systems that are serializable (Sitharam et al. 2019, p. 145 and 152). This includes an ordered processing of the constraint graph to create a construction plan or creating a triangular equation system. Complex systems exist which are not serializable thus need a more sophisticated solver. These systems are called “variational” (Sitharam et al. 2019, p. 145) as their parts are mutually dependent. This is usually the case whenever the number of included dependencies is significantly increased.

Another significant property is the existence of solutions. In the case of exactly one solution of the CSP the system is regarded as well-constraint. This is the intended state in a point-based modeling approach. Over-constraint (no possible solution) and especially well-constraint systems can usually be handled by all solving algorithms. In contrast to this, under-constraint systems suffer from the multiple solution problem. This is also referred to as the *root identification problem* regarding CSP represented as an equation system. The problem is the non-existence of a criteria for choosing one solution from the set of solutions. Although Shimizu et al. (1997) state that the user usually sets too less or too many constraints. In this paper it is assumed that under-constraint systems are the intended standard case as the set-based design proclaims. The well-constraint case occurs as the special case when a single final solution is found and the design process finishes.

2.2 Interval Arithmetic

The representation of intervals and their arithmetic was introduced by Moore (1966). There exist various publications, research projects and also a standard (IEEE Std 1788-2015) which is based on the floating-point number standard IEEE Std 754-2008. The main theorem in the calculation with intervals is the inclusion isotonicity of the projection. Every function has to guarantee the inclusion of the solution despite of any rounding errors or discontinuity. Dependent on the function and the variant of arithmetic, the operation is not necessarily bi-total apart from rounding errors. This is usually the case for arithmetics only supporting exactly one interval as a result for a function. Variants for interval arithmetic can be mainly classified in "traditional" interval arithmetic which results in a maximum of one interval and real numbers as bounds and the extended interval arithmetic which can have infinite bounds and supports results of more than one interval (Kulisch 2013, p. 140). The extended interval arithmetic can handle divisions by intervals including 0 more accurately by introducing more cases for divisions. This is also true for e.g. the square root function.

An important effect in the calculation of intervals is the interval dependency problem. It occurs whenever a variable with an interval value is used more than once in a formula or calculation sequence. For example, using the variable $A = [-2, 2]$ in a calculation of $A^2 = [0, 4]$ leads to a different result than multiplying the variable separately $A \cdot A = [-4, 4]$. The square function considers A to be the same variable, whereas the multiplication does not consider the obvious dependency of the two factors. This leads to an overestimation of the result. The interval dependency problem is the main difference between computation with intervals and with single real numbers, especially in the evaluation of results.

2.3 Interval Constraint Satisfaction Problem

Interval constraint systems are a special case of numeric constraint systems. Every variable is defined for the domain $\mathbb{IR}$ and constraints describe the arithmetic relation between variables. The vector of all values of each and every variable in an interval constraint system is called *box* (Moore et al. 2009, p. 15). A box spans in the n-dimensional space. Different queries arise to an interval constraint system and solving these queries is usually affected by the interval dependency problem. Possible queries are: Finding one arbitrary solution, finding the range of valid values of one or more variables, finding the minimum or maximum of a function also known as rigorous optimization. Searching for the range of all variables is the analogion to searching the ranges of parameters in a geometric constraint system. The quality of a box of values for a constraint system can be categorized by a certain level of consistency.
Lower consistencies, like *arc-consistencies* (Mackworth 1981; Miguel et al. 2001) and *box-consistencies* do not consider multiple occurrences of variables and thus the interval dependency problem. In contrast to these lower consistencies, the more rigorous *hull-consistencies* do consider them. The *kB-consistency* guarantees that the intervals of k-1 other variables are consistent to a variable (Lhomme 1993). This leads to the *(n+1)B-consistency* where n is the number of all variables. This is also called the *global hull-consistency* (da Cruz 2003, p. 81) and guarantees that the lower and upper bound of every interval in a box is a solution to the interval constraint satisfaction problem and all other solutions lay in between those bounds. Although, approaches exist which can compute the solution space regarding a certain precision (Fränzle et al. 2007), this paper focus on the global hull-consistency which can be computed with a reduced effort.

3. Existing Approaches

According to Bettig and Hoffmann (2011), computing the valid values of parameters is an open question of GCSPs. A former approach for polygons is presented by Hoffmann and Kim (2001). The presented algorithm is actually only applicable to linear 1-dimensional problems. It computes the range of a single dimensional constraint which is going to be adjusted. The extended approach by van der Meiden (2008) can be used for 2-dimensional cases with distances and angles. His goal is the computation of the valid parameter range of exactly one so-called variant parameter. He uses a constructive graph-based approach by computing special points where the variant parameter has critical values. These are used to determine the minimum and maximum of the range. Hidalgo Garcia (2013, chapter 4) examined the work of Meiden and proofed that the minimum and maximum can be determined but also disjunctive domains.

An approach for using intervals in modeling and solving GCSPs have been introduced by Nahm et al. (2006). They used a prototype of a CAD software for modeling geometric and non-geometric data in early stages of design under a strong uncertainness. They used an interval propagation algorithm which is strongly limited as it cannot solve equations simultaneously though is not applicable for the general case to create the global hull-consistency.

Wang et al. (2007) also used constraint-based modeling with intervals for geometry objects. They solve the equation system by piece-wise linearization with the Gauss-Seidel method. This can narrow intervals, but suffers from the interval dependency problem and cannot create the global hull-consistency in every case. Their presented example is solvable with the simpler HC4 algorithm developed by Benhamou et al. (1999). Kirchner and Huhnt (2018) used the HC4's sub algorithm HC4Revise to compute the global hull for tree-structured constraint graphs which are proven to be free from the interval dependency problem (Benhamou et al. 1999).

In summary, there is no known approach yet for computing the global hull-consistency efficiently and apply it for the computation of valid ranges of all parameters for a GCSP. These ranges are defined by a lower bound and an upper bound which are each part of at least one solution.

4. Proposed Approach

The presented concept includes the transformation of geometric constraints to numeric equations including all parameters as possible interval values. The graph-based representation of the parameters and constraints is transformed to a set of equations and variables. Each constraint is represented by one or more equations and each parameter represents one variable. An example for a transformed equation is given in figure 1.

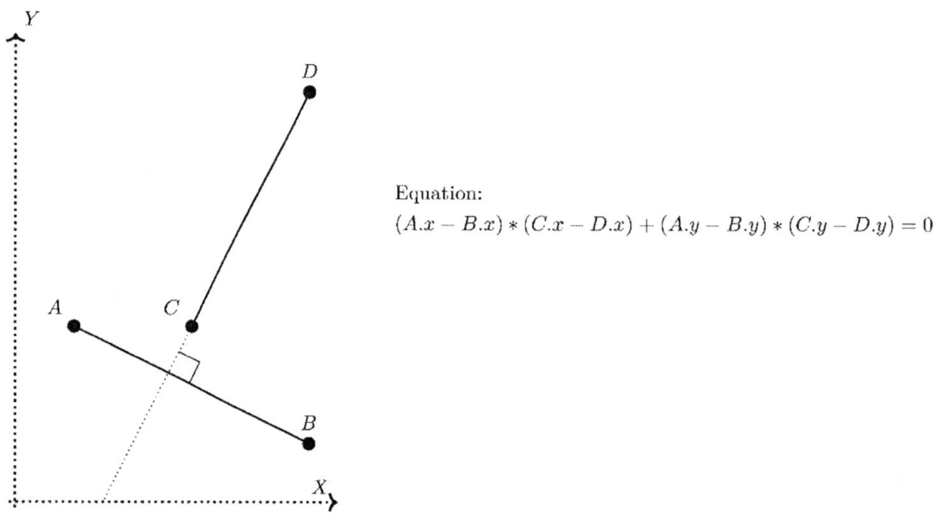

Figure 1: *Orthogonal constraint* for two lines and its equation after transformation.

As common geometric constraints are based on non-linear equations the resulting equation system is non-linear. Additional non-geometric constraints can also be included as equations. It is possible to have more, equal or less variables than equations as this is covered by all chosen algorithms.

The used interval computation library has to support at least the basic mathematical operations and functions like *square* or *square root*. This is the minimal set for the most common geometric constraints. Additionally, set operations like union and intersection are required. For effective solving of interval constraint systems the implementation has to be capable of computing the inverse functions of all operators and functions. An optional requirement which improves the solving process is the differentiation of every equation. This can be realized by automatic differentiation.

The main algorithm to compute the lower and upper bound of each parameter is the *global hull* by da Cruz (2003). This is an efficient algorithm to compute the *(n+1)B-consistency* for an arbitrary case independently of the structure of the constraint graph. The main algorithm uses a set of subalgorithms for reducing the search space. The subalgorithms are heuristics to accelerate the steps to exclude certain parts of the search space which are proven to not include a solution. As there exists a variety of usable heuristics, the proposed approach includes the well-known algorithms *HC4* (Benhamou et al. 1999) and *Interval Newton method*. The Interval Newton method is the interval extension of the Newton-Raphson method considering the first derivative for in- and exclusions.

5. Results

5.1 Implementation Details

The implementation uses a self-developed Java library for interval arithmetic and operations based on the multiple-precision datatype *BigDecimal* of the Java standard. The multiple-precision approach is noticeably slower, but it offers more control over rounding modes and precision in mathematical operations. This is necessary as the control of rounding modes for native IEEE754- floating-point datatypes is not supported by the Java language. The lack of speed is acceptable for research, but is not intended to be used in end-user software. The library also includes the support for extended interval arithmetic which supports more sophisticated case distinction for operations like division or square root. Especially division which is crucial for the *Interval Newton method* leads to disjunctive interval with a reduced overestimation in the intermediate results.

The implemented geometry model is a boundary representation (B-rep) coupled with parameters and constraints. The basic shapes polygon, line and boundary are used to create solids with faces. Only points include a parameter for each coordinate. Extended shapes like e.g. rectangles can be constructed by adding parameters and constraints to basic shapes. Every shape can be assigned to one *functional unit*. Every *functional unit* might represent a digital building element or another element of design or modelling purpose. The objects also can carry a set of parameters which are connected to the parameters of the contained shapes.

A number of geometric constraints is implemented including e.g. parallel lines or orthogonal lines. Additionally, arithmetic constraints for further constraining parameter values are available. They include e.g. the basic mathematic operations and the equality constraint.

Although the parameters, shapes, functional units, constraints and assignment relations are part of a graph representation for analyzation and visualization purposes, a graph is not a requirement for the algorithms. The essential data needed for the computation consists of the equations and variable included in the set of constraints.

5.2 Applied Example

The algorithm was successfully applied to different models like the examples given by Hoffmann and Kim (2001) or Wang et al. (2007). The results correspond with each other.

An example in detail is based on the widely used parametric model of an *extruded rectangular wall*. This is similar to the *IfcWallStandardCase* in the straight case as described by IFC4.2. The wall is described by its *thickness* and *height* and two points forming a line in an XY-plane for placement. These parameters are sufficient for the creation of a geometric representation. The parameter *length* is also added and represents the distance between the two points – P_1 and P_2 – forming the placement line. For a valid solid the points P_3 and P_4 are needed to form the base rectangle with P_1 and P_2 and P_5, P_6, P_7 and P_8 to form the top rectangle. The four side faces are also rectangles formed by pairs of points each from the base and the top. A 3-dimensional sketch is shown in figure 2.

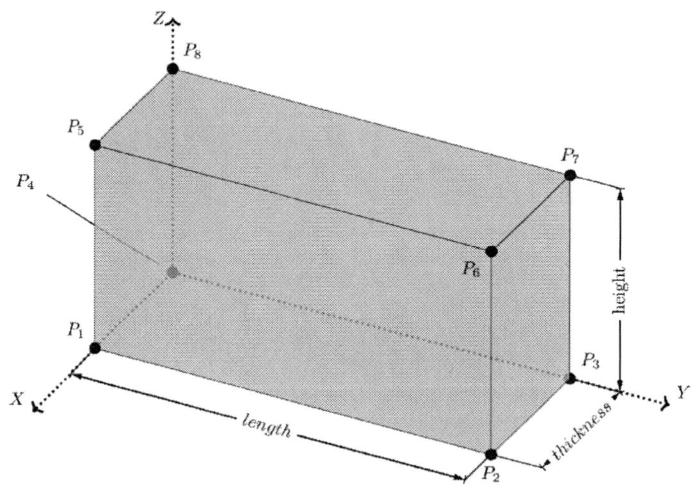

Figure 2: The parameters and vertices of the example *extruded rectangular wall*.

The included constraints for modelling are: orthogonally with oriented distance parameter between line and point in a XY-plane (Orth-O-Dist-XY), oriented distance parameter in z-direction (O-Dist-Z), XY-coordinates of two points equal (Eq-XY), distance parameter of two points (Dist-XY). The constraint graph is shown in figure 3.

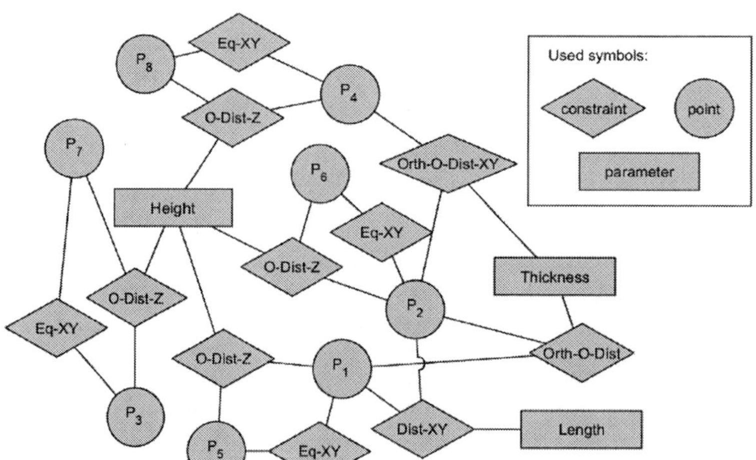

Figure 3: The constraint graph of the example *extruded rectangular wall* including the interrelationships between points, constraints and parameters.

Please note, this is one possible constraint graph. A set of possible variants for constraints in a parametric model of the extruded rectangular wall exists. They share the same parametric behavior.

The example includes 27 variables (3 coordinates for each of the 8 points and 3 parameters for the wall) and 27 equations. A computational run with initial values and the resulting global hull is given in table 1. The computation was limited to the third decimal place.

Table 1: Selected variables and their initial values and their value after computation for the example.

Variable	Initial value	Computed global hull
$P_1.x$	[3]	[3]
$P_1.y$	[0, 1]	[0, 1]
$P_2.x$	[3, 4]	[3, 4]
$P_2.y$	[5]	[5]
$P_3.x$	]- ∞, ∞[	[3.39, 3.710]
$P_3.y$	]- ∞, ∞[	[5, 5.15]
$P_4.x$	]- ∞, ∞[	[2.39, 2.709[
$P_4.y$	]- ∞, ∞[	[0, 1.15]
Thickness	[0.3, 0.6]	[0.3, 0.6]
Height	[2.2]	[2.2]
Length	]0, ∞[	[4, 5.099]

The computed global hull corresponds with the expected results. Because of the freedom of P_1 in x- and P_2 in y- direction the length of the wall is computed with the lower bound of 4 and the upper bound of 5.099 as the wall can be placed vertically or slightly diagonally. The possible diagonal placement and $\overrightarrow{P_3P_4}$ always has to be parallel to $\overrightarrow{P_1P_2}$ by a distance of the thickness, results in intervals instead of single values for the coordinates of P_3 and P_4.

6. Conclusion and Outlook

This paper presents a solution on the problem of computing ranges of parameters for arbitrary geometric constraint systems. The computational result is equivalent to the *(n+1)B-consistency.* The solution transforms the geometric constraints to a set of equations and combines existing algorithms for interval computation to find the relevant solutions for the lower and upper bound of ranges. This is approach can handle under-constraint and well-constraint systems for non-linear equations. The results are promising, although a valid comparison to existing approaches is still missing.

This way of modeling using intervals and constraints requires a change in the way on how to create and work with parametric models. It requires the user to approach an intended solution by exploring the design solutions and is similar to set-based design.

The limit of this approach is the computational effort which is unpredictable for complex models as it depends on the used heuristics and the structure of the constraint system. This means a solution to an apparently complex system is found in a short period of time, but there exist simple examples which can take a long time in the worst case. This is usually the case if a large part of the solution space has to be checked, because it can't be excluded early. Another limit is the requirement of partly continuous mathematical functions excluding piecewise-defined functions. The fixed set of geometry objects for one computation is inherent and limits the applications. The approach does not include models which can have parameters that change the geometric topology e.g. the number and the different types of geometry objects and parameters. This is limited because all constraints have to be transformable to an equation system with a fixed number of variables and equations before the computation can start.

There are different directions of research to pursue. One obvious option is using this approach for parametric studies of different engineering domains. This is promising as it makes it possible to compute valid ranges of input parameters for given intervals of output parameters. Also, bigger models have to be created and get tested. The used algorithms are suitable for concurrent computation, but the performance has not been systematically investigated. Optimizations in code are assumed to increase the computational efficiency noticeably. This also has to be compared to existing interval arithmetic libraries and approaches.

An open question is the applicability of the entire set-based approach. This would require further research on proper visualizations of the solution space, comparison of different solutions and analyzing and querying of constraint systems for certain solutions.

Remarks

This work is a part of a PhD thesis published 2021 only available in German language:
Kirchner, J.V. (2021). Wissensintegrierende Modellierung der Geometrie von Bauwerken mit Intervallen und Constraints für Parameter. TU Berlin. Available at: https://depositonce.tu-berlin.de/handle/11303/12690

References

Benhamou, F., Goualard, F., Granvilliers, L. and Puget, J.-F. (1999). Revising Hull and Box Consistency. In: Logic Programming: The 1999 International Conference, Las Cruces, New Mexico, USA, November 29 - December 4, 1999. MIT press, pp. 230–244.

Bettig, B., Bapat, V. and Bharadwaj, B. (2005). Limitations of parametric operators for supporting systematic design. In: Proceedings of the ASME International Design Engineering Technical Conferences and Computers and Information in Engineering Conference - DETC2005, 5. pp. 131–142.

Bettig, B. and Hoffmann, C.M. (2011). Geometric Constraint Solving in Parametric Computer-Aided Design. In. J. Comput. Inf. Sci. Eng. 11, 021001 (9 pages).

da Cruz, J.C.F.R. (2003). Constraint reasoning for differential models. PhD Thesis. Universidade Nova de Lisboa, Lisboa.

Fränzle, M., Herde, C., Teige, T., Ratschan, S. and Schubert, T. (2007). Efficient Solving of Large Non-linear Arithmetic Constraint Systems with Complex Boolean Structure. In: Journal on Satisfiability, Boolean Modeling and Computation 1(3–4). pp. 209-236.

Gil, N., Beckman, S. and Tommelein, I.D. (2008). Upstream Problem Solving Under Uncertainty and Ambiguity: Evidence from Airport Expansion Projects. In: IEEE Transactions on Engineering Management 55. pp. 508-522.

Hidalgo Garcia, M.R. (2013). Geometric constraint solving in a dynamic geometry framework (PhD Dissertation). Universitat Politècnica de Catalunya, Barcelona.

Hoffmann, C.M. and Kim, K.-J. (2001). Towards valid parametric CAD models. In: Computer-Aided Design, 33(1), pp. 81–90.

Hoffmann, C.M. and Joan-Arinyo, R. (2005). A Brief on Constraint Solving. In: Computer-Aided Design and Applications 2. pp. 655–663.

Institute of Electrical and Electronics Engineers [IEEE] (2008). IEEE 754-2008 - Standard for Floating-Point Arithmetic.

Institute of Electrical and Electronics Engineers [IEEE] (2015). IEEE 1788-2015 - Standard for Interval Arithmetic.

Joan-Arinyo, R. (2009). Basics on Geometric Constraint Solving. In: Proceedings of 13th Encuentros de Geometría Computacional (EGC09). Presented at the Encuentros de Geometría Computacional (EGC09, Zaragoza (Spain).

Kirchner, J. and Huhnt, W. (2018). Benefits and Limits of Interval Constraints in Acyclic Constraint Graphs for Geometric Modeling. In: Proceeding of the 17th International Conference on Computing in Civil and Building Engineering. Computing in Civil and Building Engineering (ICCCBE) 2018. Tampere, Finland. pp. 716–723.

Kreinovich, V. and Lakeyev, A.V. (1996). Linear interval equations: Computing enclosures with bounded relative or absolute overestimation is NP-hard. In: Reliable Computing, 2(4). pp. 341–350.

Kulisch, U. (2013). Computer Arithmetic and Validity, Theory, Implementation, and Applications. De Gruyter, Berlin, Boston.

Lhomme, O. (1993). Consistency Techniques for Numeric CSPs. In: Proceedings of the 13th International Joint Conference on Artificial Intelligence - Volume 1, IJCAI'93. Morgan Kaufmann Publishers Inc., San Francisco, CA, USA. pp. 232–238.

Liker, J.K., Sobek, D.K., Ward A.C. and Cristiano J.J. (1996). Involving Suppliers in Product Development in the United States and Japan: Evidence for Set-Based Concurrent Engineering. In: IEEE Transactions on Engineering Management 43 (2), pp. 165–178.

Mackworth, A.K. (1981). Consistency in Networks of Relations. In: Webber, B.L., Nilsson, N.J. (Eds.), Readings in Artificial Intelligence. Morgan Kaufmann, pp. 69–78. https://doi.org/10.1016/B978-0-934613-03-3.50009-X

Miguel, I. and Shen, Q. (2001). Solution Techniques for Constraint Satisfaction Problems: Foundations. In: Artificial Intelligence Review. 15(4), pp. 243–267.

Moore, R.E. (1966). Interval analysis. Prentice-Hall, Englewood Cliffs, NJ.

Moore, R.E., Kearfott, R.B. and Cloud, M.J. (2009). Introduction to Interval Analysis. Society for Industrial and Applied Mathematics, Philadelphia, PA, USA.

Nahm, Y.-E. and Ishikawa, H. (2006). A new 3D-CAD system for set-based parametric design'. In: The International Journal of Advanced Manufacturing Technology, 29(1–2). pp. 137–150.

Shah, J.J. (2001). Designing with Parametric CAD: Classification and comparison of construction techniques. In Geometric Modelling. New York: Springer Science+Business Media, pp. 53–68.

Shimizu, S. and Numao, M. (1997). Constraint-based design for 3D shapes. In Artificial Intelligence, Artificial Intelligence Research in Japan 91. pp. 51–69.

Sitharam, M. and St. John, A., Sidman, J. (2019). Handbook of geometric constraint systems principles. CRC Press, Taylor & Francis Group, Boca Raton.

Valdes, F., Gentry, R., Eastman, C. and Forrest, S. (2016). Applying Systems Modeling Approaches to Building Construction. In: Proceeding of the 33th International Symposium on Automation and Robotics in Construction. Presented at the 33th International Symposium on Automation and Robotics in Construction, Auburn, AL, USA.

van der Meiden, H.A. (2008). Semantics of Families of Objects. PhD Thesis. Technische Universiteit Delft.

Yannou, B., Yvars, P.-A., Hoyle, C. and Chen, W. (2013). Set-based design by simulation of usage scenario coverage. In: Journal of Engineering Design 24, pp. 575–603.

Wang, Y. and Nnaji, B.O. (2007). Solving Interval Constraints by Linearization in Computer-Aided Design. In: Reliable Computing, 13(2). pp. 211–244.

Linking Early Design Stages with Physical Simulations using Machine Learning
Structural Analysis Feedback of Architectural Design Sketches

Rasoulzadeh S., Senk V., Kovacic I., Reisinger J., Füssl J., Hensel M.
TU Wien, Austria
shervin.rasoulzadeh@tuwien.ac.at

Abstract. State-of-the-art workflows within Architecture, Engineering, and Construction (AEC) industry are still caught in sequential planning processes. Digital design tools founded in this domain often lack proper communication between different stages of design and relevant domain knowledge. Furthermore, decisions made in the early stages of design, where sketching is used to initiate, develop, and communicate ideas, heavily impact later stages, offering the need for fast feedback to the architectural designer to proceed with adequate knowledge regarding design implications. Accordingly, this paper presents research on a novel AEC workflow based on a 4D sketching application targeted for architectural design as a form-finding tool coupled with two modules: (1) *Shape Inference* module, which is aided by machine learning enabling automatic surface mesh modelling from sketches, and (2) *Structural Analysis* module which provides fast feedback with respect to the mechanical performance of the model. The proposed workflow is a step towards a platform integrating implicit and explicit criteria in the early stages of design, allowing a more informed design leading to increased design quality.

1. Introduction

Architecture, Engineering, and Construction (AEC) shapes our built environment, having substantial environmental, cultural and economic influence on society. However, among the least digitised industries, it is still caught in silo-thinking and sequential planning processes, as experts from different disciplines must work together and communicate with each other throughout different stages of the design. Moreover, the flow of information exchange between these domain-experts with various domain-knowledge within current workflows has been challenging, thus, deflecting optimised progression. In this context, Architecture, Computer Science, Engineering, and Mathematics disciplines can be connected to develop advanced computational design tools to combine implicit (e.g. aesthetical, cultural, or emotional) and explicit knowledge (e.g. functional, environmental, economic), bringing radical innovations. One such innovation can be brought by introducing a workflow that allows fast feedback already in the early stages of design.

Considering the overall workflow, many critical decisions can occur when a design is in its most rough form, namely a sketch (Mahoney, 2018). Sketching is used to initiate, develop, and communicate ideas while allowing the architectural designer to easily tap into his/her intuition to ideate and explore the solution space. In the early stages of design, sketching serves as a visual thinking and architectural form-finding process to the designer and, subsequently, as a visual reference for a computer-aided design (CAD) modelling expert. Moreover, the modelling procedure allows further communication with other downstream processes, such as structural analysis and computer-aided engineering (CAE) simulations (Eissen et al, 2008, Yu et al, 2021). However, the 3D modelling process is often too time-consuming, and simultaneously, the design intention might not be captured accurately and can be misinterpreted. Also, on the other hand, structural analysis is an essential part of the design, which studies and predicts the behaviour of structure's fitness subject to different loads, materials, etc, which is usually not

https://doi.org/10.7146/aul.455.c212

taken into account in the early stages of design. Therefore, reconciling these various domain experts can cause delays, conflicts, and undesirable design compromises.

In this setting, a workflow targeting the early stages of design can address two main challenges. First, the workflow should capture the design intention behind the various parts of the sketch and subsequently translate it into an appropriate (non-) parametric geometry format to be used in different softwares without requiring a modelling expert. Recent advances in Machine Learning (ML) have demonstrated an increasing ability regarding surface modelling and shape reconstruction from sketch data which can be taken into account for this purpose. Second, fast feedback provision with respect to the mechanical performance of the model is of great importance in unfolding the strength and weaknesses of the structure. Such feedback enables the architectural designer to modify his/her design accordingly in the early stages, where the design is still amenable to substantial improvements.

Building upon the above statements, this paper introduces a novel AEC workflow coupled with computational support, enabling the integration of digital design and structural analysis tools in the early stages of design aided by ML, resulting in quick iteration over the design cycle, increased design quality, and better supervision of structural implications of the design in the early stages. This workflow is based on a developed 4D sketching application with Unity Engine targeted for architectural design as a form-finding tool simulating traditional sketching behaviour with paper and pen but allowing the sketch creation in 3D space through tablet and stylus while capturing temporal data as of the fourth dimension. It is noteworthy that the sketch creation is guided by different geometric shapes that are used as canvases for stroke projection. The workflow starts by sketching an architectural element followed by passing the sketch to the *Shape Inference* module, which outputs the reconstructed surface mesh of the sketch. Hence, the reconstructed surface mesh is processed in the *Structural Analysis* module, whereby feedback based on the mechanical performance of the design is sent back to the sketching application. As a proof of concept, the most fundamental architectural element, namely a wall, is used throughout the pipeline to demonstrate the efficiency of the proposed workflow.

This paper is structured as follows. First, a brief overview of the state-of-the-art on novel AEC workflows targeting early stages of design and sketching applications taking the structural analysis part into account is given. Then, the proposed workflow, along with its two main modules, including the *Shape Inference* and *Structural Analysis* and come along- required pre-processing and post-processing steps are explained thoroughly. However, details of the sketching application and its main interaction techniques other than the type of data it provides is not explained as it is not in the scope of this paper. Finally, the current state of the workflow is discussed, and an overview of the future outlooks is given.

2. Related Works

Various researches have been targeting the early stages of design to automate and integrate modelling and performance simulations. In the context of 3D sketches, (Mahoney et al, 2018) presents the prototype of a 3D sketching system to enhance the design exploration in the early stages. The prototype is aided by machine learning which enables the translation of sketch into an intermediate description followed by a reconstruction function that translates this description into a 3D form. The reconstruction function and a set of libraries containing various geometric elements enable the designer to refine the solution space and produce different outputs from the same sketch. Another recent work is CASSIE (Yu et al, 2021), a conceptual modelling system leveraging freehand mid-air gestures coupled with a neatening framework producing a connected 3D curve network from the sketch. The curve network is subsequently surfaced, providing an output amenable for presentation, structural analysis, or manufacturing.

A few sketching systems integrating structural analysis have been introduced as well. However, they only work with 2D sketches and are developed for mainly educational purposes. The FEAsy (Murugappan et al. 2007), is a sketch-based environment for structural analysis in the early stages of design in which users can transform, simulate, and analyse their finite element models through freehand sketching within this environment. The tool is coupled with a beautification module, which simplifies and represents the sketch in a more meaningful way prior to the finite element analysis. STRAT (Peschel et al, 2008) is another tool for solving truss problems. Using the freehand sketch of the truss, this tool allows the designer to determine unknown forces in it with the aid of a sketch recognition system.
Many researches address supporting the architectural designer in the early stages of design throughout structural recommendations and performance simulations. (Ampanavos et al, 2021) trained a Convolutional Neural Network (CNN), which iteratively generates structural design solutions for the sketches of the plans accompanied by real-time guidance before formalisation into CAD software. Other works used ML as surrogate models to speed-up simulations that are time-consuming to be employed in the early stages of design. (Nie et al, 2020) uses a CNN for predicting stress fields in 2D linear elastic cantilevered structures. Successively, (Jiang et al, 2021) achieved a fast mechanical analysis by introducing a new network architecture called StressGAN for predicting 2D von Mises stress distributions in solid structures. However, in contrast to recent works in this area that either focus on a specific stage of the design flow such as modelling, or only work with certain types of (non-) parametric geometries in terms of dimension, this paper presents a workflow where automation of modelling and structural analysis happens within 3D space which is relatively more challenging. Simultaneously, connectivity between different stages of design is prioritised to reach a harmonious integration of sketching, modelling, and structural simulations.

3. Proposed Workflow: From Shape Inference to Structural Analysis Feedback

The proposed workflow begins with 3D sketching within the developed sketching application by an architectural designer. The sketch's 3D polylines and the associated temporal data are recorded throughout the sketching procedure. Afterwards, as the sketching finishes, the sketch's constituent 3D polylines are sent into the *Shape Inference* module for surface mesh inference. The employed reconstruction algorithm in this module digests point cloud data as input. Thus, the 3D polylines must be converted into a 3D point cloud in the pre-processing step. Subsequently, the *Shape Inference* module outputs the reconstructed surface mesh of the original sketch. Given that the surface mesh will be further processed in the *Structural Analysis* module, the outputted surface mesh must be post-processed to create an appropriate input format for the aforementioned module. As the obtained surface mesh is in 3D format, it must be transformed into a volume mesh prior to being sent to the *Structural Analysis* module. Furthermore, boundary conditions, loads, and material information are added to the volume mesh before the finite-element analysis (FEA) starts off. Ultimately, the output of this late module, including the displacements and stresses, is linked and sent back to the sketching application to be further visualised by the designer. The visualisation assists the architectural designer so he/she can improve the design in an acknowledged way regarding the structural implications of his/her design in the early stages. Depicted in the Figure 1, the general overview of the key steps in the proposed workflow can be seen.
In the subsequent sections, the surface reconstruction algorithm employed in the *Shape Inference* and its theoretical background are explained thoroughly. Additionally, the pre-processing and post-processing steps that come along with the *Shape Inference* module are discussed. Finally, the *Structural Analysis* module operations and linkage of its output back to the sketching application is described subsequently.

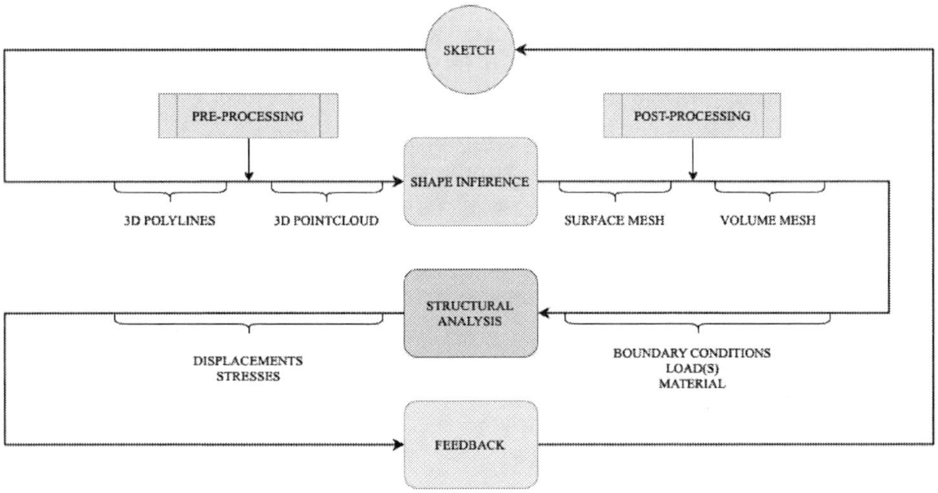

Figure 1: Overview of the proposed workflow containing two main modules allowing fast structural analysis feedback in the early stages of design.

3.1 Shape Inference

Once the sketching part is finished, the artist-drawn sketch must be converted into the intended 3D geometric format suitable for other downstream (non-) parametric and engineering applications. Extensively Artificial Intelligence (AI)-based surface mesh reconstruction algorithms have been developed for such a scenario, aiding 3D shape reconstruction from 2D and 3D sketches (Xu et al, 2014, Guillard et al, 2021). The 3D polylines drawn in the sketching application in our framework can be easily converted into a point cloud. Therefore, surface mesh reconstruction algorithms using point cloud data as input are straightforward and reasonable choices to embark on. To do so, a surface mesh reconstruction algorithm called Points2Surf (Erler et al, 2020) is leveraged to obtain a solid surface mesh of the sketched wall. In contrast to other Machine Learning (ML)-based surface reconstruction algorithms (Vakalopoulou et al, 2018, Park et al, 2019), Points2Surf is patch-based and independent from classes, leading to a better generalisation ability on unseen inputs, making it a reasonable option to get started.

In order to create a proper input format from the sketch data to be fed to this algorithm, specific steps need to be performed as pre-processing. In addition, a post-processing procedure must generate suitable mesh data for structural analysis. Each of these is described in more detail in the following.

Pre-Processing

In order to utilise the Points2Surf algorithm, firstly, the sketched wall must be converted into a point cloud from its constituent 3D polylines. To locate 3D points along the drawn 3D polylines, at every frame at which the Unity Engine's Update function gets called, the contact point of the ray originating from the camera intersecting the drawing surface is recorded and stored as a 3D point coordinate. Accordingly, a 3D point cloud of the whole sketch is obtained by merging the individual 3D polylines' point clouds into one (see Figure 2). Also, prior to feeding the point cloud into the Points2Surf network, as part of the pre-processing, the point cloud must be centred at the origin and scaled uniformly to fit within the unit cube. Additionally, within the developed sketching application, while sketching 3D polylines, the designer can set the width parameter for the brush based on his/her willingness, giving thickness to the sketched element. However, due to the nature of the point sampling strategy of the sketch, this thickness parameter is discarded. The absence of the explicit thickness in the point cloud creates a problem for the Points2Surf reconstruction algorithm since it is trained on solid objects with front and back sides. To solve this issue, normal vectors along the point cloud of the sketch are estimated, and points are moved along them to give the point cloud a slight implicit thickness. Normal estimation is done by finding adjacent points and calculating their principal axis using covariance analysis. The covariance analysis algorithm outputs two opposite directions as the normal candidates making them not consistently oriented across the point cloud. In that case, normals are aligned with respect to the tangent planes computed from the point cloud (Hoppe et al, 1992).

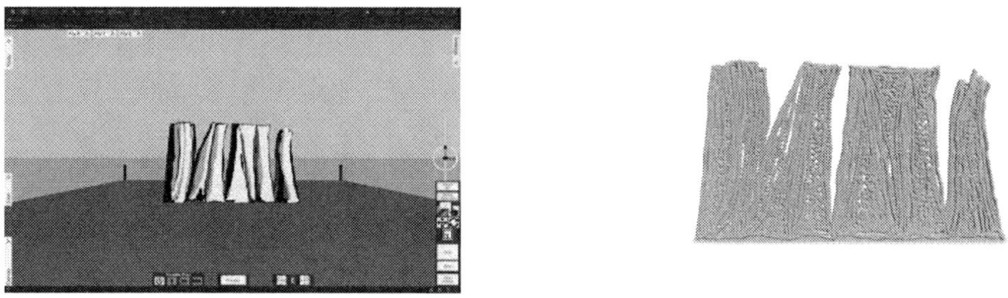

(a) (b)

Figure 2: (a) The sketch of a wall drawn in the sketching application, and (b) The corresponding obtained point cloud.

Points2Surf

As previously stated, the aim is to reconstruct a surface mesh from a 3D point cloud $P = \{p_1, p_2, \ldots, p_N\}$. The authors of Points2Surf take zero-set of the Signed Distance Function (SDF) f_S as a suitable representation for surfaces for training a neural network:

$$S = L_0(f_S) = \{x \in R^3 \mid f_S(x) = 0\} \tag{1}$$

The approach taken in Points2Surf consists of the point cloud fed into a neural network with an encoder-decoder architecture, generating a latent vector and approximating the SDF through encoder and decoder, respectively:

$$f_S(x) \approx \widetilde{f_P}(x) = s(z), \; with \; z = e(P) \tag{2}$$

where z is the latent vector obtained through the encoder e from the point cloud P, and s is the decoder conditioned on the latent vector z. However, encoding a surface with a single latent vector affects the accuracy and generalisation ability of the network. Consequently, the authors propose factorising the SDF into two factors: absolute distance f_S^d and sign of the distance f_S^s, where each of them is estimated through separate encoders e^d and e^s, respectively. To estimate the absolute distance at a query point x, local neighbourhood p^d from the point cloud P is chosen and fed to encoder e^d. Furthermore, since the interior/exterior of the surface cannot be reliably determined from a local neighbourhood, encoder e^s is trained on a global subsample p^s computed from the point cloud P for every query point x to estimate the sign of the distance. Moreover, the authors found out that instead of having two separate decoders for each, sharing information between the two latent vectors z^d and z^s benefits the network, resulting in the following formulation:

$$\left(\widetilde{f_P^d}(x), \widetilde{f_P^s}(x)\right) = s(z^d, z^s),\ with\ z^d = e^d(p^d)\ and\ z_x^s = e^s(p^s) \tag{3}$$

where s is the decoder containing the z^d and z^s as its inputs, outputting the distance $\widetilde{f^d}$ and the sign of the distance $\widetilde{f^s}$. Afterwards, the surface S can be reconstructed by applying the Marching Cubes (Lorensen et al, 1987) to the estimated SDF $\widetilde{f^d} \times \widetilde{f^s}$. Figure 3 demonstrates the overview of Points2Surf architecture.

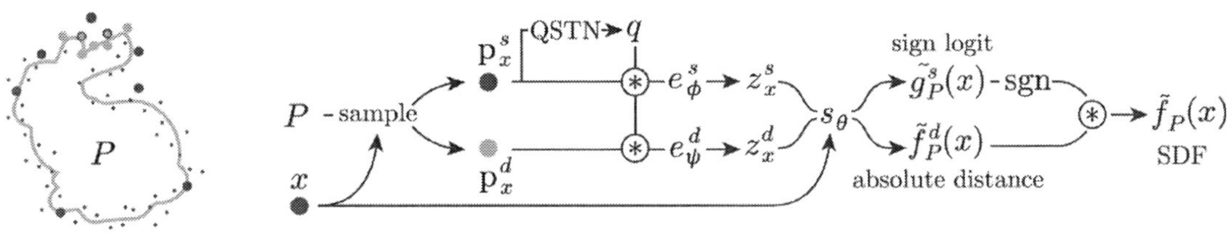

Figure 3: Points2Surf architecture. Image taken from (Erler et al. 2020).

The network architecture used for encoders e^d and e^s are the same as the PointNet (Qi et al, 2017), where a feature representation for each point is computed through a 5-layer Multi Layer Perceptron (MLP) neural network . Also, the decoder s consists of a 4-layer MLP that takes as input the concatenated feature vectors z^d and z^s and outputs the two aforementioned SDF factors. Assuming the ground-truth surfaces are available during the training for supervision, the above network is trained in an end-to-end manner regressing the distance and classifying the sign as positive or negative based on the interiority and exteriority, respectively. Two separate loss functions are used for the distance and the sign of the distance for the training procedure. Firstly, L_2-based regression is used for the distance:

$$L^d(x, P, S) = \left|tanh\left(\left|\widetilde{f^d}(x)\right|\right) - tanh\left(|d(x, S)|\right)\right|_2^2 \tag{4}$$

where $d(.,.)$ is the ground-truth distance between the query point x and surface S. Secondly, for sign of the distance classification, the binary cross-entropy loss H is used as follows:

$$L^s(x, P, S) = H\left(\sigma\left(\widetilde{f^s}(x)\right), [f_S(x) > 0]\right) \tag{5}$$

where σ is the logistic function converting the sign logits to probabilities, and $[f_S(x) > 0]$ is equal to 1 when x resides in the exterior of the surface and is equal to 0 otherwise. Altogether, the network is optimised with the following loss function compromising of the summation over these two losses for all shapes and query points of the training set:

$$\sum_{(P,S)\in S}\sum_{x\in X_S} L^d(x, P, S) + L^s(x, P, S) \tag{6}$$

The dataset that has been chosen to train the network on is the ABC dataset (Koch et al, 2019). This dataset includes a collection of one million CAD models. The authors of the Points2Surf have picked 4950 clean watertight meshes for training and 100 meshes for validation and test sets. Ultimately, for the inference on the point clouds of the sketches drawn in the developed sketching application, we have chosen and utilised the best pre-trained model based on the ablation results trained for 250 epochs. Depicted in Figure 4, a curved wall sketch's 3D polylines, its 3D point cloud representation, and the reconstructed surface mesh by the Points2Surf algorithm can be seen.

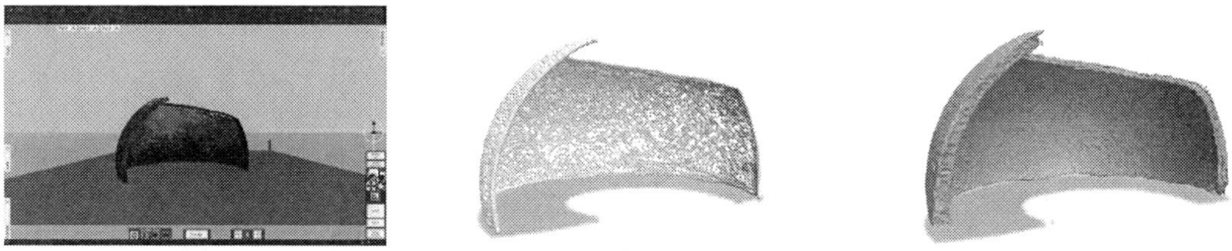

(a) (b) (c)

Figure 4: (a) The sketch of the curved wall drawn in the developed sketching application, (b) The point cloud of it, and (c) The reconstructed surface mesh.

Post-Processing

To translate the obtained surface mesh via Points2Surf into a format suitable for structural analysis, several post-processing steps must be employed, as discussed next. The reconstructed surface mesh may not be smooth enough and contain noise over its entirety, given that the density of the sampled points might differ in different parts of the sketch as the drawing speed varies. Due to the nature of the sampling strategy within the UnityEngine that is employed in the pre-processing step, very fast sketching of 3D polylines may leave empty areas in the 3D point cloud of them, and thus, the reconstructed surface mesh might be rugged. To solve this challenge, Laplacian smoothing (Vollmer et al, 1999) is employed to remove the noise and smooth the surface mesh. After smoothing, verifying the watertightness of the surface mesh is required. A watertight mesh can be defined as a mesh that is edge manifold, vertex manifold and not self-intersecting. A non-manifold triangle mesh is necessary to be able to carry out the mechanical structural analysis using finite element-based methods. Thus, the approach introduced in the ManifoldPlus (Huang et al, 2020) is adopted to convert the reconstructed surface mesh into a watertight one. ManifoldPlus extracts watertight manifolds from surface meshes using the exterior faces between the occupied and the empty voxels and a projection-based optimisation method. Subsequently, the reconstructed surface mesh is prepared for the application of suitable boundary conditions required for the structural analysis. Within this context, it is considered that the virtual ground that exists in the sketching application is the surface where boundary conditions are prescribed. Therefore, the surface mesh has been levelled at its bottom part, a feature that might not automatically exist due to the absence of domain knowledge encoded in the Points2Surf reconstruction method. To enforce planarity, the reconstructed surface mesh is sliced with a plane and capped subsequently, see Figure 5, for the reconstructed surface mesh and its corresponding smoothed variant with a planar bottom.

(a) (b)

(c) (d)

Figure 5: The reconstructed surface mesh of a curved wall viewed from different angles (top-row) and its corresponding smoothed variant with a planar bottom (bottom-row).

Tetrahedralization

Finally, the smoothed, watertight surface mesh with a planar bottom is translated into an analysis-ready volume mesh using the TetWild (Hu et al, 2018) engine, a quite robust engine that does not require any user interaction. The quality of the resulting volume mesh is a direct function of the target mesh size, controllable by a tolerance parameter, denoting how much deviation from the initial surface mesh is permitted. Figure 6 shows the curved wall discretised with first-order linear tetrahedral elements obtained by the TetWild engine.

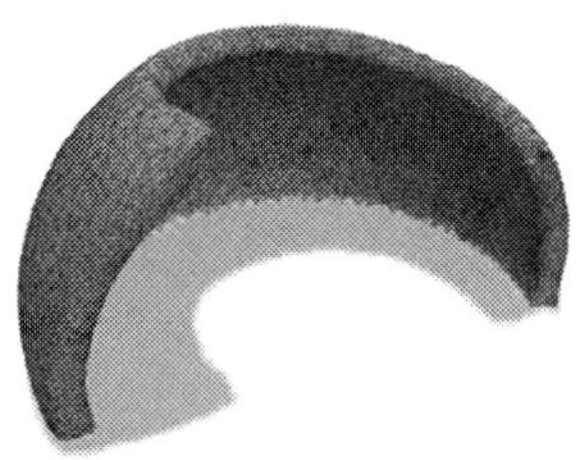

Figure 6: The volume mesh of the curved wall generated by the TetWild engine.

3.2 Structural Analysis

The finite element method is used to analyse the response of the sketched structure and assess its mechanical performance. Apart from the geometrical features, which are well defined by the post-processed volume mesh, the definition of material behaviour, boundary conditions and external loads are required together with the selection of an appropriate FE solution strategy.

Problem Definition

Regarding the definition of the material behaviour, we are currently working on implementing a material database in the sketching application as well as developing a micromechanics-based model to predict elastic properties for a wide range of bio-composites. In future, the user will have the possibility to select a broad range of different materials. So far, the materials used for our testing scenarios are described with isotropic, linear elastic constitutive models.

The material behaviour is thus fully defined by two parameters only, the Young's modulus along with the Poisson's ratio. The limitation to linear elastic material models is made to provide FE solutions almost in real-time and, thus, allowing for rapid feedback to the designer. Naturally, it is possible to extend the material database and the underlying models at any time, e.g. by taking direction-dependency and nonlinear material behaviour into account.

Displacement boundary conditions, as displayed in Figure 7(a), are automatically applied at the bottom surface, which is therefore made planar, as described in the previous section. In more detail, a fixed boundary is considered, where all displacement degrees of freedom in the 3D space (u_x, u_y, u_z) are restricted and therefore set to zero for every node. All other surfaces are considered free surfaces.

At last, external loads have to be defined. For this purpose, we focused on deadweight first, where only the density of the material in the database has to be additionally taken into account. Furthermore, in the first step, point loads are added at predefined positions to resemble selected loading states of interest, as illustrated in Figure 7(b). At this point, this is done manually within the FE software ABAQUS, for reasons to test the consistency and functionality of the proposed workflow. Subsequently, an automatic linking of the sketching tool and the FE program should take place via Python code. This allows the designer to define any loading and to mechanically pre-test his design already in the sketching application.

(a) (b)

Figure 7: (a) Visualisation of the displacement boundary conditions at the bottom surface and (b) placement of a concentrated load on a predefined position (node) on the wall. So far, for the calculations, the implicit ABAQUS/Standard solver is used. The computed output variables involve the 3D nodal displacements as well as 3D stress- and strain fields of the whole body, which can be transferred back to the sketching application.

Linking the Output Back to the Sketching Application

Computation results, such as the comparison between initial undeformed and deformed configuration (obtained by adding the computed displacements to the original nodal coordinates) are again visualised in the sketching application, as seen in Figure 8. For this purpose, the structure is converted back to a surface mesh. A heat map and a legend are also added to highlight the zones with large displacements. Other modelling results which can be visualised are stresses and strains in every direction, principal stresses, plastic strains (if plastic material behaviour is considered) or any other output fields of common FE software. Figure 8 shows the visualisation of the von Mises stresses – a common stress quantity governing yield for ductile materials such as steel.

This graphical illustration helps the designer to immediately assess the mechanical performance of the sketched structure. If certain displacements are particularly large, or stresses exceed the material strength, the designer can immediately react, e.g. by changing the geometry, the used material, or by adding additional support to the structure.

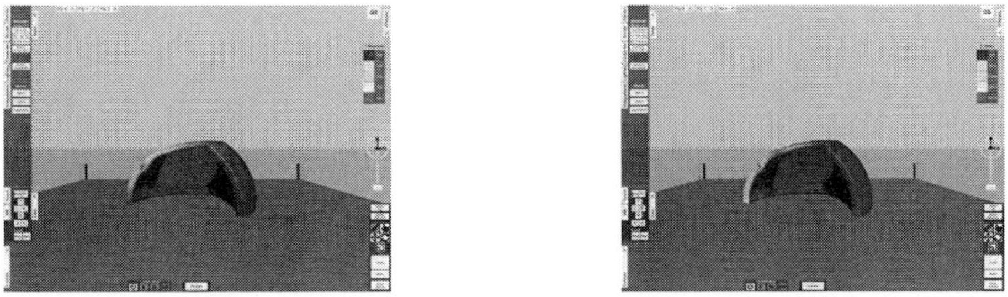

(a) (b)

Figure 8: (a) Deformed configuration with highlighted displacements as well as (b) Deformed configuration with visualised von Mises stresses.

4. Conclusion and Future Work

The early stages of design are mainly the process of exploration and ideation. It is also well understood that the decisions made at this stage have a significant impact down the line. However, lack of proper communication among disciplines as well as data and information losses between design stages makes it time-consuming and simultaneously results in a decreased design quality. As a step toward improving state-of-the-art workflows within AEC industry, this paper introduces and showcases a novel workflow automating the geometry creation followed by fast structural analysis feedback provision at the early stages of design where sketching is used for form-finding. Further improvements are envisioned at different parts of the proposed workflow. Primarily, regarding the *Shape Inference* module, a more sophisticated approach based on machine learning capturing design intention directly from 3D polylines and its coupled attributes such as timestamp, pressure, tilt, etc, generating parametric geometry is quite interesting and challenging to be further researched on and developed. Moreover, regarding the *Structural Analysis* module, just the boundary conditions are detected automatically and transferred to ABAQUS so far, while additional information such as material and loads can be recognised and carried to this module as well. In the future, we will be able to draw fixed boundaries, sketch loads and select materials from a database already within the sketching tool. Also, the integration of warnings shall be implemented, for instance, if displacements or stresses exceed certain critical values. It is also intended to integrate the *Shape Inference* and *Structural Analysis* modules and codes directly into the sketching application, to not rely on third-party programming interfaces and softwares, making it more of a unified tool. At last, the geometry can be exported to be further used in different CAD and computer graphics tools for tasks such as lighting simulations, paneling, and structural optimization.

Acknowledgements

The research is supported by grant F77 (SFB “Advanced Computational Design”, subprojects SP2 and SP8) of the Austrian Science Fund (FWF). Moreover, the authors thank the following project partners for providing valuable feedback:

- SFB, Subproject SP2, Integrating AEC Domain Knowledge - Synthesis 2.0, Peter Ferschin, Ingrid Erb, and Balint Istvan Kovacs
- SFB, Subproject SP8, Markus Lukacevic, and Markus Königsberger.

References

Ampanavos, S., Nourbakhsh, M. and Cheng, C.Y., (2021). Structural Design Recommendations in the Early Design Phase using Machine Learning. *arXiv preprint arXiv:2107.08567*.

Eissen, J.J. and Steur, G.N.R.E., (2008). Sketching, drawing techniques for product designers. Ye-Eun Publishing Co.

Erler, P., Guerrero, P., Ohrhallinger, S., Mitra, N.J. and Wimmer, M., (2020), August. Points2surf learning implicit surfaces from point clouds. In *European Conference on Computer Vision* (pp. 108-124). Springer, Cham.

Guillard, B., Remelli, E., Yvernay, P. and Fua, P., (2021). Sketch2Mesh: Reconstructing and Editing 3D Shapes from Sketches. In *Proceedings of the IEEE/CVF International Conference on Computer Vision* (pp. 13023-13032).

Hoppe, H., DeRose, T., Duchamp, T., McDonald, J. and Stuetzle, W., (1992), July. Surface reconstruction from unorganized points. In *Proceedings of the 19th annual conference on computer graphics and interactive techniques* (pp. 71-78).

Hu, Y., Zhou, Q., Gao, X., Jacobson, A., Zorin, D. and Panozzo, D., (2018). Tetrahedral meshing in the wild. *ACM Trans. Graph.*, *37*(4), pp.60-1.

Huang, J., Zhou, Y. and Guibas, L., (2020). Manifoldplus: A robust and scalable watertight manifold surface generation method for triangle soups. *arXiv preprint arXiv:2005.11621.*

Jiang, H., Nie, Z., Yeo, R., Farimani, A.B. and Kara, L.B.,(2021). Stressgan: A generative deep learning model for two-dimensional stress distribution prediction. *Journal of Applied Mechanics*, *88*(5).

Koch, S., Matveev, A., Jiang, Z., Williams, F., Artemov, A., Burnaev, E., Alexa, M., Zorin, D. and Panozzo, D., (2019). Abc: A big cad model dataset for geometric deep learning. In *Proceedings of the IEEE/CVF Conference on Computer Vision and Pattern Recognition* (pp. 9601-9611).

Lorensen, W.E. and Cline, H.E., (1987). Marching cubes: A high resolution 3D surface construction algorithm. *ACM siggraph computer graphics*, *21*(4), pp.163-169.

Mahoney, J.M., (2018). THE V-SKETCH SYSTEM, MACHINE ASSISTED DESIGN EXPLORATION IN VIRTUAL REALITY.

Murugappan, S. and Ramani, K., (2009), January. Feasy: a sketch-based interface integrating structural analysis in early design. In *International Design Engineering Technical Conferences and Computers and Information in Engineering Conference* (Vol. 48999, pp. 743-752).

Nie, Z., Jiang, H. and Kara, L.B., (2020). Stress field prediction in cantilevered structures using convolutional neural networks. *Journal of Computing and Information Science in Engineering*, *20*(1), p.011002.

Park, J.J., Florence, P., Straub, J., Newcombe, R. and Lovegrove, S., (2019). Deepsdf: Learning continuous signed distance functions for shape representation. In *Proceedings of the IEEE/CVF Conference on Computer Vision and Pattern Recognition* (pp. 165-174).

Peschel, J.M. and Hammond, T.A., (2008), September. STRAT: a Sketched-truss Recognition and Analysis Tool. In *DMS* (pp. 282-287).

Qi, C.R., Su, H., Mo, K. and Guibas, L.J., (2017). Pointnet: Deep learning on point sets for 3d classification and segmentation. In *Proceedings of the IEEE conference on computer vision and pattern recognition* (pp. 652-660).

Vakalopoulou, M., Chassagnon, G., Bus, N., Marini, R., Zacharaki, E.I., Revel, M.P. and Paragios, N., (2018), September. Atlasnet: Multi-atlas non-linear deep networks for medical image segmentation. In *International Conference on Medical Image Computing and Computer-Assisted Intervention* (pp. 658-666). Springer, Cham.

Vollmer, J., Mencl, R. and Mueller, H., (1999), September. Improved laplacian smoothing of noisy surface meshes. In *Computer graphics forum* (Vol. 18, No. 3, pp. 131-138). Oxford, UK and Boston, USA: Blackwell Publishers Ltd.

Xu, B., Chang, W., Sheffer, A., Bousseau, A., McCrae, J. and Singh, K., (2014). True2Form: 3D curve networks from 2D sketches via selective regularization. *ACM Transactions on Graphics*, *33*(4).

Yu, E., Arora, R., Stanko, T., Bærentzen, J.A., Singh, K. and Bousseau, A., (2021), May. Cassie: Curve and surface sketching in immersive environments. In *Proceedings of the 2021 CHI Conference on Human Factors in Computing Systems* (pp. 1-14).

Automated Qualitative Rule Extraction Based on Bidirectional Long Short-Term Memory Model

Zhu X.[1], Li H.[1], Xiong G.[1], Song H.[2]
[1]Cardiff University, United Kingdom, [2]Dalian Maritime University, China
ZhuX29@cardiff.ac.uk

Abstract. Digital transformation in the construction industry demands smart compliance checking against relevant standards to ensure high-quality project delivery. Due to the diverse characteristics, the qualitative rule extraction for standards remains labour intensive. Therefore, an efficient and automated rule extraction method is pivotal. The artificial neural network has been widely used for textual feature extraction in recent years. In this paper, the authors construct an automated rule extractor based on a bidirectional Long short-term memory (LSTM) neural network model, which can automate the extraction of qualitative rules in textual standards and achieves an accuracy of 96.5% in actual tests. The automated rule extractor can greatly improve the efficiency of converting unstructured textual rules to structured data. This approach can establish the basis for knowledge mining of qualitative standards as well as the development of large-scale compliance checking systems.

1. Introduction

Research on the automated extraction of rules from standards has been carried out since the 1960s (Xue and Zhang, 2021). Rules are accepted principles or instructions that state the way things are or should be done, which normally can be classified as quantitative or qualitative according to their quantifiability (Marsal-Llacuna, 2018). Taking the provisions of IBC 2015 in Table 1 as an example, quantitative rules in standards are usually expressed directly through specific numerical values with units of measurement, which can be easily recognised by regular expression matching. As it is challenging to quantify the qualitative rules (provision 2 in Table 1), the requirements are generally described in a textual manner. This purely textual description is distinguished by its variety of forms, flexibility of structure, and logical complexity, which increases the difficulties in rule localization and feature identification when extracting qualitative rules automatically (ul Hassan and Le, 2020).

Table 1: Three examples of the IBC 2015 provisions

Number	Description	Type
1	The fire separation distance between a building with polypropylene siding and the adjacent building shall be not less than 10 feet (3048 mm) (Clause 1402.12.2)	Quantitative rule
2	Exterior walls, and the associated openings, shall be designed and constructed to resist safely the superimposed loads. (Clause 1403.3)	Qualitative rule
3	The purpose of this code is to establish the minimum requirements to provide a reasonable level of safety, public health, and general welfare through structural strength… (Clause 101.3)	Explanation of rules

For the engineering domain, several rule-based and machine learning extraction algorithms have been proposed in academia (Gunjan and Bhattacharyya, 2021). Compared to the rule-

https://doi.org/10.7146/aul.455.c213

based methods which are inflexible, under-generalized and time-consuming, machine learning-based algorithms are generally more efficient but less accurate (Hailesilassie, 2016). Thus, the dominant rule extraction method in the engineering domain is still manual. With the continuous development and improvement of standards, manual extraction gradually falls short in two scenarios: multi-standards comparison and administration of complex engineering projects such as quality assurance and process management. On other hand, the rule-based and the machine learning-based approaches cannot meet the demands of the industry either, due to their incapability in efficiency and accuracy.

The authors have therefore developed a rule extractor based on a bi-directional LSTM model that enables fast, accurate and efficient automated mining of qualitative rules. To develop the rule extractor, the authors manually created a textual dataset of rules and enhanced it with data augmentation methods to fulfill a uniform sample distribution and then further improved the reliability and objectivity of the dataset through the Delphi method. After that, this dataset was then trained to produce word vectors representing the probability distributions of their correspondence in the engineering domain and adopted in the training of a bidirectional LSTM neural network to form the rule extractor. The trained rule extractor eventually achieved 98% accuracy on the test set and 96.5% accuracy in an actual validation of a qualitative standard.

An automated rule extractor can significantly reduce the proportion of manual work involved in rule extraction and process a large number of texts of standards in a short period. So, the arises of an automated rule extractor make it possible to check compliance among multiple qualitative standards and to conduct large-scale knowledge mining for qualitative standards in the engineering domain.

2. Related Work

2.1 Overview of Rule Extraction Algorithms

The keyword method is considered the most basic rule extraction method by identifying target vocabularies (Bednár, 2017), examples are the IF-THEN rule and the M-of-N rule. An improved approach is to leverage libraries of domain-specific languages, especially knowledge from domain experts. However, the accuracy of the keyword method lacks generalisability and highly relies on the libraries provided (Dragoni et al. 2016).

With the development of machine learning, some more intelligent techniques for rule extraction have been developed. Machine learning-based methods can be classified into heuristic approaches, regression-based approaches and artificial neural network approaches (Gunjan and Bhattacharyya, 2021). In heuristics, decision tree ensembles (DTEs) such as random forest (RF) give high prediction accuracy while being regarded as black-box models (Abellán et al., 2018). Support vector machine (SVM), as one of the regression-based approaches, exhibits good prediction performance when applied to several publicly available data. The downside is that it requires a pre-defined training model and falls short of scalability (Barakat and Bradley, 2010).

Artificial neural networks (ANN) are more advanced machine learning methodologies for rule extraction which can be categorised into decompositional, pedagogical and eclectic approaches, as proposed by Andrews et al. (1995). The decompositional method works by synthesising the activation rules, along with weights and biases of the hidden layers of the neural network. The pedagogical rule extraction works by matching the input-output relationship to the way that neural networks interpret it (Gethsiyal Augasta and Kathirvalavakumar, 2012). While the eclectic approach is a hybrid between pedagogical and decompositional methods, it generally analysis the ANN at the individual unit level but extracts rules at the global level (Hruschka and Ebecken, 2006). A decompositional technique is substantially more translucent compared with pedagogical algorithms, but it can be time-consuming as it is delivered layer by layer (Zarlenga et al., 2021). While in terms of computational limitation and execution time, the pedagogical approach usually delivers more performance than the decompositional.

2.2 Delphi Method

The Delphi method is a structured decision support technique that aims to obtain relatively objective information, opinions and insights through the independent and iterative subjective judgment of multiple experts in the information collection process (Hsu and Sandford, 2007). The survey team conducted multiple rounds of consultation with selected expert groups through anonymous approaches and then compiled the expert opinions from each round. This process is repeated several times until there is a convergence of opinion, resulting in a more consistent and reliable conclusion or solution.

2.3 Data Augmentation

Data augmentation techniques were originally applied in the field of computer vision, where the core approach was to create new image data by panning, rotating, compressing and adjusting the colour of an image (Xie et al., 2022). Unlike image data, data in natural language is discrete. Therefore, it is not feasible to perform a direct and simple transformation of the input data, which would most likely change the original meaning of the sentence. Currently, the two categories of text data augmentation methods commonly used in natural language processing are text representation-oriented augmentation and text-oriented augmentation. Text representation-oriented augmentation focuses on the processing of the feature representation of the original text, while original text-oriented augmentation is carried out by replacing synonyms or deleting words in the original text (Shorten et al., 2021). Back translation is a typical method of text-oriented augmentation, which re-translates content from the target language back to its source language in literal terms to obtain a sentence with a similar meaning but in a different expression (Edunov et al., 2018). This method enables not only the substitution of synonyms and the addition or deletion of words but also the reconstruction of the word order in sentences. Thus, back-translation is a very effective and reliable approach to augmenting textual data.

2.4 LSTM Neural Network

Long short-term memory (LSTM) neural networks are a special type of recurrent neural network (RNN) model, which is widely utilized in natural language processing and time-series prediction (Hochreiter and Schmidhuber, 1997). In contrast to RNNs, LSTMs introduce the concept of cell state and control the update of information on cell states through gate states, thus solving the problem of long-term dependencies. As a consequence, LSTM models can acquire better performance on feature learning of long sequences. In natural language, the meaning of a word or sentence is not only influenced by the previous content but is also related to the following content (Schuster and Paliwal, 1997). A bidirectional LSTM model that learns features from both forward and backward directions can capture more information and obtain better training results.

3. Methodology

The automated extractor of the qualitative rule is essentially a binary classifier trained from a neural network model. The underlying principle of qualitative rule extraction is similar to that of sentiment classification in natural language processing, in that the neural network model is trained with a large number of annotated rule texts to learn the sequential and lexical features of the textual rules, thus achieving the identification and extraction of qualitative rules.

Therefore, this research followed the training process of neural network models, including six main steps: dataset creation, data pre-processing, word vector embedding, neural network model construction, data loading, training and validation. The specific flowchart of this research is shown in Figure 1.

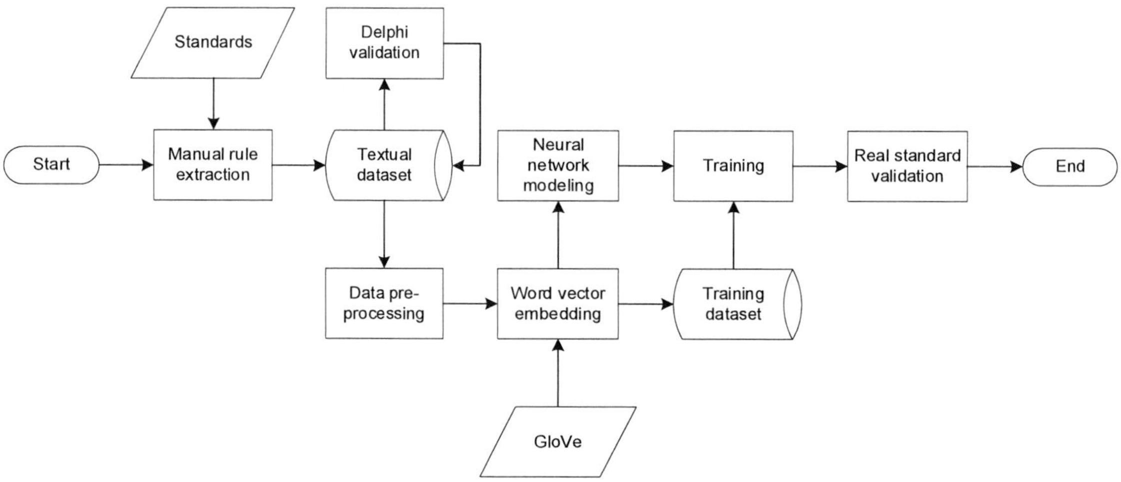

Figure 1: The development flowchart for an automated qualitative rule extractor

As all the qualitative rules in the dataset were manually extracted from the standard files, the labels of the rule samples in the dataset are inevitably subjective. In this research, the authors adopted the Delphi method to validate the labels of the rule samples to improve the objectivity and reliability of the dataset. To address the problem of uneven data distribution, the authors applied the Back Translation method to optimise the dataset and further improve the robustness and generalisation of the trained model. Considering that most of the qualitative rules in the dataset are derived from engineering standards, the authors embedded words in the dataset with word vectors trained from the lexicon of the engineering domain to achieve higher accuracy. At the end of this research, the trained model was validated using a specific engineering standard to investigate the actual performance of the extractor.

Due to space limitations, this paper only focuses on solving the problem of locating and identifying qualitative rules in the standard. The extracted rules still retain the original sentence format, which is the same as the unextracted rules in Table 3. The extraction of entities and relationships within the qualitative rules and the transformation to computer-processable rules will be further illustrated in the following papers.

4. Case Study

4.1 Text Dataset Creation

For the qualitative rule extractor in this research, there is no open dataset that fully satisfies the experimental requirements. The author, therefore, chose to manually build a small sample dataset and combine it with textual data augmentation methods to develop a dataset that is suitable for training. To ensure that the extractor not only can solve the research problem but also has sufficient generalisation capabilities, the research group manually extracted 826 rule samples from 6 international and national engineering standards, which are listed in Table 2. These standards cover a wide range of aspects of the building and construction domain, including quality management, energy management, information management process, building design, etc.

Table 2: Engineering standards included in the rule dataset.

Standard Code	Description	Published by	No. of Rules extracted
ISO 9001	Quality management systems Requirements	ISO[a]	216
ISO 14001	Environmental management systems -Requirements with guidance for use	ISO	169
ISO 50001	Energy management systems - Requirements with guidance for use	ISO	153
ISO 19650-1	Organization and digitization of information about buildings and civil engineering works, including building information modeling (BIM)	ISO	199
2015 IBC	International Building Code	ICC[b]	48
GB/T 51212	Unified standard for building information modeling	MOHURD[c]	41

[a]International Organization for Standardization, [b]ICC - International Code Council, [c]MOHURD – Ministry of Housing and Urban-Rural Development of China

4.2 Data Augmentation

After completing the initial extraction of the qualitative rules, there were 826 samples in the dataset, containing 573 rule samples and 253 non-rule samples. In general, the number of rule texts in the standard file is more than the number of non-rule texts. Currently, it is generally accepted that 1000 samples per category are required to be collected to achieve more accurate results when training neural network models for classification. In other words, there should be 2000 samples in the dataset of this research, including 1000 qualitative rule samples and 1000 non-rule samples. To meet the requirement of sample size, the authors chose to utilize back translation in data augmentation techniques to expand the dataset and balance the number of positive and negative samples. In the experimental process, the research group selected the more commonly used French and Mandarin as intermediate languages to implement the back translation of the samples. The specific procedure was as follows.

1) Count the number of positive and negative samples to be augmented
2) Randomly select a corresponding number of positive and negative samples in the dataset according to the statistical results
3) The selected samples were translated into French and Mandarin one by one with the help of a third-party translator (Google translation), and then translated back into English by another translator (DeepL) to become the translated samples.
4) The newly translated samples were compared with the original samples, and if their expressions were different, the translated samples were added to the dataset as augmented samples.

The augmented rule dataset contains 2000 samples, of which 1000 are positive rule samples and 1000 are negative non-rule samples. The dataset developed in this research can be accessed through https://gitlab.com/LonelyRanger/rules-extraction.git

4.3 Delphi Dataset Validation

The problem of small sample size and uneven sample distribution in the dataset has been addressed utilizing data augmentation. Another issue that needs to be addressed is the reliability of the samples and labels in the dataset. In this research, the research team followed the Delphi method to bring together five experts with a deep understanding of engineering standards to validate the samples and labels in the dataset. The validation process was as follows.

1) The full sample and label data underwent the first round of expert group validation.
2) The research group collates and tallies the validation results from the expert group. For samples where all experts agree, they can pass the validation directly. If more than half of the experts agree on the sample, the research group modifies the sample appropriately based on the experts' opinions and then validates it in the next round. If the sample passes the validation by only a few experts, a new sample of the same label type is generated by data augmentation to replace the original sample and is validated in the next round.
3) All adjusted samples were subjected to the above two steps of validation again until all experts came to an agreement.

In this research, after completing four rounds of validation and modification, the five experts reach an agreement on the qualitative rules and labels for the dataset. At this point, the 2000 samples in the dataset possessed a high degree of objectivity and reliability.

4.4 Textual Data Pre-processing

In this research, the pre-processing of the textual data is divided into four steps: (1) removing non-textual parts of the samples, such as punctuation, special characters, etc.; (2) splitting the rule samples into sequences consisting of individual words using the word splitting function; (3) removing stop words from the individual sample sequences. (4) counting the characteristics of the data set, such as the number of samples, the maximum sequence length, the size of the lexicon, etc. The rule samples in the dataset are all derived from standard clauses, which have a normative presentation. Therefore, noise removal and text normalisation are not necessary for the pre-processing stage of this research.

4.5 Word Embedding

Text is a piece of unstructured data information that cannot be directly computed. Word embedding is a digital text representation method that transforms unstructured textual data into structured data that can be recognised and computed. The more mainstream methods currently utilize word vectors (Word2vec, GloVe (Pennington et al., 2014)) pre-trained on large corpora as word representations. This research is aimed at the engineering domain, where the probability distribution of words is somewhat different from that of the larger corpus. The pre-trained GloVe word vector is adopted as the initial value for word embedding and modified by the backpropagation algorithm during the training process according to the distribution pattern of the vocabulary in the dataset, which can make it more consistent with the probability distribution of the vocabulary in the engineering domain.

4.6 Neural Network Training

According to the statistics of the text pre-processing stage, the maximum length of the sample sequences in the dataset was 52 and the average length was 23.56. Considering the advantages of LSTM models in long sequence learning, the authors selected a bidirectional LSTM model as the training model for the rule extractor. The bidirectional LSTM model in this research is composed of one embedding layer, two LSTM layers and one Dense layer, containing a total of 303,775 trainable parameters. The model structure is shown in Figure 2. Each LSTM layer is followed by a dropout layer with dropout rates of 0.5 and 0.25, respectively.

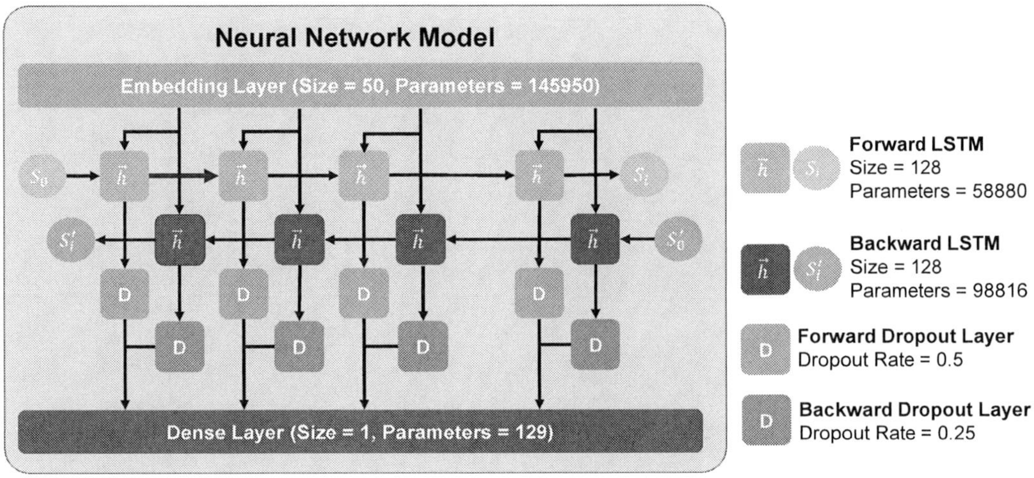

Figure 2: Structure of the neural network model for automated qualitative rule extraction

For the partitioning of the dataset, the authors applied random sampling to divide the entire dataset into a training set, a validation set and a test set in the ratio of 6:2:2. The hyperparameters of the neural network model, such as batch size, trainable layer size and dropout rate, are set based on the authors' previous experimental experience in neural network model training. In addition, neural network models with these hyperparameters are widely used in various natural language processing tasks and usually perform well in learning. Another hyperparameter, epoch, cannot be predicted before training. Given the low diversity of the dataset, the authors determined to train the model with 10 epochs, 20 epochs and 30 epochs to investigate the detailed training performance of the model.

4.7 Actual Standards Validation

The dataset in this research was built manually by the research group. Hence, the textual feature distribution may slightly differ from the real standard file, which is possibly lead to a deviation in the actual performance of the rule extractor. Therefore, the generalisation error of the rule extractor is required to be verified through actual tests after the model has been trained. The authors use the trained extractor to extract qualitative rules from a new engineering standard (ISO19650-2) and compare the automatic extraction results with those of the manual extraction by experts to evaluate the performance of the rule extractor in practice.

5. Result

To find a better performing training epoch, the authors trained the model for 10 epochs, 20 epochs and 30 epochs, and observed the changes in loss and accuracy during training. As shown in Figure 3, after 10 epochs of training, the loss of the model underwent a continuous decline, which indicates that the model did not reach the optimal training state. After 20 epochs of training, the loss of the model is still decreasing but gradually stabilizing, suggesting that the model is close to the optimal state. After 30 training epochs, the model reached its optimal state, with both loss and accuracy fluctuating within a small range. The trained model achieved a final accuracy of 98% on the test set.

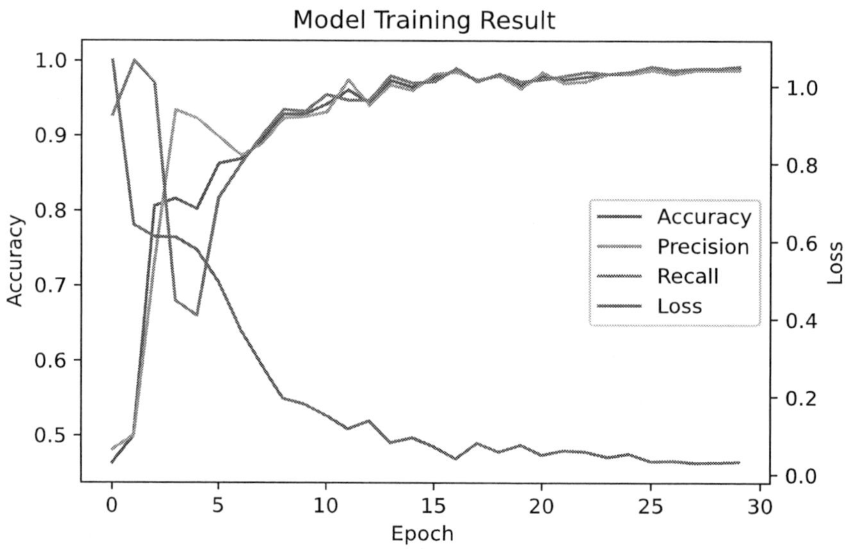

Figure 3: Training results under different training epochs

In the session of the actual standards validation, the expert group manually extracted a total of 228 qualitative rules from ISO19650-2. Relatively, the trained rule extractor extracted 220 rules from ISO19650, which achieved an accuracy rate of 96.5%. The eight missing qualitative rules are listed in Table 3. The rule extractor can therefore be tentatively concluded to have a good performance in the qualitative rule extraction for engineering standards.

Table 3: List of the 8 unextracted rules in the actual standard validation.

Number	Description of Unextracted Rules
1	The national standards organizations of the following countries are bound to implement this European Standard.
2	Each member body interested in a subject for which a technical committee has been established has the right to be represented on that committee.
3	ISO shall not be held responsible for identifying any or all such patent rights.
4	This document is applicable to built assets and construction projects of all sizes and all levels of complexity.
5	The amount of thought involved, the time taken to complete it and the need for supporting evidence will depend on the complexity of the project.
6	This document can be used by any appointing party.
7	The appointing party's defined information exchange points within each of the principal work stages are to be used in defining the project's information requirements.
8	It is recommended that this is done as a separate appointment before procurement of any other appointed party starts.

6. Discussion

The diverse features of qualitative rules make it a challenge for traditional algorithms to identify and locate rules. The manual extraction of rules is essentially a way of summarising the features of the text in the standards through human comprehension, thus achieving accurate recognition of the rules. This style of learning is mechanistically identical to the training of artificial neural networks that mimic the human brain's nervous system. Therefore, theoretically it is possible to enable automated rule extraction by training artificial neural networks. Compared with an open language environment, the expression and description of the rules in the standards are more normative, which implies the textual features are more distinct. Consequently, the trained neural network model was able to acquire a high accuracy on the test set.

In addition to the training results of the model itself, the actual performance of the rule extractor is also closely related to the quality of the dataset. Only if the dataset has a similar sample distribution to that of the application environment can the extractor acquire an accuracy close to the test set in actual applications. Through this research, the authors provide researchers who are facing similar problems with a solution to quickly build reliable small sample domain datasets.

In the actual standard validation, the rule extractor achieves an accuracy of 96%, which indicates that the rule extractor can automate rule extraction to some extent, and significantly reduce the manual work involved. However, given the nature of the rule extraction task, the extractor can only fully substitute manual extraction if its extraction accuracy is close to 100%. As can be seen from Table 3, the rule extractor has some deficiencies in the recognition of rules with a weak feature. This may be caused by the non-linearity of the activation function. In this research, the Softmax function is utilised as the activation function for output, which may be not sensitive enough for a weak feature. The research group will try some other activation functions to improve the recognition performance in future research. In addition, the use of abbreviations (unextracted rule 3) results in the loss of semantic information in the context, which may affect the recognition of qualitative rules to some extent.

In the experimental process of this study, the selection of the neural network model and the setting of some of the hyperparameters are based on the authors' previous research experience. Consequently, further research is needed on model selection and the setting of hyperparameters to obtain the best training performance. In addition, there is also room for further reduction of the generalisation error of the rule dataset.

Although this research focuses on qualitative rules in the engineering domain, the authors believe that this rule extractor is essentially capable of extracting rules from other domains due to their similarities in textual characteristics. For a more accurate result, transfer learning can be applied with this rule extractor as a pre-training model.

7. Conclusion

Automated extraction of qualitative rules is a pressing challenge in the research of engineering. In this research, the authors built a highly reliable domain dataset employing data augmentation and Delphi expert validation, and further developed an automated qualitative rule extractor by training a bi-directional LSTM model on this dataset. The extractor achieves an accuracy of 96.5% on the actual standards test and is therefore primed for application to practical tasks. For future work, alternative artificial neural network models and hyperparameters can be investigated for potential improvement in accuracy. It is expected that the automated rule extractors can replace traditional manual extraction methods to a certain extent and largely improve the efficiency of transforming unstructured textual rules into structured rules. The realisation of automated extraction of qualitative rules is of great significance for the future establishment of large-scale semantic rule knowledge bases and multi-standard compliance checking systems.

References

Abellán, J., Mantas, C.J., Castellano, J.G. and Moral-García, S. (2018). Increasing diversity in random forest learning algorithm via imprecise probabilities. Expert Systems with Applications 97, pp. 228–243. doi: 10.1016/J.ESWA.2017.12.029.

Andrews, R., Diederich, J. and Tickle, A.B. (1995). Survey and critique of techniques for extracting rules from trained artificial neural networks. Knowledge-Based Systems 8(6), pp. 373–389. doi: 10.1016/0950-7051(96)81920-4.

Barakat, N. and Bradley, A.P. (2010). Rule extraction from support vector machines: A review. Neurocomputing 74(1–3), pp. 178–190. doi: 10.1016/J.NEUCOM.2010.02.016.

Bednár, P. (2017). Vocabulary matching for information extraction language. In: 2017 IEEE 15th International Symposium on Applied Machine Intelligence and Informatics (SAMI)., pp. 149–152. doi: 10.1109/SAMI.2017.7880292.

Dragoni, M., Villata, S., Rizzi, W. and Governatori, G. (2016). Combining Natural Language Processing Approaches for Rule Extraction from Legal Documents. In: AI Approaches to the Complexity of Legal Systems., pp. 287–300. Available at: https://wordnet.princeton.edu/ [Accessed: 25 February 2022].

Edunov, S., Ott, M., Auli, M. and Grangier, D. (2018). Understanding Back-Translation at Scale. In: Proceedings of the 2018 Conference on Empirical Methods in Natural Language Processing, EMNLP 2018. Association for Computational Linguistics, pp. 489–500. Available at: https://arxiv.org/abs/1808.09381v2 [Accessed: 15 February 2022].

Gethsiyal Augasta, M. and Kathirvalavakumar, T. (2012). Rule extraction from neural networks; A comparative study. In: International Conference on Pattern Recognition, Informatics and Medical Engineering (PRIME-2012)., pp. 404–408. doi: 10.1109/ICPRIME.2012.6208380.

Gunjan, A. and Bhattacharyya, S. (2021). A Brief Review of Intelligent Rule Extraction Techniques. Advances in Intelligent Systems and Computing 1333 AISC, pp. 115–122. doi: 10.1007/978-981-33-6966-5_12.

Hailesilassie, T. (2016). Rule Extraction Algorithm for Deep Neural Networks: A Review. IJCSIS) International Journal of Computer Science and Information Security 14(7), pp. 376–381. Available at: https://sites.google.com/site/ijcsis/ [Accessed: 23 February 2022].

Hochreiter, S. and Schmidhuber, J. (1997). Long Short-Term Memory. Neural Computation 9(8), pp. 1735–1780. Available at: https://direct.mit.edu/neco/article/9/8/1735/6109/Long-Short-Term-Memory [Accessed: 23 February 2022].

Hruschka, E.R. and Ebecken, N.F.F. (2006). Extracting rules from multilayer perceptrons in classification problems: A clustering-based approach. Neurocomputing 70(1–3), pp. 384–397. doi: 10.1016/J.NEUCOM.2005.12.127.

Hsu, C.-C. and Sandford, B. (2007). The Delphi Technique: Making Sense of Consensus. Practical Assessment, Research, and Evaluation 12. doi: 10.7275/PDZ9-TH90.

Marsal-Llacuna, M.L. (2018). The standards evolution: A pioneering Meta-standard framework architecture as a novel self-conformity assessment and learning tool. Computer Standards & Interfaces 55, pp. 106–115. doi: 10.1016/J.CSI.2017.06.002.

Pennington, J., Socher, R. and Manning, C.D. (2014). GloVe: Global Vectors for Word Representation. In: Proceedings of the 2014 Conference on Empirical Methods in Natural Language Processing (EMNLP)., pp. 1532–1543. Available at: http://nlp. [Accessed: 16 February 2022].

Schuster, M. and Paliwal, K.K. (1997). Bidirectional recurrent neural networks. IEEE Transactions on Signal Processing 45(11), pp. 2673–2681. doi: 10.1109/78.650093.

Shorten, C., Khoshgoftaar, T.M. and Furht, B. (2021). Text Data Augmentation for Deep Learning. Journal of Big Data 8(1). Available at: https://doi.org/10.1186/s40537-021-00492-0.

ul Hassan, F. and Le, T. (2020). Automated Requirements Identification from Construction Contract Documents Using Natural Language Processing. Journal of Legal Affairs and Dispute Resolution in Engineering and Construction 12(2). Available at: https://orcid.org [Accessed: 23 February 2022].

Xie, Q., Dai, Z., Hovy, E., Luong, M.-T. and Le, Q. V. (2022). Unsupervised Data Augmentation for Consistency Training. In: 34th Conference on Neural Information Processing Systems (NeurIPS 2020). Available at: https://github.com/google-research/uda. [Accessed: 14 February 2022].

Xue, X. and Zhang, J. (2021). Part-of-speech tagging of building codes empowered by deep learning and transformational rules. Advanced Engineering Informatics 47. doi: 10.1016/J.AEI.2020.101235.

Zarlenga, M.E., Shams, Z. and Jamnik, M. (2021). Efficient Decompositional Rule Extraction for Deep Neural Networks. arXiv e-prints , p. arXiv:2111.12628. Available at: https://github.com/mateoespinosa/remix.

Factors contributing to measurement uncertainty of HVAC-enabled demand flexibility in grid-interactive commercial buildings

Vindel E.[1], Akinci B.[1], Bergés M.[1], Kavvada O.[2], Gavan V.[2]
[1] Carnegie Mellon University, USA, [2] ENGIE Lab CRIGEN, France
evindel@cmu.edu

Abstract. The importance of evaluating the performance of electric power demand flexibility in buildings has increased in recent years due to the expected participation of demand resources in reliability-based grid services. All demand flexibility assessments involve a degree of uncertainty when measuring the magnitude of demand response events, due to the uncertainty in the counterfactual load estimation. The objective of this work is to understand how distinct factors contribute to uncertainty in measuring HVAC-enabled demand response in buildings. More specifically, we will vary two factors that are known to contribute to the uncertainty of the observed event: choice of baseline model and choice of assessment boundary. The practical implication of our analysis is to contribute to the design of improved measurement and verification protocols for demand flexibility in buildings.

1. Introduction

1.1 Overview

The value of electric power demand flexibility as a quantifiable and reliable grid resource is increasing with a modernizing electric grid. This is evident by the active participation of demand resources in energy and ancillary services markets within different regulatory bodies (FERC, 2021). Buildings are the largest part of these demand resources and the deployment of grid-interactive technologies in this sector is anticipated (Neukomm, Nubbe and Fares, 2019). A fundamental technology requirement for this transition is the development of improved performance assessments and trustworthy metrics that quantify their demand flexibility (Satchwell *et al.*, 2021). Current measurement and verification (M&V) protocols were designed for an electric grid that benefited from but did not depend on demand flexibility. Performance assessments are critical for reliable system support, transparent financial settlements and, overall increasing the trustworthiness of demand resources (Goldberg and Agnew, 2013). The challenge in designing performance assessment protocols is that it involves the estimation of the unaltered baseline load, and this step inevitably introduces error between the real load modification and the measured load modification. Moreover, the effects of these errors are event-specific due to the varying accuracy of baseline models. The main approach to reduce the uncertainty, when measuring the real load modification, is to improve prediction accuracy through the choice of baseline model. Another known approach involves the choice of assessment boundary (i.e., level at which the demand flexibility is documented) which can improve the accuracy when measuring an event. These choices play a significant role in the design of M&V protocols and are the source of investigation for this paper. The objective of this work is to understand how the choice of baseline model and assessment boundary contribute to the measurement uncertainty of demand flexibility events. We will narrow our focus to heating ventilation and air conditioning (HVAC) flexibility in commercial buildings as it accounts for a substantial portion of flexible electricity consumption in the building sector (Roth and Reyna, 2019). Furthermore, we will extend the analysis to different climate zones (ASHRAE, 2019), given that HVAC demand flexibility heavily depends on this factor. The understanding of how these factors contribute to measurement uncertainty of demand flexibility

https://doi.org/10.7146/aul.455.c214

events can provide insight into the design of improved M&V protocols tailored to different requirements and applications.

1.2 Existing Research

Understanding the sources of measurement uncertainty for demand flexibility (DF) events has been an important topic in the design of M&V protocols (KEMA-XENERGY, 2003). As this problem is inherent to the value of demand flexibility, studies on comparing the accuracy of baseline models are common in settings beyond academic research (KEMA, 2011; Nexant, 2017). Various demand flexibility baseline models have been proposed, but they all generally fall into the following categories: averaging, simple regression, and machine learning (Amasyali and El-Gohary, 2018). Of these, averaging models cover the majority of industry practice (IRC (ISO/RTO Council), 2018). Simple regression models, such as the time-of-the-week and temperature model, have been proposed with an improved accuracy over averaging models (Taylor and Mathieu, 2015). Additionally, machine learning models, in recent years, joined the conversation due to their increased prediction accuracy (Zhang *et al.*, 2021).

Although literature for more accurate baseline models is ample, studies of the effect of baseline prediction on DF measurements is scarcer. Some works have investigated the uncertainty introduced by the source and frequency of the input data used on the model prediction (Coughlin *et al.*, 2009; Granderson and Price, 2014). Similarly, a more recent work explored the bias of common baseline models when evaluating peak electricity load reduction (Granderson *et al.*, 2021). One of the strengths of these studies is the use of real building experimental results as opposed to simulated. However, the main drawback is that the obtained results are not contextualized by the magnitude of potential DF events. A study that does have this context, evaluated the variability of DF measurements when using a specific time-of-the-week and outdoor air temperature baseline model (Mathieu, Callaway and Kiliccote, 2011). One primary finding is that DF measurement error is primarily driven by baseline model error. However, validation of the source and magnitude of this error was complicated due to the comparison being done on only 95 observations throughout multiple buildings.

The other factor explored in this study is the choice of assessment boundary on which to measure the DF event. The assessment boundary refers to the measurement level at which the DF event is documented (Schiller, Schwartz and Murphy, 2020). Although there are a few options for the assessment boundary, in this work we will focus on the HVAC and total building electricity consumption. The main difference between the two is that the building energy consumption is the combination of HVAC load and all other loads. The intuition is that, in some circumstances, divorcing controllable and non-controllable loads (i.e., sub-metering) has the potential to improve the accuracy of the measurement (Cappers *et al.*, 2013). The mechanisms through which this could be true is two-fold. First, baseline models can have a more accurate fit at the HVAC boundary than total building because the explanatory variables commonly used have a more direct relation to power. Second, load modifications have a larger relative impact at more granular assessment boundaries. Several works have studied the accuracy trade-offs of submetering to obtain more accurate DF assessments (Ji *et al.*, 2016; Lei, Mathieu and Jain, 2021). However, these studies start with the assumption that the HVAC boundary will be more accurate and do not explore the trade-offs when compared to using total building power. It is also important to note, that there are studies that have found that the choice of assessment boundary is inconsequential (Motegi *et al.*, 2004).

In this work, we cover the influence of these two factors by generating an extensive simulation dataset on which we empirically analyze their effects on measured DF events. There are four primary distinctions from prior works. First, we expand the comparison to five different baseline models including averaging, simple regression, and machine learning. Second, we document the accuracy tradeoffs of the total building and HVAC assessment boundary. Third, we apply various performance metrics relative to the magnitude of the simulated events. Fourth, we analyze these factors for five different ASHRAE climate zones (ASHRAE, 2019). The expected outcome of these results is to inform the design of future M&V protocols.

2. Proposed Approach

To evaluate how the selected factors affect measurement uncertainty of demand flexibility we will first generate a dataset of simulated events. We will leverage this dataset to empirically analyze the contribution of each factor to measurement uncertainty. For clarity in comparison, we will group each building model instance as the following triple `(Climate, Assessment Boundary, Baseline Model)` and our dataset will consist of 50 such triples (5 climates × 2 boundaries × 5 baseline models). A visual abstract of the factors explored is shown in Figure 1. Section 2.1 describes the data generation process including a description of the building model used and the procedure to create the demand flexibility events. Section 2.2 describes the selected baseline models, description of the input features used, and the training/testing methodology model fitting. Section 2.3 summarizes the evaluation metrics used to compare the results from the triple instantiations. Finally, Section 2.4 condenses the key steps of the experimental plan to generate the data and calculate the proposed evaluation metrics.

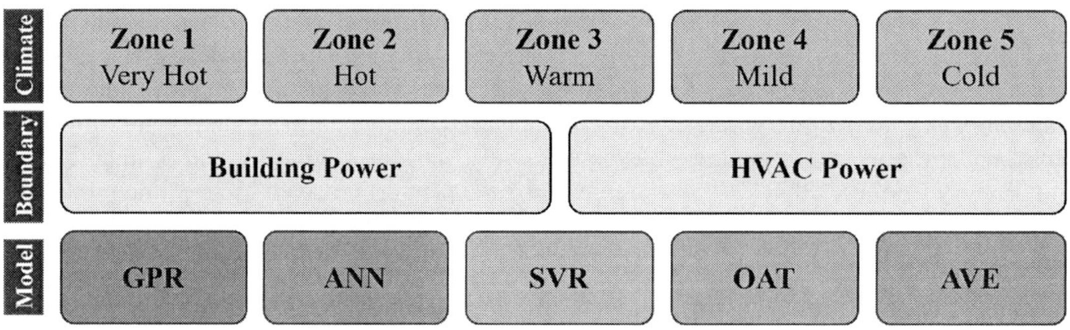

Figure 1: Factors explored - Climate Zone, Baseline Model, and Assessment Boundary (GPR – Gaussian Process Regression, ANN – Artificial Neural Network, SVR – Support Vector Regression, OAT- Time-of-week and outdoor temperature model, AVE – Mid4of6 Averaging Model)

2.1 Model Description

The selected testbed model to generate the dataset is the office building from the *Modelica Buildings Library* (Wetter *et al.*, 2014) equipped with a variable air volume (VAV) reheat system with an implementation of the control sequence *VAV 2A2-21232*. It consists of a five-zone layout shaped after one floor of the DOE Medium Office standard prototype building (Goel *et al.*, 2014). Because this model only simulates HVAC load, we simulate all other non-controllable loads (e.g., plug loads, lighting loads, etc.) as proportional to building occupancy and scaled accordingly. The occupancy was obtained from a separate agent-based stochastic occupancy simulator for office buildings (Chen, Hong and Luo, 2018). The same stochastic occupancy data is also used to model the internal thermal load that the HVAC simulation uses to balance thermal loads in the building. The simulation timestep is selected as 15 minutes given that it is a common resolution for the evaluation of demand resources (IRC (ISO/RTO Council), 2018). For demand flexibility we generate *load shedding events* through a +2°F global thermostat reset for 1-hour duration for every hour during the occupied hours (Vindel *et al.*,

2021). The evaluation period is 90 summer days, not including weekends or holidays. The selected period ensures the HVAC system is operating in cooling mode and the power consumption is engaged by both the fans and chiller.

2.2 Baseline Models

We select five candidate baseline models commonly used for building energy forecasting for demand flexibility M&V. Averaging-based models are commonly used in practice of which we select the Mid4of6 model (AVE) for this evaluation (KEMA, 2011). This model averages the load of the six most recent valid days, excluding the days with the highest and lowest energy consumption. The rest of the models evaluated are regression-based models. The simplest of these models is a piecewise linear model (OAT) that uses a time-of-the-week indicator and outdoor air temperature to predict electric load (Mathieu, Callaway and Kiliccote, 2011). The three remaining models are supervised machine learning models: artificial neural network (ANN, feed-forward, 4 hidden layers, 10-neurons per layer, sigmoid activation), support vector regression (SVR, radial basis function kernel, ε =0.1), and Gaussian process regression (GPR, squared-exponential kernel). The input features for all machine learning models are the same: outdoor air temperature, direct normal irradiance, global horizontal irradiance, relative humidity, time-of-day indicator. The test/train split for all regression-based models was obtained by generating two random datasets from geographically close weather files within the same climate zones as shown in Table 1 (ASHRAE, 2019). Note that a comparison between these machine learning models is difficult because of the variety of architectures and initialization parameters. However, for this work, our aim is not to optimize these model design decisions but to perform an initial comparison of the outputs and strengths of each model.

Table 1: Test/Train Split Weather Data for Regression-based Models

Climate Zone	1, Very Hot	2, Hot	3, Warm	4, Mild	5, Cold
Train Data	Miami, FL	Houston, TX	Atlanta, GA	Baltimore, MD	Chicago, IL
Test Data	Kendall, FL	San Antonio, TX	Athens, GA	Arlington, VA	Aurora, IL

2.3 Evaluation Metrics

The metrics we want to calculate are related to the difference between the observed shed and the real shed. Therefore, in this context, we consider the real shed, the measurand and the observed shed as the measurement. For smart grid applications, two metrics used are the median absolute percentage error (MdAPE) and the normalized mean bias error (NMBE). The first one measures the relative error of the observed measurement, accounting for the variability in the magnitude of the real shed events. We select the median, over the more common mean of the absolute percentage error, to filter out the effect of outlier events with very low magnitude sheds. The metric NMBE, on the other hand, indicates whether a particular baseline model instance generates a biased measurement of the real shed event. Positive values for NMBE indicate that the observed shed is lower than the real shed, and the opposite for negative values. Additionally, we calculate a metric called the reliability threshold estimate (REL). This reliability-inspired metric roughly estimates the frequency of a model falling within a specified threshold (Aman, Simmhan and Prasanna, 2015). For distributed energy resources participating in reliability-based grid services (e.g., contingency reserves) a commonly used threshold is ε = 10% (Aman, Simmhan and Prasanna, 2015). A negative REL value indicates that most events were higher than the threshold, and value of -1 indicates that all events are beyond the threshold. The opposite holds for positive values of REL. To evaluate the performance of the baseline models, independent of the simulated DF events, we will calculate the CVRMSE. Note that this metric is relative to the load (P_i) and not to the magnitude of individual events. For reference, values for CVRMSE less than 25% are considered an acceptable fit for the measurement of energy and demand savings (ASHRAE, 2014).

Table 2: Selected Evaluation Metrics

	Metric	Target	Equation
(1)	Median Absolute Percentage Error (%)	Event	$\text{MdAPE} = \text{median}\left(\left\lvert\frac{y_i - \hat{y}_i}{y_i}\right\rvert \text{ for } 1, \ldots, n\right) \times 100\%$
(2)	Normalized Mean Bias Error (%)	Event	$\text{NMBE} = \frac{1}{n}\sum_{i=1}^{n}\frac{y_i - \hat{y}_i}{y_i} \times 100\%$
(3)	Reliability Threshold Estimate (-)	Event	$\text{REL} = \frac{1}{n}\sum_{i=1}^{n} C(y_i, \hat{y}_i)$ $C(y_i, \hat{y}_i, \varepsilon) = \begin{cases} 1, & \text{if } \lvert y_i - \hat{y}_i\rvert / y_i < \varepsilon \\ 0, & \text{if } \lvert y_i - \hat{y}_i\rvert / y_i = \varepsilon \\ -1, & \text{if } \lvert y_i - \hat{y}_i\rvert / y_i > \varepsilon \end{cases}$
(4)	Coefficient of Variance RMSE (%)	Load	$\text{CVRMSE} = \frac{1}{\bar{P}}\sqrt{\frac{1}{n}\sum_{i}^{n}\left(P_i - \hat{P}_i\right)^2} \times 100\%$

2.4 Experiment Plan

A summary of the designed experimental plan and evaluation is presented in the steps below, and applied to all the selected climate zones:

1. Simulate the building operation generating data for both nominal and load shedding events. Repeat this step for both training and testing weather conditions.
2. Record electricity consumption for HVAC system and building total. Record all input features: outdoor air temperature, direct normal irradiance, global horizontal irradiance, relative humidity, time-of-day indicator.
3. Using the nominal power consumption for the training weather, for both assessment boundaries, fit regression-based baseline models with their respective input features.
4. Calculate the CVRMSE metric (Equation (4)) using the predicted baseline load for each model on both the test and training sets.
5. Compute the measured sheds and real sheds by subtracting the average hourly difference between the true baseline consumption and observed load, as well as the predicted baseline consumption and observed load.
6. Calculate all other evaluation metrics (Equations (1)- (3)) for all combinations of baseline model and assessment boundary.

3. Results and Discussions

The discussions are divided into two sections. Section 3.1 reports and analyses the baseline model results of all the triple instances. Section 3.2 interprets the results relative to the modelled demand flexibility events. The source code for the results presented and the dataset generated is hosted in a public repo in GitHub (https://github.com/INFERLab/DFUncertain-EGICE22/).

3.1 Baseline Model Performance

The performance of all baseline model instances is summarized in Figure 2. The results shown in this section are not connected to the modeled demand flexibility events and are only a reflection of the baseline model fit using Equation (4). For all modeled instances, HVAC consumption was less than 50% of total building power consumption (44%,44%,42%,40% and 37% for climate zones 1-5 respectively). The average Coefficient of Variation of the Root Mean Square Error (CVRMSE) for the building assessment boundary, for all models, is 6.95% and 8.90% for training and testing respectively. For the HVAC boundary the average CVRMSE for training and testing are 8.22% and 11.50%. Additionally, the maximum CVRMSE value for any triple instance is 24.47%. As mentioned earlier, some guidelines suggests that CVRMSE values below 25% are considered a good model fit (ASHRAE, 2014). Hence, by this guideline, all models performed below this minimum performance threshold. In fact, on the test data, 90% of triples had CVRMSE < 15%. Another observation is that using the CVRMSE metric, the HVAC assessment boundary performed slightly worse than the building boundary. This is primarily because the metric is associated with the magnitude of the total electricity consumption. Hence the same magnitude error has different CVRMSE values at different assessment boundaries.

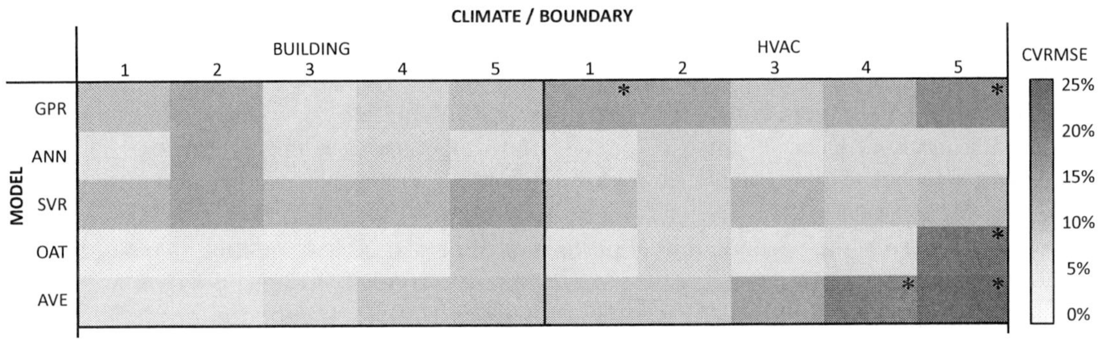

Figure 2 Baseline Model Performance Summary on Test Dataset (CVRMSE > 15% marked with *)

The performance of all models did not appear to consistently vary by climate zones. One notable exception to this finding is the AVE model at the HVAC boundary, and less so at the building boundary. The AVE model performs progressively worse when going from a hotter to a colder climate. The reason for this is that climate zones defined as "cold" have significantly more variability in daily environmental conditions than other climates that are consistently hot. Because of the inductive bias of AVE-type models, intra-day variability is expected to hinder performance. A similar decrease in performance was not observed for all other models. This is an interesting finding, particularly for the HVAC boundary, given that the power consumption is directly affected by weather conditions. For building power, the relations between environmental input features and power are less direct. The OAT model has the best performance for all climate zones at the building boundary. One explanation for this could be that this model captures the schedule-nature of all non-controllable loads by generating an independent model for each timestep. Although our dataset has a stochastic input for the non-controllable loads, these are derived from a scheduled input. This limitation is not particular to our model, but a general drawback of most building energy models. The ANN model was the best performing model using HVAC power consumption. One explanation for this is that the ANN model is able to capture the non-linear behavior of HVAC consumption better than the OAT linear model. Although the GPR model has a lower performance than the ANN and OAT model, one of the advantages of this model is that it outputs uncertainty measures over predictions. The trade-off in performance for certain applications could be compensated by the probabilistic output of the model.

3.2 Event-specific Performance

As described earlier, we model events by generating synthetic load shed events through a 1-hour global thermostat reset. For each event, we can calculate a real shed (y_i) by subtracting the average real baseline load and the DF event load for the 1-hour period. It is essential to emphasize that the real shed value is independent of assessment boundary. When the baseline model outputs a prediction for the baseline load, at either boundary, we can calculate a measured load shed ($\hat{y}_i$) by subtracting the average predicted load and the DF event load. Finally, for each event, we calculate the relative error ($((y_i - \hat{y}_i)/\, y_i) \times 100\%$). For example, let us assume that a DF event is calculated to have a 20kW average real shed magnitude. If the baseline model underpredicts the baseline load by 4kW, meaning that the measured shed is 16kW, the relative event error is +20%. A boxplot distribution of the relative event error for all triples is shown for the testing data in Figure 3.

The choice of figure as a boxplot distribution is to show the variability in relative event error. While most relative errors are close to 0% the variance of the distribution provides a visual of the expected measurement uncertainty. Figure *3* has limits for relative event error capped at +200% and -200%. Although there are events with relative errors beyond these thresholds (only 2.25% of events), they were considered outliers when calculating the interquartile range of the boxplot distribution. These events are outside the range because they were low magnitude events and not because of significant baseline model error. Not surprisingly, the model performance discussed in Section 3.1 is a good predictor of the performance when measuring DF events. However, the baseline model performance measured by Equation (4) is not able to capture the large gap in event-specific performance driven by the choice of assessment boundary. For all models, measuring the events using an HVAC power baseline model resulted in lower error on average. More specifically, for the test data this constituted in a reduction in MdAPE from 34% to 21%, on average. Regardless of the assessment boundary, in reference to these experiments, the MdAPE values can be considered high for certain grid services. Similar conclusions have been obtained regarding the expected measurement error for demand resources (Mathieu, Callaway and Kiliccote, 2011). Nevertheless, the true magnitude of the expected relative error should be subject to a more comprehensive study than the one presented.

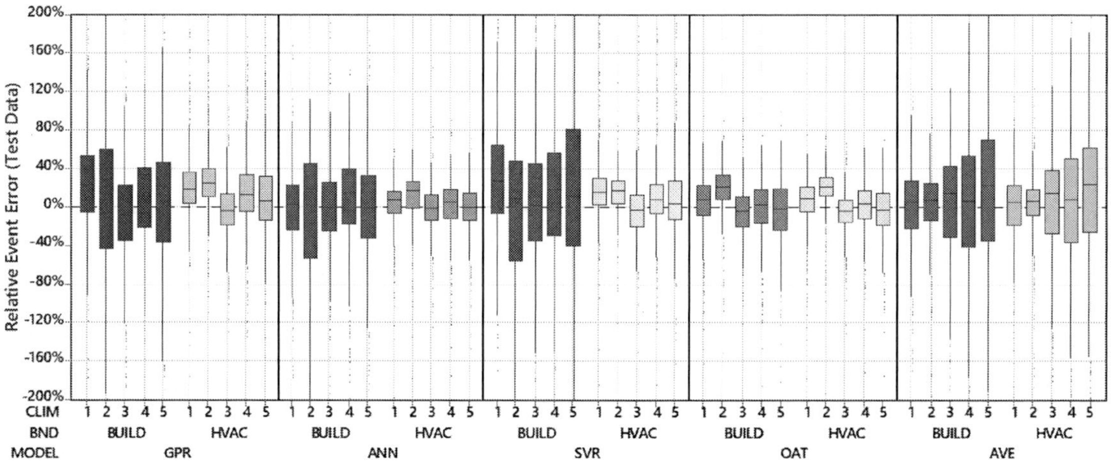

Figure 3 Boxplot distribution of relative event errors for all triple instances for Test Dataset

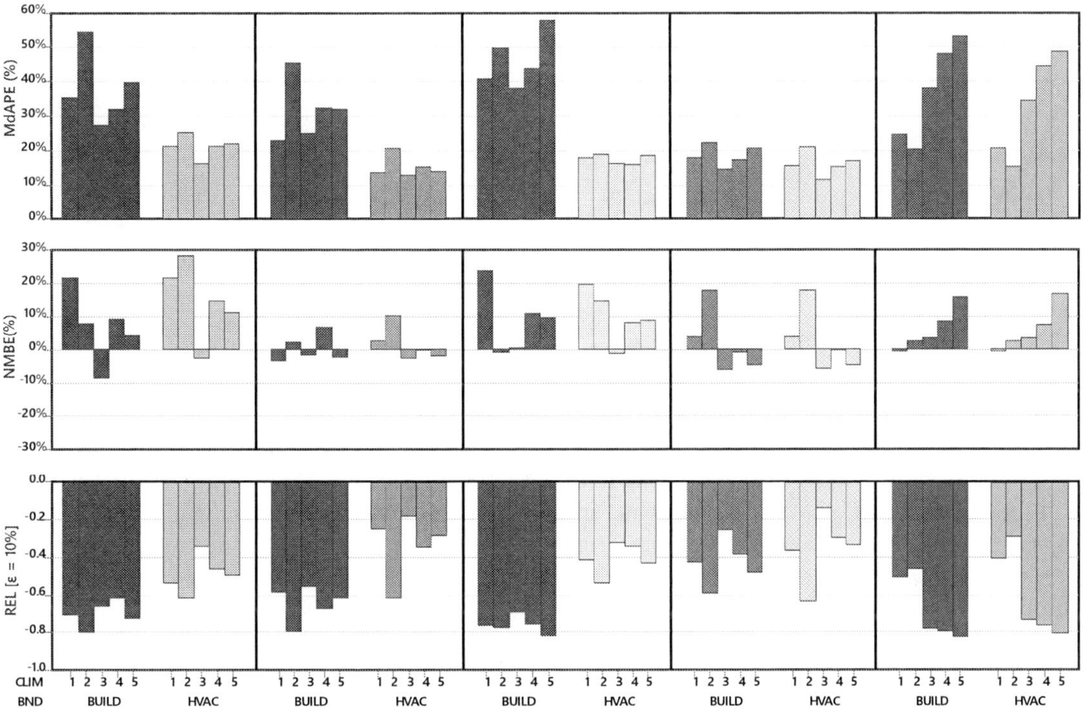

Figure 4 Event-specific metrics for Test Dataset

Figure 4 summarizes the event-specific metrics for the test dataset. As mentioned before, the MdAPE pane visually recapitulates the improvement in measurement accuracy when using the HVAC assessment boundary. Overall measurement bias is an important factor given that under/over-estimation of DF events have different implications for a grid service. In our experiments, most models exhibit low bias (i.e., NMBE close to 0%). However, for some models, we find that there is a tendency of a positive bias. In other words, the measured shed is less than the real shed. Interestingly, this conclusion agrees with existing research studies that state that baseline models tend to understate the achieved load reductions (Coughlin *et al.*, 2009; Granderson *et al.*, 2021). This could result in a systematically lower compensation for the building that provided the services. Finally, the low values for the REL metric expose existing limitations of demand flexibility as a reliability resource. For all instances, a measured event was found more likely to be beyond the 10% threshold used for the REL metric. This is represented by all triple instances having a negative REL value. This motivates the need for more accurate baseline models, or other non-baseline methods to achieve the minimum performance thresholds required by certain grid services.

4. Conclusion

In this paper we present an analysis of how the choice of baseline model and assessment boundary affect the measurement uncertainty of demand flexibility events. We generate an extensive dataset of simulated demand flexibility events by varying these two factors for five different climate zones. Lastly, we calculate performance metrics on this dataset to compare the performance of each instance. In our analysis we found several conclusions:

- Baseline error performance metrics alone, without the context of the magnitude of the demand flexibility events, are not a good indicator of the expected event measurement error.

- More accurate event measurements can be obtained by using the HVAC assessment boundary than using the building assessment boundary. This comprises of an event MdAPE reduction from 34% to 21%, on average.
- The choice of baseline model should be made considering the assessment boundary. For example, averaging models can be appropriate for hotter climates at the building boundary, while machine learning approaches can be more accurate for variable climates at the HVAC boundary.
- Although most models exhibit low bias, some models tend to underrepresent the magnitude of the real event.

We identify several avenues for future work. Given that measurement uncertainty is inherent and unavoidable for demand flexibility, we recognize the need for methods that communicate the expected uncertainty associated with specific events. This can help improve the trust of grid operators when leveraging demand resources for reliability. Furthermore, in this work we do not explore the aggregate assessment boundary. Measurement uncertainty at the aggregate level has the potential to be lower given that it can be reduced over a large population of buildings. Measurement uncertainty at this boundary has the potential to be lower than the ones explored in this work. Finally, extending this analysis to real building data is necessary because there can be added uncertainties that cannot be accounted with a simulation model.

Acknowledgements

This material is based upon work partially funded by ENGIE Lab Crigen, (CSAI)

References

Aman, S., Simmhan, Y. and Prasanna, V.K. (2015) "Holistic Measures for Evaluating Prediction Models in Smart Grids," *IEEE Transactions on Knowledge and Data Engineering*, 27(2), pp. 475–488. doi:10.1109/TKDE.2014.2327022.

Amasyali, K. and El-Gohary, N.M. (2018) "A review of data-driven building energy consumption prediction studies," *Renewable and Sustainable Energy Reviews*, 81(April 2017), pp. 1192–1205. doi:10.1016/j.rser.2017.04.095.

ASHRAE (2014) "Measurement of Energy, Demand, and Water Savings," *ASHRAE Guideline 14-2014*, pp. 1–150. Available at: www.ashrae.org%0Awww.ashrae.org/technology.

ASHRAE (2019) "ANSI/ASHRAE/IES Standard 90.1-2019 Energy Standard for Buildings Except Low-Rise Residential Buildings." Atlanta, GA: ASHRAE.

Cappers, P., MacDonald, J., Goldman, C. and Ma, O. (2013) "An assessment of market and policy barriers for demand response providing ancillary services in U.S. electricity markets," *Energy Policy*, 62, pp. 1031–1039. doi:10.1016/j.enpol.2013.08.003.

Chen, Y., Hong, T. and Luo, X. (2018) "An agent-based stochastic Occupancy Simulator," *Building Simulation*, 11(1), pp. 37–49. doi:10.1007/s12273-017-0379-7.

Coughlin, K., Piette, M.A., Goldman, C. and Kiliccote, S. (2009) "Statistical analysis of baseline load models for non-residential buildings," *Energy and Buildings*, 41(4), pp. 374–381. doi:10.1016/j.enbuild.2008.11.002.

FERC (2021) *2021 Assessment of Demand Response and Advanced Metering, Federal Energy Regulatory Commission*. Available at: http://www.ferc.gov/legal/staff-reports/2013/oct-demand-response.pdf.

Goel, S., Rosenberg, M., Athalye, R., Xie, Y., Wang, W., Hart, R., Zhang, J. and Mendon, V. (2014) *Enhancements to ASHRAE Standard 90.1 Prototype Building Models*. doi:10.2172/1764628.

Goldberg, M. and Agnew, G.K. (2013) *Measurement and Verification for Demand Response National Forum of the National Action Plan on Demand Response*.

Granderson, J., Sharma, M., Crowe, E., Jump, D., Fernandes, S., Touzani, S. and Johnson, D. (2021) "Assessment of Model-Based peak electric consumption prediction for commercial buildings," *Energy and Buildings*, 245, p. 111031. doi:10.1016/j.enbuild.2021.111031.

Granderson, J. and Price, P.N. (2014) "Development and application of a statistical methodology to evaluate the predictive accuracy of building energy baseline models," *Energy*, 66, pp. 981–990. doi:10.1016/j.energy.2014.01.074.

IRC (ISO/RTO Council) (2018) "North American Wholesale Electricity Demand Response Program Comparison."

Ji, Y., Xu, P., Duan, P. and Lu, X. (2016) "Estimating hourly cooling load in commercial buildings using a thermal network model and electricity submetering data," *Applied Energy*, 169, pp. 309–323. doi:10.1016/j.apenergy.2016.02.036.

KEMA (2011) "PJM Empirical Analysis of Demand Response Baseline Methods." Clarke Lake, MI: KEMA Inc.

KEMA-XENERGY (2003) "Protocol Development for Demand Response Calculation — Findings and Recommendations," (February).

Lei, S., Mathieu, J.L. and Jain, R.K. (2021) "Performance of Existing Methods in Baselining Demand Response From Commercial Building HVAC Fans," *ASME Journal of Engineering for Sustainable Buildings and Cities*, 2(2), pp. 1–13. doi:10.1115/1.4050999.

Mathieu, J.L., Callaway, D.S. and Kiliccote, S. (2011) "Variability in automated responses of commercial buildings and industrial facilities to dynamic electricity prices," *Energy and Buildings*, 43(12), pp. 3322–3330. doi:10.1016/j.enbuild.2011.08.020.

Motegi, N., Piette, M.A., Watson, D.S., Sezgen, O. and ten Hope, L. (2004) "Measurement and Evaluation Techniques for Automated Demand Response Demonstration," in *2004 ACEEE Summer Study on Energy Efficiency in Buildings, Pacific Grove, CA*.

Neukomm, M., Nubbe, V. and Fares, R. (2019) *Grid-Interactive Efficient Buildings*. doi:10.2172/1508212.

Nexant (2017) "California ISO Baseline Accuracy Assessment," p. 59.

Roth, A. and Reyna, J. (2019) *Grid-Interactive Efficient Buildings Technical Report Series: Whole-Building Controls, Sensors, Modeling, and Analytics*. Golden, CO (United States). doi:10.2172/1580329.

Satchwell, A.J., Piette, M.A., Khandekar, A., Granderson, J., Frick, N.M., Hledik, R., Faruqui, A., Lam, L., Ross, S., Cohen, J., Wang, K., Urigwe, D., Delurey, D., Neukomm, M. and Nemtzow, D. (2021) *A National Roadmap for Grid-Interactive Efficient Buildings*.

Schiller, S.R., Schwartz, L. and Murphy, S. (2020) *Performance Assessments of Demand Flexibility from Grid-interactive Efficient Buildings: Issues and Considerations*.

Taylor, J.A. and Mathieu, J.L. (2015) "Uncertainty in Demand Response—Identification, Estimation, and Learning," in *The Operations Research Revolution*. INFORMS, pp. 56–70. doi:10.1287/educ.2015.0137.

Vindel, E., Bergés, M., Akinci, B. and Kavvada, O. (2021) "Demand flexibility potential model for multi-zone commercial buildings using internal HVAC system states," in *Proceedings of the 8th ACM International Conference on Systems for Energy-Efficient Buildings, Cities, and Transportation*. New York, NY, USA: ACM, pp. 176–179. doi:10.1145/3486611.3486654.

Wetter, M., Zuo, W., Nouidui, T.S. and Pang, X. (2014) "Modelica Buildings library," *Journal of Building Performance Simulation*, 7(4), pp. 253–270. doi:10.1080/19401493.2013.765506.

Zhang, L., Wen, J., Li, Y., Chen, J., Ye, Y., Fu, Y. and Livingood, W. (2021) "A review of machine learning in building load prediction," *Applied Energy*, 285(July 2020), p. 116452. doi:10.1016/j.apenergy.2021.116452.

The Role of Simulation in Digital Twin Construction

Yeung T., Martinez J., Sharoni L., Sacks R.
Virtual Construction Laboratory, Technion – Israel Institute of Technology, Israel
timsonyeung@campus.technion.ac.il

Abstract. Fostered by advances in digital twin and onsite monitoring technologies, the paradigm of Digital Twin Construction (DTC) has emerged as a comprehensive mode of construction that proposes a data-driven lean production planning and control workflow, leveraging project status and design intent information to make proactive production system design changes. Simulation plays an essential role in the DTC paradigm as a provider of predictive situational awareness (SA), a mechanism for data-driven continuous improvement, and an enabler of future autonomous real-time production control systems in construction projects. In this paper, we outline these modes of use of simulation, discuss potential barriers to implementing simulation in DTC workflows, and propose a set of criteria to evaluate a simulation tool's applicability to DTC.

1. Introduction

Digital Twin Construction (DTC) is a new data-centric mode of construction management in which information and monitoring technologies are applied in a lean closed-loop planning and control system (Sacks et al., 2020). DTC leverages concepts and technologies from Building Information Modeling (BIM), Lean construction, Digital twins, and Artificial intelligence (AI) to capture project status and intent information in a digital twin information system (DTIS). As a result, the information system can provide production planners at all levels with accurate, comprehensive, and timely situational awareness of the past and present, as well as enabling projections of future status. Moreover, DTC-derived information systems may empower production planners to develop ongoing work with smoother and more reliable flows, less waste, enhanced safety, and lower risks.

Construction simulation is the discipline of building and experimenting with computer-based representations of construction systems to understand their primary behavior (AbouRizk 2010). Simulation applications range from earth-moving to high-rise construction. In production planning, simulation allows production planners to determine the potential range of impact of proposed changes before implementation. This aspect minimizes uncertainty during decision-making by providing production planners with insights about what may happen on site. In current practice, simulation provides information for the *Act* step of iterative planning and control cycles in line with the Plan-Do-Check-Act (PDCA) cycle (Deming, 2000).

As currently conceived, future DTC systems will automate the *Check* step of the PDCA cycle - monitoring of construction operations on and off site and interpretation of the resulting data streams to produce information that supports planners' situational awareness (SA). In DTC, simulation is applied on the basis of accurate and up-to-date project status information, enhancing its ability to support the *Act* step: predictive assessment and comparison of the likely outcomes and risks of the current baseline production plan to those of any possible alternative plans. The role of simulation in this context is to provide forward-projecting SA. However, it can also serve as a mechanism for data-driven continuous improvement and an enabler of future autonomous real-time production control systems in construction projects. In this paper, we outline these modes of use of simulation,

https://doi.org/10.7146/aul.455.c215

discuss potential barriers to implementing simulation in DTC workflows, and propose a set of criteria to evaluate a simulation tool's applicability to DTC.

2. DTC Conceptual Model and Workflow

A DTC information system depicts the physical status of a building or infrastructure. DTC development requires holistic thinking about the ontological and epistemological dimensions of digital twins for construction, the information, technology, process and management elements, and the relationships among them.

DTC embodies the conceptual space of the information used in the DTC flow along three orthogonal conceptual axes (for details see Figure 3 in Sacks et al. 2020). The physical–virtual axis relates the physical information inherent in the building itself to its intended design and the process information (planning). The product and process axis distinguishes between the information stored in the design BIM model's objects, their properties, and their relationships, on one hand, and construction plans, on the other. The Intent -status axis relates future-looking design and plan information (what we plan to do) to past-looking project status information (what we have done). The information of the future state of a building is described in the design and in the construction plan for the components of the building that have not yet been built. This is called Project Intent Information (PII), representing the as-designed and as-planned aspects of the project. The information about the past states of a building and its construction process records what was done and how it was done. This as-built product and as-performed process information is called Project Status Information (PSI).

A DTC workflow involves all the system components, information stores, information processing functions, and monitoring technologies according to three concentric control workflow cycles: short-term production planning, medium-term production system design, and long-term continuous improvement. Figure 2 lays out the DTC workflow:

- At the start of a construction project, designers work from a project brief to design a building to fulfill the owner's functional requirements. This is closely followed, in an iterative fashion, with construction planning. The design product and the planning process are contained in the PII. Where designers and planners predict the likely performance of their designs and plans using the PII and codified design knowledge, the results obtained are knowledge about the behavior of the building and its project, collectively called Project Intent Knowledge (PIK).
- As construction progresses and data accumulate, the Interpret function uses complex event processing (CEP) to comprehend what was done and what resources were consumed during this process. The information that is generated describes the PSI. Events may be classified using diverse methods such as rule inferencing or machine learning algorithms.
- In the next step, an 'evaluate' function compares the actual to the intended, the PII to the PSI. The output of this function is called Project Status Knowledge (PSK). PSK supports decisions and actions that lead to value judgments about the current status. Appropriate data visualization tools are needed to communicate the project status, design intent or production plan deviations, and any other anomalies (not shown in the figure).
- At this stage, designers and planners can propose changes to the product design or the production plan in response to the status knowledge, and apply their decisions to update the PII, thus completing the PDCA cycle. The updated PII continues to govern operations in the

construction itself, and the planning and control cycle is repeated until the completion of the project. Finally, all the collected information and knowledge (PII, PIK, PSI, and PSK) are archived.

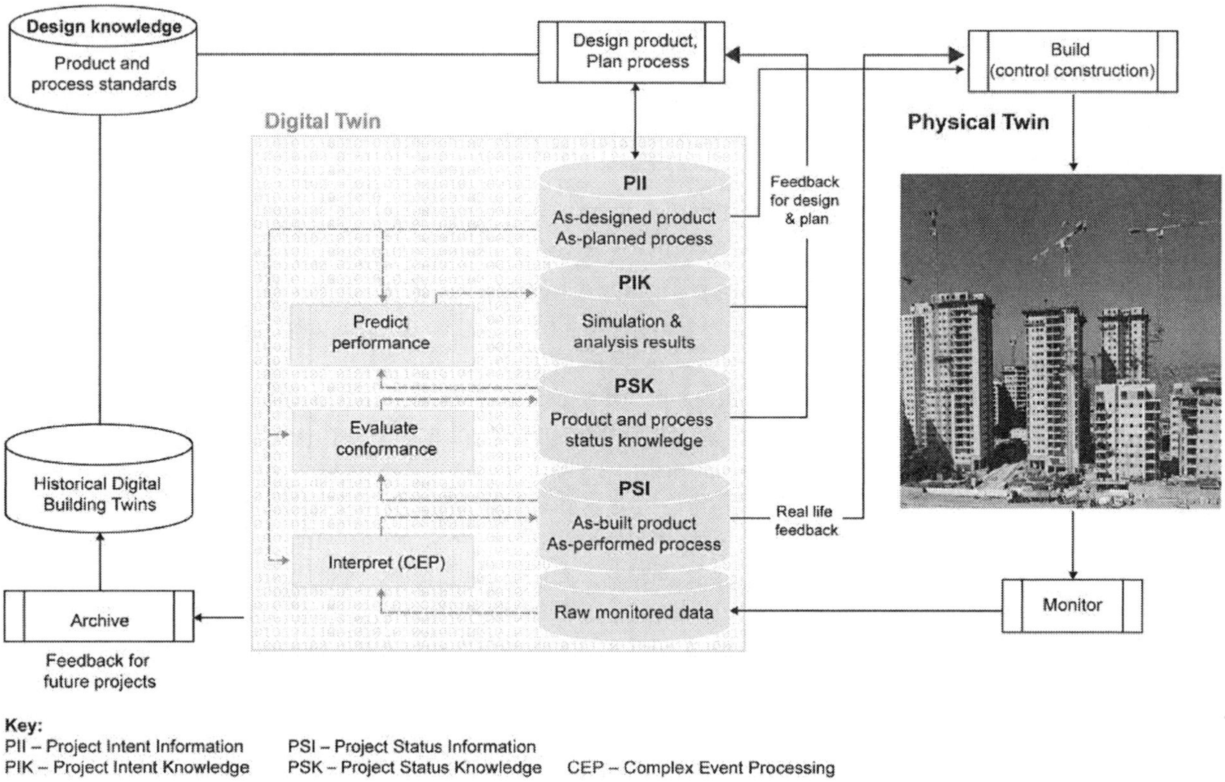

Figure 1: DTC workflow (from Sacks et al. 2020).

3. Role of Simulation in DTC

The previous section explained the fundamental role of a DTC information system in enhancing planners' situational awareness. This corresponds to the *Check* step of the PDCA cycle. The role of simulation in DTC is to help planners optimize their decisions concerning any necessary changes to the product design or to the process plans by leveraging a computer's capability to process the status data to predict how possible decisions might play out going forward. The goal is to provide what are sometimes termed 'actionable insights' (Thalheim et al., 2017) for the *Act* step of the PDCA cycle. In this section, we outline three ways that simulation can contribute to the DTC production planning and control workflow.

3.1. As a Provider of Predictive Situational Awareness

***Central Claim**: Simulation's basic role in DTC is to provide future-projecting situational awareness for proactive production planning and control.*

Predictive situational awareness (SA), or level 3 forward-projecting SA as proposed by Endsley (1995), grants planners the ability to project the future behaviours and risks of a production system. This is achieved through comprehension of the current situation and knowledge of the status and dynamics of the system. In the DTC workflow, simulation can work hand-in-hand with the DTIS to provide predictive SA. It can help planners understand the current trajectory of the project and explore what-if scenarios.

Figure 2 outlines a workflow in DTC where the information system can explore alternative production plans' outcomes and performances through simulation and provide recommendations to planners on the course of actions that can improve the outcome of the project. In large complex projects, simulation may offer the planner an alternative plan (AP) that they hadn't considered before. Grounded on PSI and PII, the system can generate alternative production plans from starting points that are within planners' degree of freedom in product and process changes (Martinez et al., 2022), while also leveraging knowledge from historical DT databases. An AP consists of the work breakdown schedule (a hierarchy of work packages, activities, tasks that capture the construction methods and group the building product element parts that are constructed in each one), the location breakdown schedule (a hierarchy of zones and locations in which work is assigned), a planned construction and material delivery time schedule, labor assignments, equipment utilization, product information requirements, and site safety information. The APs are then simulated to project the range of their probable outcomes, which are stored as PIK. APs' performances are assessed with respect to planners' objectives using multi-criteria evaluation methods. Planners may explore additional scenarios in a closed-loop optimization cycle. Finally, the system presents all simulated APs with probability distributions of their behaviors/characteristics (i.e. how safe, reliable, costly, fast, resilient, and/or lean they are). The APs that best meet the planners' objectives can be recommended to them. The chosen AP will be updated into the PII as the new baseline plan.

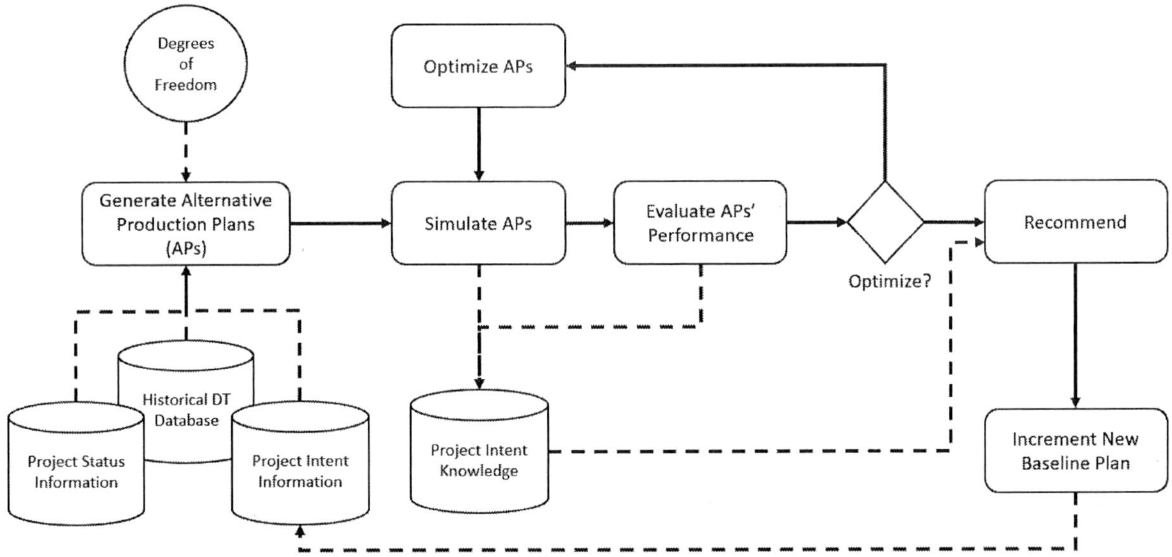

Figure 2: Generation of alternative production system designs and production plans, simulation, evaluation, and optimization.

3.2. As a Mechanism for Rapid Continuous Improvement

***Central Claim**: Simulation can enable continuous improvement by evaluating the outcomes of decisions made in Virtual Design and Construction (VDC) (product and process design) and in* *medium to long term lookahead planning (production system design) by enabling iterative optimization through virtual PDCA cycles.*

In the previous mode, simulation served to provide short-term predictions of a construction production system's function subject to a set of planning decisions made within the scope of planners' degrees of freedom of action. However, simulation can equally well evaluate possible alternatives that emerge from considerations of alternative product designs and alternative production system designs. These evaluations can be applied to enable continuous improvement, as comparisons between the outcomes of alternative choices can be used to guide medium- and long-term decisions within a current project or within future projects, where medium to long term planning concerns a three to six weeks lookahead, depending on the project type and size.

In the DTC paradigm, a virtual PDCA cycle can be created by using simulation as a validation mechanism that forecasts future behaviors and risks of a given production system over time. Product design changes are common throughout the construction process, whether due to customizations introduced by clients or due to engineering detailing conflicts. These changes can cause ripple effects to the production system and the production plan, and construction methods and sequences might need to be reconsidered.

In a conventional implementation of the PDCA cycle for a construction project (Figure 3), planners perform production planning and control and deliver the production plan as PII to the construction site as the *Plan* step of PDCA. The construction team executes the plan based on the given information as the *Do* step. Information about the as-built product and the as-performed processes that produced is collected from the site, typically through manual documentation, and in turn provides planners with level 2 SA, a comprehension of current situation (Endsley, 1995). Planners can use this SA to evaluate the performance of the production system (*Check*) and make management decisions, which are the appropriate changes to the product and production system design to improve project performance, as the *Act* step of PDCA.

Meanwhile, simulation coupled with the DTC information system supports a virtual PDCA optimization loop within the overall PDCA cycle (Figure 4). *Planning* and *acting* in the DTC workflow involves a closed-loop virtual PDCA cycle that begins with reacting to the project status through virtual prototyping of the construction project in VDC (Li et al., 2008), and production system design (*virtual* Act) followed by production planning and control (*virtual Plan*) to generate an alternative PII. This PII is simulated (*virtual Do*) to generate simulated PSI, which can be then be evaluated against the alternative PII to *check* whether the proposed changes are predicted to fulfill its intended goals. This understanding provides planners with level 3 predictive SA as PIK. They can build upon this newly discovered insight to perform multiple iterations of this virtual PDCA cycle to optimize their solution until they arrive at a satisfactory solution as the new PII for construction. PSI can be generated in the DTC information system through automated monitoring of the construction site and interpretation of the data streams. Then the DTC information system performs evaluation on the PSI and PII collectively to generate knowledge on the current status of the project (level 2 SA), which can be used as a basis for the next overall PDCA cycle.

Thanks to simulation as part of the virtual PDCA cycle, planners can learn and continuously improve their proposed systems and products without suffering real-world consequences of failure. They can test any building design, construction method, and production system from any point forward in time, understand how the production system would behave, what are the risks, where are the bottlenecks, where are the wastes, will the proposed changes have the intended effect?

While simulation can enable the virtual PDCA cycle in any standard production planning workflow, virtual PDCA cycles in DTC workflows offer significantly greater improvement opportunities. As discussed above, the DTC information system can provide planners with current information and knowledge on the as-built product and the as-performed processes that they can use as the basis for planning. In current planning workflows, planners predominantly rely on their expert experience to construct their initial solutions, often leading to misjudgment on the feasibility and effectiveness of their solutions. Meanwhile, planners in the DTC workflow are empowered to create more reliable plans by building upon the PSK provided by the DTC information system. Guided by an understanding of the project status from its inception to the current point in time, planners will be better equipped to create plans that address the quality, safety, and productivity issues occurring on the construction site while maintaining realistic expectations on the implementation feasibility.

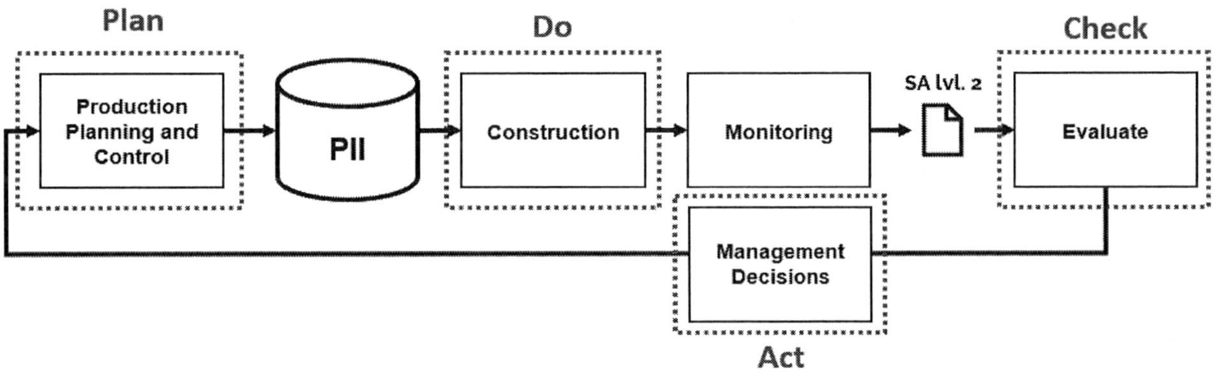

Figure 3: Conventional PDCA cycle

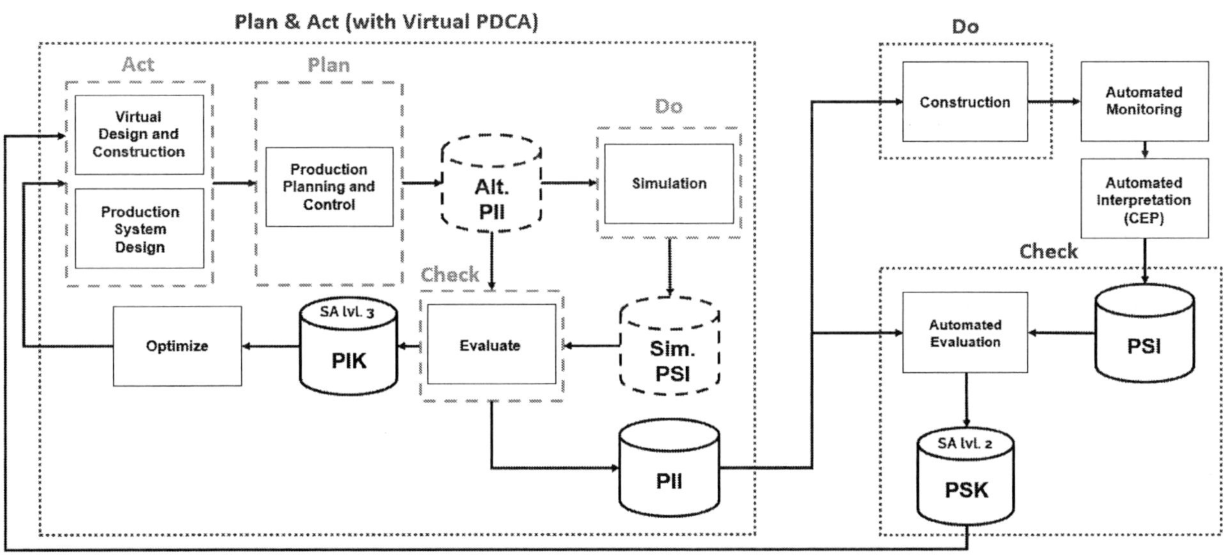

Figure 4: Virtual PDCA in DTC. The virtual cycle is iterated within the control cycle.

Within a typical planning window, planners can perform many iterations of VDC, explore many different alternative designs and construction plans, optimize them based on feedback from simulation results, and develop proactive strategies to mitigate uncertainty and risks that may arise in the solution that they choose. Without simulation, planners can at most consider the known-

known factors. With simulation, they can develop understanding of the potential impacts of known-unknown factors. In other words, simulation can serve as a virtual simulator of their specific construction site in the current control cycle, allowing them to iteratively optimize their solutions with validation feedback. The virtual PDCA workflow could potentially reduce the feedback cycle sufficiently to support continuous learning, thus maximizing learning opportunities and producing better planners in the long run.

Furthermore, by using archived project records for education and training, construction planners could be trained in much the same way as aircraft simulators are used to prepare pilots for the unexpected, making them more resilient when things do go wrong.

3.3. As an Enabler of Autonomous Real-Time Production Control Systems

Central Claim: *Predictive feedback provided by simulation is not only helpful for contemporary human-centric production planning and control workflows, it will also play an integral role in future autonomous real-time production control systems in construction projects.*

"The function of real-time production control is to adapt the production system to the changing environment, while preserving efficiency with respect to cost, time, and quality requirements. Real-time production control systems provide decisions for specific problems associated with part manufacturing, quality control, material provision, internal logistics, resource maintenance, and personnel allocation" (Pfeiffer et al., 2008).

In manufacturing, simulation has been used extensively as a component of real-time production control systems. As the DTC paradigm and its supporting technologies continue to evolve, we can contemplate a future construction site with features that may resemble manufacturing in terms of real-time production control.

Currently, production control remains a challenging task for construction planners. Not only are production managers struggling to consistently optimize their control decisions, their scale of "real-time" uses the units of days and/or weeks, far from the minute to minute, second to second real-time control in manufacturing. Three things are needed for autonomous real-time production control systems to work in construction: a) real-time status of the production system, b) a method to evaluate decisions/actions, and c) behavior models of production system components. Real-time status can be provided by the DTC information system, as conceived in the BIM2TWIN project ("BIM2TWIN," 2022); evaluation and optimization of alternative decisions require simulation.

As discussed above, the predictive feedback provided by simulation within a DTC information system can be used to generate data defining forward-projecting situational awareness and stored within the PIK. This is not only useful for product and production system design in medium- and long-term planning, it is also beneficial to short-term production control. Given the complexity of construction projects and the large scales of their production systems, human planners find it challenging to perform proper, optimized production control in construction. Autonomous agents that are fully integrated with the information system and can execute simulations can achieve real-time production control with optimized decision-making based on full comprehension of the production system status and foreknowledge of the likely implications of their possible actions.

4. Evaluating Simulations for DTC

There is a wide range of computer simulation tools available for use in construction. The tools vary in their scope, input requirements, output information, modelling approaches, system compatibility, and intended workflows. Hence, it is not trivial for researchers and practitioners to judge a simulation tool's applicability to the DTC workflow, i.e., how well it can fulfil the roles outlined in the previous section. Evaluation requires a method that examines the fundamental characteristics of simulation tools relevant to the DTC planning and control workflow. To address this need, we propose a set of criteria as a basis for future evaluations.

Five primary criteria are defined in Table 1. These concern the elementary features of a simulation tool that characterize its general quality. In addition to the primary criteria, we define seven secondary criteria in Table 2 to evaluate how well a simulation tool can leverage the DTC information system and support simulation's three modes of use outlined in Section 3.

Table 1: Primary criteria for evaluating a simulation tool's applicability to DTC.

Criterion	Description
Relevance	How well the output of the tool satisfies the intended purposes, which, in the context of this paper, are the three modes of use in Section 3
Explainability	How well the results of the simulation can be interpreted by the user transparently and justifiably
Comprehensiveness	How thorough has the simulation taken into account the expected and unexpected events that can occur
Resolution	The level of decomposition of the production system and processes into their components
Fidelity	The extent to which the elements of the simulation faithfully imitate the characteristics and behaviors of their real-world counterpart
Reusability	How applicable the simulation is to different types of construction projects in different geographical locations

Table 2: Secondary Criteria for evaluating a simulation tool's applicability to DTC.

Criterion	Description
Flexibility	How capable the simulation is in changing its structure, i.e., how modular the simulation is
Extensibility	How easy it is to model new production system components (methods, products, and resources) into the simulation
Calibratability	The extent to which the simulation can be calibrated based on project status information, i.e., how many parameters can be calibrated in the simulation
Automatability	To what extent can the process of simulation model adjustment, calibration, extension, and alignment be automated
Stochasticity	The extent to which the simulation models events and behaviors stochastically with probability distributions
BIM Integration	How much BIM information is leveraged in the simulation

5. Potential Barriers in Implementing Simulation in DTC

DTC information system and workflows as outlined here require simulation functionalities capabilities beyond those common in state-of-the-art applications in construction. While computer simulation's value to production planning and control is well understood, its ability to integrate with the DTC information system to provide actionable insight for human planners and autonomous control systems remains to be demonstrated. Moreover, as Abdelmegid et al. (2020) pointed out, computer simulation has not gained widespread adoption by the construction industry, despite its usefulness having been proven by research efforts in the past four decades. Hence, it is reasonable to expect that simulation implementation in the DTC workflow will face many of the same barriers of simulation adoption in the industry today. Below, we discuss four major barriers shared by the DTC paradigm and ways to address these barriers.

The amount and nature of input and output data requirements – A significant quantity of data is required from the site to create an accurate model. Due to a lack of practical methods to provide updated and meaningful data during construction to capture changes in the production system, most construction simulations depend on historical data to overcome the information gap, affecting the reliability and credibility of the model. Moreover, data collection tools and workflows often vary from project to project, This inconsistency has led to missing, limited, or faulty data that causes difficulties in statistically characterizing construction processes through random distributions. DTC information systems, which integrate onsite monitoring technology with digital twin information processing, will support an automated data collection and processing framework that can replace the traditional manual and tedious process and boost simulation models' ability to maintain synchronization with the project status.

Sophisticated nature of simulation outputs – Statistical tables and charts are the typical outputs of a construction simulation model. These have been identified as unfit for current data management systems and visualization techniques for construction. For a simulation to make a meaningful contribution to planners' situational awareness, the explainability of the simulation output must be given adequate attention to avoid the "black-box effect" perception towards simulation that is prevalent among construction practitioners.

The long cycle time of simulation studies – The process of developing a construction simulation model from scratch is highly time-consuming for both modelers and construction stakeholders. Researchers such as (AbouRizk, 2010) have highlighted that the average time to construct a model in simulation studies is likely to exceed the duration of the construction project of interest, discouraging industry partners from adopting simulation as a decision-support tool. This barrier can potentially be overcome in DTC. Through a data schema that standardizes project status and intent information requirement, the DTC information system can support a modeling framework that automatically and parametrically constructs the simulation model according to the as-designed product and the as-planned production system, while project status knowledge can be used to calibrate the model to reflect system behaviors.

Limitations in construction simulation tools and methods – This barrier is the most frequently reported factor that hinders adoption of construction in simulation. Current simulation tools are reported to be incapable of capturing the reality of the construction systems (Leite et al., 2016). Modelers have made unrealistic assumptions and simplifications when adopting modeling strategies and tools from other disciplines (such as manufacturing). The complexity of modern construction systems increases the potential for inaccurate conceptualization of the construction operations and flows, further extending the gap between academic and industry. This barrier cannot be overcome by technology alone. Rather, it requires close collaborations between researchers and practitioners to model and validate behaviors of the production system guided by a robust and comprehensive framework that leverages information from the DTC information system and is supported by a lean understanding of the production system such as Transformation-Flow-Value views, variability, and waste.

6. Conclusion

The emerging DTC paradigm empowers human planners and future autonomous production control systems to make optimized decisions based on situational awareness of current project status and potential future states. Supported by onsite monitoring technologies and predictive simulation, planners in the DTC workflow can thoroughly explore alternative plans and designs and arrive at optimal solutions through virtual PDCA cycles. Simulation has three essential roles in the DTC workflow: as a provider of predictive situational awareness (SA), as a mechanism for data-driven continuous improvement, and as an enabler of future autonomous real-time production control systems in construction projects. We have proposed a set of criteria to evaluate a simulation tool's applicability to DTC and identified four potential barriers to implementing simulation in DTC. In ongoing work in the BIM2TWIN project, we are building a prototype tool to compile and run simulations as part of a virtual PDCA cycle.

Acknowledgement

This work was funded in part by BIM2TWIN project of the European Union's Horizon 2020 research and innovation programme under grant agreement no. 958398. The authors thank our BIM2TWIN colleagues from Fira Oy, SPADA and IDP for their support in the ongoing research on simulation and process prediction in the framework of DTC.

References

Abdelmegid, M.A., González, V.A., Poshdar, M., O'Sullivan, M., Walker, C.G., Ying, F., (2020). Barriers to adopting simulation modelling in construction industry. Autom. Constr. 111, 103046. https://doi.org/10/gnhm8b

AbouRizk, S., (2010). Role of Simulation in Construction Engineering and Management. J. Constr. Eng. Manag. 136, 1140–1153. https://doi.org/10/dhbd32

BIM2TWIN [WWW Document], (2022). . BIM2TWIN. URL https://bim2twin.eu/ (accessed 2.27.22).

Deming, W.E., (2000). Out of the Crisis, MIT Press. Massachusetts Institute of Technology, Center for Advanced Engineering Study.

Endsley, M.R., (1995). Toward a Theory of Situation Awareness in Dynamic Systems. Hum. Factors J. Hum. Factors Ergon. Soc. 37, 32–64. https://doi.org/10.1518/001872095779049543

Leite, F., Cho, Y., Behzadan, A.H., Lee, S., Choe, S., Fang, Y., Akhavian, R., Hwang, S., (2016). Visualization, Information Modeling, and Simulation: Grand Challenges in the Construction Industry. J. Comput. Civ. Eng. 30, 04016035. https://doi.org/10.1061/(ASCE)CP.1943-5487.0000604

Li, H., Huang, T., Kong, C.W., Guo, H.L., Baldwin, A., Chan, N., Wong, J., (2008). Integrating design and construction through virtual prototyping. Autom. Constr. 17, 915–922. https://doi.org/10/dnft75

Martinez, J.R., Yeung, T., Sacks, R., (2022). Scope of action of production planners in the context of Digital Twin Construction. Presented at the 12th International Conference on Construction in the 21st Century, Al-Zaytoonah University, Amman, Jordan, p. 12 pps.

Pfeiffer, A., Kádár, B., Monostori, L., Karnok, D., (2008). Simulation as one of the core technologies for digital enterprises: assessment of hybrid rescheduling methods. Int. J. Comput. Integr. Manuf. 21, 206–214. https://doi.org/10.1080/09511920701607717

Sacks, R., Brilakis, I., Pikas, E., Xie, H.S., Girolami, M., (2020). Construction with digital twin information systems. Data-Centric Eng. 1, e14. https://doi.org/10.1017/dce.2020.16

Thalheim, J., Rodrigues, A., Akkus, I.E., Bhatotia, P., Chen, R., Viswanath, B., Jiao, L., Fetzer, C., (2017). Sieve: actionable insights from monitored metrics in distributed systems, in: Proceedings of the 18th ACM/IFIP/USENIX Middleware Conference. Presented at the Middleware '17: 18th International Middleware Conference, ACM, Las Vegas Nevada, pp. 14–27. https://doi.org/10.1145/3135974.3135977

Leveraging Textual Information for Knowledge Graph-oriented Machine Learning: A Case Study in the Construction Industry

Shahinmoghadam M. [1], Motamedi A. [1], Soltani M.M. [2]
[1] École de technologie supérieure, Canada, [2] Toronto, Canada
Mehrzad.Shahinmoghadam.1@ens.etsmtl.ca, Ali.Motamedi@etsmtl.ca, mo_solta@encs.concordia.ca

Abstract. The proven power of Knowledge Graphs (KGs) to effectively represent lexical and semantic information about numerous and heterogeneous entities and their interconnectedness has led to the growing recognition of their potential in engineering disciplines. Meanwhile, a greater focus has been placed on graph embedding techniques to derive dense vector representations of KGs. Such representations could enable the use of conventional machine learning techniques over the content of KGs. However, in the context of building engineering, the quality of the graph embeddings could be problematic, mainly due to the relatively small size of the KGs that are created for individual buildings. This paper aims to investigate the effectiveness of applying KG embedding methods when the elements of the building are described narrowly within the KG. The results of our experiments confirm that proper use of data transformation techniques can significantly improve the quality of the feature representation for downstream tasks.

1. Introduction

Due to the ubiquitous presence of graph (network) structures in many real-world phenomena, graph-oriented analytics has been the subject of interest in many fields of research (Goyal and Ferrara, 2018). Recently, both academia and industry practitioners have shown an increased interest in the notion of Knowledge Graphs (KGs). In general terms, a KG can be defined as a structured representation of facts about real-world or abstract subjects (Ji et al., 2022). Each KG is composed of nodes and edges (entities and relationships) which jointly represent facts (semantic descriptions) about different subjects in an explicit and machine-readable format.

Successful applications of Knowledge Graphs (KGs) for purposes including but not limited to context-aware information retrieval and question-answering over knowledge bases, has attracted considerable attention in various engineering disciplines. The construction and building engineering sector have been no exception to this trend. The added value of KGs and their potential for open exchange and management of the built environment data has been most recently highlighted in (Pauwels et al., 2022).

Despite their vast expressive power to represent knowledge in a structured way, manipulation of KGs is challenging for purposes such as statistical learning (Wang et al., 2017). To address these challenges, a fast-growing volume of research has been dedicated to represent the entities of the KG in the form of numerical vectors. In the context of graph analytics, this approach is known as graph embedding. Representation of the KG components in low-dimensional vector spaces will significantly facilitate applicability of the machine learning methods over the content of the KG. This way, further knowledge can be extracted from KGs when symbolic inference mechanisms are incapable of or inefficient in doing so.

The effectiveness of the existing graph embedding techniques has been under investigation in various domains (e.g., bioinformatics, social network analysis) and the results have been encouraging (Goyal and Ferrara, 2018). Moreover, researchers have proposed novel embedding techniques that are customized to specifically cope with the content of KGs. However, the majority of the existing embedding techniques have been tested with large-scale graphs that usually contain billions of facts (Rossi et al., 2021), while the average size of a KG that is

https://doi.org/10.7146/aul.455.c216

constructed for an individual building (or small group of buildings) will be significantly smaller in scale. Moreover, the structural pattern of a building KG may be quite different from open-domain KGs such as Wikidata. Hence, the applicability of the KG embedding techniques in the context of building engineering remains questionable.

This paper aims to address the above-mentioned issue by examining the quality of the results of applying existing KG embedding algorithms over small-sized building KGs. To meet this objective, a case study approach was adopted. First, a working dataset was created whose content was extracted from existing reference models, which had originally been developed for building engineering intentions. Subsequently, a set of experiments were carried out with the purpose of deriving the embeddings of the building graph to be used as the input to a node classification model. The results of our experiments showed that despite the possibility of encountering challenges within the downstream machine learning phase (e.g., reduced applicability of linear models), careful curation of the embeddings (e.g., kernel approximation) can significantly improve the effectiveness of the derived feature vector for supervised/unsupervised learning. The remainder of the paper describes the required background, methods used, and experiments conducted, followed by the discussion and conclusion.

2. Background

2.1 KG definition and characteristics

Following the recent successful adoption of KGs in various domains of practice, the volume of research publications on KGs has been increasing (Hogan et al., 2021). Despite the previous research efforts made to provide a widely-accepted formal definition of KGs, no such definition currently exists within the literature (Ji et al., 2022). Yet, in a general sense, a KG can be viewed as a graph composed of nodes and edges, which together provide formal descriptions of the entities of interest and their interconnectedness (Ehrlinger and Wöß, 2016; Hogan et al., 2021). In some of the reference publications, the incorporation of the KG content into formal ontologies and the use of the semantic reasoners has been essential to the definition of KGs (Ehrlinger and Wöß, 2016). Thanks to the reasoning power of formal ontologies, numerous implicit relationships can be automatically inferred and added to the original KG as new factual statements. Regardless of the way a KG is created, one of its outstanding potentials is its ability to preserve the "context" in data representation. The explicit representation of contextual correspondences within a KG provides the possibility of interpreting the data from different perspectives (Hogan et al., 2021). This is of great value to the development of various types of context-aware applications (information/knowledge retrieval, recommender systems, industrial chatbots, etc.)

2.2 KGs in the built environment

Most recently, Pauwels et al. (Pauwels et al., 2022) elaborated on the notion of KGs for the built environment. In their work, researchers put a significant weight on the principles of "linked data" and "semantic web" technologies, e.g., OWL (Web Ontology Language (McGuinness and Van Harmelen, 2004)) and RDF (Resource Description Framework (Lassila and Swick, 1998)). Thanks to the availability of the mature ontologies that currently exist for the built environment, KGs can be constructed practically to represent facts about the design, construction, and operation of the real-world built entities. The nodes of such KGs can refer to both real-world entities (e.g., a physical space) or virtual ones (e.g., average floor temperature sensor (Balaji et al., 2018)), while the edges of the KG make reference to the semantic relationships that exist between the entities of the building. When incorporated into formal ontologies such as ifcOWL (buildingSMART, 2022), each pair of nodes linked via an edge (known as a triple) expresses a "fact" about the building, in an explicit and formal (machine-readable) manner. However, the inclusion of detailed geometric descriptions as well as sensory observations in KGs is associated with considerable complexities and inefficiencies (Pauwels et al., 2022). Hence, from a practical perspective, the content of the KGs that are constructed for the built environments will mainly consist of lexical and semantic descriptions. Nevertheless, a large amount of valuable (semantic) information can be still represented within KGs that will be of great value to knowledge extraction purposes.

2.3 KG representation learning

The key motivation behind our current study is that with the help of the "semantic embedding" techniques, the contextualized information contained in the built environment KGs can be exploited for knowledge extraction using machine learning methods. Semantic embedding can be defined as encoding the semantics of the data (KG content in our case) into numeric vector representations (Bengio et al., 2013). In other words, KG embedding techniques can be used to generate a feature vector by which the textual information contained in KGs can be represented in a numeric form. Recently, there has been a growing interest in developing semantic embedding techniques that can effectively cope with the particular characteristics of KGs (i.e., dealing with lexical and semantic information). One of the relatively recent algorithms in this regard is RDF2Vec (Ristoski et al., 2019), which was originally proposed to learn vector representation of RDF-formatted KGs. However, the effectiveness of the existing techniques has been mostly tested over large-scale open-domain KGs (e.g., Freebase (Bollacker et al., 2008) and Wikidata (Vrandečić and Krötzsch, 2014)), and rarely investigated in construction and building engineering research.

2.4 Research gap and objectives

Given the relatively significant small size of the KGs that are created for individual built environments, compared to the size of the open-domain benchmark KGs, the applicability of the existing KG-embedding techniques for the built environment needs to be carefully investigated. This study set out to contribute to filling this gap by focusing on the RDF-formatted KGs that are built for individual buildings. Our main objective is to investigate the applicability of the RDF2Vec method by examining the usability of the generated embeddings in a node classification scenario.

3. Methods and materials

3.1 Data preparation

To create a working dataset for the purpose of this study, we used two of the reference building models that are publicly available at ("BrickSchema.org", 2022). These reference models, serialized in RDF format, are primarily intended for building engineering research purposes. They are representative examples of the use of the Brick schema (ontology) to deliver rich semantic descriptions of a building's physical, logical and virtual assets and their relationships ("BrickSchema.org", n.d.). Among the five reference models that were available at the time of our study (early January 2022), we selected the "Gates Hillman Center" (GHC) and "Engineering Building Unit 3B" (EBU) models, which contained approximately 35,000 and

8,000 relationships, respectively. The percentage of mapping the building's actual data points to the entities of the used schema (Brick ontology) for the GHC and EBU models were 99% and 96%, respectively. The rationale behind the selection of these two models was to reinforce the validity of the results by performing our experiments using two datasets that were different in size. A summary of the description of the models is provided in Table 1. More details on the characteristics of the actual buildings and their associated semantic model can be found in (Balaji et al., 2018).

Table 1: Summary of the description of the data.

General description	Description of the semantic models (KGs)			Description of the created datasets (Target class statistics)			
	Graph nodes	**Total relationships**	**Unique relationships**	**Train/Test samples**	**Point/ subclass**	**Location/ subclass**	**Equipment/ subclass**
Gates Hillman Center (GHC); 217k (ft^2) floor space, Built 2009	≈ 9.6k	≈ 35.7k	9	1452 364	934 Sensor	475 Room	447 VAV (variable air volume)
Engineering Building Unit 3B (EBU); 150k (ft^2) floor space, Built 2004	≈ 6.1k	≈ 8.4k	4	576 145	238 Sensor	246 Room	237 Damper

Several SPARQL queries were conducted, over the two models mentioned above, to create two distinct datasets for the entities of interest, i.e., the entities for which the embeddings were calculated. Three distinct types, namely "Point", "Location", and "Equipment", were considered as the target classes for the development of the datasets. It should be noted that for the "type" relationships, the original models only contained triples that indicated the subclasses of the three mentioned target classes. For example, while the model contained type relationships indicating the "Room" class, the fact that a room is a subclass of the "Location" class was absent from the model. Finally, each created dataset was split into a training set (80% of samples) and test set (20% of samples). The summary of the statistics for each created dataset can be seen in Table 1.

3.2 Approach

A summary of our approach towards the experimental evaluations conducted in this study is shown in Figure 1. Description of the three main modules depicted in the figure is given as follows:

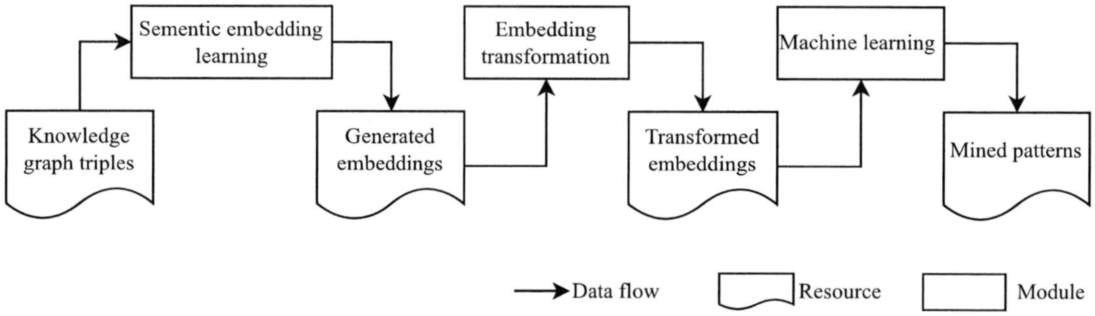

Figure 1: Proposed approach.

Semantic embedding learning. As mentioned in the previous section, we used the RDF2Vec algorithm to generate the embeddings for the instances of points, locations, and equipment in the created datasets. A Python implementation of RDF2vec (Vandewiele et al., 2020) was used in this study to calculate the KG embeddings. For all experiments, the size of the embeddings was set to 100. In other words, at each round of embedding calculation, a feature vector with 100 dimensions was learned to represent the entities of interest in a continuous vector space.

Embedding transformation. In the proposed approach, the embedding transformation module is responsible for maintaining the applicability of the generated embeddings for downstream tasks such as node classification as intended in the current study, as well as other tasks (e.g., exploratory data analysis, link prediction, etc.). Both linear and non-linear data transformation methods were considered for our embedding transformation module. In particular, we considered the following algorithms:

Principal Component Analysis (PCA). As one of the most popular dimensionality reduction techniques, PCA was considered for the removal of those dimensions from the generated embeddings that express insignificant rates of explained variance among the data points. Using PCA, non-representative dimensions can be removed from the feature vector (noise reduction), which in turn can improve the overall computational performance for downstream machine learning. Moreover, 2D/3D visualizations of the embeddings based on the identified principal components can be used to intuitively observe the discriminative power of the learned vector representation.

Kernel Principal Component Analysis (Kernel PCA). Despite its recognized strengths, there are many probable occasions in which linear PCA fails to find the linear separation between the dissimilar instances of the data. To tackle this issue, we considered the use of kernel approximation methods to find a projection of the embeddings (in higher dimensions) that allows for them to be linearly separated.

t-SNE (t-distributed Stochastic Neighbor Embedding). T-SNE is highly effective for the 2D/3D visualization of high-dimensional data (Van der Maaten and Hinton, 2008). Given the relatively large size of the embeddings generated for each dataset (100 dimensions), we first used the t-SNE algorithm to intuitively observe the distance at which the dissimilar embeddings (node types) were clustered apart from each other.

Node classification. The ultimate goal of our node classification module is to assign a distinct "type label" to an unseen building node entity. In particular, the objective is to construct a model that takes the transformed (pre-processed) embeddings of a node that is a joint product of the two previous modules as input and gives a label of the class to which the node belongs to (object type) as output. With reference to the experimental setup that was used in this study for dataset creation, each node can only belong to one of the "Point", "Location", or "Equipment" classes.

For the sake of model development, we tested the predictive performance of three different algorithms each from a different group of supervised learning methods. In particular, we used "Logistic Regression", "Random Forest", and "Multi-layer Perceptron" algorithms, which belong to linear, ensemble, and neural network machine learning models, respectively. For the sake of the evaluation metrics, we computed "accuracy score" and "F1-score" (harmonic mean of precision and recall) to compare the prediction performance of each trained model.

4. Results and discussion

4.1 Experiments

Before we address the experimental results, it should be noted that the codes and created datasets will be made available by request, for the benefit of the community and to ensure the reproducibility of the reported results. Moreover, it should be mentioned that the main purpose of this case study has been to highlight the potential benefits of KG embeddings for machine learning purposes in an industrial setting. Hence, an in-depth comparison of the existing techniques to derive and transform the embeddings, as well as hyper-parameter tuning for the methods used in the present work will be left to future research.

In the first step of our experimental evaluations, we calculated the embeddings for the two datasets that were created for the purpose of this study. Figure 2 shows the results of the use of t-SNE to deliver 2D visualizations of the generated embeddings for GHC and EBU datasets, respectively. A closer look at Figure 2 reveals two key observations: First, the embeddings derived for none of the datasets were clustered quite far apart, thereby restraining the linear separation of the dissimilar classes. Second, while the distribution of the GHC embeddings follows a perceptible (circular) pattern, the embeddings generated for the EBU dataset seem to be more arbitrary.

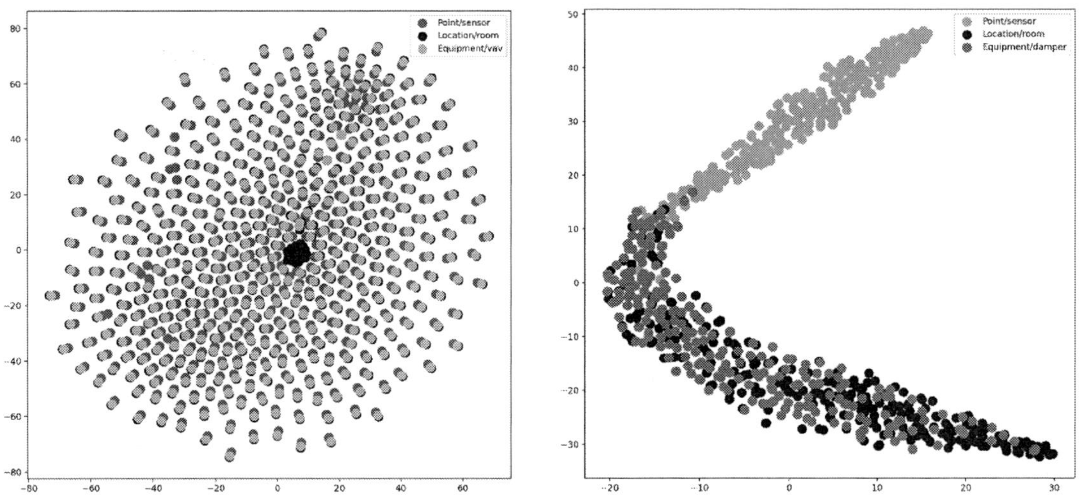

Figure 2: t-SNE visualization of embeddings for GHC (left) and EBU (right) datasets.

To find a plausible explanation for the dissimilar behaviour of the two datasets, we looked at the underlying structure of the KGs upon which the embeddings were generated. As one can see from Table 1, while 9 unique relationships can be found in the GHC model, only 4 unique relationships were used to describe the entities of the EBU semantic model. Moreover, the ratio of total relationships to nodes, for the GHC model ($\approx$ 35.7/9.6), is almost three times higher than that of the EBU model ($\approx$ 8.4/6.1). Based on these comparisons it can be argued that the granularity of the semantic descriptions within the GHC model has been higher, comparatively. To further reinforce our argument, we conducted an exploratory analysis by running multiple queries (SPARQL queries) over the reference models (KGs). The results of our analysis confirmed that the structure of the description of the entities in the used KGs is comparatively different from each other, in terms of both syntactic and semantic characteristics. For example, while up to 6 unique relationships were used to describe the room entities inside the GHC model, only 2 relationships were used within the EBU model for the same purpose. Hence, it can be concluded that different "modelling patterns", i.e., using different terminology and structures to describe the entities of a building within a KG can lead to varying behaviours of the derived embeddings. However, answering the question of which modelling pattern leads to better data representation requires profound research considerations and is beyond the scope of the present study.

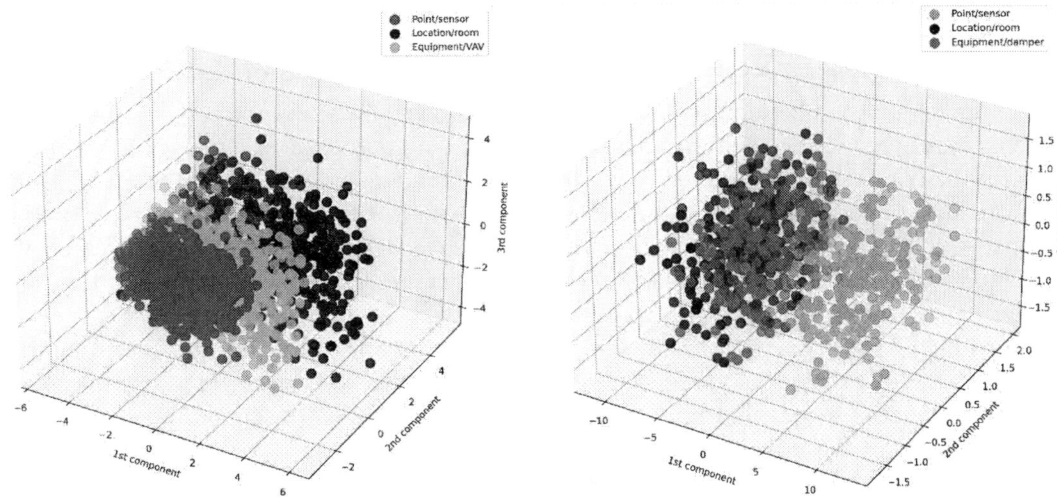

Figure 3: PCA-based transformation of embeddings for GHC (left) and EBU (right) datasets.

As mentioned in section 3.2, we considered the use of both linear and non-linear projection methods to improve the quality of the feature representation. The plots depicted in Figure 3 and Figure 4 show the results of the use of linear and kernel PCA, respectively, to deliver 3D visualizations of the transformed embeddings. As one can see from the comparison of the plots in Figure 3 and Figure 4, the used methods show competitive discriminative power. To quantitatively compare the quality of the feature representations, we calculated the variance of the projected samples. This step was taken to identify feature representation with lower variance as it points to a denser representation, which will be more favourable for statistical learning purposes. The results confirmed that for both datasets, kernel approximation outperformed linear PCA, in terms of delivering dense representations (see Table 2).

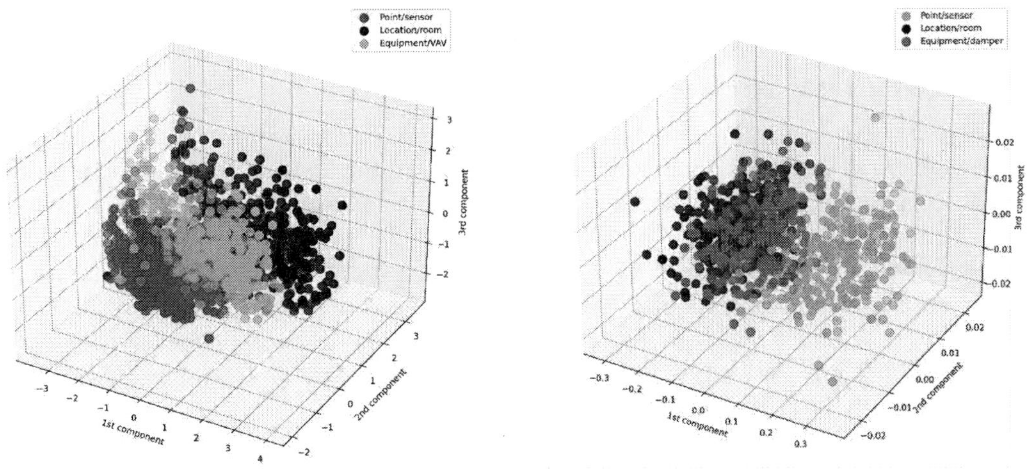

Figure 4: Kernel approximation of embeddings for GHC (left) and EBU (right) datasets.

Table 2: Variance of the transformed embeddings calculated for 1st to 3rd principal components.

	Linear PCA	Kernel PCA
GHC dataset	2.96	1.21
EBU dataset	9.9	0.01

Subsequent to obtaining encouraging results with the use of kernel PCA to find the projection of the generated embeddings in higher dimensions, the next step was to perform a dimensionality reduction step. To identify the effective number of principal components to be used for the representation of the training data, we used a base classifier (i.e., a Random Forest model with 100 decision trees) and observed the quality of the predictions as we changed the number of the components. As a result of taking this step, the size of the feature vector was set to 80 and 100 for the GHC and EBU samples, respectively. Hence, prior to the training and testing of our node classification models, we reduced the dimension of the feature vectors (embeddings) to decrease noise and improve the computational performance. After training three distinct classification models for each dataset, the test sets were introduced to the developed models to evaluate the quality of their predictions. The prediction performance scores of the trained models are presented in Table 3.

Table 3: Summary of the node classification results.

	Tested with GHC dataset			**Tested with EBU dataset**		
	Random Forest	**Logistic Regression**	**ML-Perceptron**	**Random Forest**	**Logistic Regression**	**ML-Perceptron**
Accuracy	0.91	0.96	0.95	0.76	0.76	0.79
F1-score	0.91	0.96	0.95	0.76	0.75	0.78

It is apparent from Table 3 that the accuracy of the predictions made by the models that were trained with the GHC data is higher than that of those made by the models that were trained with the EBU dataset. The different size of the data used to train the two sets of the models can be mentioned as an immediate explanation for this observation. However, with reference to our earlier discussion of the effect of the structural differences in KG creation (e.g., granularity of the semantic descriptions), it is strongly possible that the lower performance of the models that were trained with EBU data, stems from the quality of the content of the KG.

4.2 Implications to research and practice

The results of testing our trained models confirmed that relatively accurate predictions of object types could be realized based purely on the embeddings of the lexical and semantic information that exist for a building entity inside the KG. Given the small size of the used KGs, in addition to the narrow semantic descriptions that existed for the building entities inside the KGs (particularly for the case of the EBU model), it can be concluded that even minimalistic semantic descriptions inside the individual building KGs can effectively contribute to the identification of latent semantic patterns. These findings can be of important value to various lines of research in the built environment. In particular, the research on the notion of Building Information Modelling (BIM), which has been traditionally abundant with rule-based approaches, can be advanced with the help of KG-oriented machine learning techniques for context-aware machine learning. In this respect, semantic enrichment of the building information models is one of the areas with the most potential in which KG embeddings can be used to facilitate machine learning from graph-structured linked sources of building data. Among other worthwhile applications, context-aware information retrieval and Question-Answering systems for the built environment can benefit from KGs and their embeddings. In fact, the learned embeddings could be used for the unsupervised clustering of the content of the building KGs. Then, by assigning relevant semantic tags to the identified clusters, the required information can be searched through contextually relevant information that is contained inside the most relevant clusters. Moreover, given the importance of query relaxation/approximation for effective discovery of meaningful information from semantic building models (Bennani et al., 2021), KG embeddings can be of value in this regard, as previous research has shown encouraging results in other domains (Mai et al., 2020; Wang et al., 2018).

Finally, the key implications and values of our findings to research and practice can be summarized as follows: To the best of our knowledge, this work is among the very few existing papers that investigate the effectiveness of KG embedding techniques in the context of building engineering, while these techniques can have considerable implications in the realm of building analytics. In fact, while KGs can provide valuable background knowledge about the building, the corresponding embeddings provide ready-to-use numeric representations of that knowledge in continuous vector spaces. This allows the background knowledge about the building to be incorporated for downstream machine-learning tasks. Most importantly, with the absence of the building's geometry and operational time-series data in the KG (see section 2), entity embeddings can be used to generate vector representations of the lexical and semantic information that is contained in the KG, thereby facilitating "context-aware building analytics".

5. Conclusion

This study set out to investigate the usefulness of applying KG embedding techniques to individual building KGs. Our results provided quantitative evidence that semantic representation learning techniques in combination with careful pre-processing of the learned embeddings can enable the use of machine learning techniques to find latent semantic patterns from the lexical content of the building KGs. We also found that the modelling pattern used to create a building KG, i.e., word synthesis and choice of the semantic relationships, is an important determinant of the quality of the generated embeddings (feature vector). Hence, the identification of best modelling practices for KG creation for individual buildings is an important direction for future research. Another important direction for future research would be to investigate the effectiveness of KG embedding methods for applications such as context-aware information retrieval and Question-Answering from building KGs.

References

Balaji, B., Bhattacharya, A., Fierro, G., Gao, J., Gluck, J., Hong, D., Johansen, A., Koh, J., Ploennigs, J., Agarwal, Y. and Bergés, M. (2018), "Brick: Metadata schema for portable smart building applications", Applied Energy, Vol. 226, pp. 1273–1292.

Bengio, Y., Courville, A. and Vincent, P. (2013), "Representation Learning: A Review and New Perspectives", IEEE Transactions on Pattern Analysis and Machine Intelligence, presented at the IEEE Transactions on Pattern Analysis and Machine Intelligence, Vol. 35 No. 8, pp. 1798–1828.

Bennani, I.L., Prakash, A.K., Zafiris, M., Paul, L., Roa, C.D., Raftery, P., Pritoni, M. and Fierro, G. (2021), "Query relaxation for portable brick-based applications", Proceedings of the 8th ACM International Conference on Systems for Energy-Efficient Buildings, Cities, and Transportation, Association for Computing Machinery, New York, NY, USA, pp. 150–159.

Bollacker, K., Evans, C., Paritosh, P., Sturge, T. and Taylor, J. (2008), "Freebase: a collaboratively created graph database for structuring human knowledge", Proceedings of the 2008 ACM SIGMOD International Conference on Management of Data, Association for Computing Machinery, New York, NY, USA, pp. 1247–1250.

"BrickSchema.org". (2022), available at: https://brickschema.org/ (accessed 23 February 2022).

buildingSMART. (2022), "ifcOWL", BuildingSMART Technical, available at: https://technical.buildingsmart.org/standards/ifc/ifc-formats/ifcowl/ (accessed 23 February 2022).

Ehrlinger, L. and Wöß, W. (2016), "Towards a definition of knowledge graphs", SEMANTiCS (Posters, Demos, SuCCESS), Citeseer, Vol. 48 No. 1–4, p. 2.

Vandewiele, G., Steenwinckel, B., Agozzino, T., Weyns, M., Bonte, P., Ongenae, F., & De Turck, F. (2020), "pyRDF2Vec: Python Implementation and Extension of RDF2Vec", IDLab, https://github.com/IBCNServices/pyRDF2Vec. Goyal, P. and Ferrara, E. (2018), "Graph embedding techniques, applications, and performance: A survey", Knowledge-Based Systems, Vol. 151, pp. 78–94.

Hogan, A., Blomqvist, E., Cochez, M., D'amato, C., Melo, G.D., Gutierrez, C., Kirrane, S., Gayo, J.E.L., Navigli, R., Neumaier, S. and Ngomo, A.C.N.,. (2021), "Knowledge Graphs", ACM Computing Surveys, Vol. 54 No. 4, p. 71:1-71:37.

Ji, S., Pan, S., Cambria, E., Marttinen, P. and Yu, P.S. (2022), "A Survey on Knowledge Graphs: Representation, Acquisition, and Applications", IEEE Transactions on Neural Networks and Learning Systems, presented at the IEEE Transactions on Neural Networks and Learning Systems, Vol. 33 No. 2, pp. 494–514.

Lassila, O., & Swick, R. R. (1998), "Resource description framework (RDF) model and syntax specification".

Mai, G., Yan, B., Janowicz, K. and Zhu, R. (2020), "Relaxing Unanswerable Geographic Questions Using A Spatially Explicit Knowledge Graph Embedding Model", in Kyriakidis, P., Hadjimitsis, D., Skarlatos, D. and Mansourian, A. (Eds.), Geospatial Technologies for Local and Regional Development, Springer International Publishing, Cham, pp. 21–39.

McGuinness, D. L., & Van Harmelen, F. (2004). "OWL web ontology language overview", W3C recommendation, 10(10), 2004.

Pauwels, P., Costin, A. and Rasmussen, M.H. (2022), "Knowledge Graphs and Linked Data for the Built Environment", in Bolpagni, M., Gavina, R. and Ribeiro, D. (Eds.), Industry 4.0 for the Built Environment: Methodologies, Technologies and Skills, Springer International Publishing, Cham, pp. 157–183.

Ristoski, P., Rosati, J., Di Noia, T., De Leone, R. and Paulheim, H. (2019), "RDF2Vec: RDF graph embeddings and their applications", Semantic Web, IOS Press, Vol. 10 No. 4, pp. 721–752.

Rossi, A., Barbosa, D., Firmani, D., Matinata, A. and Merialdo, P. (2021), "Knowledge Graph Embedding for Link Prediction: A Comparative Analysis", ACM Transactions on Knowledge Discovery from Data, Vol. 15 No. 2, p. 14:1-14:49.

Van der Maaten, L. and Hinton, G. (2008), "Visualizing data using t-SNE", Journal of Machine Learning Research, Vol. 9 No. 11.

Vrandečić, D. and Krötzsch, M. (2014), "Wikidata: a free collaborative knowledgebase", Communications of the ACM, ACM New York, NY, USA, Vol. 57 No. 10, pp. 78–85.

Wang, M., Wang, R., Liu, J., Chen, Y., Zhang, L. and Qi, G. (2018), "Towards empty answers in SPARQL: approximating querying with RDF embedding", International Semantic Web Conference, Springer, pp. 513–529.

Wang, Q., Mao, Z., Wang, B. and Guo, L. (2017), "Knowledge Graph Embedding: A Survey of Approaches and Applications", IEEE Transactions on Knowledge and Data Engineering, presented at the IEEE Transactions on Knowledge and Data Engineering, Vol. 29 No. 12, pp. 2724–2743.

Reconstruction of Wind Turbine Blade Geometry and Shape Matching of Airfoil Profiles to Point Clouds

Bermek M., Gentry R.
Georgia Institute of Technology, USA
mbermek@gatech.edu

Abstract. Wind Turbine Blades have a limited operation life due to safety and performance concerns. At the end of this cycle, these massive composite structures still retain more than sufficient structural capacity for architectural and infrastructure re-use applications. Re-Wind research group develops ideas and technologies for at scale solutions of accumulating blade waste problem. Blade Machine (BM) is the software workflow used in construction of reliable digital twins for these objects. We share the results of turbine blade geometry reconstructions from 3D point clouds using a knowledge-based approach. With necessary adjustments the described method can be generalized for application in a vast array of objects in the built environment for surveying or re-use.

1. Introduction

Wind-turbine blades are monolithic fiber-reinforced polymer (FRP) structures built to withstand immense loads applied by wind. As these components perform in high-speed motion, they are operated for a restricted lifespan to ensure predictable performance. At the end of this period, the wind blades are decommissioned but retain significant residual structural capacity for lower demand applications.

Recycling of Turbine Blades are associated with such high energy and labor costs that the current practice is abandonment in landfills, incineration followed by landfill, or in the best-case cement kiln co-processing. This latter happens in limited locations and at a small scale. All these methods are energy inefficient and contribute to CO_2 emissions.(Deeney et al., 2021) Considering the expected volume of cumulative blade waste is projected to reach 43 million tons,(Liu and Barlow, 2017) adaptive reuse offers an efficient alternative by prolonging the life-cycle of turbine blades. (Nagle et al., 2022)

The Re-Wind project focuses on developing adaptive re-use ideas for the de-commissioned wind blades. Adaptive re-use ideas such as high voltage electrical power structures (Alshannaq et al., 2019) pedestrian bridges (Leahy et al., 2021) and housing (Bank et al., 2018) (Gentry et al., 2020) have been proposed by the Re-Wind team. Unlike incineration and disposal, re-use applications require accurate and intricate CAD, structural engineering, and CAM models to facilitate the re-design and re-engineering processes.

The collection of tools and methods used to build these models is referred to as Blade Machine (BM). This paper focuses on the problem of building surface-based virtual models from point clouds of turbine blades.

Turbine blade manufacturing sector is highly competitive. Most designers and manufacturers keep specifications for their products secret. By the time the blades are decommissioned, specifications and shop drawings are often lost as they are not retained in public repositories. As Figure 1 indicates, one data model Re-Wind project has developed relies on structured manufacturing documentation. Yet due to the scarcity of this type of information, this method is not globally applicable.

https://doi.org/10.7146/aul.455.c217

The Blade Machine workflow starts downstream of the acquisition of point clouds. Due to their scale and non-uniform geometry, objects like wind blades fall into an underdeveloped niche regarding reality capture and Scan-to-BIM research.

For practical purposes and modularity BM is articulated in four phases. (Figure 1.) These are:

- Phase 1: Point cloud orientation, cleanup, airfoil recognition, AeroDyn output and skeleton model.
- Phase 2: Structural topology assertation, surface model generation and structural segmentation.
- Phase 3: Calculation of composite section properties for engineering analysis and back-calculation of section stresses from external 3D frame analysis.
- Phase 4: Mesh generation for finite element analysis. Generation of solid models for re-fabrication tasks such as CNC blade cutting and drilling.

This paper focuses on the considerations and methods of the Phase 1 of Blade Machine implementation – focusing on digital reconstruction of complex geometry.

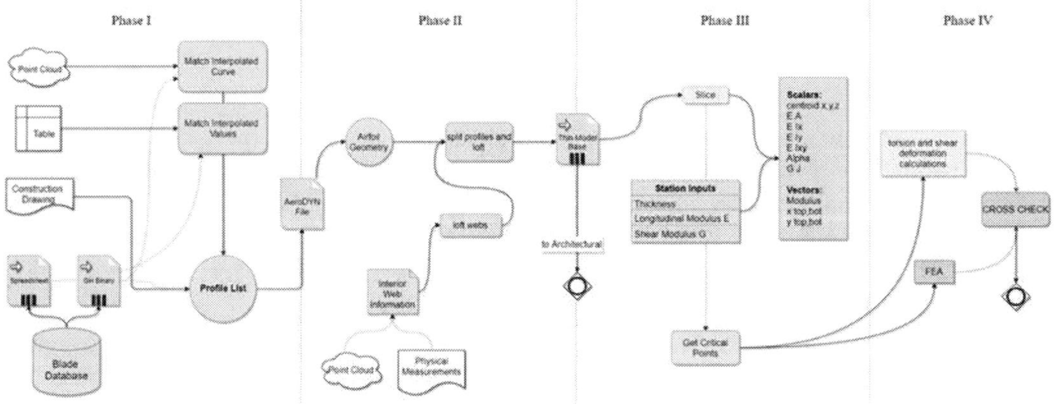

Figure 1: Blade Machine workflow.

2. Concepts and Approach

An initial method for digital reconstruction of a wind-blade has been presented in Tasistro-Hart et al. (2019). This method relied on genetic optimization algorithms to find best-fit matches of airfoil sections in synthetic point clouds generated from digital models. The method worked well in the tests cases but proved unreliable noisy real-world point clouds obtained with laser scanning and photogrammetry.

Some of these artifacts in the sample scans were noisy data, non-uniform sampling due to skewed perspective and loss of resolution, missing data due to occlusion, and adjacent but otherwise unrelated objects captured. A second type of artifact that can be introduced in post-processing is erroneous alignment of partial point clouds.

Another change in BM software, after the initial publication, was the definition of the geometry around an internal curvilinear reference axis defined by section geometry. This facilitates the formatting of the information to industry standards such as AeroDyn. (Moriarty and Hansen, 2005, Jonkman et al., 2015)

2.1 Point Clouds

Given the limited information available regarding the fabrication geometry of turbine blades, reality capture methods are used to obtain product geometry. Common methods for objects of similar scale are stereo-photogrammetry, Structure from Motion (SFM), and laser or lidar scanning. These survey models provide point clouds and can contain information ranging from object color to surface normals.

Point clouds are useful tools to store information collected in the field about the “as is” conditions of large objects. No-Contact methods for their acquisition are cheap and fast to use and can produce highly detailed results. Point clouds are data intense; this makes them require large storage, information transfer, and processing capabilities. There are many methods used to reconstruct the geometries found within point clouds. (Berger et al., 2017)

Our choice of CAD software was Rhinoceros 3D, because of its easily scriptable add-on Grasshopper. Grasshopper 3D provides an intuitive Visual Programming Language interface with the CAD software. Furthermore, common open-source point cloud processing software such as CloudCompare and MeshLab can interface with this environment directly through components.

Workarounds, plugins, and additional scripting have been kept to a minimum to maintain portability. While their use for algorithms requiring iterations and looping were inevitable in the general BM workflow, the operations described in this paper can be implemented without resorting to such extensions.

Segmentation is an umbrella term for methods used to distinguish homogeneous clusters of points that are geometrically significant. Again, there are many emerging methods regarding segmentation. (Nguyen and Le, 2013)

To achieve a dimensional reduction of the segmentation problem, our method leverages product knowledge specific to airfoils within the context of turbine blade manufacturing. We adopt a hybrid (graph and geometry based) shape retrieval method as the internal feature around which our sections are searched for (blade axis) is not a physical entity that can be captured.(Tangelder and Veltkamp, 2007)

The difficulty in parametrization of these sections, coupled with the lack of information available for creation of training and testing sets, precludes the application of other established methods of segmentation.(Agapaki and Brilakis, 2022)

We use a proxy database of pre-encoded airfoils to match. The blade database lets the user choose to develop continuous geometries through spline interpolations. The possibility of using NURBS geometry allows for non-linear interpolation, smaller model sizes, and continuous surface models depending on the needs of the downstream use.

2.2 Turbine Blade Geometry

Blade turbine geometry presents many challenges; both in construction and the survey of the artifact. Overall, these are cantilever beam type geometries with variable sections. The length of the object is markedly larger than the other dimensions. Most of the large-scale re-use proposals take advantage of the length of these objects. This characteristic lends itself to a dimensional reduction where we consider the overall geometry as a series of sections lying along a curve developing in the major dimension.

We assume the scanned object to be monolithic. This is true for global reconstructions but does not account for internal or subsurface components. These components are populated into the model in later phases of the workflow to build high fidelity digital proxies. The exterior is a concatenation of cylindrical, ruled, or lofted surfaces. Sections found in the initial phase are utilized to recreate these considering construction methods and aerodynamic geometries. Variable section segmenting and rebuilding is a transferrable workflow to different applications. Some of these are already applied in MEP construction tracking. (Bosché et al., 2014)

For the sake of brevity internal structures of turbine blades will not be detailed in this article. Yet whenever possible these scans provide a valuable alternative to destructive testing and are integrated to the model in later stages of BM workflow.

2.3 Airfoils:

The cross-sectional shapes of our turbines are referred to as Airfoils. These shapes produce an aerodynamic force while interacting with fluids in relative motion. These curves confer lift and drag properties to the blade combined with the twist governing the angle of attack along its length. (Bertin and Smith, 1998, Biot, 1942)

Airfoils are characterized by a rounder Leading Edge (LE) and a sharper Trailing Edge (TE). The names derive from the order in which these sections are designed to encounter oncoming airflow. (Hau, 2013)

Two geometrically significant curves span between these two points. The straight line running across these is referred to as the airfoil's chord line and is the basis for measuring the relative chord length and the thickness. The second one is the camber line. The difference in the shell geometry between the two halves delimited by the camber line in non-symmetric airfoils creates a pressure difference between the two sides. These sides are named the Low Pressure (LP) side and High Pressure (HP) side. The camber line traverses the middle points between the HP and LP sides on stations developed orthogonally to the chord line. The chord line can intersect the outer shell, and the camber line is contained within the airfoil save for the intersections with the TE and LE points. And while the former is the directrix of an orthogonal basis the latter is the median curve used to distinguish between HP and LP sides. The two lines are coincident in symmetric sections. Low pressure side presents a convex form while the high-pressure side is convex on LE and concave on TE portions.

In the spatial development of a turbine blade, the chord lines —or their projections to the world X-Y plane— generally present a sequential rotation along the blade axis to give desired angles of attack (AoA) to the different sections along the length of the blade. This is called the Twist of the blade.

Airfoils are classified, published, or held as proprietary knowledge by diverse organizations. Depending on the compiling or publishing entity's specifications, airfoils are grouped in families sharing similar characteristics.

2.4 Axial development

A cartesian coordinate system that allows for localized coordinate definitions through linear mappings is widely implemented in computer graphics applications of CAD interfaces. The former is called Global, or World Coordinate System (GCS) and the latter is named Local or User Coordinate System (LCS).

In blade design and construction, the ideal Z axis of GCS is also referred to as "Pitch Axis". Airfoil sections lie on a curvilinear Blade Axis instead. Understanding the approximate nature of this convention is critical to be able to recreate the actual state of a decommissioned blade or establish a new design.

In short, the section curves defining the shell geometry lie in planes not necessarily parallel or aligned, and each host plane has its unique linear mapping of roto-translation from world coordinates. This nonlinear development is to accommodate for deflections and aerodynamic properties. The pre-bend serves to avoid collisions with the support tower under wind load, while the twist is conditioned for the large part by aerodynamic factors.

The coordinate transformations maintain $xi \perp yi \perp zi \; \forall \; \Pi i$ (orthonormal) and origin Oi $\forall \; \Pi i \in \gamma$ where the curve $\boldsymbol{\gamma}$ represents the blade axis. Within this definition the origin (Oi) of the plane can be an arbitrary point if it maintains a fixed relation to section geometry in each plane. We pick this point to be the intersection of the chord line and the line of maximum thickness perpendicular to the chord.

The assumption is that the resulting shell form of the turbine blade is constructed around a succession of airfoil profiles lying on planes arranged along the blade axis with plane normals tangent to the blade axis. These sections, remain in sequence if projected to the pitch (world Z) axis, parallel to the root (world X-Y) plane.

This, as previously noted, is one of the main differences from previously described segmentation methods. By specifying a curve instead of a series of offsets from and arbitrary pitch axis position we can reduce oblique plane problems into planar problems.

3. Blade Machine Point Cloud Processing:

3.1 Rebuilding Sections

In contrast to other methods such as rebuilding from technical drawings or tabulated data, point cloud segmentation starts with the spatial configuration already schematized. The cluster of points and related information is already geometrically tractable within a processing or modelling software. Human operators can approach the surveyed object intuitively for manual cleanup processes and automated geometric processing benefits from standardized formats of point cloud representation.

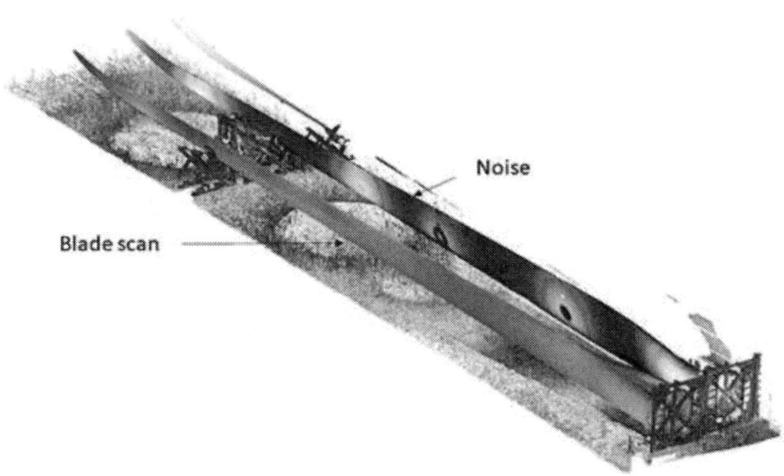

Figure 2: A Blade scan as stitched. Prior to cleanup.

As the geometries are distinguishable from other artificial or natural structures and color information can be hosted with the point cloud, the operator can easily identify the parts constituting the turbine blade proper and perform a manual cleanup. Once the turbine blade is isolated the cloud is imported in Rhinoceros 3D. Figure 2 displays the configuration of a field scan prior to cleanup.

The scan, depending on the configuration of the objects in the field, or initial registration of multiple scans can result oriented arbitrarily in the coordinate space of the CAD software. We rely on features common to turbine blades and reorient the point set to a conventional configuration for ease of visualization and simplification of later operations.

A typical sequence of operations can be summed up as follows:

1. Orienting the Point Cloud
2. Dimensional Reduction
3. Cross section reconstruction
4. Procrustean Matching

Throughout the process we rely on a series of geometric definitions repeatedly. These are convex hulls, minimum bounding boxes, and rectangles (MBB and MBR), and rotating calipers method to go from the former to the latter.

Initially we use rough approximations to find a bounding box around our point cloud that is representative of the dimensionality of our turbine blade. This is a rectangular prism with one dimension significantly larger than the other two. One definite way of finding the MBB is through the 3d extension of the convex hull and rotating calipers method (O'Rourke, 1985), yet a high density point cloud can cause this process to be onerous. As the time complexity for this method is cubic.

The iterative search for a small volume bounding box can be structured as an optimization problem that can start from and already reduced search space if the extreme points of the point cloud are taken and the initial bounding box is oriented through the two farthest pair of points. We can rely on an approximate search to find extreme regions to probe. We can then proceed to identify features of a typical turbine blade. The root and the tip. These two ends vary in the size of their imprint drastically and once we identify the root plane, knowing in which half space the tip is situated can provide us with a normal vector to align with the Pitch Axis, represented as the Z in the GCS of the CAD model space.

Following this, GCS oriented MBB edges provide us with directions by simple measurement of their lengths. The longest represents the pitch axis, the second one provides the direction of the maximum chord (to align with GCS X axis) and the shortest yields an approximate thickness. Similar searches in the extreme regions located along these yield, in the same manner as the root and tip, the LE-TE orientation, where the region corresponding to the LE will have a larger imprint than the one corresponding to the TE.

The interpolation of a good approximate for the blade axis lets us constrain our subsequent feature and geometry searches to planes. Planar searches reduce the complexity of operations and yield more clarity in the nature of the operations for the user.

Point clouds are sectioned by defining a plane and filtering out the points with a distance above a set threshold in the direction of the plane normal. This method does not account for duplicates and crowding, so a simple averaging of point coordinates yields results that are biased away from section centroids. Compounded with the variability of point densities between different regions in scans this can throw off any approximation. Thus, we execute a cleanup of the points.

Averaging points within a tolerance is useful in avoiding crowding and reducing the complexity arising from compaction of points within the intercepted volume. Once we reach sufficient homogeneity in distribution of points around the airfoil profile, we proceed to rebuild the section. Figure 3 indicates how centroids in different stages of reconstruction can show a bias due to scan artifacts.

3.2 Profile rebuilding

The point set is used to define the convex hull of the captured section. Convex hull is the smallest convex point set that contains all the members of the point set. The perimeter of this set provides us with valuable information used in matching our found airfoils to catalogued ones. First, the length of the perimeter is probed for distribution and average distance of points along the constituting edges. If there are aberrations in distribution the section is subject to corrective operations.

In a complete scan the longest edge commonly corresponds to the concave section of the HP side TE. This edge is then used to rebuild the concavity by way of a basis change. This secant is then replaced by the rebuilt concave profile to yield the airfoil shape. The points are then checked for deviations in distance from the concave profile and the profile is fitted within tolerance limits according to the average. Figure 3, shows a comparison of the convex and concave hulls and relative centroids.

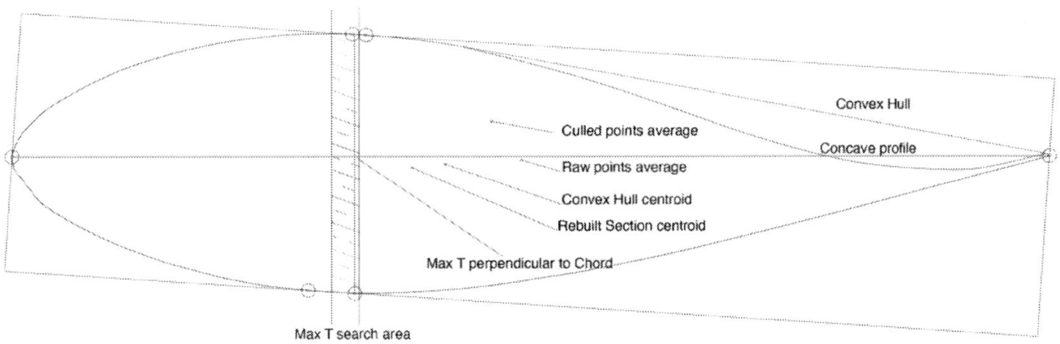

Figure 3: Rebuilt profile with Chord and Arbitrary MBR.

When the distribution of points indicates a lack of sampling for a given segment, the neighbors of the segment are used to interpolate a curve that will approximate the curve expected to be found in the region of the turbine blade. Once these gaps are patched, the search for the airfoil properties starts.

Our search relies on the observation that once the MBR is constructed around an airfoil there will be 5 or 6 intersections between this and the concave hull. The intersections along the short edges of the MBR yield the chord. As previously mentioned, while the MBR problem can be approached as an optimization problem with a clear minimum; with the two calipers method we can reduce our search space.

Freeman and Shapira (1975) prove that MBR must have one side parallel to one of the hull edges. This means that if we have a set of arbitrarily oriented MBRs in the direction of all the sides of our convex hull, the smallest area rectangle will be the absolute MBR. Toussaint (1983) provides a two-caliper approach that solves the problem in O(n) using two rotating calipers as this foregoes the linear search for MBR area at the end of the alignment procedure. The extension to 3D of this concept is not a naive search as the 2d approach. The MBB must have at least two adjacent faces flush with edges of the enclosed polyhedron. (O'Rourke, 1985)

Once the chord is intercepted, we redraw the MBR oriented along the chord to intercept a perpendicular chord and thickness combination. The second chord is not necessarily coincident with the first one yet after the second iteration we converge on the best approximation for the chord.

At this point we have a normal for the plane within which our section resides, and we have a chord and a reconstructed concave hull. Our set of airfoils to match with are organized and stored in a database where every entry has information with regards to its label, family of pertinence, Chord-to-Thickness ratio, position of maximum thickness projected on the chord, TE type alongside a polyline and a cubic spline interpolation.

All the geometric features are represented such that the chord of the stored airfoil is a unitized line starting at the LE and reaching TE. So, we can assume that every chord line we intercept from our sections is an applied vector on the LE-TE line, starting at LE. Thus, the length of the chord line is the uniform scale factor for the matching of known airfoil shapes to found airfoil shapes. Figure 4 displays information extracted from a very low-resolution scan.

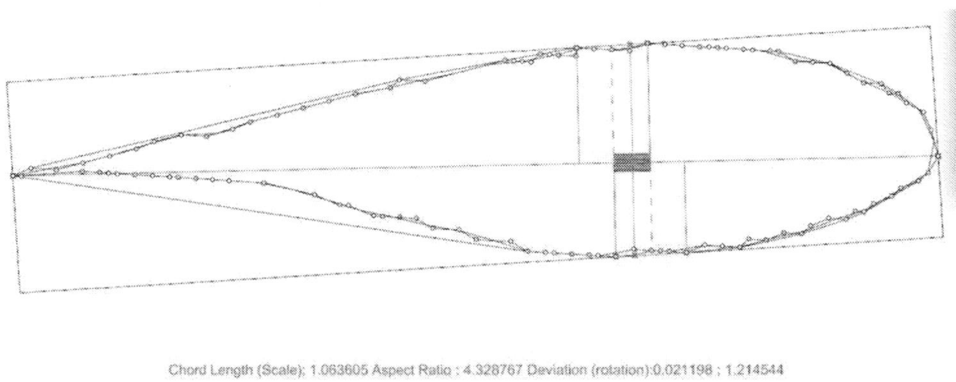

Figure 4: Depicting rotation and scaling factors derived from found section.

This kind of matching, where only translation, rotation and uniform scaling are allowed is referred to as Procrustean Matching. It maintains the shape of profiles that will be compared. In plane the operation requires a 2D translation vector and two scalars. One for rotation and one for scale scaling. The 3D extension of the same where we move our unitized profile to a plane along the blade axis requires 7 factors. One 3D Translation vector, another 3D rotation vector and again the scaling factor. This transformation, commonly used in geodesy is named Helmert Transform or seven-parameter transformation. Initial and final shape have a similarity relation.(Helmert, 1875, Helmert, 1876)

BM software has been developed with the possibility of going through each step manually. When the results of this automated workflow are compared with a manually matched turbine blade scan, the matches are compatible with what other researchers in the Re-Wind team have previously established. Figure 3 shows a comparison between values obtained by human or in different stages of automated search.

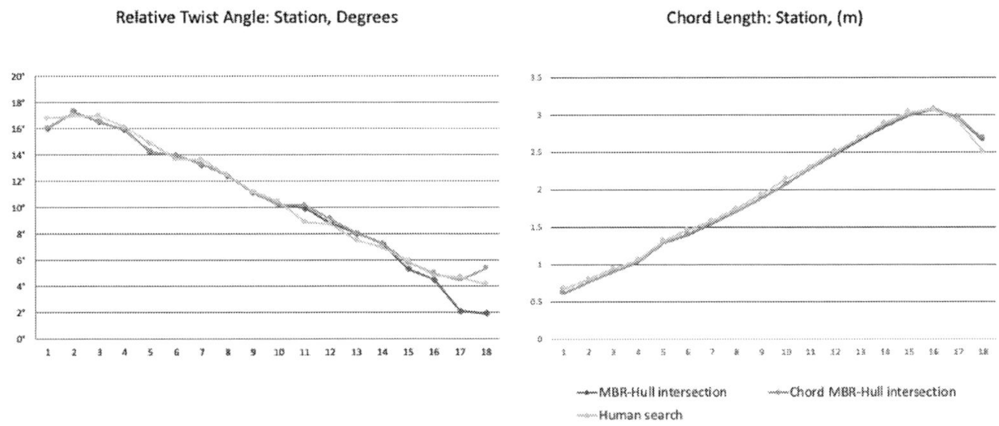

Figure 5. Comparison of automated and human searches for chords

3.3 Region Calculus

Having already extracted the Chord-to-Thickness ratio, through comparison of our chord oriented MBR's sides, we can filter our database for airfoils that have similar proportions. This is a numerical operation to help limit the number of candidates to which will have to apply transformations and region algebra to find the closest match.

Establishing objective comparison parameters are essential to evaluate similarity between shapes. Expressed in Region Connection Calculus (RCC) terms the relationship between shapes being matched present Partial Overlap (PO) or more rarely Tangential Proper Part (TPP and TPPi) relations. (Randell et al., 1992)

For each comparison, following the uniform scaling and alignment along LE-TE coordinates, we extract a series of resulting regions. Assuming Region A is the found airfoil and Region B is the candidate, we calculate the area of the overlap ($A \cap B$) and overflow ($A^c \cup B^c$). In DE-9IM terms these correspond to $I(a) \cap I(b)$ for the former and $I[(a) \cap E(b)] \cup [E(a) \cap I(b)]$ for the latter. Figure 6 shows PO conditions with 3 different candidates.

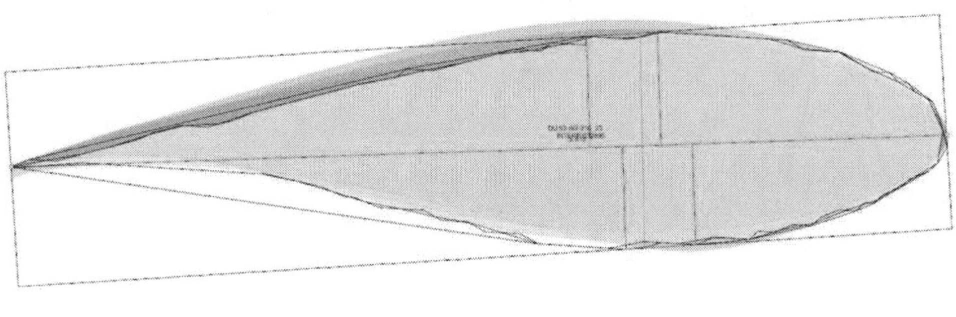

Figure 6: Demonstrating intersection or overlap in cyan and union of complements or overflow in orange

The selected candidates are sorted by a ranking where overlap area proportional to the area of shape A is a bonus and the overflow areas proportional to the area of shape A are penalties. The best fit airfoil is then selected and roto-translated to the initial position of the section in the GCS of the CAD system to rebuild the turbine blade hull.

The final configuration is output in a geometric model, an AeroDYN formatted spreadsheet and a list of blade axis tangent vectors at a pre-set location within the section.

4. Conclusions and Future Work:

Rebuilding of the idealized shape is useful for a global structural analysis, and large-scale volume representation. These can be utilized for property analyses to establish feasibility of re-use for given applications.

Through a comparative analysis of the idealized shape and the actual point cloud scan, we can identify damage, deformations, and missing sections. Idealized shape model can be also used as a substrate to encode additional information such as unexpected artifacts. Once the ideal form is constructed production of a planar mapping to annotate visual observations is a trivial task.

The modular dataflow provides the possibility of alternating or substituting rule-based automation with human operators. With the limited amount of information given the current level of necessity in reverse engineering turbine blades it is not very feasible to imagine a vast availability of examples. Making use of these recorded sections can be valuable. In the future a systematic collection of these errors and results can constitute a training set.

Acknowledgements

This research was funded by the National Science Foundation (NSF) under grants 2016409, 1701413, and 1701694; by InvestNI/Department for the Economy (DfE) under grant 16/US/3334 and by Science Foundation Ireland (SFI) under grant USI-116 as part of the US-Ireland Tripartite research program.

References

Agapaki, E. & Brilakis, I. (2022). Geometric Digital Twinning of Industrial Facilities: Retrieval of Industrial Shapes. *arXiv preprint arXiv:2202.04834.*

Alshannaq, A., Scott, D., Bank, L., Bermek, M. & Gentry, R. (2019). Structural Re-Use of De-Commissioned Wind Turbine Blades in Civil Engineering Applications. *Journal Name: Proceedings, American Society for Composites 2019 Annual Meeting*, Medium: X.

Bank, L. C., Arias, F. R., Yazdanbakhsh, A., Gentry, T. R., Al-Haddad, T., Chen, J.-F. & Morrow, R. (2018). Concepts for reusing composite materials from decommissioned wind turbine blades in affordable housing. *Recycling,* 3, 3.

Berger, M., Tagliasacchi, A., Seversky, L. M., Alliez, P., Guennebaud, G., Levine, J. A., Sharf, A. & Silva, C. T. A survey of surface reconstruction from point clouds. Computer Graphics Forum, (2017). Wiley Online Library, 301-329.

Bertin, J. J. & Smith, M. L. (1998). *Aerodynamics for engineers*, Prentice Hall New Jersey.

Biot, M. A. (1942). Some simplified methods in airfoil theory. *Journal of the Aeronautical Sciences,* 9, 185-190.

Bosché, F., Guillemet, A., Turkan, Y., Haas, C. T. & Haas, R. (2014). Tracking the built status of MEP works: Assessing the value of a Scan-vs-BIM system. *Journal of computing in civil engineering,* 28, 05014004.

Deeney, P., Nagle, A. J., Gough, F., Lemmertz, H., Delaney, E. L., Mckinley, J. M., Graham, C., Leahy, P. G., Dunphy, N. P. & Mullally, G. (2021). End-of-Life alternatives for wind turbine blades: Sustainability Indices based on the UN sustainable development goals. *Resources, Conservation and Recycling,* 171, 105642.

Freeman, H. & Shapira, R. (1975). Determining the minimum-area encasing rectangle for an arbitrary closed curve. *Communications of the ACM,* 18, 409-413.

Gentry, T. R., Al-Haddad, T., Bank, L. C., Arias, F. R., Nagle, A. & Leahy, P. (2020). Structural Analysis of a Roof Extracted from a Wind Turbine Blade. *Journal of Architectural Engineering,* 26, 04020040.

Hau, E. (2013). *Wind turbines: fundamentals, technologies, application, economics*, Springer Science & Business Media.

Helmert, F. R. (1875). Über die Berechnung des wahrscheinlichen Fehlers aus einer endlichen Anzahl wahrer Beobachtungsfehler. *Z. Math. U. Physik,* 20, 300-303.

Helmert, F. R. (1876). Ueber die Wahrscheinlichkeit der Potenzsummen der Beobachtungsfehler und über einige damit im Zusammenhange stehende Fragen. *Zeitschrift für Mathematik und Physik,* 21, 102-219.

Jonkman, J. M., Hayman, G., Jonkman, B., Damiani, R. & Murray, R. (2015). AeroDyn v15 user's guide and theory manual. *NREL Draft Report.*

Leahy, P. G., Zhang, Z., Nagle, A. J., Ruane, K., Delaney, E., Mckinley, J., Bank, L. & Gentry, T. R. Greenway pedestrian and cycle bridges from repurposed wind turbine blades. Proceedings of ITRN 2021, University of Limerick, (2021). Irish Transport Research Network (ITRN), 1-8.

Liu, P. & Barlow, C. Y. (2017). Wind turbine blade waste in 2050. *Waste Management,* 62, 229-240.

Moriarty, P. J. & Hansen, A. C. (2005). AeroDyn theory manual. National Renewable Energy Lab., Golden, CO (US).

Nagle, A. J., Mullally, G., Leahy, P. G. & Dunphy, N. P. (2022). Life cycle assessment of the use of decommissioned wind blades in second life applications. *Journal of Environmental Management,* 302.

Nguyen, A. & Le, B. 3D point cloud segmentation: A survey. 2013 6th IEEE conference on robotics, automation and mechatronics (RAM), (2013). IEEE, 225-230.

O'rourke, J. (1985). Finding minimal enclosing boxes. *International journal of computer & information sciences,* 14, 183-199.

Randell, D. A., Cui, Z. & Cohn, A. G. (1992). A spatial logic based on regions and connection. *KR,* 92, 165-176.

Tangelder, J. W. H. & Veltkamp, R. C. (2007). A survey of content based 3D shape retrieval methods. *Multimedia Tools and Applications,* 39, 441.

Tasistro-Hart, B., Al-Haddad, T., Bank, L. C. & Gentry, R. (2019). Reconstruction of wind turbine blade geometry and Internal structure from point cloud data. *Computing in Civil Engineering 2019: Data, Sensing, and Analytics.* American Society of Civil Engineers Reston, VA.

Toussaint, G. T. (1983). Solving geometric problems with the rotating calipers. *Proc. IEEE Melecon.*

Nonintrusive Behavioral Sensing and Analytics for Supporting Human-Centered Building Energy Efficiency

Huang K., Liu K.
Stevens Institute of Technology, U.S.A.
Kaijian.Liu@stevens.edu

Abstract. Occupant behavior is a significant factor affecting building energy use and occupant comfort. Capturing occupant behavior, therefore, holds great promise toward human-centered building energy efficiency. However, existing methods for behavioral sensing and analytics are mainly based on intrusive sensing techniques (e.g., visual and acoustic sensing), which are known for infringing occupant privacy and have limited applicability. As such, the authors propose a novel nonintrusive approach for behavioral sensing and analytics. It uses (1) environmental chemical sensing to detect air composition changes caused by occupant behaviors, and (2) machine learning to learn from the air data to extract behavior information (e.g., occupancy and behavior type). This paper focuses on presenting the proposed approach and its evaluation in extracting occupancy information. The preliminary experimental results show that the proposed approach achieved an accuracy of 64.59% in sensing and analyzing occupancy, indicating the potential of the nonintrusive approach in supporting human-centered energy efficiency.

1. Introduction

Buildings represent a source of enormous untapped energy efficiency potential. In the past decade, building energy intensity (energy use per square meter) has declined at an annual rate of around 1% (International Energy Agency, 2020). Nevertheless, the full potential of building energy efficiency has not yet been achieved. As estimated by the Internal Energy Agency (IEA), building energy intensity in 2030 needs to be 45% less than that in 2020, in order to tap into the full efficiency potential to achieve the universal energy access goal by the United Nations (International Energy Agency, 2021). The development of building energy codes and advancement in high-efficiency energy technology have contributed to the improvement of building energy efficiency, but are not sufficient to harness its full potential. Buildings are complex sociotechnical systems with dynamic human-building interactions (Lumpkin et al., 2020). Because of the differences in the behaviors of building occupants, buildings often have significant variances in energy computation, even if they are designed under the same codes and equipped with the same energy technology (Van den Brom et al., 2019). Recent studies (e.g., Paone and Bacher, 2018; Jang and Kang, 2016; Rafsanjani and Ahn, 2016), thus, emphasize the importance of sensing and analyzing occupant behavior and incorporating the behavior into energy optimization for human-centered building energy efficiency to harness the untapped efficiency potential.

However, sensing and analyzing occupant behavior is challenging because of two primary reasons. First, occupant behavior is of high diversity. As people spend on average more than 90% of their time indoors (Al horr et al., 2016), the diverse types of human behavior that exist in the universe occur frequently in buildings. The behaviors of occupants in buildings include energy-use behaviors (e.g., adjusting thermostats, opening/closing windows, turning on/off lights, using electric appliances, etc.) and non-energy-use behaviors (e.g., leisure, office, and occupational behavior). Each high-level non-energy-use behavior has a multitude of sub-types. For example, leisure behavior includes reading, entertaining, cooking, etc. The diverse types of occupant behavior to be captured significantly challenge the capability of behavioral sensing systems. Second, occupant behavior is privacy-sensitive. Occupants generally do not prefer and

https://doi.org/10.7146/aul.455.c218

even are against being directly monitored. Studies (e.g., Tomah et al., 2016) show that occupant privacy is one of the most significant concerns in the era of urbanization and digitalization. Protecting occupant privacy becomes even more important in buildings, because buildings are private environments where people live, work, and study on a day-to-day basis. Hence, while we attempt to deploy sensing and analytics techniques to monitor occupants and their behavior, we must protect their privacy.

To address these challenges, the authors propose a novel nonintrusive behavioral sensing and analytics approach for supporting human-centered building energy efficiency. The proposed approach leverages (1) environmental chemical sensing to detect air composition changes caused by different types of occupant behavior, without collecting sensitive private information from occupants, and (2) machine learning to learn from the air data to extract occupant behavior information (e.g., occupancy and behavior type). This paper, as a pilot study, focuses on presenting a proof-of-concept prototype developed to evaluate the feasibility of the proposed nonintrusive approach. The prototype includes two primary components: (1) a CO_2 sensor-based nonintrusive sensing system for collecting CO_2 concentration data, and (2) a bidirectional long short-term memory (bi-LSTM)-based information extraction model for extracting occupancy information from the collected concentration data.

2. State of the Art and Knowledge Gaps

A body of research efforts have been untaken to sense and analyze occupant behavior using various techniques, including wearable sensors, object sensors, and cameras. Despite the importance of these efforts, two primary knowledge gaps are identified. First, there is a lack of methods that can sense and analyze the large number of occupant behavior types that exist. Existing behavioral sensing methods mainly rely on sensing techniques that are specialized in sensing certain types of behaviors. For example, wearable sensors, in addition to their adherence problems (e.g., people stop using wearable sensors with time), mainly leverage accelerometers to capture behaviors with distinctive motion patterns, such as different phases of exercising (Walker et al., 2016). Object sensors, such as Wi-Fi, passive infrared (PIR) sensors, and smart meters, provide a limited amount of behavioral information. For instance, Wi-Fi mainly captures the locations of occupants to derive occupant behaviors (Ding et al., 2021). However, location information alone is not enough because different behaviors can occur at the same location. PIR sensors mainly capture the motion of occupants (Yan et al., 2018), but are not able to detect occupant behaviors that are relatively stationary. Smart meters mainly monitor the energy use of electronic devices to analyze occupant behaviors in close connections with such devices (e.g., working) and are, thus, limited in sensing and analyzing behaviors that do not involve the use of electronic devices (Razavi et al., 2019).

Second, there is a lack of methods for nonintrusive behavioral sensing and analytics. Occupants value their privacy, especially in indoor environments. As such, there is an evident need to conduct behavioral sensing and analytics in a nonintrusive manner to protect occupancy privacy. Visual sensing using cameras, compared to other sensing techniques such as those discussed above, is more capable of sensing different types of occupancy behavior. However, despite its advantages, visual sensing is often criticized for its privacy infringement issues, because it collects sensitive private information from occupants (e.g., facial features, body shape, etc.). Although there are privacy protection techniques (e.g., face blurring), people still feel uncomfortable under visual monitoring. For example, in many cases, people do not want to be monitored by video cameras even though they are informed that key visual features in the images frames of videos are anonymized, the images are 100% secure, and no other parties will have access to the images (Xu and Pombo, 2019).

3. Proposed Nonintrusive Behavioral Sensing and Analytics Approach

To address the aforementioned knowledge gaps, the authors propose a novel nonintrusive behavioral sensing and analytics approach. The proposed approach leverages (1) environmental chemical sensors to nonintrusively sense occupant behavior based on air composition changes caused by occupant presence and occupant behaviors, without collecting any sensitive and private personal information; and (2) machine learning to learn from the air composition data to analyze and extract information that describes occupancy and occupant behavior (both energy-use and non-energy-use behavior). To evaluate the feasibility of the proposed approach, this paper, as a pilot study, focuses on presenting a proof-of-concept prototype, which leverages CO_2 sensor-based nonintrusive sensing system and supervised deep learning for sensing and analyzing occupancy information. The prototype includes two primary components: nonintrusive behavioral sensing, and nonintrusive behavioral analytics.

3.1 Nonintrusive Behavioral Sensing

In this paper, the nonintrusive behavioral sensing was conducted using a CO_2 sensor-based sensing system. A CO_2 sensor was chosen and used in this pilot study because of three primary reasons. First, CO_2 sensors are economical and are already equipped in most buildings. Second, CO_2 sensors have a wide detection range, which allows for detecting CO_2 concentration changes in all directions of an indoor space. Third, more importantly, the sensors only collect CO_2 concentrations and do not collect any sensitive and private personal information from occupants (e.g., facial and body features). The development of the sensing system included two primary steps: sensing system design, and sensing system calibration.

Sensing System Design. The design of the proposed CO_2 sensor-based sensing system is depicted in Figure 1. The sensing system includes a breadboard, an analog-digital converter, a general-purpose input/output (GPIO) extension board, and a Raspberry Pi. The CO_2 sensor is a metal oxide semiconductor (MOS)-based sensor for collecting CO_2 concentrations in the hosting environment. It includes a variable resistor to respond to and sense different levels of CO_2 concentrations and a load resistor to control the sensitivity and accuracy of the sensor in responding to CO_2 concentration changes. The CO_2 concentrations collected by the sensor are in the form of analog signals, which are converted to digital signals by the analog-digital signal converter (a MCP 3008 chip in the design). The GPIO board transfers the digital signals into a machine-readable format and transmits the signals to a central processing unit (CPU) on the Raspberry Pi (which is a microcomputer with a graphic interface) for data storage.

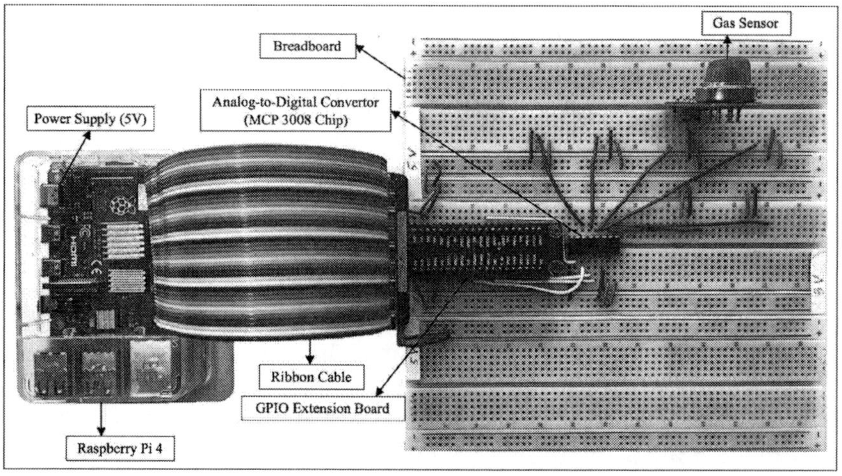

Figure 1: Design of Proposed Nonintrusive Sensing System.

Sensing System Calibration. The CO_2 sensor needs to be calibrated to establish a baseline CO_2 concentration in the clean air. Without the calibration, the sensor would use the CO_2 concentration level at the time of deploying the sensing system in the hosting environment as the baseline, which could result in improper sensing of CO_2 concentrations (e.g., concentrations that are lower than the concentration level at the deployment). The calibration aims to fix the resistance of the variable resistor to establish a resistance baseline according to the CO_2 concentration in the clean air. The sensor was calibrated by (1) pre-heating the sensor for 24 hours without any data collection, (2) placing the sensor in a clean air environment (i.e., in a natural landscape), and (3) monitoring the resistance value until it becomes fixed to complete the calibration process.

3.2 Nonintrusive Behavioral Analytics

Nonintrusive behavior analytics aims to learn from the data collected using environmental chemical sensors to extract occupant behavior information. This paper focuses on extracting occupancy information from CO_2 concentration data collected using the sensing system (as per Section 3.1). The analytics includes three components: outlier removal, data standardization, and deep learning.

Outlier Removal. Outlier removal was conducted to remove CO_2 concentration data instances that deviate significantly from the other instances in the dataset. Two sources of outliers were identified: sensor malfunctions caused by the fluctuations in the conditions of the hosting environment (e.g., drastic humidity and temperature changes), and sensor overreactions (e.g., a sudden surge in CO_2 concentrations caused by occupants directly exhaling to the sensor). Such outliers skew the distribution of the data and thus negatively affect the performance of the subsequent machine learning. As such, outliers were removed using the Pauta criterion (Li et al., 2016). The Pauta criterion was used because it is the standard outlier removal method for normally distributed data, such as the CO_2 concentration data in this study. As per Equation (1), a data instance is considered as an outlier and thus removed, if the residual error between the instance and the mean of all the instances is greater than 3σ. In Equation (1), X is arithmetic mean of all data instances in the dataset, X_b is a data instance, V_b is residual error, and σ is standard deviation of all data instances.

$$|V_b| = |X_b - X| > 3\sigma \quad (1)$$

Data Standardization. Data standardization was conducted to scale the data in a way that the scaled data can center around a mean of zero. Data standardization allows training more robust machine learning models and was, thus, conducted in this study. The standard score (also referred to as the z-score), which is a numerical measure that describes the relationship between a data instance and the mean of all the data instances, was chosen for the standardization. The CO_2 concentration data were standardized using Equation (2), where X is arithmetic mean of all data instances in the dataset, X_b is a data instance, σ is standard deviation of all data instances, and Z_b is the z-score of data instance X_b (which represents the standardized value for X_b).

$$Z_b = (X_b - X) / \sigma \quad (2)$$

Deep Learning. A deep learning architecture was developed to learn from the standardized CO_2 concentration data to extract occupancy information. It learns from CO_2 concentrations from past and the current time intervals to predict the occupancy at the current time interval. As shown in Figure 2, the architecture includes three layers: an input layer, a bi-directional long short-term memory (bi-LSTM) layer, and a softmax output layer.

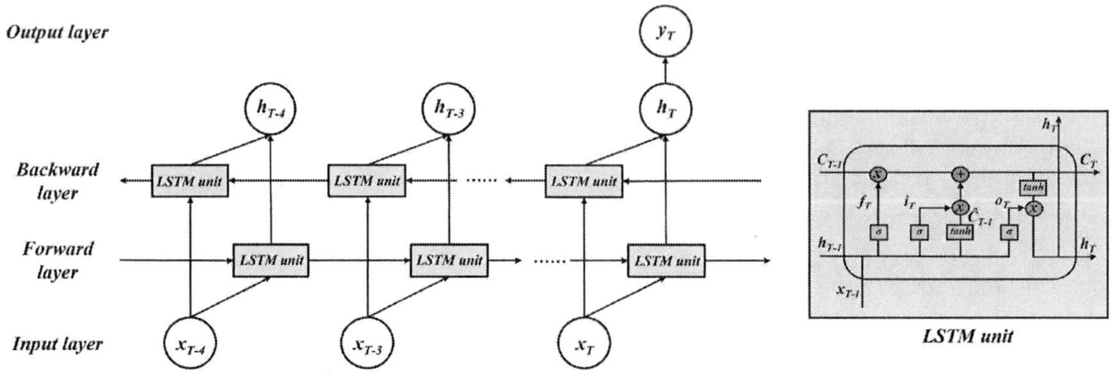

Figure 2: Learning Architecture for Extracting Occupancy Information from CO_2 Data.

The input layer takes vectors of CO_2 concentrations at consecutive time intervals as input, e.g., {*T-4, T-3, T-2, T-1, T*}. In this study, a vector includes CO_2 concentrations collected within a one-minute time interval. CO_2 concentrations from previous intervals were also used to extract the occupancy information at the current interval *T*, because this allows enriching the features used for the extraction and capturing the sequential and temporal changes in the concentrations to inform the extraction. The LSTM layer maps each input vector into a hidden representation in a way that the temporal dynamics connecting the data and the nonlinear dynamics of the data are captured by the hidden representation. LSTM is a special recurrent neural network that includes "gate" structures to regulate the flow of information in the network. As shown in Figure 2, LSTM includes three "gate" structures: a forget gate to decide which values of the previous state h_{T-1} and input x_{T-1} need to be preserved/remembered, an input gate to decide which values of the conveyor belt need to be preserved, and an output gate to decide what flows from the conveyor belt C_{T-1} to the state h_T. In this study, a bi-LSTM layer was used, because it allows for capturing the flow of information about CO_2 concentrations in both forward and backward directions to increase the amount of information (e.g., about temporal dynamics and nonlinearity) captured in the hidden representations for improved performance of occupancy information extraction. The output layer is a dense layer with the softmax activation function. The softmax function is a normalized exponential function to normalize the output of the learning architecture to a probability distribution over the desired output classes (i.e., occupancy categories in this study).

4. Nonintrusive Behavioral Sensing and Analytics Prototype Implementation

The behavioral sensing and analytics methods were implemented to develop a prototype system for evaluating the performance of the proposed nonintrusive approach. The implementation included four steps: (1) data collection, (2) dataset preparation, (3) algorithm implementation, and (4) performance evaluation.

Data Collection. The method presented in Section 3.1 was followed to develop a CO_2 sensor-based behavioral sensing system. The developed sensing system was instrumented in an office room for a week (from November 23 to November 30, 2021). The room, which is a fan-shaped room with a radius of 14.8ft and located on the campus of Stevens Institute of Technology, serves as an office for five graduate students. Figure 3 shows the raw CO_2 concertation data collected.

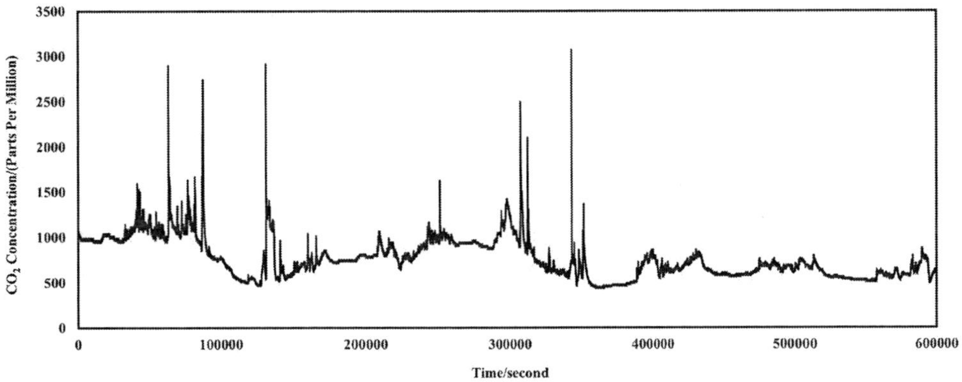

Figure 3: Collected Raw CO_2 Concentration Data.

Dataset Preparation. Dataset preparation included dataset creation and human annotation. To create the dataset, the raw time-series concentration data, as shown in Figure 3, were segmented into a set of non-overlapping intervals, where an interval has a width of one minute and includes a total of 30 concentration readings (sampling frequency = two seconds). A 'sliding window' approach with a timestep of five was then used to create individual inputs for the learning architecture. For example, to extract the occupancy information at time interval *T*, the input included the concentration readings in intervals *T-4*, *T-3*, *T-2*, *T-1*, and *T*. The input used to extract occupancy information at *T+1* included the readings at intervals at *T-3*, *T-2*, *T-1*, *T*, and *T+1*. Thus, the created dataset includes a total of 9,996 individual inputs. The dataset was randomly split into a training set and a testing set at a ratio of 7:3. Human annotation was conducted to mark-up the entire dataset with gold standard occupancy information. An office entrance and exit log was used to prepare the gold standard. The time of entrance and exit of an individual was manually recorded on the log, to count the gold standard occupancy for each time interval.

Algorithm Implementation. The nonintrusive behavioral analytics algorithm (as per Section 3.2) was implemented to train an occupancy information extraction model. The implementation was conducted using Keras (Keras, 2022), which is an open-source software library that provides a Python interface for artificial neural networks. The training included three steps. First, the hyperparameters for the learning algorithm were defined, as per Table 1. Second, the algorithm was initially trained for 1,000 epochs to identify the optimal number of epoch to avoid overfitting and underfiting. Based on the analysis of the relationship between training loss (categorical cross-entropy loss, as per Table 1) and trainng epoch number, the optimal epoch was identified as 700. As seen in Figure 4, the training loss after 700 epoches started become unstable, indicating model overfitting. Third, the algorithm was retrained using 700 epochs, resuling in a final extraction model.

Table 1: Hyperparameters of Nonintrusive Behavioral Analytics Algorithm.

Hyperparameter	Parameter Value
Batch size	32
Optimizer	Adam
Hidden representation/output layer dimension	250/6
Activation function of output layer	Softmax
Loss function	Categorical cross-entropy

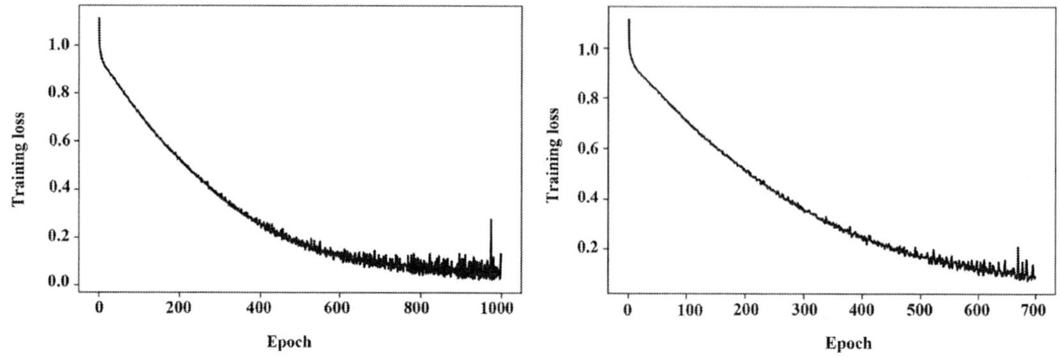

Figure 4: Training Loss against Training Epoch.

Performance Evaluation. The performance of the occupancy information extraction model was evaluated using four metrics: accuracy, precision, recall, and F-1 score. Accuracy, as per Equation (3), is the percentage of the number of correctly-extracted occupancy instances out of the number of all extracted occupancy instances. For each occupancy category: precision, as per Equation (4), is the percentage of the number of correctly-extracted occupancy instances out of the number of all extracted occupancy instances for the category; recall, as per Equation (5), is the percentage of the number of correctly-extracted occupancy instances out of the number of instances that should be extracted for the category; and F-1 score, as per Equation (6), is the harmonic mean of the precision and recall. In Equations (3-5), *TP* is true positive, *TN* is true negative, *FP* is false positive, and *FN* is false negative.

$$Accuracy = \frac{TP + TN}{TP + TN + FP + FN} \quad (3)$$

$$Precision = \frac{TP}{TP + FP} \quad (4)$$

$$Recall = \frac{TP}{TP + FN} \quad (5)$$

$$F\text{-}1\ score = \frac{2 \times (Recall \times Precision)}{(Recall + Precision)} \quad (6)$$

5. Preliminary Experimental Results and Discussion

Table 2 summarizes the performance results for sensing and analyzing occupancy using the proposed nonintrusive approach. Overall, using a CO_2 sensor-based sensing system and bi-LSTM, the proposed approach achieved an accuracy of 64.59% in extracting occupancy information. The preliminary results show the promise of the proposed approach in sensing and analyzing occupant behavior in a nonintrusive and hence more user-acceptable way.

Two main sources of errors were identified. First, from the sensing perspective, only one type of environmental chemical sensors, CO_2 sensor, was used in this pilot study. However, the results show that only using this single-type sensor is not sufficient for behavioral sensing and analytics (e.g., extracting occupancy information). As per Figure 5, the CO_2 data exhibit a high degree of with-in class variance. For example, when the gold standard occupancy category is "4", the CO_2 concentrations sometimes show consistent periodical changes around a standardized parts per million (PPM) of -0.25. In some other cases, for the same category, the CO_2 concentrations show drastic changes (e.g., surging abruptly to a standardized PPM of 0.75). Such a high degree of with-in class variances could be attributed to two reasons. On one hand, the sensing performance of environmental chemical sensors, such as the CO_2 sensor, can be affected by many factors in the hosting environment, such as ventilation, temperature, humidity, etc. For example, different humidity conditions may result in different sensor readings even when the occupancy remains the same. On the other hand, CO_2 concentrations alone are not fully indicative of occupancy. For instance, CO_2 may increase or decrease its concentration indoor due to window opening. In such cases, the collective patterns of multiple types of gases, such as CO and ethanol, may provide more discriminative information for machine learning to better extract occupancy information. As a result of such with-in class variances, some CO_2 concentration patterns that are different from other patterns used for model training but are for the same occupancy category were not captured and learned, which led to extraction errors. In their future work, the authors plan to incorporate additional sensors into the nonintrusive sensing system to capture the factors affecting the sensing performance (e.g., humidity, temperature, and lighting sensors) and other types of gases that are also indicative of occupancy and occupant behavior (e.g., ethanol, methane, and butane sensors).

Table 2: Performance Results for Nonintrusive Occupancy Sensing and Analytics.

		Gold Standard Occupancy						Performance Result			
		0	1	2	3	4	5	Precision	Recall	F-1 score	Accuracy
Extracted Occupancy	0	1,104	76	89	58	14	39	80.00%	82.95%	81.45%	64.59%
	1	53	115	79	28	2	7	40.49%	34.12%	37.04%	
	2	60	88	335	94	8	4	56.88%	55.10%	55.97%	
	3	58	49	95	328	18	15	58.26%	60.97%	59.58%	
	4	27	1	2	23	24	11	27.27%	30.77%	28.92%	
	5	29	8	8	7	12	31	32.63%	28.97%	30.69%	

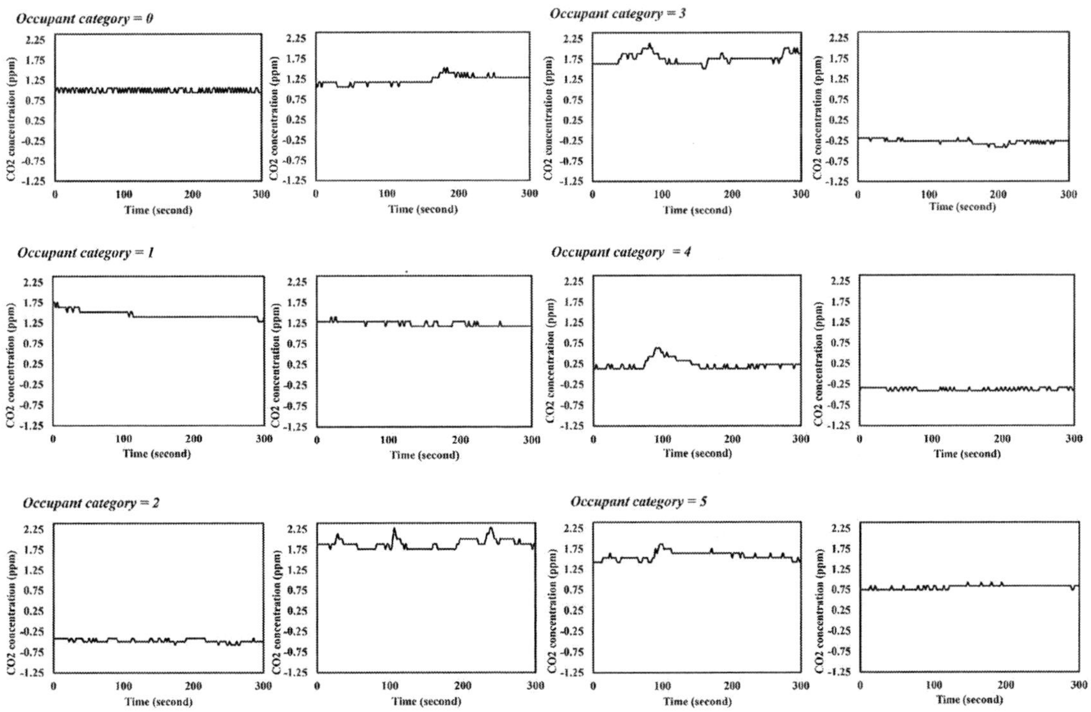

Figure 5: Examples of with-in Class Variances in CO_2 Concentration Data.

Second, from the machine learning perspective, the class imbalance and the ambiguity between adjacent occupancy categories also contributed the extraction errors. On one hand, as shown in Table 2, the occupancy categories/classes are naturally imbalanced. For example, the percentages of instances in occupancy categories "0" to "5" are 44.38%, 11.24%, 20.27%, 17.94%, 2.6%, 3.57%, respectively. Such class imbalance caused instances in the majority classes (e.g., occupancy categories "2" and "3") get sufficiently learned at the cost of insufficiently learning from those in the minority classes (e.g., occupancy categories "4" and "5"). On the other hand, the ambiguity between adjacent occupancy categories posed challenges for the extraction model to correctly extract occupancy information. For example, as shown in Table 2, a total of 94 instances, which belong to category "3", were incorrectly extracted into category "2". One of the primary reasons for such ambiguity could be the similarity between CO_2 patterns in adjacent categories. For example, as shown in Figure 5, the ranges and patterns of CO_2 concentrations for categories "2" and "3" are highly similar. In their future work, in addition to leveraging more types of sensors in the sensing systems to address the ambiguity, the authors also plan to incorporate data balancing methods (e.g., cost-sensitive learning) in the proposed behavioral analytics to address the class imbalance problem.

6. Conclusions and Future Work

In this paper, the authors proposed a novel nonintrusive approach for occupant behavioral sensing and analytics to better support human-centered building energy efficiency. The significance of this paper lies in that the paper is among the first to investigate the use of environmental chemical sensors to sense and analyze occupant behaviors in a truly nonintrusive way. The proposed approach senses and analyzes air composition changes caused by occupancy and occupant behaviors to enable the extraction of occupant behavior information. Such a novel nonintrusive approach would allow for capturing diverse occupant behaviors while significantly mitigating the privacy concerns raised by building instrumentations. A prototype system, which includes a CO_2 sensor-based sensing system and a bi-LSTM-based occupancy information extraction model, was developed in this pilot study to evaluate the feasibility of the proposed nonintrusive approach. The prototype was implemented in sensing and analyzing CO_2 concentrations to extract occupancy information. The preliminary results show that the proposed approach achieved an accuracy of 64.59% in extracting occupancy information from CO_2 concentration data. The results show the potential of the proposed approach in better sensing and analyzing occupant behavior (including energy-use and non-energy-use behaviors) for human-centered energy efficiency.

In their future work, the authors plan to focus their research efforts on two main directions. First, incorporating multi-type environmental chemical sensors into the proposed nonintrusive sensing system to improve the capability of the behavioral sensing. Such sensors include sensors for sensing multiple types of gases (e.g., ethanol, ammonia, hydrogen sulfide, etc.) and sensors for sensing ambient conditions (e.g., temperature, relative humidity, etc.). Second, developing real-time, cost-sensitive machine learning methods that can extract information about occupancy and occupant behavior for multi-zone and multi-occupancy buildings in real time. This effort would offer opportunities for real-time, human-centered building operation and control to simultaneously maximize energy efficiency and improve occupant comforts.

References

Al horr, Y., Arif, M., Katafygiotou, M., Mazroei, A., Kaushik, A. and Elsarrag, E. (2016). Impact of indoor environmental quality on occupant well-being and comfort: A review of the literature. International Journal of Sustainable Built Environment. 5(1), pp. 1–11.

Keras (2022). Keras, Keras website, https://keras.io, accessed March 2022.

Ding, X., Jiang, T., Zhong, Y., Huang, Y. and Li, Z. (2021). Wi-Fi-based location-independent human activity recognition via meta learning. Sensors. 21(8), p. 2654.

IEA (2020). Tracking Buildings 2020, The International Energy Agency website, https://www.iea.org/reports/tracking-buildings-2020, accessed February 2022.

IEA (2021). Tracking Buildings 2021, The International Energy Agency website, https://www.iea.org/reports/tracking-buildings-2021, accessed February 2022.

Jang, H. and Kang, J. (2016). A stochastic model of integrating occupant behaviour into energy simulation with respect to actual energy consumption in high-rise apartment buildings. Energy and Buildings. 121, pp. 205–216.

Lumpkin, D.R., Horton, W.T. and Sinfield, J. v. (2020). Holistic synergy analysis for building subsystem performance and innovation opportunities. Building and Environment. 178, p. 106908.

Li, L., Wen, Z. and Wang, Z. (2016). Outlier detection and correction during the process of groundwater lever monitoring base on Pauta criterion with self-learning and smooth processing. In: Zhang, L., Song, X., Wu, Y. (Eds.). Theory, Methodology, Tools and Applications for Modeling and Simulation of Complex Systems, Singapore: Springer, pp. 497–503.

Paone, A. and Bacher, J.P. (2018). The impact of building occupant behavior on energy efficiency and methods to influence it: A review of the state of the art. Energies. 11(4).

Rafsanjani, H.N. and Ahn, C. (2016). Linking building energy-load variations with occupants' energy-use behaviors in commercial buildings: Non-intrusive occupant load monitoring (NIOLM). Procedia Engineering. 145, pp. 532–539.

Razavi, R., Gharipour, A., Fleury, M. and Akpan, I.J. (2019). Occupancy detection of residential buildings using smart meter data: A large-scale study. Energy and Buildings. 183, pp. 195–208.

Tomah, A.N., Ismail, H.B. and Abed, A. (2016). The concept of privacy and its effects on residential layout and design: Amman as a case study. Habitat International. 53, pp. 1–7.

Van den Brom, P., Hansen, A.R., Gram-Hanssen, K., Meijer, A. and Visscher, H. (2019). Variances in residential heating consumption – Importance of building characteristics and occupants analysed by movers and stayers. Applied Energy. 250, pp. 713–728.

Walker, R.K., Hickey, A.M. and Freedson, P.S. (2016). Advantages and limitations of wearable activity trackers: Considerations for patients and clinicians. Clinical Journal of Oncology Nursing. 20(6).

Xu, L. and Pombo, N. (2019). Human behavior prediction though noninvasive and privacy-preserving internet of things (IoT) assisted monitoring. In: 2019 IEEE 5th World Forum on Internet of Things (WF-IoT), 2019, Limerick, Ireland.

Yan, J., Lou, P., Li, R., Hu, J. and Xiong, J. (2018). Research on the multiple factors influencing human identification based on pyroelectric infrared sensors. Sensors. 18(2), p. 604.

Platology: A Digital Twin Ontology Suite for the Complete Lifecycle of Infrastructure

Khan R[1]., Tomar R[1]., Hartmann T[2]., Ungureanu L[2]., Chacón R[3]., Ibrahim A[1].
[1]DigitalTwin Technology GmbH, Germany, [2]Technische Universität Berlin, Germany, [3]Universitat Politècnica de Catalunya, Spain
rehan.khan@digitaltwin.technology

Abstract. The construction industry will have to present compelling solutions to achieve the UN societal development goals (SDG). A digital twin has the potential to revolutionize the design, construction, and performance of civil infrastructure assets across the environment. This paper proposes an ontology mapping the physical objects with required attributes aiming to augment built infrastructure development throughout their complete lifecycle in the context of cyber-physical synchronicity of the digital twin paradigm. This research is conducted within the framework of the H2020 project ASHVIN, aiming to develop a real-time Digital Twin for the Design, Construction, and Operation phase of the infrastructure. The proposed "Platology" ontology suite will encompass physical assets and processes of an infrastructure's lifecycle and the possibility for accurate version, configuration, and state management to form a bidirectional communication path between the physical and the virtual.

1. Introduction

The European Union (EU) is embarking on a unique stage of history with significant challenges at its helm such as climate change, rapidly expanding urban areas, deteriorating infrastructure, and a significant need to reduce carbon emissions to which buildings and construction contribute around 40%. The Architecture, Engineering, Construction (AEC) industry being one of the largest consumers of natural resources and generators of waste in addition to being one of the least digitalized sectors has a significant role to play (Kovacic et al., 2020). In order to cope with the above-mentioned challenges, the commitment to the digital transformation of the European construction industry is not only ineluctable but critical in delivering sustainable solutions and meeting the objectives of the European Green Deal (European Construction Sector Observatory, 2021).

Digital solutions are widely used across the construction industry focusing on automating processes across different phases of the infrastructure's lifecycle. Although these systems yield considerable improvements, they largely remain detached from one another. Digital Twins (DTs) offer coherent solutions by integrating many technologies and methodologies to create an effective living system (Boje et al., 2020). In this research study the definition set out for a digital twin is that it is "a digital replica of a building or infrastructure system together with possibilities to accurately simulate its multi-physics behavior (think of structural, energy, etc.) with additional possibilities to represent all important processes through its development lifecycle."

A digital twin (DT) for built infrastructure, as a means to link digital models and simulations with real-world data, opens new possibilities for improving productivity, resource efficiency, and safety. The physical and digital elements of a construction DT involve heterogeneous data formats & different information capturing methods thus resulting in an undefined conceptual framework. The need for holistic thinking is advocated by (Sacks et al., 2020) to incorporate new processes and technologies for a construction DT, which can be attained through the logical approach of ontology and knowledge representation thereby also establishing a

https://doi.org/10.7146/aul.455.c219

conceptual framework. An ontology defines a common vocabulary for a domain with a formal representation of concepts and relations, from the construction DT perspective these can be basic information and technology elements, the relation between them, and their individual and collective functions. Therefore, this paper introduces a systemization of core concepts for the development of an ontology for a digital twin of an infrastructure project through its lifecycle in the form of an ontology suite called "Platology". The paper begins with the introduction and motivation, followed by the review of existing literature related to knowledge representation of digital twins and relevant ontologies. Section 3 summarizes the methodology adopted for ontology specification. Followed by Section 4 presenting Platology. Lastly, the discussion and conclusions are epitomized in Sections 5 and 6.

2. Literature Review

This section contemplates previous research on digital twin knowledge representation and relevant ontology works to give a background and reference for the development of Platology.

2.1 Knowledge Representation for Digital Twins

Digital Twin is a term that was coined in 2003 at the University of Michigan's Executive Course on Product Lifecycle Management (Grieves, 2014). Although at that time the concept was not mature enough due to technological limitations, it has resurfaced in recent years and has become more mature and definitive as the world becomes more interconnected. Despite the fact that the concept of DT was introduced by Grieves in 2003, it was revisited by the National Aeronautics and Space Administration (NASA) in 2012 defining it as "integrated multi-physics, multi-scale, probabilistic, simulation of a system that mirrors the life of its twin promptly using historical data, real-time sensor data, and available physical models". This is still the most used definition of a digital twin in academic publications (Glaessgen and Stargel, 2012).

DTs are essentially nourished by bidirectional interaction between the physical and virtual spheres and therefore establish new possibilities. Data management is decisive for the development and maintenance of any information system, DT being one such concept requires data management to address challenges such as data variety, data mining, and DT dynamics between the virtual and physical spaces (Singh et al., 2021). Ontologies as the basis for the application of semantic web and linked data technologies are a well-established approach for leveraging data and information sources (Zhong et al., 2015). An ontology supports the development of formalized knowledge representation and is essentially an explicit representation of concepts, terminologies, and relationships existing in a particular domain (Gruber, 1995). Ontologies formalize complex engineering knowledge allowing humans and computers to understand and exploit domain knowledge. Furthermore, with knowledge mapping and logic as its basis, it can assist the automation of routine engineering tasks alongside providing computational solutions to complex tasks (Hartmann and Trappey, 2020).

2.2 Knowledge Representation for a Construction Digital Twin

The formulation of workflow for a construction-centred DT system is fragmented and is built upon fundamentals of computing in construction, construction monitoring technologies, and lean construction (Sacks et al., 2020). Recent studies have explored data-driven representations and ontological dimensions of DTs for construction. Sacks et al., (2020) introduced a conceptual evaluation on the characterization of information systems for digital twin construction (DTC) along 4 dimensions explicitly: physical-virtual, product-process, intent-status, data information-knowledge decisions. As a result, by basic classification of information entities into virtual or physical, product or processes, and intended or realized aspects, they establish the required ontological dimensions of digital twins for construction. On the other hand, (Fjeld, 2020) proposed a six-level framework Digital Twin Maturity Index (DTMI) based on the degree of automation and degree of integration between the physical and virtual starting with a Static Twin (Level 100) to an Intelligent Twin at Level 500 with each level possessing the features of lower maturity levels. The contemplated incremental and data-driven approach envisions a process of learning and simulation of several scenarios to become a fully autonomous twin. Further building upon work by Fjeld, (Mêda et al., 2021) advocated the use of digital data templates (DDT) and digital building logbooks (DBL) within the framework of incremental DTC to establish maturity levels that streamline the digital transformation of construction for a circular economy.

2.3 Ontologies for an Infrastructure's Lifecycle

Within the AEC industry, the use of semantic web technologies in the form of ontology development has increased over the years (Pauwels et al., 2018). Ontological studies have focussed on mapping knowledge discretely during the design, construction, and operational phase of an infrastructure's lifecycle. At the initial design phase, Niknam and Karshenas (2017) present a BIM design ontology (BIMDO) approach to conceptualizing the design properties of building elements with further integration with cost-estimation and scheduling knowledge bases to create a resource use profile during the design and planning phase of an infrastructure's lifecycle. In addition, some ontologies have conceptualized the construction stage of an infrastructure's lifecycle. A recent research study by (Zheng et al., 2021) adduces an ontology set of digital construction ontologies (DiCon) formalizing and integrating construction workflow domain information with data from heterogeneous sources and information systems for an organised representation of multi-context data within the digital construction context. Research by Gregor and Tibaut (2020) proposes an ontology-based method for information creation for the digital twin of buildings with its core built on the existing Building Topology Ontology (BOT). Intending to minimize human assistance and processing of raw point cloud data, the authors introduce a BOT-driven approach to translate point cloud data to ontology data (individuals and their object and data properties), which can be further formatted to establish the automated scan-to-BIM aspect for a digital twin. In addition, a study by Liu et al. (2021) introduces the Building Concrete Monitoring (BCOM) ontology mapping the information schema for monitoring of concrete work, concrete curing, and testing of concrete properties. Furthermore, the use of an information container holding information about concrete works and linking it to the IFC-based building model enables possibilities for information flow between the construction and operation phase for the further development of digital twin and asset management.

In the operational phase of the infrastructure, the use of an ontology to model the environment adds richness for intelligent exploitation. (Zhong et al., 2018) developed an ontology-based framework for integration of building information from BIM, building environment monitoring through sensors, and regulatory information based on building regulation and design requirements to automate compliance checking during the monitoring phase of the building's lifecycle. Researchers (Ait-Lamallam et al., 2021) detail an ontological approach IFCInfra4OM for the standardisation of road infrastructure BIM during the operation and maintenance phase of highways through the integration of monitored data into the 3D model to establish a highway information model to manage project data during the operational phase of the highway infrastructure.

Platology envisions to conceptualize the entire lifecycle of infrastructure digital twin, but in this research study, the construction phase is given greater emphasis.

3. Methodology

The name Platology draws inspiration from the ancient Greek philosopher Plato who in his work explained an ontological dualism in which there are two worlds, essentially depicting a DT which is a bridge between real and virtual worlds. In his work, Plato introduces the Theory of Forms which consists of two worlds. The Sensible World consists of individual realities and existence in the realm of material and space things thus representing the real world. Whereas the Intelligible World is the world of eternal and invisible realities called Ideas (or "Forms") hence characterizing a virtual world (Burt, 1889). Therefore, the ontology presented in this paper introduces Plato's ontological dualism as a concept underlying DT by illustrating the applicability of the ontology through a knowledge domain aimed at mapping the real physical assets involved in the construction lifecycle and their bi-directional communication with their virtual replicas. Platology is the basis for the ASHVIN platform which represents an open-source real-time DT platform integrating IoT, image technologies, a set of tools, and demonstrated procedures aimed at productivity, cost, and safety for the European construction industry. Figure 1 represents the envisioned data mapping for the ASHVIN digital twin platform. Platology provides a knowledge base for the development of the ASHVIN platform and its DT toolbox. The deliverable D7.1 within the ASHVIN project (Łukaszewska, 2021) gives an extensive insight into the implementation of the ASHVIN platform and tools to be validated on the real-life demonstration projects.

This section presents the methodology adopted to develop Platology. The ontology development is based on the guidelines described by the METHONTOLOGY approach (Fernández-López et al., 1997) which stresses on the processes of knowledge acquisition, conceptualization, implementation, and evaluation.

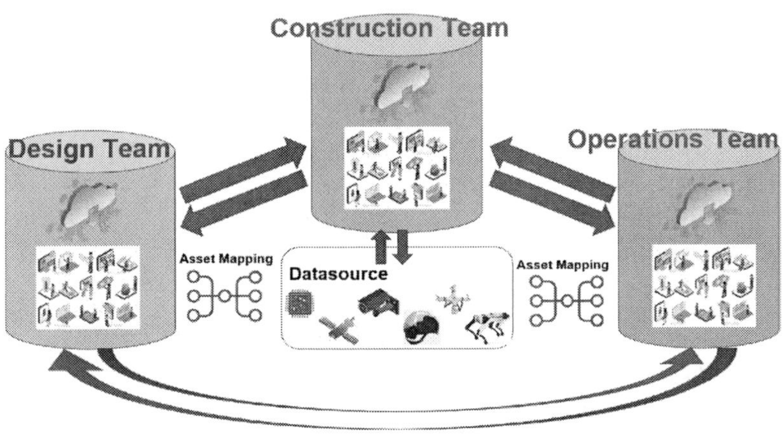

Figure 1: Envisioned data flow for ASHVIN platform.

3.1 Ontology specification

The objective of ontology specification is to give explicit information about the aim and scope of the targeted ontologies and ascertain the intended end-users and requirements of the ontology. This can be established through a list of questions called competency questions that the knowledge base based on the particular ontology should be able to address (Grüninger and

Fox, 1995). Thus, this section presents the specification of Platology using natural language and a set of competency questions (CQs).

What is the purpose? The purpose of Platology is to formalize concepts related to connectivity and information creation between the physical and virtual for an infrastructure DT during its entire lifecycle to enable collaboration among different disciplines through an iterative and coordinated exchange of information.

What is the scope? Platology will cover concepts and relations related to the representation of physical world objects on the construction site during its lifecycle & the IoT enabled sensors and their communication to facilitate a state-of-the-art DT platform. It will further provide a basis for the development of specific toolkits quantified in the research project.

Who are the end-users? The envisioned end-users include those directly using the ontology such as digital twin tech providers, IoT developers, and digital solution providers in the construction industry, alongside European standardization bodies. The indirect users could be those primarily involved in the construction industry such as construction managers, construction workers, architects & designers.

3.2 Knowledge Acquirement and Conceptualization

Knowledge acquisition is needful to determine relevant concepts for the ontology and its domain for developing a class hierarchy and setting class properties. Identification of relevant terms is guided by the specification and competency questions presented in the previous section. The acquirement of knowledge is based on literature review, case studies for digital twins in AEC, and brainstorming with project partners.

For knowledge regarding DTs in construction (Mêda et al., 2021; Sacks et al., 2020) provide implicit knowledge for ontology development. For construction monitoring aspect of the ontology (Boje et al., 2020; Mêda et al., 2021) have been used to develop the classes and sub-classes of Platology. To make the digital twin models of buildings and infrastructure machine-readable, only geometric data is not fully sufficient, instead semantic data consideration is very important as has been shown also as a part in Figure 4. To properly describe and structure this specific information, multiple data modelling concepts are currently being applied. Platology considers the most important data modelling notations and concepts (Borrmann et al., 2015).

4. Platology

Platology encompasses the systemization of physical and digital assets for an infrastructure digital twin through its entire lifecycle (Design, Construction & Operation). The conceptualization is done through a phase-wise approach through the complete lifecycle for the DT of an infrastructure. As illustrated in Figure 2 each *InfrastructureDigitalTwin* during its lifecycle has a *DesignPhase*, *ConstructionPhase*, and *OperationPhase*. Developing an ontology to represent each of these phases could result in a complex, large, and probably unpractical approach. Therefore, the Platology ontology suite mainly consists of three ontologies DesDT, ConDT, and OpDT ontologies for the design, construction, and operation stages respectively for a digital twin of civil infrastructure. For this research study, the construction phase is focused upon to develop the ontological model for the construction phase DT and to limit the scope of demonstration in this paper.

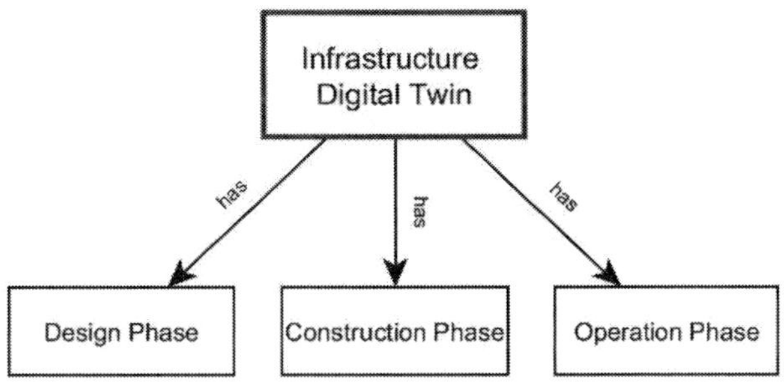

Figure 2: Platology suite with phase-wise lifecycle representation.

4.1 ConDT Ontology

The main classes of construction digital twin ontology (ConDT) comprise of general concepts which are common for a construction DT. The concepts illustrated in Figure 3 capture the domain knowledge of the digital twin of infrastructure during the construction phase. The *PhysicalStructure*, *Processes,* and *DigitalModel* are part of a construction DT and make up the core. Also, the construction DT generates *Outcomes* that can be categorized as the benefits generated due to the implementation of DT during the construction phase. Similarly, the digital twin has *DataResources* which fuel the DT during the construction phase of an infrastructure's lifecycle.

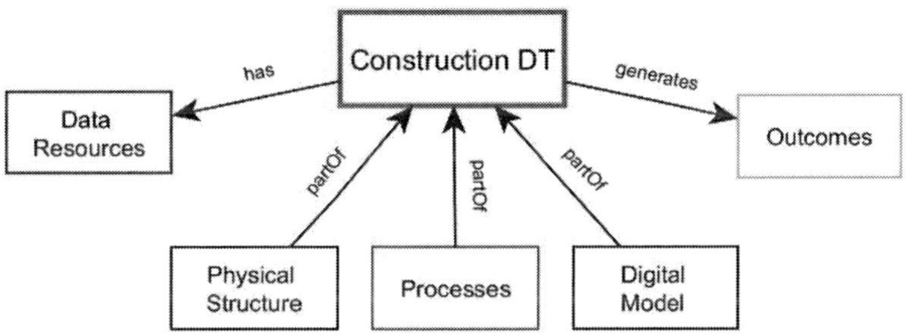

Figure 3: ConDT ontology and its sub-classes.

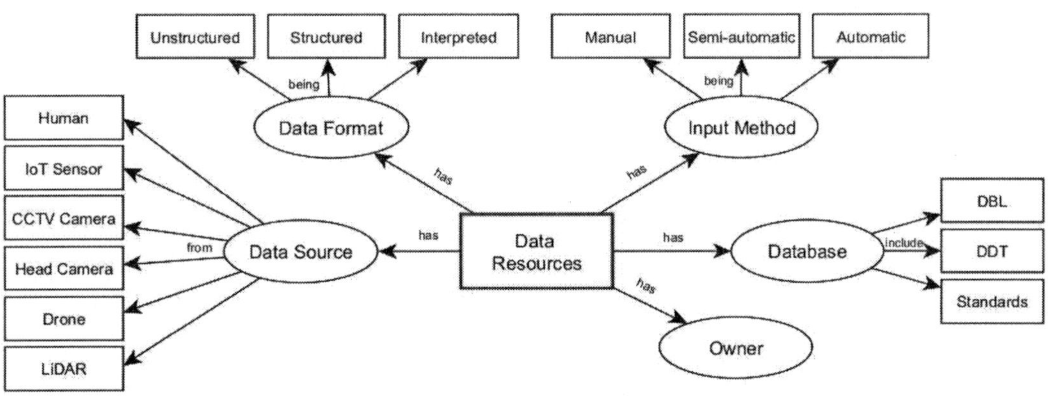

Figure 4: *DataResources* class and knowledge block for different dimensions.

As shown in Figure 4, the *DataResources* class has five main concepts named *DataSource*, *DataFormat*, *InputMethod*, *Database,* and *Owner*. This ontology integrates the dimension of data resources from the ontological framework proposed by Barth et al. (2020) and also incorporates the possible dimensions related to data for a construction DT. The sub-classes *DataFormat* and *InputMethod* show the type of data format and the automation level of data collection. Additionally, the data resources can include a *Database* that can consist of relevant standards, historical data, digital building logbooks (DBL), and digital data templates that can augment data-driven construction for the deployment of digital twins (Mêda et al., 2021).

The *Processes* class essentially represents the processes required to define the workflow for construction centered on digital twins and form the link between the physical structure and the digital model of a construction DT. Figure 5 depicts the relevant processes such as *ConfigurationManagement* to maintain consistency among requirements, design, configured items & associated construction, *ConstructionSimulation* for simulation of construction sequence & activities and *LeanPlanning* to support lean project planning.

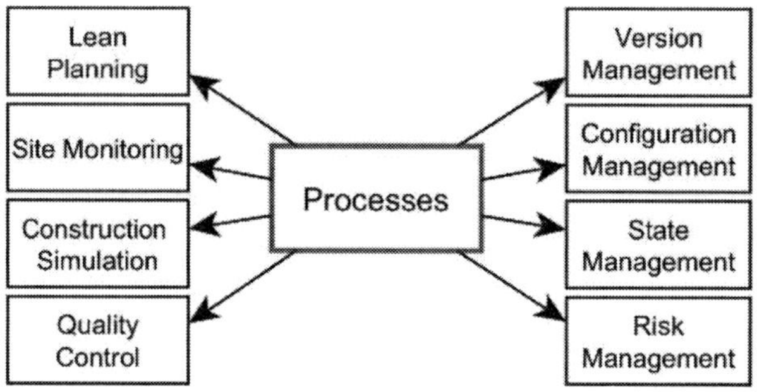

Figure 5: Processes representation for a construction DT.

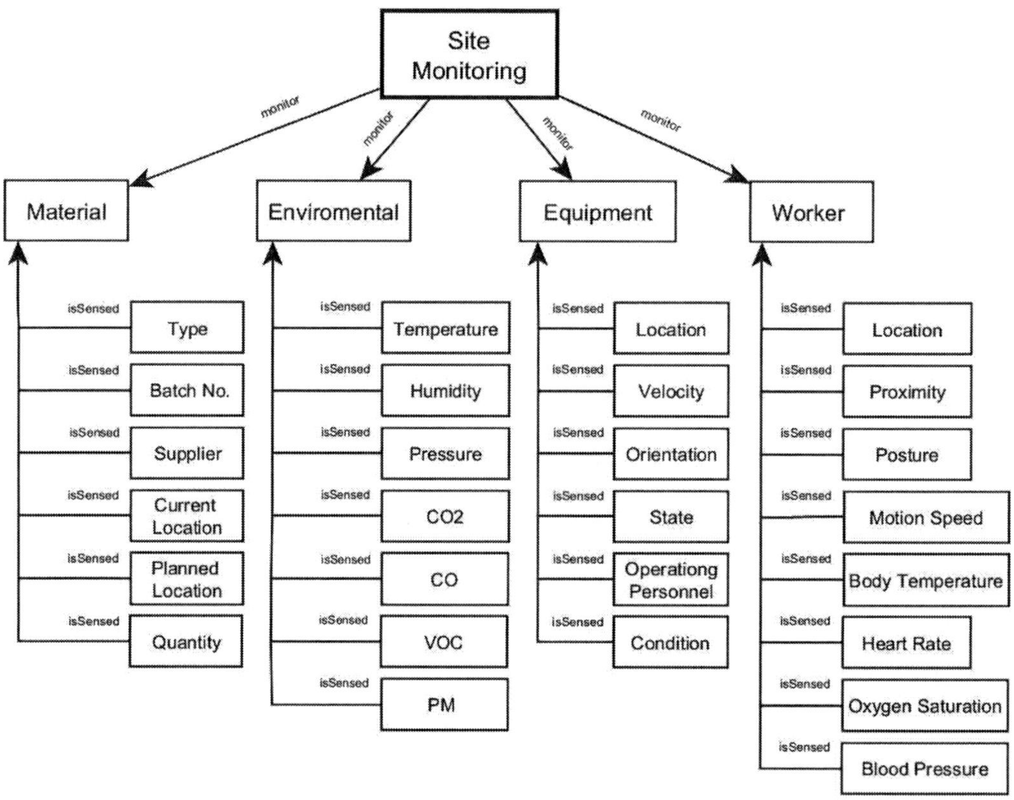

Figure 6: Site monitoring conceptualization.

To support a DT, a sensored construction site is necessary to monitor construction material, environment, equipment or machines, and workers (Calvetti et al., 2020). Figure 6 conceptualizes the dimensions of the process *SiteMonitoring* for various aspects that are monitored such as *Material*, *Environmental*, *Equipment*, and *Worker*. Each dimension has parameters that can be sensed to enable data collection and analysis. Monitoring of equipment through parameters such as *Location*, *State,* and *Condition* facilitates better allocation of resources and optimization of equipment usage.

Figure 7 illustrates the outcomes generated through DT application enabling productive, resource efficient, and safe construction. Each outcome (*Productivity*, *ResourceEfficiency*, *Safety*, and *Cost*) has performance indicators (PI) identified for planning and controlling construction activities. Each sub-class of *Outcomes* has PI which contributes to its implementation. The PI were identified to support the implementation during construction works on ASHVIN demonstration projects and ASHVIN tools.

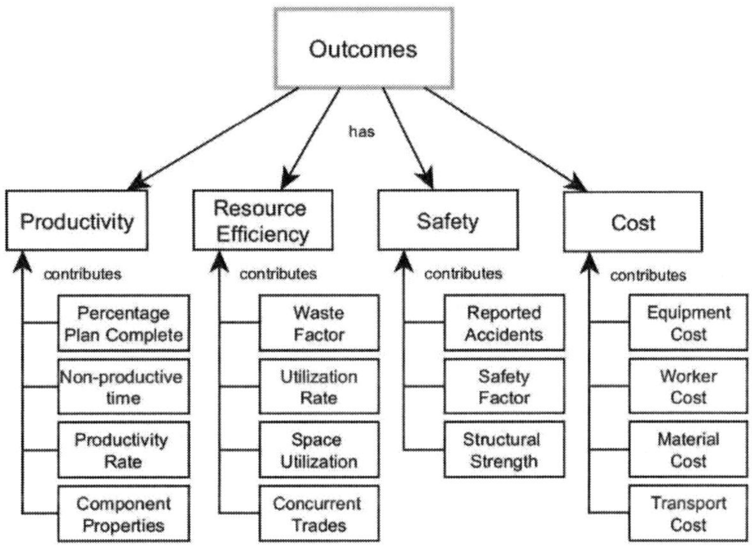

Figure 7: DT-related outcomes for the construction phase.

5. Discussion

The proposed Platology aims to conceptualize knowledge and concepts related to DT of civil infrastructure through their entire lifecycle. In this research paper, the construction phase is given emphasis, and attributes concerning DT of a construction site are defined in the form of an ontology ConDT. The knowledge systemization of the design and operation phases alongside information exchange between these phases based on the incorporation of interoperability task within ASHVIN planned under future research will enrich the ontological model to enable a semantic real-time DT platform for civil infrastructures. Future research work shall include validation of Platology and ConDT to verify its competency against the problems identified. The knowledge base Platology is tailored to be applicable across demos-sites within the research project ASHVIN. With further instantiation for a few selected demos-sites (Table 1), the knowledge base will enrich its potential. Future activities also include implementing Platology using OWL/RDF to develop a machine-readable model.

Moreover, ConDT ontology doesn't conceptualize details regarding the physical process of the construction site, ontologies such as Building Topology Ontology (BOT) defining core concepts of a building can be used to connect with ConDT ontology and will be part of future work. Also, the processes forming the link between the digital and physical part of a DT can be explored more in detail, with only the *SiteMonitoring* process conceptualized in this study. The proposed approach will evolve, as the development of the DT in terms of applicability is still at the outset and research along with real cases in the particular area are just emerging. Thus, the addition of new dimensions or refining the definition outlined in this paper is highly plausible.

Table 1: Real-world infrastructure projects under the ASHVIN consortium.

Infrastructure project	Lifecycle (Phase)	Location
Kineum office building	Construction	Gothenburg, Sweden
Logistic hall	Construction	Rinteln, Germany
Highspeed railway bridges	Monitoring	Spain

6. Conclusion

This paper advocates and outlines an approach for the conceptualization of knowledge for digital twins of civil infrastructure projects through their entire lifecycle. The linkage between objects existing in the physical world (construction (sub-) products, the environment, construction machinery) and their virtual replicas and simulations for a DT is vital. The knowledge systemization of this aspect has not been widely explored. Hence the motivation for the proposed ontology is to contribute towards a common understanding of the dimensions of the construction digital twins. The proposed ontology and framework support researchers and professionals in structuring and positioning their construction DT activities with their manifold benefits and communicating with internal and external stakeholders. Furthermore, the ConDT ontology provides a conceptual view of information, physical and virtual parameters of construction that can aid in the formulation of a real-time digital twin platform for construction.

Acknowledgements

This research project is funded under the European Union's program Horizon 2020 research and innovation programme under grant agreement no 958161.

References

Ait-Lamallam, S., Sebari, I., Yaagoubi, R., Doukari, O., 2021. IFCInfra4OM: An ontology to integrate operation and maintenance information in highway information modelling. ISPRS International Journal of Geo-Information 10.

Barth, L., Ehrat, M., Fuchs, R., Haarmann, J., 2020. Systematization of Digital Twins: Ontology and Conceptual Frameworkenvironment. In: Proceedings of the 2020 The 3rd International Conference on Information Science and System. ICST, pp. 13–23.

Boje, C., Guerriero, A., Kubicki, S., Rezgui, Y., 2020. Towards a semantic Construction Digital Twin: Directions for future research. Automation in Construction 114.

Borrmann, A., König, M., Koch, C., Beetz, J., 2015. Chapter 3 Data Modeling. In: Building Information Modeling.

Burt, B.C., 1889. A BRIEF HISTORY OF GREEK PHILOSOPHY. Boston, Ginn & Co.

Calvetti, D., Mêda, P., Gonçalves, M.C., Sousa, H., 2020. Worker 4.0: The future of sensored construction sites. Buildings 10.

European Construction Sector Observatory, 2021. Digitalisation in the construction sector. Brussels.

Fernández-López, M., Gómez-Perez, A., Juristo, N., 1997. METHONTOLOGY: from Ontological Art towards Ontological Engineering. In: Proceedings of the AAAI-97 Spring Symposium. pp. 33–40.

Fjeld, T.M.B., 2020. Digital Twin-Towards a joint understanding within the AEC/FM sector. Norwegian University of Science and Technology, Trondheim.

Glaessgen, E.H., Stargel, D.S., 2012. The Digital Twin Paradigm for Future NASA and U.S. Air Force Vehicles.

Gregor, M., Tibaut, A., 2020. Ontology based information creation approach for digital twins: Early-stage findings. In: Studies in Computational Intelligence. Springer Verlag, pp. 405–413.

Grieves, M., 2014. Digital Twin: Manufacturing Excellence through Virtual Factory Replication. Whitepaper.

Gruber, T.R., 1995. Toward Principles for the Design of Ontologies Used for Knowledge Sharing? International Journal of Human-Computer Studies 43, 907–928.

Grüninger, M., Fox, M.S., 1995. Methodology for the Design and Evaluation of Ontologies. In: Proceedings of the Workshop on Basic Ontological Issues in Knowledge Sharing, ICJAI-95. Montreal.

Hartmann, T., Trappey, A., 2020. Advanced Engineering Informatics - Philosophical and methodological foundations with examples from civil and construction engineering. Developments in the Built Environment 4, 100020.

Kovacic, I., Honic, M., Sreckovic, M., 2020. Digital Platform for Circular Economy in AEC Industry, Engineering Project Organization Journal.

Liu, L., Hagedorn, P., König, M., 2021. An Ontology integrating As-Built Information for Infrastructure Asset management using BIM and Semantic Web. In: 2021 European Conference on Computing in Construction.

Łukaszewska, A., 2021. D7.1 ASHVIN TECHNOLOGY DEMONSTRATION PLAN [WWW Document]. URL https://zenodo.org/record/5542985 (accessed 4.18.22).

Mêda, P., Calvetti, D., Hjelseth, E., Sousa, H., 2021. Incremental digital twin conceptualisations targeting data-driven circular construction. Buildings 11, 554.

Niknam, M., Karshenas, S., 2017. A Shared Ontology Approach to Semantic Representation of BIM Data. Automation in Construction 80.

Pauwels, P., Poveda-Villalón, M., Sicilia, Á., Euzenat, J., 2018. Semantic technologies and interoperability in the built environment. Semantic Web 9, 731–734.

Sacks, R., Brilakis, I., Pikas, E., Xie, H.S., Girolami, M., 2020. Construction with digital twin information systems. Data-Centric Engineering 1, e14.

Singh, S., Shehab, E., Higgins, N., Fowler, K., Reynolds, D., Erkoyuncu, J.A., Gadd, P., 2021. Data management for developing digital twin ontology model. Proceedings of the Institution of Mechanical Engineers, Part B: Journal of Engineering Manufacture 235, 2323–2337.

Zheng, Y., Törmä, S., Seppänen, O., 2021. A shared ontology suite for digital construction workflow. Automation in Construction 132.

Zhong, B., Gan, C., Luo, H., Xing, X., 2018. Ontology-based framework for building environmental monitoring and compliance checking under BIM environment. Building and Environment 141, 127–142.

Zhong, B.T., Ding, L.Y., Love, P.E.D., Luo, H.B., 2015. An ontological approach for technical plan definition and verification in construction. Automation in Construction 55, 47–57.

A Framework for Virtual Prototyping-Based Design of Operator Support System for Construction Equipment

Vahdatikhaki F., Makarov D., Miller S., Doree A.
University of Twente, the Netherlands
f.vahdatikhaki@utwente.nl

Abstract. Improper design of construction equipment operator support systems can lead to the erosion of operators' trust and ultimately failed adoption. Because keeping the end users in the development process is time-consuming and costly, this is seldom done. To address this issue, a new virtual reality-based framework is proposed in this study. In this framework, designers of the operator guidance system utilize a Virtual Prototyping (VP) platform of the guidance system to receive feedback from the end-users. VP platform allows end-users to have an immersive experience with the front-end system and provide feedback without requiring the designers to make a substantial investment in the design of the back-end structure. This framework is applied to a case of a compaction guidance system. It is demonstrated that VR simulators are able to serve as a technology assessment platform that allows end-users to open transparent and substantive dialogues about the system with the designers.

1 Introduction

In recent years, owing to the rapid development of information technologies, many real-time support systems are developed to help operators of construction equipment improve their performances by allowing them to base their strategies on real data rather than their experiential base (Teizer et al. 2010, Vahdatikhaki and Hammad 2015, Wang and Razavi 2016, Park et al. 2017). These Operator Support Systems (OSSs) deploy sensors and real-time location systems to collect data about the equipment status (Langroodi et al. 2021) and the surroundings of the equipment (Park et al. 2017) and provide the operator with different levels of guidance, e.g., the presence of workers in the blind spot, the best strategy for the next movement, etc. The positive contribution of these systems to the safety, productivity, and quality of construction operations is amply demonstrated in the literature (Lee et al. 2009, Lee et al. 2012, Feng et al. 2015).

The main limitation of the current body of knowledge in equipment operator support systems is that the main focus is usually placed on the technical dimensions of these systems, i.e., methods in which data are collected and translated to relevant information. In doing so, very little attention was paid to the user interface aspect of such systems. This is a major oversight because the successful adaption of these technologies in practice heavily predicates on the acceptance by the operators and without a proper strategy for the Human-Computer Interaction (HCI) of these systems operator acceptance is seldom achieved (Son et al., 2012, Liu et al. 2018).

The HCI-sensitive design of OSS requires the active engagement of operators in the design cycle to ensure that not only operators needs are properly addressed by the system, i.e., from the functional requirements perspective, but also the system does not pose an operational challenge to the operators, in terms of usability and cognitive load. Nevertheless, the user-engaged OSS design in the construction industry is very challenging due to the following reasons: (1) For the users to be able to interact and experiment with OSSs, they need to be exposed to working prototypes of the systems. These working prototype needs to have a certain level of stability and maturity before they can be used for the experimentation; otherwise, the

https://doi.org/10.7146/aul.455.c220

operators cannot focus on the usability aspect of the OSS for feedback. However, when the prototypes are developed to this level of maturity, the cost of modifying the system architecture based on the feedback from the end-users is high; (2) Given the high cost of construction equipment, the tight schedule on which equipment operators work, and the strict liability mechanisms, operators are hardly ever willing to compromise the project by pay attention to OSSs, in fear of being held accountable for subpar quality; and (3) Construction operators normally function in a largely intuition-driven and experience-oriented working ecosystem. As such, their interaction with OSSs is usually characterized by the sheer lack of trust in the systems, especially when OSSs are not compatible with operators' intuition.

Virtual Prototyping (VP) has been long applied in other industries and domains to address the above-mentioned issues (Wang 2002, Alberto and Puerta 2007, Kim et al. 2011). To apply the VP concept, a virtual replica of a system/product is developed using virtual reality to allow users to interact with the design artifact safely and securely. While VP has been also used in the construction industry mainly in the building and infrastructure sector (Li et al. 2008, Li et al. 2012) , e.g., through the use of Building Information Modeling (BIM), it has rarely been used for the user-engaged design of construction equipment OSS.

Therefore, this research proposes a framework for the VP-based design of construction equipment OSSs. In this framework, Virtual Reality (VR)-based simulators are used to communicate the design intent and alternatives with the end-users. To this end, a case study of compaction OSS is used to demonstrate the feasibility and effectiveness of the proposed framework. It should be highlighted that the present work is based on the generalization of the previous work of the authors which reported on the specific design issue with respect to compaction OSSs (Makarov et al. 2021). In this research, the result of the same case study is used but from the lens of assessing the feasibility and usefulness of using VP in the design of construction OSSs.

The remainder of this paper is structured as follows. First, the proposed framework is presented. This is then followed by the case study. Finally, the conclusions and future work are presented.

2 Proposed Framework

Figure 1 presents the overview of the proposed framework. As shown in this figure, the framework consists of three main phases, namely, identification of user requirements, development of virtual prototyping platform, and assessment and analysis. These phases need to be followed sequentially in order to gain an insight into the usability, as well as, usefulness aspect of the construction equipment OSSs.

2.1 Identification of User Requirements

The first phase in the proposed framework is largely based on the model-based systems engineering's principle (Madani and Sievers 2018). The first step in the process is to identify the stakeholders of the system. It should be highlighted that given the scope of construction equipment OSSs, the main stakeholders are operators, construction workers, site safety managers, and project managers. Operators are important because they are the direct users of the system; they need to interact with the system, analyze the information, develop strategies and execute them. Therefore, they are the main stakeholder of not only the content but also the interface design of OSSs. Workers play a role because one of the main goals of equipment OSSs is to improve the safety of the construction sites by avoiding collisions with the workers. Thus, although they do not directly interact with the system, the functionality of the system impacts their work environment tremendously. From this perspective, the workers are more concerned with the content of OSSs to make sure information pertinent to their safety is reflected in the systems. The site safety managers also have a stake in these systems because they want to make sure OSSs can contribute effectively to the global safety of the construction site. From this standpoint, the site safety managers adopt a more holistic view towards safety (as compared to workers) and have an interest in the fleet-level and crew-level safety rather than the individual-level performance of the system. Project managers, on the other hand, have yet more global view of OSSs because they expect the system to contribute not only to improved safety but also productivity, cost, and product/process quality. They have a strong impact on the definition of the scope of OSSs to shape them as all-around support systems. Other players can also play a role in setting the requirement of systems, such as client (quality perspective), government (sustainability perspective), etc. It is the role of the system designers to identify the stakeholders and determine to what extent and when they need to be involved in the design and testing of OSSs.

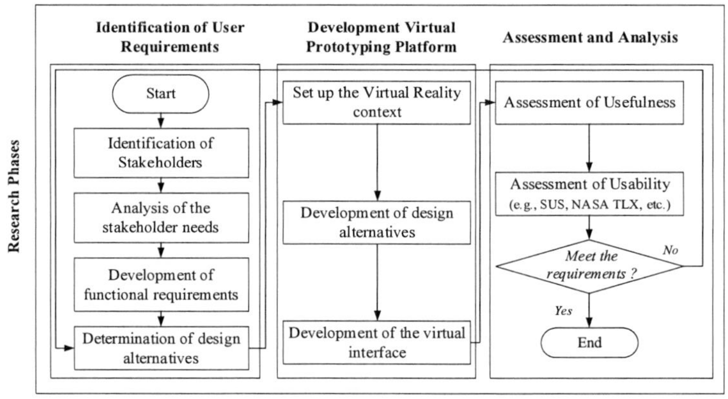

Figure 1: Overview of the proposed framework

Upon the identification of the stakeholders, it is important to identify their needs from the OSS. The identification of the needs can be best done through interviews and workshops with the stakeholders. It is important to note that at this level the needs are required to be expressed in terms of high-level expectations and aspirations (e.g., the system should improve safety).

It is important because a detailed dialogue about the system at this stage may create more confusion as there can be contradictory views of the system among the stakeholders, which can be easily detected if the discussion is kept at the needs level.

The next step in this phase is to identify the functional requirements of the OSS. In this step, the specific features that the OSS needs to deliver to address the needs of the users will be derived by the designer. This includes requirements such as the OSS needs to warn the presence of nearby workers.

Once the functional requirements are set up, the designer needs to develop several different alternatives for the OSSs in terms of how the functional requirements are materialized. This can for instance be about whether the warning against nearby workers is generated in terms of an audio warning, visual warning, or a combination. The designer needs to develop a list of all the alternatives and have them ready for development in the next phase of the framework.

2.2 Development of VP platform

Once the alternative designs are determined, the designer needs to set up the VP platform. VP platform consists of the context, user interface of the OSS, and the VR user interaction, as shown in Figure 2.

Context refers to the overall environment that simulates the condition of the construction site in the VP platform. The previous work of the authors provides a comprehensive description of the context for a realistic VR environment and how it can be generated (Vahdatikhaki et al. 2019). In short, the context includes the geometry of the site, the location, and movement of other equipment/workers, permanent and temporary structures, etc. These elements of the context can be either (1) hypothetical (i.e., built from scratch) or (2) data-driven (i.e., virtual reconstruction of the actual site), as explained by Vahdatikhaki et al. (2019). In doing so, BIM models, publicly available GIS data, LiDAR 3D point clouds, and other 2D and 3D drawings of the construction site can be used to build a realistic context. Also, the tracking data of equipment from past projects, if available, can be deployed to better represent the dynamic aspects of the construction site. Based on the authors' extensive field observations, it is very important to bear in mind that it is very difficult to ask operators (especially with years of experience) to make a distinction between the content and presentation of information in the virtual OSS. The general tendency of the operators is to view the entire system as a single unit. Therefore, incongruities between the actual and virtual context can significantly distract the operators and derail the whole discussion over the OSS usability. Besides, to allow operators to better experience the features of OSS, it is important to build a context that can showcase the full functionality of the OSS design.

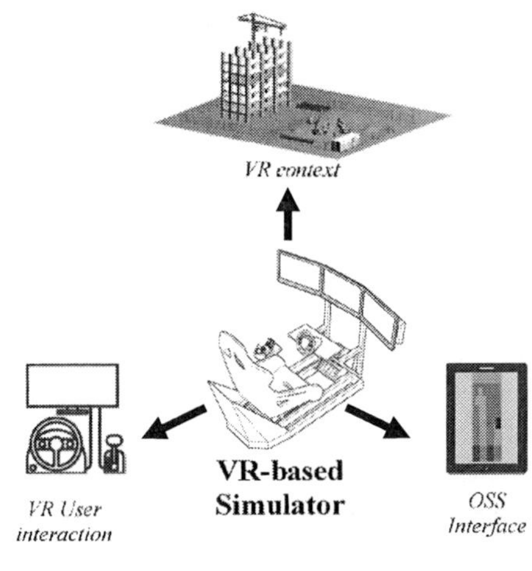

Figure 2: Components of VP for OSS design

Other than the context, the designer needs to determine the VR interaction mechanism. Depending on the type of equipment for which OSS is being designed, a steering wheel, joysticks, and pedals can be used to replicate the cockpit. As for the screen, either a multi-screen monitor setup or a VR headset can be used. While VR headset can offer a better immersive experience, it imposes higher graphical requirements on the system (i.e., to reduce VR sickness) and also pose a technical challenge with respect to tracking and visualizing the hand motions of the operator. For an accurate interaction between the control units and the virtual equipment in the VP platform, it is important to rig the 3D model and capture all the controllable degrees of freedom of the equipment.

Given that the main purpose of developing VP for equipment OSS is to allow end-users to assess the usability of the OSS, it is important to develop the OSS interface as realistic to the design intent as possible. The interface should capture the graphical and audio characteristics of the ultimate design and in general should provide the operator with the pieces of information needed to improve safety, productivity, sustainability, and quality of the operation (depending on the needs determined in Phase 1). Similar to the case of context, the accuracy of the OSS design is vital to have a substantive dialogue with the operators. It is also important to note that other than the Graphical User Interface (GUI) aspect of OSS, it is important to capture the context-system interaction of the OSS as much as possible. In other words, for the user interface to be deemed realistic it should accurately and realistically represent the impact of user decisions, which is manifested in the interaction with the control unit of the VP platform, on the context. Therefore, it is important to make both the interface and context dynamic.

By incorporating the above-mentioned components, the designer should develop different design alternatives in the VP platform.

2.3 Assessment and Analysis

The last stage of the proposed framework is to assess the developed OSS from the usability perspective. To this end, experiment sessions need to be arranged with the potential respondent to allow them to use and interact with the VP platform and compare different alternatives. It would be a good practice to combine new end users with some of the stakeholders who participated in Phase 1. This would allow to assess the extent to which the designed OSS alternatives can globally address the end-users' needs. A statistically significant difference in the assessment by the new and recurring participants can suggest an incomprehensive representation of the end-users' needs.

In essence, the usability of the OSS can be assessed mainly in terms of how easy-to-understand and easy-to-work-with the OSS is. These can be assessed through a number of criteria. System Usability Scale (SUS) is a popular framework that is designed to assess the usability of industrial systems through a set of standard questions (Brooke 1996). Among applications in many domains, SUS is used in the automotive industry for similar purposes (Li et al. 2017).

In addition to SUS, the National Aeronautics and Space Administration's Task Load Index (NASA TLX) method is widely used to gather and assess subjective workload scores based on a weighted average of ratings of six factors: mental demand, physical demand, temporal demand, own performance, effort, and frustration level (Hart 2006). NASA TLX can be used to assess the extent to which OSS cognitively overloads the users. This is an important criterion because construction equipment OSSs are largely designed for application in real-time. Inundation of operators with information in the cockpit can either become counter-productive and distractive or erode the willingness of the operators to use the system in practice.

Table 1 presents the list of usability questions proposed by this research. This list adapted the basic questions from NASA TLX and SUS to make them more specific for construction equipment OSSs. Also, on top of these two well-known questionnaires, several other customized questions can be asked to assess more construction-specific dimensions of OSSs. The users can use the Likert scale to express the extent to which they agree or disagree with each of the statements, where (1) completely disagree, (2) disagree, (3) neutral, (4) agree, (5) completely agree.

On top of these specific questions, the designer needs to investigate the extent to which the developed designs satisfy the needs expressed in Phase 1 of the framework. Therefore, the recurring participants were presented with the list of needs and asked about to what extent they think the developed designs satisfy their needs for the operation. In other words, the usefulness of the developed OSS needs to be assessed separately through the comparison of the functionalities of the OSS with the high-level needs of the operators.

Table 1: Usability assessment of Construction Equipment OSS [adapted from Makarov et al. (2021)]

Criteria	Question	Source
Reusable	The provided support encourages you to interact with it frequently	SUS & NASA TLX
Clear	The provided support provides clear information	
Comprehensible	The provided support use understandable visuals	
Easy to use	The provided support provides information that is easy to follow	
Actionable	Looking at the provided information, you know what you need to do	
Non-overloading	The provided support does not overload you with information	
Non-distractive	The provided support provides information in a non-distracting manner	
3D visualization	You would rather have the information in 3D	Customized
Helpful	The provided support helps in the decision making	
Assistive	The provided support helps to find points of attention in the operation	
Instructive	The provided support helps improve your skills	
Informative	The provided support helps improve your knowledge about the operation	
Explicative	The provided support helps see how other operators are working	
Collaborative	The provided support helps collaborate with other operators	
Effective	The provided support helps achieve higher quality operation/final product	
Supportive	The provided support helps make faster decisions about your strategy	
Recommendable	You recommend the use of the system	

3 Implementation and Case study

To assess the feasibility of the proposed framework, the case of compaction OSS for asphalt was used in this study. It is important to mention in the compaction operations, the operators of rollers need to perform a certain number of compaction passes on the hot asphalt at a specific temperature range to ensure effective and efficient compaction of the asphalt. Over/under-compaction or compaction at the temperature above/below the prescribed thresholds increase the chance of not meeting the design density requirements and the chance of premature road failure. That is why it is important to assist the operators of rollers in developing their compaction strategies through the use of compaction OSSs.

In the domain of compaction OSS, the de facto standard for OSSs is based on the provision of descriptive guidance which merely collects real-time temperature and compaction count and presents the results to the operators as contour plots, as shown in Figure 3. This mode of support is however likely to cause cognitive overload. Because operators are expected to analyze two pieces of information concurrently to draw a strategy and this should be done on top of paying regular attention to equipment conditions, other pieces of equipment, and safety.

However, based on the lessons learned from the mining and agriculture industries, it seems important for the compaction OSSs to transition to a more prescriptive mode of guidance. In the more prescriptive modes, operators can be provided with more processed information in form of a compaction priority index (Makarov et al. 2019) or a suggested compaction trajectory. At the same time, one can argue that a more prescriptive system can agitate the operators through claiming part of the control of the operation and giving them the impression that their trade is becoming de-professionalized. This can be a serious adoption barrier that may hamper the use of prescriptive systems. Therefore, it seems essential that before the development of compaction OSS is pushed any further, a thorough usability analysis of various alternatives is carried out.

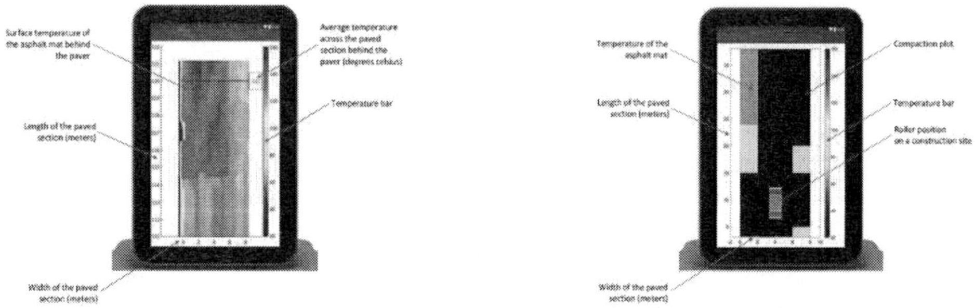

(a) *(b)*

Figure 3: Common representation of (a) temperature and (b) compaction count [adapted from Makarov et al. (2021)]

For the above-mentioned reason, the proposed framework was applied. The requirement of the compaction OSS was determined through several informal discussions with the operators and project managers. It is therefore concluded that the main requirements of compaction OSSs are to (1) provide relevant information that can quickly guide the operators as to which part of the asphalt mat needs to be paid more attention at any given time; (2) the provided information should be easy to follow and non-distractive with clear color coding; (3) the placement of the screen in the cockpit should not hamper the normal operation; (4) the provided information should relate to their previous experience or otherwise operators need to be trained for the use of OSS; and (5) the presentation of data on the compaction OSS should follow the industry standard to make sure there are no fundamental differences in how different OSSs should be used. Based on these requirements, three different alternatives were developed for the compaction OSSs. The first type of OSS is similar to the de facto case of the descriptive system presented in Figure 3. The second alternative, which is called semi-guidance, merges the compaction and temperature plots into a compaction priority map as shown in Figure 4(a). Different colors indicate different levels of priority attached to the corresponding parts of the asphalt mat. In the last alternative, which is called guidance compaction OSS, the priority map is further analyzed and processed to recommend a compaction trajectory to the operators, as shown in Figure 4(b). The details of these three alternatives are presented in detail in the previous work of the authors and therefore not repeated here for brevity (Makarov et al. 2021).

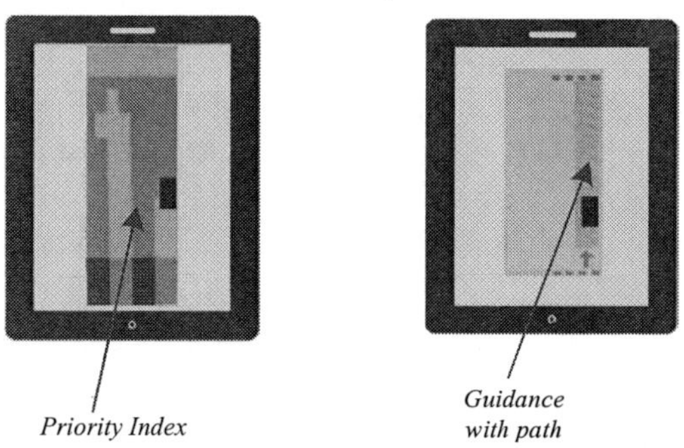

(a) *(b)*

Figure 4: (a) semi-guidance and (b) guidance compaction OSSs [adapted from Makarov et al. (2021)]

These three alternatives were developed in a VR scenario that was built in Unity 3D (2022). Figure 5 shows a snapshot of this scenario. The three alternative OSSs were developed inside the scene to enable operators to easily toggle between the three alternatives and experiment with them.

(a)

(b)

Figure 5: Developed (a) VR scenario, and (b) hardware

Several workshops with a total of 50 participants were held to assess the usability of different OSSs. The questionnaire presented in Table 1 was used for the assessment. The details of how different OSSs were perceived by the operators are provided in the previous work of the author (Makarov et al. 2021) and because it is out of the scope of the present research, it is excluded from this paper. Instead, this paper focuses more on the evaluation of the suitability of the VP platform for the assessment of equipment OSSs. To this end, a separate questionnaire was prepared and shared with the participant, as shown in Table 2. As shown in this table, this questionnaire is more focused on the suitability of the developed VP platform for the assessment of equipment OSS. Participants were asked to use the 5-point Likert scale to express the extent to which they agree with each of the statements in the questionnaire.

Table 2: Questionnaire about the assessment of PV platform [adapted from Makarov et al. (2021)]

Question	Category
VP is an appropriate medium to evaluate/compare different OSS solutions	Adequate
VP helps you prepare for future work with real machine	Preparative
VP represents scene and equipment realistically	Realistic
VP can be used to explore and evaluate different working scenarios	Work analysis
VP can be used to express your wishes, expectations, and suggestions about OSS	Communication value
VP can be used to test your operational strategy before actual projects	Planning value
VP can be used to assess your skills and progress	Development tracking
Do you recommend using the VP platform to your peers for education?	Education value
Do you recommend using the VP platform for the evaluation of new technologies?	Technology assessment
The VP platform provides sufficient feedback on your performance	Formative
The use of all control elements (wheel, pedals, and buttons) is easy	Easy to use
VP platform can be more realistic with use of additional joysticks & VR goggles	Enhancing Control
VP platform can be more realistic with the use of additional sound accompaniment	Enhancing Audio

3.1 Results

Figure 6 presents the results of the validation. As shown in this chart, the VP platform is found to be adequate for the purpose of assessing different OSSs, with an average score of 3.3. It is also generally appreciated as a platform for the assessment of new technologies in this domain (average score of 3.4). The platform is found to be easy to use (average score of 3.46) and has added value for application as a planning tool before the actual construction operations (average score of 3.5).

Having said that, there are certain applications for which the VP platform was not perceived as suitable, at least in the current shape of the proposal. For instance, the operators found the depth of the feedback provided to them at the end of using the VP platform insufficient (average score of 2.88). Also, although they saw the potential, the details of the developed VP were not deemed sufficient for the use as an educational tool, i.e., training simulator (average score of 2.9). This can be also attributed to the relatively low realism of the simulator (average score of 2.84). This, again, highlights the significance of the point mentioned earlier in Section 2.2 about the importance of having high contextual realism in the VP platform. Part of this low realism was associated with the inadequate control units of the VP platform (average score of 3.8) and also the absence of realistic audio (average score of 3.6).

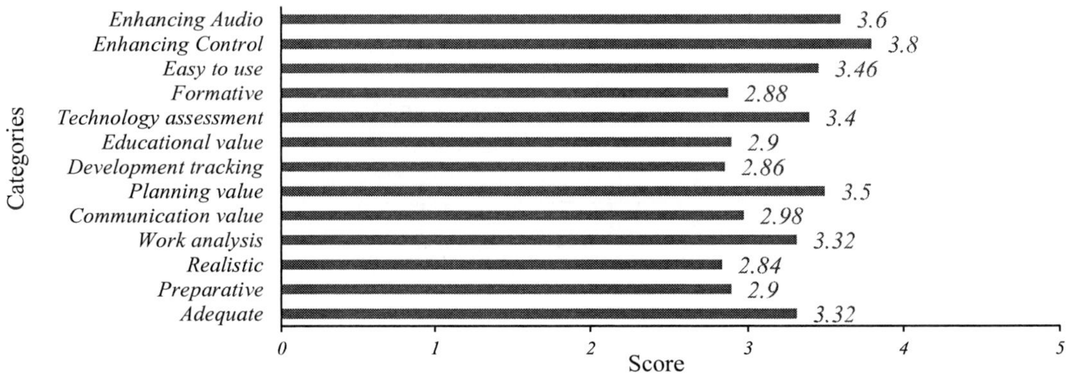

Figure 6: Results of the Assessment of the VP platform

4 Conclusions

The present paper proposed a framework for the use of virtual prototyping for the assessment of various construction equipment operator support systems. The framework starts by exploring the needs of the operators and other stakeholders and proceed to the steps required for the technical development of the VR simulator. In the end, a set of customized questions are proposed to assess the usability of the designed OSS.

Overall, the developed framework is shown to be feasible and useful for the assessment of construction equipment OSSs in a safe and secure environment. Although in the current shape the developed prototype was not deemed ready, overall the VP platform was found to have potentials for applications in the planning, work analysis, and training of construction operations. In general, it is also observed that the VP platform can streamline the design cycle and allow designers to access wider demographics for the testing of their new design concepts. Using the proposed VP platform users can be actively engaged in the design cycle of the equipment OSSs and have their needs and concerns taken into account in the system design at the earlier phases of design.

In the future, the authors would like to focus on the enhanced realism of the VP platform and assess it for other pieces of equipment too. Additionally, by better linking the data from the actual construction projects to the VR environment, the Digital Twin concept can be further extended into the domain of technology assessment and training.

References

Alberto J., Puerta A. (2007). State of the art of the virtual reality applied to design and manufacturing processes, Int J. Adv. Manuf.Technol. 33, pp. 866–874.

Brooke J. (1996). SUS: a "quick and dirty" usability scale, in: Usabiliyt Evaluation In Industry, CRC

Press.

Feng C., Dong S., Lundeen K.M., Xiao Y., Kamat V.R. (2015). Vision-Based Articulated Machine Pose Estimation for Excavation Monitoring and Guidance, in: Proceedings of the International Symposium on Automation and Robotics in Construction.

Hart S.G. (2006). Nasa-Task Load Index (NASA-TLX); 20 Years Later, In: Proceedings of the human factors and ergonomics society annual meeting, Los Angeles, CA.

Kim C., Lee C., Lehto M.R., Yun M.H. (2011). Affective evaluation of user impressions using virtual product prototyping, Human Factors and Ergonomics in Manufacturing & Service Industries. 21 pp. 1–13.

Langroodi A.K., Vahdatikhaki F., Doree A. (2021). Activity recognition of construction equipment using fractional random forest, Automation in Construction. 122.

Lee G., Cho J., Ham S., Lee T., Lee G., Yun S.-H., Yang H.-J. (2012). A BIM- and sensor-based tower crane navigation system for blind lifts, Automation in Construction. 26, pp. 1–10.

Lee G., Kim H.-H., Lee C.-J., Ham S.-I., Yun S.-H., Cho H., Kim B.K., Kim G.T., Kim K. (2009). A laser-technology-based lifting-path tracking system for a robotic tower crane, Automation in Construction. 18, pp. 865–874.

Li H., Chan N.K.Y., Huang T., Skitmore M., Yang J., (2012). Virtual prototyping for planning bridge construction, Automation in Construction. 27, pp. 1–10.

Li H., Huang T., Kong C.W., Guo H.L., Baldwin A., Chan N., Wong J. (2008). Integrating design and construction through virtual prototyping, Automation in Construction. 17, pp. 915–922.

Liu D., Lu W., Niu Y. (2018). Extended Technology-Acceptance Model to Make Smart Construction Systems Successful, Journal of Construction Engineering and Management. 144.

Li R., Chen Y.V., Sha C., Lu Z. (2017). Effects of interface layout on the usability of in-Vehicle information systems and driving safety, Displays. 49, pp. 124–132.

Madni A.M., Sievers M. (2018). Model-based systems engineering: Motivation, current status, and research opportunities, Systems Engineering. 21 172–190. doi:10.1002/SYS.21438.

Makarov D., Miller S., Vahdatikhaki F., Doree A. (2019). Comprehensive Real-time Pavement Operation Support System Using Machine-to-Machine Communication, International Journal of Pavement Research and Technology. 13(1), pp. 93-107.

Makarov D., Vahdatikhaki F., Miller S., Mowlaei S., Dorée A. (2021). Usability assessment of compaction operator support systems using virtual prototyping, Automation in Construction. 129.

Park J., Yang, X. Cho Y.K., Seo J. (2017). Improving dynamic proximity sensing and processing for smart work-zone safety, Automation in Construction. 84, pp. 111–120.

Son H., Park Y., Kim C., Chou J.S. (2012). Toward an understanding of construction professionals' acceptance of mobile computing devices in South Korea: An extension of the technology acceptance model, Automation in Construction. 28, pp. 82–90.

Teizer J., Allread B.S., Fullerton C.E., Hinze J. (2010). Autonomous pro-active real-time construction worker and equipment operator proximity safety alert system, Automation in Construction. 19, pp. 630–640.

Unity 3D, (2022). Unity Technologies. https://unity.com/

Vahdatikhaki F., El Ammari K., Langroodi A.K., Miller S., Hammad A., Doree A. (2019). Beyond data visualization: A context-realistic construction equipment training simulators, Automation in Construction. 106.

Vahdatikhaki F., Hammad A. (2015). Dynamic equipment workspace generation for improving earthwork safety using real-time location system, Advanced Engineering Informatics. 29, pp. 459–471.

Wang G.G. (2002). Definition and Review of Virtual Prototyping, Journal of Computing and Information Science in Engineering. 2 pp. 232–236.

Wang J., Razavi S.N. (2016). Low False Alarm Rate Model for Unsafe-Proximity Detection in Construction, Journal of Computing in Civil Engineering. 30.

Integration of Wave-Based Non-Destructive Survey Results into BIM Models

Artus M.[1], Schickert M.[2], Lai J.[1], Koch C[1].

[1]Bauhaus-Universität Weimar Germany, [2]MFPA life cycle material engineering Weimar Germany
mathias.artus@uni-weimar.de

Abstract. Aging bridges and rising load indices induce increases in bridge deterioration. Several nationalities conduct non-destructive testing (NDT) methods to analyze current bridge conditions. Traditional practice relies on exchanging plans and reports. However, sufficient planning and interpretation of NDT surveys require comprehensive building information. Building Information Modeling (BIM) has become an established concept for design, planning, and construction of buildings and structures. Combining the concept of BIM and NDT promises benefits in case of planning and performing surveys and interpret resultant data. This paper describes a framework that incorporates building information, inspection data, and data of wave-based surveys, for instance ultrasonic and Ground Penetrating Radar (GPR), to allow in-depth building assessment.

1. Introduction

The European Commission asserted an increase of road freight transport in recent years that led to a higher load on road bridges (Directorate-General for Mobility and Transport, 2021). Hence, bridge load capacities have to be checked to enhance bridges' life-time (Bundesministerium für Verkehr und digitale Infrastruktur, 2020). In Germany, heuristic load capacity analyses are based on historical information about materials and construction processes (Bundesministerium für Verkehr, Bau und Stadtentwicklung, 2011). Additional surveys, for example Non-Destructive Testing (NDT), provide detailed and up to date information about the structural quality of the bridge. Results from NDT surveys may prove or disprove assumptions made earlier, and hence, allow precise statements about bridge load capacities. This information may be utilized when supporting decisions about required maintenance actions or repair. Subsequently, financial properties may be invested in a more targeted manner.

German guidelines for inspections define visual inspections as basic processes examining bridge conditions. Some defects, for example, extensive moisture penetration or cracks exceeding defined thresholds reason an in-depth investigation, such as structural or material analyses (Deutsches Institut für Normung, 1999; Bundesministerium für Verkehr, Bau und Stadtentwicklung, 2017). The inspector assumes defects and decides about further investigations, such as a radar survey analyzing moisture penetration or localize tension ducts (Taffe, Stoppel and Wiggenhauser, 2010). The test engineer receives the order of the NDT method in conjunction with plans and inspection reports, which are the basis for testing engineers who perform personal on-site inspections and arrange the surveys. During a third visit on-site, the engineer performs the survey, and finally, all survey results are interpreted and send back as a report. This workflow is error prone and time consuming because its paper-based data exchange.

Interpretation of the data requires the relation between survey results and building information, for example, a correct interpretation of radar images requires knowledge about component dimensions and as-designed positions of reinforcement and tendon ducts. BIM models include all required geometric and semantic information (Borrmann, König, Koch and Beetz, 2018). Based on the conceptual definitions of BIM, the open standard of the Industry Foundation

https://doi.org/10.7146/aul.455.c221

Classes (IFC) has been defined (International Organization for Standardization, 2018). Since the planning of Inspections and NDT needs not be based on the actual structural situation, the as-built model is required as a starting point, as opposed to the as-planned model. Results of NDT surveys may reveal defects, that have to be incorporated in the BIM model, hence, a data model for defects is required as well.

Although novel developments define a standardized data exchange for the NDT sector, e.g., the Standard Practice for Digital Imaging and Communication in Nondestructive Evaluation DICONDE (ASTM, 2016), exchanging data in practice is performed via reports and 2D CAD files. Niederleithinger and Vrana (2021) emphasized the necessity for combining BIM and NDT to provide quality assurance data to engineers and inspectors. Contradictory to that, Braml, Wimmer, Maack, Küttenbaum, Kuhn, Reingruber, Gordt and Hamm (2021) used an ontological approach to link building and sensor data. They remarked in their paper that BIM for bridges is too coarse, and hence, they used a different method to include building data. A detailed explanation about required building information is missing, as well as a detailed description on how they store and transfer building and sensor data. Schickert, Koch, Kremp and Bonitz (2020) improved the perception and ease interpretation of NDT results by using Augmented Reality (AR) for visualization. However, the underlying building model consisted only of a CAD model of the test specimen. Based on prior work, a workflow to establish the combination of building information in the form of BIM and NDT data was proposed by (Schickert, Artus, Lai and Kremp, 2021). However, definitions of required data for planning and interpretation tasks are missing up to now. In summary, a comprehensive method combining BIM and NDT is desirable. This study aims to develop a framework that provides building information to the testing engineer for planning surveys, integrating and interpreting results. To limit the scope, this paper focuses on wave-based NDT surveys, such as Ultrasonic and Ground Penetrating Radar (GPR) because they are often used to analyze bridges.

This study focuses on the following research questions.

- Which building and damage information is required to plan and interpret radar surveys?
- How can this information be incorporated into existing BIM models?
- How can the required information be visualized to ease planning and interpretation?

2. Parameter Definition for Wave-Based Surveys

Wave-based surveys are used to measure internal parameters of concrete components or structures, e.g., localize internal objects of concrete components, measure layer thicknesses, or to do qualitative checks of moisture penetration. Wave-based surveys use, for example, radar or ultrasonic waves. Independently from the wave type, a transmitter sends one or multiple waves into the survey object and a receiver receives the waves reflected at material transitions. Raw measurement data consists of amplitudes over time and is called a single track. Within this single track, reflections can be identified, and hence, the transit time for the signal and its reflections are calculated. Based on the transit times and the propagation velocity of the signal, positions of medium transitions are calculated. Several measurements alongside a line on the surface of a component may be combined to measure the profile or cross section of a component. To retrieve 3-dimensional data, a grid of measurements on the component's surface is combined. The visualization of a line and a grid is called B-Scan and C-Scan respectively. Furthermore, grid data may be visualized as 3-dimensional geometry as shown by Figure 1 right.

Later interpretation of this data, such as the localization of tendon ducts, requires knowledge about the as-built building or structure. This leads to a chicken-and-egg problem because the radar survey aims to measure the positions of reinforcement and layers, but, on the other hand, needs the as-planned positions of these parts in order to evaluate their measurements. Hence, some information, which can be delivered by BIM, are positions of tendon ducts, reinforcement, and information about layers in components. This data is already part of BIM (Borrmann, König, Koch and Beetz, 2018).

Furthermore, surveys based on waves are influenced by surface defects such as cracks, spalling, or delamination. These data is not included in conventional BIM models. Artus and Koch (2020) developed BIM extensions to incorporate damage information, which is called Damage Information Modeling (DIM). These DIM models contain geometric information about defects that enables engineers to inspect a bridge in the office in order to prepare on-site surveys. Further data is necessary to properly combine survey results, damage, and building models.

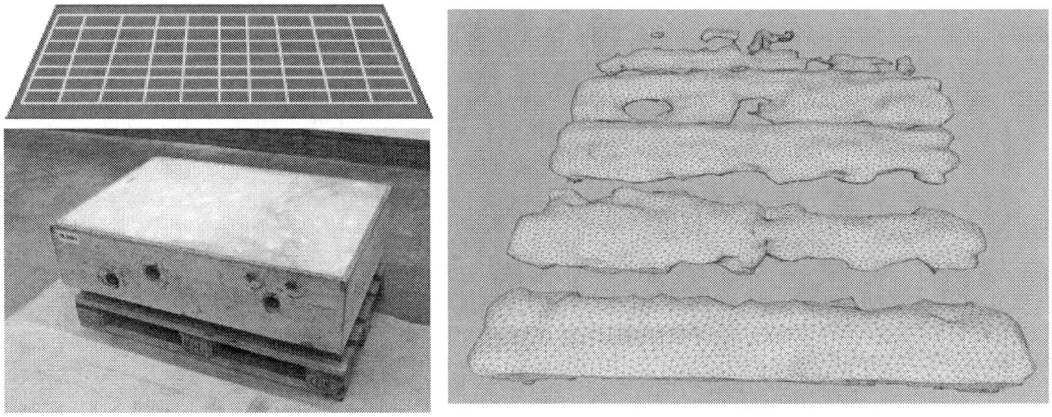

Figure 1: Scan grid (top left) of a surface of a test specimen (bottom left) and resultant 3D reconstruction of measurement results of back wall (right). The holes occur because of shadowing effects.

Table 1 shows an overview of the proposed parameters required for survey planning. Based on the test objective and the post-processing of the signal, different test results and visualizations may be generated, for example, measuring the radar reflection on a single line or in a grid using a B- or C-Scan, respectively. The component and structure ID are necessary to identify the structure and component of the survey. The test objective defines the aim of the survey that could be measurement of thickness of components, layers, or shells, localization of reinforcement, tension-ducts, or anchors, registration of voids or imperfections, or analysis of moisture, salt content, or homogeneity of the component. Additional descriptions, such as special setups or processes, are stored in the survey description. Survey start and end contain the timestamps of the survey, which includes planning, performing, and data analyses. Furthermore, the test result time specifies the time stamp when the data has been collected. A position based on Global Positioning System (GPS) data or other geographic information and the orientation of the measurement results are stored in the survey location. Textual descriptions of the component and test objective are optional. Finally, the inspection area and possible defects are required.

For visualization and assessment, data from Table 1 shall be exchanged via IFC files. An *IfcTask* represents a survey with related time information and responsibilities. Structure and component identifiers are the Global Unique Identifiers (GUID) of the entire structure and component respectively. The survey location, weather condition, test object condition, and test objective description are stored within an *IfcPropertySet.* Surface defects are covered by the aforementioned concept of DIM, and hence, are stored as *IfcVoidingFeature*. Last open point is the inspection area. In general, BIM and IFC offer possibilities to include geometries. However, the problem is which entity is used in conjunction with the geometry. Inspection areas may be understood as spatial zones, which is similar to a lighting or thermal zone using *IfcSpatialZone.* GPR tests a component from the surface, hence, the inspection area can be understood as a 2D plane or, if the depth of the scan is considered, as a cuboid.

Table 1: Overview of planning parameters.

Parameter name	Data type
Structure ID	String
Component ID	String
Test objective	Enumeration
Testing engineers	Actor [1:n]
Survey description	String
Survey start	Date time
Survey end	Date time
Survey location	String
Weather condition	String
Test object condition	String
Test objective description	String
Inspection area	Plane or spatial geometry
Surface defects	Subtraction or solid geometry

Furthermore, inspection results have to be integrated into the BIM model. Table 2 shows an overview of mandatory test result data for a wave-based survey. Information about the device, such as manufacturer and model, are required to consider device specific parameters. The test result summary is a textual summary of from the engineer and the coordinate system provides information about the local coordinate system of the test results depending on the coordinate system of the building. A comprehensive description of result parameters for ground penetrating radar may be found in Deutsche Gesellschaft für Zerstörungsfreie Prüfung e.V. (2008).

3. Modeling in IFC and Visualization

All result data has to be integrated into the BIM model and linked to related components. Both could be directly integrated into the BIM model but the result data may include multiple components. This leads to two possible solutions, either splitting up the geometry into several geometries or simply include the result as external reference. If the geometry is split and directly included, external references are omitted but some information could be misleading because of missing parts of the results, and hence, significance is compromised. Furthermore, it is preferred to include the results as external references. 2D and 3D result data may be included as external references and the results are kept in the CAD format provided and are integrated via document references. In case of later inquiries or verification of the test data, the raw data is important, which consists of vectors and matrices. Storing matrices and vectors in IFC is possible but impractical, so a reference to the location of the raw data is included in the IFC file.

Table 2: Overview of result data of wave-based surveys.

Parameter name	Data type
Device manufacturer	String
Device model	String
Device serial number	String
Test result time	Date time
2D test results	Image (as reference)
3D test results	Solid geometry (as reference)
Test result coordinate system	6-dimensional vector (position and orientation)
Test result summary	String

Except the 2D and 3D test results, the data may be stored as *IfcPropertySet* in relation to the survey. One approach to include 2D test results into IFC files would be to use textures. However, B- and C-scans represent material or layer information from below the surface, hence, using these result images as textures on the component surface would be misleading. The resulting images may be added as a document to the inspection area. Correct positioning of 3D result data from grid scans is mandatory for subsequent interpretation. Traditionally, engineers use a visible point at the structure or component to describe the measurement location, for example, 2 meters from the upper left corner of the pier to the right and 1 meter downwards. This positioning has to be transformed and included into the BIM model as shown in Table 1 by the attribute test result coordinate system.

Figure 3 shows an excerpt of the IFC file created with the test result as proxy #39115 and the survey result as document reference #39128. The label "Survey result" as object type for the proxy helps to identify elements that are results. Another possibility is to use a type object, which has the advantage to carry more information. Using the document association #39131 the STL file is linked to the tested component, which is not part of the excerpt, and related properties. STL files are CAD files without dimensioning; hence, this dimensioning has to be delivered additionally. Last, the property 'Image type' indicates that the related document contains 3-dimensional geometric information. Figure 3 shows the second excerpt of the IFC file with the testing engineer (#39137) and the weather condition during the survey (#39140).

The prototype for a BIM viewer has been developed using Unity in combination with IfcOpenShell (IfcOpenShell, 2015) and xBIM (Lockley, Benghi and Černý, 2017). Figure 4 shows an overview of the implementation and data processing pipeline. After selecting the IFC file, IfcOpenShell generates an OBJ file that can be loaded by the Unity application at runtime. In parallel, xBim.Essentials are used to read the IFC file into the memory and provide access to available semantic information.

```
#39115=IFCPROXY('3o0qbRQDP5MRKKu45U1K_6',#39116,
    'GPR test result','3D Test result of GPR survey',
    'Survey result',#39126,$,.PRODUCT.,$);
#39128=IFCDOCUMENTREFERENCE('da1s1d1_ascii_Linsen.stl',
    '1fI_EeNvCEO_1iYeKFZsVA','sd','sd',$);
#39129=IFCPROPERTYSET('3MfYz00HfAwucWalt6hbd2',#39116,
    'File Parameter',$,(#39130,#39132));
#39130=IFCPROPERTYSINGLEVALUE('Model Scaling',$,
    IFCIDENTIFIER('Meter'),$);
#39132=IFCPROPERTYSINGLEVALUE('Image Type',$,
    IFCIDENTIFIER('Image_3D'),$);
#39131=IFCRELASSOCIATESDOCUMENT('1RS$3mF1XEjh9wwMItwRWB',
    #39116,'Related Parameters','Connect related parameters.',
    (#39115,#39129),#39128);
```

Figure 2: Excerpt of an example IFC file with the test result as proxy (#39115) and the related STL file as reference (#39128).

```
#39133=IFCTASK('1g7QA_8LmkahfwvLcbanAQ',#39116,
    'Radar survey',$,'Non-destructive Testing','2022-US-42',
    $,'finished','Radar survey on-site',.F.,0,
    #39134,.USERDEFINED.);
#39134=IFCTASKTIME('Radar survey time',.MEASURED.,$,
    .ELAPSEDTIME.,$,$,$,$,$,$,$,$,$,.F.,$,'5d',
    '2022-02-22T08:15:00','2022-02-28T09:00:00',$,
    IFCREAL(100));
#39135=IFCRELASSIGNSTOPROCESS('1-yeVHSLz0W1YPLEYCJQfA',#39116,$,
    $,(#39115),.PRODUCT.,#39133,$);
#39136=IFCACTOR('0TBDQzdFeEunoqbfunjIYw',#39116,$,$,
    'Testing Engineer',#39137);
#39137=IFCPERSON('42/3141','Gropius','Walter',$,$,$,#39138,
    $);
#39138=IFCACTORROLE(.ENGINEER.,$,'Testing Engineer');
#39139=IFCPROPERTYSET('01_HQ7Oz10iNua2bPmAtQA',#39116,
    'Survey information',$,(#39140));
#39140=IFCPROPERTYSINGLEVALUE('Weather Condition',$,
    IFCLABEL('Cloudy, slight rain'),$);
```

Figure 3: Excerpt of an example IFC file with the testing engineer (#39137) and the weather condition (#39140).

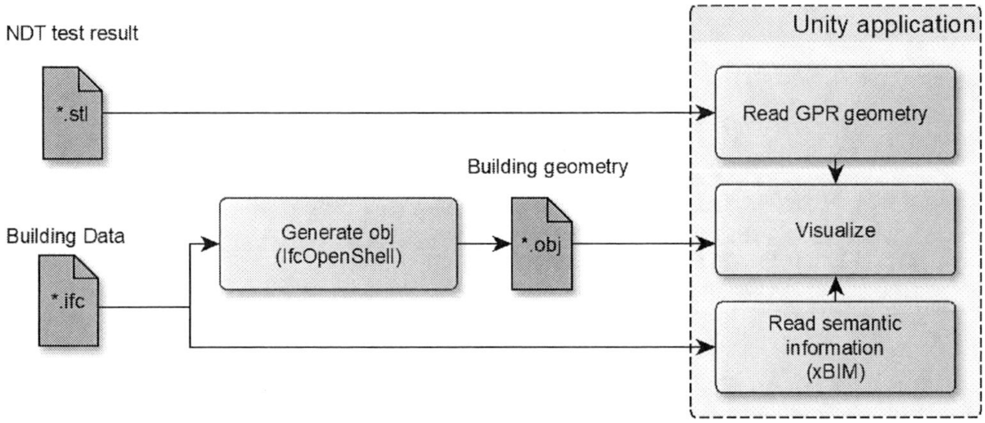

Figure 4: Implementation and data processing in the application.

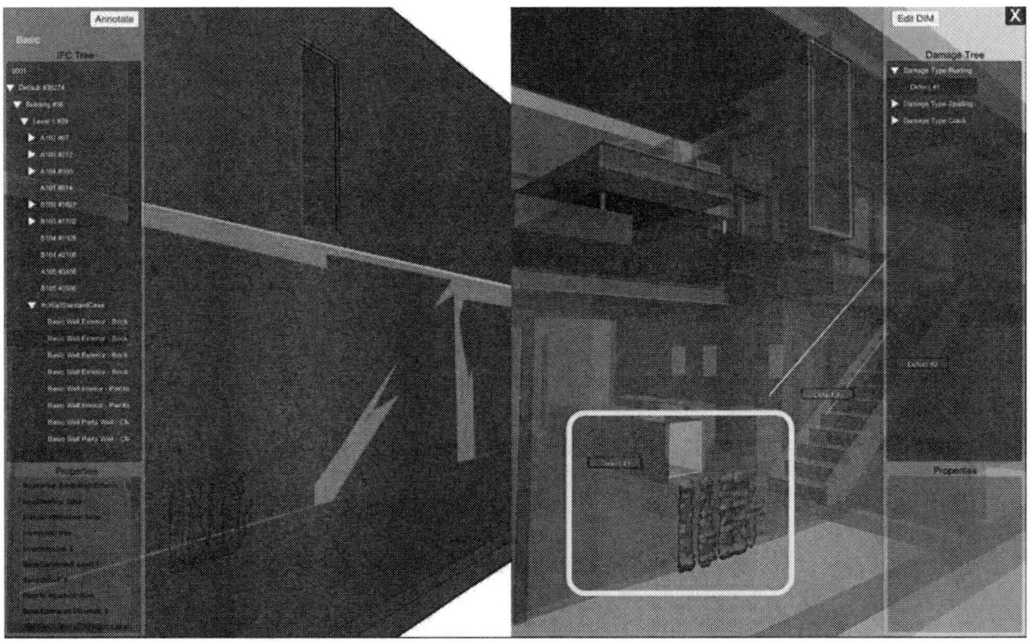

Figure 5: Screenshot of the developed prototype for visualizing material defects.

Based on the naming conventions and the document reference, the file is interpreted and visualized as shown in Figure 5. The red body is the same geometry as shown in Figure 5, right. Since wave-base surveys provide information about the interior of components the visualization requires transparency to represent this. However, transparency worsens the perception of localization. This has led to a split screen solution visualizing the building without transparency on the left and with transparency on the right. Looking on the left, the user can identify what is in the foreground and what in the background and on the right, survey results are visible colored in red. Also, a tree view of the building is to be seen on the far left and the far right list shows registered defects within the model.

4. Conclusion

On the one hand, appropriate evaluation of GPR test results requires information about the tested structure or building and BIM provides this information. On the other hand, instead of utilizing existing building information, engineers go on-site to plan NDT surveys. Subsequently, the visualization of test results is limited to images and CAD files lacking interconnection to the tested building or component. A proper visualization that combines both, building information and test results, promises better perception and eases interpretation.

This study aimed to develop a data model that links wave-based survey information and test results with existing building information. In addition to process, building, and damage information, test results are stored as 2D images or 3D geometries. Instead of including this result data directly into the BIM model, they are linked via document references. The implementation of this model has been done by using the open IFC standard for data exchange and Unity for visualization. Finally, the visualization of the test data in relation to the building data reveals the reason of observed reflections, and hence, eases the interpretation.

This study aimed to develop a data model to link NDT and building data. However, according to (Borrmann, König, Koch and Beetz, 2018) a standardized terminology is required as well. Furthermore, instead of using paper based reports, CAD files, and images for data exchange, the building's NDT sector requires a standardized data exchange definition, such as the IFC format for BIM, to keep up with digitization. A more general problem is the discussion about the data that should be included in IFC and data that should be referenced only. NDT survey acquire dynamic data of structures and buildings similar to sensors used for structural health monitoring. Future work has to identify criteria that help to decide if supplemental data is included into IFC files directly or referenced only.

5. References

Artus, M. and Koch, C. (2020), Modeling Geometry and Semantics of Physical Damages using IFC, paper presented at Workshop on Intelligent Computing in Engineering, 1.7.-04.07.2020, Berlin (digital).

ASTM (2016), Standard Practice for Digital Imaging and Communication in Nondestructive Evaluation (DICONDE) No. E2339-15, available at: https://www.astm.org/e2339-15.html (accessed 11 January 2022).

Borrmann, A., König, M., Koch, C. and Beetz, J. (Eds.) (2018), Building Information Modeling: Technology Foundations and Industry Practice, 2nd ed., Springer International Publishing, Cham.

Braml, T., Wimmer, J., Maack, S., Küttenbaum, S., Kuhn, T., Reingruber, M., Gordt, A. and Hamm, J. (2021), Datenablage als Grundlage für den digitalen Zwilling eines Bauwerks – Verwaltungsschale BBox, in Krieger, J. (Ed.), 1. Fachkongress Digitale Transformation im Lebenszyklus der Verkehrsinfrastruktur: Fachtagung über Planung, Bau, Betrieb von Brücken, Tunneln, Straßen digital Tagungshandbuch 2021, expert, Tübingen, pp. 75–84.

Bundesministerium für Verkehr und digitale Infrastruktur (2020), Stand der Modernisierung von Straßenbrücken der Bundesfernstraßen, Berlin.

Bundesministerium für Verkehr, Bau und Stadtentwicklung (2011), Richtlinie zur Nachrechnung von Straßenbrücken im Bestand (Nachrechnungsrichtlinie), available at:

https://www.bast.de/BASt_2017/DE/Ingenieurbau/Publikationen/Regelwerke/Entwurf/Nachrechnungsrichtlinie-Ausgabe-5_2011.pdf;jsessionid=6EA06626A2B940AE90920BAE6AF3BE2C.live21304?__blob=publicationFile&v=1 (accessed 1 February 2019).

Bundesministerium für Verkehr, Bau und Stadtentwicklung (2017), Leitfaden für Objektbezogene Schadensanalyse (OSA).

Deutsche Gesellschaft für Zerstörungsfreie Prüfung e.V. (2008), Merkblatt B10: Merkblatt über das Radarverfahren zur Zerstörungsfreien Prüfung im Bauwesen.

Deutsches Institut für Normung (1999), DIN 1076: Ingenieurbauwerke im Zuge von Straßen und Wegen Überwachung und Prüfung No. 1076.

Directorate-General for Mobility and Transport (European Commission) (2021), EU transport in figures: Statistical pocketbook 2021.

IfcOpenShell (2015), IfcConvert, available at: http://ifcopenshell.org/ifcconvert (accessed 8 February 2021).

International Organization for Standardization (ISO) (2018), ISO 16739-1:2018-11: Industry Foundation Classes (IFC) für den Datenaustausch in der Bauwirtschaft und im Anlagenmanagement - Teil 1: Datenschema, Vol. 25.040.40 No. ISO 16739-1, 2018-11, Beuth.

Lockley, S., Benghi, C. and Černý, M. (2017), Xbim.Essentials: a library for interoperable building information applications, The Journal of Open Source Software, Vol. 2 No. 20, p. 473.

Niederleithinger, E. and Vrana, J. (2021), ZfPBau 4.0 – Herausforderungen an die ZfP im Bauwesen im Rahmen der Digitalisierung, in Krieger, J. (Ed.), 1. Fachkongress Digitale Transformation im Lebenszyklus der Verkehrsinfrastruktur: Fachtagung über Planung, Bau, Betrieb von Brücken, Tunneln, Straßen digital Tagungshandbuch 2021, expert, Tübingen, pp. 187–190.

Schickert, M., Artus, M., Lai, J.P.H. and Kremp, F. (2021), Integration und Visualisierung von Zustandsdaten in digitalen Bauwerksmodellen - Konzepte und Realisierungen, in Krieger, J. (Ed.), 1. Fachkongress Digitale Transformation im Lebenszyklus der Verkehrsinfrastruktur: Fachtagung über Planung, Bau, Betrieb von Brücken, Tunneln, Straßen digital Tagungshandbuch 2021, expert, Tübingen, pp. 381–389.

Schickert, M., Koch, C., Kremp, F. and Bonitz, F. (2020), Visualisierung von Ultraschall- und Radar-Abbildungen durch Augmented Reality, paper presented at Fachtagung Bauwerksdiagnose, 2020-02-13, Berlin.

Taffe, A., Stoppel, M. and Wiggenhauser, H. (2010), Zerstörungsfreie Prüfverfahren im Bauwesen (ZfPBau), available at: http://www.dgzfp.de/Portals/bauwerksprfg2010/BB/V03-04.pdf (accessed 15 November 2021).

SFS-A68: a dataset for the segmentation of space functions in apartment buildings

Ziaee A., Suter G.
TU Wien, Austria
amir.ziaee@tuwien.ac.at

Abstract. Analyzing building models for usable area, building safety, or energy analysis requires function classification data of spaces and related objects. Automated space function classification is desirable to reduce input model preparation effort and errors. Existing space function classifiers use space feature vectors or space connectivity graphs as input. The application of deep learning (DL) image segmentation methods to space function classification has not been studied. As an initial step towards addressing this gap, we present a dataset, SFS-A68, that consists of input and ground truth images generated from 68 digital 3D models of space layouts of apartment buildings. The dataset is suitable for developing DL models for space function segmentation. We use the dataset to train and evaluate an experimental space function segmentation network based on transfer learning and training from scratch. Test results confirm the applicability of DL image segmentation for space function classification.

1. Introduction

Building information modeling (BIM) authoring systems support detailed analysis of usable area, building safety, or energy analysis (e.g., Autodesk, 2021). Accurate analysis requires function classification data for spaces and related objects. Usually, these data need to be manually entered by end-users. They may also be lost in data exchanges between BIM authoring software (Lai et al., 2019). This is problematic because it can lead to input errors and inaccurate analysis. Furthermore, input preparation is time-consuming, particularly for large and functionally diverse buildings. Automating the space function classification task is desirable because it can help reduce input preparation effort and input errors and improve the accuracy of building analysis results.

To automate classification tasks in BIM, researchers have explored the application of supervised Machine Learning (ML) and Deep Learning (DL) methods (Section 2). Segmentation, as the most well-known capability of supervised ML and DL, can classify a variety of object classes at the pixel level of an image (Long et al., 2015). While DL segmentation methods have been developed to segment building and furnishing elements in point clouds (Ma, Czerniawski and Leite, 2020; Emunds et al., 2021), their application to space function classification has not been studied. A fundamental challenge is to develop suitable datasets to train and evaluate segmentation models. To address this issue, we present a dataset, SFS-A68, that consists of input and ground truth images generated from 68 digital 3D models of space layouts of apartment buildings (Ziaee, Suter and Barada, 2022). We use the dataset to train and evaluate an experimental space function segmentation network based on transfer learning (Tan et al., 2018) and training from scratch. We follow a general ML and DL workflow (Figure 1) consisting of problem formulation, data collection, pre-processing, construction, validation, and model deployment (Eisler and Meyer, 2020).

First, we define space function classification as a semantic segmentation problem. We choose space functions in apartment buildings as an application domain. Apartments are typically

https://doi.org/10.7146/aul.455.c222

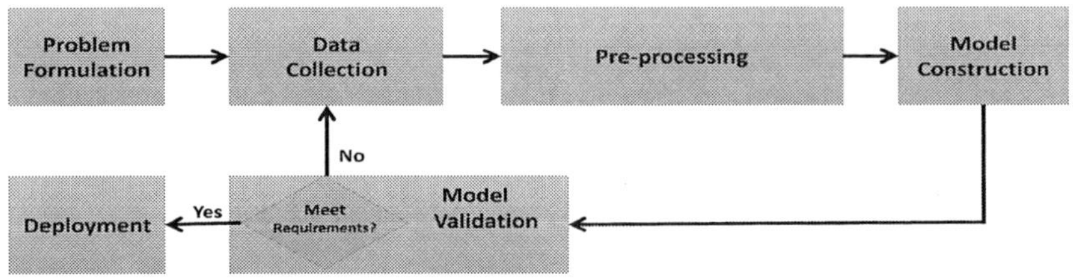

Figure 1: Machine Learning and Deep Learning workflow (Eisler and Meyer, 2020).

diverse in space areas, functions, and accessibility (Heckmann and Schneider, 2011), making them suitable to explore the application potential of segmentation models. Next, we describe the data collection workflow which we have adopted to develop our dataset. The workflow involves selecting buildings, interpreting their floor plans, modeling space layouts in BIM authoring or CAD systems, and data quality verification. Layouts are pre-processed according to the input requirements for space function segmentation. We describe how vector images of layout models are automatically converted to raster images. Layout elements are colored consistently by their class in these images. We have used the dataset to train and validate a space function segmentation network based on transfer learning and training from scratch. We present initial results obtained from testing the network's capability to predict space functions. Deployment of the space function segmentation network in a BIM analysis application is beyond the scope of this study. It would require the post-processing of prediction images. In this step, a predicted class or a list of predicted classes would need to be extracted for each space from all pixels in a prediction image that carry class prediction data for that space. Information about predicted classes would be passed to the BIM analysis application to modify space labels in the building model accordingly.

2. Related work

Classification methods for BIM can be categorized into rule-based, ML-based, and DL-based methods. Rule-based classification involves rule sets to encapsulate domain knowledge. For example, Belsky et al. (2016) introduced a rule language to classify objects based on their properties and spatial relationships. Bloch and Sacks (2018) developed rules on single or pairwise room features to classify space functions in apartment buildings. Examples for features include room area, accessibility, or the number of windows in a room. Suter (2022) developed space ontologies encoded in the Ontology Web Language (OWL) and used a general-purpose OWL semantic reasoner to infer space functions of given space layouts. Rule-based methods are limited because knowledge needs to be encoded explicitly. Developing robust and non-contradictory rules is a challenging task that requires domain and programming expertise. For space function classification, the accuracy of rule-based methods may be lower than ML and DL methods (Bloch and Sacks, 2018).

By contrast, supervised ML and DL are data-driven methods. They use a set of inputs with their associated labels or ground truths to train a model that can be used to classify new inputs. A key difference between the two methods is that DL has the capability to extract features automatically. De las Heras et al. (2014) proposed a two-step pipeline to interpret floor plan images. In the first step, walls, doors, and windows are segmented using supervised ML. In the second step, a wall junction graph is derived, and room regions are identified as cycles in the graph. Bloch and Sacks (2018) applied supervised ML with iteration to classify space functions in apartments. Their artificial neural network (ANN) classifier uses features of individual spaces, including floor area and the number of doors, and space connectivity features as input. The ANN was trained to classify 15 space functions for a dataset of 150 spaces from 32 similar apartments.

Applications of DL methods in BIM include semantic segmentation of building interiors. Ma, Czerniawski and Leite (2020) created DL models to segment building and furnishing element classes in point clouds of non-residential interior spaces. Synthetic point clouds were generated from BIM models using BIM authoring and CAD software. Leonhardt et al. (2020) converted geometries of objects in room scenes to synthetic point clouds to train a DL neural network for 3D object classification and segmentation. IFCNet is a dataset consisting of approximately 19'000 instances of 65 IFC classes (Emunds et al., 2021). Instance images were created from multiple viewpoints and passed as input to a Multi-View Convolutional Neural Network (MVCNN) to learn shape descriptors. Wang, Sacks and Yeung (2022) developed a Graph Neural Network (GNN) model that classifies eight apartment space functions. A dataset was created that consists of spatial connectivity graphs for 224 apartment layouts from three countries.

Existing work indicates a significant potential for ML and DL methods to address classification needs in BIM in general and space function classification in particular. Existing space function classifiers use space feature vectors or space connectivity graphs as input (Bloch and Sacks, 2018; Wang, Sacks and Yeung, 2022). However, the applicability of DL image segmentation methods to space function classification has not been studied. This gap appears significant because DL image segmentation methods have been applied successfully in many domains (Minaee et al., 2020). Our SFS-A68 dataset provides a basis for developing novel space function classifiers that use such methods.

3. Problem formulation

We aim to segment space function classes in images of space layout models of apartment buildings. Examples for space function classes are 'LivingRoom', 'Kitchen', 'Loggia' and 'Elevator'. There are two variants of the problem: semantic and instance space function segmentation. The task of semantic space function segmentation is to assign each pixel in a space layout image to a space function class. Instance segmentation assigns each space pixel to a space instance of a space function class. In this study, we focus on semantic space function segmentation. We aim to develop DL image segmentation networks for semantic space function segmentation (Figure 2).

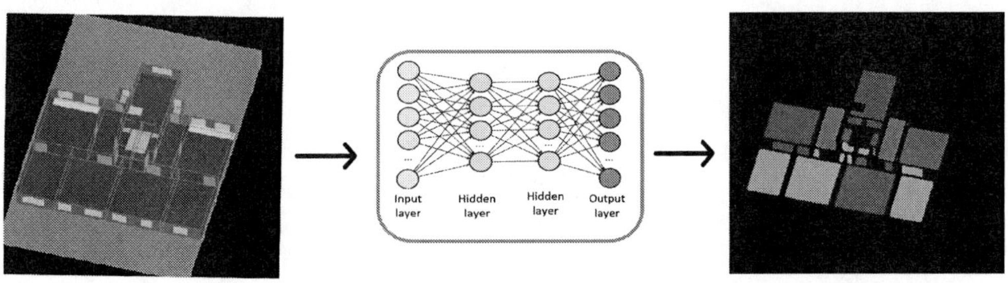

(a) Input image (b) Space function segmentation network (c) Output image

Figure 2: Space function segmentation network.

To train a space function segmentation network, we need input images of space layouts with dimensions H x W x 3 as uniformly scaling two-dimensional RGB images and corresponding ground truth images with dimensions H x W x N, where N corresponds to the number of space function classes. Each layout element in an input image is colored according to a unique class color (Table 1, left column). Space element classes may be helpful as metadata to determine space function classes. For example, a 'Bathroom' may contain a 'SanitaryElement'.

Each pixel in a ground truth image is assigned to a space function class. Space function classes in apartment buildings that are classified by the space function segmentation network are shown in Table 1, right column. Circulation spaces, such as stairways or elevators, are classified because we aim to classify complete floors rather than individual apartments. We have identified 22 space function classes for the apartment buildings in our dataset. Since existing space classification systems, such as UniClass and OmniClass (NBS, 2020; CSI, 2010), currently do not cover all required classes, we defined a class hierarchy that meets our needs.

Table 1: Class hierarchies.

Layout element classes		Space function classes		
Name	**Count**	**Name**	**Count [-]**	**[%]**
Space		Space		
InternalSpace	2'296	**ResidentialSpace**		
ExternalSpace	223	CommunalSpace		
SpaceElement		DiningRoom	3	0.1
SpaceContainedElement		FamilyRoom	6	0.2
CirculationElement		LivingRoom	275	10.9
FlightOfStairs		PrivateSpace		
Landing		Bedroom	495	19.7
FurnishingElement		MasterBedroom	23	0.9
KitchenElement		BoxRoom	2	0.1
SanitaryElement		HomeOffice	8	0.3
EquipmentElement		**ServiceSpace**		
HomeAppliance		Shaft	401	15.9
TextileCareAppliance		StorageRoom	83	3.3
SpaceEnclosingElement		WalkInCloset	2	0.1
Opening		SanitarySpace		
Partition		Bathroom	301	11.9
Window		Toilet	150	6.0
Door		Kitchen	25	1.0
RegularDoor		LaundryRoom	117	4.6
UnitDoor		**CirculationSpace**		
ElevatorDoor		VerticalCirculationSpace		
		Elevator	84	3.3
		Stairway	70	2.8
		HorizontalCirculationSpace		
		Entrance	75	3.0
		Hallway	11	0.4
		MainHallway	19	0.8
		InternalHallway	145	5.8
		External		
		AccessBalcony	19	0.8
		Loggia	108	4.3
		Air	96	3.8

4. Data collection

The SFS-A68 dataset is derived from source data comprising 68 digital 3D models of space layouts of apartment buildings designed or built in the years 1952-2019. Master of Architecture students at TU Wien created the models for an Architectural Morphology course taught by the second author. Each layout model represents a complete or partial floor plan. In total, source data cover 275 apartments of varying types (Table 2). 52% of apartments are 2-Room or 3-Room apartments.

Table 2. Apartment types in the SFS-A68 dataset.

Type	Count [-]	[%]
Apartment	275	100
1-Room Apartment	17	6
2-Room Apartment	65	24
3-Room Apartment	78	28
4-Room Apartment	53	19
5-Room Apartment	49	18
>5-Room Apartment	13	5

Students selected floor plans from a variety of sources, including books and professional journals on apartment design and architecture websites (Heckmann and Schneider, 2011; Plataforma Networks, 2022). 78% of floor plans are from buildings in Austria, Germany, and Switzerland, and 22% from 10 countries in Europe, the USA, and Southern America, respectively. Students created space layout models in BIM authoring (2021) or CAD (2015-2020) software by following a four-step workflow.

In the first step, an apartment building is selected. The building must be well documented. At a minimum, floor plans must be available either in raster image or vector drawing formats, and their scales must be known. Floor plans and related data are considered ground truth.

In the second step, floor plans of a selected apartment building are interpreted. Ambiguous features in floor plans are identified and resolved. For example, the physical separation between a living room and a hallway or a kitchen may be partial or non-existent.

In the third step, a layout model is created using BIM authoring or CAD software for a selected floor plan. The model is exported as an IFC file and imported into the Space Modeling System (SMS; Suter, 2022). SMS extracts space data from the IFC file and simplifies the shapes of space elements. For example, window shapes are converted from a multiple Brep to a single face representation. A label editor in SMS is used to semi-automatically label layout elements according to Table 1. A detailed description of this step is given in (Suter, 2022).

In the fourth step, the data quality of the layout model and labels is verified. Typical inconsistencies include missing doors or layout elements with inaccurate labels. The data quality of each layout model in the SFS-A68 dataset was verified independently against ground truth floor plans by a teaching assistant and the second author, who both have an architectural background.

5. Pre-processing

3D space layout models are converted to SVG images where layout element regions are colored by layout element class. Next, the colored SVGs are converted to PNG raster images that can be used as input or ground truth to train space function segmentation networks. Each image pixel value is normalized to make non-zero gradients less frequent during training and help networks learn faster.

5.1 Conversion to SVG

SMS converts a 3D space layout model to two Scalable Vector Graphics (SVG) images whose elements are colored by their class. SVG is a W3C standard for 2D graphics based on XML syntax (W3C, 2018). It supports vector objects, such as paths (regions), raster images, and text. A benefit of the SVG format for the pre-processing workflow is that the appearance of image elements can be defined in linked Cascading Style Sheet (CSS) style sheets. SMS projects 3D layout elements on the XY plane of the layout model's local coordinate system. Layout element faces are converted to regions. Each region has a class attribute whose value is populated with the class of its layout element. A style is defined for each layout element class in a CSS style sheet. It has properties for stroke thickness and fill color. Each layout element class has a unique fill color (Table 1). As a result, SVG images of layout models generated by SMS are colored consistently. A single CSS style sheet is used to color all SVG images for input and ground truth. Each space region in an input image is colored as 'InternalSpace' or 'ExternalSpace' while a region for a ground truth image is colored by its function class. Space elements are colored according to their classes in each input image.

5.2 Conversion to PNG

SVG images are converted to raster images. The PNG raster image format is chosen for this study. We use the Wand library (ImageMagick Studio, 2021) to convert an SVG image for input or ground truth to a corresponding PNG image. The shape of an input image returned by the procedure is Height x Width x [R, G, B]. For ground truth, all space regions are iteratively extracted for each space function class from the SVG image, and then they are converted to a PNG image with shape Height x Width x Number of Space Function Classes.

5.3 Normalization

Normalization is widely used in the data pre-processing steps of DL models to decrease a model's training time and prevent model weights from increasing during training such that networks converge faster. Scaling of pixel channels from the [0, 255] range to ranges [0, 1] and [-1, 1] are two commonly used approaches to ensure that each pixel has a similar data distribution (Huang et al., 2020). The first scaling approach is known as normalization and is applied to a ground truth image using Otsu's thresholding function in the OpenCV library after Gaussian filtering (Bradski, 2000). Subsequently, binary masks are created for the ground truth image. In a binary mask, 0 represents a background pixel, and 1 represents a foreground space function class pixel. The second scaling approach is known as standardization. It shifts the data distribution to have a mean of zero and a standard deviation of one unit. It is performed per pixel as shown in Equation 1:

$$X' = (X / \mu) - \sigma \qquad (1)$$

where X' is the normalized pixel, μ and σ are the mean and the standard deviation over all channels, respectively (Huang et al., 2020).

6. Model construction

Applying the pre-processing workflow to each layout results in a dataset comprised of 68 standardized input images with their corresponding normalized ground truth images. Since the dataset used to train a model must be different from the one used to evaluate its performance, the SFS-A8 dataset is split into a training and a testing dataset with a ratio of 80% (54 layouts) to 20% (14 layouts). In this study, we do not perform hyperparameter fine-tuning, which requires a validation dataset. Therefore, the training dataset is used to train the space function segmentation network and the test dataset to evaluate it.

The U-Net (Siddique et al., 2021) architecture is chosen to segment space function classes. It is a fully convolutional network consisting of an encoder-decoder with a skip connector from the encoder to the decoder. The encoder's task is to downsample and gradually reduce the spatial dimension for feature extraction, and the decoder's task is to restore image details and spatial dimension by up-sampling. We decided to use Training from Scratch (TfS U-Net) and Transfer Learning (TL U-Net) as two approaches for training the U-Net. Transfer learning (Tan et al., 2018) is useful when available training data are limited, thereby saving resources and improving the accuracy and training time of new models. The typical approach to perform transfer learning with a segmentation network is to use a pre-trained classification model as an encoder and build a decoder on top of it. The decoder is trained first, followed by the encoder, and finally, both are trained on a small data set. Transfer learning the space function segmentation model is done as follows:

1. **Select a pre-trained classification model:** VGG16 (Simonyan and Zisserman, 2014), which was trained on a large dataset called ImageNet (Deng et al., 2009), was chosen as the U-net encoder because it has fewer convolutional layers between max-pooling layers, which more closely matches the original U-net structure and therefore training is faster.
2. **Create a decoder:** A decoder is created on top of the encoder by adding three blocks, where each block is consists of skip connection, convolution, batch normalization, LeakyRelu (Xu et al., 2015), deconvolution, batch normalization, and LeakyRelu. Skip connections were used to connect the encoder layers to the decoder blocks. The output number of the decoder's last layer corresponds to the number of space function classes in the dataset.
3. **Train the model:** A strategy was developed to train the decoder and encoder. The strategy consists of three steps:
    1. Train the decoder with a learning rate of 0.001 and an epoch number of 100, while the pre-trained U2-Net encoder layers are frozen.
    2. Unfreeze all the encoder layers and train them with a learning rate of 0.0001 and an epoch number of 100 while the decoder layers are frozen.
    3. Unfreeze both the decoder and encoder and train them simultaneously with a learning rate of 0.00009 and an epoch number of 100.

To train U-net from scratch, we used the developed training strategy in reverse order, starting with the third step with a learning rate of 0.001, then the second step with a learning rate of 0.0001, and finally the first step with a learning rate of 0.0001. Since the training dataset is small and different from the dataset of the pre-trained model, in each training step, input and ground truth images are augmented by resizing to H+30 × W+30 as well as random rotation and flipping vertically and horizontally, followed by cropping to H × W. During training of the networks, an Adam optimizer (Zhang, 2018) is used to minimize the binary cross-entropy loss (Equation 2):

$$L =-\frac{1}{N}\sum_{i=1}^{N} y_i * log\,\hat{y}_i + \left(1 - y_i\right) * log\left(1 - \hat{y}_i\right) \qquad (2)$$

where y_i is the corresponding target value of the i-th scalar value in the network output ($\hat{y}_i$), and N is the number of scalar values in the model output.

7. Model validation

The outputs of the space function segmentation models for the test dataset are evaluated by Intersection over Union (IoU) and total error metrics (Long et al., 2015). IoU quantifies the percent overlap between ground truth and prediction output based on Equation 3:

$$IoU = \frac{TP}{TP + FP + FN} \qquad (3)$$

where TP is the number of true-positive pixels, FP is the number of false-positive pixels, and FN is the number of false-negative pixels. Total error computes the number of all incorrect pixels divided by the total number of pixels based on Equation 4:

$$Total\ Error = \frac{FN + FP}{FN+FP+TN+TP} \qquad (4)$$

where TN is the number of true-negative pixels. Evaluation results for the test dataset are given in Table 3. IoU values are computed only for classes that are present in a test layout's ground truth. For example, 'FamilyRoom' and 'WalkInCloset' are not present in any test layout, and therefore no IoU values are reported for these classes. Examples from the test dataset are shown in Figure 5.

Table 3: Intersection over Union (IoU) and Total Error for the test dataset. IoU is computed only for classes that are present in a test layout's ground truth.

Class	Number of test layouts with class	IoU		Total Error	
		TfS U-Net	TL U-Net	TfS U-Net	TL U-Net
DiningRoom	1	0.00	0.33	0.000	0.000
FamilyRoom	0	n/a	n/a	0.000	0.000
LivingRoom	14	0.35	0.94	0.057	0.005
Bedroom	13	0.00	0.90	0.044	0.004
MasterBedRoom	5	0.00	0.60	0.007	0.002
BoxRoom	1	0.00	0.89	0.001	0.000
HomeOffice	1	0.00	0.75	0.001	0.000
Shaft	12	0.00	0.05	0.001	0.001
StorageRoom	6	0.00	0.25	0.001	0.001
WalkInCloset	0	n/a	n/a	0.000	0.000
BathRoom	14	0.00	0.71	0.009	0.003
Toilet	9	0.00	0.19	0.001	0.001
Kitchen	8	0.00	0.82	0.007	0.001
LaundryRoom	4	0.00	0.09	0.001	0.001
Elevator	12	0.00	0.69	0.002	0.001
Stairway	11	0.00	0.82	0.009	0.001
Entrance	6	0.00	0.59	0.005	0.002
Hallway	1	0.00	0.53	0.000	0.000
MainHallway	3	0.00	0.70	0.002	0.001
InternalHallway	6	0.00	0.44	0.005	0.002
AccessBalcony	3	0.00	0.90	0.006	0.001
Loggia	3	0.00	0.90	0.002	0.000

8. Discussion

The results show that the TL U-Net model outperforms the TfS U-Net model for IoU and Total Error metrics for all space function classes. The TfS U-Net model only predicts the 'LivingRoom' class. It does not make predictions for the other classes (Figure 5d). The training dataset appears too small for training from scratch.

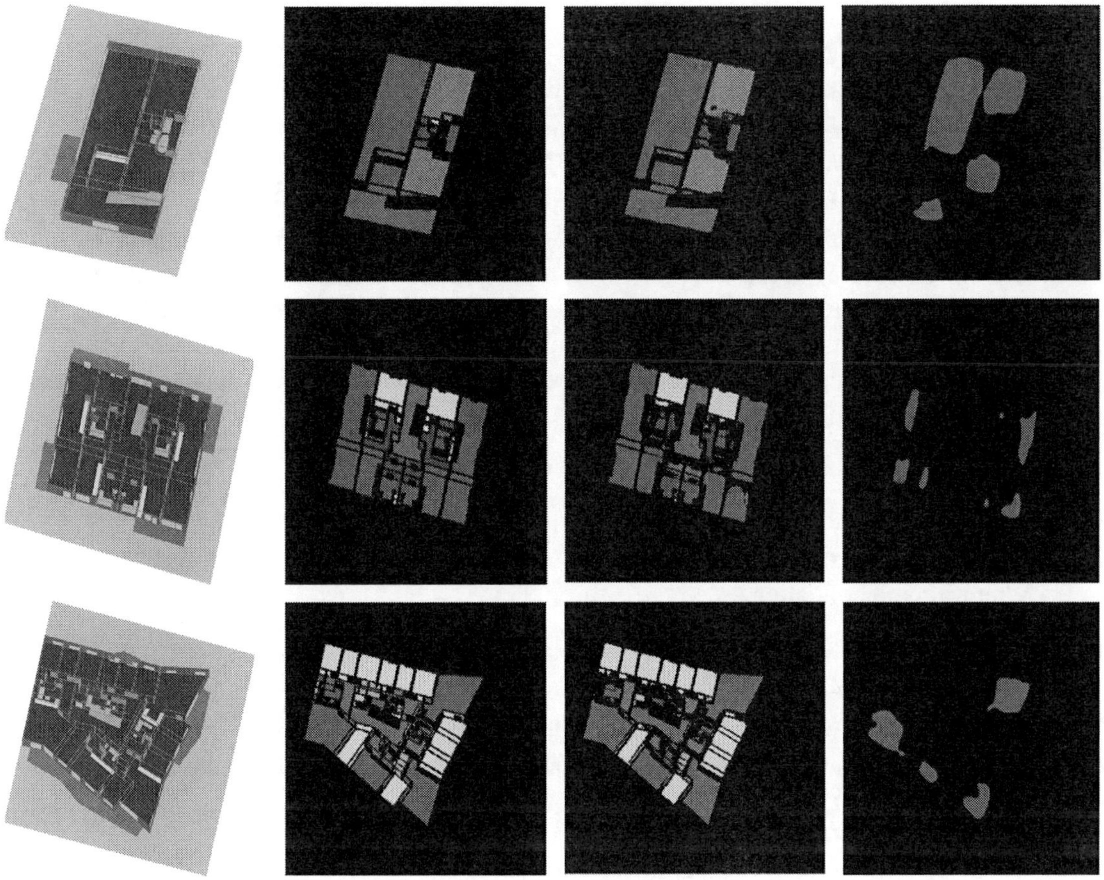

(a) Input layout (b) Ground truth (c) TL U-Net prediction (d) TfS U-Net prediction

Figure 5: Test dataset examples.

The TL U-Net model makes predictions for all classes, but significant performance differences exist. IoU values are highest (IoU>=0.9) for 'LivingRoom', 'Bedroom', and external spaces. They are the lowest (IoU<=0.25) for small service spaces. This result is qualitatively similar to an existing space function classification model (Wong, Sacks, and Yeung, 2022), even though the number of predicted classes and the DL method used differ from the TfS U-Net model. IoU values do not appear to depend on the frequency of classes in the SFS-A68 dataset. For example, only 5.1% of spaces in the SFS-A68 dataset are 'Loggia' or 'AccessBalcony' spaces (Table 1), but the TfS U-Net model is better at predicting these classes than 'Shaft' spaces, which make up 15.9% of spaces. As an explanation, 'Loggia' and 'AccessBalcony' spaces are larger, and they (or their context) may have more salient features than 'Shaft' spaces.

The SFS-A68 dataset currently has two main limitations. First, layout images are created by projection from a single, fixed viewpoint only. Instead, suppose the dataset included images taken from multiple viewpoints of the space layout models, similar to Edmunds et al. (2021). In that case, a space function segmentation network may more easily detect certain features, such as doors or windows. Second, as 78% of buildings are located in the German-speaking region of Europe, the dataset is not well balanced regarding geography, climate, culture, or building codes. We aim to address these limitations in future versions of the dataset.

9. Conclusion

We presented a dataset for space function segmentation in apartment buildings. We plan to extend the dataset to further increase the diversity of space layouts, particularly regarding location. Since SMS is a general-purpose layout modeling system, it could be used to create similar datasets for other building types, such as office buildings or schools.

We used the dataset to develop segmentation models based on transfer learning and training from scratch. In future work, we plan to compare the performance of different DL model architectures, including hyperparameter fine-tuning. Moreover, the influence of space elements or viewpoints on model performance needs to be investigated. Finally, we will explore how predictions of a space function segmentation network can be deployed in BIM analysis applications.

Acknowledgments

The authors gratefully acknowledge support by Grant Austrian Science Fund (FWF): I 5171-N, Mihael Barada, and participants in course '259.428-2021S Architectural Morphology' at TU Wien for data collection.

References

Autodesk (2021) Revit 2021 User's Guide. [Online] Available: https://knowledge.autodesk.com/support/revit-products [Accessed 11 April 2022]

Belsky, M., Sacks, R. and Brilakis, I. (2016). Semantic enrichment for building information modeling. Computer-Aided Civil and Infrastructure Engineering, 31, 261–274. https://doi.org/10.1111/mice.12128

Bloch, T. and Sacks, R. (2018) Comparing machine learning and rule-based inferencing for semantic enrichment of BIM models. Automation in Construction, 91, 256–272. https://doi.org/10.1016/j.autcon.2018.03.018

Bradski, G. (2000) The OpenCV library. Dr. Dobb's Journal: Software Tools for the Professional Programmer, 25, 120–123.

CSI (2010) OmniClass Construction Classification System (OCCS), Table 13: Spaces by Function. [Online] Available: https://www.csiresources.org/standards/omniclass [Accessed 11 April 2022]

De las Heras, L. S.-P., Ahmed, S., Liwicki, M., Valveny, E. and Sanchez, G. (2014) Statistical segmentation and structural recognition for floor plan interpretation. International Journal on Document Analysis and Recognition (IJDAR), 17, 221–237. https://doi.org/10.1007/s10032-013-0215-2

Deng, J., Dong, W., Socher, R., Li, L.J., Li, K. and Fei-Fei, L. (2009) Imagenet: A large-scale hierarchical image database. In 2009 IEEE Conference on Computer Vision and Pattern Recognition, 248-255. https://doi.org/10.1109/CVPR.2009.5206848

Eisler, S. and Meyer, J. (2020) Visual Analytics and Human Involvement in Machine Learning. arXiv preprint arXiv:2005.06057. https://doi.org/10.48550/arXiv.2005.06057

Emunds, C., Pauen, N., Richter, V., Frisch, J. and Van Treeck, C. (2021) IFCNet: A Benchmark Dataset for IFC Entity Classification. arXiv preprint arXiv:2106.09712. https://doi.org/10.48550/arXiv.2106.09712

Heckmann, O. and Schneider, F. (2011) Grundrissatlas Wohnungsbau, Birkhäuser.

Huang, L., Qin, J., Zhou, Y., Zhu, F., Liu, L. and Shao, L. (2020) Normalization techniques in training DNNs: Methodology, analysis and application. arXiv preprint arXiv:2009.12836. https://doi.org/10.48550/arXiv.2009.12836

Lai, H., Deng, X. and Chang, T.-Y. P. (2019) BIM-based platform for collaborative building design and project management. Journal of Computing in Civil Engineering, 33, 05019001. https://doi.org/10.1061/(ASCE)CP.1943-5487.0000830

Leonhardt, M., Pauen, N., Kirnats, L., Joost, J. N., Frisch, J. and Van Treeck, C. (2020) Implementierung von KI-basierten Referenzprozessen für die computergestützte Objekterkennung im Gebäude. BauSIM, September, 599–606. https://doi.org/10.18154/RWTH-2020-10846

Long, J., Shelhamer, E. and Darrell, T. (2015) Fully convolutional networks for semantic segmentation. In Proceedings of the IEEE Conference on Computer Vision and Pattern Recognition, 3431-3440. https://doi.org/10.1109/CVPR.2015.7298965

Ma, J. W., Czerniawski, T., and Leite, F. (2020) Semantic segmentation of point clouds of building interiors with deep learning: Augmenting training datasets with synthetic BIM-based point clouds. Automation in Construction, 113, 103144. https://doi.org/10.1016/j.autcon.2020.103144

Minaee, S., Boykov, Y.Y., Porikli, F., Plaza, A.J., Kehtarnavaz, N. and Terzopoulos, D. (2021) Image segmentation using deep learning: A survey. IEEE Transactions on Pattern Analysis and Machine Intelligence. https://doi.org/10.1109/TPAMI.2021.3059968

NBS (2020) UniClass, Table SL - Spaces/ locations. [Online] Available: https://www.thenbs.com/-/media/uk/files/xls/uniclass/2020-10/uniclass2015_sl_v1_18.xlsx?la=en [Accessed 11 April 2022]

Plataforma Networks, (2022) ArchDaily. [Online] Available: https://www.archdaily.com [Accessed 11 April 2022]

Siddique, N., Paheding, S., Elkin, C. P. and Devabhaktuni, V. (2021) U-net and its variants for medical image segmentation: A review of theory and applications. IEEE Access. https://doi.org/10.1109/ACCESS.2021.3086020

Simonyan, K. and Zisserman, A. (2014) Very deep convolutional networks for large-scale image recognition. arXiv preprint arXiv:1409.1556. https://doi.org/10.48550/arXiv.1409.1556

Suter, G. (2022) Modeling multiple space views for schematic building design using space ontologies and layout transformation operations. Automation in Construction, 134, 104041. https://doi.org/10.1016/j.autcon.2021.104041

Tan, C., Sun, F., Kong, T., Zhang, W., Yang, C. and Liu, C. (2018) A survey on deep transfer learning. International Conference on Artificial Neural Networks. 270–279. https://doi.org/10.48550/arXiv.1808.01974

ImageMagick Studio (2021) ImageMagick. [Online] Available: https://imagemagick.org/ [Accessed 11 April 2022]

W3C (2018) Scalable Vector Graphics (SVG) 2 Candidate Recommendation. [Online] Available: https://www.w3.org/TR/SVG2/ [Accessed 11 April 2022]

Wang, Z., Sacks, R. and Yeung, T., (2022) Exploring graph neural networks for semantic enrichment: Room type classification. Automation in Construction, 134, 104039. https://doi.org/10.1016/j.autcon.2021.104039

Xu, B., Wang, N., Chen, T. and LI, M. (2015) Empirical evaluation of rectified activations in convolutional network. arXiv preprint arXiv:1505.00853. https://doi.org/10.48550/arXiv.1505.00853

Ziaee, A., Suter, G. and Barada, M. (2022) SFS-A68: a dataset for the segmentation of space functions in apartment buildings. [Online] Available: https://doi.org/10.5281/zenodo.6426871 [Accessed 11 April 2022]

Zhang, Z. (2018) Improved Adam optimizer for deep neural networks. IEEE/ACM 26th International Symposium on Quality of Service (IWQoS), 2018. IEEE, 1-2. https://doi.org/10.1109/IWQoS.2018.8624183

A Multi-Scenario Crowd Data Synthesis Based On Building Information Modeling

Huang H.[1], Gao G.[1,2], Ke Z.[1], Peng C.[1], Gu M. [1,2]
[1]School of Software, Tsinghua University, Beijing, China, [2]Beijing National Research Center for Information Science and Technology(BNRist), Tsinghua University, Beijing, China
gaoge@tsinghua.edu.cn

Abstract. Deep learning methods have proven to be effective in the field of crowd analysis recently. Nonetheless, the performance of deep learning models is affected by the inadequacy of training datasets. Because of policy implications and privacy restrictions, crowd data is commonly difficult to access. In order to overcome the difficulty of insufficient dataset, the previous work used to synthesize labelled crowd data in outdoor scenes and virtual games. However, these methods perform data synthesis with limited environmental information and inflexible crowd rules, usually in unauthentic environment. In this paper, a tool for synthesizing crowd data in BIM models with multiple scenes is proposed. This tool can make full use of the comprehensive information of real-world buildings, and conduct crowd simulations by setting behavior rules. The synthesized dataset is used for data augmentation for crowd analysis problems and the experimental results clearly confirm the effectiveness of the tool.

1. Introduction

In recent years, deep learning has become a technology area of great interest. A large number of models based on deep learning algorithms have emerged in the field of computer vision. These deep learning models help solve some crowd analysis problems that are difficult for traditional methods, including crowd detection (Liu et al.,2019), trajectory prediction (Huang et al.,2019), pose estimation (Kocabas et al.,2019), crowd counting (Liu et al.,2019) and so on. However, the efficient training of deep learning models relies on a large amount of labeled data. The production of datasets requires high-quality raw data and accurate labeling information, which is time-consuming and laborious. Data is also increasingly difficult to access because of policy implications and privacy restrictions. Currently, the performance of models in crowd trajectory prediction, crowd counting and other tasks is insufficient partly due to the shortage of training datasets. In order to improve the performance of crowd analysis models, researchers tried to develop some alternative methods to acquire datasets. Recently, synthetic datasets are widely used in deep learning field to improve model performance.

For crowd data synthesis, some researchers have developed data collectors and annotators to generate large-scale crowd data from games. And other researchers consider using graphics simulators to generate crowd data in real scenes. Some datasets (Richter et al.,2016; Richter et al.,2017; Wang et al.,2019) collect virtual scenes through GTA5 (a computer game) and then automate the annotation. Specifically, Richter et al(2016) reconstructs the communication between the game and the graphics hardware and successfully completes semantic annotation of the game data while the game code is not available. Richter et al(2017) proposes a new middleware construct that receives render commands from the game. Then, the data obtained by the middleware is annotated by the system in real time, and finally the usable dataset is generated. Wang et al(2019) develops a data collector and annotator that could generate synthetic labeled crowd scenes. Moreover, the method (Wang et al.,2019) is not limited by the characteristics of GTA5 (population limitation) through a split-and-splice strategy, which enables it to produce complex crowded scenarios. A mixed reality dataset was proposed by Cheung et al(2018), which combined background images of the real world with synthetic

https://doi.org/10.7146/aul.455.c223

pedestrians for pedestrian detection. Chai et al(2020) uses neural network model to successfully generate a continuous crowd video with diverse crowd behaviors. A crowd data synthesis tool based on real image scene is proposed by Khadka et al(2020). Based on graphics tools, the real image scenes can be used to generate data sets for a variety of computer vision-related problems. The results of quantitative crowd analysis confirm the success of using synthetic data to train and test networks.

However, these datasets focus on graphical generation and ignore the impact of the environment and crowd movement rules. In previous works, crowd data is generated in empty outdoor scenes or in virtual games, wherefore the source of pedestrian environmental information is either the virtual world, or a few images with limited information. Moreover, the rules of crowd behavior are not static, but change according to environmental information and crowd status. Since the game code is not available, the crowd movement rules are hard-coded and cannot be changed according to the environment. In addition, due to the incomplete information, the previous works only synthesize the crowd from a single and partial perspective, which leads to poor generality and reusability.

In this paper, therefore, a tool for generating crowd data in real buildings with multiple scenes is proposed. By utilizing real world building information models (Eastman et al.,2008) rich in geometric and semantic information, our tool bridges the gap between the real world and the virtual environment. Since there are industrial standards for Building Information Modeling software, we can obtain a large amount of realistic data in an efficient way, so as to greatly increase the credibility of the generated data. Besides, Multi-scenario crowd simulation allows crowd behavior rules to be set by users. The simulation results can be combined with building information models to render realistic crowd data and provide a credible ground reality and annotation. In addition, datasets synthesized with our tools has complete crowd behavior data and environmental information and can be directly used for various complex computer vision tasks, such as trajectory prediction, crowd counting, and other indoor tasks.

To the best of our knowledge, our work is the first to generate indoor crowd data on the basis of real-world buildings. Several key contributions of our work are:

• The novel tool extracts information from industry-standard realistic building models that can be obtained in bulk and with authenticity.

• According to the simulation results, the tool can use graphical rendering to synthesize datasets of various crowd analysis problems, which are automatically labeled.

• The data generated by the tool can improve the results of existing crowd analysis tasks, and related new crowd analysis problems can also be proposed.

2. Methodology

In this section, the proposed tool algorithm flow and implementation method are described. BIM model information is firstly extracted, followed by the completion of multi-agent population simulation. Then, the indoor crowd data is synthesized and stored. Figure 1 shows the architecture of the proposed tool.

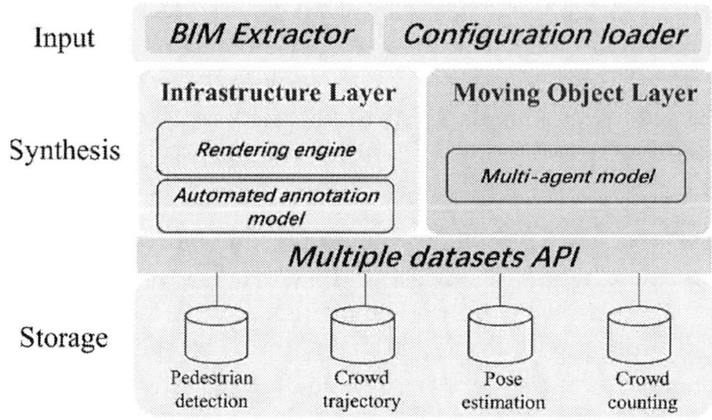

Figure 1: System architecture

2.1 Information extraction from BIM models

Building information modelling is the 3D CAD modelling technology for various buildings widely used in Architecture, Engineering, and Construction (AEC) (Eastman et al.,2008) industries. It stores real-world buildings in digital form, including geometric information and semantic information. The Industry Foundation Classes (IFC) data format is the internationally accepted specification for BIM, and thus used as the building model format in this study.

We mainly extract the geometric information of the building and the semantic information of each component (such as doors, walls, rooms and spaces) from the BIM model to form our navigation map, as shown in Figure 2. The geometric information helps us to obtain the boundaries of spaces and products in buildings. And the semantic information can help us get the passability and risk coefficient of different areas. We specifically discuss BIM information extraction process as follows.

Geometric information. As a part of a navigational map, any building component with a shape can be a pedestrian-accessible space (e.g., stair) or a pedestrian-inaccessible space (e.g., wall). Through the geometry information provided in BIM, we can calculate the bounding box of the 3d building components and place them in local placement.

Semantic information. In traditional maps, semantic information is generally ignored. However, in the process of crowd simulation, the state of component (e.g., locked door) or space (e.g., private room) will have a great influence on the simulation results. And some of the building components may affect the mobility of people.

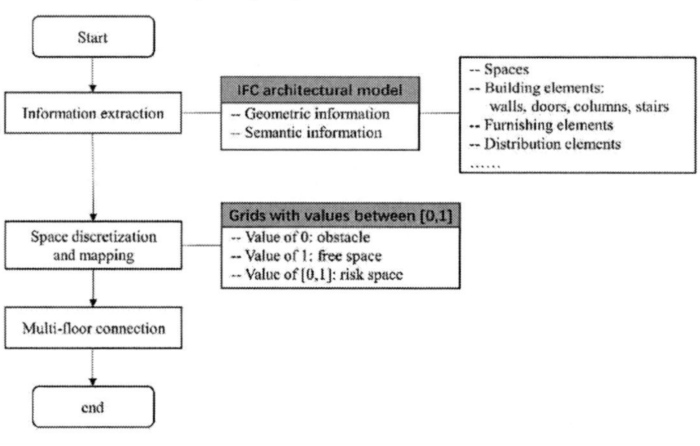

Figure 2: General data flow for BIM extraction

Once BIM information extraction is completed, the building indoor map with rich semantic information is constructed. Figure 3 shows the overall appearance of a BIM model and Figure 4 shows the internal perspective of this BIM model.

Figure 3: The facade of a BIM model

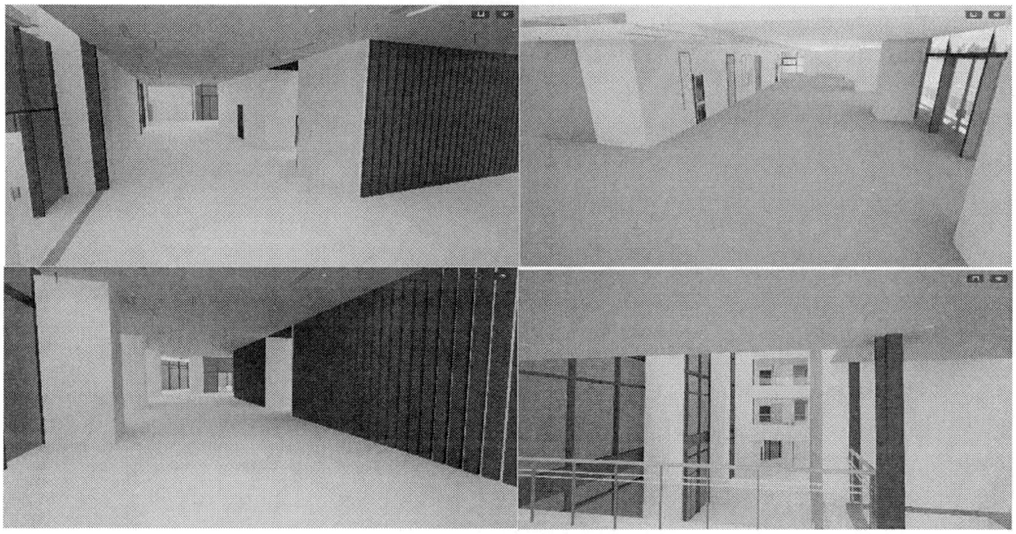

Figure 4: The internal perspectives of a BIM model

2.2 Multi-scenario crowd simulation

Multi-agent methods (Sharma et al.,2018) are often used to simulate the complex behavior of various groups. The rules of multi-agents can be defined by users, which is proven to be reliable in crowd simulation. In this section, we use the multi-agent model to simulate individuals with independent consciousness. Moreover, we set up different multi-agent targets to meet the needs of different scenarios. In crowd simulation, human attributes are assigned to the agent, including age, moving speed, occupied space and random fall factors. In addition, different behavior rules are designed according to different scenes, so that agents can properly interact with other agents and the environment. Figure 5 shows the flow of multi-agent simulation process.

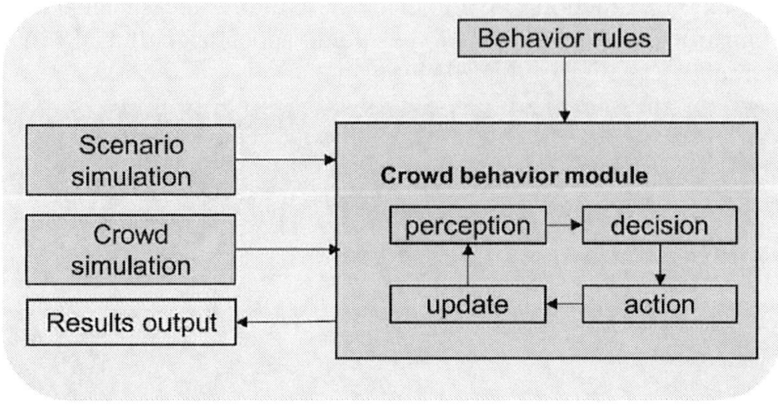

Figure 5: Multi-agent simulation process

For this simulation algorithm, some configuration parameters such as population distribution, age ratio and simulation scenarios are inputted by users. After the configuration file is set up, the tool could perform crowd simulation in normal and emergency situations. The scenario of the normal situation is to generate the crowd data in the daily operation process of the building. It has no specific purpose and is suitable for general computer vision tasks. The scenario of the emergency situation is to generate the crowd data in the condition of a critical event.

After completing the simulation, the tool will get a series of continuous agent coordinates and state results. The result of an agent is represented by a quad vector:

$$a = \{(X^t, Y^t, Z^t, S^t | t \in T)\} \tag{1}$$

where (X^t, Y^t, Z^t, S^t) is the agent's position and current state at time t. In this quad, X^t and Y^t are plane coordinates, expressed in absolute coordinates. Since the elevation of the agent in the building is consistent with that of the floor on which the agent is located, the height coordinate Z^t directly adopts the elevation of the floor. S^t is the current state of the agent, which is very important for subsequent data synthesis. Table 1 lists all possible states of the agent.

Table 1: The state category of the agent.

S	State of the agent
0	Resting
1	Walking
2	Falling
3	Running
4	Talking

The simulation results of all the agents are denoted by

$$A = \{a_i | i = 1,2, \dots, N\} \tag{2}$$

2.3 Data generation

Unlike generating datasets from game data or simple pictures, environment information and crowd information are fully accessible and computable in our tool. Comprehensive information makes it possible to annotate datasets accurately and automatically.

Specifically, the simulation results will be rendered in BIM model scenes as crowd information. Whereafter, the tool will record rendering results from multiple indoor perspectives to produce video or images. According to different dataset requirements, the tool extracts, combines and calculates the corresponding information from the crowd simulation results, and automatically complete the annotation of the dataset. The process of data generation is shown in Figure 6.

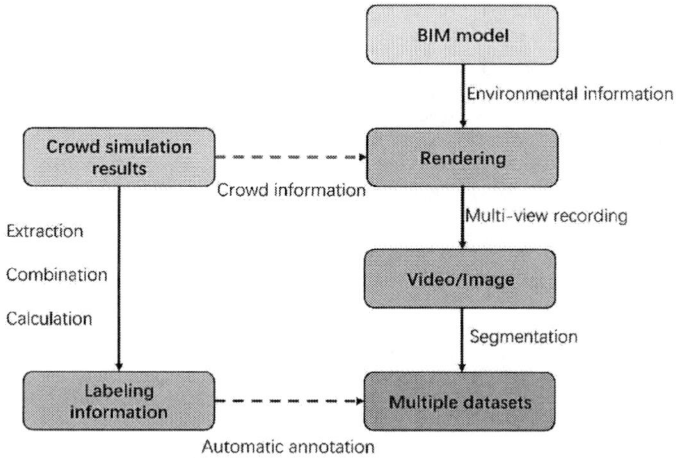

Figure 6: The process of data generation

This tool builds multiple datasets for the following four tasks: 1) pedestrian detection, 2) trajectory prediction, 3) pose estimation, and 4) crowd counting.

Pedestrian detection. Crowd detection needs to collect datasets with human body bounding box information. The tool calculates the bounding box at different times according to the size and state of the agent from the simulation results, and then automatically labels the bounding box of the coordinate where the agent is located.

Trajectory prediction. Trajectory prediction requires pedestrian trajectory data within a period of time, which is expressed as:

$$traj = \{(X^t, Y^t | t \in T)\} \tag{3}$$

As we can see, the crowd simulation result is almost the same as the trajectory dataset. In the tool, the trajectory of the crowd can be easily obtained by extracting the trails of moving people in the field of view.

Pose estimation. In the pose estimation task, the joint positions of the human body need to be used. Since the crowd is rendered in 3D by the graphics renderer, the tool can directly get the joint positions of the crowd from graphical engine. Therefore, the acquired joint sites can be labeled into the video or images.

Crowd counting. The head coordinates of the crowd can be obtained from the rendering results, and the tool will automatically label the crowd in the field of view to get a crowd counting datasets.

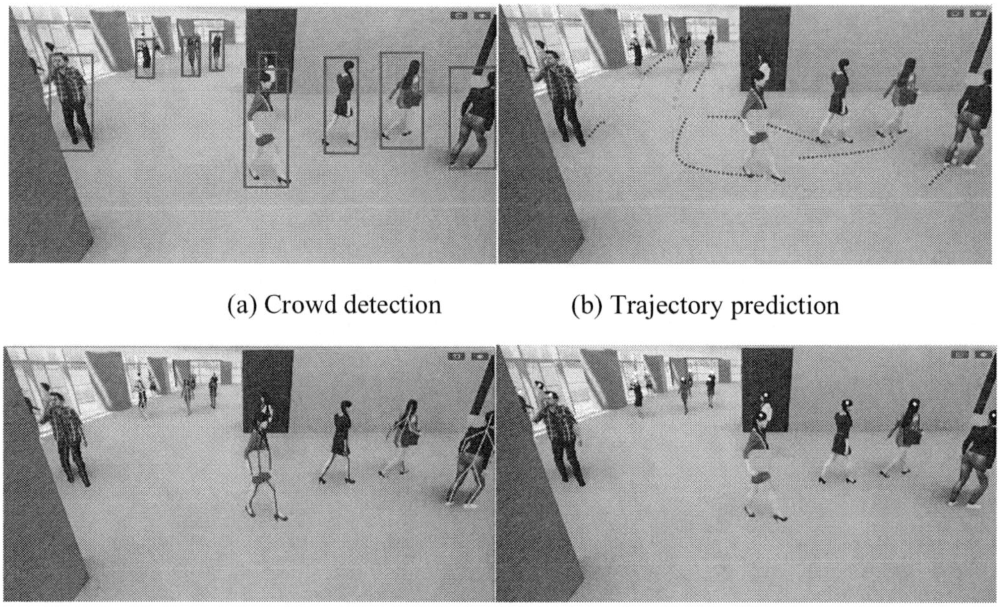

(a) Crowd detection (b) Trajectory prediction

(c) Pose estimation (d) Crowd counting

Figure 7: Datasets generated by our tool

3. Evaluation

Trajectory prediction is a popular task in crowd analysis. In this section, we conducted experiments on two relevant datasets: ETH (Pellegrini et al.,2010) and UCY (Lerner et al.,2007). These datasets contain different types of scenes: Zara1, Zara2, Univ, Eth, and Hotel. We chose Social-BiGAT (Kosaraju et al.,2019) and Sophie (Sadeghian et al.,2019) as the experimental network architectures to confirm the improvement on trajectory prediction with our synthetic data. Both networks use the combination of scene information and social information for trajectory prediction.

In the model test phase, the models observe the crowd trajectory in the past 3.2 seconds, and then predict the trajectory in the next 4.8 seconds. Two metrics will be used to evaluate the performance of the experiment: average displacement error (ADE) (Pellegrini et al.,2009), and final displacement error (FDE) (Alahi et al.,2016). Both are used to evaluate the average distance between the true trajectory and the predicted result.

In order to prove the effectiveness of synthetic data, we pre-trained the models with synthetic data, and compared with the original performance. The results of the experiments are shown in Table 2.

As expected we see that both the networks trained with synthetic data outperform those trained without synthetic data. It is proved that our synthetic data can improve the performance of crowd trajectory prediction, regardless of the network structure.

Table 2: ADE/FDE for Social-BiGAT and Sophie, with and without synthetic data (*lower values are better)

Dataset	Social-BiGAT		Sophie	
	(without)	(with)	(without)	(with)
ETH	0.69/1.29	**0.65/1.19**	0.70/1.43	**0.66/1.37**
HOTEL	0.49/1.01	**0.33/0.98**	0.76/1.67	**0.63/1.42**
UNIV	0.55/1.32	**0.51/1.30**	0.54/1.24	**0.47/1.11**
ZARA1	0.30/0.62	**0.25/0.55**	0.30/0.63	**0.24/0.47**
ZARA2	0.36/0.75	0.38/0.81	0.38/0.78	**0.31/0.67**
AVG	0.48/1.00	**0.42/0.96**	0.54/1.15	**0.46/1.01**

4. Conclusion

In this paper, we have proposed a novel tool to synthesize crowd data in real buildings. Our tool leverages geometric and semantic information of BIM models, while enabling crowd simulations, using multi-agent method. The tool renders and records the crowd simulation results in the BIM model. To synthesize multiple datasets for different tasks, the corresponding information is extracted from the crowd simulation results to complete automatic annotation of the dataset. We showed that the synthetic datasets could help improve the results of crowd-related tasks and provide a research foundation for future indoor crowd-related tasks.

Our tool provides a new and efficient way to synthesize data. But it relies on artificial rules for crowd behavior, which requires the expertise of its users. In the future, we will consider data-driven methods to automatically obtain crowd action rules in different scenarios and lower the threshold for using tools.

5. Acknowledgements

This work was supported by the 2019 MIIT Industrial Internet Innovation and Development Project "BIM Software Industry Standardization and Public Service Platform".

References

Liu, S., Huang, D., and Wang, Y. (2019). Adaptive nms: Refining pedestrian detection in a crowd. In Proceedings of the IEEE/CVF conference on computer vision and pattern recognition., pp. 6459-6468.

Huang, Y., Bi, H., Li, Z., Mao, T., and Wang, Z. (2019). Stgat: Modeling spatial-temporal interactions for human trajectory prediction. In Proceedings of the IEEE/CVF international conference on computer vision., pp. 6272-6281.

Kocabas, M., Karagoz, S., and Akbas, E. (2018). Multiposenet: Fast multi-person pose estimation using pose residual network. In Proceedings of the European conference on computer vision., pp. 417-433.

Liu, W., Salzmann, M., and Fua, P. (2019). Context-aware crowd counting. In Proceedings of the IEEE/CVF Conference on Computer Vision and Pattern Recognition., pp. 5099-5108.

Richter, S. R., Vineet, V., Roth, S., and Koltun, V. (2016, October). Playing for data: Ground truth from computer games. In European conference on computer vision., pp. 102-118.

Richter, S. R., Hayder, Z., and Koltun, V. (2017). Playing for benchmarks. In Proceedings of the IEEE International Conference on Computer Vision., pp. 2213-2222.

Wang, Q., Gao, J., Lin, W., and Yuan, Y. (2019). Learning from synthetic data for crowd counting in the wild. In Proceedings of the IEEE/CVF Conference on computer vision and pattern recognition., pp. 8198-8207.

Cheung, E., Wong, A., Bera, A., and Manocha, D. (2018, April). MixedPeds: pedestrian detection in unannotated videos using synthetically generated human-agents for training. In Proceedings of the AAAI Conference on Artificial Intelligence, 32.

Chai, L., Liu, Y., Liu, W., Han, G., and He, S. (2020). CrowdGAN: Identity-free Interactive Crowd Video Generation and Beyond. IEEE Transactions on Pattern Analysis and Machine Intelligence, 01, pp.1-1.

Khadka, A., Remagnino, P., and Argyriou, V. (2020, May). Synthetic crowd and pedestrian generator for deep learning problems. In ICASSP 2020-2020 IEEE International Conference on Acoustics, Speech and Signal Processing (ICASSP)., pp. 4052-4056.

Eastman, C., Teicholz, P., Sacks, R., Liston, K., and Handbook, B. I. M. (2008). A Guide to Building Information Modeling for Owners, Managers, Architects, Engineers, Contractors, and Fabricators

BuildingSMART Industry Foundation Classes (IFC). http://www.buildingsmart-tech.org/specifications/ifc-overview/. Accessed 30 Sept 2018

Sharma, S., Ogunlana, K., Scribner, D., and Grynovicki, J. (2018). Modeling human behavior during emergency evacuation using intelligent agents: A multi-agent simulation approach. Information Systems Frontiers, 20(4), pp. 741-757.

Pellegrini, S., Ess, A., and Gool, L. V. (2010, September). Improving data association by joint modeling of pedestrian trajectories and groupings. In European conference on computer vision., pp. 452-465.

Lerner, A., Chrysanthou, Y., and Lischinski, D. (2007, September). Crowds by example. In Computer graphics forum, 26, 3, pp. 655-664.

Kosaraju, V., Sadeghian, A., Martín-Martín, R., Reid, I., Rezatofighi, H., and Savarese, S. (2019). Social-bigat: Multimodal trajectory forecasting using bicycle-gan and graph attention networks. Advances in Neural Information Processing Systems, 32.

Sadeghian, A., Kosaraju, V., Sadeghian, A., Hirose, N., Rezatofighi, H., and Savarese, S. (2019). Sophie: An attentive gan for predicting paths compliant to social and physical constraints. In Proceedings of the IEEE/CVF Conference on Computer Vision and Pattern Recognition., pp. 1349-1358.

Pellegrini, S., Ess, A., Schindler, K., and Van Gool, L. (2009, September). You'll never walk alone: Modeling social behavior for multi-target tracking. In 2009 IEEE 12th international conference on computer vision., pp. 261-268.

Alahi, A., Goel, K., Ramanathan, V., Robicquet, A., Fei-Fei, L., and Savarese, S. (2016). Social lstm: Human trajectory prediction in crowded spaces. In Proceedings of the IEEE conference on computer vision and pattern recognition., pp. 961-971.

New ways of data governance for construction? Decentralized Data Marketplaces as Web3 concept just around the corner.

Bucher D. F., Hall D. M.
ETH Zurich, Switzerland
bucher@ibi.baug.ethz.ch

Abstract. In the upcoming era of distributed technological integration known as Web3, the built environment will need to adapt. Solving the most significant social, environmental and economic challenges will likely require new approaches to data sharing and efficient data management. This will need to occur within organizations, across software tools, and between partners. However, today's approach of data fragmentation and a scattered system of data islands prevent efficient data usage in the construction industry. The question that now arises is whether the decentralized marketplace approach has the potential to make construction data sets more uniform, efficient, and usable for all stakeholders through distributed technological integration. Therefore, this paper's contribution is to provide a conceptual starting point and possible research stream approach towards this question. Doing so by outlining current data management challenges and discussing them in comparison with already existing web3 approaches in research and industry.

1. Introduction

In today's digital economy, data is considered as one of the most important assets for businesses and society in general. New technological developments, such as mobile computing, the Internet of Things (IoT) and many more, lead to a continuous increase of applications, creating enormous potential added value for companies by generating information. They represent the foundation of a data-driven economy, the so-called data economy, on whose foundation new types of digital services and even new business models are emerging (Farboodi and Veldkamp, 2021). More and more industries are recognizing the benefits of data and its aggregation. Unfortunately, the Architecture, Engineering, and Construction (AEC) industry tends not to be one of them (Yan *et al.*, 2020).

To successfully manage a construction project's planning, construction, and operation stages, intensive and continuous communication is necessary among its stakeholders (Homayouni *et al.*, 2010). Throughout the life cycle of a project, these ongoing communications are often accompanied by the generation of large amounts of data in various formats and characteristics. The utilized data are no longer limited to governed database records but include data in non-traditional standard formats. Resulting in files containing data in structured, semi-structured, or unstructured formats whose complexity makes data processing and usability increasingly challenging.

In addition, the collaboration process is characterized by fragmentation, non-standardized collaboration, and actors and skills (Hall *et al.*, 2018). As a result, while the process of data handover between phases and the effective transfer of data is of significant value, it presents substantial challenges to industry practitioners. The critical issue in the field has been, and remains, how to achieve interoperability among the multiple models and multiple tools used throughout the different phases of a project (Poirier *et al.*, 2014).

To date, the majority of research on AEC data management, interoperability, and exchange operates with an underlying assumption that the data exchange and data flow occurs within a centralized system (centralized databases & control monopoly of platforms). However, the current growth of decentralized web3 approaches to data management and exchange provides

https://doi.org/10.7146/aul.455.c224

an opportunity to understand how a decentralized data marketplace approach might evolve in construction. To further explore this concept, this paper conducts a comparative review in order to address the following questions:

- What are the data management approaches and applications of recent years in construction?
- How has there already been an influence of web3 concepts of the current state of data management practices in construction?
- What are decentralized data marketplaces, how have they been applied in other industries, and how do they offer a novel approach to solving current barriers in construction?
- How do decentralized data marketplaces compare to past centralized data management strategies?

2. Data Management Challenges in Construction

Today, the industry faces a major challenge to improve the efficiency and effectiveness of the integrated design and construction process (Lee *et al.*, 2005). In particular, the industry today is at a point where data and information must permeate a multi-layered and complex system in a machine-readable manner. This can be considered from three perspectives.

Figure 1: Perspectives on Data Management Challenges

2.1 Lifecycle Management of Data

Projects in the construction industry are characterized by many stakeholders from different companies and disciplines involved across different life cycle stages (Wu and Zhang, 2019). Therefore, continuous and intensive data generation and document exchange are essential for successfully handing over information between phases. As the project progresses, the volume of data continues to increase. Empirical data shows that individual file sizes currently range from megabytes to gigabytes, with a clear trend toward increasing file sizes.

Despite the long life cycle of decades of buildings, the actual life cycle of project data is short, concentrated in the design and construction phases (Huang *et al.*, 2021). Data is often constantly revised until the completion of a construction process, then delivered, archived, and occasionally accessed thereafter for building operations or facility management. Over time, they transition from an active to an inactive state. Therefore, it would be beneficial for companies and organizations to bring all project data under their control. The data becomes a real asset that can be used throughout the building lifecycle, especially for building operations and maintenance.

2.2 Data Silos and Islands of Automation

Driven by digital transformation, the industry increasingly uses Building Information Modeling (BIM), integrative methodologies, and corresponding digital tools (Klinc and Turk, 2019). The total amount of data in a construction project is often enormous, located in encapsulated systems with different formats and forming so-called silos of information (Corry *et al.*, 2014). Scholars and practitioners argue that data integration and its democratizing are the key factors for improving data management in construction.

With its numerous specialist disciplines and interdisciplinary dependencies, the construction industry resulted in an ecosystem of variety of software tools. These tools are tailored for different tasks and, in most cases, work well independently in their application domain. However, the challenge repeatedly referred to is that this ecosystem forms a landscape of islands of automation (Hannus *et al.*, 1997). Applications control their specific data without inherently sharing them with others. Therefore, the collaboration between architects, engineers, and contractors is still constrained by the heterogeneity of application models in general and the often lack of defined collaboration processes. There is hardly any possibility to use information from architectural design and the ongoing construction process to analyze the quality of construction works (Scherer and Schapke, 2011).

2.3 Information Loss and Interoperability

Interoperability is a recognized paradigm for connecting heterogeneous data systems into synergistic entities that enable more efficient use of information resources. If based on open standards, whether for file-based or server-based data exchange, it has many theoretical benefits.

Existing technologies can connect data in a federated environment, making it increasingly easy for stakeholders to access the information they need. However, the quality of the available information is also a decisive factor in determining its usefulness. The information exchange still heavily relies on the handover of files, for example, the 2D drawings and 3D models of a project. Such files are not machine-readable inherently, which means the information cannot be comprehensively interpreted and processed by computers. The information consistency can only be checked manually.

Moreover, the changes across disciplines and phases are time-consuming and costly. Errors are hard to detect and cause more significant problems in the further phases of the project. This inconsistency of information exchange is known as information loss. It is estimated that disorganized and poorly managed information, or a lack of linkage between documents and information, is often one of the leading causes of construction time delays.

Two commonly reported interdependent hurdles for achieving the interoperability of integrated building information within the construction industry have been the fragmented industry actor landscape and the heterogeneous adoption of IT among these actors (Laakso *et al.*, 2012). In addition, Abanda (2015) defined three types of interoperability barriers; conceptual, technological, and organizational.

2.4 Current Data Management Approaches in Construction

The AEC industry is solving the outlined challenges above by accelerating its digital progress rather on an application-specific level, i.e., with the advent and application of various digital technologies such as Building Information Modeling (BIM) or pertinent platforms. Therefore, several efforts have been made to promote BIM creation, sharing, integration, collaboration, and knowledge management throughout the lifecycle of a project. Two different types of methods for interoperability and collaboration based on BIM have been introduced.

The first approach is methods based on ontologies and semantic web concepts. Specific domain ontologies improve collaboration and decision-making by representing problem-solving domains for different disciplines. The second approach is based on the Industry Foundation Classes (IFC) format. IFC enables different participants, provided with heterogenic systems and applications, to simplify their exchange of information and enhance collaboration (Ismail *et al.*, 2017).

On a more technological level, cloud computing and platformization offer new opportunities for data management in the AEC industry. This can enable for example, a cloud-based common data environment (CDE). A CDE is a collaborative and integrative data platform solution for construction stakeholders that can serve individual projects while connecting enterprise-level processes. CDE applications begin with the planning phase but can act as the single source of data further along the lifecycle of an asset and for different purposes (Valra *et al.*, 2021). For example, Honic (2019) proposed how a CDE could digitally map an object with material passports to capture and store data for building materials and products. In a broader perspective, Bucher and Hall (2020) proposed that using linked data and ontologies can enable a three-dimensional ecosystem consisting of CDE's and digital mock-up platforms (e.g., digital twins).

Despite their potential, the widescale adoption of BIM and related concepts has been delayed as companies struggle with the lack of full internal and external data integration (Ullah *et al.*, 2019). Although most agree that new technologies such as BIM and CDEs are important, implementation still suffers from fragmented systematic data integration and weakening interoperability. Hence, there is a need for a common data foundation that can be used efficiently in a vendor-neutral way. In addition, there is a lack of a technological solution that democratizes access to data in a wide range of areas.

3. Web3 in the Construction Industry

3.1 Overview of Web3

Using the idea of a more autonomous, intelligent, and open internet, the inventor of the World Wide Web, Tim Berners-Lee, coined the term for today's web 3.0 as the semantic web (Berners-Lee and Hendler, 2001). This emerging concept offers a way to improve current data organization and management methodologies. The underlying principle is to categorize and store information in such a way that a system can learn what a particular piece of data means. In other words, data is being organized in such a way that programs are capable of understanding it in the same way a human would, enabling them to generate and share better content. Furthermore, the semantic web propagates an increased decentralization of information, focusing on consistency and accessibility (Staab and Stuckenschmidt, 2006).

Today, the content of the Web is designed to be consumed and interpreted by humans. However, most of this content cannot be automatically combined, aggregated, and condensed into new statements. Automatic processing by computers requires additional forms of data, called metadata, or data about data. Web3 is therefore understood by making web content readable by machines. To do this, new data distribution protocols are being developed that actively work together to form a fundamental network that enables artificial intelligence. A duality is thus emerging so that the web is no longer just a means to an end but also a network for non-human communication and automated data exchange.

Data within web 3.0 will be connected in a decentralized manner. This represents an evolution from the current generation of the Internet (web 2.0), where data is mainly stored in centralized repositories and encapsulated in documents (Alabdulwahhab, 2018). Representing a similar situation as in the construction industry. While earlier approaches to automatically linking data from different sources required the laborious creation of global metadata systems, newer approaches proclaim a data format that makes it easier to link data. The concept of directly connected data is termed *Linked Data*. In the past, expensive data integration has been a stumbling block in data publishing. In fact, to integrate two data sources, both semantics and syntax must be aligned. *Linked Data* is therefore built on a set of design principles to provide machine-readable data on the Web for use by the network.

In addition to machine-readable data, web 3.0 also creates the opportunity for storage and provision by decentralized systems (Jara *et al.*, 2014). For example IPFS aims to solve the web data's typical availability problems, such as the limited lifetime of content, firewall blocks, and out-of-business services (Benet, 2014). It uses cryptographic checksums of file contents to address and link data, which originates in GIT, BitTorrent, and distributed hash tables.

While the development of IPFS is primarily aimed at file systems, so-called blockchain databases can transform conventional storage systems. The advantages of such blockchain-like technology are decentralized control, tamper resistance, value generation, and transmission (Orjuela *et al.*, 2021). Research and use of these technologies are mostly missing in construction, whereas it seems interesting to replace current cloud-based, highly centralized solutions with such approaches. Therefore, future research approaches should not only be on technological feasibility but also the consideration of the fundamental redesign of today's data organization as well as its impact on data availability.

3.2 Approaches to Web3 in Construction

Construction scholarship and consulting reports have identified the advantages of web 3.0 concepts over the past decade. For example, (Pauwels *et al.*, 2011) formulate why and how web of data technologies (e.g., rdf, owl) can be beneficial for BIM. They outline use cases and their benefits situated in interoperability, linking data and logical inference. Farghaly (2018) formulated a framework for how the transfer of BIM model data to Asset Information Model (AIM) platforms might proceed. By defining a process map and connecting existing ontologies, this work aims to improve building assets information management.

Various ontologies have been developed so far. Generic ontologies such as ifcOWL can map the established IFC data structure (Pauwels *et al.*, 2017). Specific ontologies approach different data sets commonly used for building services engineering or cost calculations. However, the use of ontologies for multi-domain BIM methodologies is only just emerging (Rasmussen *et al.*, 2019).

In addition, the use of commonly used tools such as the CDE is being investigated by scholars from a more decentralized, web-based point of view (Tao *et al.*, 2021). Werbrouck (2019) formulated a CDE using decentralized data structures. Structuring information based on linked data and a web-wide graph opens up the possibility for digital agents to semantically interpret and use this data with minimal human intervention. In this regard, Oraskari (2018) discussed the possibility of federated building models in a collaborative AEC/FM setting. Based on the limitations of cloud data, i.e., limited content lifetime, limited resources, blocking firewalls, and unavailable services, this study addresses both the benefits and limitations of IPFS technology for implementing linked building data. Poinet (2021) pioneered an innovative open-source data framework to address the interoperability challenge. Introduced as *speckle,* the framework allows users to establish a flexible and data-driven dialogue between stakeholders in the design phase. Namely, the basic schema structure is not restricted to proprietary or industry-standard formats. However, it allows defining one's own domain-specific object models.

Overall, Web3 approaches in the construction industry are flawed in one respect. Even though they promise interoperability and vendor-neutral data access, most implementation are still technologically centralized (Soman *et al.,* 2020). This can create a barrier to stakeholder participation when technologies are still highly dependent on specific cloud platforms owned by others. There is a need for an open access, vendor-neutral, and decentralized data foundation. Furthermore, it should be added that specifically the use of ontologies and linked data approaches offers a possibility to link heterogeneous data sets. Nevertheless, in principle, these technologies do not create a system that incentivizes data sharing and seamless collaboration across phases and between actors.

4. Decentralized Data Marketplaces and Data Governance

4.1 Overview and Application in other Industries

In other industries, businesses and organizations have realized that data-driven decisions are far more effective than the traditional trial and error methods and intuitions (Frazzon *et al.*, 2018). As a result, they started generating data out of every operation and started analyzing the data to figure out opportunities to perform better, accelerate growth and enhance operational efficiency. But, similar to the construction industry, these data are often kept in data silos. The data owned by one organization can be useful for another, but unfortunately, sharing data between organizations is not stimulated. In addition, if data is generated and collected, one can observe a gap between the use and collection of this data. On the one hand, data collectors accumulate data from producers such as sensors, machines, and users. On the other hand, there are various data consumers such as analytics tools, artificial intelligence platforms, and models.

In recent years, numerous digital solutions have emerged whose primary business model is trading raw and processed data and offering data-related services. They exist as both centralized and decentralized. In other words: data sale has been practiced for a long time, but the data marketplace is a relatively new business model and refers to an intermediary service for data exchange (Ghosh, 2018). Most digital data marketplaces tend to have a centralized structure. Today's platforms provide an infrastructure for data exchange by acting as a digital intermediary. In addition, the marketplace operator acts as an overview agent, brings together supply and demand, and coordinates pricing. In this context, it is not possible to exclude that platform operators may abuse their control over the platform infrastructure and manipulate the market for their benefit. Data exchange and trade in the construction industry are primarily between different system actors, i.e., companies. Studies show that the business models of B2B platforms have not been able to show the same economic effects as the platforms in the B2C sector. The possible reason for this is a lack of trust (Hunhevicz and Hall, 2019). As a result, most platform users in the B2B sector try to create and operate their own platforms. Moreover, there is usually no exchange of information between individual platforms, which means that positive network effects no longer come into play.

Different researchers show that decentralized systems help increase trust in data and its processing. No entity takes a superior role. Therefore, the participants can trade with each other and exchange information that would otherwise not be shared while providing privacy, anonymity, transparency, and access control. These solutions often possess an in-built trust layer that enables data providers and consumers to build value on top of a trustless and censorship-resistant protocol, which promotes an open platform where anyone can join and add value to the network and community. By using blockchain, or more general, distributed ledger technology as the censorship-resistant building block, such concepts of marketplaces developed primarily from using specific parts of this technology (smart contracts). There are a few examples to mention here.

The most well-known project, *Ocean Protocol*, offers two main services (Ocean Protocol Foundation, 2020). A *Data Ecosystem Platform* and a decentralized *Data Marketplace*. The former facilitates control of data access, allowing owners to upload and store their data while retaining full control when monetizing the data for buyers. The data marketplace facilitates the selling and buying of data by connecting sellers and buyers around the world.

Another project is the *Enigma* (rebranded *Secret*) data marketplace (Zyskind *et al.,* 2015). It vision to complement a blockchain of any kind with an off-chain data network. Introduced as a decentralized privacy-preserving content management and data exchange protocol, it leverages the privacy guarantees of a specific trust network for data encryption and access management, as well as the decentralized data storage solution of IPFS.

Streamr focuses on the open and fair exchange of real-time data (Streamr, 2017). The marketplace offers access to paid and free data sources. The uniqueness is that the data is collected via an off-chain network, whereby larger amounts of data can be processed efficiently. However, the solution currently runs on a centralized structure which leads to the emergence of a superior third party.

Various research has examined the differences between centralized approaches of specific platforms such as data marketplaces and decentralized approaches. As a result, a decentralized approach enables the following benefits.

- Independency of any central server hosted by a third party (Ranchal *et al.*, 2010)
- Resistance to data tampering (Aniello *et al.*, 2017)
- Minimal manipulation of ratings and references (Shakeret al., 2021)
- No monopoly power of market platform operators (Vergne, 2020)
- Peer-to-peer data connections with seamless payments (Ramachandran *et al.*, 2018)

5. Discussion

As introduced above, the AEC industry has been diagnosed with some lack of digital systemic changes to reduce the industry' data fragmentation, improve communication efficiency and effectiveness, and reduce the high costs due to lack of data democratization among its system participants. Over the decades, many researchers working on changing this status quo have proposed many techniques and methods to improve data management issues, and a series of guiding standards and specifications have been developed in standardization organizations. However, these outcomes are often based on multiple perspectives, from different stakeholders' points of view, tailored to their countries, fields, and organizations' characteristics.

The high productivity of academic results does not imply that they can directly interface with reality and impact. On the one hand, new technologies leading the industry need to be popularized, learned, and understood by more practitioners. On the other hand, professional knowledge is constantly being cited in the process of ambiguity; many new technologies arise, are interrelated, may replace each other, or may function together. This difficulty highlights a certain impasse and the desirability of a completely new approach.

This approach, in the context of decentralized data marketplace and their potential application to construction industry challenges (see section 1.2) are twofold.

On the one hand, using a marketplace, decentralized or not, offers a certain impact on the quality of the submitted data. A particular quality standard needs to be met for successfully sharing or selling datasets. This standard can be defined by a central authority or a peer-to-peer mechanism. On the other hand, seamless access to a data distribution protocol allows the data to remain in a kind of silo solution, but the project phase dependency partially fades as the silo is part of a larger network. This gives a natural incentive or intrinsic motivation for the efficient handling, and cross-phase use of generated data within a company since breaking clear phase transitions no longer reduces the value of the data.

Decentralized data marketplaces operate similarly to their centralized counterparts. The key difference is the level of privacy and security provided by having two decentralized components in the web3 technology stack. In other words, the data owners have a secure and smooth access to their data, while maintaining privacy and confidentiality. This is because ownership never shifts to a central entity, meaning the data creator is paid for the data, not an intermediary. As a result, participants in the network are motivated to make their data available collaboratively while at the same time benefiting monetarily. In addition, as described above, incentive mechanisms encourage data providers to adhere to a particular data format standard. A decentralized approach reinforces that since intermediaries do not co-benefit from a data transaction compared to a centralized solution.

Moreover, the decentralized architecture based on the web3 technology stack offers the advantage that the implementation of an incentive system is simpler due to the characteristics of the decentralized trust layer

6. Conclusion

This paper attempted to encourage a discussion on the use of decentralized data marketplaces and provide a line of reasoning for further research on decentralized data marketplaces in construction. This by highlighting that data management in the construction industry still has certain limitations, although well advanced and addressed with various approaches. Therefore, whether these specific marketplaces offer a possible solution for further developing data governance and improving data-based, collaborative efficiency in construction, this contribution represents a first thought-starter in this direction. Still, these approaches have not yet been studied in detail, especially for the underlying data storage systems and different data characteristics. More detailed implications and impacts are therefore to be elaborated in future research.

7. Acknowledgment

This research is part of Future Cities Lab Global Module A1- Circular Future Cities, conducted at the Future Cities Lab Global at the ETH hub of Singapore-ETH Centre, which was established collaboratively between ETH Zurich and the National Research Foundation Singapore.

References

Abanda, F.H., Vidalakis, C., Oti, A.H. and Tah, J.H.M. (2015) 'A critical analysis of Building Information Modelling systems used in construction projects', *Advances in Engineering Software*, 90, pp. 183–201. doi:10.1016/j.advengsoft.2015.08.009.

Alabdulwahhab, F.A. (2018) 'Web 3.0: The Decentralized Web Blockchain networks and Protocol Innovation', in *2018 1st International Conference on Computer Applications & Information Security (ICCAIS)*. IEEE, pp. 1–4. doi:10.1109/CAIS.2018.8441990.

Aniello, L., Baldoni, R., Gaetani, E., Lombardi, F., Margheri, A. and Sassone, V. (2017) 'A Prototype Evaluation of a Tamper-Resistant High Performance Blockchain-Based Transaction Log for a Distributed Database', in *2017 13th European Dependable Computing Conference (EDCC)*. IEEE, pp. 151–154. doi:10.1109/EDCC.2017.31.

Benet, J. (2014) 'IPFS - Content Addressed, Versioned, P2P File System'. Available at: https://arxiv.org/abs/1407.3561v1 (Accessed: 3 September 2021).

Berners-Lee, T. and Hendler, J. (2001) 'Publishing on the semantic web', *Nature*, 410(6832), pp. 1023–1024. doi:10.1038/35074206.

Bucher, D.F. and Hall, D.M. (2020) 'Common data environment within the AEC ecosystem: Moving collaborative platforms beyond the open versus closed dichotomy', in *EG-ICE 2020 Workshop on Intelligent Computing in Engineering, Proceedings*, pp. 491–500. doi:10.3929/ethz-b-000447240.

Corry, E., O'Donnell, J., Curry, E., Coakley, D., Pauwels, P. and Keane, M. (2014) 'Using semantic web technologies to access soft AEC data', *Advanced Engineering Informatics*, 28(4), pp. 370–380. doi:10.1016/j.aei.2014.05.002.

Farboodi, M. and Veldkamp, L. (2021) *A Growth Model of the Data Economy*. Cambridge, MA. doi:10.3386/w28427.

Farghaly, K., Abanda, F.H., Vidalakis, C. and Wood, G. (2018) 'Taxonomy for BIM and Asset Management Semantic Interoperability', *Journal of Management in Engineering*, 34(4), p. 04018012. doi:10.1061/(asce)me.1943-5479.0000610.

Frazzon, E.M., Kück, M. and Freitag, M. (2018) 'Data-driven production control for complex and dynamic manufacturing systems', *CIRP Annals*, 67(1), pp. 515–518. doi:10.1016/J.CIRP.2018.04.033.

Ghosh, H. (2018) 'Data Marketplace as a Platform for Sharing Scientific Data', in. Springer, Singapore, pp. 99–105. doi:10.1007/978-981-10-7515-5_7.

Hall, D.M., Algiers, A. and Levitt, R.E. (2018) 'Identifying the Role of Supply Chain Integration Practices in the Adoption of Systemic Innovations', *Journal of Management in Engineering*, 34(6), p. 04018030. doi:10.1061/(ASCE)ME.1943-5479.0000640.

Hannus, M., Penttila, H. and Silén, P. (1997) *Islands of Automation in Construction*. Available at: http://cic.vtt.fi/hannus/islands/index.html.

Homayouni, H., Neff, G. and Dossick, C.S. (2010) 'Theoretical categories of successful collaboration and BIM implementation within the AEC industry', in *Construction Research Congress 2010: Innovation for Reshaping Construction Practice - Proceedings of the 2010 Construction Research Congress*, pp. 778–788. doi:10.1061/41109(373)78.

Honic, M., Kovacic, I., Sibenik, G. and Rechberger, H. (2019) 'Data- and stakeholder management framework for the implementation of BIM-based Material Passports', *Journal of Building Engineering*, 23, pp. 341–350. doi:10.1016/j.jobe.2019.01.017.

Huang, Y., Shi, Q., Zuo, J., Pena-Mora, F. and Chen, J. (2021) 'Research Status and Challenges of Data-Driven Construction Project Management in the Big Data Context', *Advances in Civil Engineering*. Edited by W. Yi, 2021, pp. 1–19. doi:10.1155/2021/6674980.

Hunhevicz, J.J. and Hall, D.M. (2019) 'Managing mistrust in construction using DLT: a review of use-case categories for technical decisions', *Proceedings of the 2019 European Conference for Computing in Construction*, 1, pp. 100–109. doi:10.35490/ec3.2019.171.

Ismail, A., Nahar, A. and Scherer, R. (2017) 'Application of graph databases and graph theory concepts for advanced analysing of BIM models based on IFC standard', in *Digital Proceedings of the 24th EG-ICE International Workshop on Intelligent Computing in Engineering 2017*, pp. 146–157. Available at: https://www.researchgate.net/publication/318600860 (Accessed: 18 August 2021).

Jara, A.J., Olivieri, A.C., Bocchi, Y., Jung, M., Kastner, W. and Skarmeta, A.F. (2014) 'Semantic Web of Things: an analysis of the application semantics for the IoT moving towards the IoT convergence', *International Journal of Web and Grid Services*, 10(2/3), p. 244. doi:10.1504/IJWGS.2014.060260.

Klinc, R. and Turk, Ž. (2019) 'Construction 4.0 – Digital Transformation of one the oldest industries', 21(3), pp. 292–410. doi:10.15458/ebr.92.

Laakso, M. and Kiviniemi, A. (2012) 'The IFC standard - A review of history, development, and standardization', *Electronic Journal of Information Technology in Construction*, 17, pp. 134–161.

Lee, a, Aouad, G., Cooper, R., Fu, C., Marshall-Ponting, a J., Tah, J.H.M. and Wu, S. (2005) *nD modelling-a driver or enabler for construction improvement?, RICS Research Paper Series, RICS, London*. Available at: http://usir.salford.ac.uk/621/ (Accessed: 23 February 2022).

Ocean Protocol Foundation (2020) *Technical Whitepaper*.

Oraskari, J., Beetz, J., Caad, L. and Törmä, S. (2018) 'Federated Building Models in collaborative AEC/FM settings using IPFS', in *International Conference on Computing in Civil and Building EngineeringInternational Conference on Computing in Civil and Building Engineering*. Available at: https://www.w3.org/wiki/SparqlEndpoints (Accessed: 10 September 2020).

Orjuela, K.G., Gaona-García, P.A. and Marin, C.E.M. (2021) 'Towards an agriculture solution for product supply chain using blockchain: case study Agro-chain with BigchainDB', *Acta Agriculturae Scandinavica, Section B — Soil & Plant Science*, 71(1), pp. 1–16. doi:10.1080/09064710.2020.1840618.

Pauwels, P., Krijnen, T., Terkaj, W. and Beetz, J. (2017) 'Enhancing the ifcOWL ontology with an alternative representation for geometric data', *Automation in Construction*, 80, pp. 77–94. doi:10.1016/J.AUTCON.2017.03.001.

Pauwels, P., De Meyer, R. and Van Campenhout, J. (2011) 'Interoperability for the Design and Construction Industry through Semantic Web Technology', in *Lecture Notes in Computer Science (including subseries Lecture Notes in Artificial Intelligence and Lecture Notes in Bioinformatics)*, pp. 143–158. doi:10.1007/978-3-642-23017-2_10.

Poinet, P., Stefanescu, D. and Papadonikolaki, E. (2021) 'Collaborative Workflows and Version Control Through Open-Source and Distributed Common Data Environment', in *Lecture Notes in Civil Engineering*. Springer, pp. 228–247. doi:10.1007/978-3-030-51295-8_18.

Poirier, E.A., Forgues, D. and Staub-French, S. (2014) 'Dimensions of Interoperability in the AEC Industry', in *Construction Research Congress 2014*. Reston, VA: American Society of Civil Engineers, pp. 1987–1996. doi:10.1061/9780784413517.203.

Ramachandran, G.S., Radhakrishnan, R. and Krishnamachari, B. (2018) 'Towards a Decentralized Data Marketplace for Smart Cities', in *2018 IEEE International Smart Cities Conference (ISC2)*. IEEE, pp. 1–8. doi:10.1109/ISC2.2018.8656952.

Ranchal, R., Bhargava, B., Othmane, L. Ben, Lilien, L., Kim, A., Kang, M. and Linderman, M. (2010) 'Protection of Identity Information in Cloud Computing without Trusted Third Party', in *2010 29th IEEE Symposium on Reliable Distributed Systems*. IEEE, pp. 368–372. doi:10.1109/SRDS.2010.57.

Rasmussen, M.H., Lefrançois, M., Schneider, G.F. and Pauwels, P. (2019) 'BOT: the Building Topology Ontology of the W3C Linked Building Data Group', *Semantic Web Journal* [Preprint]. Available at: https://www.microsoft.com/microsoft-365/ (Accessed: 21 July 2020).

Scherer, R.J. and Schapke, S.-E. (2011) 'A distributed multi-model-based Management Information System for simulation and decision-making on construction projects', *Advanced Engineering Informatics*, 25(4), pp. 582–599. doi:10.1016/j.aei.2011.08.007.

Shaker, M., Shams Aliee, F. and Fotohi, R. (2021) 'Online rating system development using blockchain-based distributed ledger technology', *Wireless Networks*, 27(3), pp. 1715–1737. doi:10.1007/s11276-020-02514-w.

Soman, R.K. and Whyte, J.K. (2020) 'Codification Challenges for Data Science in Construction', *Journal of Construction Engineering and Management*, 146(7), p. 04020072. doi:10.1061/(ASCE)CO.1943-7862.0001846.

Staab, S. and Stuckenschmidt, H. (2006) *Semantic web and peer-to-peer decentralized management and exchange of knowledge and information, Semantic Web and Peer-to-Peer: Decentralized Management and Exchange of Knowledge and Information*. doi:10.1007/3-540-28347-1.

Streamr (2017) *Whitepaper - Unstoppable Data for Unstoppable Apps: DATAcoin by Streams*.

Tao, X., Das, M., Liu, Y. and Cheng, J.C.P. (2021) 'Distributed common data environment using blockchain and Interplanetary File System for secure BIM-based collaborative design', *Automation in Construction*, 130, p. 103851. doi:10.1016/j.autcon.2021.103851.

Ullah, K., Lill, I. and Witt, E. (2019) 'An overview of BIM adoption in the construction industry: Benefits and barriers', in *Emerald Reach Proceedings Series*. Emerald Publishing Limited, pp. 297–303. doi:10.1108/S2516-285320190000002052.

Valra, A., Madeddu, D., Chiappetti, J. and Farina, D. (2021) 'The BIM Management System: A Common Data Environment Using Linked Data to Support the Efficient Renovation in Buildings', *Proceedings*, 65(1), p. 18. doi:10.3390/proceedings2020065018.

Vergne, J. (2020) 'Decentralized vs. Distributed Organization: Blockchain, Machine Learning and the Future of the Digital Platform', *Organization Theory*, 1(4), p. 263178772097705. doi:10.1177/2631787720977052.

Werbrouck, J., Pauwels, P., Beetz, J. and van Berlo, L. (2019) 'Towards a Decentralised Common Data Environment using Linked Building Data and the Solid Ecosystem', *Advances in ICT in Design, Construction and Management in Architecture, Engineering, Construction and Operations (AECO) : Proceedings of the 36th CIB W78 2019 Conference*, (September), pp. 113–123. Available at: https://biblio.ugent.be/publication/8633673 (Accessed: 24 September 2021).

Wu, J. and Zhang, J. (2019) 'New Automated BIM Object Classification Method to Support BIM Interoperability', *Journal of Computing in Civil Engineering*, 33(5). doi:10.1061/(ASCE)CP.1943-5487.0000858.

Yan, H., Yang, N., Peng, Y. and Ren, Y. (2020) 'Data mining in the construction industry: Present status, opportunities, and future trends', *Automation in Construction*, 119, p. 103331. doi:10.1016/j.autcon.2020.103331.

Zyskind, G., Nathan, O. and Alex, P. (2015) *Whitepaper - Enigma: Dectralized Computation Platform with Guaranteed Privacy*.

Self-supervised Learning Approach for Excavator Activity Recognition Using Contrastive Video Representation

Ghelmani A., Hammad A.
Concordia University, Canada
amin.hammad@concordia.ca

Abstract. Detecting construction equipment and classifying their activities are important steps for evaluating their performance and productivity on construction sites. To this end, many automated activity monitoring frameworks based on computer vision have been developed. However, most of the current state-of-the-art activity recognition methods for construction equipment are based on supervised deep learning methods. A major drawback of these approaches is that large, annotated datasets are required for each equipment and activity. To address this problem, this work adapts and customizes the self-supervised, spatiotemporal contrastive video representation learning method for excavator activity recognition. Self-supervised methods use the spatiotemporal information present in video frames as a source of information for pre-training a deep neural network without labels, which is then fine-tuned using a few labeled data. The results show the potential of this method, obtaining the recognition accuracy of 84.6% while using only 10% of the labeled data in an available dataset.

1. Introduction

The traditional way of monitoring the activities of various construction equipment is time consuming and labor intensive, especially on large construction sites (C. Chen et al., 2020). Considering that a major step in any large scale construction project is earthmoving operations, excavator activity monitoring would enable site managers to make more informed decisions by providing them with the productivity and work cycle duration information (C. Chen et al., 2020). Examples of such decisions include resource allocation, scheduling, and path planning (Kim et al., 2018).

Recently, with the abundant use of surveillance cameras in construction sites (Kim and Chi, 2019), various automated vision-based activity recognition methods have been proposed (Luo et al., 2020; C. Chen et al., 2020; Kim and Chi, 2019). Convolutional Neural Networks (CNN) are the main building block in all vision-based deep learning methods. For instance, Roberts and Golparvar-Fard (2019) applied a Hidden Markov Model (HMM) on the detection outputs of a CNN network to detect, track, and identify the activities of excavators and dump trucks. Kim and Chi (2020) combined CNN and Long Short-Term Memory (LSTM) architectures for activity recognition of excavators and dump trucks, while Slaton et al. (2020) used CNN and LSTM combination for detecting the sequential activities of excavators and roller compactors.

The main limitation of above-mentioned 2D CNN-based methods is the separate extraction of spatial and temporal features (Li et al., 2020), which limits the efficiency of deep learning models to extract spatiotemporal data simultaneously. 3D CNN-based methods however, incorporate the spatiotemporal data extraction into a single architecture, which alleviates the above limitation. Chen et al. (2020) proposed a three-stage excavator activity recognition method in which excavators are first detected and tracked in consecutive frames. Then, the tracked frames are input into a 3D CNN network for activity recognition. Lou et al. (2020) used the You Only Look Once (YOLOv3) network in a multi-stage framework for worker activity recognition. Recently, Jung et al. (2021) proposed a single-stage architecture by combining 3D

https://doi.org/10.7146/aul.455.c225

CNN with attention mechanism for detecting the activities of multiple construction equipment, while Torabi et al. (2021) used a single-stage architecture called You Only Watch Once 53 (YOWO53) for worker activity recognition. The current state-of-the-art methods for equipment and worker activity recognition, while achieving high performance, are based on supervised deep learning methods, which require large annotated datasets for each equipment/worker and each activity. Particularly, the fact that various types of construction equipment exist on the site, often varying in different phases of the project (Kim and Chi, 2021), poses major challenges for the development of a general supervised activity recognition method.

One possible approach for avoiding the time-consuming and error-prone process of data annotation is using self-supervised methods. In recent years, many self-supervised methods have been proposed for learning visual features from large-scale unlabeled image and video datasets (Jing and Tian, 2021). A popular approach in self-supervised methods is to define a pretext task as the learning objective of the neural network, by which the output label is created from the input data itself (i.e., self-supervision). For instance, some self-supervised video representation learning methods exploit the sampling rate and playback speed information (Cho et al., 2020; Feichtenhofer et al., 2019; Yao et al., 2020), in which a model is trained to maintain the consistency between different representations of the same video at different sampling rates. Another common approach is to use the temporal order of frames or clips (Misra et al., 2016; Xu et al., 2019). Misra et al. (2016) proposed a temporal order verification task in which the model predicts whether or not the input frames have been shuffled or are in the correct order. Xu et al. (2019) extended this task by selecting short clips from an input video and training a model to predict the sequential order of input clips.

Recently, contrastive learning-based self-supervised approaches have obtained the state-of-the-art performance (T. Chen et al., 2020; Grill et al., 2020). In contrastive learning, the pretext task is to have the model produce consistent representations for different augmentations of the same input while increasing the difference with the augmentations of other inputs. Qian et al. (2021) proposed a spatiotemporal contrastive video representation learning (CVRL) method, which uses contrastive learning on spatiotemporally augmented clips extracted from the input video. Compared with supervised methods, self-supervised approaches are able to achieve similar performance (T. Chen et al., 2020) while requiring far less labeled training data.

The main goal of this paper is to adapt and customize the self-supervised CVRL method for the task of excavator activity recognition. To this end, the CVRL method is first trained on a large dataset of unlabeled excavator activities collected from YouTube and local construction sites. Then, it is fine-tuned on a limited annotated dataset. While several works have tried to address the problem of construction equipment detection using limited datasets (Kim and Chi, 2021; Xiao et al., 2021), to the best of authors' knowledge this study is the first attempt to address the problem of excavator activity recognition using self-supervised approaches.

2. Methodology

The general framework in which self-supervised methods are applied is comprised of three main phases. The first phase is to use the selected self-supervised learning (SSL) method to pre-train a neural network. The second phase is to use the pre-trained neural network in the down-stream task to obtain high performance with a small, labeled dataset. Finally, the third phase is to test the performance of the model trained in previous two phases on the never-before-seen test data. CVRL (Qian et al., 2021) is a self-supervised contrastive video representation learning method. Self-supervised contrastive approaches, in general, try to minimize the distance between the outputs of the model for two different augmentations of the same video, while maximizing their distance with the outputs of the model for augmentations of other videos. In this manner, the model is expected to extract context similarity in the input data without supervision (i.e., labels) (Jing and Tian, 2021). The pre-training phase using the CVRL method is done in five consecutive steps of temporal augmentation, spatial augmentation, clip encoding, projection, and loss calculation (Figure 1). The details of each step are provided in the following paragraphs.

Considering that augmentations are at the core of contrastive approaches, the quality of the learnt representations is determined, in large part, by the choice of the applied augmentations. To this end, and to exploit the spatiotemporal information present in the videos, CVRL proposes a novel temporal augmentation method in which for an input video of length T, two clips with the temporal distance of Δt are extracted, where Δt is sampled from a linearly decreasing distribution over $[0, T]$. The intuition behind using this distribution, which discourages large Δt values, is to model the decrease in temporal correlation between extracted clips as the temporal distance between them increases. After sampling two temporally augmented clips from each video, in the second step the spatial augmentations of random cropping, resizing, horizontal flipping, color jittering, gray scaling, and Gaussian blurring are applied in a consistent manner to all of the frames in a clip (e.g., all of them are horizontally flipped).

In the third step, the two augmented clips are input to the selected backbone model to obtain their respective encoding (i.e., representation). CVRL uses the common 3D ResNet (Hara et al., 2018) model as the backbone architecture. In contrastive learning, the model is trained to be invariant to the augmentations applied to be able to produce consistent representations for clips extracted from the same input video. However, information such as the color or object orientation might be important for down-stream tasks. Therefore, in the fourth step, encoding of each extracted clip is passed into a multi-layer projection head to map the encoded representations into an m-dimensional space. The use of projection head during training improves down-stream performance by limiting the effect of augmentation invariance to the projection output, on which the contrastive loss is calculated (T. Chen et al., 2020). Projection head is only used during the self-supervised training step and is later discarded. Customizing the projection space dimension plays a crucial balancing role between the quality of the learnt representation during the pre-training phase, and the performance of the model on down-stream tasks. A detailed inspection of the effect of different projection dimensions is presented in Section 3.3.

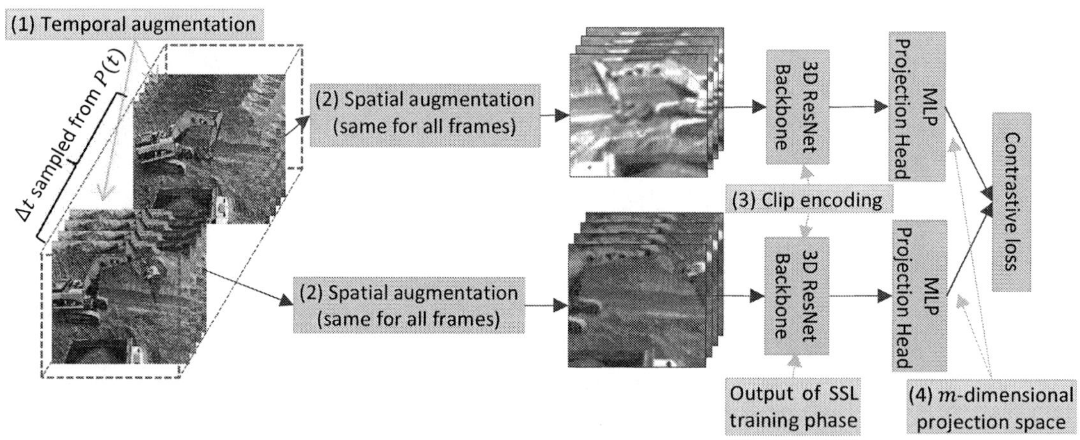

Figure 1: Self-supervised pre-training of 3D ResNet backbone.

The final step is to calculate the contrastive loss. CVRL uses the InfoNCE loss (Oord et al., 2019) on the spatiotemporally augmented clips. To apply the contrastive loss, given a batch of N input videos, two augmented clips are extracted from each video, resulting in $2N$ final clips per batch. For a positive pair of clips, i.e., a pair of augmented clips extracted from a single video, the rest of the $2(N-1)$ clips in the batch are treated as negative samples. Assuming z_i and z_j are a positive pair, the contrastive loss for this pair is calculated using Equation (1).

$$\mathcal{L}_i = -\,log\frac{exp(sim(z_i, z_j)/\tau)}{\sum_{k=1}^{2N} \mathbb{1}_{k\neq i}\, exp(sim(z_i, z_k)/\tau)} \quad (1)$$

Where, $sim(z_i, z_j)$ represents the cosine similarity between two vectors, and $\mathbb{1}_{k\neq i}$ denotes an indicator function which equals 1 when $k \neq i$ and 0 when $k = i$. τ is the temperature parameter which improves the performance of the model by increasing or decreasing its confidence in the output prediction (Hinton et al., 2015). Considering that τ changes the output class probabilities, it affects the calculated loss and subsequently the entire training process. Hence, careful adjustment of this hyperparameter is required for the given dataset and activity classes to obtain the best performance possible, as presented in Section 3.3. Finally, Equation 1 computes the loss for a positive pair of (i, j) clips, the total batch loss is calculated over all positive pairs, both (i, j) and (j, i), in a batch. Considering that in contrastive learning the model learns by comparing the data in each batch, the size of batch plays a crucial role on the quality of the learnt representations (T. Chen et al., 2020). As such, careful customization of this value for the dataset at hand is of paramount importance as shown in Section 3.3.

After self-supervised training, to evaluate the quality of the pre-trained backbone, the most common approach is linear evaluation (T. Chen et al., 2020; Oord et al., 2019). In linear evaluation, the weights of the pre-trained backbone are frozen and a linear classifier is trained on top of the backbone. Considering the limited learning capacity of a linear classifier, the test accuracy in linear evaluation is a proxy for the quality of the representation learnt by the backbone network. In CVRL, backbone network output is ℓ_2 normalized before being fed into the linear classifier. Prediction loss is then calculated using the output of the linear classifier and the true data label.

Finally, test data are used to obtain the final performance of the model. Following a common practice (Feichtenhofer et al., 2019), during testing ten clips are extracted from each input video by uniformly sampling along the temporal dimension. For each clip, the shorter spatial side is scaled to a size of n pixels and three $n \times n$ crops are then taken along the longer spatial dimension to cover the entire frame, as an approximation to fully convolutional testing. The size n, is selected based on the frame size of the videos in the dataset and the input size of the model. Before predicting an activity class for the input video, the output of the softmax layer for the 30 views (10 clips $\times$ 3 crops) is averaged over. Afterwards, this averaged softmax value is used to obtain the predicted class of the model and the final test accuracy.

3. Experiments

3.1 Dataset Description

The experiments were conducted on an excavator video dataset, collected from various sources including local construction sites, YouTube, and videos used in similar research works (Roberts and Golparvar-Fard, 2019). The excavator activities in the dataset include digging, swinging, and loading. The collected videos are from more than 25 different construction sites to add more diversity to the collected dataset by including various site conditions, camera viewpoints, scales, and colors of the excavators. The overall statistics of the dataset are presented in Table 1 and examples of each activity are shown in Figure 2.

Table 1: Statistics of the Collected Excavator Dataset.

Activity Type	Number of Videos	Number of frames	Average video clip length (sec)
Digging	295	64,436	7.28
Swinging	476	51,441	3.60
Loading	321	51,632	5.36
Total	1,060	163,295	5.13

(a) Digging (b) Swinging (c) Loading

Figure 2: Samples from the Collected Dataset.

3.2 Implementation Details

The original CVRL method uses SGD optimization. However, in this work it was found that ADAM optimization algorithm yields better performance. As such, ADAM optimization algorithm with an initial learning rate of 0.16 is used. The learning rate is linearly warmed-up for 5 epochs followed by a half-period cosine learning rate decay strategy. The training is done using two NVIDIA RTX A6000 GPUs. Due to GPU memory limitations, a maximum batch size of 256 videos (512 augmented clips) is considered. During self-supervised training, two 16-frame clips with a temporal stride of 2 are extracted from each video. To increase the variation in the applied spatial augmentations, horizontal flip, color jittering, and gray scaling are only applied 50%, 80%, and 20% of the time, respectively. The initial dimension of the projection space is set to 128 and the self-supervised training is performed for 300 epochs, with the temperature parameter set to 0.1. In contrast to the spatial augmentations applied during the self-supervised pre-training, during linear evaluation, only cropping, resizing, and flipping augmentations are applied.

For linear evaluation, 32-frame clips with a temporal stride of 2 are used, and the training is carried out for 100 epochs with a batch size of 256 videos. The testing is done using the 30 view approach described in Section 2 with a crop size of 256×256 per clip. Training, evaluation, and testing data ratios are 80%, 10%, and 10%, respectively. More specifically, during self-supervised pre-training, 80% of the data, without labels, are used to pre-train the 3D ResNet backbone model. During the linear evaluation, the backbone weights are frozen, and the 10% evaluation data are used to train the linear classifier added on top of the backbone. Finally, the performance of the overall framework is evaluated using the 10% test dataset, that was not used in any of the previous two phases, to obtain a more accurate metric for the performance of the trained model.

3.3 Experimental Results

The results of linear evaluation on the test dataset for different configurations of the hyperparameters are shown in Table 2 using the common top-1 accuracy metric. In deep learning classification tasks, the final layer of a neural network (softmax), outputs a probability for each class and the final prediction of the network is obtained by finding the class that the network considers to be the most probable (top-1 accuracy). The initial hyperparameters in this work were originally selected in accordance with the hyperparameters suggested in the CVRL work. However, considering the differences between the excavator dataset used in this work and the Kinetics-400 (Kay et al., 2017) and Kinetics-600 (Carreira et al., 2018) human activity datasets used in the CVLR paper, a thorough ablation study on different configurations of hyperparameters was carried out.

Table 2: Linear Evaluation Results.

Batch size	Temperature	Projection dim.	Learning rate	Top-1 Acc. (%)
32	0.1	128	0.16	59.5
64	0.1	128	0.16	66.2
128	0.1	128	0.16	75.5
256	0.1	128	0.16	81.9
256	**0.05**	128	0.16	80.3
256	**0.1**	128	0.16	81.9
256	**0.5**	128	0.16	67.7
256	0.1	**64**	0.16	78.1
256	0.1	**128**	0.16	81.9
256	0.1	**256**	0.16	73.8
256	0.1	128	**0.32**	70.1
256	0.1	128	**0.16**	81.9
256	0.1	128	**0.1**	**84.6**
256	0.1	128	**0.08**	83.3

As mentioned in Section 2, batch size plays a crucial role in the final performance of contrastive learning-based methods, due to the comparison done between positive and negative samples in each batch. As such, batch size is the first considered hyperparameter to customize for the available excavator dataset and activity classes. It can be seen from the results that the performance of CVRL steadily improves with increasing batch size as has been shown in other contrastive methods (Oord et al., 2019; Tian et al., 2020). Given the role of temperature parameter in the loss calculation and consequently, the entire training process, the temperature parameter is the next considered hyperparameter to customize. The importance and role of temperature parameter is also evident by the large variations in the final performance of the model for different values. It can be seen in Table 2 that the best performance is obtained for temperature parameter of 0.1 while for the value of 0.5 the performance drops significantly.

The third considered hyperparameter is the projection dimension. As explained in Section 2, the trade-off between the quality of the pre-trained model and down-stream performance, is determined by careful selection of the projection dimension. To this end, different dimensions for the projection space were also tested, with the projection dimension of 128 obtaining the best performance. Finally, changing the learning rate shows that the best performance is achieved with the learning rate of 0.1, which differs from the learning rate suggested by the CVRL work (0.32) by a large margin. Considering the significant difference between the performance of the model for learning rate values of 0.16 and 0.32 and the iterative approach of hyperparameter customization in deep learning methods, the results for the customization of batch size, temperature, and projection dimension hyperparameters are reported using the learning rate of 0.16. However, during the final customization of the learning rate hyperparameter, it is observed that the learning rate of 0.1 yields the best performance.

It should be noted that as described in Section 3.2, only 10% of the dataset is used during linear evaluation phase, while the results shown in Table 2 are obtained using the never-before-seen test dataset. Hence, the CVRL model is able to obtain a high activity recognition accuracy of 84.6% while reducing the labeled data requirement by a factor of 10. More generally, the results in Table 2 demonstrate the efficiency and applicability of using self-supervised approaches in the construction domain.

4. Conclusion and future work

In this work, the spatiotemporal Contrastive Video Representation Learning (CVRL) method was adapted and customized to the task of excavator activity recognition on construction sites. Extensive linear evaluation of the model and ablation analysis of various hyperparameters demonstrated the promising performance of the CVRL method, by obtaining the top-1 activity classification accuracy of 84.6% while using only 10% of the labeled data from the available dataset. More generally, the results show the applicability of using self-supervised methods for equipment activity recognition in the construction domain.

Considering that the main advantage of the self-supervised approach is reducing the number of required labeled data, the future work includes addressing the problem of recognizing the activities of multiple equipment, which can enhance the applicability of vision-based monitoring during multiple phases of construction projects. Furthermore, while only 10% of the labeled dataset was used in this paper, a more detailed analysis of the ratio of labeled data used and the final classification accuracy of the model can further clarify the advantages and limitations of self-supervised approaches.

References

Carreira, J., Noland, E., Banki-Horvath, A., Hillier, C., Zisserman, A. (2018). A Short Note about Kinetics-600, arXiv:1808.01340.

Chen, C., Zhu, Z., Hammad, A. (2020). Automated excavators activity recognition and productivity analysis from construction site surveillance videos, Autom. Constr. 110, 103045. https://doi.org/10.1016/j.autcon.2019.103045

Chen, T., Kornblith, S., Norouzi, M., Hinton, G. (2020). A Simple Framework for Contrastive Learning of Visual Representations. In: Proceedings of the 37th International Conference on Machine Learning. PMLR, pp. 1597–1607.

Cho, H., Kim, T., Chang, H.J., Hwang, W. (2020). Self-supervised spatio-temporal representation learning using variable playback speed prediction, ArXiv Prepr. arXiv:2003.02692.

Feichtenhofer, C., Fan, H., Malik, J., He, K. (2019). SlowFast Networks for Video Recognition. Presented at the Proceedings of the IEEE/CVF International Conference on Computer Vision, pp. 6202–6211.

Grill, J.B., Strub, F., Altché, F., Tallec, C., Richemond, P.H., Buchatskaya, E., Doersch, C., Pires, B.A., Guo, Z.D., Azar, M.G., Piot, B., Kavukcuoglu, K., Munos, R., Valko, M. (2020). Bootstrap your own latent: A new approach to self-supervised Learning, arXiv:2006.07733.

Hara, K., Kataoka, H., Satoh, Y. (2018). Can Spatiotemporal 3D CNNs Retrace the History of 2D CNNs and ImageNet? Presented at the Proceedings of the IEEE Conference on Computer Vision and Pattern Recognition, pp. 6546–6555.

Hinton, G., Vinyals, O., Dean, J. (2015). Distilling the Knowledge in a Neural Network, ArXiv Prepr. arXiv:1503.02531.

Jing, L., Tian, Y. (2021). Self-Supervised Visual Feature Learning with Deep Neural Networks: A Survey, IEEE Trans. Pattern Anal. Mach. Intell. 43, 4037–4058. https://doi.org/10.1109/TPAMI.2020.2992393

Jung, S., Jeoung, J., Kang, H., Hong, T. (2021). 3D convolutional neural network-based one-stage model for real-time action detection in video of construction equipment, Comput.-Aided Civ. Infrastruct. Eng. 37, 126–142. https://doi.org/10.1111/mice.12695

Kay, W., Carreira, J., Simonyan, K., Zhang, B., Hillier, C., Vijayanarasimhan, S., Viola, F., Green, T., Back, T., Natsev, P., Suleyman, M., Zisserman, A. (2017). The Kinetics Human Action Video Dataset, arXiv:1705.06950.

Kim, J., Chi, S. (2021). A few-shot learning approach for database-free vision-based monitoring on construction sites, Autom. Constr. 124, 103566. https://doi.org/10.1016/j.autcon.2021.103566

Kim, J., Chi, S. (2020). Multi-camera vision-based productivity monitoring of earthmoving operations, Autom. Constr. 112, 103121. https://doi.org/10.1016/j.autcon.2020.103121

Kim, J., Chi, S. (2019). Action recognition of earthmoving excavators based on sequential pattern analysis of visual features and operation cycles, Autom. Constr. 104, 255–264. https://doi.org/10.1016/j.autcon.2019.03.025

Kim, J., Chi, S., Seo, J. (2018). Interaction analysis for vision-based activity identification of earthmoving excavators and dump trucks, Autom. Constr. 87, 297–308. https://doi.org/10.1016/j.autcon.2017.12.016

Li, J., Liu, X., Zhang, W., Zhang, M., Song, J., Sebe, N. (2020). Spatio-Temporal Attention Networks for Action Recognition and Detection, IEEE Trans. Multimed. 22, 2990–3001. https://doi.org/10.1109/TMM.2020.2965434

Luo, X., Li, H., Yu, Y., Zhou, C., Cao, D. (2020). Combining deep features and activity context to improve recognition of activities of workers in groups, Comput.-Aided Civ. Infrastruct. Eng. 35, 965–978. https://doi.org/10.1111/mice.12538

Misra, I., Zitnick, C.L., Hebert, M. (2016). Shuffle and Learn: Unsupervised Learning Using Temporal Order Verification. In: Computer Vision – ECCV 2016. Presented at the European Conference on Computer Vision, Springer, Cham, pp. 527–544. https://doi.org/10.1007/978-3-319-46448-0_32

Oord, A. van den, Li, Y., Vinyals, O. (2019). Representation Learning with Contrastive Predictive Coding, ArXiv Prepr. arXiv:1807.03748.

Qian, R., Meng, T., Gong, B., Yang, M.-H., Wang, H., Belongie, S., Cui, Y. (2021). Spatiotemporal Contrastive Video Representation Learning. Presented at the Proceedings of the IEEE/CVF Conference on Computer Vision and Pattern Recognition, pp. 6964–6974.

Roberts, D., Golparvar-Fard, M. (2019). End-to-end vision-based detection, tracking and activity analysis of earthmoving equipment filmed at ground level, Autom. Constr. 105, 102811.

Slaton, T., Hernandez, C., Akhavian, R. (2020). Construction activity recognition with convolutional recurrent networks, Autom. Constr. 113, 103138. https://doi.org/10.1016/j.autcon.2020.103138

Tian, Y., Krishnan, D., Isola, P. (2020). Contrastive Multiview Coding. In: Computer Vision – ECCV 2020, Lecture Notes in Computer Science. Springer International Publishing, pp. 776–794. https://doi.org/10.1007/978-3-030-58621-8_45

Torabi, G., Hammad, A., Bouguila, N. (2021). Joint Detection And Activity Recognition Of Construction Workers Using Convolutional Neural Networks. Presented at the 2021 European Conference on Computing in Construction, pp. 212–219. https://doi.org/10.35490/EC3.2021.197

Xiao, B., Zhang, Y., Chen, Y., Yin, X. (2021). A semi-supervised learning detection method for vision-based monitoring of construction sites by integrating teacher-student networks and data augmentation, Adv. Eng. Inform. 50, 101372. https://doi.org/10.1016/j.aei.2021.101372

Xu, D., Xiao, J., Zhao, Z., Shao, J., Xie, D., Zhuang, Y. (2019). Self-Supervised Spatiotemporal Learning via Video Clip Order Prediction. Presented at the Proceedings of the IEEE/CVF Conference on Computer Vision and Pattern Recognition, pp. 10334–10343.

Yao, Y., Liu, C., Luo, D., Zhou, Y., Ye, Q. (2020). Video Playback Rate Perception for Self-Supervised Spatio-Temporal Representation Learning. Presented at the Proceedings of the IEEE/CVF Conference on Computer Vision and Pattern Recognition, pp. 6548–6557.

Design and Development of Heritage Building Information Model (HBIM) Database to Support Maintenance

Chen W., Yuan J., Luo H.
School of Civil and Hydraulic Engineering, Huazhong University of Science and Technology, China
weiya_chen@hust.edu.cn

Abstract. HBIM is an important and useful asset for historical building protection. It has significant advantages in the digital structured archiving of building structures and materials, which has been widely used and studied. This paper proposes a novel framework of HBIM database, which can be further divided into four parts: architectural status database, construction technique database, pathology database and featured element database. We integrated all kinds of data during the whole update process into the HBIM platform, and present in detail the content and organization of each constituting part. This HBIM database is timely updated and maintained to keep all information from the beginning to the end of the update process, so as to provide an important basis for better use and maintenance of historical buildings.

1. Introduction

Historical buildings are part of national history and an important carrier of cultural value, which is difficult to be recovered once damaged. Due to the long time span of historical buildings, many original design drawings and construction technologies have been lost, and it is difficult to determine their current status in term of structure safety. This brings great challenges to the renewal and maintenance of historical buildings. Although the Chinese government has proposed to strengthen the protection of historical buildings, a large number of them have lost their historical and cultural values in the process of renewal and maintenance during nationwide urbanization, which brings many challenges for the protection of historical buildings.

In order to solve the problem that the elements of historical features are damaged in the process of renewal and maintenance of historical buildings, digital and information technology is gradually adopted in this process. Building digital database to keep historical data in archives is one of the common methods for assisting the repair and protection of historical buildings at present.

As a basic tool in the AEC industry, BIM is the preferred tool to integrate building information from different sources, usually being used as an important approach of digital construction. Being a rich data repository of building facilities, BIM supports different tasks in the whole building's life cycle. Because there are special historical and cultural characteristics in historical buildings compared with general buildings, building information model technology for the special attributes of historical building protection is added on the basis of the technical core of BIM, and the concept of HBIM is born.

This paper proposes a framework of HBIM database, adding the historical and cultural attributes of buildings on the basis of the data information covered by BIM, and integrating various data in the whole process of historical building renewal project, so as to provide an important basis for the protection and repair of historical buildings.

The paper is structured as the following. Section 2 introduces the development process of HBIM theory and practice and the related work on how to build HBIM database. Section 3 introduces the HBIM database framework and its specific content proposed in this paper.

https://doi.org/10.7146/aul.455.c226

Section 4 takes a typical historical building in Wuhan named “Bagong house” as an example to show the HBIM database established in this paper. Finally, section 5 addresses the benefits, disadvantages, and delivers innovative recommendations based on the presented case study results.

2. Literature Review

2.1 HBIM Theory and Practice

For the theory and practice of BIM in the field of historical building protection, Arayici Y., Murphy M. and Fai S. had important research in the early stage.

From 2009 to 2017, Murphy M. and Mcgovern E. of the University of Dublin Ireland, took Henrietta street in Dublin as an example, putting forward the concept of HBIM (Murphy and Keenaghan, 2009), the technical framework of HBIM (Murphy and Mcgovern, 2009), the combined application of HIBM and GIS (Dore and Murphy, 2012), and how to convert BIM model data into a web-based game engine platform for popularization and use successively (Murphy and Corns, 2017).

Another major researcher is Fai S. (2013) from Carlton University in Canada, who mainly studies the application of BIM in cultural heritage information recording, and also has explored the process, implementation standards and application of achievements of HBIM.

Above all, the application research related to HBIM in recent ten years covers the basic concept, framework, construction process, combined use with other technologies and application promotion. However, in many cases, HBIM still stands as a tool for three-dimensional display of oblique photography and BIM, it can only be used for the auxiliary display of urban planning scheme and cannot reflect the specific historical information, let alone achieving further useful functions.

2.2 Establishing HBIM Database

Regarding the establishment of HBIM database, Zhou Hongbo (2017) puts forward the construction scheme of BIM database through the study of IFC Standard, and studies the methods of adding, modifying and deleting components in BIM component library. Sun Weichao (2012) explores the modeling idea of various components of ancient buildings on the Revit platform. From the perspective of the mapping relationship between knowledge ontology and HBIM, Shang Dunjiang (2021) proposes the HBIM data information structure based on 5W1H model for architectural heritage data information collection, and built an architectural heritage evaluation management framework based on HBIM-MR technology (MR refers to mixed reality). HBIM-MR is used to evaluate and manage architectural heritage through historical building information model data in virtual environment. Li Shujing (2014) proposes a new information collection method of "type tree + structure tree" for the information collection of cultural relics buildings, and tries to use BIM technology for the repair of these buildings.

As summarized above, most of the current research on HBIM database only focuses on a certain type of building data, such as building elements. There is relatively few research on the integration of different types and different stages of attribute data during the renewal of historical buildings.

In order to solve this problem, this paper proposes a framework of HBIM database to store more types of data, including building status, pathology, construction techniques and featured elements, which may be involved in the protection and repair of historical buildings.

3. Method

3.1 Establishment of HBIM Database

Conceptually, HBIM database is based on BIM with elements of historical features attached. To build HBIM multi-dimensional structured database, we need to identify and extract the historical feature elements of buildings, and keep their spatial structure. BIM is used to store these elements and bind them with time and space attributes in the next step. When the database is initialized, it will continue to evolve with the advancement of the renewal project.

Depending on the data source, the data collected are divided into four sub sections, which are as follows: element database, construction techniques database, pathology database and architectural status database.

The framework of HBIM database is shown in Figure 1.

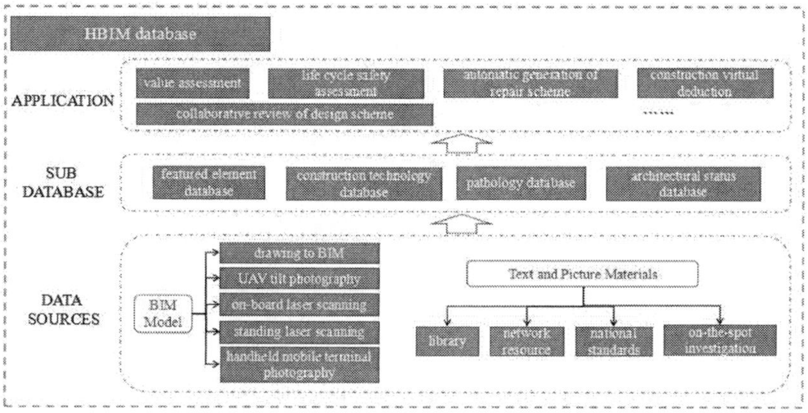

Figure 1: The framework of HBIM database.

3.1.1 Database of Featured Element

Building elements refer to the various elements of a building. For a historical building, its elements can always reflect the typical style characteristics of historical times. The element database is made up by information of featured elements of historical buildings, such as material properties, shape and size, design style, artistic features, etc., which can scientifically guide the construction, protection and repair of these elements.

In order to effectively store the featured element information of historical buildings digitally, the following three steps are taken to build the this database:

- Obtain the point cloud data reflecting the overall structure of the historical building and each featured element through laser scanner to build point cloud models.
- Fuse the overall point cloud model of historical buildings and the single point cloud model of each featured element to obtain the three-dimensional point cloud model of historical buildings.
- Transform the 3D historical building point cloud model into the corresponding BIM model, code different kinds of elements and give relevant attributes to form the

featured element database of historical buildings.

3.1.2 Database of Construction Technique

The construction technique database stores the construction and repair technologies used in the renewal of historical buildings, including repair construction technique standards and characteristic practices. In this database, the construction technique is divided into four types: special repair construction, building repair construction, structural repair construction and facility repair construction. Each type of construction technique is further subdivided according to the different repair contents. The repair of different parts of the building is described in detail from three aspects: current situation, repair objectives and technical measures. Finally, the establishment of the construction technique database is completed by collecting the text materials, videos and images of the repair construction process.

3.1.3 Database of Architectural Pathology

The building pathology in this paper refers to the combination of construction quality accidents and quality defects.

To establish a pathology database, firstly we divide pathologies into three categories according to the subjects as follows: building pathology, structural pathology and equipment pathology. And then the pathologies are further subdivided according to the location and manifestation of the pathology. The specific classification is shown in Figure 2.

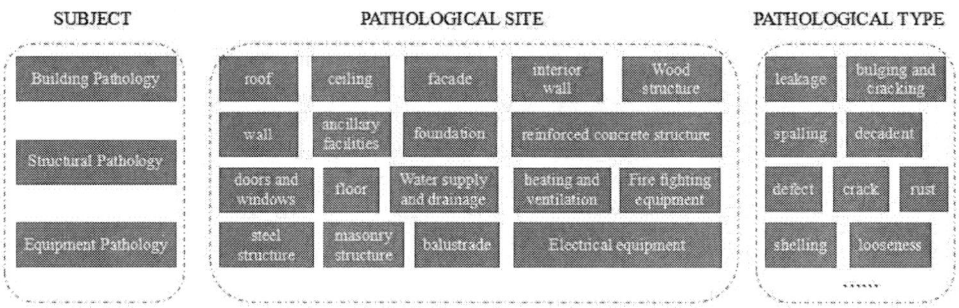

Figure 2: Contents in architectural pathology database.

Finally, a pathology database is established, which contains the information of pathology types, pathology distribution, pathology formation mechanism and deterioration mechanism, etc. All data are derived from architectural pathology and the real conditions of historical buildings obtained on site.

3.1.4 Database of Architectural Status

The architectural status database collects and summarizes various data of historical buildings to provide a strong guarantee for surveillance and repair. At the same time, it also serves as basic data to assist in generating planning schemes for building renewal and utilization. Data in the current database includes the material of a single historical building: geographical location, block overview, building overview, historical evolution, preservation value, design documents, four-dimensional model, drawing information, etc. At the same time, it also includes the current laws, regulations and standards related to the preservation and repair of historical buildings.

These data come from historical building preservation plans, relevant records on the network, national codes and standards, and data collected on site. The database sets up a series of architectural attributes to structure and integrate these scattered data from different sources for reference for subsequent preservation and repair.

3.2 BIM Modeling in Complex Scenes

3.2.1 With Design Drawings

When there are mapping drawings of historical buildings, the method of "drawing to BIM" is used. "Drawing to BIM" is to convert an existing 2D architectural drawing to a 3D model, which is based on the architectural information given on the architectural surveying and mapping drawings, and directly constructs the three-dimensional model in a BIM software such as Revit.

3.2.2 Without Design Drawings

When there is no mapping drawing of historical buildings, we need to take different methods to obtain drawings according to the different scales and accuracy that are to be measured. Generally, we adopt four mapping methods: UAV tilt photography (for a wide area), mobile laser scanning (for indoor complex space), terrestrial laser scanning (for near ground space) and handheld mobile terminal photography (for featured elements) according to the different scope of application.

4. Case Study

4.1 Architectural overview

Bagong house is one of the first-class excellent historical buildings in Wuhan, located in the Russian concession of Hankou. It is a Renaissance building with brick concrete structure, and is designed by Jingming foreign firm, a British funded company.

Figure 3: "Xiao Bagong House" and "Da Bagong House" in 2015.

4.2 BIM Modeling

The BIM model of Bagong house is generated by the method of "Drawing to BIM", and the modeler manually constructs the BIM model in Revit software according to the data of scanned two-dimensional architectural drawings. Then, the modeler renders the BIM model to make it more in line with the architectural reality, and finally integrates the rendered model into the platform.

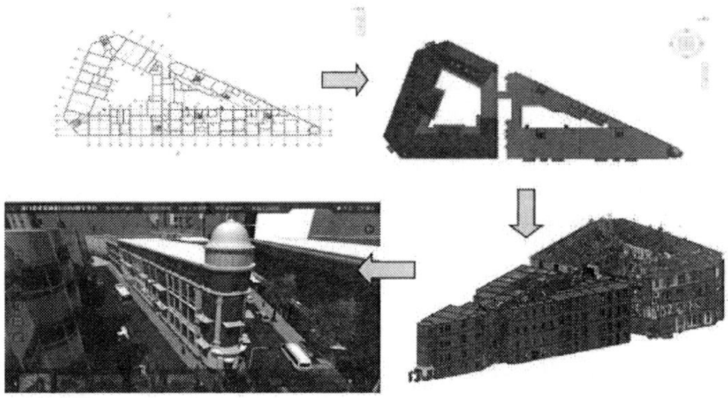

Figure 4: BIM modeling process of "Bagong House".

4.3 HBIM Database of Bagong House

4.3.1 Featured Element Database

The identification of featured elements of Bagong house is mainly based on the contents of historical building protection plans. For example, the railing in Figure 5 is the key protection part specified in the plan. Through the description of the current situation in the plan, it can be seen that the style, shape and decoration of the component have certain historical and artistic value, which can reflect the construction style of Jingming foreign firm, the builder of Bagong house at that time to a certain extent. Therefore, the component is regarded as one of the featured elements of Bagong house, and put it into the featured element database.

Figure 5: Stair handrail of "Bagong House" (Current situation: the handrail column capital is exquisitely carved, the body of the column is carved with petal decoration, and the top is pumpkin shaped. The right column also has bowl decoration above the pumpkin shape).

After determining which components are the featured elements we need, laser scanner is used to obtain the point cloud data of the elements, and then the 3D model of the elements is obtained. Then the 3D model of elements and attribute information (such as name, distribution, current situation, material, size, etc.) are collected for coding. Repeat the above operations for all featured elements to make a collection, and you can get the featured element database of Bagong house, as shown in Figure 6.

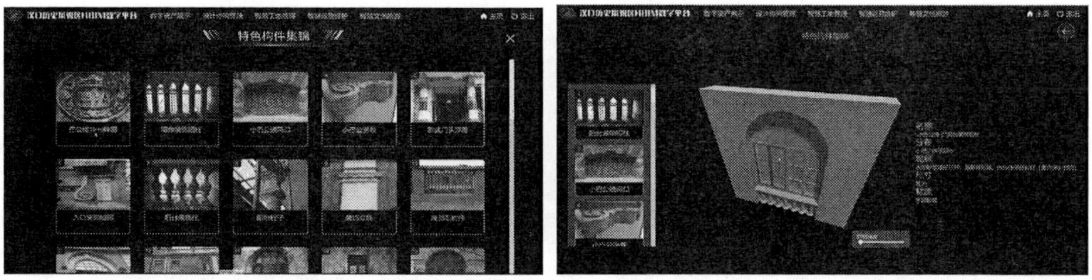

Figure 6: Snapshot of featured element database of "Bagong House".

4.3.2 Construction Technique Database

The repair of different parts of the building is described in detail from three aspects: current situation, repair objectives and technical measures. Some repair technologies with special requirements are also recorded in the database. As shown in Table 1, take the repair measures of grass reinforced gray floor as an example.

Table 1: Repair measures of grass reinforced gray floor.

Three aspects	Concrete content	Status picture
present situation	The floor of the indoor toilet and kitchen of Bagong house is grass reinforced ash leveling floor, that is, straw stems are added to the "foreign ash", which can increase the tensile force and ductility of the ash and prevent wall cracking.	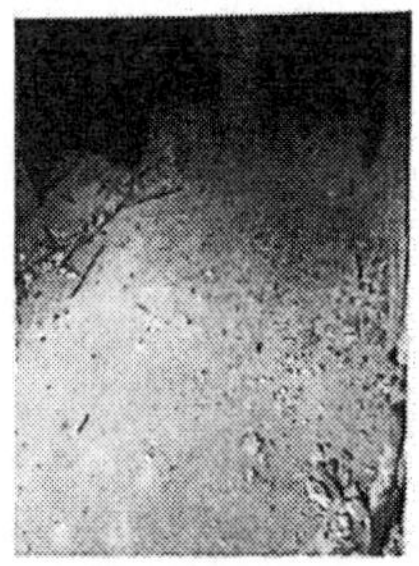
repair target	After the repair of Bagong house, it is mainly used for office and boutique hotel. The toilet function is still used and floor tiles are used.	
technical measures	The grass reinforced gray floor has serious damage problems such as exposed reinforcement, corrosion of reinforcement, serious carbonization and pulverization of cement, which can be removed and rebuilt according to the actual situation of the site. For the floor slab that does not meet the demolition conditions, the method of external bonding carbon fiber shall be adopted for reinforcement.	

In order to more intuitively describe the repair technique, we recorded the complete repair technique as a video at the construction site and also stored it in the construction technique database, so as to provide reference for the future repair of the building or the repair and renewal of other historical buildings.

4.3.3 Architectural Pathology Database

The pathology data of Bagong house are mostly from the protection plans of historical buildings and on-site shooting. We classify the pathology data of Bagong house according to the previously divided pathology types, and fill these data into the corresponding types for detailed description (including picture description and text description), as shown in Figure 7.

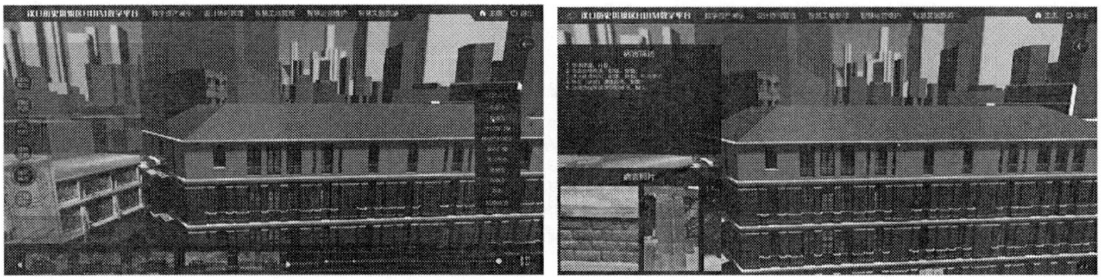

Figure 7: Snapshot of pathology database of "Bagong House" (Classify the pathologies existing in "Bagong house" according to the classification standards, and store the pathology data in the database. Click the pathology name in the list on the right to view the corresponding photos, coordinates, disease description, etc).

4.3.4 Architectural Status Database

For the architectural status database of Bagong house, we firstly make a template according to the relevant attributes of historical buildings, and then filled the text or image data obtained from various ways into the template according to a certain format, so as to complete the structure of the data for computer search and use.

Figure 8 shows the current situation of Bagong house in HBIM database.

Figure 8: Snapshot of architectural status database of "Bagong House".

5. Conclusion

Digital archiving of historical building materials is an urgent need at present. The HBIM database framework proposed in this paper integrates the current situation, featured elements, repair technique and pathology of historical buildings, and comprehensively integrates the data that may be needed in the renewal project of historical buildings and stores them in a BIM model. Different from the traditional building management using BIM model, it deeply excavates the unique historical and cultural elements of historical buildings, which can effectively reflect the heritage value of the building to a certain extent, and can continuously record the historical building data and assist its operation and maintenance during the process of heritage preservation and utilization.

However, the current HBIM database still faces some limitations. Although the database stores a large number of construction data from various sources, there may still have data loss and errors due to the limitations of manual collection. Therefore, more intelligent means should be considered to improve the process of data collection in the future.

Funding

This work was supported by NSFC under Grant 72001086.

References

Murphy M., Keenaghan G., Mcgovern E., (2009). A Flexible Web Based Learning Tool for Construction and Surveying Students Using Building Information Modelling and Laser Scanning.

Murphy M., Mcgovern E., Pavia S., (2009). Historic building information modelling (HBIM). pp.311-327.

Murphy M., Mcgovern E., Pavia S., (2012). Historic Building Information Modelling - Adding Intelligence to Laser and Image Based Surveys. ISPRS-International Archives of the Photogrammetry. Remote Sensing and Spatial Information Sciences, pp. 1-7.

Dore C., Murphy M., (2012). Integration of Historic Building Information Modeling (HBIM) and 3D GIS for recording and managing cultural heritage sites: International Conference on Virtual Systems and Multimedia.

Murphy M., Corns A., Cahill J., (2017). Developing Historic Building Information Modelling Guidelines and Procedures for Architectural Heritage in Ireland, pp. 539-546.

Fai S., Sydor M., (2013). Building Information Modelling and the documentation of architectural heritage: Between the 'typical' and the 'specific, International Journal of Dermatology. pp.705-710.

Zhou H., (2017). Research on BIM component library based on IFC Standard. JOURNAL OF GRAPHICS, pp. 589-595.

Sun W., (2012). Design of ancient building information model system based on Revit architecture. School of architecture, Tianjin University.

Shang D., Xu B., (2021). Application of HBIM-MR technology in architectural heritage evaluation and management from the perspective of Ontology. Construction economy, pp. 93-97.

Li S., (2014). Collection and expression of architectural heritage information based on BIM Technology under the background of information surveying and mapping. School of architecture, Tianjin University.

Point Cloud-Based Concrete Surface Defect Semantic Segmentation Using Modified PointNet++

Bolourian N., Hammad A., Ghelmani A.
Concordia University, Canada
amin.hammad@concordia.ca

Abstract. Structural inspection is essential to improve the safety and sustainability of infrastructure systems, such as bridges. Therefore, several technologies have been developed to detect defects automatically and accurately. For example, instead of using naked eye for bridge surface defect detection, which is subjective and risky, Light Detection and Ranging can collect high-quality 3D point clouds. This paper presents the Surface Normal Enhanced PointNet++ (SNEPointNet++), which is a modified version of the well-known PointNet++ method applied to the task of concrete surface defect detection. To this end, a point cloud dataset from three bridges in Montreal was collected, annotated, and classified into the three classes of cracks, spalls, and no-defects. Based on the comparison between the results (IoU) from the proposed method and similar research done on the same dataset, there are at least 54% and 13% performance improvements in detecting cracks and spalls, respectively.

1 Introduction

Structural inspection is essential to improve the sustainability and safety of infrastructure systems (e.g., bridges). Therefore, several technologies have been recently developed to detect defects automatically and accurately. Light Detection and Ranging (LiDAR) scanners have proven their benefits in identifying surface defects of bridges, such as cracks and spalls. Olsen et al. (2010) proposed a slicing analysis to quantify the spalling volume of large-scale structural elements based on the cross-sectional slices of the point cloud data. Other approaches based on damage-sensitive features such as curvature (Teza et al., 2009), distance and gradient (Liu et al., 2010), and surface normal (Guldur and Hajjar, 2017) have also been proposed. For localization and quantification of concrete surface spalls, Kim et al. (2015) introduced a new automated technique using Terrestrial Laser Scanner (TLS), which was applicable for defects larger than 4 mm in depth. Guldur et al. (2015) first used both graph-based and surface normal-based methods considering RGB and XYZ coordinates of points to detect the defects, and then applied clustering to group the defect points into individual defects. Those methods are sensitive to noise, uneven density, and complicated structures (Te et al., 2018).

Recently, the use of Deep Learning (DL)-based methods has been increasing in the construction industry. DL is applied for classification, semantic segmentation, and instance segmentation of point clouds. In terms of bridge inspection, DL classification aims to investigate the existence of defects without giving further information about their location or boundary. Compared to classification, semantic segmentation is more detailed requiring each point to be labeled individually and each class can be visualized with a specific color. Instance segmentation provides an even more detailed analysis by segmenting the points and assigning an ID to each instance in a class (Hafiz and Bhat, 2020).

Qi et al. (2017a) presented the first novel point-based method, called PointNet, to learn the features of each point using shared Multilayer Perceptrons (MLPs), which is a supplement of feedforward network, and global features using symmetrical pooling functions. However, PointNet has two main shortcomings: (1) lack of local context learning and (2) translation invariance limitation (Qi et al., 2017b). To overcome these limitations, in another work Qi et

https://doi.org/10.7146/aul.455.c227

al. (2017b) proposed PointNet++, which has hierarchical feature learning by using multiple vanilla PointNet learners with different scales.

This paper aims to take advantage of both point cloud data and DL-based semantic segmentation to detect concrete surface defects by applying a modified version of a well-known DL method, called PointNet++ (Qi et al., 2017b). The proposed method is called Surface Normal Enhanced PointNet++ (SNEPointNet++).

2 Methodology

PointNet++ architecture can be categorized into two main sections: (1) Sampling and grouping, (2) feature propagation. The goal of the sampling and grouping section is to address the two main limitations of lack of local context and translation invariance in the original PointNet paper. To this end, first a set of center points are sampled from input data using the furthest-point sampling algorithm, then neighboring points around each sampled center point are determined and grouped using query ball. While this approach includes the local context, since the density of point clouds is not unified in all parts of a real dataset, the resulting neighborhood may vary depending on the selected center points (translation variance). To address this problem, PointNet++ employs multi-scale and multi-resolution grouping. Finally, each center point and its corresponding neighborhood are input into the Vanilla PointNet to obtain local features. After obtaining the desired features, in the second section the features are propagated back into the original input size so as to obtain the label of each point (segmentation). To this end, interpolation layers are required, corresponding to the sampling and grouping layers used in the previous section. Furthermore, the output of each interpolation layer is first concatenated with the input of the corresponding sampling and grouping layer through skip connections, for improved performance, before being fed into a unit PointNet. Finally, the extracted features are passed through two fully connected PointNet units to obtain the label of each point.

Considering that PointNet++ semantic segmentation method was originally designed to detect indoor building elements, it cannot be applied in an off-the-shelf manner to the task of concrete bridge defect detection. As such, four main aspects differentiate this study from the original one, as explained below.

1. Creating a large high-quality point cloud dataset

A sufficient point cloud dataset is a key issue in the point-based semantic segmentation of surface defects. Unlike point clouds, many images of concrete cracks and spalls are available online, which can be used for training a DL model. Strict safety regulations, availability, and accessibility complications in scanning a bridge are the main reasons for the lack of point cloud datasets. Therefore, this study aims to provide a high-quality point cloud dataset to be used in surface defect detection by different groups of researchers. Furthermore, several data augmentation approaches such as shifting, flipping, and rotating can be applied to generate a bigger dataset based on the available one. In this work, the collected point clouds were tripled by flipping vertically and horizontally, however, rotation was not applied because it can alter the characteristics of some defects (e.g. orientation of shear cracks)

2. Redefining the attributes of points to better capture the main features of defects

Unlike the original PointNet++, finding two identical elements in one class is impossible, which causes some difficulties in the learning process. However, almost all cracks and spalls have two main characteristics; they are deeper and darker than their adjacent areas. Therefore, if trained properly, the network can learn to use these defining characteristics to distinguish between different types of defects and improve its performance.

This study proposes using normal vectors, as an input feature for training SNEPointNet++, in addition to the point location and color features, which are collected during scanning. The use of normal vectors for spall localization has also been suggested in other works such as Kim et al. (2015), which developed a methodology based on the changes in the depth and normal vectors of defects. Ideally, the normal vector of the no-defect area and the deepest point of a defect are perpendicular to the XZ plane, and the deviation between two adjacent normal vectors, identifying the potential presence of a defect. In the original PointNet++ work, the normalized coordinate values of (*X'*, *Y'*, *Z'*) are also used, which provide the network with the relative location of each point. However, since the changes in depth indicate defect existence and Y' dedicates the depth of each point, only this feature is employed in SNEPointNet++. It is computed based on Equation 1 (Qi et al., 2017a).

$$Y' = y_i / y_{max} \tag{1}$$

where y_{max} is the maximum value of y_i in each segment. As shown in Figure 1, a reference plane matching the damaged surface is used to calculate the depth of the points of the defect (y_i) with respect to that surface. It can be seen that the value of Y' increases with the depth of the defect. As such, in the SNEPointNet++ method, each point is represented by a 10-dimensional vector with values of x, y, z, R, G, B, N_x, N_y, N_z, and Y'.

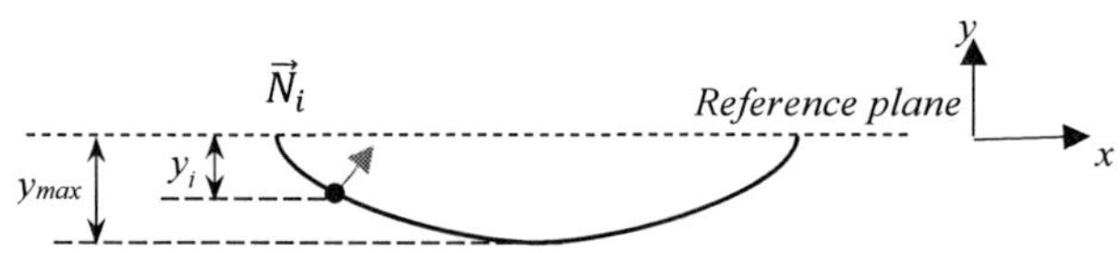

Figure 1: Cross Section of a Sample of Normal Vector and Depth of a Defect Point.

It should be noted that unlike the original PointNet++, in SNEPointNet++, 2D convolving for wrapping the dataset is performed on the XZ surface using the blocks with the given size.

3. Addressing the issue of imbalanced data for priority classes

The imbalanced class distribution is one of the main challenges in this research. Because not only the number of defects in each class but also their size are much different. Moreover, the largest part of the dataset belongs to the no defect class, which has the least priority. As a result, a weighted softmax cross-entropy loss function is applied to increase the contribution of the minority classes (spalls and cracks), which have priority.

4. Applying sensitivity analysis to adjust the hyperparameters in order to better capture the features of small defects.

The hyperparameters related to the network architecture and the dataset should be adjusted in case of using different datasets and attributes. The range of each hyperparameter is selected to cover the most promising values. The two main hyperparameters, which are considered in this paper are number of sub-layers and sampling size of each sublayer. Sub-layers in PointNet++ are responsible for extracting the features from the sampled and grouped points. The learning capacity of a neural network increases exponentially with its depth (i.e., number of sub-layers) and polynomialy with its width (i.e., number of nodes) (Montufar et al., 2014). Therefore, a sensitivity analysis on the number of sub-layers is performed to obtain the optimal performance.

On the other hand, multiple sampling sizes is one of the advantages of PointNet++. Deeper network makes the opportunity of increasing the variety of sampling sizes. Although all defects are small, their sizes vary in a wide range. Therefore, the sampling sizes should satisfy large spalls as well as small cracks.

The best combination of hyperparameters are selected based on the following three performance metrics, which are computed using Equations 2-4.

$$Precision = TP/(TP + FP) \tag{2}$$

$$Recall = TP/(TP + FN) \tag{3}$$

$$IoU = TP/(FP + TP + FN) \tag{4}$$

where TP, FN, TN, and FP represent True Positive, False Negative, True Negative, and False Positive, respectively.

3 Case Study

3.1 Data Collection and Preparation

The input of the proposed method, which is the 3D point cloud dataset, was scanned from four reinforced concrete bridges in Montreal using a FARO Focus3D scanner (FARO Technologies Inc., 2012). The 3D Faro laser scanner is equipped by a camera, which automatically captures images during scanning and detects the color of each point. CloudCompare (Girardeau-Montaut, 2020) is a 3D point cloud processing software. Afterwards, the scanned point clouds were registered and the irrelevant points (i.e., buildings, trees) were removed. Then, several parts were segmented out of the scanned bridge surface, and the *Z*-axis of the canonical coordinate system was set in the vertical direction. Normal vectors were calculated and three attributes (N_x, N_y, and N_z) were added to each point. Finally, the point cloud was manually annotated and labeled into three classes: cracks, spalls, and no-defect. The statistical information of the dataset is summarized in Table 1. Figure 2 demonstrates the distribution of the dataset based on segment density.

Table 1: Statistics of the Annotated Dataset Before Augmentation.

Dataset	Number of segments	Number of points	Cracks		spalls		No-defect
			Number of cracks	Number of points	Number of spalls	Number of points	Number of points
Training & Evaluation	81	21,313,285	475	182,430	588	1,252,551	19,878,304
Testing	21	5,628,620	120	64,269	185	682,614	4,881,737
Total	102	26,941,905	595	246,699	773	1,935,165	24,760,041

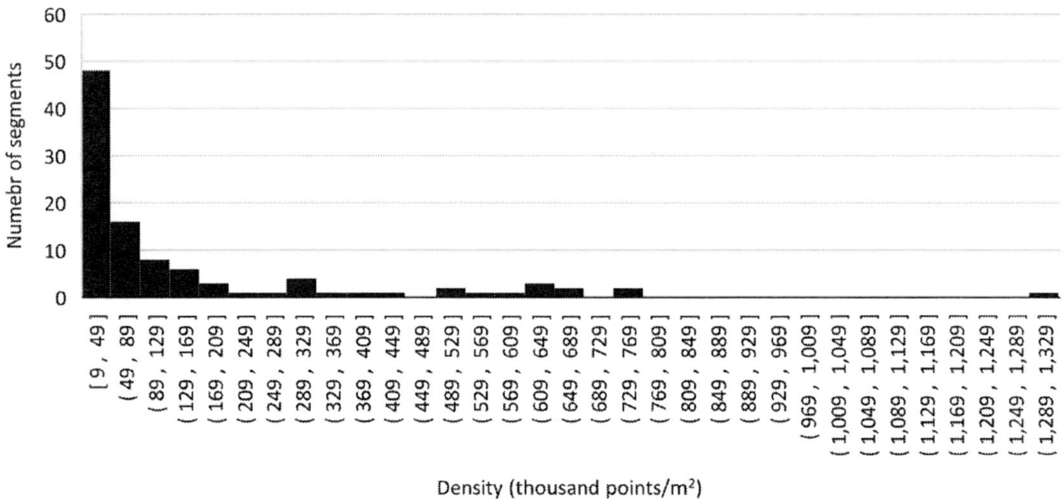

Figure 2: Distribution of Dataset Segments Based on Density.

The prepared dataset is further tripled in size by flipping the original dataset once horizontally and once vertically (Figure 3). The implementation and model training were performed using TensorFlow-GPU 1.15.1, python 3.6, and Cuda 11.0. The point cloud dataset attributes and the corresponding labels were concatenated and stored into *NumPy* format files. Then, the annotated point clouds were wrapped and normalized inside the blocks and saved in HDF5 format. The number of points in each block and block sizes variables can be adjusted in this step.

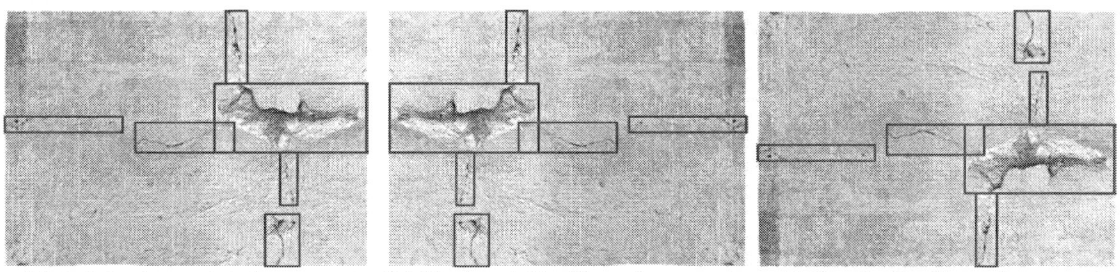

(a) Original annotated segment (b) Horizontally flipped segment (c) Vertically flipped segment

Figure 3: Data Augmentation.

3.2 Training and Testing

Data processing was performed on a LAMBDA workstation, with 3 NVIDIA RTX A6000 GPUs and an AMD Ryzer Threadripper 3960x 24-core CPU. Most of the algorithms are developed in Python 3.8. The number of batches and initial learning rate were assumed 24 and 1e-3, respectively. The learning rate decayed 50% every eight epochs until the minimum value of 1e-5 was reached.

The original network includes two sets of 4-layer networks. In this study, four, five, and six sublayers were considered to find the effective depth. The widths of defects vary between 0.2 cm (i.e., hairline cracks) and 50 cm (i.e., severe spalls). Therefore, a relatively wide range of 2.5 cm to 50 cm was considered for the sampling size of each sub-layer. The five sublayers with the sampling sizes of 2.5 cm, 5 cm, 10 cm, 20 cm, and 30 cm resulted in the most efficient network performance in terms of both crack and spall semantic segmentation. The testing results and the architecture of SNEPointNet++ are shown in Table 2 and Figure 4, respectively.

Table 2: Testing Results (%).

Sampling size in each layer (cm)					**Cracks**			**Spalls**		
1	**2**	**3**	**4**	**5**	**Precision**	**Recall**	**IoU**	**Precision**	**Recall**	**IoU**
2.5	5	10	20	30	73.3	93.0	69.2	89.9	92.0	82.5

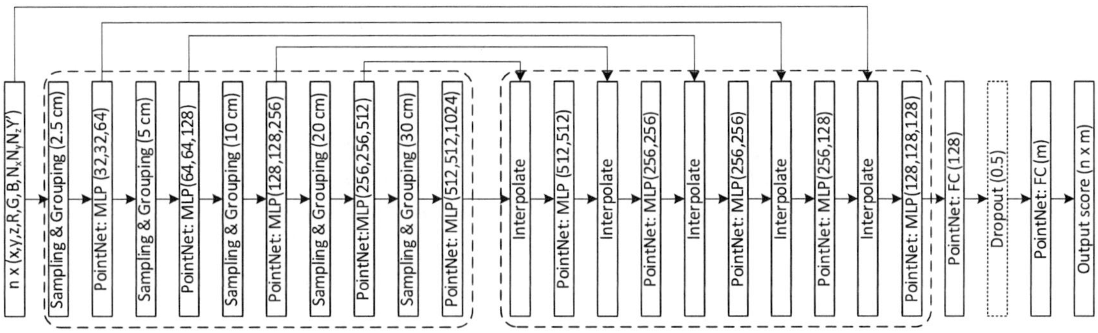

Figure 4: Architecture of SNEPointNet++.

4 Discussion

The recent image-based methods have reached around 98% (Le et al., 2021) to 99% (Vignesh et al., 2021) recalls in concrete surface defect classification. However, classification is not the appropriate approach to find the semantic information of each point individually, which is the objective of this research.

Compared to the recent image-based semantic segmentation methods, SNEPointNet++ results in 1-6% (Hoskere et al., 2020; Fu et al., 2021; Wang et al., 2022) and 1% higher IoU (Hoskere et al., 2020) in terms of crack and spall detection, respectively. Although Lee et al. (2019) trained a model with the highest precision in crack semantic segmentation, SNEPointNet++ leads to 19% higher recall.

To compare point cloud-based surface defect detection methods, they are categorized into three groups based on the types of defects (i.e., cracks, spalls, and both). The crack detection methods are incomparable because of using different scales (i.e., error) or visualization to show the results. Although the dataset of Valença et al. (2017) included the cracks with 0.1 mm to 4 mm thickness, the minimum detectable crack width was 1 mm. Turkan et al. (2018) proposed the only DL-based method in this category, which is not comparable due to showing the results based on error.

In the case of spall detection, the best result of Kim et al. (2017) was 92% average recall and 97 % average precision for ten samples with the sizes between 10 mm × 10 mm × 4 mm and 100 mm × 100 mm × 7 mm. Due to scanning larger spalls in an ideal situation in terms of incidence angle and distance, better results are expected.

The last group, which belongs to spall and crack detection methods, includes two studies. Unlike Guldur and Hajjar (2017) method, adapted DGCNN (Bahreini and Hammad, 2021) and SNEPointNet++ were evaluated using the same dataset. The IoU results show that the efficiency of SNEPointNet++ is 10% and 24% higher than adapted DGCNN in terms of spall and crack detection, respectively.

5 Conclusions and Future Work

This paper presents a DL-based automated method for detecting two types of concrete surface semantic segmentation, including cracks and spalls, using point clouds. The basic benefits of PointNet++ are: (1) considering the features related to both images (i.e., RGB) and point cloud (i.e., x, y, z); (2) not converting point clouds into other representations (i.e., voxels, images); (3) considering both local and global features; and (4) using multi-scale and multi-resolution samples. However, applying the original PointNet++ does not result in high performance, and fundamental modifications are required based on the nature of defects and collected dataset.

The contributions of this paper are: (1) Creating a large high-quality point cloud dataset, available upon request, for future research in concrete surface defect detection; and (2) Developing SNEPointNet++, which is a DL point-based semantic segmentation method for concrete surface defect detection. The proposed method is a modified version of PointNet++ to focus on two main characteristics of surface defects: normal vector and depth.

The proposed technique is successfully validated through a dataset of four bridges in Montreal, Canada, which was tripled by augmentation. This dataset includes 1,785 cracks and 2,319 spalls with a minimum width of 2 mm and 5 mm, respectively. SNEPointNet++ can detect cracks and spalls with 93% (IoU: 69%) and 92% (IoU:83%) recalls, respectively. It can be concluded that considering the nature, size, and patterns of the classes is vital to train a high-performance model. Using different settings for the scanning quality and resolution during the data collection, and having the segments with different densities make SNEPointNet++ invariant to these factors. However, a high-quality dataset is still required to have an accurate defect annotation.

As mentioned above, the lack of a huge dataset, which is crucial to train an accurate model, can be considered as the main limitation of this research. Moreover, the available dataset is limited to the surfaces of the bridge piers and abutments. Therefore, the model is not trained for curved surfaces. Despite using the weighted loss function for learning, the effect of the class-imbalanced dataset on the results cannot be fully eliminated. As future work, the dataset can be expanded by scanning more bridges, using other augmentation approaches, and generating synthetic point cloud datasets. Furthermore, instance segmentation can be applied to extract the individual defects. Future work could also define more classes based on the level of severity, such as small, medium, and severe spalls. In addition, future work will aim to investigate the effect of RGB on the performance of SNEPointNet++ by training the network without color feature and comparing the results with the network outputs of this paper.

References

Bahreini, F., Hammad, A. (2021). Point Cloud Semantic Segmentation of Concrete Surface Defects Using Dynamic Graph CNN. In: 38th International Symposium on Automation and Robotics in Construction. pp. 379–386.

FARO Technologies Inc. (2012). Faro Laser Scanner Focus 3D X 130 -NEO-Tech.

Fu, H., Meng, D., Li, W., Wang, Y. (2021). Bridge Crack Semantic Segmentation Based on Improved Deeplabv3+, J. Mar. Sci. Eng. 9, 671.

Guldur, B., Hajjar, J.F. (2017). Laser-based surface damage detection and quantification using predicted surface properties, Autom. Constr. 83, pp. 285–302. https://doi.org/10.1016/j.autcon.2017.08.004

Guldur, B., Yan, Y., Hajjar, J.F. (2015). Condition Assessment of Bridges Using Terrestrial Laser Scanners. In: Structures Congress. pp. 355–366.

Hafiz, A.M., Bhat, G.M. (2020). A survey on instance segmentation: state of the art., International journal of multimedia information retrieval 9, pp. 171–189. https://doi.org/doi.org/10.1007/s13735-020-00195-x

Hoskere, V., Narazaki, Y., Hoang, T.A., Spencer Jr., B.F. (2020). MaDnet: multi-task semantic segmentation of multiple types of structural materials and damage in images of civil infrastructure, J. Civ. Struct. Health Monit. 10, pp. 757–773.

Kim, M.K., Sohn, H., Chang, C.-C. (2015). Localization and Quantification of Concrete Spalling Defects Using Terrestrial Laser Scanning, J. Comput. Civ. Eng. 29, pp. 1–12. https://doi.org/10.1061/(ASCE)CP.1943-5487.0000415

Le, T.-T., Nguyen, V.-H., Le, M.V. (2021). Development of Deep Learning Model for the Recognition of Cracks on Concrete Surfaces, Appl. Comput. Intell. Soft Comput., e8858545. https://doi.org/10.1155/2021/8858545

Lee, D., Kim, J., Lee, D. (2019). Robust concrete crack detection using deep learning-based semantic segmentation, Int. J. Aeronaut. Space Sci. 20, pp. 287–299.

Liu, W., Chen, S., Boyajian, D., Hauser, E. (2010). Application of 3D LiDAR scan of a bridge under static load testing, Mater. Eval. 68, pp. 1359–1367.

Montufar, G.F., Pascanu, R., Cho, K., Bengio, Y. (2014). On the number of linear regions of deep neural networks, Adv. Neural Inf. Process. Syst. 27, pp. 1–9.

Olsen, M.J., Kuester, F., Chang, B.J., Hutchinson, T.C. (2010). Terrestrial Laser Scanning-Based Structural Damage Assessment, J. Comput. Civ. Eng. 24, pp. 264–272. https://doi.org/10.1061/(asce)cp.1943-5487.0000028

Qi, C.R., Su, H., Mo, K., Guibas, L.J. (2017a). Pointnet: Deep learning on point sets for 3d classification and segmentation. In: Computer Vision and Pattern Recognition (CVPR). IEEE, Honolulu, HI, USA, pp. 4–23. https://doi.org/10.1109/CVPR.2017.16

Qi, C.R., Yi, L., Su, H., Guibas, L.J. (2017b). PointNet++: Deep Hierarchical Feature Learning on Point Sets in a Metric Space, Adv. Neural Inf. Process. Syst. pp. 1–14.

Te, G., Hu, W., Zheng, A., Guo, Z. (2018). Rgcnn: Regularized graph CNN for point cloud segmentation. In: The 26th ACM International Conference on Multimedia. Seoul, Republic of Korea, pp. 746–754. https://doi.org/10.1145/3240508.3240621

Teza, G., Galgaro, A., Moro, F. (2009). Contactless recognition of concrete surface damage from laser scanning and curvature computation, Non-Destr. Test. Eval. Int. 42, pp. 240–249. https://doi.org/10.1016/j.ndteint.2008.10.009

Turkan, Y., Hong, J., Laflamme, S., Puri, N. (2018). Adaptive wavelet neural network for terrestrial laser scanner-based crack detection, Autom. Constr. 94, pp. 191–202. https://doi.org/10.1016/j.autcon.2018.06.017

Valença, J., Puente, I., Júlio, E., González-Jorge, H., Arias-Sánchez, P. (2017). Assessment of cracks on concrete bridges using image processing supported by laser scanning survey, Constr. Build. Mater. 146, pp. 668–678. https://doi.org/10.1016/j.conbuildmat.2017.04.096

Vignesh, R., Narenthiran, B., Manivannan, S., Arul Murugan, R., RajKumar, V. (2021). Concrete Bridge Crack Detection Using Convolutional Neural Network. In: Materials, Design, and Manufacturing for Sustainable Environment. Springer, pp. 797–812.

Wang, J., Liu, Y., Nie, X., Mo, Y.L. (2022). Deep convolutional neural networks for semantic segmentation of cracks, Struct. Control Health Monit. 29, e2850.

Evaluating the Performance of Deep Learning in Segmenting Google Street View Imagery for Transportation Infrastructure Condition Assessment

Wei Y., Liu K.
Stevens Institute of Technology, U.S.A.
Kaijian.Liu@stevens.edu

Abstract. Understanding the relationships between the condition of transportation infrastructure and the well-being of citizens in society is of significant importance towards restoring the aging and deteriorating transportation infrastructure in a way that enhances well-being. However, attaining such understanding is challenging because it relies on large-scale transportation infrastructure condition assessment. The broad spatial coverage of Google Street View (GSV) imagery offers a unique opportunity for such large-scale assessment. However, despite the richness of deep learning methods that can segment and recognize transportation infrastructure assets from GSV imagery for subsequent condition assessment, the performance of these methods typically varies. As such, this paper focuses on conducting performance evaluation of representative deep learning-based image segmentation methods to identify the optimal methods for recognizing transportation assets from GSV imagery. The preliminary evaluation results show that the ResNet + UNet and MobileNet + UNet methods achieved the highest intersection over union (IOU) of 0.87.

1. Introduction

The aging and deteriorating transportation infrastructure has disproportionate impacts on the well-being of citizens in society. For example, according to the American Society of Civil Engineers' Infrastructure Report Card, more than 40% of the U.S. transportation infrastructure, such as roadways and highways, is in poor or mediocre condition (American Society of Civil Engineers, 2022a). Such poor conditions result in unreliable and inefficient transportation services, increased travel time and costs for businesses and households, and, in turn, lead to higher prices for goods and lower disposable household income (American Society of Civil Engineers, 2022b). Consequently, the well-being of people gets negatively affected as resources necessary to maintain and improve well-being become less accessible and affordable. Most often, the negative impacts on well-being get passed along disproportionately to people from traditionally underserved groups (American Society of Civil Engineers, 2022b).

There is, therefore, an evident need to quantitatively understand the relationships between the condition of transportation infrastructure and the well-being of citizens. Such an understanding would allow for restoring transportation infrastructure in a way that equitably enhances the well-being of different population groups in society. However, attaining the understanding is challenging because it requires assessing the condition of transportation infrastructure at a large scale (e.g., the city scale). Existing methods for transportation infrastructure condition assessment typically do not scale well. Visual assessment by human inspectors, although it is still common in practice, is too costly and time-consuming to be conducted at scale (Yeum et al., 2021). On the other hand, recent advancement in automated condition assessment technology has largely reduced human involvement in the assessment process. Such technologies include visual imaging, ground penetrating radar, infrared thermography, LiDAR, and hyperspectral imaging. For example, ground penetrating radar has been used to assess the thickness of road pavements

https://doi.org/10.7146/aul.455.c228

(Willett et al., 2006). Visual imaging, infrared thermography, and hyperspectral imaging technologies have been used to assess the conditions of road damages, such as cracks and delamination (Schnebele et al., 2015). However, these technologies have not been widely applied because of technology adoption barriers. Studies (e.g., Li et al., 2017) show that initial investments in assessment equipment and subsequent costs of training professional equipment operators are currently the principal factors hindering the wide adoption and application of these automated condition assessment technologies in practice.

The availability of Google Street View (GSV) imagery offers a great promise for large-scale transportation infrastructure condition assessment. First, GSV imagery is readily and publicly accessible. This advantage liberates transportation agencies from investing in new equipment and training specialized operators and, thus, largely eliminates technology adoption barriers. Second, GSV imagery covers transportation assets in almost any place around the world. Currently, GSV can already provide images that cover more than 10 million miles of roads in the world (Raman, 2017). The broad spatial coverage of GSV imagery lends itself a unique edge in conducting large-scale condition assessment. Third, GSV imagery is of high resolution. GSV images are usually taken using high-resolution camera systems, such as 20MP cameras. The high resolution not only allows for accurately segmenting and recognizing transportation assets from GSV images, but also enables the detection, localization, and quantification of damages on the recognized assets.

However, despite the promise of GSV imagery, there is a lack of studies that evaluate the performance of different deep learning methods in segmenting transportation infrastructure assets from GSV images. Such an evaluation is critical to identify the optimal learning methods that can be used to better conduct the segmentation to support subsequent condition assessment (i.e., damage detection, localization, and quantification). Existing research efforts have focused on images captured using hand-held cameras or cameras mounted unmanned aerial vehicles (UAVs). For a few studies that use GSV images, they are mainly committed to a single learning method and are limited in additionally comparing other alternative methods. To address this limitation, this paper focuses on conducting performance evaluation of representative deep learning-based segmentation methods to identify the optimal ones for segmenting transportation assets from GSV imagery. In the remainder of this paper, the evaluation methodology is introduced in detail, and the evaluation results are discussed.

2. State of the Art and Knowledge Gaps

A body of research efforts have been undertaken in the field of image-based transportation infrastructure condition assessment. According to recent survey studies by Spencer et al., (2019), existing image-based assessment methods mostly rely on images captured using hand-held cameras or cameras mounted on unmanned aerial vehicles (UAVs). For example, recent studies (e.g., Li et al., 2019; Sukanya et al., 2020; and Mahmud et al., 2021) have focused on detecting and segmenting roads from images captured using UAVs. However, a limited number of studies have explored the use of GSV imagery for condition assessment of transportation infrastructure. Recent studies that used GSV imagery for the assessment include Ma et al., (2017) and Alipour and Harris (2020).

However, despite the importance of existing research, there is a lack of understanding of the performances of different deep leaning-based image segmentation methods in segmenting transportation infrastructure assets from GSV images. Such an understanding is critical to identify the optimal learning methods that can reliably segment transportation assets from GSV images to support subsequent condition assessment. On one hand, existing research efforts have focused on comparing and understanding the performances of different learning methods in segmenting general objects (e.g., humans, trees, and sky in natural scenes) from general images rather than GSV images. For example, Ahmed et al., (2020) evaluated the performance of several representative deep learning methods in segmenting humans from top-view images. However, the comparison results achieved using general images typically do not generalize to GSV images because, compared to general images, GSV images are often associated with severe occlusions (e.g., roads occluded by traveling vehicles) and are captured in dynamically changing environments (e.g., sunny days with an abundant amount of lights vs. cloudy/rainy days without decent lights). On the other hand, existing studies that use GSV images for transportation infrastructure condition assessment are limited in comparing alternative deep learning methods. For example, Ma et al., (2017) leveraged convolutional neural networks to detect pavement damages from GSV images; Campbell et al., (2019) used MobileNet to detect traffic signs from GSV images; and Alipour and Harris (2020) exploited deep residual networks (ResNet) to detect road defects from GSV images. However, these studies are committed to using a single learning method and did not additionally compare the performance of the chosen method to other deep learning-based segmentation methods. They are, thus, limited in identifying optimal methods for GSV-based transportation asset segmentation.

3. Evaluation Methodology

An evaluation methodology was developed and followed to evaluate the performance of representative deep learning methods in segmenting transportation infrastructure assets from GSV images. The methodology included three main steps: (1) data preparation, (2) deep learning method selection, and (3) deep learning method implementation and evaluation.

3.1 Data Preparation

Data preparation aimed to create a dataset with annotations for deep learning-based segmentation algorithm training and evaluation. Data preparation included four steps. First, a dataset, which includes a total of 500 GSV images, was created. The images were purposively sampled from main streets in Manhattan, New York City (NYC), so that each image captures key transportation infrastructure assets such as roads, sidewalks, bike lanes, and vehicles. Images for NYC were used in this study because road/street scenes in NYC are typically more complex than those in other cities, making the use of such images more suitable in comparing different segmentation algorithms. Figure 1 shows a sample of collected GSV images. Second, image preprocessing was conducted to resize raw images into the same size of 256 by 256 to allow for mini-batch-based segmentation model training. Third, the resized images were manually annotated using the Visual Geometry Group Image Annotator, which is a commonly used annotation tool for adding class labels to each pixel in an image. Each image pixel was annotated into one of the five classes that cover key transportation asset categories, including "Road", "Sidewalk", "Bike Lane", "Vehicle", and "Background". Fourth, the dataset was split into a training set and a testing set at a ratio of 4:1, which is a commonly used ratio in image segmentation. The annotations in the testing set were used for evaluation purposes only.

Figure 1: Examples of Google Street View (GSV) Images.

3.2 Deep Learning Method Selection

Deep learning method selection aimed to select representative deep learning methods (for image segmentation) for the subsequent performance evaluation. The selection included two steps. First, representative deep learning methods for extracting visual features from images were selected. The selection focused on convolutional neural networks (CNN)-based feature extraction methods, because CNN is one of the most successful and widely used architecture for visual feature extraction. Based on the survey study by Minaee et al., (2020), four well-known CNN-based feature extraction methods were selected, including convolutional neural networks (CNN) (Fukushima, 1980), very deep convolutional networks (VGG) (Simonyan et al., 2015), residual neural networks (ResNet) (He et al., 2015), and MobileNet (Howard et al., 2017). Second, representative deep learning methods for learning from extracted visual features to segment images into pre-defined segmentation classes were selected. Four representative methods were selected, including fully convolutional networks (FCN)-8 (Long et al., 2015), FCN-32 (Long et al., 2015), SegNet (Badrinarayanan et al., 2015), and UNet (Ronneberger et al., 2015). FCNs were selected because they are one of the first deep learning methods for image segmentation and have been commonly used as a benchmark (Minaee et al., 2020). SegNet was selected because, unlike traditional FCN (which leverages a shallow network architecture for up-sampling), it uses a decoder network that includes multiple up-sampling layers and a pixel-wise classification layer for segmentation. Each up-sampling layer uses the pooling indices from its corresponding down-sampling layer to conduct non-linear up-sampling without the need to learn how to up-sample. Such an up-sampling architecture configuration allows for reducing the number of parameters to be learned to improve the performance of segmentation models. UNet was selected because it leverages a contracting path with down-sampling to capture visual contexts and an expanding path with multiple up-sampling layers that also use down-sampled feature maps as input to capture visual patterns to enable precise localization and segmentation. The use of the two paths allows for using a small number of training images to achieve more precise segmentation.

3.3 Deep Learning Method Implementation and Evaluation

The selected deep learning methods were implemented to develop models for segmenting GSV images into the pre-defined segmentation class (i.e., "Road", "Sidewalk", "Bike Lane", "Vehicle", and "Background"). The implementation included three steps. First, the selected visual feature extraction methods were implemented. Figure 2 shows the specific deep learning architecture used to implement each extraction method. Second, the selected segmentation methods were implemented. Figure 3 shows the specific learning architecture used to implement each segmentation method. In a segmentation learning architecture, a visual feature extraction architecture was used as an "encoder" to down-sample raw input images to extract feature maps, and the "decoder" architecture of the selected segmentation method was used to up-sample the feature maps for pixel-wise classification/segmentation. For example, in the CNN + FCN-32 architecture, the CNN architecture was used to extract feature maps, and the 32X up-sampling layer in the FCN-32 was used to up-sample the feature maps from the 5th pooling block of the CNN for pixel-wise classification. As a result, a total of 16 segmentation models were implemented, and each model was implemented using a combination of a selected visual feature extraction method and a selected segment method. The Python code implementation from Divam (2019) was used for the implementation. Third, the segmentation models were separately trained using the training dataset. During the model training, the training pixel accuracy was monitored to ensure that the model is fully trained to converge. Pixel accuracy, as per Equation (1), is the ratio of the number of correctly segmented pixels to the total number of pixels. In Equation (1), C is the number of pre-defined segmentation classes, and P_{ij} is number of pixels of class i that are classified as class j. Figure 4 shows the training pixel accuracy against the training epoch for each model. As per Figure 4, at epoch = 10, the training pixel accuracy for each segmentation model was over 90% and became stable, which indicates that the model is trained to converge.

	CNN	VGG	ResNet	MobileNet
Pool 1	Zero Padding 3x3, 64 Conv. BatchNorm. ReLU Activation MaxPooling	3x3, 64 Conv. 3x3, 64 Conv. MaxPooling	Zero Padding 7x7, 64 Conv.	3x3, 32, Conv. Block 64, Depthwise Conv. Block
Pool 2	Zero Padding 3x3, 128 Conv. BatchNorm. ReLU Activation MaxPooling	3x3, 128 Conv. 3x3, 128 Conv. MaxPooling	3x3, 64-64-256, Conv. Block 3x3, 64-64-256, Identity Block 3x3, 64-64-256, Identity Block	128, Depthwise Conv. Block 128, Depthwise Conv. Block
Pool 3	Zero Padding 3x3, 256 Conv. BatchNorm. ReLU Activation MaxPooling	3x3, 256 Conv. 3x3, 256 Conv. 3x3, 256 Conv. MaxPooling	3x3, 256-256-1024, Conv. Block 3x3, 256-256-1024, Identity Block 3x3, 256-256-1024, Identity Block 3x3, 256-256-1024, Identity Block 3x3, 256-256-1024, Identity Block 3x3, 256-256-1024, Identity Block	256, Depthwise Conv. Block 256, Depthwise Conv. Block
Pool 4	Zero Padding 3x3, 256 Conv. BatchNorm. ReLU Activation MaxPooling	3x3, 512 Conv. 3x3, 512 Conv. 3x3, 512 Conv. MaxPooling	3x3, 256-256-1024, Conv. Block 3x3, 256-256-1024, Identity Block 3x3, 256-256-1024, Identity Block 3x3, 256-256-1024, Identity Block 3x3, 256-256-1024, Identity Block	512, Depthwise Conv. Block 512, Depthwise Conv. Block 512, Depthwise Conv. Block 512, Depthwise Conv. Block 512, Depthwise Conv. Block
Pool 5	Zero Padding 3x3, 256 Conv. BatchNorm. ReLU Activation MaxPooling	3x3, 512 Conv. 3x3, 512 Conv. 3x3, 512 Conv. MaxPooling	3x3, 512-512-2048, Conv. Block 3x3, 512-512-2048, Identity Block 3x3, 512-512-2048, Identity Block	1024, Depthwise Conv. Block 1024, Depthwise Conv. Block

Figure 2: Learning Architectures for the Selected Deep Learning-based Visual Feature Extraction Methods.

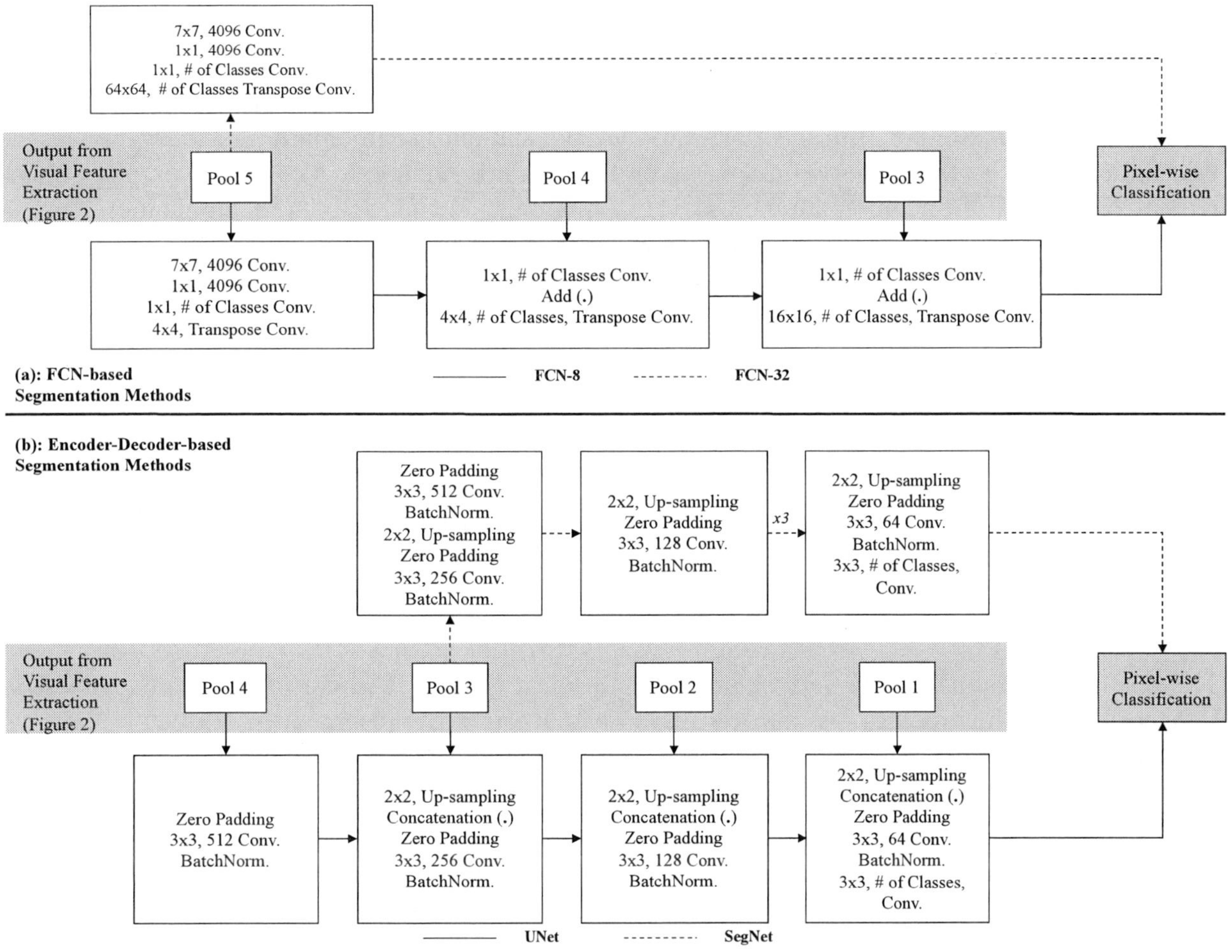

Figure 3: Learning Architectures for Selected Deep Learning-based Segmentation Methods.

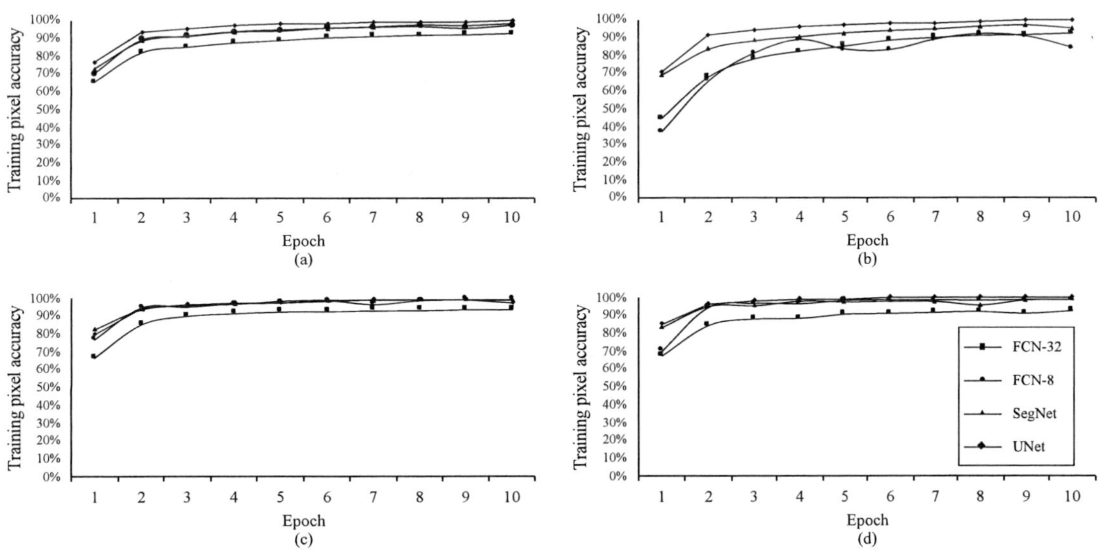

Figure 4: Training Pixel Accuracy of Segmentation Models: (a) CNN-based Models, (b) VGG-based Models, (c) ResNet-based Models, and (d) MobileNet-based Models.

The trained segmentation models were evaluated using two commonly used metrics for image segmentation: class-wise intersection over union (IOU) and mean IOU. For each segmentation class, class-wise IOU, as per Equation (2), is the ratio of the area of intersection between the classified segmentation map for the class and the gold standard segmentation map for the class to the area of union between the two maps. Mean IOU, as per Equation (3), is the average of class-wise IOUs over all the segmentation classes. In Equations (2) and (3), *i* is a segmentation class, *A* is classified segmentation map for class *i*, and *B* is gold standard segmentation map for the class *i*.

$$Accuracy = \frac{\sum_{i=0}^{C} P_{ii}}{\sum_{i=0}^{C}\sum_{j=0}^{C} P_{ij}} \quad (1)$$

$$Class\text{-}wise\ IOU(i) = \frac{|A \cap B|}{|A \cup B|} \quad (2)$$

$$Mean\ IOU = \frac{1}{C}\sum_{i=0}^{C} Class\text{-}wise\ IOU(i) \quad (3)$$

4. Evaluation Results and Discussion

The results for evaluating the performance of the selected deep learning methods in segmenting transportation infrastructure assets from GSV imagery are presented in Table 1. Overall, compared to the other combinations of the feature extraction and segmentation methods, the combinations ResNet + UNet and MobileNet + UNet achieved the highest mean IOU of 0.87.

Two important observations are drawn from the evaluation results. First, using skip connections and separable depthwise convolutions are important strategies to extract representative visual features from GSV images to support subsequent transportation asset segmentation. As seen in Table 1, the ResNet-based and MobileNet-based models achieved an average mean IOU (across all the segmentation methods) of 0.82 and 0.82, respectively. The CNN-based and VGG-based models only achieved an average mean IOU of 0.76 and 0.64, respectively. ResNet uses a set of residual blocks (i.e., convolution and identify blocks, as per Figure 2), which formulate the output layers of each block to learn residual functions with reference to the layer inputs. Such a residual learning configuration allows for substantially increasing the depth of the networks to better capture distinctive visual features, yet without negatively affecting the efficiency and performance of model optimization. On the other hand, MobileNet utilizes depthwise separable convolutional layers, which apply a separate filter only at one input channel (instead of at multiple channels at once). Depthwise separable convolution layers can generate outputs same as those generated by traditional convolution layers, but they require much less parameters to reduce the size of the model and improve the performance of feature extraction. The evaluation results also suggest that incorporating depthwise separable convolutions into residual blocks could allow for benefiting from the advantages of both ResNet and MobileNet to further improve the performance of visual feature extraction from GSV images.

Second, concatenating down-sampled feature maps and up-sampled feature maps to further up-sample the maps for pixel-wise classification shows effectiveness in segmenting transportation infrastructure assets from GSV images. As seen in Table 1, the UNet-based models achieved an average mean IOU (across all the feature extraction methods) of 0.85, which is higher than the IOUs by the FCN-32-based, FCN-8-based, and SegNet-based models (IOU = 0.57, 0.80 and 0.82, respectively). SegNet, compared to FCN-8, achieved a slightly higher IOU. This could be because SegNet uses more up-sampling and transpose convolution operations than FCN-8. UNet, compared to SegNet, further conducts convolutions on the concatenated feature maps (i.e., up-sampled maps and their corresponding down-sampled maps), which allows UNet to achieve a 3% higher IOU than SegNet. The evaluation results, thus, suggest that encoder-decoder-based segmentation methods, such as SegNet and UNet, are generally more effective than FCN-based methods in segmenting transportation assets from GSV images. In future research efforts, other types of encoder-decoder-based methods, such as VNet and WNet, can be evaluated to assess if they can further improve the performance of GSV image segmentation.

Table 1: Results for Evaluating the Performance of Deep Learning Methods in Segmenting Transportation Infrastructure Assets from GSV Images.

Feature extraction method	Segmentation method	Class-wise IOU					Mean IOU
		Background	Road	Sidewalk	Vehicle	Bike Lane	
CNN	FCN8	0.86	0.89	0.72	0.45	0.82	0.75
	FCN32	0.82	0.86	0.70	0.39	0.71	0.70
	UNet	0.95	0.86	0.87	0.53	0.82	0.81
	SegNet	0.90	0.91	0.79	0.50	0.85	0.79
VGG	FCN8	0.89	0.92	0.79	0.45	0.86	0.78
	FCN32	0.49	0.27	0.05	0.00	0.00	0.15
	UNet	0.96	0.93	0.54	0.55	0.92	0.84
	SegNet	0.91	0.90	0.76	0.51	0.85	0.79
ResNet	FCN8	0.95	0.96	0.86	0.55	0.91	0.84
	FCN32	0.81	0.87	0.71	0.38	0.76	0.71
	UNet	0.98	0.97	0.91	0.58	0.93	0.87
	SegNet	0.95	0.94	0.59	0.56	0.90	0.85
MobileNet	FCN8	0.93	0.94	0.85	0.54	0.88	0.83
	FCN32	0.83	0.88	0.75	0.43	0.75	0.73
	UNet	0.98	0.97	0.90	0.58	0.93	0.87
	SegNet	0.95	0.94	0.59	0.56	0.90	0.85

5. Conclusions, Limitations, and Future Work

In this paper, a set of representative deep learning methods were evaluated in segmenting transportation infrastructure assets from GSV images. The evaluation results show that the ResNet + UNet and MobileNet + UNet methods achieved the highest mean IOU of 0.87 – indicating the suitability of these methods for segmenting transportation assets from GSV images. In addition, two conclusions were also drawn from the results. First, incorporating depthwise separable convolutions into residual blocks could allow for better extracting distinctive visual features from GSV images to support subsequent segmentation. Second, encoder-decoder-based methods are more suitable than FCN-based methods in segmenting GSV images.

Two main limitations of this study are acknowledged. First, as a pilot study, this paper focused on evaluating CNN-based feature extraction methods and FCN-based and encoder-decoder-based segmentation methods. Other methods, such as multiscale and pyramid network-based and attention-based methods, were not evaluated. In their future work, by following the evaluation methodology presented in this paper, the authors plan to further evaluate the performance of other prominent deep learning methods in segmenting GSV images. Second, the size of the dataset used in the evaluation is limited. For example, the dataset in this study mainly covers transportation assets in Manhattan, NYC, but does not cover other areas in the nation. A larger and more diverse GSV dataset can be curated and used for evaluation in the future.

In their future work, the authors will focus their research efforts on three main directions. First, developing a new deep learning-based image segmentation method, based on the findings of this study, to better segment transportation assets from GSV images. The segmentation is the first step toward large-scale transportation infrastructure condition assessment. Hence, the segmentation method to be developed will need to achieve an IOU of over 95% to reduce the number of errors propagating into the subsequent assessment steps. In addition to GSV images, the method will also be applied to segment transportation assets from images captured by the cameras on autonomous vehicles and/or reported by citizens. Such images would also be valuable for transportation infrastructure condition assessment, because they are more dynamic and can better capture update-to-date infrastructure conditions. Second, developing new deep learning methods for detecting, localizing, and quantifying transportation asset damages in the segmented images that include key transportation assets (instead of assessing damages using unsegmented images to improve performance of damage condition assessment). Third, conducting data-driven investigations to understand the relationship between transportation infrastructure condition and citizen well-being to support well-being informed infrastructure investment decision making.

References

Ahmed, I., Ahmad, M., Khan, F.A., Asif, M. (2020). Comparison of deep-learning-based segmentation models: Using top view person images, IEEE Access, 8, pp. 136361136373.

Alipour, M., Harris, D.K. (2020). A big data analytics strategy for scalable urban infrastructure condition assessment using semi-supervised multi-transform self-training, Journal of Civil Structural Health Monitoring, 10 (2), pp. 313–332.

American Society of Civil Engineers (2022a). Report Card for America's Infrastructure, https://infrastructurereportcard.org/, accessed January 2022.

American Society of Civil Engineers (2022b). Failure to Act Economic Reports, https://infrastructurereportcard.org/resources/failure-to-act-economic-reports/, accessed January 2022.

Badrinarayanan, V., Kendall, A., Cipolla, R. (2017). Segnet: A deep convolutional encoder-decoder architecture for image segmentation, IEEE Transactions on Pattern Analysis and Machine Intelligence, 39 (12), pp. 2481–2495.

Campbell, A., Both, A., Sun, Q.C. (2019). Detecting and mapping traffic signs from Google Street View images using deep learning and GIS, Computers, Environment and Urban Systems, 77, p. 101350.

Divam, G (2019). A Beginner's Guide to Deep Learning Based Semantic Segmentation Using Keras, https://divamgupta.com/image-segmentation/2019/06/06/deep-learning-semantic-segmentation-keras.html, accessed December 2021.

Fukushima, K., Miyake, S. (1980). Neocognitron: A self-organizing neural network model for a mechanism of visual pattern recognition, Biological Cybernetics, 36, pp. 193–202.

He, K., Zhang, X., Ren, S. and Sun, J. (2016). Deep residual learning for image recognition. In: IEEE Conference on Computer Vision and Pattern Recognition, 2016, Las Vegas, NV.

Howard, A.G., Zhu, M., Chen, B., Kalenichenko, D., Wang, W., Weyand, T., Andreetto, M. and Adam, H. (2017). Mobilenets: Efficient convolutional neural networks for mobile vision applications. arXiv preprint arXiv: 1704.04861.

Li, M., Faghri, A., Ozden, A., Yue, Y. (2017). Economic feasibility study for pavement monitoring using synthetic aperture radar-based satellite remote sensing: Cost-benefit analysis, Transportation Research Record, 2645 (1), pp. 1–11.

Li, Y., Peng, B., He, L., Fan, K., Tong, L. (2019). Road segmentation of unmanned aerial vehicle remote sensing images using adversarial network with multiscale context aggregation, IEEE Journal of Selected Topics in Applied Earth Observations and Remote Sensing, 12 (7), pp. 2279–2287.

Long, J., Shelhamer, E. and Darrell, T. (2015). Fully convolutional networks for semantic segmentation. In: IEEE Conference on Computer Vision and Pattern Recognition, 2015, Boston, MA.

Ma, K., Hoai, M. and Samaras, D. (2017). Large-scale continual road inspection: Visual infrastructure assessment in the wild. In: British Machine Vision Conference, 2017, London, United Kingdom.

Mahmud, M.N., Osman, M.K., Ismail, A.P., Ahmad, F., Ahmad, K.A. and Ibrahim, A. (2021). Road image segmentation using unmanned aerial vehicle images and DeepLab V3+ semantic segmentation model. In: 11th IEEE International Conference on Control System, Computing and Engineering, 2021, Penang, Malaysia.

Minaee, S., Boykov, Y.Y., Porikli, F., Plaza, A.J., Kehtarnavaz, N. and Terzopoulos, D. (2021). Image segmentation using deep learning: A survey. IEEE Transactions on Pattern Analysis and Machine Intelligence.

Raman A (2017). Cheers to Street View 10th birthday! https://www.blog.google/products/maps/cheers-street-views-10th-birthday/, accessed August 2021.

Ronneberger, O., Fischer, P. and Brox, T. (2015). U-Net: Convolutional networks for biomedical image segmentation. In: International Conference on Medical Image Computing and Computer-Assisted Intervention, 2015, Munich, Germany.

Schnebele, E., Tanyu, B.F., Cervone, G., Waters, N. (2015). Review of remote sensing methodologies for pavement management and assessment, European Transport Research Review, 7 (2), pp. 1–19.

Simonyan, K. and Zisserman, A. (2014). Very deep convolutional networks for large-scale image recognition. arXiv preprint arXiv: 1409.1556.

Spencer Jr, B.F., Hoskere, V., Narazaki, Y. (2019). Advances in computer vision-based civil infrastructure inspection and monitoring, Engineering, 5 (2), pp. 199–222.

Sukanya and G. Dubey. (2020). Segmentation and detection of road region in aerial images using hybrid CNN-random field algorithm. In: 10th International Conference on Cloud Computing, Data Science & Engineering, 2020, Uttar Pradesh, India.

Willett, D.A., Mahboub, K.C., Rister, B. (2006). Accuracy of ground-penetrating radar for pavement-layer thickness analysis, Journal of Transportation Engineering, 132 (1), pp. 96–103.

Yeum, C.M., Choi, J., Dyke, S.J. (2019). Automated region-of-interest localization and classification for vision-based visual assessment of civil infrastructure, Structural Health Monitoring, 18 (3), pp. 675–689.

Fake it till you make it: training deep neural networks for worker detection using synthetic data

Tohidifar, A., Saffari S. F., Kim D.
University of Toronto, Canada
civdaeho.kim@utoronto.ca

Abstract. The construction industry's productivity and safety have long been a source of concern, while the broad use of deep neural network (DNN)-based visual AI has transformed other industries. Automation and digitalization powered by DNN provide intriguing answers; yet the lack of high-quality, diversified data prevents the construction sector from leveraging the benefits. This paper presents a novel computational framework that enables synthetic data generation for DNN training to overcome the time-consuming manual data collection and avoid data privacy problems. The suggested framework uses graphics engines to create a virtual duplicate of the construction site that generates non-real yet realistic visuals. The proposed framework randomizes crucial scene elements such as worker pose, clothes, camera viewpoint, and lighting conditions to enhance the variety of the synthetic dataset. The findings of this study present promising potential of synthetic data in DNN training.

1. Introduction

Accounting for 13 percent of global GDP, construction, an industry that provides infrastructure essential to daily life, is one of the largest industries worldwide (Oxford Economics, 2021). Despite its vital importance, the construction industry is facing several challenges. It is renowned as the least automated (Neythalath et al., 2021), experiencing significant safety (Zhou et al., 2015) and productivity problems (Dixit et al., 2019). In recent years, Deep Neural Network (DNN)-based visual Artificial Intelligence (AI), under the umbrella term of Industry 4.0, made its way into different industries and improved the productivity and safety of the work environments (Chien et al., 2020). In spite of DNNs' promises in other industries, significant challenges hinder the construction industry from reaping the benefits (Rao et al., 2022). On the one hand, the construction sites' dynamic, complex, and unstructured nature demand a higher level of AI than other industries (Daeho Kim et al., 2020; Laufer Alexander et al., 2008). On the other hand, the unavailability of data and privacy concerns around the collected data (Akinosho et al., 2020) raised significant hindrances to the widespread adoption of DNN-based visual AI in the construction industry. Even though many recent studies focused on applying DNNs, the development of field-applicable models appears to be over-ambitious (Bang et al., 2019). Insufficient high-quality and diversified data in construction studies resulted in incomplete and overfitted models, ultimately limiting the accuracy and scalability of DNN solutions (Grosse et al., 2021).

To address the data shortage of DNN solutions, a significant portion of previous studies were focused on the manual collection and labelling of data. However, manual labelling is laborious, time-consuming, and expensive (Assadzadeh et al., 2022). While the exact costs of labelling construction data remain unknown, the scale of the problem can be conveyed by looking at the crowdsourcing data labelling services. Semantic segmentation provided by Google Cloud would incur 0.87 USD per class for a single image (Dahun Kim et al., 2020). Besides the prohibitively time-consuming nature of manual data collection, the collected data is susceptible to human error and biases (Assadzadeh et al., 2022). Incorrect annotations would decrease the accuracy of experiments (Xiao and Kang, 2021). Since training high-quality DNNs require millions of labelled data, notable investments from both time and expenses are involved in the manual collection, labelling, and ensuring the quality of the data.

https://doi.org/10.7146/aul.455.c229

An essential element of DNNs' prosperity in other industries is the availability of publicly shared datasets and access to a benchmarking system. Comparative benchmarking, however, in the construction industry is limited due to the lack of willingness of stakeholders to share project datasets (Hwang et al., 2018). The stratified analysis showed that practitioners are primarily unsatisfied with the level of data sharing among stakeholders in the construction industry (Ayodele and Kahimo-shakantu, 2021). Furthermore, recording personal visual data has brought privacy concerns (Akinosho et al., 2020). Ethical issues regarding privacy are of concern in many countries, which resulted in the passing of strict laws to protect privacy (Fabbri et al., 2021). In light of the recent General Data Protection Regulation (GDPR), which applies to all companies holding EU citizen data, care must be taken with data sources (Koops, 2014). Ethical issues regarding privacy are also critical in the US. As an instance of privacy concerns, datasets for re-identification modules of DukeMTMC were taken offline recently (Fabbri et al., 2021; Ristani et al., 2016).

One possible solution to the data limitation issue is to leverage the available computational power to augment or synthesize data. The research community has already recognized the potential of synthetic data created by powerful graphical engines to compensate for the data shortage (Amato et al., 2019; Bousmalis et al., 2017) and create non-real, but real-looking comparative benchmarking (Fabbri et al., 2021). However, promising as it may seem, the potential of computer-generated data for training DNNs in the construction domain remained uninspected. There is a lack of understanding of DNNs' behaviour when trained with synthetic data, specifically in the construction domain. No study has been conducted regarding the feasibility of training DNNs only using synthetic data to understand construction workers. We do not know how the realism of synthetic images impacts the DNNs performance. In addition, there is no consensus about the optimal size of the synthetic dataset to achieve state-of-the-art performance. Would privacy be an issue? Should synthetic images include occluded and cluttered scenes? These are the questions that remained unanswered. As a preliminary step toward extensive experiments to answer the above questions, this study aims to develop a computational method of synthetic data generation for human workers in construction scenes and to visually verify the performance of synthetic data-trained DNN on real construction images.

Section 2 reviews the related works to the objective of the study and highlights the current state of the art and their limitations. Section 3 elaborates on the proposed method for synthetic data generation and explains the adapted DNN model. Training details, real-world validation dataset, and the employed evaluation metrics, along with achieved results are presented in Section 4. Lastly, the research contributions and limitations are covered in Section 5.

2. Related works

To tackle the data limitation and privacy concerns, two mainstream research can be seen: (i) data augmentation and (ii) synthetic data generation.

2.1 Data Augmentation

Data augmentation is an approach that utilizes the available dataset to augment or increase the dataset size by introducing linear transformations, interpolations and distortion, and probabilistic approaches (Delgado and Oyedele, 2021). Linear transformation approaches can be applied when the features of the datasets are not affected by alterations. Since images are transformation invariant, linear transformation techniques such as cropping, flipping, and altering the colour space are easy and efficient methods to be implemented (Shorten and Khoshgoftaar, 2019). Interpolations and distortion methods introduce non-linear distortions and randomness to augmented data. This method has shown to be effective in shallow and deep neural networks (Delgado and Oyedele, 2021). Probabilistic methods, on the other hand, generate new data considering the distribution of the variables in the training set instances in a probabilistic manner (Delgado and Oyedele, 2021). To properly handle the probabilistic characteristic of a new dataset, this method is usually combined with deep learning models with probabilistic characteristics. Although many studies advocate the efficacy of data augmentation, this method do not augment new content to the dataset and is limited in the stimulation of the model's parameters during training (Luo et al., 2020, 2018). Moreover, it might discard important information that is essential as the labels. The label-preserving augmentation is of more concern when multiple images are being combined. Therefore, the scope of where and when these transformations can be applied is relatively limited (Shorten and Khoshgoftaar, 2019).

2.2 Synthetic Data

Another approach to increase the data size and quality is to generate synthetic data. In this approach, the computational powers are leveraged to simulate new data from analogous mediums. One of the most renowned pieces of work in this domain is the flying chairs study (Dosovitskiy et al., 2015). The proposed method of this study uses 3 dimensional (3D) models of chairs in a virtual world and generates synthetic images. Generated synthetic images are proven to be effective in improving DNN training. Since labels are extracted automatically in this approach, data generation is a seamless effort (Neuhausen et al., 2020); thus, an unlimited number of synthetic data is accessible as seen in the SYNTHIA dataset (Ros et al., 2016).

Despite the wide application of synthetic data in other disciplines, construction-related research expressed interest lately. With the rapid increase in the prevalence of building information modelling (BIM) (Alvanchi et al., 2021), research is underway to generate synthetic data from BIM. Acharya used the indoor images derived from BIM as training data for a deep learning network that estimates the pose of a camera (Acharya et al., 2019). Ma et al. (Ma et al., 2020) used synthetic point clouds obtained from BIM as the training data for point cloud segmentation networks. Hong et al. (Hong et al., 2021) employed BIM to construct a synthetic dataset that contains the annotation information of infrastructure elements. BIM-powered synthetic data generation is, inevitably, limited in scope to the building components. Human workers and equipment, as one of the most essential entities in productivity and safety of the construction site, are neglected in this approach.

To incorporate human workers and equipment in the synthetic data generation process, recent studies used 3D virtual models of construction sites. Soltani et al. (Soltani et al., 2018) applied 3D modelling tools to generate automatically labelled synthetic training images. They used virtual images of construction resources extracted from various views for training by using a 3D excavator model. Kim and Kim (Kim and Kim, 2018) reconstructed a 3D model of a concrete mixer truck using the multi-view stereo algorithm to generate synthetic data. Following the same approach, Mahmood et al. (Mahmood et al., 2022) developed a synthetic dataset for training DNN models that estimated the 3D pose of an excavator. In a very recent study by Neuhausen et al (Neuhausen et al., 2020), synthetically generated images are leveraged to train DNNs with a focus on human worker detection and tracking model. A comparative study of the developed model on both synthetic and real-world data identified the synthetic images as a viable solution for vision-based DNN training. Although synthetic data are applied widely out of the construction industry, there exists a promising potential to be used in construction-related activities. In an attempt to investigate the capabilities of synthetic data on DNN training, this study uses the human workers images at virtual construction site to train a worker detection model.

3. Training a deep neural network using synthetic construction images

Following the promising results of prior studies in the computer vision domain (Fabbri et al., 2021), this study adopts a graphical engine (Blender (2022)) to simulate a virtual construction site. The virtual construction site is then used to render diversified images from various scenarios of construction activities. Figure 1 illustrates different parts of the proposed framework.

The first part of the framework is to build and prepare a construction worker avatar. In this part, a human worker conducts multiple construction activities. The worker's body motion is collected using the motion capture suit. This capturing method records the movement of all the body joints and anonymizes the worker that has done the activity. Meanwhile, a 3-dimensional (3D) avatar of the human worker is modelled. Both the motion information and the worker avatar are input to the graphical engines. In the second part, the 3D models of the buildings under construction are extracted from both points clouds or BIM models.

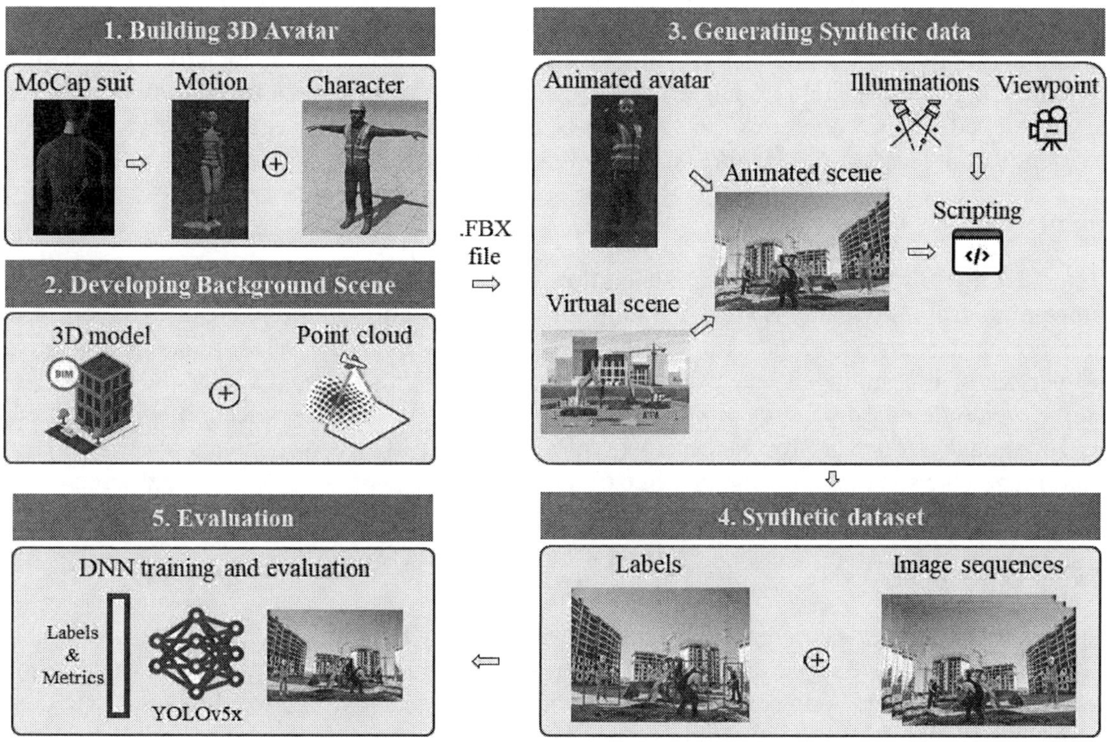

Figure 1. Synthetic data generation framework

In the third part, the collected information of the body joints' movements is augmented into a 3D worker avatar, to create an animated worker in the virtual environment. By placing multiple characters of animated avatars conducting various construction tasks on the developed digital construction replica, an animated construction scene is generated. By scripting into the graphical engine, we automatically randomized the camera location, its viewpoint in the digital world, and lighting conditions. By randomizing the scene, multiple screenplays are generated in the virtual world. Rendering each of these screenplays produces sequences of images. Since all the manipulations take place on a graphical engine, extraction of entities' exact information is a seamless procedure. By using the scripting capability, the required ground truth labels are extracted from the virtual world as the last step of the third part. In the fourth part, rendered image sequences along with ground truth labels are organized as training and validation datasets. The fifth part of the framework uses the synthetic dataset to train DNN models for worker detection.

3.1 Dataset Generation

The synthetic data generation process of this study is comprised of three different processes: namely, screenplay settings, renderings, and label generations. This section will elaborate more on each process.

Screenplays

The first process is the screenplay design, which provides the basis for synthetic image generation. The screenplay contains the arrangement of everything that is seen on the scene, including locations, and avatars' actions. To design screenplays, we manually placed animated avatars in different locations of the scene and randomized the location and viewpoint of the camera. Three different construction-related activities of walking, digging, and coordinating are assigned to the workers. Two unique worker avatars are also used in our screenplays. To obtain diversified viewpoints in the synthetic dataset, we randomized the location of the camera within a range of 35 meters from a target worker. The target worker is a specific avatar selected to be tracked by the camera in the scene. It is critical to have the target avatar to ensure the existence of at least a single worker in every rendered image.

Rendering

After setting up screenplays, we simulated the virtual construction scene and rendered various viewpoints from the scene. By randomizing the camera location in the scene and rendering the animation of avatars, we generated 41 screenplays. Each of the screenplays yields image sequences of the animated construction site, from different viewpoints. For the case of this study, we rendered 14 seconds of screenplays at a rate of 10 frames per second, which resulted in 140 image sequences for each screenplay. To obtain as diverse images as possible, we randomized the sun direction and daytime of the recordings. By rendering all of the screenplays, we were able to generate 5,740 images with a click of a single button within two days.

Label generation

Since graphical engines are used in this framework, every rendered image comes with precise information about the scene. Blender's data structure enables the extraction of 3D annotations of visible or occluded body parts, 2D and 3D bounding boxes, instance segmentation, and depth maps (see Figure 2). While this study sufficed to the exploitation of the 2D bounding boxes for worker detection in the scene, there exists a significant potential in using the generated labels.

3.2 Statistical Analysis of the synthetic data

The synthetic dataset of this study is rendered as a Full HD image sequence. Each image contains 5.2 people per frame on average, totalling more than 30K bounding boxes. The distance of the avatars from the camera in the scene ranged from 5 to 100 meters, which resulted in bounding boxes with dimensions from 0.1 to 400 pixels.

3.3 Worker detection model

This study adopts pre-trained YOLOv5 (Jocher et al., 2022) as the worker detection model. Pre-trained YOLOv5 is trained on the COCO dataset (Lin et al., 2014), where the inputs are labelled in 80 object categories. Although the pre-trained YOLO can detect the persons, the process of fine-tuning the model with synthetic images is essential for multiple reasons. Firstly, the major difference of context in construction-related images with the COCO dataset reduces the performance of the pre-trained model in construction scenes. The construction contexts contain images such as equipment and workers and the backgrounds are usually cluttered. However, the COCO images are mostly captured out of the construction sites, with very controlled illumination and backgrounds (Kim et al., 2019). Secondly, the pre-trained network is not compatible with various camera viewpoints. This is due to the limited variation in the COCO dataset. For example, an image of persons captured with a UAV has a completely different appearance and scale than the person presented in the COCO dataset, which in turn, puzzles the convolutional layers and deteriorates the localization performance of the pre-trained model. To incorporate a wider range of viewpoints, this study fine tunned the model with diversified synthetic images. Another essential factor is the overfitting problem. Since the YOLO model has a very high level of complexity and considering that the COCO dataset is not suitable for construction worker detection, there is a need for a huge, labelled image dataset of construction workers to avoid overfitting. Therefore, this study adopts the pre-trained YOLO as the initial point and fine tunned with synthetic images.

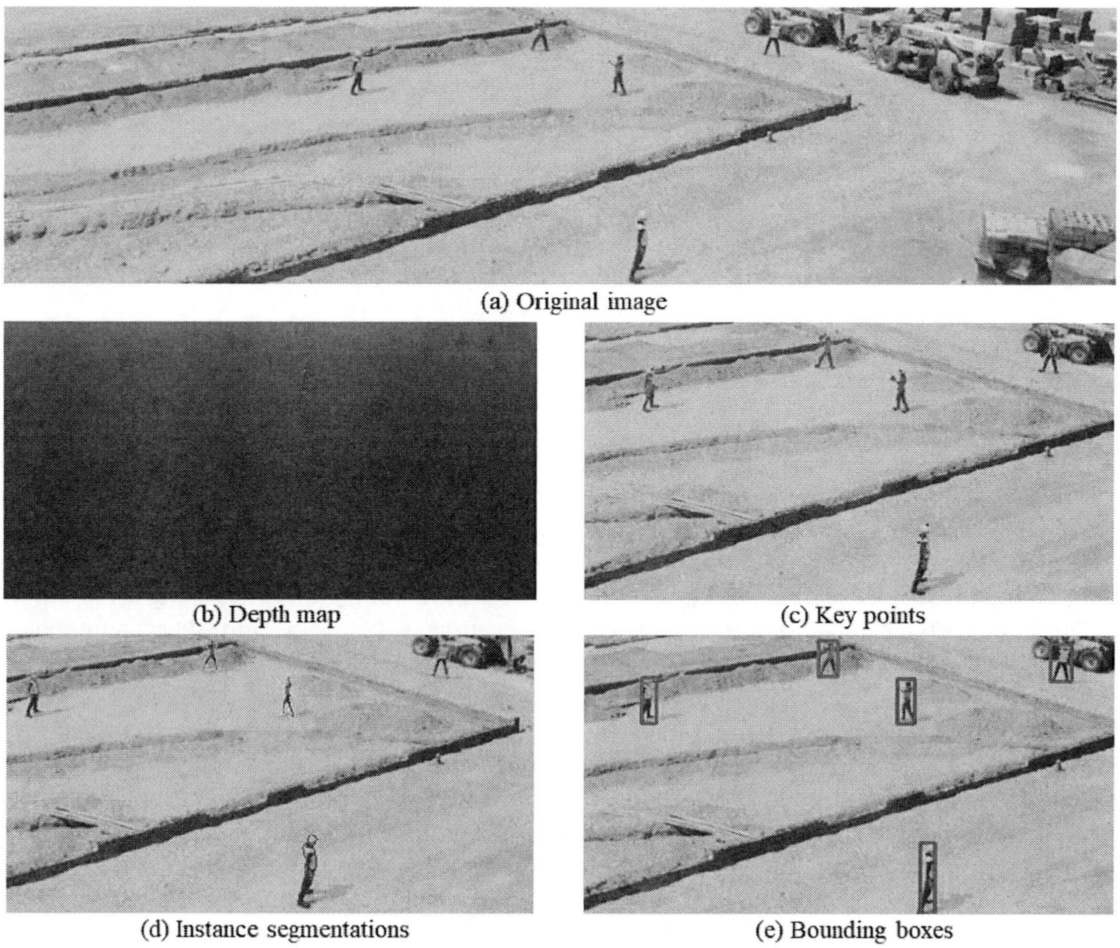

Figure 2. Sample of synthetic data

4. Experimental details and results

The Generalized Intersection of Unions (GIoU) is used as the bounding box regression loss function. GIoU is adapted in YOLOv5 to address the inaccurate calculation of non-overlapping bounding boxes. Further details of the GIoU loss function can be found in (Wang et al., 2021). For training the model, we used Stochastic Gradient Descent (SGD) optimizer. As a fine-tuning process, all of the pre-trained model's layers were completely unfrozen and all the pre-trained weights of the network were used as an initialization point. After unfreezing all the layers, the model is trained for 50 epochs with an initial learning rate of 1e-2 while using cosine annealing the final learning was decreased to 1e-4. The momentum of the optimizer and weight decay was set to 0.937 and 5e-4 respectively. Figure 3 illustrates the learning curve of the model fine-tuned on synthetic data for 50 epochs with a batch size of 4. Decrease of loss by increasing epochs in both training and validation set in the learning curve is an absolute indication that synthetic data enables DNN training.

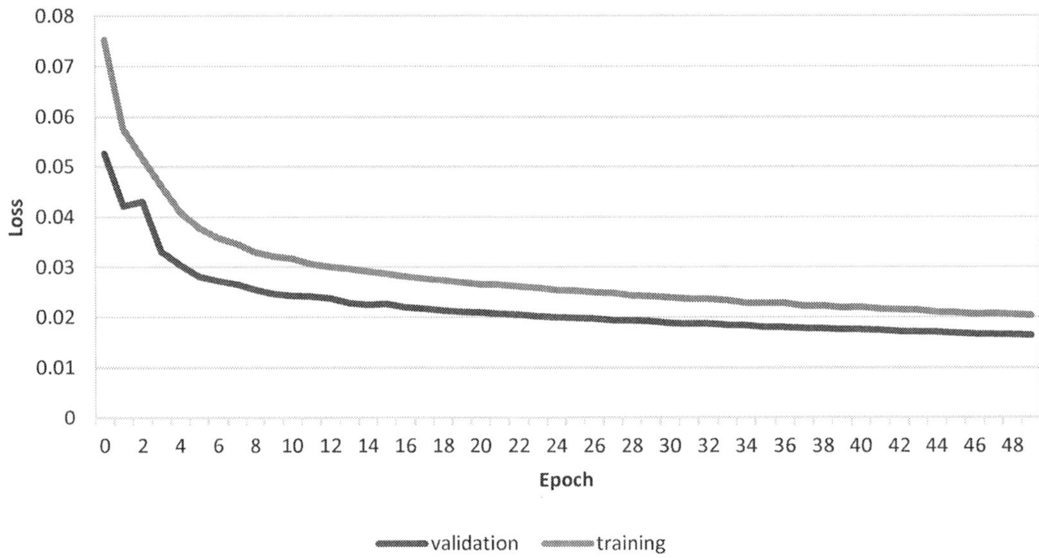

Figure 3. The learning curve of the model trained on the synthetic dataset

For visual verification, this study used the publicly available dataset of Moving Objects in Construction Sites (MOCS) (Xuehui et al., 2021). This dataset contains 41,668 images of 13 categories of construction mobile objects. Concerning the scope of this research, images containing workers are filtered out of the MOCS validation set, which yielded 3,091 images as benchmarking data for this research. Figure 4 illustrates several detection results of the synthetic data-trained model on real construction images (i.e., MOCS validation set). As shown in Figure 4, it successfully detected construction workers in diverse scenarios and at varying scales. Given that this model was trained only with synthetic data, the detection results are an indication of the great potential of synthetic data in DNN training. It should be noted that the fine-tuned model used in this experiment did not reach the optimum performance since it was trained with a very limited amount of synthetic data (i.e., 5,740 images). With the incorporation of a wider range of 3D backgrounds, worker motions, and avatar colours in data generation, the model would have another chance to improve its performance. Our follow-up study will address it, establishing a complete training set of synthetic construction images, and conducting a quantitative evaluation on real test images. This study will lay a stepping stone to non-real but real-looking image-driven DNN training.

Figure 4. Sample prediction for the model trained on synthetic images

5. Conclusion

The productivity and safety of the construction industry have continuously experienced staggering challenges, while the widespread adoption of DNN-based visual AI revolutionized other industries. DNN-powered automation and digitization offer promising solutions; however, the unavailability of high-quality and diversified data prohibitively hinders the construction industry from reaping the benefits. To address the time-consuming manual data collection process and avoid data privacy concerns, this study proposes a novel computational framework that enables synthetic data generation for DNN training. The proposed framework leverages the power of graphical engines to develop a virtual replica of the construction site and renders non-real but real-looking images. To increase the diversity of the synthetic dataset, the proposed framework randomizes critical features of the scene, such as the worker's pose, clothing, camera viewpoint, lighting condition, and sun direction. Although numerous questions remained intact, the results of this study indicated the potential and applicability of computer-generated synthetic images in the development of high-quality, field applicable DNNs. Further research should be conducted to address critical questions such as understanding DNNs' behaviour when trained with synthetic data, exploring the impact of synthetic image realism on DNN performance, examining the feasibility of training DNNs for pose estimation, semantic segmentation, depth estimation and activity recognition, and determining the optimal size of the synthetic dataset. Moreover, the creation of a virtual construction site involved the manual placement of avatars in pre-defined locations in the scene. Although this procedure can be automated, this study limited its scope to the manual placement of avatars in the scene. Leveraging the agent-based simulations can be a suitable approach toward automation of the avatar placement in the scene.

References

Acharya, D., Khoshelham, K., Winter, S. (2019). BIM-PoseNet: Indoor camera localisation using a 3D indoor model and deep learning from synthetic images. ISPRS J Photogramm 150, 245–258. https://doi.org/10.1016/j.isprsjprs.2019.02.020

Akinosho, T.D., Oyedele, L.O., Bilal, M., Ajayi, A.O., Delgado, M.D., Akinade, O.O., Ahmed, A.A. (2020). Deep learning in the construction industry: A review of present status and future innovations. J. Build. Eng. 32, 101827. https://doi.org/10.1016/j.jobe.2020.101827

Alvanchi, A., TohidiFar, A., Mousavi, M., Azad, R., Rokooei, S. (2021). A critical study of the existing issues in manufacturing maintenance systems: Can BIM fill the gap? Comput Ind 131, 103484. https://doi.org/10.1016/j.compind.2021.103484

Amato, G., Ciampi, L., Falchi, F., Gennaro, C., Messina, N. (2019). Learning Pedestrian Detection from Virtual Worlds, in: Ricci, E., Rota Bulò, S., Snoek, C., Lanz, O., Messelodi, S., Sebe, N. (Eds.), Image Analysis and Processing – ICIAP, Springer International Publishing, Cham, pp. 302–312.

Assadzadeh, A., Arashpour, M., Brilakis, I., Ngo, T., Konstantinou, E. (2022). Vision-based excavator pose estimation using synthetically generated datasets with domain randomization. Autom Constr 134, 104089. https://doi.org/10.1016/j.autcon.2021.104089

Ayodele, T., Kahimo-shakantu, K. (2021). Data Sharing in the Construction Industry: An Assessment of Stakeholders' Perception, in: International Conference on Infrastructure Development and Investment Strategies for Africa.

Bang, S., Park, S., Kim, Hongjo, Kim, Hyoungkwan (2019). Encoder–decoder network for pixel-level road crack detection in black-box images. Comput-Aided Civ Inf 34, 713–727. https://doi.org/10.1111/mice.12440

Blender (2022). URL https://www.blender.org/ (accessed 10 April 2022).

Bousmalis, K., Silberman, N., Dohan, D., Erhan, D., Krishnan, D. (2017). Unsupervised pixel-level domain adaptation with generative adversarial networks, in: Proceedings of the IEEE conference on computer vision and pattern recognition, pp. 3722–3731.

Chien, C.-F., Dauzère-Pérès, S., Huh, W.T., Jang, Y.J., Morrison, J.R. (2020). Artificial intelligence in manufacturing and logistics systems: algorithms, applications, and case studies. Int. J. Prod. Res. 58, 2730–2731. https://doi.org/10.1080/00207543.2020.1752488

Delgado, J.M.D., Oyedele, L. (2021). Deep learning with small datasets: using autoencoders to address limited datasets in construction management. Appl. Soft Comput. 112, 107836. https://doi.org/10.1016/j.asoc.2021.107836

Dixit, S., Mandal, S.N., Thanikal, J.V., Saurabh, K. (2019). Evolution of studies in construction productivity: A systematic literature review (2006–2017). Ain Shams Eng. J. 10, 555–564. https://doi.org/10.1016/j.asej.2018.10.010

Dosovitskiy, A., Fischer, P., Ilg, E., Hausser, P., Hazirbas, C., Golkov, V., Van Der Smagt, P., Cremers, D., Brox, T. (2015). Flownet: Learning optical flow with convolutional networks, in: Proceedings of the IEEE International Conference on Computer Vision (ICCV), pp. 2758–2766.

Fabbri, M., Brasó, G., Maugeri, G., Cetintas, O., Gasparini, R., Ošep, A., Calderara, S., Leal-Taixé, L., Cucchiara, R. (2021). MOTSynth: How Can Synthetic Data Help Pedestrian

Detection and Tracking?, in: Proceedings of the IEEE/CVF International Conference on Computer Vision, pp. 10849–10859.

Grosse, K., Lee, T., Biggio, B., Park, Y., Backes, M., Molloy, I. (2021). Backdoor Smoothing: Demystifying Backdoor Attacks on Deep Neural Networks.

Hong, Y., Park, S., Kim, Hongjo, Kim, Hyoungkwan (2021). Synthetic data generation using building information models. Autom. Constr. 130, 103871. https://doi.org/10.1016/j.autcon.2021.103871

Hwang, S., Jebelli, H., Choi, B., Choi, M., Lee, S. (2018). Measuring Workers' Emotional State during Construction Tasks Using Wearable EEG. J. Constr. Eng. Manag. 144, 04018050. https://doi.org/10.1061/(ASCE)CO.1943-7862.0001506

Jocher, G., Chaurasia, A., Stoken, A., Borovec, J., NanoCode012, Kwon, Y., TaoXie, Fang, J., imyhxy, Michael, K., Lorna, V, A., Montes, D., Nadar, J., Laughing, tkianai, yxNONG, Skalski, P., Wang, Z., Hogan, A., et al. (2022). ultralytics/yolov5: v6.1 - TensorRT, TensorFlow Edge TPU and OpenVINO Export and Inference. https://doi.org/10.5281/zenodo.6222936

Kim, D., Liu, M., Lee, S., Kamat, V.R. (2019). Remote proximity monitoring between mobile construction resources using camera-mounted UAVs. Autom Constr 99, 168–182. https://doi.org/10.1016/j.autcon.2018.12.014

Kim, Dahun, Woo, S., Lee, J.-Y., Kweon, I.S. (2020). Video panoptic segmentation, in: Proceedings of the IEEE/CVF Conference on Computer Vision and Pattern Recognition, pp. 9859–9868.

Kim, Daeho, Lee, S., Kamat, V.R. (2020). Proximity Prediction of Mobile Objects to Prevent Contact-Driven Accidents in Co-Robotic Construction. J. Comput. Civ. Eng. 34, 04020022. https://doi.org/10.1061/(ASCE)CP.1943-5487.0000899

Kim, Hongjo, Kim, Hyoungkwan (2018). 3D reconstruction of a concrete mixer truck for training object detectors. Autom. Constr. 88, 23–30. https://doi.org/10.1016/j.autcon.2017.12.034

Koops, B.-J. (2014). The trouble with European data protection law. Int. Data Priv. Law 4, 250–261. https://doi.org/10.1093/idpl/ipu023

Laufer Alexander, Shapira Aviad, Telem Dory (2008). Communicating in Dynamic Conditions: How Do On-Site Construction Project Managers Do It? J Manage Eng 24, 75–86. https://doi.org/10.1061/(ASCE)0742-597X(2008)24:2(75)

Lin, T.-Y., Maire, M., Belongie, S., Hays, J., Perona, P., Ramanan, D., Dollár, P., Zitnick, C.L. (2014). Microsoft COCO: Common Objects in Context, in: Fleet, D., Pajdla, T., Schiele, B., Tuytelaars, T. (Eds.), European conference on computer vision (ECCV), Springer International Publishing, Cham, Switzerland, pp. 740–755.

Luo, H., Wang, M., Wong, P.K.-Y., Cheng, J.C.P. (2020). Full body pose estimation of construction equipment using computer vision and deep learning techniques. Autom. Constr. 110, 103016. https://doi.org/10.1016/j.autcon.2019.103016

Luo, X., Li, H., Cao, D., Yu, Y., Yang, X., Huang, T. (2018). Towards efficient and objective work sampling: Recognizing workers' activities in site surveillance videos with two-stream convolutional networks. Autom. Constr. 94, 360–370. https://doi.org/10.1016/j.autcon.2018.07.011

Ma, J.W., Czerniawski, T., Leite, F. (2020). Semantic segmentation of point clouds of building interiors with deep learning: Augmenting training datasets with synthetic BIM-based point clouds. Autom. Constr. 113, 103144. https://doi.org/10.1016/j.autcon.2020.103144

Mahmood, B., Han, S., Seo, J. (2022). Implementation experiments on convolutional neural network training using synthetic images for 3D pose estimation of an excavator on real images. Autom. Constr. 133, 103996. https://doi.org/10.1016/j.autcon.2021.103996

Neuhausen, M., Herbers, P., König, M. (2020). Using Synthetic Data to Improve and Evaluate the Tracking Performance of Construction Workers on Site. Appl. Sci. 10, 4948. https://doi.org/10.3390/app10144948

Neythalath, N., Søndergaard, A., Bærentzen, J.A. (2021). Adaptive robotic manufacturing using higher order knowledge systems. Autom. Constr. 127, 103702. https://doi.org/10.1016/j.autcon.2021.103702

Oxford Economics (2021). Future of Construction: A Global Forecast for Construction to 2030. Oxford Economics. https://www.oxfordeconomics.com/resource/future-of-construction/

Rao, T.V.N., Gaddam, A., Kurni, M., Saritha, K. (2022). Reliance on Artificial Intelligence, Machine Learning and Deep Learning in the Era of Industry 4.0, in: Smart Healthcare System Design, John Wiley & Sons, Ltd, pp. 281–299. https://doi.org/10.1002/9781119792253.ch12

Ristani, E., Solera, F., Zou, R., Cucchiara, R., Tomasi, C. (2016). Performance Measures and a Data Set for Multi-target, Multi-camera Tracking, in: Hua, G., Jégou, H. (Eds.), European conference on computer vision (ECCV), Springer International Publishing, Cham, pp. 17–35.

Ros, G., Sellart, L., Materzynska, J., Vazquez, D., Lopez, A.M. (2016). The synthia dataset: A large collection of synthetic images for semantic segmentation of urban scenes, in: Proceedings of the IEEE conference on computer vision and pattern recognition, pp. 3234–3243.

Shorten, C., Khoshgoftaar, T.M. (2019). A survey on Image Data Augmentation for Deep Learning. J. Big Data 6, 60. https://doi.org/10.1186/s40537-019-0197-0

Soltani, M., Zhu, Z., Hammad, A. (2018). Framework for Location Data Fusion and Pose Estimation of Excavators Using Stereo Vision. J. Comput. Civ. Eng. 32, 04018045. https://doi.org/10.1061/(ASCE)CP.1943-5487.0000783

Wang, Z., Wu, Y., Yang, L., Thirunavukarasu, A., Evison, C., Zhao, Y. (2021). Fast Personal Protective Equipment Detection for Real Construction Sites Using Deep Learning Approaches. Sensors 21. https://doi.org/10.3390/s21103478

Xiao, B., Kang, S.-C. (2021). Development of an Image Data Set of Construction Machines for Deep Learning Object Detection. J. Comput. Civ. Eng. 35, 05020005. https://doi.org/10.1061/(ASCE)CP.1943-5487.0000945

Xuehui, A., Li, Z., Zuguang, L., Chengzhi, W., Pengfei, L., Zhiwei, L. (2021). Dataset and benchmark for detecting moving objects in construction sites. Autom. Constr. 122, 103482. https://doi.org/10.1016/j.autcon.2020.103482

Zhou, Z., Goh, Y.M., Li, Q. (2015). Overview and analysis of safety management studies in the construction industry. Saf. Sci. 72, 337–350. https://doi.org/10.1016/j.ssci.2014.10.006

BIM standards and classification systems in data validation

Jensen F., Gade P.
University College of Northern Denmark, Denmark
1075459@ucn.dk

Abstract. Digitalisation has been proven vital to transition the construction industry into more sustainable ways of working. One of the ways the construction industry is digitalising is through Building Information Modelling. An important part of BIM is consistent and trustworthy data. However, effective automation of BIM data validation remains an issue for the construction industry. This paper uses a semi-structured literature review to investigate the use and challenges for BIM standards and building classification systems in relation to BIM data validation. To better understand what is hindering the development and successful implementation of these standards as data validation content. Findings from the review highlight multiple challenges hindering the implementation of standardised data validation workflows in the construction industry. It also shows that software vendors have an important role, where they must provide platform facilities that better support the heterogeneity of rules needed for the construction industry.

1. Introduction

Better quality data is vital to achieving changes and helping the transition to more sustainable practices in the construction industry (CI) (Designing Buildings Ltd., 2021). Digital technologies, like BIM, are necessary to achieve these goals. To deliver high-quality BIM data, compliance checking becomes important (EU BIM Task Group, 2017). However, the language of BIM is built on shifting sands. Terms and definitions have changed over time and will continue to adapt and evolve. The world of BIM is complicated and sometimes confusing. Too often terms are used in contexts that blur their meaning. If BIM data validation, is to be simplified, we must refer to common reference points, such as standards, that "anchor" our approach. Data validation is generally defined as an activity aimed at verifying whether the value of a data item comes from the given set of acceptable values, to ensure a certain level of quality of the data (Zio *et al.*, 2016). Data validation in relation to the CI is also referred to as compliance checking or model checking and is a means to check the project data deliverables against those specified in the project requirements (Amor and Dimyadi, 2021). Data validation ensures that the information delivered at a particular project stage is correct and in accordance with the responsibilities of the party who have delivered it. This helps to ensure interoperability, which is a characteristic of good quality data (SDG, 2018). However, interoperability has been identified as one of the main barriers to data exchange in the CI (A. Poirier, Forgues and Staub-French, 2014; Castro-Lacouture, Irizarry and Ashuri, 2014, pp. 1987–1996).

To ensure interoperable data, the data must be consistently validated before it is shared and used. This paper focuses on the initial pre-check which can be used to ensure reliable data for subsequent code checking and BIM-based analysis (Ciribini et al., 2014). To do so, standardised templates (also called rulesets) become essential to definite and store validation rules in a machine-readable and reusable format. Templates can help to reduce manual errors and automate workflows, by providing predefined and verified content. In its essence, data validation templates share a lot of commonalities with data templates for construction objects, as defined in ISO 23387:2020. These data templates provide a data structure used to ensure that construction objects are machine-readable, versatile, and consistent, so they can be used in

https://doi.org/10.7146/aul.455.c230

different software. By structuring rules and requirements in a data validation template, the information can be used to check and verify the BIM models and objects.

Standardisation of data validation templates becomes an important part of ensuring data interoperability. Because standards and building classification systems, establish a consensus and provide a formula on the best way of doing something. This enables an unambiguous exchange of information, facilitates better communication, and better exchange of information between different stakeholders. In general, the purpose of data validation templates becomes to standardise and automate how BIM data is checked, to enable consistency and interoperability. However, there seems to be a missing connection between BIM standards and their availability in current data validation workflows used in the CI. Therefore, this study aims to answer the research question:

"Given the importance of standardised workflows, what are the current challenges for the efficient use of BIM standards and building classification systems as part of BIM data validation templates?".

To answer the research question a semi-structured literature review (SSLR) was conducted. The SSLR investigates the importance and challenges regarding BIM standards and building classification systems in relation to BIM data validation in the CI. To better understand what is hindering the development and successful implementation of these standards as data validation content. In addition, grey literature is used to collect information that is produced outside traditional publishing, including existing information about data validation solutions and initiatives, for example from buildingSMART. Grey literature is used to help describe more current information concerning the research area and provide important contributions not found within commercially published literature, to provide a more balanced view of the evidence (Paez, 2017). The literature review is conducted as initial research to better understand how BIM standards can become specific in BIM data validation templates, as the current standards and guidelines are experienced as vague and don't facilitate practical solutions for data validation in the CI.

2. Methodology

A semi-systematic literature review is used as a structured procedure to identify and synthesise relevant sources to obtain a comprehensive overview of the literature published for the specific research question and create new knowledge by compiling the existing works (Snyder, 2019). Additional grey literature is used to identify the current solutions and initiatives concerning BIM standards and building classification systems for the purpose of data validation in the CI. The semi-structured approach is used because of the diverse disciplines and various groups of researchers involved in the CI, which can hinder a successful full systematic review process (Wong *et al.*, 2013).

The SSLR is performed in 4 steps: (1) designing the review, (2) conducting the review, (3) analysis, and (4) writing up the review (Tranfield, Denyer and Smart, 2003; Snyder, 2019). The selected databases were Science Direct, Scopus and Semantic Scholar, with the search being limited to results in English language, in the period from 2015 to 2022. This period was chosen because of the speed at which both BIM standards and data validation in general, is developing and advancing in the CI. The grey literature was found through a web search using Google and Google Scholar. However, as grey literature is not published in peer-reviewed publications and comes in varying quality, the use of this literature must be done with caution (Paez, 2017). The grey literature is combined with the findings from the literature, with the purpose of better understanding how BIM standards and building classification systems can become specific to data validation as templates, and the related challenges. Based on the research question, relevant keywords are identified, and a search is performed in the selected databases. From the objective of the research, the keywords identified were 'BIM', 'AEC', 'data validation', 'classification' and 'standard'. Alternative search terms (Table 1) were also searched to ensure adequate coverage of the literature.

Table 1: Search terms.

Keyword	Search terms
BIM	'BIM', 'Building Information Modelling', 'VDC', 'Virtual design and construction', '3D modelling'
AEC	'AEC', 'AEC-FM', 'Architecture, Engineering and Construction', 'Architect*', 'Engineer*', 'Construction industry', 'Construction'
Data validation	'Data validation', 'validation', 'model checking', 'checking'
Classification	'Classification', 'Classifications'
Standard	'Standard*', 'BIM standard'

From the database search, 335 publications were found using the search strings in Table 2, with the inclusion criteria being articles published between 2015 and 2022 and in English language.

Table 2: Search strings.

Database	Search string	Number of results
Science Direct	(BIM OR VDC) AND (AEC OR Construction) AND (Validation OR Checking) AND ((Classification) OR (Standards OR "BIM standards"))	34
Scopus	(BIM OR "Building Information Modelling" OR VDC OR Virtual design and construction OR "3D modelling") AND (AEC OR AEC-FM OR "Architecture, Engineering and Construction" OR "Architect*" OR "Engineer*" OR "Construction industry" OR "Construction") AND ("Data validation" OR Validation OR "Model checking" OR Checking) AND ((Classification*) OR (Standard* OR "BIM standard*"))	88
Semantic Scholar	BIM Construction Data Validation Model Checking Classification Standard	213

The results collected from the database search were then filtered by the exclusion criteria based on their title, abstract and keywords. The exclusion criteria are articles that are not related to the construction industry, articles that do not consider BIM standards and/or building classification systems, articles that do not concern data validation/model checking for BIM data, and non-peer-reviewed publications and whitepapers. To keep track of the collected publications in the qualification of the search results, a research protocol is used. The research protocol contains the title, author, year, number of citations, abstract, and keywords.

By assessing the articles based on the inclusion and exclusion criteria, 55 publications were selected. Additionally, further relevant literature was collected by checking the references of the collected publications (snowball approach). From the final list of articles, a thematic analysis was performed similarly to a qualitative approach (Ward, House and Hamer, 2009). The thematic analysis was carried out in 4 phases: (1) initialisation, (2) construction, (3) rectification, and (4) finalisation, as described by Ward, House and Hamer (2009). In the initial phase, the articles were read through while reflective notes and coding were performed, by letting themes emerge naturally. In the construction phase, the codes were compared and organised in terms of similarities and differences in relation to the research question. In the rectification phase, the data was checked and confirmed by connecting themes and subthemes and integrating these with each other. The analysis was finalised by developing a "storyline" to create a coherent story answering the research question.

3. Results

The SSLR findings have been categorised into four main topics: (1) BIM standards and (2) building classification systems in relation to BIM data validation. Followed by (3) standardisation of BIM data validation, and finally (4) identified themes related to challenges that are hindering standardised data validation templates in the CI. These themes include insufficient data and data requirements, a current approach prioritising experts, and the challenges of expressing complex rules in a machine-readable format.

3.1 BIM Standards

From the SSLR it is found that BIM standards are developed by international, national, and regional organisations, and by businesses or other organisations for their internal use. They can also be developed by a consortium of businesses to address a specific marketplace need, or by government departments to support regulations (ISO, 2021). These BIM standards are usually adopted through the consensus of organisations involved with the technology and are rarely mandated by a national government agency (Sacks, Gurevich and Shrestha, 2016). The use of BIM standards should enable all project participants to collaborate efficiently, and share compatible BIM models and information (Ganah and Lea, 2021). However, detailed descriptions or guidelines on how data validation should be carried out appear to be missing.

International BIM standards. On an international level, different organisations are working on the creation of international BIM standards. An international standard is a high-level principle-based standard developed in collaboration with other relevant bodies. They define the structure and mechanisms of BIM data exchange. By doing so, standards facilitate communication which is critical when working across domains, disciplines, and national boundaries. The main international organisations identified in the literature were ISO (International Organization for Standardization) and buildingSMART. With buildingSMART being a leading authority behind open standards like the IFC file format and is heavily involved in the internationalisation of the common approach to data interoperability and open BIM.

National BIM standards. On a national level, it is found that government and industry bodies assist in the production of BIM standards. BIM implementation plans are dictated by the government, initiatives in the CI, or a combination of both. Meanwhile, some countries (including the United States, the United Kingdom, France and Denmark) have also issued national BIM mandates on government projects (McAuley, Hore and West, 2017). The development and promotion of BIM standards are found to be driven by national real estate agencies and CI organisations (Ganah and Lea, 2021), to facilitate better outcomes on BIM projects. Overall, multiple national actors are seen working on a variety of standards, creating a growing number of standards for the CI.

3.2 Building classification systems

Building classification systems are identified as one of the tools used to digitalise construction data, by facilitating a way of structuring the BIM information so it can be managed and sorted (CoBuilder, 2021). During data validation processes, building classification systems (like UniClass) become essential. They provide a means to describe construction elements and their interrelationships in a standardised and machine-readable way, which is necessary for templates to work. Classification systems enable query and check of sharply targeted sets of BIM data, without requiring a BIM expert and proprietary software (Sattler *et al.*, 2019). However, research undertaken by Jin Wu and Jiansong Zhang (2018, p. 2) on automating the classification of BIM objects showed that automated BIM object classification and error-free classification is an approach that is currently difficult given the associated complexities in creating the necessary rule sets to do so (Heaton, Parlikad and Schooling, 2019, p. 184). Therefore, it becomes necessary to apply standardised classification systems from the beginning of a project. In that way, manual and time-consuming tasks of selecting individual objects and classifying them can be removed, which become a decisive factor for automating data validation workflow.

3.3 Automating data validation with standardised templates

Data validation is a means to ensure that data is correct, complete, and compliant. However, there is no standard on how to check BIM projects against requirements (Lee, Solihin and Eastman, 2019; Lee, Eastman and Solihin, 2021). Therefore, a major part of the data validation process is rule definitions. Rules can be developed not only by standards and building classification systems but also by multiple other sources such as codes, best practice guidelines, and project-based requirements (Dimyadi, Solihin and Hjelseth, 2016). To create these data validation templates, different actors are working on interpreting BIM standards, building codes and other requirements for the CI. The purpose become to facilitate tools and templates that automate and improve the data validation workflow, which can lead to financial savings and increased quality in construction projects. However, the CI is still challenged when it comes to the flow of digital information on projects. Because different stakeholders are responsible for different domains of design, construction, and operation, the supply chain is complex and generates large amounts of information. This information can get misinterpreted or even lost in exchanges or handovers (DSCiBE, 2014). This is further complicated when some data is being shared using unstructured formats (PDF, XLS) or sometimes 3rd-party solutions. The use of recognised standards can help enable interoperability within the entire supply chain on a construction project (DSCiBE, 2014). In addition, large software companies can also influence how CI actors participate in the digital supply chain, by having the tools on the market which support a certain way of working (E.g., Autodesk Revit and BIM 360). However, this creates a risk of bottlenecks for data exchange which can diminish the advantages of digital supply chains (DSCiBE, 2014), because software solutions might contradict standards and guidelines.

From an EU perspective, the digital standardisation of the CI is led by the European body CEN. The Technical Committee TE/442 oversees the standardisation work concerning all information in the built environment. Among the first open BIM standards adopted by the CEN were the ISO 12006-3:2007, ISO 16739:2013 and ISO 29481-2:2012 from the buildingSMART International standards. According to DSCiBE (2014), these three standards are widely known as the three pillars of interoperability and set out a common format for data exchange, data-semantic concepts, data relations and a standard for specifying required information. The ISO 29481 can also be used for guidance when developing data validation templates according to Hjelseth (2015). An example of an international initiative, which is standardising data validation templates is found from buildingSMART. buildingSMART is currently developing the buildingSMART Data Dictionary (bSSD). The bSDD hosts standards, classifications, properties, allowed values, units, and translations, and can be used to access different standards to enrich BIM models. Furthermore, it can also be used for checking data validity and compliance (buildingSMART, 2021). On a national level, initiatives are also found. For example, the BART (Byggeriet's Automatic Rule Check) project in Denmark is researching how to translate project-specific requirements into machine-readable rules for construction. It is working on creating templates for checking whether the requirements of the Building Regulations (BR18) have been complied with (Rasmussen and Schlachter, 2021). Apart from the international and national initiatives, numerous software vendors are also found working on improving data validation in the CI. Some of these solutions offer the function to create templates to remove repetitive tasks and secure high data quality through standardisation. These solutions include, but are not limited to, the Solibri Ruleset Manager, BIMvision, BEXEL Manager, and Verifi3D by Xinaps.

3.4 Challenges with data validation templates

From the SSLR a consensus is found, to standardise the data validation approach for it to be successful in the CI. There seems to be a general agreement in the literature, that manual checking is unnecessarily time-consuming and subject to error. Because the currently manual workflow relies on the accuracy, experience, and expertise of the person or people performing the checks, the results can vary and be subject to certain inaccuracies. However, the task of standardising data validation in the CI is found to be hindered by a combination of multiple challenges. This section goes through the challenges identified by the SSLR.

Data presence and naming. To begin with, different standards and national codes require different and detailed information. These pieces of information must be present in the BIM models in a certain way and be of high quality before they can be used for compliance checking (Amor and Dimyadi, 2021). Because there are different approaches to BIM, different representations of the information are created and used. For example, IFC (Industry Foundation Classes) property sets are used. Overall, different naming conventions and data formats seem to remain a fundamental problem for ensuring high data quality.

Insufficiently detailed requirements. Another challenge hindering data validation templates is the insufficiently detailed requirements in the BIM standards and guidelines. Most BIM guidelines refer to data validation, or model checking, but only highlight its importance rather than providing clear instructions regarding the way forward (Choi, Lee and Kim, 2020, p. 3). Choi et al. (2020) report that detailed components and the methodology for quality control are lacking and therefore limitations are found when adopting these guidelines into machine-readable templates for data validation.

Machine-readable compliance. One of the main challenges identified in the literature is the fact that BIM standards and similar documents are typically written in human-oriented languages. To enable automated data validation, the content needs to be translated into a machine-readable format, which requires interpretation of the data. This is further complicated, when the documents are often expressed in a way, which is very different from the expressions used in BIM. Depending on the specific case, expert knowledge is often required to interpret the meaning or semantics of the BIM standards and requirements. The interpretation must take into account the intent, base and hidden assumptions assumed general knowledge of the subjects, and dependencies with other rules (Solihin and Eastman, 2015). This implies that the specification of rules can be a task of its own (Dimyadi, Solihin and Hjelseth, 2016), which makes the data validation process time- and resource-heavy. The creation of machine-readable templates also involves testing and verification of the content, to confirm it is solid and it can be trustworthy, adding more work to the process.

Proprietary data. Since current templates are often found to be created by specialists, the result is often a black-box representation with no guarantee of the translation being 100 % equivalent to the original version (Amor and Dimyadi, 2021). In general, the use of siloed data approaches, and hard-coded expressions, risks resulting in less quality and failure during use. Besides and associated with silos, there are also loss of information, loss of knowledge and wasted effort (Pedro Mêda, Hipólito Sousa and Eilif Hjelseth, 2020). Furthermore, custom machine-readable versions of a standard or code also constitute an additional version, which might not be automatically connected to the source. This version also has to be maintained, adding additional costs (Amor and Dimyadi, 2021) and the risk of human errors and data consistency issues (Lee, Solihin and Eastman, 2019). When a data validation template is written in a proprietary language, it requires in-depth knowledge of the technical structures to utilise.

The complexity of rules. Another challenge identified, hindering the successful implementation of data validation templates, is the complexities inherent in the rules themselves. Combined with the breadth of conditions to which they need to apply. Due to the high number of different BIM standards, classification systems and codes, there is a theoretically infinite number of rules that can be defined. Combined with the limitation of the technical expression of rule templates, more advanced data validation is often hindered due to the complexity of the rule expressions themselves. To be able to handle large and diverse amounts of BIM requirements and data, each rule or class of rules must apply to a subset of the data to make it tractable (Solihin and Eastman, 2015). However, defining formalised rules that address all possible values, properties, and relationships is still complex and demanding (Lee, Solihin and Eastman, 2019). This is made further difficult since there currently is no standardised way of creating a machine-interpretable version of codes and BIM standards. Therefore it is critical to have an effective method for translating and distributing machine-readable versions (Amor and Dimyadi, 2021). This can systematise the rules and templates to make the task of data validation tractable (Solihin and Eastman, 2015).

4. Discussion

In the SSLR it is found that BIM implementation in the EU has reached a high level of maturity. However, the EU countries need to share best practices because non-standardised approaches will lead to a fragmented market where information is being siloed (Charef *et al.*, 2019). As BIM has become the industry norm, templates (rulesets) become increasingly important for model coordination and data validation. If these templates are to be successful, they need to be based on standards.

4.1 BIM standards and building classification system

This review shows that BIM standards and building classification systems are dictated by geographic factors and many of them are inherited from standards that previously served 2D workflows. The BIM standards and building classification systems become specific at a project and discipline level within a country. Individual organisations agree to BIM requirements on a project basis, these project requirements are adapted in accordance with the client's scope of services. Therefore, the development and refinement of standards specific to 3D workflows are still in progress. This would appear to be linked to a workflow, which is partly digitalised but still relies on manual checking for the purpose of data validation. Though many of these standards are similar, they remain different, which can lead to confusion and mistakes when having to apply different standards on multiple different projects. This can make it difficult to easily ensure that deliverables are following the agreed standard (Sacks, Gurevich and Shrestha, 2016). In the end, there is a risk of making the standards and requirements seen as more of a burden than an asset, if the documentation isn't clear. In general, it is found that while BIM has led to improvements in projects the benefits have not been fully realised. However, templates can still help minimise errors by automating repetitive parts of the data validation process.

4.2 Automating data validation with standardised templates

A high number of BIM standards and building classification systems exist and more are still being developed on both national and international levels. These standards can be used for data validation of BIM data in the CI. However, digital tools and templates are needed to support data validation because manual checking is unnecessarily time-consuming and subject to error. An example of a current initiative is the bSDD, which removes the human translation and interpretation process from the equation and uses a machine-readable format from the beginning. These initiatives are an important step towards a standardised approach to data and data validation in the CI. By combining systems in databases like bSDD, solutions to name mapping and object naming problems can be found. For example, bSDD provides standardised data templates for national classification systems (Like UniClass) and application-specific standards (Like IfcAirport). When the bSDD gets to a point where it also supports fully developed Information Delivery Manuals (IDMs), software vendors can connect to the bSDD database. This opens the door for end-users to access and use international harmonised templates for the purpose of data validation in the CI. This can potentially enable the use of a single source of truth format, which is both human and machine-readable. Development of such standardised tools and templates is needed to support data validation of BIM data, to ensure high data quality. For such solutions to be a success, the role of software vendors becomes increasingly important. The software vendors must adapt and facilitate these standards, to make the content available for the end-users in the CI. The software vendors must provide platform facilities that better support the heterogeneity of rules needed for the CI (Solihin and Eastman, 2015). However, this adoption still seems to be hindered by the challenges such as those identified in the SSLR. In addition, it seems like those developing the data validation tools are not involved in the creation of the standards. Therefore, each tool is at risk of becoming a standalone solution without connection to a standardised approach including an open data format.

In general, the current approach to data validation within the CI seems to be a stronghold for "experts" resulting in a siloed workflow based on individual capabilities rather than collective cooperation. The true potential of open BIM is not fully served by this approach. Creating machine-readable versions of BIM standards or codes is currently a high-cost process undertaken by experts. Instead, data validation needs to be made more accessible to all participants in the CI. As highlighted by Hjelseth (2015), model checking software in the CI is still a specialist tool, operated by a limited number of professionals. Hjelseth (2015) further argues that for improved information exchange and project-based collaboration the role of data validation becomes critically important. Though, the process is hindered by different factors, as highlighted in the SSLR. For BIM standards, their commonality is that they are written in a human-oriented language. This entails the requirement of significant domain knowledge to interpret these standards into a machine-readable format, that allows for digital data validation. Furthermore, existing data validation templates are often written in a proprietary language and limited in their capabilities due to the complexity of the rules themselves and the breadth of conditions to which they need to apply. In short, data validation is still the domain of industry experts, and the currently manual workflow relies on the accuracy, experience, and expertise of the person or people performing the checks. As of now, the automated data validation process still needs to rely on human input and decisions to achieve trustworthy results. This semi-automated workflow was also identified by Dimyadi and Amor (2013).

5. Conclusion

BIM standards have the potential to be defined into a machine-readable template format that allows for improved, and to some degree automated, data validation. This gives opportunities to data validation solution providers, to provide flexible tools that enable BIM standards and building classification systems for the purpose of simplifying the approach to data validation in the CI. Templates can be a way of making data validation faster and more accessible to all participants in a construction project, by creating a standardised and reliable data validation process. BIM standards and classification systems are of the highest importance in the creation of these templates, to reach a successful data validation process. For a collaborative use of BIM standards, different naming conventions across countries must be considered. Instead of each country and software vendor creating siloed formats and standards, international standards need to facilitate a common approach, to minimise errors, improve collaboration and increase interoperability in the end. These standards must still be specific enough to create practical and machine-readable solutions. While the current standards and guidelines seem vague and don't facilitate practical solutions for data validation in the CI, but only describe and highlight the importance of data validation. Further research is suggested to investigate how software vendors can adapt to and connect with current BIM standards to meet the end-users needs and enable standardised data validation workflows across the CI.

References

A. Poirier, E., Forgues, D. and Staub-French, S. (2014). 'Dimensions of Interoperability in the AEC Industry'. Available at: https://ascelibrary.org/doi/pdf/10.1061/9780784413517.203.

Amor, R. and Dimyadi, J. (2021). 'The promise of automated compliance checking', Developments in the Built Environment, 5(December 2020). doi: 10.1016/j.dibe.2020.100039.

buildingSMART (2021). buildingSMART Data Dictionary. Available at: https://www.buildingsmart.org/users/services/buildingsmart-data-dictionary/ (Accessed: 29 September 2021).

Castro-Lacouture, D., Irizarry, J. and Ashuri, B. (2014). 'Construction Research Congress 2014: Construction in a Global Network'. Available at: https://ascelibrary.org/doi/book/10.1061/9780784413517.

Charef, R., Emmitt, S., Alaka, H., Fouchal, F. (2019). 'Building Information Modelling adoption in the European Union: An overview', Journal of Building Engineering, 25. doi: 10.1016/j.jobe.2019.100777.

Choi, J., Lee, S. and Kim, I. (2020). 'Development of quality control requirements for improving the quality of architectural design based on bim', Applied Sciences (Switzerland), 10(20), pp. 1–25. doi: 10.3390/app10207074.

Ciribini, A. L. C., Ventura, S. M. and Bolpagn, M. (2014) 'Informative content validation is the key to success in a BIM-based project', Creative Commons Attribution– NonCommercial 3.0, 1(6), pp. 87–111. doi: 10.14609/Ti.

CoBuilder (2021). What Is A Data Template (DT)? Available at:

https://cobuilder.com/en/what-is-a-data-template/ (Accessed: 18 November 2021).

Designing Buildings Ltd. (2021). Digitalisation in Construction. Available at: https://www.designingbuildings.co.uk/wiki/Digitalisation_in_Construction (Accessed: 19 October 2021).

Dimyadi, J. and Amor, R. (2013). 'Automated Building Code Compliance Checking. Where is it at?', Proceedings of the CIB World Building Congress 2013 and Architectural Management & Integrated Design and Delivery Solutions (AMIDDS), (380), pp. 172–185. doi: 10.13140/2.1.4920.4161.

Dimyadi, J., Solihin, W. and Hjelseth, E. (2016). 'Classification of BIM-based Model checking concepts', Journal of Information Technology in Construction, 21(October), pp. 354–370.

DSCiBE (2014) 'Digital Supply Chains - Data Driven Collaboration', pp. 1–67. Available at: https://www.gs1.org/sites/default/files/digitalsupplychainsdatadrivencollaboration.pdf.

EU BIM Task Group (2017). EU BIM Task Group, Handbook for the introduction of Building Information Modelling by the European Public Sector. Available at: http://www.eubim.eu/handbook/ (Accessed: 13 December 2021).

Ganah, A. and Lea, G. (2021). 'A Global Analysis of BIM Standards Across the Globe: A Critical Review', 1(July 2021), pp. 52–60. Available at: https://jpmm.um.edu.my/index.php/JPMP/article/view/29153.

Heaton, J., Parlikad, A. K. and Schooling, J. (2019). 'Design and development of BIM models to support operations and maintenance', Computers in Industry, 111, pp. 172–186. doi: 10.1016/j.compind.2019.08.001.

Hjelseth, E. (2015). 'BIM-based model checking (BMC)', Building Information Modeling: Applications and Practices, (March), pp. 33–61. doi: 10.1061/9780784413982.ch02.

ISO (2021). 'ISO'. Available at: https://www.iso.org/sites/ConsumersStandards/1_standards.html (Accessed: 14 September 2021).

Lee, Y.-C., Eastman, C. M. and Solihin, W. (2021). 'Rules and validation processes for interoperable BIM data exchange', Journal of Computational Design and Engineering, 8(1), pp. 97–114. doi: 10.1093/jcde/qwaa064.

Lee, Y. C., Solihin, W. and Eastman, C. M. (2019). 'The Mechanism and Challenges of Validating a Building Information Model regarding data exchange standards', Automation in Construction, 100(December 2017), pp. 118–128. doi: 10.1016/j.autcon.2018.12.025.

McAuley, B., Hore, A. and West, R. (2017). 'Global BIM Study', BICP Irish BIM Study, 4, pp. 78–81. Available at: https://arrow.dit.ie/beschconart.

Paez, A. (2017). 'Gray literature: An important resource in systematic reviews'.

Pedro Mêda, Hipólito Sousa and Eilif Hjelseth (2020). 'Data Templates - Traceability and Digital Record Through Project Life-Cycle'.

Rasmussen, M. H. and Schlachter, A. (2021). 'Automated Rule Checking: What is state of the art, and how can it be translated into the Danish context?' Available at: https://bartbyg.dk/.

Sacks, R., Gurevich, U. and Shrestha, P. (2016). 'A review of Building Information Modeling protocols, guides and standards for Large construction clients', Journal of Information Technology in Construction, 21(July), pp. 479–503.

Sattler, L., Lamouri, S., Pellerin, R., Maigne, T. (2019). 'Interoperability aims in building information modeling exchanges: A literature review', IFAC-PapersOnLine, 52(13), pp. 271–276. doi: 10.1016/j.ifacol.2019.11.180.

SDG (2018). SDG Knowledge Weekly: Data, Indicators and Statistics for Sustainable

Development. Available at: http://sdg.iisd.org/commentary/policy-briefs/sdg-knowledge-weekly-data-indicators-and-statistics-for-sustainable-development/ (Accessed: 13 December 2021).

Snyder, H. (2019). 'Literature review as a research methodology: An overview and guidelines', Journal of Business Research, 104(August), pp. 333–339. doi: 10.1016/j.jbusres.2019.07.039.

Solihin, W. and Eastman, C. (2015). 'Classification of rules for automated BIM rule checking development', Automation in Construction, 53, pp. 69–82. doi: 10.1016/j.autcon.2015.03.003.

Tranfield, D., Denyer, D. and Smart, P. (2003). Towards a Methodology for Developing Evidence-Informed Management Knowledge by Means of Systematic Review*, British Journal of Management.

Ward, V., House, A. and Hamer, S. (2009). 'Developing a framework for transferring knowledge into action: A thematic analysis of the literature', Journal of Health Services Research and Policy, 14(3), pp. 156–164. doi: 10.1258/jhsrp.2009.008120.

Wong, G., Greenhalgh, T., Westhorp, G., Buckingham, J. (2013). 'RAMESES publication standards: Meta-narrative reviews', Journal of Advanced Nursing, 69(5), pp. 987–1004. doi: 10.1111/jan.12092.

Wu, J. and Zhang, J. (2018). 'Automated BIM Object Classification to Support BIM Interoperability', Construction Research Congress 2018: Sustainable Design and Construction and Education - Selected Papers from the Construction Research Congress 2018, 2018-April, pp. 706–715. doi: 10.1061/9780784481301.070.

Zio, M. Di, Fursova, N., Gelsema, T., Gießing, S., Guarnera, U., Petrauskienė, J., Quenselvon Kalben, L., Scanu, M., K.O. ten Bosch, Mark van der Loo, Walsdorfer, K. (2016). 'Methodology for data validation 1.0 Essnet Validat Foundation', (June), pp. 0–75. Available at: https://ec.europa.eu/eurostat/cros/system/files/methodology_for_data_validation_v1.0_rev-2016-06_final.pdf.

BIM-based fall hazard ontology and benchmark model for comparison of automated prevention through design approaches in construction safety

Johansen K.W. [1], Schultz C. [2], Teizer J. [3]
[1]Department of Civil and Architectural Engineering, Aarhus University, Denmark
[2]Department of Electrical and Computer Engineering, Aarhus University, Denmark
[3]Department of Civil and Mechanical Engineering, Technical University of Denmark, Denmark
Kwj@cae.au.dk

Abstract. Due to the continuous changes in its complex and dynamic work environment, work in the construction industry is one of the most dangerous. Many of the existing workplace safety planning techniques are still based on 2D drawings and manual expertise. This effort is cumbersome as the progressing work quickly results in outdated safety plans. Researchers have put much effort into automating the planning process, but their result's soundness and completeness are incomparable. This work describes our BIM-based ontology of construction hazards and mitigation interventions for fall from height hazards based on EU and US regulations. We extract the variations of the rules and capture the concepts in spatial artifacts. We carefully created a benchmark model that allows for soundness and correctness assessment which enables comparison of different automated PTD approaches.

1. Introduction

Construction is one of the most dangerous industries due to the continuous change in the environment (Pinto et al., 2011). Over time, the previously safest route may have turned into a very dangerous route, e.g., because of changes in the tower cranes planned tasks, missing fall protection equipment, or debris in the designated pedestrian walk path. Consequently, the workers are responsible and must be aware of, consider, and adapt to new hazardous situations that may not be a part of the safety plan due to the low temporal resolution adopted when undertaking initial safety planning. Safety planning is currently a manual and labour-intensive task. In particular, the standard planning process only covers the overall site layout in a coarse temporal resolution because it would be impossible to generate a new safety plan on every state change of the construction site. The lack of temporal precision and, therefore, the demand for the workers to take over the situation planning, result in thought-provoking statistics.

Furthermore, current manual safety assessment is done on an overall procedure, typically once at the beginning of a construction project and often based on 2D cad drawings of the construction site and building layout. Additionally, safety planning may be subject to human biases, and the safety expert may even oversee potential hazards. Often, it is chosen to make the complete construction site, including indoor areas, subject to an injunction of hardhats even though only parts of the construction site are subject to *strike from the above* hazards. Finally, the overall request may result in safety equipment fatigue.

A report on labour statistics in the US from (BLS, 2020) shows that fatalities in the private construction industry correspond to 21.2% (1008) of fatalities (4764). Furthermore, the report indicates that the predominant reason for fatalities in the construction industry is falls, slips, and trips, which correspond to 36.5% (368). These findings motivate the research and development of automated safety design and planning, also referred to as Prevention Through Design and Planning (PtD/P). With the emerging research of automating the task, manual work is reduced, and consequently, the temporal resolution is expectedly rising. Furthermore, an automated programming-based approach may be less biased and prone to produce errors

https://doi.org/10.7146/aul.455.c231

depending on the accuracy of the rule implementation. In general, assessment of truth is a non-trivial task but especially a comparison of the automated approaches.

To get the full benefit of an automated approach, it needs to be sufficiently fast and operate on an updated version of the Project Intent Information (PII) considering the current stage of the construction site captured in the Project Status Knowledge (PSK). PII and PSK are introduced in (Sacks et al., 2020) as a part of the Digital Twin (DT) concept. In our previous work (Teizer et al., 2022), we outline a holistic approach to interact with a DT in PtD/P and other safety aspects. The emergence of DT is an enabling factor for automated safety design and planning, where the temporal precision can be enhanced. It also enables further insight into the historical data of the construction crew and specific scenarios that need extra attention in the design.

The current research in the domain of automated safety design and planning is often based on individual models, which makes the comparison of approaches complicated. Furthermore, it is our understanding that a common standardized approach of defining hazards in construction would be beneficial in combination with a benchmark model that can be used for correctness assessment. Our research questions for this study are therefore:

RQ 1 Can we formalize *fall from height* hazards as defined in Germany, Denmark, and the US construction safety regulations, where considered mitigation strategies are guardrails and cover boards using spatial artifacts extracted from building information models?

RQ 2 Would such a formalization be accessible to industry practitioners and readily exploited in current workflows?

RQ 3 Can various approaches to formalizing fall safety hazards be put on a "level playing field" so strategies can be directly compared in terms of soundness and completeness?

In addressing these research questions our contributions in this paper are:

C1 We present a new concept and formal definition of a shared benchmark BIM model, with a precise formal definition of sound and complete *fall from height* analysis.

C2 We develop a new, freely available benchmark BIM model, with the precise sound and complete analysis according to DK, DE, and US construction safety standards facilitating a "success" score calculation by following our prescribed safety criteria.

2. Related Work

The domain of construction code and regulation checking is an ongoing research topic. The most commonly investigated rule is regarding *fall from heights* hazards as these are responsible for most fatalities in the construction industry (Collins et al., 2014; Li et al., 2022; Melzner et al., 2013; Schwabe et al., 2019). To explore automated prevention through design, one must first define a link between the construction regulation and the Building Information Model (BIM) and afterward define the logic that can check whether the regulation is violated in a given BIM model. The drive behind the efforts has been the fact that the current practices are cumbersome and affected by manual assessment. With the emergence of Digital Twins (DT), the knowledge gap between the current state of the construction site and planning has been made smaller. As presented in DTCS (Teizer et al., 2022), the digital twin and automated safety assessment even allow the decision-makers at the construction site to analyze different approaches in terms of cost, time, safety fitness, etc., before making a choice.

2.1. Linking construction safety codes to building information models

We need a way of formally capturing construction regulations and building codes such that the computer can (1) interpret the natural language formulation of the content and (2) link this content to concepts in BIM for automated safety analysis in construction. There are several construction safety ontologies that capture object concepts and their relationships (Lu et al., 2015; Wang and Boukamp, 2011; Zhang et al., 2015a; Zhou et al., 2016). Some of these ontologies are used for safety rule checking, i.e., to determine if some safety hazards are present in the BIM model under investigation. The above examples successfully point out the areas where the safety expert needs to be cautious and apply temporary prevention equipment. However, these automated approaches are not applied in actual construction hazard planning, which may be due to a lack of knowledge and descriptiveness of ontologies.

2.2. Construction hazard identification

Takim et al. (2016) and Zhang et al. (2015b) are examples of automated fall hazard identification, which are based on maximum elevation height, and maximum slab openings, that are allowed before prevention measures must be applied. In Tekbas and Guven (2020), the prevention measures are injected into the BIM model using Dynamo, the Revit programming interface. Even though those mentioned above are already significant contributions, their correctness and soundness cannot be assessed without going through the identified hazards individually. The reason is that there is no easy way to compare the results of the different approaches in an environment that contains identified edge cases. Another reason is that the algorithms are often benchmarked on the number of identified hazards but not compared to the number of existing hazards. Benchmarking is commonly used in other domains such as machine learning and computer vision, where a portion of the data, i.e., test data, is used as ground truth to assess the correctness and soundness of a trained model (Deng et al., 2009; Xuehui et al., 2021). The adoption of benchmarking provides the stakeholders with a deeper insight into the quality of the hazard identification provided.

3. Methodology

By comparing different approaches to defining domain languages for construction safety analysis and assessment, we have chosen to follow a similar approach to the one presented in (Zhang et al., 2015a) and later adopted in (Li et al., 2022). The approach is based on IDEF5 (Peraketh et al., 1994), which consists of five subsequent steps that will generate three resulting outputs, i.e., a graphical representation of the ontology language, a structured text representation, and a procedure with a guideline for information extraction.

3.1. Step 1: Organizing and Scoping

The purpose of initiating a formal standardization of a construction safety domain language is to provide an approach that can be used in our future research and the community to streamline the efforts on automated construction safety assessment. We initiate the domain language with the most straightforward and predominant spatial artifact (i.e., *movement*, *fall*, and *fall hazard space*) and envision the vocabulary extending over time when work progresses in the community. We base our ontology on the Industrial Foundation Classes (IFC) to permit interoperability. Additionally, the IFC structure is similar to graph databases used in the emerging Digital Twins (DTs).

3.2. Step 2: Data Collection

We collect the natural language formulation of the construction safety codes from the European Union, Denmark, Germany, and the US regulation. We have chosen the EU regulation to get an overview of Europe, Denmark (where we are located), and Germany to compare similarities within the European countries. Besides the European regulations, we have chosen to consider the US regulations as it should reveal differences and similarities between the two continents.

3.3. Step 3: Data Analysis

Based on each of our chosen country and continent regulations, we extract two kinds of information: (1) their definition of when fall protective equipment must be applied, (2) The dimensions of hazard space for different mitigation strategies, and (3) example implementations of fall protection systems. The extracted and analyzed information is assumed to make our ontology applicable for at least the included countries and continents.

3.4. Step 4: Initial Ontology Development

Our initial ontology is based on the current state of the art, which we refine to ensure further applicability and consensus in the research domain. The ontology focuses on fall hazard scenarios. Based on our data analysis (step 3), we extract the variating factors and define a vocabulary of variables that we extract from the regulation. Subsequently, we define the ontology using spatial artifacts and the vocabulary. Additionally, we propose a strategy to integrate the spatial artifacts into IFC, which exclusively depends on existing IFC-classes, meaning that the ontology is compliant with the IFC4 tools and workflows.

3.5. Step 5: Ontology Refinement and Validation

To refine and validate our ontology, we develop a benchmark model. Based on the regulations, we carefully create scenarios that will, or will not, require fall hazard mitigation equipment depending on the regulation. We are utilizing the benchmark model to validate our ontology and expectedly refine it during this process. Additionally, we will refine the ontology based on other continents and countries and feedback from practitioners in future research studies.

4. Otology development

4.1. Safety regulation collection and analysis

We analyze the European (ES, 2018), Danish (BFA, 2020), German (BG-Bau, 2021), and US regulations (OSHA, 2019). To ensure that the proposed ontology is representative, we extract the factors that are present in them. We compile the variating factors into a vocabulary and extract their values for comparison, as shown in Table 1. Figure 1 shows a graphical representation of the vocabulary variables, which are limited to *falls from height*, where mitigation approaches include safety guardrails and cover panels. Hence, we are not investigating safety nets.

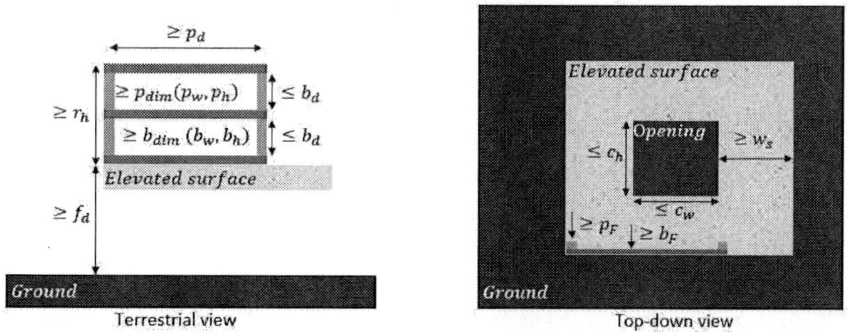

Figure 1: Illustration of values in Table 1 (horizontal boards colored in red and vertical poles in grey)

4.2. Definition of ontology for fall from heights

After extracting the variables that change in the European, Danish, German, and US regulations, we define our ontology that captures the construction regulation. Our ontology shown in Figure

2 is based on spatial artifacts, which captures concepts pertaining to human experience and behaviour as semantically rich regions of empty space. In a BIM model, spatial artefacts are derived from IfcElements and their spatial relationships. Depending on the point of view, the surface of a slab (for example) may simultaneously introduce a walkable space, fall space, and tumbling space. Thus, extraction of the spatial artifacts is based on the construction regulation, the element relationships according to specific points of view, the location of the IfcElement instance, and the geometry of the IfcElement instance; the location and geometry are extracted from instance's IfcProductRepresentation. Additionally, the relationship between spatial artifacts may introduce *hazard spaces*, e.g., Fall hazard space. Each hazard is mitigated via mitigation equipment, which is a subclass of IfcElement. The individual mitigation strategies have test procedures specified in the safety regulation. The test procedure indirectly captures the attributes of the mitigation system, e.g., dimensions, pole- and bord distances, etc.

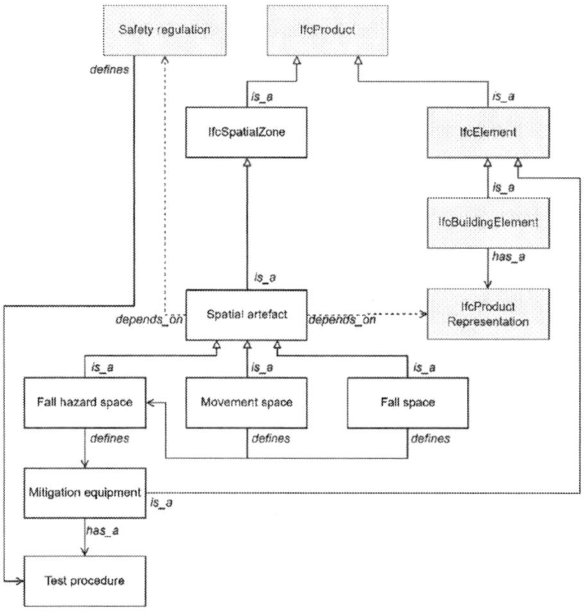

Figure 2: Diagram of our BIM-based ontology of construction hazards and mitigation interventions.

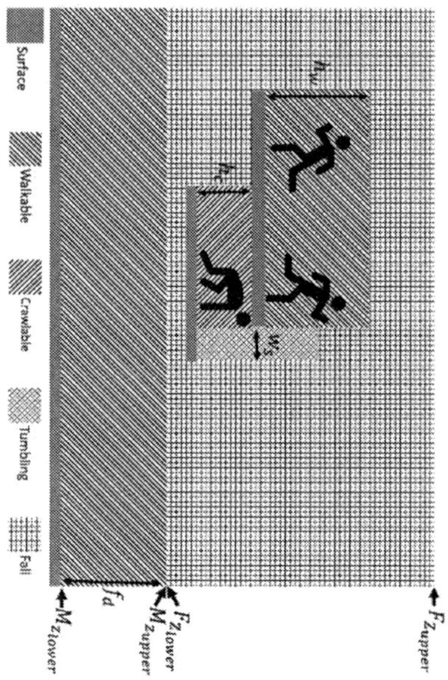

Figure 3: Illustration of spatial artefacts extracted from IfcElements.

Figure 4: Leading edge.

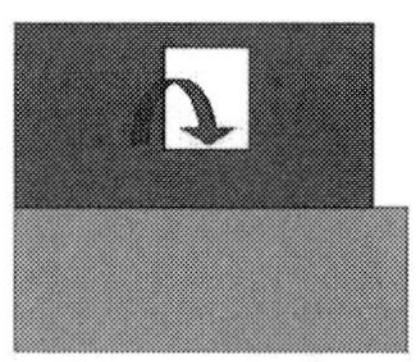

Figure 5: Offset leading edge.

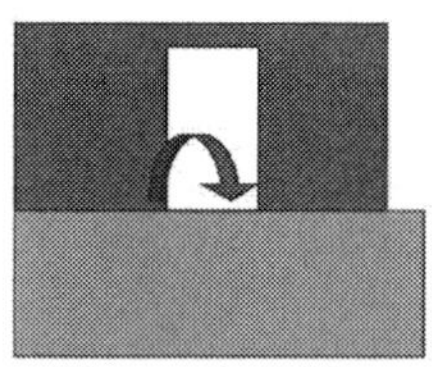

Figure 6: Offset top leading edge.

Figure 7: Tumbling space.

4.3. Integration into Industry Foundation Classes

Figure 3 presents our latest version of IFC integration, which is based on the work presented in (Li et al., 2022). The integration utilizes the IfcProperty class and the IfcRelReferencedInSpatialStructure class to capture information about which products in the BIM model directly generate a given spatial artifact. This version is fully compliant with IFC4 and can be processed by all IFC4 compliant tools. Each spatial artifact is implemented as an instance of the IfcSpatialZone class. The spatial artifact type is expressed as an instance of IfcProperty that selects an enumerated value.

Table 1: Variable vocabulary defined through analysis of scoped regulations.

Natural language formulations	Attribute	Symbol	US	EU	German	Danish
The minimum distance, from an elevated surface to a lower surface which an item or a human being could fall onto, which would require a form of fall protection equipment.	Fall distance	f_d	1,8m	1m	1m	1m
The minimum width of a surface, which an agent is allowed to be present on	Surface width	w_s	56cm	60cm	60 cm	60cm
The minimum Height of a space, which is considered walkable	Walk height	h_w	NA	NA	NA	NA
Minimum height of a space considered crawlable	Crawl height	h_c	NA	NA	NA	NA
Maximum width of hole in a surface, where chosen mitigation will be a coverboard, i.e., maximum width of cover boards	Cover width	c_w	1m	NA	NA	NA
Maximum height of hole in a surface, where chosen mitigation will be a coverboard, i.e., maximum height of cover boards	Cover height	c_h	1m	NA	NA	NA
Minimum height of guardrail (aka., Safety railing, safety barrier)	Railing height	r_h	1,1m	1m	1m	1m
Maximum distance between vertical poles of guardrail installation	Pole distance	p_d	2,4m	NA	2m	2,25m
Maximum distance between horizontal boards in guardrail installation	Board distance	b_d	$r_h/2$	0,47m	0,47m	0,47m
Best practice width of applied vertical poles in guardrail installation	Pole width	p_w	5cm	NA	3cm	4,5cm
Best practice height of applied vertical poles in guardrail installation	Pole height	p_h	10cm	NA	15cm	7cm
Best practice width of applied horizontal boards/rails in guardrail installation	Board width	b_w	2,5cm	NA	3cm	3,2cm
Best practice height of applied horizontal boards/rails in guardrail installation	Board height	b_h	15cm	NA	15cm	15cm
Minimum continues force that vertical poles in guardrail installation should withstand	Pole force	p_f	890N	300N	300N	300N
Minimum continues force that horizontal boards in guardrail installation should withstand	Board force	b_f	890N	300N	300N	300N

Table 2: Overview and description of spatial artifacts for fall hazard identification and analysis.

Spatial Artefact	Specialized subclasses	Description	Illustration	Constraints
Movement space		Regions in which an agent (e.g., construction worker, manager, and visitor) can travel.		
	Crawlable space	Regions in which an agent can travel crawling.	Figure 3	$h_c \leq height < h_w \ and \ width \geq w_s$
	Walkable space	Regions in which an agent can travel upright	Figure 3	$height = h_w \ and \ width \geq w_s$
Fall space		Regions in which an object or agent will fall by f_d.	Figure 3	$F_{z_{lower}} = M_{z_{lower}} + f_d$
Fall hazard spaces		Regions in which an agent is subject to a fall hazard		
	Leading edge space	Regions where the movement space in its full height intersects with a fall space	Figure 4	$M_{z_{lower}} \geq F_{z_{lower}} \wedge M_{z_{upper}} \leq F_{z_{upper}}$
	Offset leading-edge space	Regions where a portion of the movement space intersects with a fall space	Figure 5	$M_{z_{lower}} + offset_{lower} < M_{z_{lower}} + r_h$
	Offset top leading-edge space	Regions where a portion of the movement space intersects with a fall space	Figure 6	$M_{z_{upper}} - offset_{upper} < M_{z_{lower}} + h_c$
	Tumbling space	Regions in which an agent can tumble over fall prevention equipment on lower surface	Figure 7	$z_{upperSurface} - z_{lowerSurface} < f_d \wedge width_{lowerSurface} < w_s$

The enumeration of spatial artifact types is implemented as an instance of IfcPropertyEnumeration, with the name "PEnum_SpatialArtefactType". The relationship with existing products in the IFC model that are used to directly generate the spatial artefact is expressed via an instance of IfcRelReferencedInSpatialStructure; for example, a slab on which a person can walk may be used to derive a movement space.

For representing mitigation strategies (e.g., coverings, harnesses, safety nets) we adopt a similar approach by creating instances of the existing class IfcCivilElement and assigning a property enumerated value (with a custom property enumeration listing the mitigation strategies) to indicate the mitigation strategy class.

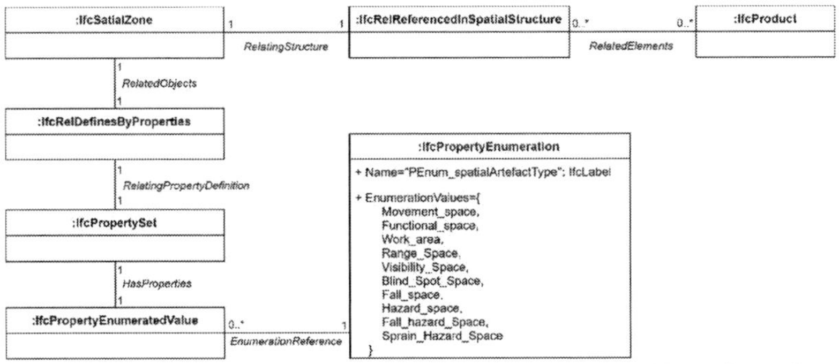

Figure 8: UML class diagram depicting how instances of spatial artifacts for safety analysis are expressed in standard IFC4.

4.4. Validation of ontology

Figure 11 shows the results of our automated approach of prevention through design, specifically for fall hazard identification and prevention. The algorithm is running on an IFC file exported from CAD software. The result, which is also IFC-format, is imported into the same CAD software for subsequent internal correctness and soundness assessment. As part of future work, the ontology will be further validated in a series of studies and workshops where industry experts are interviewed to assess the analysis soundness and completeness, and to assess how this analysis fits into their current practices, workflows, and tools. Additionally, we will assess the expandability, portability, and scalability of our approach, e.g., by extending the current coverage to other continents and hazard types.

5. Definition of the benchmark model

Figure 9 shows the benchmark model that has been carefully designed to include edge case scenarios of the regulations that have been investigated for this work. Specifically, it consists of two parts separated by the stamped line. The first part in front of the dashed line shown in the detailed view in Figure 9 is designed such that the first platform's elevation (f_d) is below the threshold for all analysed regulations, the second platform's elevation (f_d) is high enough to be subject to the EU regulation, and the third platform's elevation is subject to both EU and US regulation. Additionally, the platforms have been designed with smaller outgoing platforms, whose widths (w_s) are chosen to be subject to individual regulations, described in the figure. Lastly the platforms include two openings, where one is bigger than the allowable coverable dimensions (c_w and c_h) stated for the US regulation; i.e. the larger opening requires guardrails, and the other smaller opening requires a covering. This dimension is not stated for the EU regulation, and it is assumed to have the same measure requirements. The other part of the model (behind the stamped line) is designed to capture special cases such as openings in walls and slabs, leading edges, coverable gabs, tumbling spaces, leading edges that are non-orthogonal to the model space, and obstacles in the movement space.

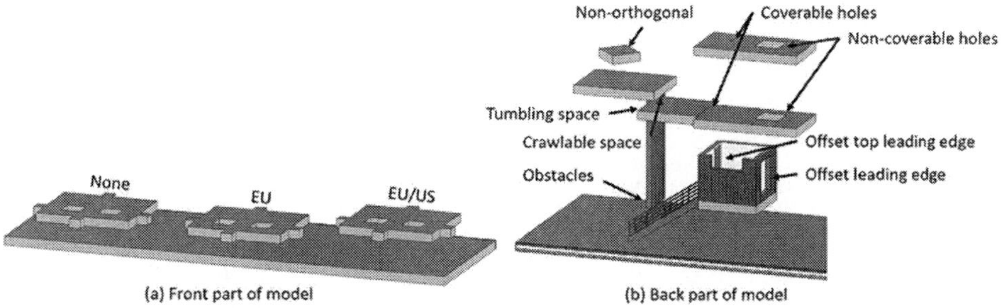

Figure 9: 3D view of benchmark model (a) front and (b) back with description of included scenarios.

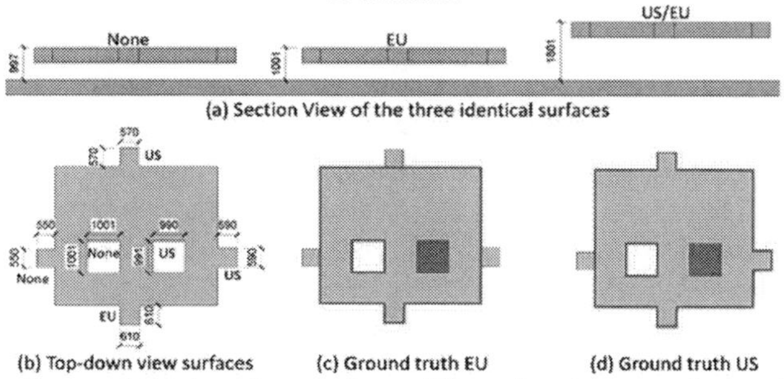

Figure 10: (a) 2D section and (b) top-down view of f_d and w_s in scenarios and their application in (c) EU and (d) US regulations from Figure 9 (a).

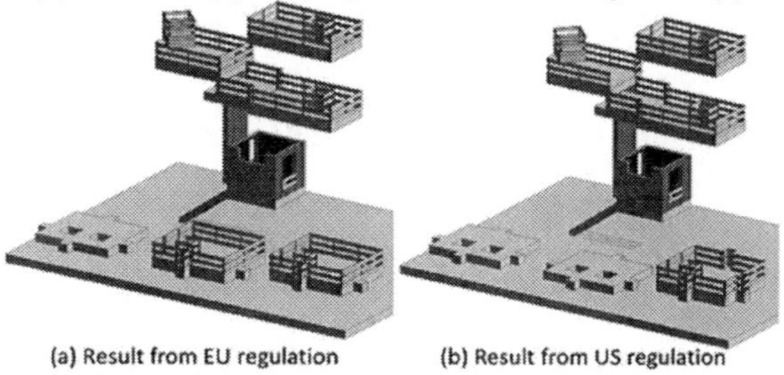

Figure 11: Safe design based on (a) EU regulation and (B) US regulation.

6. Discussion

We have created the ontology based on the *fall from height* safety regulations of two regions, Europe and the US. Additionally, we have performed internal validation through an internal safety expert assessment. This assessment will be extended in future work to incorporate external industry practitioners. Furthermore, the ontology will be tested against other countries and continents.

We provide a benchmark model consisting of two parts: the front part, which contains edge cases of the analysed regulations, and the back part, which consists of different IfcElements that create the various spatial artifacts described in our ontology. The benchmark model does not yet contain any sloped surfaces, which is another aspect to be addressed in future research.

The ontology and benchmark model have been developed to be utilized in our own prevention through design algorithm. We have included the results in Figure 11, but as this is not the main contribution, we have not described this in detail. Nevertheless, it has been the basis for the internal soundness and completeness assessment. This has been done on the input (regulation, benchmark model, and ontology) and output (safety enhanced model). One final direction we are pursuing is automatically generating benchmark BIM models directly from a formal logic-based description of hazards (such as *falls from height*), taking inspiration from automated test case generation in software engineering (Larsen et al., 2010), spatial grammars and generative design (Mckay et al., 2012), and declarative spatial reasoning (Bhatt et al., 2011; Schultz et al.,

2017). This will involve adapting notions of equivalence class partitioning, boundary testing, and coverage to the construction safety domain, e.g., what we refer to as *edge cases* corresponds to strategies in boundary testing.

7. Conclusion

We analyzed the construction regulations pertaining to *falls from height*, specifically for cases where guardrails and cover panels are used as a mitigation measure. We formalized the rules and their variating factors into tangible definitions using spatial artifacts that can be extracted from building information models. Our ontology has been defined in close relation to Industry Foundation Classes, and its integration has been proposed such that our work is accessible and exploitable in industry practitioners' current workflows and tools. Additionally, we provide a freely available benchmark model for comparing different PTD approaches in the community.

Our future research will include case studies that can determine the soundness, completeness, expandability, portability, and scalability of our approach, focusing on the design aspect. Furthermore, we envision extending this with planning, which incorporate timing (scheduling) and processes (tasks and their dependencies). We invite the community to take part in the investigation of these topics to drive the efforts of streamlined contributions.

Acknowledgement

The research presented in this paper has received funding from the European Union's Horizon 2020 research and innovation program under grant agreements no. 958398 and no. 958310.

References

BFA, B. for B.& A., (2020). Håndbogen - Arbejdsmiljø i bygge og anlæg. Branchearbejdsmiljørådet for Bygge & Anlæg.

BG-Bau, (2021). Absturzsicherungen auf Baustellen Seitenschutz/Absperrungen | BG BAU - Berufsgenossenschaft der Bauwirtschaft. URL https://www.bgbau.de (accessed 2.11.22).

Bhatt, M., Lee, J., Schultz, C., 2011. CLP(QS): A Declarative Spatial Reasoning Framework. pp. 210–230. https://doi.org/10.1007/978-3-642-23196-4_12

BLS, B. of labour statistics, (2020). Fatal occupational injuries by industry and event or exposure, all United States. URL https://www.bls.gov/iif/oshwc/cfoi/cftb0340.htm#cfoi_at_a1.f.2 (accessed 2.16.22).

Collins, R., Zhang, S., Kim, K., Teizer, J., (2014). Integration of Safety Risk Factors in BIM for Scaffolding Construction 307–314. https://doi.org/10.1061/9780784413616.039

Deng, J., Dong, W., Socher, R., Li, L.-J., Li, K., Fei-Fei, L., (2009). ImageNet: A large-scale hierarchical image database, in: 2009 IEEE Conference on Computer Vision and Pattern Recognition. Presented at the 2009 IEEE Conference on Computer Vision and Pattern Recognition, pp. 248–255. https://doi.org/10.1109/CVPR.2009.5206848

ES, E. standards, (2018). Temporary edge protection systems - DS_EN 13374_2013+A1_2018.

Larsen, P.G., Lausdahl, K., Battle, N., (2010). Combinatorial Testing for VDM, in: 2010 8th IEEE International Conference on Software Engineering and Formal Methods. Presented at the 2010 8th IEEE International Conference on Software Engineering and Formal Methods, pp. 278–285. https://doi.org/10.1109/SEFM.2010.32

Li, B., Schultz, C., Teizer, J., Golovina, O., Melzner, J., (2022). Towards a unifying domain model of construction safety, health and well-being: SafeConDM. Adv. Eng. Inform. 51, 101487. https://doi.org/10.1016/j.aei.2021.101487

Lu, Y., Li, Q., Zhou, Z., Deng, Y., (2015). Ontology-based knowledge modeling for automated construction safety checking. Saf. Sci. 79, 11–18. https://doi.org/10.1016/j.ssci.2015.05.008

Mckay, A., Chase, S., Shea, K., Chau, H.H., (2012). Spatial grammar implementation: From theory to useable software. Artif. Intell. Eng. Des. Anal. Manuf. 26, 143–159. https://doi.org/10.1017/S0890060412000042

Melzner, J., Zhang, S., Teizer, J., Bargstädt, H.-J., (2013). A case study on automated safety compliance checking to assist fall protection design and planning in building information models. Constr. Manag. Econ. 31, 661–674. https://doi.org/10.1080/01446193.2013.780662

OSHA, (2019). 1910.29 - Fall protection systems and falling object protection-criteria and practices. | Occupational Safety and Health Administration. URL https://www.osha.gov/laws-regs/regulations/standardnumber/1910/1910.29 (accessed 2.11.22).

Peraketh, B., Menzel, C.P., Mayer, R.J., Fillion, F., Futrell, M.T., (1994). Ontology Capture Method (IDEF5).: Defense Technical Information Center, Fort Belvoir, VA. https://doi.org/10.21236/ADA288442

Pinto, A., Nunes, I.L., Ribeiro, R.A., (2011). Occupational risk assessment in construction industry – Overview and reflection. Saf. Sci. 49, 616–624. https://doi.org/10.1016/j.ssci.2011.01.003

Sacks, R., Brilakis, I., Pikas, E., Xie, H.S., Girolami, M., (2020). Construction with digital twin information systems. Data-Centric Eng. 1. https://doi.org/10.1017/dce.2020.16

Schultz, C., Bhatt, M., Borrmann, A., (2017). Bridging qualitative spatial constraints and feature-based parametric modelling: Expressing visibility and movement constraints. Adv Eng Inform. https://doi.org/10.1016/J.AEI.2015.10.004

Schwabe, K., Teizer, J., König, M., (2019). Applying rule-based model-checking to construction site layout planning tasks. Autom. Constr. 97, 205–219. https://doi.org/10.1016/j.autcon.2018.10.012

Takim, R., Zulkifli, M.H., Nawawi, A.H., (2016). Integration of Automated Safety Rule Checking (ASRC) System for Safety Planning BIM-Based Projects in Malaysia. Procedia - Soc. Behav. Sci., ASEAN-Turkey ASLI QoL2015: AicQoL2015Jakarta, Indonesia, 25–27 April 2015 222, 103–110. https://doi.org/10.1016/j.sbspro.2016.05.195

Teizer, J., Johansen, K.W., Schultz, C., (2022). The Concept of Digital Twin for Construction Safety 1156–1165. https://doi.org/10.1061/9780784483961.121

Tekbas, G., Guven, G., (2020). BIM-Based Automated Safety Review for Fall Prevention, in: Ofluoglu, S., Ozener, O.O., Isikdag, U. (Eds.), Advances in Building Information Modeling, Communications in Computer and Information Science. Springer International Publishing, Cham, pp. 80–90. https://doi.org/10.1007/978-3-030-42852-5_7

Wang, H.-H., Boukamp, F., (2011). Ontology-Based Representation and Reasoning Framework for Supporting Job Hazard Analysis. J. Comput. Civ. Eng. 25, 442–456. https://doi.org/10.1061/(ASCE)CP.1943-5487.0000125

Xuehui, A., Li, Z., Zuguang, L., Chengzhi, W., Pengfei, L., Zhiwei, L., (2021). Dataset and benchmark for detecting moving objects in construction sites. Autom. Constr. 122, 103482. https://doi.org/10.1016/j.autcon.2020.103482

Zhang, S., Boukamp, F., Teizer, J., (2015a). Ontology-based semantic modeling of construction safety knowledge: Towards automated safety planning for job hazard analysis (JHA). Autom. Constr. 52, 29–41. https://doi.org/10.1016/j.autcon.2015.02.005

Zhang, S., Sulankivi, K., Kiviniemi, M., Romo, I., Eastman, C.M., Teizer, J., (2015b). BIM-based fall hazard identification and prevention in construction safety planning. Saf. Sci. 72, 31–45. https://doi.org/10.1016/j.ssci.2014.08.001

Zhou, Z., Goh, Y.M., Shen, L., (2016). Overview and Analysis of Ontology Studies Supporting Development of the Construction Industry. J. Comput. Civ. Eng. 30, 04016026. https://doi.org/10.1061/(ASCE)CP.1943-5487.0000594

Automating the Estimation of Productivity Metrics for Construction Workers Using Deep Learning and Kinematics

Jacobsen E. L.[1], Teizer J.[2]
[1]Department of Civil and Architectural Engineering, Aarhus University, Denmark
[2]Department of Civil and Mechanical Engineering, Techincal University Denmark, Denmark
elj@cae.au.dk

Abstract. In this study, a novel method for direct work estimation is used to classify whether a painter is performing direct work or not. The aim is to build an accurate and reliable work classification algorithm that can help monitor construction sites. The method utilizes a deep learning algorithm using convolutional and long short-term memory layers to classify multivariate time-series data collected from five inertial measurement units (IMUs) mounted on the workers' arms, torso, and legs. Three models are developed, differing in window sizes from 3 seconds to 7 seconds. The best performing model achieves an accuracy of 90% and an F1-score of 87.6%. This is the first step towards a general model that can classify productivity measures for workers on construction sites, which will be a valuable input for monitoring construction sites and future analyses.

1. Introduction

The construction industry is very labor-intensive as it consists of many manual tasks. The ability to monitor and manage both workers and activities can be an essential tool to ensure projects are within the scope of time and cost. Several publications have over the last decade shown the construction industry lacks behind other industries in terms of productivity (Neve et al., 2020; Chapman et al., 2010). The conclusions vary due to the complex nature of the construction industry and the difficulty of consistently measuring productivity. The methods used are easily biased and often lack continuity, only looking at small percentages of the construction projects' timespan. No standardization has been made for monitoring productivity, which is currently done on several levels, from project to task and worker levels. Therefore, developing methods that allow for continuous monitoring of construction worker productivity is necessary to improve construction projects' performance.

Productivity can be an intangible concept as different tasks require different actions; different tasks have different definitions of whether an action is productive. In general, construction labor productivity (CLP) can be defined as the product output per person-hour worked. Several other factors are relevant when examining productivity, but as a measure of performance, CLP has been used alone as it is a significant factor for the total project cost, as well as because it is the only factor that is conscious of its contribution (Wandahl et al., 2021). This paper (1) gives an overview of current activity recognition and productivity estimation research in construction, (2) introduces a deep learning method for productivity estimation, (3) shows the early implementation and preliminary results of the model, and (4) discusses the future work regarding the method, the current challenges, and the potential.

2. Background

CLP has been extensively studied using manual methods, especially work sampling (Araujo et al., 2020; Wandahl et al., 2021; Gouett et al., 2011). Work sampling can be used to estimate CLP due to the direct correlation between the direct work (DW) category "producing" and

https://doi.org/10.7146/aul.455.c232

productivity. Automated processes, especially machine learning methods, have also been investigated to estimate productivity using static information such as project size, worker experience, or contractual agreements (Jacobsen and Teizer, 2022). The methods differ in the modality used for activity recognition, and most publications fall into one of three categories: images/videos, audio, or kinematic data (Sherafat et al., 2020).

2.1 Computer Vision Methods

Research within computer vision has seen an increase in interest from construction research (Jacobsen and Teizer, 2022). The methods based on images and videos have also been used for activity recognition. Luo et al. (2018) developed a convolutional neural network (CNN) model based on optical flow to recognize three actions: Walking, transporting, and steel bending. Support Vector Machine (SVM) is a highly used model, which has been used for activity detection both in lab settings (Khosrowpour et al., 2014) and on actual construction sites (Liu and Golparvar-Fard, 2015; Yang et al., 2016; Khosrowpour et al., 2014). Computer-vision methods have, in most cases, seen very well-performing models due to the efforts that have been put into the field of computer-vision methods, developing robust recognition models. However, computer-vision methods have limitations. Using cameras requires a well light scene, is a stationary method, and suffers in almost every configuration, especially in dynamic work settings, from occlusions (Jacobsen and Teizer, 2021). Furthermore, storing the information needed for the supervised machine learning algorithms can be costly as the files from cameras (pictures or videos) require large amounts of storage (Sherafat et al., 2020).

2.2 Audio-based Methods

Audio-based recognition for construction workers has primarily been used for activity detection through either an array of microphones or single microphones installed on job sites. A substantial part of the publications uses SVM for activity recognition. Several different features are used across the publications. Rashid and Louis (2020) utilize four domain-specific feature sets for their classification: time-, frequency-, cepstral-, and wavelet-domain features. Their algorithm was used to classify activities: nailing with nail-gun, hammering, table-saw cutting, and drilling. Others use only cepstral features (Yang et al., 2015) or only time features (Cheng et al., 2017). As the experiments differ in activities classified, experimental setup, and data quantities, it is impossible to compare these to each other, which is also why it is impossible to state which features are the most important when using audio-based methods for classifying activities. However, Rashid and Louis (2020), who use in total 318 features, shows that for their experiments, cepstral-domain features contribute the most to the algorithm's performance and wavelet-domain features contribute the least.

2.3 Kinematic-based Methods

Kinematic signals such as orientation data, magnetic fields, acceleration, and angular velocity have been used as a basis for activity detection algorithms. These data streams are collected from sensors, for instance, inertial measurement units (IMUs). This is possible as activities often have unique kinematic patterns. Different types of machine learning algorithms have been used to classify these patterns. Joshua and Varghese (2011) used decision trees, Naïve Bayes and multilayer perceptron to classify bricklaying activities using one acceleration sensor. More recent work has investigated other methods for activity classification, such as neural networks, KNN, and SVM (Akhavian and Behzadan, 2018; Ryu et al., 2018; Yang et al., 2019). Similarly to audio-based methods, SVM is a frequently used algorithm in this domain. This could be due to its ease of implementation or the simplicity of most implementations. Some studies also utilize IMUs in combination with other datastreams, such as location (Cheng et al., 2013). Here the location is used for spatiotemporal reasoning, where zones have been predefined as working zones or material zones, to assist in classifying a movement into working, idling, walking or material handling.

3. Methods

In this section, an introduction to the proposed method for estimating direct work is given. First, the data acquisition and the pre-processing steps are explained. After introducing the initial steps, the deep learning model and the tuning investigated will be explained. Finally, the model performance will be assessed through accuracy, precision, and F1-scores.

3.1 Raw Kinematic Data and Pre-processing

The raw kinematic data is collected from five IMUs placed on the worker, as shown in Figure 1. The data is collected at 60 Hz, and six features are used for each IMU. The features are acceleration on three axes and angular velocity around three axes. 60 Hz is used for the data collection, as this is the standard output of the sensor. If the system was to be used for real-time prediction, the optimal frequency should be investigated, as this is believed to become a tradeoff between accuracy and computational efficiency. Other publications have used similar sampling frequencies (Sherafat et al., 2020)

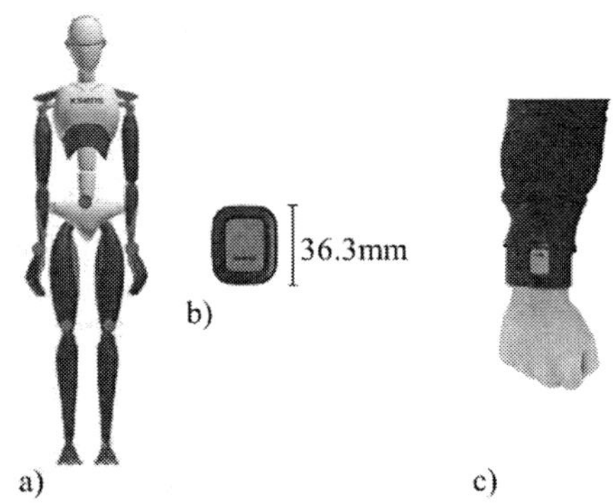

Figure 1: (a) Sensor position marked in red, (b) The sensor used for data collection, (c) Implementation on worker body

After data collection, each participants' data are combined into an array containing all features (30 in total). A fixed length sliding time window is used with 50% overlap as the input. Several window lengths have been investigated to assess how this affects performance. These configurations are window lengths of 3, 5, and 7 seconds. Each window is labelled based on video footage used as ground truth. The windows are labelled based on the amount of data that belongs to each class in the window, with the most frequent class being the overall label of the given window.

Data augmentation was implemented to increase the amount of data available for training the model. This method has been proven successful in many domains, such as activity recognition of construction machinery (Rashid and Louis, 2019). Two augmentations have been implemented: Jittering and scaling. Both of which have been done four times, with different distributions. An example of a 3 second window is shown in Figure 2.

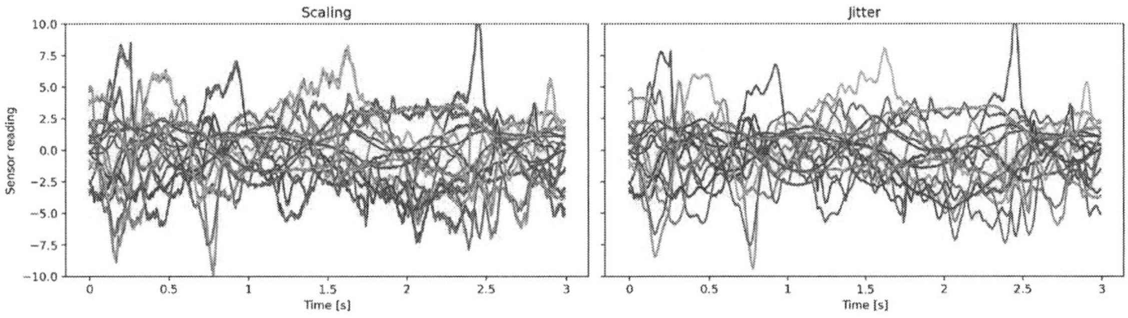

Figure 2: Data augmentation of a 3 second window. Each color represents a channel from the dataset (either acceleration or angular velocity).

3.2 Time Series Classification Model

The core of this method is a deep learning algorithm utilizing stacked convolutional layers to extract features and LSTM layers to find temporal relations in the feature maps created by the stacked convolutional layers. The convolutional layers use a 1D kernel to compute a temporal convolution of the data given by each sensor input. This kernel can be seen as a filter running over the input, filtering the data to find features. In stacked convolutional networks, the deeper layers will represent the features in more abstract ways, which have significantly impacted language processing (Krizhevsky et al., 2012) and computer vision (Jacobsen and Teizer, 2022). The method of combining convolutional layers with LSTM also has shown robust performance on human activity recognition before (Ordóñez and Roggen, 2016). The model used in this research consists of convolutional layers, each with 32 filters, whereafter the data is then reshaped into a 2D array fed into LSTM layers connected to dropout layers. Finally, the architecture uses a flatten layer followed by a dense layer before the output layer.

4. Model Evaluation and Case Study

The model evaluation is done on data of simulating painting of flat walls indoors in a research environment and could in the future act as pre-training for datasets collected in more realistic work environments. This gathered data is split into training and test data, where the training data was augmented, ultimately giving the model 8 times more data for training. Therefore, this model will allow for testing the robustness of the system before deploying it on a real work task settings on a construction site.

4.1 Data Collection

The dataset was collected in a laboratory environment, in which four sessions were completed and then combined into the final dataset. Data was in total collected for 90 minutes with the five sensors and a frequency of 60 Hz. This corresponds to 324.360 lines of data, each having 30 features. No additional features were calculated, meaning that only the features given directly from the IMU were used. The labelling was done using three classes, presented below:

1. Direct Work

   Direct work is work that physically adds value to the finished product. This creates the output previously discussed as one of the components of productivity. Examples of direct work would be painting walls, laying tiles or bricks, assembling interior elements, and installing drywall sheets.

2. Indirect Work

   Indirect work is work that is necessary but does not directly contribute to the finished product. This could be activities such as getting materials and cleaning up the workstation from the predecessor's mess.

3. Waste

   Waste is work that is not necessary because it does not contribute to the finished product. This could include waiting, toilet visits, errands away from the construction site, walking to and from break, or walking between workstations without any tools.

The challenge with this classification is that these categories are not as tangible as the classification done in earlier activity recognition work, such as classifying whether a worker is hammering, walking, or lifting something.

The task was to paint walls around a predefined location, where a camera was set up to record the task. Breaks were done when it was seen as fitting. The breaks were labelled as waste and were spent on various tasks, such as walking around, getting a cup of coffee, or sitting and reading through the instructions. The direct work class was used whenever actual painting was happening. The indirect work class was used whenever the painting roller was dipped in the tray. An image from each of the three classes can be seen in Figure 3.

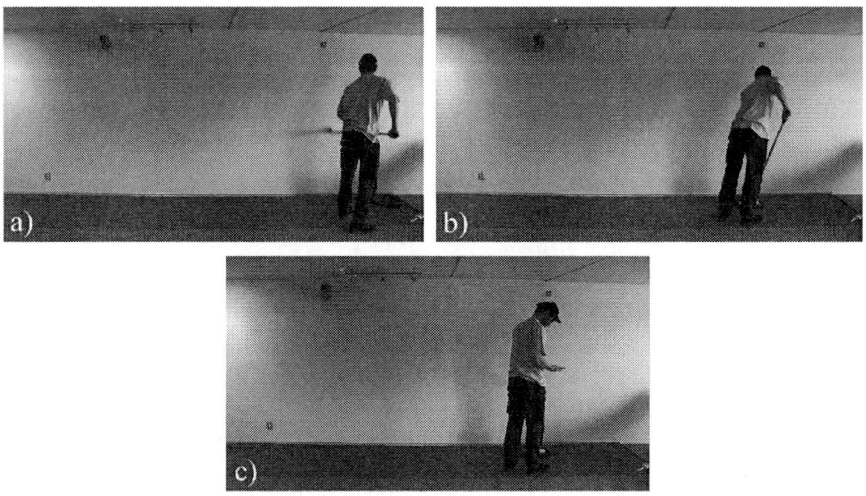

Figure 3: Ground truth recording of (a) Direct Work (painting the wall), (b) Indirect Work (picking up paint), and (c) Waste (answering incoming call).

The class distribution is shown in Table 1, where the number of occurrences for each class is shown.

Table 1: Distribution of training and test data given in windows of 3 seconds.

Class	Windows	Original training	Augmented training	Test data
Waste	1.734	1.273	10.184	461
Indirect work	587	449	3.592	138
Direct work	1.275	889	7.112	386

4.2 Implementation of Model

In the developed models, three different window lengths were used, the 7s model is shown in Figure 4, where also the labelling of the data is depicted.

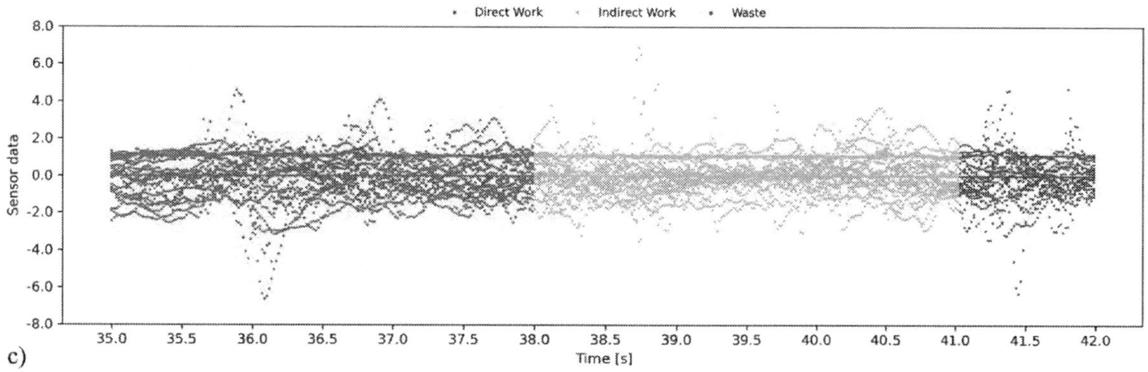

c)

Figure 4: An example showing one of the 7s windows colored based on the label's class: green is direct work, yellow is indirect work, and red is waste

The project was developed on a windows machine using Tensorflow 2.6.0 in a Python 3.9.7 environment. For the three different models, each window consisted of an array of sizes 120 x 30, 300 x 30, or 420 x 30, respectively. The models were all set to train for 50 epochs and used a learning rate of 0.001. Minor hyperparameter tuning was done to the network, specifically the number of filters on the convolutional layers, the number of convolutional layers, the dropout, and the learning rate.

4.2 Evaluation Measures

Four performance measures are used to evaluate the performance of the developed models: accuracy, precision, recall, and F1 score. Accuracy only looks if the instances are classified correctly, whereas precision and recall look into how the misclassifications are distributed. In multiclass classification, a generalization of the measures is needed (Sokolova and Lapalme, 2009) to calculate the precision (Equation 1) and recall (Equation 2). Both measures are essential for a high performing model. However, it is often challenging to maximize both measures at once. Because of this, the F1-score is often used as a combination of the two (Equation 3). In the equations tp_i is true positive for the class C_i, fp_i is false positive, fn_i is false negative, and tn_i is true negative.

$$\frac{\sum_{i=1}^{l} tp_i}{\sum_{i=1}^{l}(tp_i + fp_i)} \tag{1}$$

$$\frac{\sum_{i=1}^{l} tp_i}{\sum_{i=1}^{l}(tp_i + fn_i)} \tag{2}$$

$$\frac{2 \cdot Precision(C_i) \cdot Recall(C_i)}{Precision(C_i) + Recall(C_i)} \tag{3}$$

5. Results

For the best performing model (7s), a model training history is shown in Figure 5. The model training history is depicted for the training and validation set, where the validation dataset is taken as 20% of the training dataset. As the dataset is very simple, only consisting of a worker painting a wall, it is expected that convergence will happen quickly. As seen in Figure 5, this is the case, as the model very quickly reaches high accuracy and minimal loss.

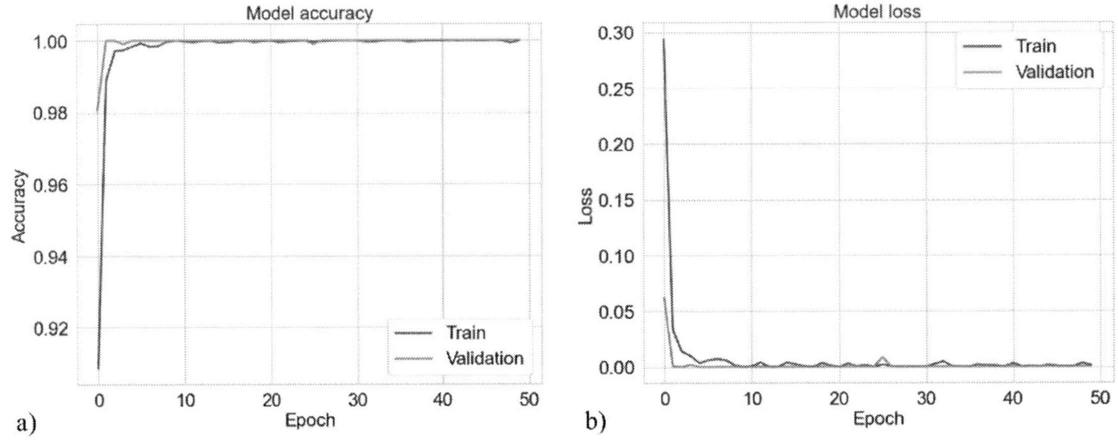

Figure 5: (a) Accuracy and (b) loss for 7s window model.

A confusion matrix is used for each of the three models to depict how well the model classifies and where it is mistaken (Figure 6).

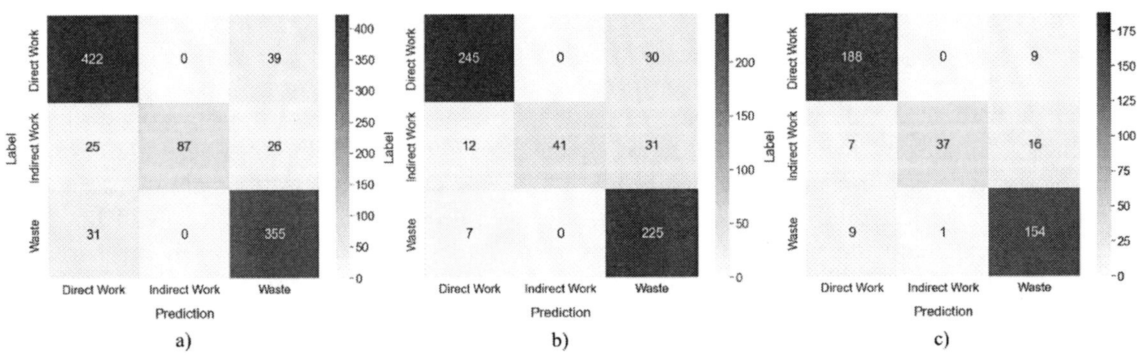

Figure 6: Confusion matrix for (a) 3s, (b) 5s, and (c) 7s windows.

All models perform satisfactorily, with the 7s model being the best among them. The accuracy ranges from 88.5% to 90%, as displayed in Table 2, where all performance measures can be seen. A general confusion from all models is with the class Indirect Work due to the imbalanced dataset. For the 3 second model, only 16.3% of the windows are in the Indirect Work class. This class imbalance could be solved by augmenting the worst represented class more than the others. All models have high precision in the Indirect Work category (100%, 100%, 97.4%, respectively), meaning that when the models predict Indirect Work, it is often or always true. The recall of Indirect Work however, is low (63%, 48.8%, 61.7% respectively). This means that whenever a worker is actually doing direct work, the model will misclassify the action in 37% to 51.2% of the time, depending on the model. All models perform well for Direct Work and Waste, with most windows being predicted to the true label and therefore having high accuracy, recall and precision. A substantial part of the windows misclassified are windows where two or even three classes are present in the same window. An initial step to increase model performance could be to exclude windows where the class distribution is above a threshold.

Table 2: Evaluation measures for deep learning models.

Model	Accuracy	Precision	Recall	F1-Score
3s window	0.885	0.909	0.822	0.863
5s window	0.865	0.905	0.767	0.885
7s window	0.900	0.919	0.837	0.876

The three models evaluated are all successful solutions to classify the productivity measures, all being close to 90% accurate. This is seen as sufficient for estimating worker productivity, as other manual methods such as work sampling use far less frequent data collection for their assessment. If the current models' classification was to be downsampled to giving one classification each minute, it is expected that this model would produce a more accurate picture of the construction site than the manual methods can.

6. Future Steps

As more trades become part of the project, it is expected that the model's performance will decrease. To combat this, hyperparameter tuning on all the individual models will be done, and new deep learning methods will be investigated. Methods such as Graph Convolutional Networks and attention-based models have seen successful implementations for timeseries problems (Zerveas et al., 2021; Heidari and Iosifidis, 2021) and could lead to robust performances for models classifying multiple trades.

The model's output is seen as a valuable input for decision-makers, and therefore, it is necessary to investigate the possibility of near real-time outputs. Having real-time outputs would make the model more valuable for the industry, as decisions could be made based on the current output of the model. Furthermore, the number of classes could be extended to distinguish between the activities, as the literature has several subgenres to the classes used in this paper. To enable real-time outputs, feature importance should be investigated, to examine what features are important and which could be left out. This would not only lead more efficient computations, but could make the setup less invasive on the worker.

In the results section, the misclassification was discussed to primarily happen in windows where two or three classes are present. Implementing a dynamic window would make this situation impossible and make the model more robust.

7. Conclusion

Estimating productivity automatically provides a more robust solution than current methods such as work sampling. CLP is a important metric for understanding a construction project. To be able to estimate the metric automatically using simple kinematics sensors allows for greater insights and allows for detailed analyses, which potentially could lead to a higher CLP. This paper provides a trained classification model based on deep learning methods, utilizing kinematics data from IMUs. The paper evaluates the effect of window sizes on the models to evaluate this hyperparameter to increase performance. Currently, the method has only been trained and tested on one task but shows good performance. Further analysis will determine how well the model generalizes to other tasks and trades.

The hyperparameter tuning of this research was minimal, and future research should focus on finding optimal parameters to enable the models to generalize. As the data is collected in a controlled environment, data collection on a construction site is planned for future evaluation of the method. Creating a high-quality kinematics dataset of human activities on construction sites is an important step for the field, as this is currently unavailable. This would also enable an evaluation of the robustness of the algorithms, enabling validation of their output in a real construction setting. The data used in this paper would be utilized for pre-training on models that should be deployed on a real construction site, which has been shown to increase the performance of models in the past (Zerveas et al., 2021).

To better understand how the model functions, it would be beneficial to use local interpretation methods to get local explanations for the classifications done by the model. This could potentially lead to pruning down the model and exclude sensors. The pruning would make for a more efficient model, as fewer computations would be needed. If the model is to be used in a real-time environment, this is seen as an essential step. The exclusion of sensors would also be beneficial, as this would mean less intrusion on the worker and make the setup less invasive.

References

Akhavian, R., Behzadan, A. H. (2012). Remote Monitoring of Dynamic Construction Processes Using Automated Equipment Tracking, *Construction Research Congress 2012,* 10.1061/9780784412329.137.

Araujo, L. O. C., Neto, N. R., Caldas, C. (2020). Analyzing the Correlation between Productivity Metrics, *Construction Research Congress 2020*, 10.1061/9780784482889.077.

Chapman, R. E., Butry, D. T., Huang, A. L. (2010). Measuring and improving U.S. construction productivity, *Proceedings of the 2010 CIB World Congress.*

Cheng, C. F., Rashidi, A., Davenport, M. A., Anderson, D. V. (2017). Acoustical Modeling of Construction Jobsites: Hardware and Software Requirements, *Computing in Civil Engineering*, 10.1061/9780784480847.044.

Cheng, T., Teizer, J., Migliaccio, G. C., Gatti, U. C. (2013). Automated task-level activity analysis through fusion of real time location sensors and worker's thoracic posture data, *Automation in Construction*, 10.1016/j.autcon.2012.08.003.

Gouett, M. C., Haas, C. T., Goodrum, P. M., Caldas, C. H. (2011). Activity Analysis for Direct-Work Rate Improvement in Construction, *Journal of Construction Engineering and Management*, 10.1061/(ASCE)CO.1943-7862.0000375.

Heidari, N., Iosifidis, A. (2021). Temporal Attention-Agumented Graph Convolutional Network for Efficeient Skeleton-Based Human Action Recognition, *Proceedings of ICPR 2020 - 25th International Conference on Pattern Recognition (ICPR),* 10.1109/ICPR48806.2021.9412091

Jacobsen, E. L., Teizer, J. (2022). Deep learning in construction: Review of applications and potential avenues, *Journal of Computing in Civil Engineering*, 10.1061/(ASCE)CP.1943-5487.0001010.

Jacobsen, E. L., Solberg, A., Golovina, O., Teizer, J. (2021). Active personalized construction safety training using run-time data collection in physical and virtual reality work environments, *Construction Innovation*, 10.1108/CI-06-2021-0113.

Joshua, L., Varghese, K. (2011). Accelerometer-Based Activity Recognition in Construction, *Journal of Computing in Civil Engineering*, 10.1061/(ASCE)CP.1943-5487.0000097.

Khosrowpour, A., Niebles, J. C., Golparvar-Fard, M. (2014). Vision-based workface assessment using depth images for activity analysis of interior construction operations, *Automation in Construction*, 10.1016/j.autcon.2014.08.003.

Liu, K., Golparvar-Fard, M. (2015). Crowdsourcing construction activity analysis from jobsite video streams, *Journal of Construction Engineering and Management*, 10.1061/(ASCE)CO.19437862.0001010.

Michel, P., Levy, O., Neubig, G. (2019). Are sixteen heads really better than one?, *33rd Conference on Neural Information Processing Systems (NeurIPS 2019),* arXiv:1905.10650.

Neve, H. H., Wandahl, S., Lindhard, S., Teizer, J., Lerche, J. (2020). Determining the Relationship between Direct Work and Construction Labor Productivity in North America: Four Decades of Insights, *Journal of Construction Engineering and Management*, 10.1061/(ASCE)CO.1943-7862.0001887.

Ordóñez, F. J., Roggen, D. (2016). Deep Convolutional and LSTM Recurrent Neural Networks for Multimodal Wearable Activity Recognition, *Sensors*, 10.3390/s16010115.

Rashid, K. M., Louis, J. (2019). Times-series data augmentation and deep learning for construction equipment activity recognition, *Advanced Engineering Informatics*, 10.1016/j.aei.2019.100944.

Rashid, K. M., Louis, J. (2020). Activity identification in modular construction using audio signals and machine learning, *Automation in Construction*, 10.1016/j.autcon.2020.103361.

Ryu, J., Seo, J., Lee, S. (2019). Automated Action Recognition Using an Accelerometer-Embedded Wristband-Type Activity Tracker, *Journal of Construction Engineering and Management*, 10.1061/(ASCE)CO.1943-7862.0001579.

Sainath, T. N., Kingsbury, B., Saon, G., Soltau, H., Mohamed, A. R., Dahl, G., Ramabhadran, B. (2015) Deep convolutional neural networks for large-scale speech tasks, *Neural Networks*, 10.1016/j.neunet.2014.08.005.

Sherafat, B., Ahn, C. R., Akhavian, R., Behzadan, A. H., Golparvar-Fard, M., et al. (2020). Automated Methods for Activity Recognition of Construction Workers and Equipment: State-of-the-Art Review, *Journal of Construction Engineering and Management*, 10.1061/(ASCE)CO.1943-7862.0001843.

Sokolova, M, Lapalme, G. (2009). A systematic analysis of performance measures for classification tasks, *Informaiton Processing and Management*, 10.1016/j.ipm.2009.03.002.

Vaswani, A., Shazeer, N., Parmar, N., Uszkoreit, J., Jones, L., et al. (2017). Attention is all you need, *31st Conference on Neural Information Processing Systems (NIPS 2017), Long Beach, CA, USA*, ArXiv:1706.03762.

Wandahl, S., Pérez, C. T., Salling, S., Neve, H. H., Lerche, J., Petersen, S. (2021). The Impact of Construction Labour Productivity on the Renovation Wave, *Construction Economics and Building*, 10.5130/AJCEB.v21i3.7688.

Yang, J, Shi, Z., Wu, Z. (2016). Vision-based action recognition of construction workers using dense trajectories, *Advanced Engineering Informatics*, 10.1016/j.aei.2016.04.009.

Yang, S., Cao, J., Wang, J. (2015). Acoustics recognition of construction equipments based on LPCC features and SVM, *34th Chinese Control Conference*, 10.1109/ChiCC.2015.7260254.

Yang, Z., Yuan, Y., Zhang, M., Zhao, X. (2019). Assessment of Construction Workers' Labor Intensity Based on Wearable Smartphone System, *Journal of Construction Engineering and Management*, 10.1061/(ASCE)CO.1943-7862.0001666.

Zerveas, G., Jayaraman, S., Patel, D., Bhamidipaty, A., Eickhoff, C. (2021). A Transformer-Based Framework for Multivariate Time Series Representation Learning, *27th ACM SIGKDD Conference on Knowledge Discovery and Data Mining (KDD '21)*, 10.1145/3447548.3467401.

Trajectory Prediction: A Review of Methods and Challenges in Construction Safety

Chronopoulos C.[1], Teizer J.[2], Esterle L.[3]
[1]Department of Civil and Architectural Engineering, Aarhus University, Denmark
[2]Department of Civil and Mechanical Engineering, Technical University of Denmark, Denmark
[3]Department of Electrical and Computer Engineering, Aarhus University, Denmark
chrichr@cae.au.dk

Abstract. This review focuses on methods for trajectory prediction of moving entities (i.e., pedestrian workers and heavy construction equipment) in construction. To the authors' knowledge it is the first review on trajectory prediction devoted to construction safety. Through a bibliometric analysis of the relevant literature, it examines the input data and prediction models used for trajectory prediction in dynamic and complex construction environments. Several techniques are available to perform prediction and their performance varies widely. Various types of data is being used, however, so far vision-based data is the major input to the models. Hence, computer-vision techniques are deployed for object tracking to infer the locations of the construction resources in almost entirely outdoor environments. This review concludes with an overview of the gaps, challenges, and future research steps for trajectory prediction relevant for researchers as well as practitioners working on reducing occupational health and safety hazards on construction sites.

1. Introduction

Construction sites are highly dynamic and constantly evolving environments. Due to the irregular environment, workers are prone to accidents mainly attributed to four key hazards, namely falls from height, struck-by heavy objects, caught-in or –between, and electrocutions. Furthermore, many construction accidents involve pedestrian workers in the proximity of static or dynamic hazards, such as unprotected leading edges, moving heavy construction equipment, or lifted crane loads. In 2019, nearly two-thirds of all construction fatal accidents in the U.S. were caused by those types of hazards also known as the 'Construction Focus Four' (CPWR, 2021). This is a reason why construction in the US remains at the top of the list of fatal accidents as it observes a 25%-share of all fatalities for the year 2019 (U.S. Bureau of Labor Statistics, 2020).

Trajectory prediction literature in the field of construction contributes mainly towards two directions. First, is the development of proactive real-time safety systems based on proximity monitoring for accident prevention. Those systems aim to provide relevant stakeholders (e.g., workers, equipment operators, safety managers) information for identifying static or dynamic hazard zones and performing safety decision-making, as well as enough response time for preventing imminent potentially hazardous events. Second, is the transition of construction to automation and autonomy where trajectory prediction is critical for safety planning and collision avoidance in human-robot collaboration.

Proximity monitoring and detection in construction sites have been a major research area, and various location tracking methods have been adopted for acquiring spatio-temporal data of onsite moving workers and equipment. For instance, radio frequency identification (RFID) technology has been adopted in proximity warning systems (Schiffbauer, 2001; Teizer et al., 2010), as well as ultra wideband (UWB) (Cheng et al., 2011; Teizer and Cheng, 2015), Bluetooth low-energy (BLE) (Lin et al., 2015; Teizer et al., 2017), Global Navigation Satellite Systems (GNSS) (Li et al., 2013; Zhang et al., 2015) and Long Range Wide Area Networks

https://doi.org/10.7146/aul.455.c233

(LoRA) (Teizer et al., 2020) for indoor and outdoor localization accordingly. More recently, vision-based systems that take advantage of modern computer vision techniques have been developed to identify the location of objects in construction site environments (Nahangi et al., 2018; Kim et al., 2020). Those studies investigated and validated the applicability of such location tracking technologies in various construction site environments and demonstrated high accuracy. However, the uncertainties in the dynamic construction environment affect the accuracy of proximity warning systems and alert frequency, reducing users' trust and potentially limiting their situational awareness (Ruff, 2006).

Regardless of when the construction sector will eventually achieve the envisioned level of autonomy, both directions are significant to ensure and reinforce the safety of workers in the dynamic and complex construction environment. The remainder of this paper is structured as follows, (a) an introduction to the methodology of the literature review, (b) quantitative results on the applications of trajectory prediction in construction as well as what input data and prediction models are used, and (c) discussion of the challenges and future directions. The main contributions of this paper are (i) identification of applications and methods for trajectory prediction used in construction, (ii) limitations and challenges of the existing studies, and (iii) future research steps in trajectory prediction for safety in construction.

2. Method

The literature review and the bibliometric analysis are based on the Scopus and Web of Science (WoS) scientific databases because of the extensive coverage of literature, the ability to export the search results as comma separated values (CSV) file for further analysis, and the support of Boolean (i.e., "AND", "OR") and proximity operators (i.e., "W/", "NEAR/") in search strings for advanced queries. The selected scientific databases have been successfully used in previous state-of-the-art review papers (Jacobsen and Teizer, 2022; Kim et al., 2019). The yielded search results have been exported in CSV file format and used for further analysis. The export contains the citation information (e.g., authors, title, and year) and, abstract and keywords.

The literature search is performed as a keyword search query by using keywords and, Boolean and proximity operators to limit the yielded results to the intended focus area. The search string consists of two parts. The first part contains the keywords "trajector*", "move*", "path" and "motion" followed by "predict*" and "forecast*" combined with the proximity operator "W/2" (or "NEAR/2 in WoS)", that is for combinations of sets of keywords within two words space. The "or" operator is used to include all keyword sets variations. The asterisk wildcard is used to indicate a character that may or may not be present in the term. The second part is focused on yielding results that are relevant to the construction sector and therefore, it includes the keyword "construction" followed by keywords such as, "worker", "site", "safety", "project" and "environment". The results are limited to publications written in English.

3. Data

The publications that were yielded from the search were first filtered by eliminating the duplicate records in the two databases. Subsequently, the results were screened to only include relevant publications. The screening was done by searching in the titles and abstracts for topics and research fields that are not in the scope of the review. These topics include for instance soil mechanics and geotechnical engineering, offshore engineering, cost estimation, and labour ergonomics, and therefore, the corresponding papers were excluded from the publications database. This resulted in a total of 49 papers that were further assessed for eligibility.

The overall review process can be described by the following stages, (i) identification of the records from the selected digital databases and duplicate elimination, (ii) screening of the initial results, (iii) eligibility assessment of the publications, and (iv) inclusion of the relevant studies (as shown in Figure 1). The analysis of the current state-of-the-art for the trajectory prediction in construction aims to shed light on two main questions: What models or methods have been used for trajectory prediction in construction in previous studies, and what type of input data are utilized? For this, the abstracts and full text of the selected publications were reviewed.

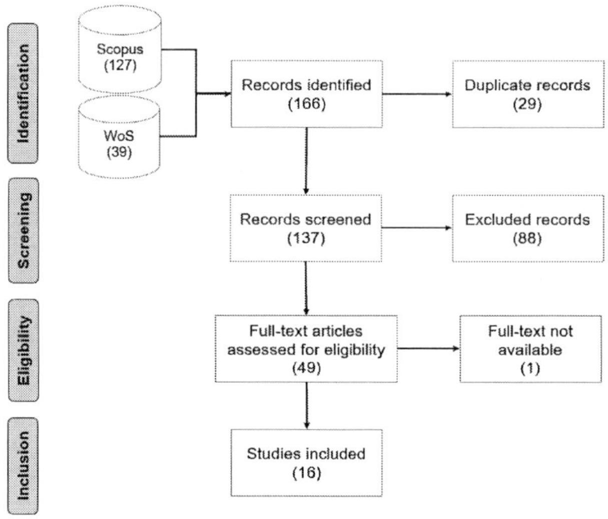

Figure 1: Stages and flow of the review process (number of publications in parentheses).

3.1 Input Data

Each publication on the topic of trajectory prediction in construction has been categorized based on the type of input data that are used by the corresponding predictive method to perform the prediction task. Regardless of the technology used, trajectory prediction requires either acquiring raw location tracking data (i.e., x, y, z coordinates over time) or inferring the location of the tracked entities indirectly, for instance, through the analysis of video-recorded footage and the application of object tracking techniques.

Therefore, the input data could be grouped into three main categories, (i) vision-based data, (ii) raw location tracking data, and (iii) point clouds. In the analysed publications, the most frequently used type of input is vision data, namely camera footage from construction sites. The cameras used in the corresponding studies are mostly stationary and less frequently embedded in moving vehicles, such as unmanned aerial vehicles (UAVs). Another type of input data used is location tracking data from GNSS devices. Lastly, 3-dimensional point cloud data from Light Detection and Ranging (LiDAR) sensors which are combined with kinematic data from inertial motion units, stroke sensors, and rotational encoders that measure force, angular rate and displacement of objects. Figure 2 shows the number of publications per type of input data.

3.2 Model

To understand how the trajectory prediction of moving workers and equipment is performed in the construction safety literature, the adopted models and methods for trajectory prediction have been investigated in the publications dataset. Deep neural networks (DNN) are commonly used for trajectory prediction. A sub-genre of DNN is recurrent neural networks (RNN) in which long short-term memory (LSTM) models are the most common for trajectory prediction problems. In other publications, Kalman filtering (KF) and hidden Markov models (HMM) are used for the prediction of workers and equipment motions. An illustration of the distribution of adopted methods in the identified publications is presented in Figure 3.

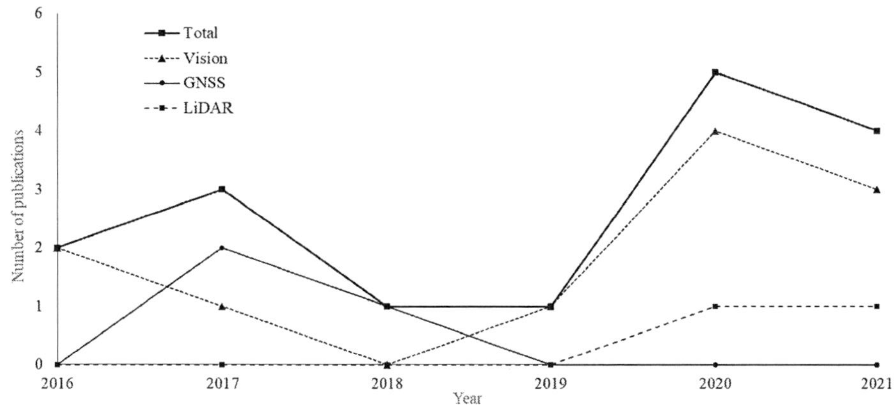

Figure 2: Publications per year and type of input data used for trajectory prediction.

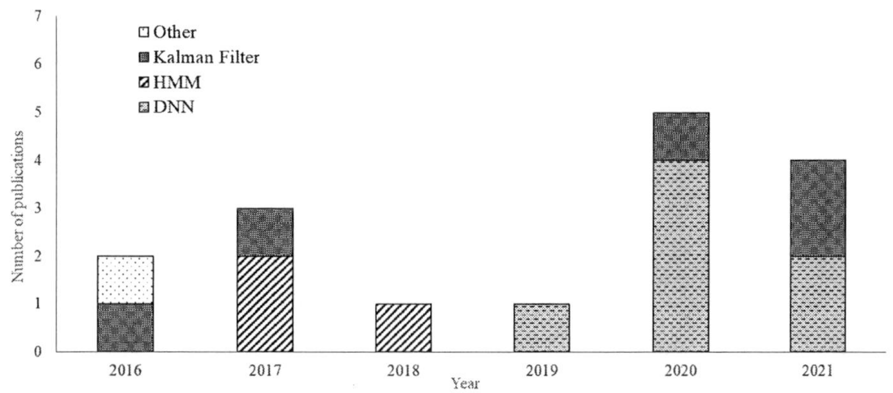

Figure 3: Publications per year and method used for trajectory prediction.

4. Results

Trajectory prediction is a critical topic in other relevant research fields, motivated and enhanced by the rapid technological advancements of the computational power as well as of the availability and cost-effectiveness of computational, sensory and data acquisition technologies.

4.1 Trajectory Prediction in Construction

Trajectory prediction in construction refers to the short-term prediction of the path followed by a moving object within 1 to 10 seconds ahead and focuses on two main directions. First, the development of proactive real-time safety systems based on proximity monitoring for accident prevention (Golovina et al., 2019), and second, the transition of construction to automation and autonomy where trajectory prediction is critical for safety planning and collision avoidance in human-robot collaboration. Although the future of automation and robotics in construction is promising (Garcia de Soto and Skibniewski, 2020), the majority of the identified publications focus on proximity monitoring for accident prevention rather than on construction automation.

Three categories of input data were found to be used for trajectory prediction in construction literature: vision-based data, raw location tracking data, and 3-dimensional point cloud data from LiDAR sensors. Similar to Jacobsen and Teizer (2022) the average time of publication (ATP) is used as a bibliographic metric. Table 1 shows the ATP for the different types of input data, prediction methods and applications in the construction literature. The most common input type, namely the vision-based data have an ATP of 2019.2, whereas the LiDAR data have the highest ATP with very limited publications. DNN models are the most commonly used and have the highest ATP contrary to the other predictive models that have also developed in the previous decades. This is arguably showing a trend in the application of DNN for trajectory prediction in construction. The three types of input data and models adopted for trajectory prediction in the identified construction literature are depicted in Table 2 and further discussed in the following sub-sections.

Table 1: Average time of publication (ATP) and number of papers for different types of input data and model adopted for trajectory prediction in construction.

Input data	ATP	Publications	Method	ATP	Publications
Vision	2019.2	11	DNN	2020.1	7
GNSS	2017.3	3	Kalman Filter	2019.0	5
LiDAR	2020.5	2	HMM	2017.3	3
			Other	2016.6	1

Table 2: Model adopted for different types of input data for trajectory prediction in construction.

Input data	DNN	Kalman Filter	HMM	Other	References
Vision				x	Rezazadeh Azar, (2016)
	x (ConvLSTM)				Bang et al., (2021)
	x (Seq2Seq LSTM)				Cai et al., (2020)
		x			Deng et al., (2021)
	x (Seq2Seq LSTM)				Hu et al., (2020)
	x (Social LSTM+GAN)				Kim et al., (2019)
	x (Social LSTM+GAN)				Kim et al., (2020)
	x (Social LSTM)				Kong et al., (2021)
		x (UKF)			Papaioannou et al., (2017)
	x (LSTM+MDN)				Tang et al., (2020)
		x			Zhu et al., (2016)
GNSS			x		Rashid and Behzadan, (2017)
			x		Rashid et al., (2017)
			x		Rashid and Behzadan, (2018)
LiDAR		x (EKF)			Rasul et al., (2020)
		x (UKF)			Rasul et al., (2021)

Vision-based Data

Video recorded footage is used for predicting the movement of workers and equipment in construction sites through vision-based object recognition. The tracked objects (i.e., workers and equipment) are identified in the frames using computer vision and the motion vector is then calculated. Short-term prediction is commonly performed based on NN models and KF, whereas HMM are less frequently applied. Zhu et al. (2016) proposed a framework for computer vision-based estimation of position and short-term prediction of workers and mobile equipment. The researchers assumed functionality with clear and of acceptable quality videos with limited occlusions, which makes the framework susceptible to input of inferior quality. To solve the tracking limitations in construction environments, Rezazaddeh Azar (2016) developed a vision-based equipment tracking algorithm for automated camera control with predictive capability by estimating the motion vector and speed of the tracked object.

To increase the accuracy of the predictive models semantic and contextual information is used combining input from other sensory technologies. Papaioannou et al. (2017) introduced a system that uses footage from CCTV camera infrastructure and data from the inertial sensors embedded on modern smartphones and applied the Social Force Model (SFM) to consider obstacles and other people in the scene, assuming that they affect the behaviour of human motion, and represent their effect as repulsive forces. Cai et al. (2020) designed an LSTM model to predict worker trajectories in construction environments, considering additional contextual information, namely the distance to the nearest neighbour, the relationship between that neighbour and the tracked worker, and the distance to destination. An LSTM network combined with mixture density network (MDN) for construction workers and equipment path prediction towards right time intervention of collision and intrusion was constructed by Tang et al. (2020). The model considers two contextual cues, namely the distance between moving and static objects and the type of objects (i.e., worker and vehicle) to predict up to 2 seconds in the future. Although the model outperforms other existing models, it is still limited by the dynamic visual occlusions due to other moving construction resources. Semantic information in the form of predefined hazard zones is also considered in the literature. Deng et al. (2021) used KF to predict the movement of workers in construction sites and the estimated trajectory is checked against a set of artificial danger zone boundaries to determine whether the prediction point lies inside or outside of the zones. Considering the occlusion limitations, the researchers performed multi-angle detection which however, is limited by the camera resolution, especially when the workers are far from the camera position. Kong et al. (2021) proposed a framework for workers' trajectory prediction in construction sites based on the Social LSTM architecture. The framework takes into consideration the workers' unsafe behaviour, defined as any movement towards predefined hazardous areas, and corrects the predicted trajectories using KF. One important shortcoming of that study is related to the validation of the pre-trained model, performed on their own dataset with limited scenarios, preventing it from being generalizable.

Only two of the identified publications focused on the future construction, where human workers and robots co-exist and collaborate. Kim et al. (2019) proposed a framework based on social generative adversarial network (S-GAN) for trajectory prediction to tackle contact-driven hazards in construction between workers and autonomous trucks. Their results showed that longer observation periods do not necessarily lead to higher prediction accuracy, due to inclusion in the prediction of less relevant time steps. In a later study, they evaluated the model on a controlled testbed, including a worker and a truck following three predefined movement patterns (Kim et al., 2020). Hu et al. (2020) expanded the application of the LSTM model developed by Cai et al. (2020), by implementing the A* path planning algorithm for autonomous robots in construction sites. However, the study validates the worker trajectory and path planning algorithms separately assuming flat ground surface.

Location Tracking Data

GNSS are satellite-based navigation technologies that depend on the satellites orbiting around the earth. Existing studies have deployed low-cost GNSS technology for tracking construction resources to enhance construction safety, planning and management (Pradhananga and Teizer, 2013; Zhang et al., 2015). GNSS data have also been used as input to trajectory prediction models in construction applications. Rashid and Behzadan (2017) developed a smartphone-based application for trajectory prediction of workers to prevent contact-driven accidents in construction sites. The underlying model is based on HMM. A risk factor is introduced and ranges between 0 and 1 depending on the angle between the trajectory and the centre of one stationary and user-defined hazard zone (Rashid et al., 2017). The model was further developed to consider one static or dynamic hazard (i.e., moving between two points) and validated it by comparing to a benchmark Polynomial Regression model, showing better prediction accuracy (Rashid and Behzadan, 2018). Both models however, are error-prone in predicting trajectories with sharp turns and are limited to a single pedestrian worker and a predefined hazard. Furthermore, the application considers outdoor construction activities due to the limitations of GNSS technologies in indoor environments. Another shortcoming is related to the large number of detected close-call events (n=369) and potential collisions (n=77) in a 30-minute experiment, which could hinder the users' situational awareness and trust in the warning system and lead to delays.

Point Clouds

Point clouds are sets of data points in space that can represent 3-dimensional objects, where each point has its own set of x, y and z coordinates. In a recent study, a LiDAR sensor was utilized to acquire point cloud data to track the positions of heavy machinery and obstacles in a construction site (Rasul et al., 2020; Rasul et al., 2021). The raw point cloud data were analysed to first detect the heavy machinery (i.e., excavator) and then perform detection and clustering of other objects (i.e., workers and machinery) of a width greater than 0.4m, which is the average chest width of a human being. The Extended Kalman Filter (EKF) was adopted for predicting the position and velocity of the moving objects, whereas the excavator's predicted working area was calculated based on kinematics analysis and data from embedded stroke sensors and a rotational encoder (Rasul et al., 2020). In a later study, they used unscented Kalman filtering (UKF) to predict the non-linear motion dynamics of the moving objects. In both studies two safety indices are defined and used, namely the time to collision (TTC), and the warning index (x) defined as the degree of potential collision risks.

5. Gaps, Challenges and Future Research

This paper reviews the problem of trajectory prediction in dynamic and complex construction environments and discusses the current applications, prediction methods and input data used for the predictive task. The following summarizes the gaps, challenges and directions for future research for trajectory prediction with a specific focus on the construction site applications:

1. Predicting the future trajectories of moving objects while incorporating human behaviour is a highly complex problem and hence it is limited to short-term prediction typically for 1-10 seconds ahead with decreasing performance when the prediction horizon increases. Previous studies improved the models' accuracy by correcting the predicted trajectories with KF, whereas other methods include construction semantic (i.e., static hazard zones) and contextual information (e.g., distance from hazards, risk factor) to achieve better performance. Trajectory prediction of moving construction resources should not neglect

pedestrian workers and their contribution to potentially hazardous events. Future research should focus on both construction heavy equipment and pedestrian workers while integrating additional construction semantic information. For instance, construction semantic information such as dynamic hazard areas, work order and construction site layout information (Chronopoulos et al., 2021) could potentially further improve the prediction performance and thus, increase the impact of the developed architectures in real construction applications.

2. Currently, trajectory prediction in construction aims to support the development of proactive real-time safety systems for accident prevention. Increasing the accuracy of prediction models is a common goal among all identified publications. However, it is important to consider the time dimension in proactive warning systems and the feedback must be shared at the desired level-of-detail at the right-time instead of in real-time (Teizer, 2016). Frequent warnings can limit the situational awareness and trust in the warning system of workers and operators (Ruff, 2006). Novel systems focusing on construction safety though trajectory prediction should ensure not only high prediction accuracy but also right-time warning functionality.
3. The current state-of –the-art of trajectory prediction in construction mostly utilizes vision-based data as input to computer-vision methods for object recognition and tracking. For this, recorded videos from cameras on-board UAVs, stationary commercial cameras, existing CCTV infrastructure and public datasets (Lerner et al., 2007) are used to train or validate the developed models. This introduces three significant issues that need to be considered in future research studies. First, is the comparability of performance metrics between models that are validated on different datasets. Second, is the absence of publicly available datasets for the construction sector to be used as benchmark for validating the developed models. Third, the use of camera-based systems in dynamic and rough construction environments is susceptible to various limitations, such as occlusions (Zhu et al., 2016), camera equipment resolution (Deng et al., 2021) and limited field-of-view (Jacobsen and Teizer, 2021), dust, weather conditions, malicious acts, and vandalisms.
4. The trajectory prediction literature in the context of construction focuses primarily on outdoor applications and thus the proposed methods including the tools, models, training and validation are structured based on that spatial assumption. However, several types of private or public construction projects take place in indoor environments, for instance buildings, underground and tunnelling projects with additional constraints (e.g., limited luminosity, dust, no network, signal or GNSS coverage) that further constrain the applicability and scalability of those methods in the aforementioned projects. Future research efforts should also include indoor or hybrid construction environments in developing and validating trajectory prediction models for construction safety.

6. Conclusion

This review paper is, to the authors' knowledge, the first that presents an overview of the trajectory prediction models for complex and dynamic construction environments. Deep neural networks are commonly used in recent studies to perform prediction compared to other methods. To increase the performance of the models, linear estimation models have been applied and integration of limited contextual and semantic information is performed. Various limitations exist and are related to the applied technologies as well as the dynamic and complex characteristics of the construction environments. The paper discusses those limitations and proposes future research steps in trajectory prediction for safety in construction. For instance, the integration of additional construction semantic information (e.g., dynamic hazard areas, work order and construction site layout information) to further improve the prediction accuracy and the consideration of right-time proactive warning systems not only in outdoor construction environments but also in indoor or hybrid construction projects.

References

Bang, S., Hong, Y. and Kim, H. (2021). Proactive proximity monitoring with instance segmentation and unmanned aerial vehicle-acquired video-frame prediction, *Computer-aided civil and infrastructure engineering*, 36(6), pp. 800–816. doi: https://www.doi.org/10.1111/mice.12672.

Cai, J., Zhang, Y., Yang, L., Cai, H. and Li, S. (2020). A context-augmented deep learning approach for worker trajectory prediction on unstructured and dynamic construction sites, *Advanced engineering informatics*, 46(101173), p. 101173. doi: https://www.doi.org/10.1016/j.aei.2020.101173.

Cheng, T., Venugopal, M., Teizer, J. and Vela, P.A. (2011). Performance evaluation of ultra wideband technology for construction resource location tracking in harsh environments, *Automation in Construction*, 20(8), pp. 1173–1184. doi: https://www.doi.org/10.1016/j.autcon.2011.05.001.

Chronopoulos, C., Johansen, K.W., Teizer, J., Schultz, C. and Esterle, L. (2021). Towards a holistic self-organised safety framework for construction, in *2021 IEEE International Conference on Autonomic Computing and Self-Organizing Systems Companion (ACSOS-C)*. IEEE. doi: https://doi.org/10.1109/ACSOS-C52956.2021.00060.

CPWR - The Center for Construction Research and Training (2021). *Fatal injury trends in the construction industry*. https://www.cpwr.com/wp-content/uploads/DataBulletin-February-2021.pdf.

Deng, H., Ou, Z. and Deng, Y. (2021). Multi-angle fusion-based safety status analysis of construction workers, *International journal of environmental research and public health*, 18(22), p. 11815.

Garcia de Soto, B. and Skibniewski, M.J. (2020). Future of Robotics and Automation in Construction. In Sawhney, A., Riley, M., and Irizarry, J. (eds.) *Construction 4.0: An innovation platform for the built environment*. Routledge, pp. 289–306.

Golovina, O., Perschewski, M., Teizer, J., König, M. (2019). Algorithm for Quantitative Analysis of Close Call Events and Personalized Feedback in Construction Safety, *Automation in Construction*, Elsevier, 99, 206-222, doi: https://doi.org/10.1016/j.autcon.2018.11.014.

Hu, D., Li, S., Cai, J. and Hu, Y. (2020). Toward intelligent workplace: Prediction-enabled proactive planning for human-robot coexistence on unstructured construction sites, in *2020 Winter Simulation Conference (WSC)*. IEEE.

Jacobsen, E.L. and Teizer, J. (2022). Deep learning in construction: Review of applications and potential avenues, *Journal of computing in civil engineering*, 36(2). doi: https://www.doi.org/10.1061/(asce)cp.1943-5487.0001010.

Kim, D., Jebelli, H., Lee, S. and Kamat, V.R. (2020). Enhancing deep neural network-based trajectory prediction: Fine-tuning and inherent movement-driven post-processing, in *Construction Research Congress 2020*. Reston, VA: American Society of Civil Engineers.

Kim, D., Lee, S. and Kamat, V.R. (2020). “Proximity prediction of mobile objects to prevent contact-driven accidents in co-robotic construction, *Journal of computing in civil engineering*, 34(4), p. 04020022. doi: https://www.doi.org/10.1061/(asce)cp.1943-5487.0000899.

Kim, D., Liu, M., Lee, S. and Kamat, V.R. (2019). Trajectory prediction of mobile construction resources toward pro-active struck-by hazard detection, in *Proceedings of the 36th International Symposium on Automation and Robotics in Construction (ISARC)*. International Association for Automation and Robotics in Construction (IAARC).

Kim, M.-K., Wang, Q. and Li, H. (2019). Non-contact sensing based geometric quality assessment of buildings and civil structures: A review, *Automation in Construction*, 100, pp. 163–179.

Kong, T., Fang, W., Love, P.E.D., Luo, H., Xu, S. and Li, H. (2021). Computer vision and long short-term memory: Learning to predict unsafe behaviour in construction, *Advanced engineering informatics*, 50(101400), p. 101400. doi: https://www.doi.org/10.1016/j.aei.2021.101400.

Lerner, A., Chrysanthou, Y. and Lischinski, D. (2007). Crowds by example, *Computer graphics forum: journal of the European Association for Computer Graphics*, 26(3), pp. 655–664. doi: https://www.doi.org/10.1111/j.1467-8659.2007.01089.x.

Li, H., Chan, G. and Skitmore, M. (2013). Integrating real time positioning systems to improve blind lifting and loading crane operations, *Construction management and economics*, 31(6), pp. 596–605.

Lin, X.-Y., Ho, T.-W., Fang, C.-C., Yen, Z.-S., Yang, B.-J. and Lai, F. (2015). A mobile indoor positioning system based on iBeacon technology, *Annual International Conference of the IEEE Engineering in Medicine and Biology Society. IEEE Engineering in Medicine and Biology Society. Annual International Conference*, 2015, pp. 4970–4973. doi: https://www.doi.org/10.1109/EMBC.2015.7319507.

Nahangi, M., Heins, A., McCabe, B. and Schoellig, A. (2018). Automated localization of UAVs in GPS-denied indoor construction environments using fiducial markers, in *Proceedings of the 35th International Symposium on Automation and Robotics in Construction (ISARC)*. International Association for Automation and Robotics in Construction (IAARC). doi: https://www.doi.org/10.22260/isarc2018/0012.

Papaioannou, S., Markham, A. and Trigoni, N. (2017). Tracking people in highly dynamic industrial environments, *IEEE transactions on mobile computing*, 16(8), pp. 2351–2365.

Pradhananga, N. and Teizer, J. (2013). Automatic spatio-temporal analysis of construction site equipment operations using GPS data, *Automation in Construction*, 29, pp. 107–122. doi: https://www.doi.org/10.1016/j.autcon.2012.09.004.

Rashid, K.M. and Behzadan, A.H. (2017). Enhancing motion trajectory prediction for site safety by incorporating attitude toward risk, in *Computing in Civil Engineering 2017*. Reston, VA: American Society of Civil Engineers.

Rashid, K.M. and Behzadan, A.H. (2018). Risk behavior-based trajectory prediction for construction site safety monitoring, *Journal of construction engineering and management*, 144(2), p. 04017106.

Rashid, K.M., Datta, S. and Behzadan, A.H. (2017). Coupling risk attitude and motion data mining in a preemtive construction safety framework, in *2017 Winter Simulation Conference (WSC)*. IEEE.

Rasul, A., Seo, J. and Khajepour, A. (2021). Development of sensing algorithms for object tracking and predictive safety evaluation of autonomous excavators, *Applied sciences (Basel, Switzerland)*, 11(14), p. 6366. doi: https://www.doi.org/10.3390/app11146366.

Rasul, A., Seo, J., Oh, K., Khajepour, A. and Reginald, N. (2020). Predicted safety algorithms for autonomous excavators using a 3D LiDAR sensor, in *2020 IEEE International Systems Conference (SysCon)*. IEEE.

Rezazadeh Azar, E. (2016). Active control of a pan-tilt-zoom camera for vision-based monitoring of equipment in construction and surface mining jobsites, in *Proceedings of the 33rd International Symposium on Automation and Robotics in Construction (ISARC)*. International Association for Automation and Robotics in Construction (IAARC).

Ruff, T. (2006). Evaluation of a radar-based proximity warning system for off-highway dump trucks, *Accident; analysis and prevention*, 38(1), pp. 92–98. doi: https://www.doi.org/10.1016/j.aap.2005.07.006.

Schiffbauer, W.H. (2001). An Active Proximity Warning System for Surface and Underground Mining Applications, in *SME Annual Meeting*.

Tang, S., Golparvar-Fard, M., Naphade, M. and Gopalakrishna, M.M. (2020). Video-based motion trajectory forecasting method for proactive construction safety monitoring systems, *Journal of computing in civil engineering*, 34(6), p. 04020041. doi: https://www.doi.org/10.1061/(asce)cp.1943-5487.0000923.

Teizer, J. (2016). The role of automation in right-time construction safety, in *Proceedings of the 33rd International Symposium on Automation and Robotics in Construction (ISARC)*. International Association for Automation and Robotics in Construction (IAARC).

Teizer, J., Allread, B.S., Fullerton, C.E. and Hinze, J. (2010). Autonomous pro-active real-time construction worker and equipment operator proximity safety alert system, *Automation in Construction*, 19(5), pp. 630–640. doi: https://www.doi.org/10.1016/j.autcon.2010.02.009.

Teizer, J. and Cheng, T. (2015). Proximity hazard indicator for workers-on-foot near miss interactions with construction equipment and geo-referenced hazard areas, *Automation in Construction*, 60, pp. 58–73. doi: https://www.doi.org/10.1016/j.autcon.2015.09.003.

Teizer, J., Neve, H., Li, H., Wandahl, S., König, J., Ochner, B., König, M. and Lerche, J. (2020). Construction resource efficiency improvement by Long Range Wide Area Network tracking and monitoring, *Automation in Construction*, 116 (103245). doi: https://www.doi.org/10.1016/j.autcon.2020.103245.

Teizer, J., Wolf, M., Golovina, O., Perschewski, M., Propach, M., Neges, M. and König, M. (2017). Internet of things (IoT) for integrating environmental and localization data in building information modeling (BIM), in *Proceedings of the 34th International Symposium on Automation and Robotics in Construction (ISARC)*. Tribun EU, s.r.o., Brno.

U.S. Bereau of Labor Statistics (2020). *Number and rate of fatal work injuries, by industry sector*. Available at: https://www.bls.gov/charts/census-of-fatal-occupational-injuries/number-and-rate-of-fatal-work-injuries-by-industry.htm (Accessed: January 10, 2022).

Zhang, S., Teizer, J., Pradhananga, N. and Eastman, C.M. (2015). Workforce location tracking to model, visualize and analyze workspace requirements in building information models for construction safety planning, *Automation in Construction*, 60, pp. 74–86. doi: https://www.doi.org/10.1016/j.autcon.2015.09.009.

Zhu, Z., Park, M.-W., Koch, C., Soltani, M., Hammad, A. and Davari, K. (2016). Predicting movements of onsite workers and mobile equipment for enhancing construction site safety, *Automation in Construction*, 68, pp. 95–101. doi: https://www.doi.org/10.1016/j.autcon.2016.04.009.

A Critical Review on Methods for the Assessment of Trainees' Performance in Virtual Reality-based Construction Safety Training

Harichandran A.[1], Teizer J.[2]
[1]Department of Civil and Architectural Engineering, Aarhus University, Denmark
[2]Department of Civil and Mechanical Engineering, Technical University of Denmark, Denmark
aparnaharichandran@cae.au.dk

Abstract. Virtual Reality (VR) is one of the transformative technologies that aid construction safety training. This study is a systematic review of literature on estimating the performance of the trainees during VR-based construction safety training. The critical analysis of the selected literature identified seven focus areas of research, often overlapping with one or more areas. The focus areas include hazard recognition training, personalised feedback, training method improvement, the effect of VR training, the efficacy of VR training, safety behaviour analysis, and automated safety analysis. Most studies focus on either training with existing scenarios for improving hazard recognition or enhancing the training method with the latest technologies or supplementary devices. The possibilities of automated data collection during VR training need to be further explored for quantitatively estimating the participant performance and analysis of close calls or safety incidents.

1. Introduction

Accident rates in the construction industry have been consistently high for decades (Bureau of Labor Statistics, 2020). Conventional classroom-based safety education and training do not adequately prepare the workforce for complex and dynamic construction sites (Wolf et al., 2022). Transformative technological solutions have been explored for improving workplace safety. Virtual Reality (VR) is one of the leading technologies that provides an immersive and interactive learning experience. A VR environment is created through stationary displays such as desktops or CAVE; head-based displays such as head-mounted displays (HMD) or smartphones; or handheld VR devices (Zhang et al., 2020). Earlier studies on construction safety training deployed stationary displays, whereas head-based displays have been widely used now.

The initial studies that featured VR environments mostly implemented it as a visualisation tool (Perlman *et al.*, 2014). The studies on the later stages compared its effectiveness with the existing training methods (Pham et al., 2018). As VR technology advances, the training methods are improved with additional devices (Kim *et al.*, 2021). There are prospects of improving training through dynamic scenario creation with the aid of digital twins (Harichandran *et al.*, 2021). However, most VR-based safety training methods estimated the participants' performance either qualitatively or through manual quantitative estimation (Han *et al.*, 2021). A few studies have explored the possibilities of inbuilt scripting capabilities of game engine software for automated data collection (Golovina *et al.*, 2019). Nevertheless, the existing studies are yet to achieve real-time performance assessment and feedback. Various aspects of VR application in the built environment have been extensively reviewed (Zhang *et al.*, 2020; Rey-Becerra *et al.*, 2021). According to the authors' knowledge, there are no comprehensive reviews that exclusively focus on estimating the performance of the trainees. The objective of this study is to conduct a systematic review of the literature on performance assessment of trainees during VR-based construction safety training. The scope of the review is limited to documents in the Scopus database published from 2011 to 2022.

https://doi.org/10.7146/aul.455.c234

2. Research Method

This study has adopted a systematic review method where the data is collected through well-defined criteria to include relevant and high-quality publications. Scopus is a literature database that encompasses various disciplines, including Virtual Reality (VR), construction management, and safety science. It also offers extensive options for a systematic search compared to other databases such as Google Scholar and Web of Science (Zhang et al., 2020). Therefore, Scopus is selected as the database for retrieving relevant publications for this study.

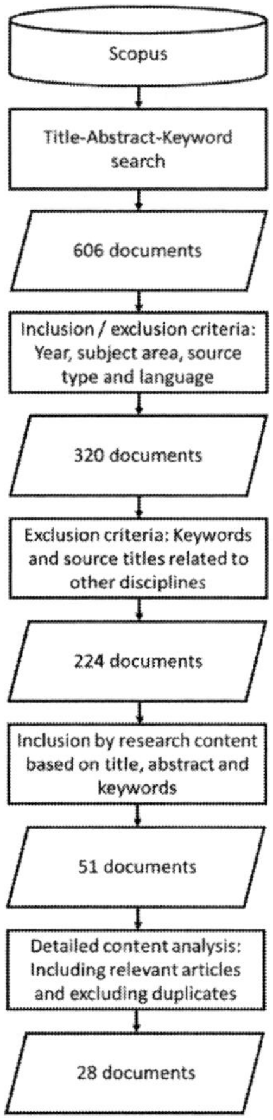

Figure 1: Method for selecting relevant literature.

The method for selecting the literature is illustrated in Figure 1. First, the publications related to VR-based construction safety training that focused on estimating the performance of the trainees were extracted by searching the 'title', 'abstract' and 'keywords of the documents. The code used for the search is: (TITLE-ABS-KEY (("virtual reality") OR ("virtual environment") OR ("serious game")) AND TITLE-ABS-KEY (("construction safety") OR ("safety training") OR ("training environment")) AND TITLE-ABS-KEY (("data collect*") OR ("collect data*") OR ("analy*") OR ("performance") OR ("feedback"))). The Boolean operator 'OR' is applied to look for alternate words or synonyms, while 'AND' is applied to include relevant literature that contains all the critical search elements. The double quotes characters ("") ensure that the words inside are searched together for avoiding irrelevant literature. The asterisk character (*) is suffixed to a term (or some terms) for retrieving results that start with its predecessor. These specifications ensured only literature relevant to the objective of the study was captured in the initial search. The initial search resulted in 606 documents which were then filtered through various inclusion and exclusion criteria. The first stage of filtering applied criteria related to year of publication, subject area, source type and language. Virtual reality and related technology are continuously evolving. Therefore, the latest ten years of research adequately represent the most relevant literature. The publications from 2011 to 2022 were considered for this study since the search was conducted in early April 2022. The subjects selected include Computer Science, Engineering, Social Sciences, Mathematics, Decision Sciences, and Business, Management and Accounting. The source type is limited to journals and conference proceedings. The language of publications is set as English. The search resulted in 320 documents after applying these criteria.

The authors observed that some of the results are medical publications related to drug safety, medical training, or clinical competence. Therefore, exclusion criteria are applied to remove documents that contain keywords related to medical research. The search after applying these criteria retrieved 224 documents related to VR research in construction safety training. The authors then intensively read the title, abstract and keywords; and scanned the outline of these documents to analyse the research content. The selected documents include 51 publications on VR for construction safety training. Finally, detailed content analysis has been performed by rigorously reviewing these publications. The authors paid attention to selecting the studies focusing on assessing the performance of the trainees in the VR environment. The conference publications later elaborated and published in peer-reviewed journals were considered duplicates and removed. The outcome of the final filtering resulted in 28 documents, and a critical analysis of these publications is presented in this study.

3. Analysis, Results and Discussion

3.1 An Overview of The Literature

The content analysis of the database search results narrowed the outcomes to 51 publications on construction safety training based on VR. The authors are interested in a subset of these studies (28 publications) that estimate the performance of the trainees in the VR environment. An overview of these publications based on the sources are provided in Table 1. The most relevant studies are published in journals such as 'Automation in Construction', 'Advanced Engineering Informatics', 'Journal of Construction Engineering and Management', and 'International Journal of Occupational Safety and Ergonomics'. The journals such as 'Accident Analysis and Prevention', 'IEEE Transactions on Visualization and Computer Graphics', and 'Safety Science' also publish equally relevant content. Early ideas, preliminary results of the ongoing research and proof of concepts are presented in conferences such as International Symposium on Automation and Robotics in Construction (ISARC) and Construction Research Congress (CRC). Notably, the proceedings of these conferences are among the top sources that offer the most number of publications. However, journal articles provide 67 – 68 per cent of the relevant literature on VR research in construction.

The number of studies on VR applications in the built environment is rising (Zhang et al., 2020) and the latest search conducted for this study also shows a similar trend for the past ten years. The current study focuses explicitly on VR applications for construction safety training. The trend of research publications from 2011 is illustrated in Figure 2. The drops at the end of the curves are due to the time at which this study is conducted. More publications can be expected towards the end of this year based on the past data. The VR has been actively explored in several construction domains, such as architectural and engineering design, project management, human behavioural studies, and engineering education. The limited number of publications observed in this study is due to the specific focus on construction safety training. Studies on other aspects of construction safety, such as inspection and planning, have been omitted. Therefore, some years (2011, 2015, 2017) may have very little or no publications on VR based safety training.

Table 1: Overview of the VR research publications in various sources.

Source of publication	Number of publications in	
	VR for construction safety training	**Trainee performance assessment**
International Symposium on Automation and Robotics in Construction (ISARC)	9	7
Automation in Construction	7	4
Advanced Engineering Informatics	5	2
Construction Research Congress (CRC)	5	1
Journal of Construction Engineering and Management	4	2
International Journal of Occupational Safety and Ergonomics	3	2
Accident Analysis and Prevention	2	2
IEEE Transactions on Visualization and Computer Graphics	2	2
Safety Science	2	1
Construction Innovation	1	1
Engineering, Construction and Architectural Management	1	1
IEEE International Conference on Architecture, Construction, Environment and Hydraulics (ICACEH)	1	1
International Journal of Engineering Education	1	1
Journal of Engineering Education	1	1
Annual Conference of the International Group for Lean Construction (IGLC)	1	0
Buildings	1	0
Institute of Industrial and Systems Engineers Annual Conference and Expo (IISE)	1	0
Journal of Civil Engineering Education	1	0
Journal of Management in Engineering	1	0
Journal of Safety Research	1	0
Procedia Engineering	1	0
Total number of publications	51	28

The distribution of publications based on the country or region is presented in Figure 3. The USA has the highest number of publications on VR-based construction safety training and studies covering trainee performance assessment. Many publications have emerged from countries such as Germany, China, Denmark, Hong Kong, and India. Most of the collaborative research was conducted within the countries or regions. This may be because VR research is highly dependent on the training facilities and lab space available. However, a few experimental studies show collaborations between countries (Choi *et al.*, 2020; Wolf *et al.*, 2022).

Figure 2: Year-wise research publications on VR based construction safety training and trainee performance assessment.

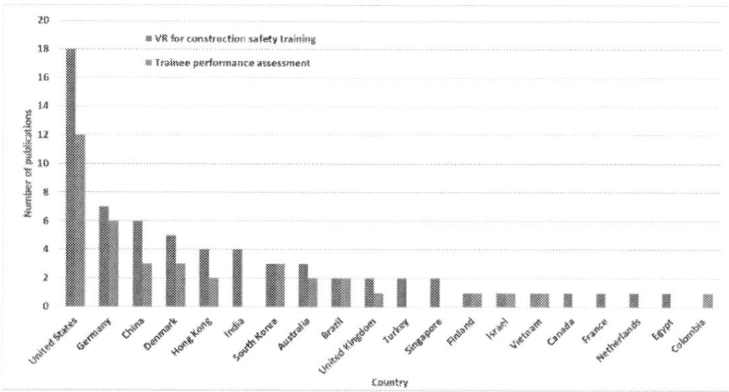

Figure 3: Distribution of VR research publications based on country or region.

3.2 Performance Assessment in Virtual Reality Training

The studies on trainee performance assessment were selected from the VR-based construction safety training publications. A systematic review of the selected research publications was conducted for in-depth analysis of the contents. The results of the content analysis are summarised in Table 2. Seven research focuses were identified: 1) training for hazard recognition (THR), 2) personalised feedback to the trainees for improving the safety performance (PFT), 3) studies that support or improve the VR based safety training (TMI), 4) effect of VR training on trainees (VRT), 5) estimating the efficacy of VR based safety training and/or benchmarking with conventional training methods (EVR), 6) analysing the safety behaviour of the trainees (SBT), 7) automatically analysing the close call events and safety incidents (ASA). The distribution of these research focus areas across the selected studies is presented in Figure 4.

From the initial applications of VR for construction safety training, the studies were focused on training the workers to identify hazards or potential hazards (Gupta and Varghese, 2020). The earlier studies merely visualised hazards and manually recorded the performance in hazard identification (Perlman *et al.*, 2014). Latest training methods involve the automatic player data collection through inbuilt C# scripts and colliders embedded in the VR training environment (Golovina *et al.*, 2019; Moelmen *et al.*, 2021). These data can be further used to provide personalised feedback to the trainees to improve their performance (Wolf et al., 2022). A few studies have focused on personalised feedback in safety training. Similarly, very little focus has been given to the automated analysis of close call events and safety incidents. The interaction between trainees and surrounding objects can be automatically recorded to generate data that will eventually aid in quantitative safety analysis (Golovina *et al.*, 2016).

Table 2: Summary of the content analysis of literature on trainee performance assessment.

Research paper	Focus of the study						
	THR	PFT	TMI	VRT	EVR	SBT	ASA
(Li et al., 2022)	X						
(Lucena and Saffaro, 2022)	X						
(Wolf et al., 2022)	X	X					
(Habibnezhad et al., 2021)			X				
(Han et al., 2021)				X			
(Kim *et al.*, 2021)					X		
(Jacobsen et al., 2021)	X	X					
(Moelmen et al., 2021)				X			
(Choi *et al.*, 2020)						X	
(Jeelani *et al.*, 2020)	X	X					
(Noghabaei and Han, 2020)	X					X	
(Chihming et al., 2020)	X		X				
(Nykänen *et al.*, 2020)					X		
(Hasanzadeh *et al.*, 2020)				X		X	
(Pedro et al., 2020)			X	X			
(Ye and König, 2019)	X		X				
(Shi et al., 2019)						X	
(Habibnezhad et al., 2019)			X	X			
(Wolf *et al.*, 2019)		X	X				
(Golovina et al., 2019)		X					X
(Pham et al., 2018)					X		
(Pinheiro et al., 2016)	X		X				
(Hilfert *et al.*, 2016)	X		X				
(Golovina *et al.*, 2016)							X
(Perlman *et al.*, 2014)	X				X		
(Albert et al., 2014)	X			X	X		
(Teizer *et al.*, 2013)			X				
(Guo et al., 2012)			X				

Several studies explore the potential of existing VR devices and supplementary devices to enhance the learning experience. Eye-tracking technology for estimating the attention of the trainees (Chihming *et al.*, 2020) and trackers for incorporating the gait movements are some examples (Habibnezhad *et al.*, 2019). Some of the studies focus on the effect of VR training on participants in terms of cognitive load, attention span and knowledge retention. Most of these studies analyse these effects based on self-assessment questionnaires or manual observation (Albert *et al.*, 2014; Han *et al.*, 2021). A few of the studies have collected run time participant data for quantitative estimation of the effect of VR training (Moelmen *et al.*, 2021). The efficacy of VR training has been estimated through statistical methods such as generalised linear mixed modelling, bivariate linear regression analysis, and multilevel modelling (Nykänen *et al.*, 2020; Kim *et al.*, 2021). Generally, the studies that focus on training efficacy involved a larger number of participants than the studies focused on hazard identification or training method improvement. Another advantage of VR-based training is exposing the trainees to unsafe situations and assessing their behaviour. Situational awareness, risk-taking behaviour or the effect of interventions can be quantitatively estimated through various measures such as time and frequency of gazing, position and heart rate measurements through external devices (Choi *et al.*, 2020; Hasanzadeh *et al.*, 2020). Even though several research directions have been explored in VR based construction safety training, the possibilities of automated data collection and analysis have not been fully explored yet.

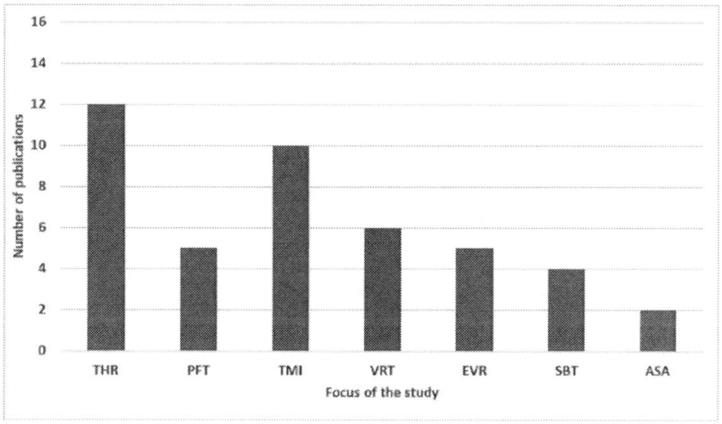

Figure 4: Research focus of studies on trainee performance assessment during VR based construction safety training.

4. Conclusions

Virtual Reality (VR) based safety training provides a more realistic and interactive learning experience than conventional classroom training. The application of VR in construction and built environments has been widely studied and reviewed. However, a study that exclusively focused on estimating the performance of the trainees during VR based construction safety training does not exist according to the authors' knowledge. This study conducts a systematic review of literature relevant to this domain. The content analysis of the Scopus database search resulted in 51 publications on construction safety training based on VR. A subset of these studies consists of 28 publications that estimate the performance of the trainees in the VR environment; they have been selected for in-depth analysis.

The selected studies were distributed into seven focus areas, often overlapping with one or more areas. The focus areas include hazard recognition training, personalised feedback, improving training methods, the effect of VR training, the efficacy of VR training, safety behaviour analysis, and automated safety analysis. Most studies focus on either training with existing scenarios for improving hazard recognition or enhancing the training method with the latest technologies or supplementary devices. The possibilities of automated data collection during VR training need to be further explored for generating a quantitative estimate of the participant performance and analysis of close calls or safety incidents. Creating dynamic training scenarios from the digital twin of the construction site is another future direction for VR based safety training.

References

Albert, A., Hallowell, M. R., Kleiner, B., Chen, A. and Golparvar-Fard, M. (2014) 'Enhancing Construction Hazard Recognition with High-Fidelity Augmented Virtuality', *Journal of Construction Engineering and Management*, 140(7), p. 04014024. doi: 10.1061/(ASCE)CO.1943-7862.0000860.

Bureau of Labor Statistics (2020) *National Census of Fatal Occupational Injuries in 2019*. Available at: www.bls.gov/iif (Accessed: 10 July 2021).

Chihming, W., Zexin, J., Yuxin, L., Songqing, H. and Zhongwei, Y. (2020) 'Investigation on the eye-tracking technology in hazard identification of building construction engineering', in *2nd IEEE International Conference on Architecture, Construction, Environment and Hydraulics (ICACEH 2020)*. Hsinchu, Taiwan, pp. 32–35. doi: 10.1109/ICACEH51803.2020.9366265.

Choi, M., Ahn, S. and Seo, J. O. (2020) 'VR-Based investigation of forklift operator situation awareness for preventing collision accidents', *Accident Analysis & Prevention*, 136, p. 105404. doi: 10.1016/J.AAP.2019.105404.

Golovina, O., Kazanci, C., Teizer, J. and König, M. (2019) 'Using serious games in virtual reality for automated close call and contact collision analysis in construction safety', in *36th International Symposium on Automation and Robotics in Construction (ISARC 2019)*. Banff, Canada, pp. 967–974. doi: 10.22260/isarc2019/0129.

Golovina, O., Teizer, J. and Pradhananga, N. (2016) 'Heat map generation for predictive safety planning: Preventing struck-by and near miss interactions between workers-on-foot and construction equipment', *Automation in Construction*, 71, pp. 99–115. doi: 10.1016/j.autcon.2016.03.008.

Guo, H., Li, H., Chan, G. and Skitmore, M. (2012) 'Using game technologies to improve the safety of construction plant operations', *Accident Analysis and Prevention*, 48, pp. 204–213. doi: 10.1016/J.AAP.2011.06.002.

Gupta, A. and Varghese, K. (2020) 'Scenario-based construction safety training platform using virtual reality', in *Proceedings of the 37th International Symposium on Automation and Robotics in Construction (ISARC 2020)*. Kitakyushu, Japan, pp. 892–899. doi: 10.22260/isarc2020/0123.

Habibnezhad, M., Puckett, J., Fardhosseini, M. S. and Pratama, L. A. (2019) 'A mixed VR and physical framework to evaluate impacts of virtual legs and elevated narrow working space on construction workers' gait pattern', in *Proceedings of the 36th International Symposium on Automation and Robotics in Construction (ISARC 2019)*. Banff, Canada, pp. 1057–1064. doi: 10.22260/ISARC2019/0141.

Habibnezhad, M., Shayesteh, S., Jebelli, H., Puckett, J. and Stentz, T. (2021)' Comparison of ironworker's fall risk assessment systems using an immersive biofeedback simulator', *Automation in Construction*, 122. doi: 10.1016/J.AUTCON.2020.103471.

Han, Y., Diao, Y., Yin, Z., Jin, R., Kangwa, J. and Ebohon, O. J. (2021) 'Immersive technology-driven investigations on influence factors of cognitive load incurred in construction site hazard recognition, analysis and decision making', *Advanced Engineering Informatics*, 48, p. 101298. doi: 10.1016/J.AEI.2021.101298.

Harichandran, A., Johansen, K. W., Jacobsen, E. L. and Teizer, J. (2021) 'A Conceptual Framework for Construction Safety Training using Dynamic Virtual Reality Games and Digital Twins', in *38th International Symposium on Automation and Robotics in Construction (ISARC2021)*. Dubai, UAE, pp. 621–628. doi: https://doi.org/10.22260/ISARC2021/0084.

Hasanzadeh, S., Polys, N. F. and De La Garza, J. M. (2020) 'Presence, Mixed Reality, and Risk-Taking Behavior: A Study in Safety Interventions', *IEEE Transactions on Visualization and Computer Graphics*, 26(5), pp. 2115–2125. doi: 10.1109/TVCG.2020.2973055.

Hilfert, T., Teizer, J. and König, M. (2016) 'First person virtual reality for evaluation and learning of construction site safety', in *33rd International Symposium on Automation and Robotics in Construction (ISARC 2016)*. Auburn, USA, pp. 200–208. doi: 10.22260/ISARC2016/0025.

Jacobsen, E. L., Solberg, A., Golovina, O. and Teizer, J. (2021) 'Active personalized construction safety training using run-time data collection in physical and virtual reality work environments', *Construction Innovation*. doi: 10.1108/CI-06-2021-0113.

Jeelani, I., Han, K. and Albert, A. (2020) 'Development of virtual reality and stereo-panoramic environments for construction safety training', *Engineering, Construction and Architectural Management*, 27(8), pp. 1853–1876. doi: 10.1108/ECAM-07-2019-0391.

Kim, N., Anderson, B. A. and Ahn, C. R. (2021) 'Reducing Risk Habituation to Struck-By Hazards in a Road Construction Environment Using Virtual Reality Behavioral Intervention', *Journal of Construction Engineering and Management*, 147(11), p. 04021157. doi: 10.1061/(ASCE)CO.1943-7862.0002187.

Li, W., Huang, H., Solomon, T., Esmaeili, B. and Yu, L. F. (2022) 'Synthesizing Personalized Construction Safety Training Scenarios for VR Training', *IEEE Transactions on Visualization and Computer Graphics*. doi: 10.1109/TVCG.2022.3150510.

Lucena, A. F. E. and Saffaro, F. A. (2022) 'Guidelines for exploring construction sites in virtual reality environments for hazard identification', *International Journal of Occupational Safety and Ergonomics*, 28(1), pp. 86–95. doi: 10.1080/10803548.2020.1728951.

Moelmen, I., Grim, H. L., Jacobsen, E. L. and Teizer, J. (2021) 'Asymmetrical Multiplayer Serious Game and Vibrotactile Haptic Feedback for Safety in Virtual Reality to Demonstrate Construction Worker Exposure to Overhead Crane Loads', in *38th International Symposium on Automation and Robotics in Construction (ISARC 2021)*. Dubai, UAE, pp. 613–620. doi: https://doi.org/10.22260/ISARC2021/0083.

Noghabaei, M. and Han, K. (2020) 'Hazard Recognition in an Immersive Virtual Environment: Framework for the Simultaneous Analysis of Visual Search and EEG Patterns', in *Construction Research Congress (CRC 2020)*. Tempe, Arizona, pp. 934–943. doi: 10.1061/9780784482865.099.

Nykänen, M., Puro, V., Tiikkaja, M., Kannisto, H., Lantto, E., Simpura, F., Uusitalo, J., Lukander, K., Räsänen, T., Heikkilä, T. and Teperi, A. M. (2020) 'Implementing and evaluating novel safety training methods for construction sector workers: Results of a randomized controlled trial', *Journal of Safety Research*, 75, pp. 205–221. doi: 10.1016/J.JSR.2020.09.015.

Pedro, A., Pham, H. C., Kim, J. U. and Park, C. (2020) 'Development and evaluation of context-based assessment system for visualization-enhanced construction safety education', *International Journal of Occupational Safety and Ergonomics*, 26(4), pp. 811–823. doi: 10.1080/10803548.2018.1553377.

Perlman, A., Sacks, R. and Barak, R. (2014) 'Hazard recognition and risk perception in construction', *Safety Science*, 64, pp. 13–21. doi: 10.1016/J.SSCI.2013.11.019.

Pham, H. C., Dao, N. N., Pedro, A., Le, Q. T., Hussain, R., Cho, S. and Park, C. S. (2018) 'Virtual field trip for mobile construction safety education using 360-degree panoramic virtual reality', *International Journal of Engineering Education*, 34(4), pp. 1174–1191. doi: https://www.ijee.ie/contents/c340418.html.

Pinheiro, R. B. O., Pradhananga, N., Jianu, R. and Orabi, W. (2016) 'Eye-tracking technology for construction safety: A feasibility study', in *33rd International Symposium on Automation and Robotics in Construction (ISARC 2016)*. Auburn, USA, pp. 282–290. doi: 10.22260/ISARC2016/0035.

Rey-Becerra, E., Barrero, L. H., Ellegast, R. and Kluge, A. (2021) 'The effectiveness of virtual safety training in work at heights: A literature review', *Applied Ergonomics*, 94, p. 103419. doi: 10.1016/J.APERGO.2021.103419.

Shi, Y., Du, J., Ahn, C. R. and Ragan, E. (2019) 'Impact assessment of reinforced learning methods on construction workers' fall risk behavior using virtual reality', *Automation in Construction*, 104, pp. 197–214. doi: 10.1016/J.AUTCON.2019.04.015.

Teizer, J., Cheng, T. and Fang, Y. (2013) 'Location tracking and data visualization technology to advance construction ironworkers' education and training in safety and productivity', *Automation in Construction*, 35, pp. 53–68. doi: 10.1016/j.autcon.2013.03.004.

Wolf, M., Teizer, J. and Ruse, J. H. (2019) 'Case study on mobile virtual reality construction training', in *Proceedings of the 36th International Symposium on Automation and Robotics in Construction (ISARC 2019)*. Banff, Canada, pp. 1231–1237. doi: 10.22260/isarc2019/0165.

Wolf, M., Teizer, J., Wolf, B., Bükrü, S. and Solberg, A. (2022) 'Investigating hazard recognition in augmented virtuality for personalized feedback in construction safety education and training', *Advanced Engineering Informatics*, 51, p. 101469. doi: 10.1016/J.AEI.2021.101469.

Ye, X. and König, M. (2019) 'Applying eye tracking in virtual construction environments to improve cognitive data collection and human-computer interaction of site hazard identification', in *Proceedings of the 36th International Symposium on Automation and Robotics in Construction (ISARC 2019)*. Banff, Canada, pp. 1073–1080. doi: 10.22260/ISARC2019/0143.

Zhang, Y., Liu, H., Kang, S. C. and Al-Hussein, M. (2020) 'Virtual reality applications for the built environment: Research trends and opportunities', *Automation in Construction*, 118. doi: 10.1016/J.AUTCON.2020.103311.

Automated Construction Payment Using Blockchain-Enabled Smart Contracts and Building Information Modelling

Matarneh, S.T.[1], Elghaish, F.[2], Rahimian, F.[3], Dawood, N.[3]

[1] Al Ahliyya Amman University, Faculty of Engineering, P.O. Box 19328, Al-Saro, Al-Salt, Amman, Jordan
[2] Queen's University Belfast, School of Natural and Built Environment, University Rd, Belfast BT7 1NN, UK
[3]Teesside University, Centre for Sustainable Engineering, Southfield Rd, Middlesbrough TS1 3BX

Abstract: The potential of blockchain in the construction sector has been recognized in existing literature, as well as its capacity to be integrated into construction projects to automate financial transactions for increased transparency, security, and control. Permissioned blockchain, according to existing research, can be utilized to create a business network among project participants due to its features being compatible with the nature of the construction sector. This article lays out a framework for introducing permissioned blockchain technology, notably Hyperledger fabric, into the construction delivery process. The suggested framework comprises explicit procedures that show how to develop a network during the pre-construction, construction, and closeout stages. The suggested framework also displays the flow of financial transactions across the envisaged financial system. Because of the capabilities of Building Information Modelling/Management (BIM) and cost planning. As a result, the framework determines the data needed to enter the blockchain financial system from 4D/5D BIM. The benefits of employing blockchain in the construction business were emphasized in a systematic literature review, which also selected the best blockchain platform. The framework can also be used by academics and industry practitioners to recognise the architecture of smart contracts (chaincode) in the construction sector, such as formulating endorsement and validation policies. Finally, the findings of this article will be used to develop a proof-of-concept prototype that will be used to test and confirm the suggested conceptual framework's applicability using a real-world case study.

1. Introduction

Blockchain is defined as a distributed ledger for the bitcoin cryptocurrency (Swan, 2015). Blockchain, on the other hand, has evolved into a full system for sharing and storing data on highly secure networks (Andoni et al., 2019). Many organisations that advocate that blockchain be used to improve the overall construction process (ICE, 2018; Lamb, 2018; Kinnaird et al., 2018). Moreover, blockchain research has become a trend during the last few years (Turk and Klinc, 2017; Li et al., 2018). Mason (2017) and Mason and Escott (2018a) emphasized the necessity of incorporating certain blockchain capabilities, such as smart contracts, into construction industry projects to automate payments. Following the researchers' recommendations, construction and engineering firms such as Arup have expressed a strong desire to integrate blockchain technology into the construction sector to improve performance in a variety of areas, including payment automation, supply chain management, and smart cities (Kinnaird et al., 2018). Furthermore, BIM has become a mandatory process in many countries. As a result, studies have looked into the integration of blockchain with BIM, such as Mathews et al. (2017a), who propose the integration for increasing trust among project participants in the construction industry. Besides, blockchain and BIM are advised for creating a comprehensive smart environment – digital built plan – for the construction industry (ICE, 2018; Lamb, 2018; Kinnaird et al., 2018).

https://doi.org/10.7146/aul.455.c235

Despite the high level of recognition for the importance of blockchain, payment automation in the construction industry has yet to be developed/presented as a practical application. The literature study is employed in this study to investigate the current state of blockchain/smart contract deployment in the construction industry and critically analyse the proposed potentials as well as the reality of the highlighted challenges. After that, a conceptual framework will be developed to outline detailed steps through the project delivery stage, such as how the blockchain consensus mechanism can be established during the pre-construction stage and how the closeout stage will be revolutionised by embracing blockchain technology. In this essence, this research aims to advance the use of blockchain and smart contracts by formulating a conceptual framework. It explains how smart contracts can be used and exploited through the project delivery process (pre-construction, construction, and closeout stage). In addition, the suggested framework takes into account the link between the BIM process and the automated payment smart contract framework's proposed workflow.

2. Blockchain in construction

The construction industry has been slow to incorporate blockchain and smart contracts in its practices. However, multiple attempts have been made to use them by constructing business models at various points of the project's lifecycle (Elghaish et al., 2021). The engineering and construction stages of blockchain research are the most active. Several studies, for example, looked at the security of payments during the engineering and construction stages and found that blockchain-based smart contracts are an effective way to resolve interim payment difficulties in building projects (Ahmadisheykhsarmast and Sonmez, 2020; Chong and Diamantopoulos, 2020; Das et al., 2020). Other research focused on construction quality information management and indicated that blockchain implementation can improve construction quality information management by allowing information traceability (Sheng et al., 2020; Zhang et al., 2020; Zhong et al., 2020). Some studies have focused on multi-stage applications and investigated blockchain applications during the entire project lifecycle. For example, Pattini et al. (2020) looked into the capabilities of blockchain in information flow management in construction projects and found that it might be useful in the design, bidding, construction, and maintenance stages. The use of blockchain and smart contracts in the construction contracting process was also highlighted. Researchers found that they have the potential to reduce transaction costs (Dakhli et al., 2019), reduce paperwork (Mason and Escott, 2018b), increase trust (Wang, 2017), facilitate immediate payment (Wang, 2017), secure payments (Salar, 2018), reduce construction disputes (Saygili et al., 2022) and improve procurement practice (Maciel, 2020).

3. Blockchain/smart contracts-BIM integration

Today information is exchanged and shared digitally in construction projects but the contracts that regulate them are often overlooked. Throughout the project's lifecycle, different stakeholders transact with each other during the project's lifecycle using collaboration platforms such as BIM with having any direct contractual relationship among themselves. As a result, there is a lack of design liability control, resulting in claims and conflicts. Furthermore, the reliance on numerous software packages by collaborative platforms such as BIM results in data exposure to third parties, data corruption, data integrity, and data loss (Pradeep et al., 2021). Various academics have looked into blockchain technology and smart contracts in order to address these challenges. According to several studies, blockchain technology has the potential to improve BIM workflows in construction projects by providing consistent and immutable design records (Nawari and Ravindran, 2019; Pattini et al., 2021; Mohammed et al., 2021). Hargaden et al. (2019) discussed the potentials of blockchain technology in the construction industry and its adoption feasibility through use cases. The authors discussed the use of smart contracts and the viability of integrating them with BIM. Fitriawijaya et al. (2019) investigated the possibility of blockchain in maintaining BIM data within the model from the design stage until the operation stage. Zheng et al. (2019) designed a "bcBIM" system where project participants exchange hash values of BIM models in blockchain as data proofs. To keep all participants informed of the project status and changes, Parn and Edwards (2019) advocated using blockchain technology in a single data environment to keep all project participants up to date on project progress and changes (CDE). Liu et al. (2019) presented a conceptual architecture for storing BIM data in a blockchain network and exchanging it for long-term collaboration during the design and construction phases. Dounas et al. (2020) developed a framework of decentralised architectural design using BIM agents connected over the Ethereum blockchain to enhance the building information modelling processes. For utilizing blockchain technology in IPD projects, Elghaish et al. (2020) developed a framework to automate financial transactions. In order to visualize the flow of information, the framework focused on connecting the three processes of IPD, blockchain, and BIM. Similarly, Hamledari and Fischer (2021) developed a methodology for monitoring project progress that that integrates blockchain/ smart contracts and robotic reality capture technologies. Erri Pradeep et al. (2021) investigated the potential of blockchain technology in information exchange to allow auditability exchanged records audits and improve design liability controlling. Suliyanti and Sari (2021) demonstrated how BIM data can be securely transferred on a blockchain utilizing Hyperledger fabric. Tao et al. (2021) discussed how blockchain might be used in conjunction with BIM to improve the collaborative design process. To secure data sharing and maintenance, the authors used the blockchain network to act as several common data environment containers. Tao et al. (2022) developed a framework for blockchain and BIM to boost design collaboration process. To ensure transparency, traceability, and immutability throughout its fragmented supply chain management, Li et al. (2022) developed a service-oriented system architecture of blockchain, IoT and BIM for the data-information-knowledge-driven supply chain management in modular construction. Finally, to improve information visibility, traceability, and boost collaboration in working environment, Wu et al. (2022) developed a blockchain-enabled IoT-BIM platform for off-site production management in modular construction.

Table 1 below shows the selected articles related to the integration of blockchain/smart contracts and BIM in construction projects. Although various attempts have been made in the previous five years to examine blockchain/smart contract applications in the BIM context, more research into payment automation utilizing these technologies is needed.

Table 1: Blockchain/smart contracts integration with BIM

Authors/Year	Method	Aim
Mathews et al. (2017b)	Literature review	To look at the possibilities of blockchain in terms of providing feasible solutions to the issue of trust in a collaborative procurement system.
Amaludin and Taharin, (2018)	Literature review	To demonstrate the benefits of using blockchain technology to solve problems in the Malaysian construction industry.
Jiang (2018)	Literature review	To explore the applications of BIM, IoT, and blockchain technologies in construction industry.
Liu et al. (2019)	Conceptual framework based on literature review	To improve data traceability and reusability for sustainable collaboration.
Parn and Edwards (2019)	Mixed methods analysis of reports review and case studies analysis	To boost building information modelling (BIM) implementation in infrastructure asset management.
Shojaei et al. (2019)	Conceptual framework based on literature review	To highlight the potential of integrating smart contracts, blockchain, and BIM.
Zheng et al. (2019)	Practical BIM system model based on blockchain in mobile cloud with big data sharing.	To present the possibility of auditing BIM data to control historical modifications.
Pradeep et al. (2020)	Literature review	To develop a set of basic functional requirements for efficient integration of blockchain and BIM tools.
Dounas et al. (2020)	Practical framework of BIM and Ethereum blockchain integration.	To improve the building information modelling processes.
Elghaish et al. (2020)	Practical framework that combines three processes of BIM, IPD, and blockchain.	To facilitate payment management and risk/reward sharing practices in IPD.
Xue and Lu (2020)	Practical framework of BIM and blockchain integration.	To track the gradual semantic modifications in BIM progress cycle.
Erri Pradeep et al. (2021)	Practical framework of blockchain and BIM using a design science research method	To define challenges facing design liability control and information security.
Hamledari and Fischer (2021)	Practical framework integrating blockchain/ smart contracts and robotic reality capture technologies.	To automate the progress of decentralized payments.
Tao et al. (2021)	Practical framework of blockchain, IPFS and a smart contract algorithm in BIM environment.	To secure decentralized design collaboration.
Li et al. (2022)	Practical framework of blockchain, IoT and BIM platform (BIBP) integration.	To the supply chain data transparency, traceability, and immutability.
Tao et al. (2022)	Practical framework for blockchain and BIM	To streamline design coordination process.
Wu et al. (2022)	Practical framework of a blockchain technology, IoT and BIM.	To provide solutions to overcome "single point of failure" problem of IoT networks.

4. Methodology

To gain a comprehensive understanding of a topic, a systematic literature review is highly recommended (Webster and Watson, 2002). Literature review supports in identifying research gaps, and to develop conceptual models to guide future research (Langley, 1999). Thus, in this study, literature review was utilized to identify research gaps and investigate potential solutions. Existing studies related to blockchain adoption in construction industry were reviewed. Then, research gaps were identified, and a conceptual framework is developed to propose a robust solution for integrating blockchain and smart contracts in BIM environment in construction projects to automate payments through the project's lifecycle.

5. Framework development

The three primary stages of a construction project are: pre-construction, construction, and closeout. There are a numerous number of transactions between various participants among these three stages. BIM provides a platform for sharing and exchanging information between different participants during the project's lifecycle. Thus, BIM should be a leverage for sharing not only project's component information, but also financial information. The existing literature review shows the potential of blockchain technology in maintaining immutable transaction records. Therefore, the blockchain technology along with smart contacts are proposed in this conceptual framework to automate payments between projects' participants among the project's lifecycle as shown in Figure 1.

Pre-construction stage:

During the pre-construction stages, project's participants decide to use the blockchain to manage financial tasks including payments, retentions, etc. Then, the endorsement policy will be developed to define the duration of implementing financial tasks, the monetary value of the construction package task, and to assign responsibilities. These established conditions will be later coded to be utilised for data validation in blockchain mechanism. This validation is called the consensus mechanism which consists of a set of algorithms to process the validation of invoked and stored data in the blockchain network (Wang et al., 2018). Defining responsibilities and roles in this stage is essential to limit the possibility of tampering any data of general blockchain. As a result, the permissioned blockchain requires a consensus process and has pre-defined counterparts. To automate the consensus mechanism, a quantified data should be available to serve as validation points. BIM has an essential role in this stage as a shared platform for each construction package prices thru the 5D BIM model. These estimated prices are linked to the timeline (4D BIM) to allow payment's scheduling for all project's parties.

Construction stage

Throughout the construction process, according to the scheduled payments, the blockchain administrator can assign who is the data sender/receiver at each payment milestone. Accordingly, the contractor performs as a data sender by sending invoices and the owner performs as a data receiver. Thus, the endorsement policy should consider the owner and architect as the main endorser for any invoked transaction. Generally, the Hyperledger fabric's consensus mechanism validates the transaction in two layers (1) endorsement policy (who should accept the transaction), and (2) the data-blocks allocation through specific channel. To validate the consensus mechanism, the agreed conditions will be checked for each block (transaction) automatically in terms of payment milestone date, the value of the invoice and the maximum amount of contract. One the transaction is validated; it will be sent to the concerned parties' ledger. BIM plays a vital role in this stage in terms of checking payment due by comparing the actual performed works again the planned works using 4D and 5D BIM. In this stage, project's parties will use smart contracts to invoke transactions to record data or request a payment. Endorsed transactions should be ordered using channels to be recorded in the correct ledger.

Close out stage

At the close out stage, the blockchain plays a significant role in closing out the project by providing a historical record of financial data. Participants can use API to invoke query transactions to get all recorded financial data. This will allow them to estimate the final payment precisely. The proposed framework suggests an automated platform for receiving, validating, recording, and displaying immutable transactions of payments through the project's lifecycle. Furthermore, the proposed framework suggests an improvement to the payment and cashflow management in construction projects by offering consistent historical transactions.

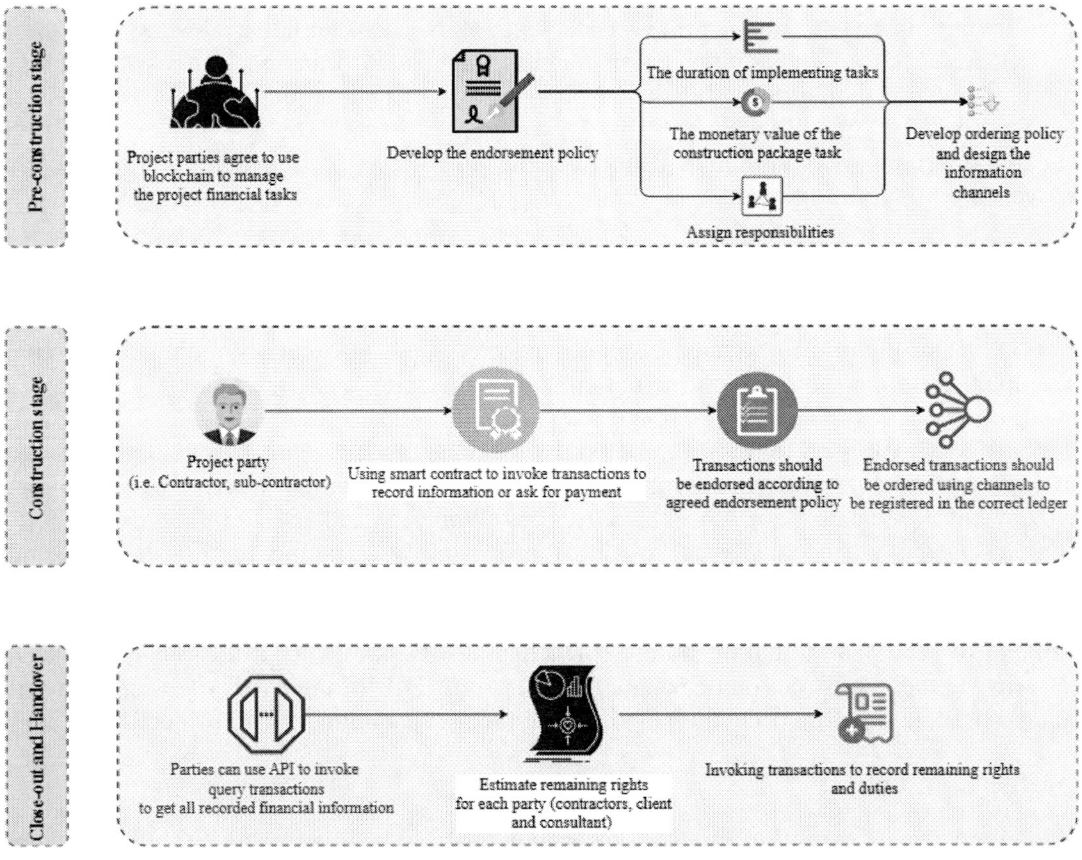

Fig. 1. The automated payment conceptual framework

Model architecture

Fig. 2 demonstrates the framework architecture with detailed tasks. Thus, it can be used as a departure point for developing a practical solution to employ permissioned blockchain, smart contracts and BIM in construction projects. This model can be a point of departure to develop practical solution-based BIM and blockchain to automate the payment process.

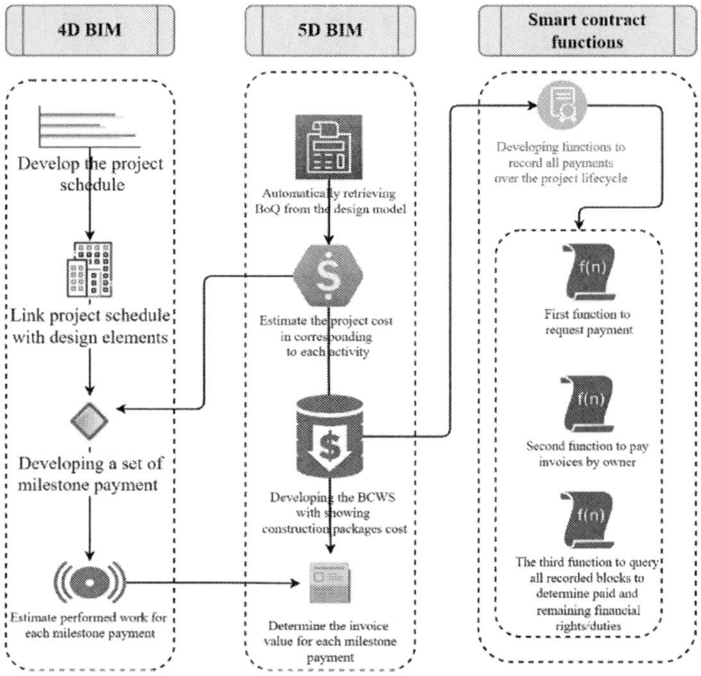

Fig. 2. The model architecture

6. Discussion and conclusion

Extant literature review survey shows that the Hyperledger fabric is a user-friendly blockchain platform for automated payments through the project's lifecycle. Given, The Hyperledger fabric is a modular consensus mechanism that allows project participants to develop a consistent mechanism relying on the project terms and conditions (Androulaki et al., 2018; Brandenburger et al., 2018; Dhillon et al., 2017), therefore, it can be used to develop a wide range of solutions to minimise fragmentation in construction process. The Hyperledger fabric's applicability originates from a partnership between Hyperledger (Linux), IBM, Oracle, and SAP, which allows for a seamless implementation (Van Mölken, 2018; Vukolić, 2016). The critical analysis of the existing research in blockchain within the construction industry focuses on developing a theoretical foundation that may be utilised as a starting point for moving forward. These theoretical bases can be extended to explore further the application of blockchain/smart contract in construction or to develop prototypes to validate the conceptual frameworks. As such, this study attempts to draw a practical application to blockchain/smart contracts by outlining the essential functional requirements during the pre-construction stage, such as establishing the consensus mechanism. In addition, the proposed framework addressed the construction stage carefully by presenting the data flow (i.e., who is the data sender and receiver). Finally, because the existing research did not give enough investigation into financial transactions during the closeout stage, the closeout stage is taken into account in this study. It is worth noting that this is where the majority of claims and disputes arise. Thus, the proposed framework suggests a set of tasks to be implemented with smart contracts to minimise potential claims and disputes. This could come to reality by exploiting the functionality of smart contracts to add more functions and record all types of financial issues (i.e., advanced payments, regular payments and retentions).

7. References

ICE, I. o. c. e. (2018). Blockchain Technology in The Construction Industry Digital Transformation For High Productivity.

Ahmadisheykhsarmast, S., & Sonmez, R. (2020). A smart contract system for security of payment of construction contracts. Automation in Construction, 120, 103401. doi:https://doi.org/10.1016/j.autcon.2020.103401.

Amaludin, A., & Taharin, M. (2018). Prospect of Blockchain Technology for Construction Project Management in Malaysia. ASM Science Journal, 11, 199-205.

Andoni, M., Robu, V., Flynn, D., Abram, S., Geach, D., Jenkins, D., . . . Peacock, A. (2019). Blockchain technology in the energy sector: A systematic review of challenges and opportunities. Renewable and Sustainable Energy Reviews, 100, 143-174. https://doi.org/10.1016/j.rser.2018.10.014.

Androulaki, E., Barger, A., Bortnikov, V., Cachin, C., Christidis, K., De Caro, A., . . . Manevich, Y. (2018). Hyperledger fabric: a distributed operating system for permissioned blockchains. Paper presented at the Proceedings of the Thirteenth EuroSys Conference. https://doi.org/10.1145/3190508.3190538

Brandenburger, M., Cachin, C., Kapitza, R., & Sorniotti, A. (2018). Blockchain and trusted computing: Problems, pitfalls, and a solution for hyperledger fabric. arXiv preprint arXiv:1805.08541.

Chong, H.-Y., & Diamantopoulos, A. (2020). Integrating advanced technologies to uphold security of payment: Data flow diagram. Automation in Construction, 114, 103158. doi:https://doi.org/10.1016/j.autcon.2020.103158

Dakhli, Z., Lafhaj, Z., & Mossman, A. (2019). The Potential of Blockchain in Building Construction. Buildings, 9(4), 77. Retrieved from https://www.mdpi.com/2075-5309/9/4/77

Das, M., Luo, H., & Cheng, J. C. P. (2020). Securing interim payments in construction projects through a blockchain-based framework. Automation in Construction, 118, 103284. doi:https://doi.org/10.1016/j.autcon.2020.103284

Dhillon, V., Metcalf, D., & Hooper, M. (2017). The hyperledger project. In Blockchain enabled applications (pp. 139-149): Springer. https://doi-org.libproxy.viko.lt/10.1007/978-1-4842-3081-7_10

Dounas, T., Lombardi, D., & Jabi, W. (2020). Framework for decentralised architectural design BIM and Blockchain integration. International Journal of Architectural Computing, 19(2), 157-173. doi:10.1177/1478077120963376

Elghaish, F., Abrishami, S., & Hosseini, M. R. (2020). Integrated project delivery with blockchain: An automated financial system. Automation in Construction, 114, 103182. doi:https://doi.org/10.1016/j.autcon.2020.103182

Elghaish, F., Hosseini, M. R., Matarneh, S., Talebi, S., Wu, S., Martek, I., . . . Ghodrati, N. (2021). Blockchain and the 'Internet of Things' for the construction industry: research trends and opportunities. Automation in Construction, 132, 103942. doi:https://doi.org/10.1016/j.autcon.2021.103942

Erri Pradeep, A. S., Yiu, T. W., Zou, Y., & Amor, R. (2021). Blockchain-aided information exchange records for design liability control and improved security. Automation in Construction, 126, 103667. doi:https://doi.org/10.1016/j.autcon.2021.103667

Fitriawijaya, A., Hsin-Hsuan T., & Taysheng, J. (2019). A blockchain approach to supply chain management in a BIM-enabled environment. Intelligent & Informed, Proceedings of the 24th International Conference of the Association for Computer-Aided Architectural Design Research in Asia (CAADRIA) 2019, Volume 2, 411-420. © 2019 and published by the Association for Computer-Aided Architectural Design Research in Asia (CAADRIA),Hong Kong.

Hamledari, H., & Fischer, M. (2021). Construction payment automation using blockchain-enabled smart contracts and robotic reality capture technologies. Automation in construction, 132, 103926. doi:https://doi.org/10.1016/j.autcon.2021.103926

Hargaden, V., Papakostas, N., Newell, A., Khavia, A., & Scanlon, A. (2019, 17-19 June 2019). The Role of Blockchain Technologies in Construction Engineering Project Management. Paper presented at the 2019 IEEE International Conference on Engineering, Technology and Innovation (ICE/ITMC).

Jiang, H. (2018). Cup-of-Water Theory: A Review on the Interaction of BIM, IoT and Blockchain During the Whole Building Lifecycle. Paper presented at the Proceedings of the 35th International Symposium on Automation and Robotics in Construction (ISARC).

Wang J.P.W., Wang, X., Shou, W. (2017). The outlook of blockchain technology for construction engineering management. Front. Eng, 4(1), 67-75. doi:10.15302/j-fem-2017006

Kinnaird, C., Geipel, M., & Bew, M. (2018). Blockchain technology: how the inventions behind bitcoin are enabling a network of trust for the built environment. London: Arup.

Lamb, K. (2018). Blockchain and Smart Contracts: What the AEC sector needs to know. https://doi.org/10.17863/CAM.26272.

Langley, A. (1999). Strategies for Theorizing from Process Data. The Academy of Management Review, 24(4), 691-710. doi:10.2307/259349.

Kassem, M., Lia, J., & Greenwood, D. (2018). Blockchain in the built environment: analysing current applications and developing an emergent framework. In Creative Construction Conference 2018 (pp. 59-66). Budapest University of Technology and Economics. doi: 10.3311/CCC2018-009.

Li, X., Lu, W., Xue, F., Wu, L., Zhao, R., Lou, J., & Xu, J. (2022). Blockchain-Enabled IoT-BIM Platform for Supply Chain Management in Modular Construction. Journal of Construction Engineering and Management, 148(2). doi:10.1061/(ASCE)CO.1943-7862.0002229.

Liu, Z., Jiang, L., Osmani, M., & Demian, P. (2019). Building Information Management (BIM) and Blockchain (BC) for Sustainable Building Design Information Management Framework. Electronics, 8(7), 724. https://www.mdpi.com/2079-9292/8/7/724.

Maciel, A. (2020). Use of blockchain for enabling Construction 4.0. In Construction 4.0 (pp. 395-418). Routledge. ISBN: 9780429398100.

Mason, J. (2017). Intelligent contracts and the construction industry. Journal of Legal Affairs and Dispute Resolution in Engineering and Construction, 9(3), 04517012.

Mason, J., & Escott, H. (2018). Smart contracts in construction: views and perceptions of stakeholders. Paper presented at the Proceedings of FIG Conference, Istanbul May 2018.

Mathews, M., Robles, D., & Bowe, B. (2017). BIM+ blockchain: A solution to the trust problem in collaboration?.

Mohammed, A., Almousa, A., Ghaithan, A., & Hadidi, L. A. (2021). The role of blockchain in improving the processes and workflows in construction projects. Applied Sciences (Switzerland), 11(19). doi:10.3390/app11198835.

Nawari, N. O., & Ravindran, S. (2019). Blockchain and the built environment: Potentials and limitations. Journal of Building Engineering, 25. doi:10.1016/j.jobe.2019.100832.

Parn, E. A., & Edwards, D. (2019). Cyber threats confronting the digital built environment. Engineering, Construction and Architectural Management, 26(2), 245-266. doi:10.1108/ECAM-03-2018-0101.

Pattini, G., Di Giuda, G. M., & Tagliabue, L. C. (2020). Blockchain application for contract schemes in the construction industry. Paper presented at the Proceedings of International Structural Engineering and Construction.

Pattini, G., Seghezzi, E., & Di Giuda, G. M. (2021). Digitalization in construction: Blockchain applicability in the industry. Paper presented at the Proceedings of International Structural Engineering and Construction. doi: 10.14455/ISEC.2021.8(1).AAE-06.

Pradeep, A. S. E., Amor, R., & Yiu, T. W. (2020). Blockchain Improving Trust in BIM Data Exchange: A Case Study on BIMCHAIN. In Construction Research Congress 2020 (pp. 1174-1183). https://doi.org/10.1061/9780784482865.124.

Salar, A., & Sönmez, R. . (2018). Smart Contracts in Construction Industry. Paper presented at the The 5th International Project and Construction Management Conference 2018 (16 - 18 Kasım 2018), North Cyprus.

Saygili, M., Mert, I. E., & Tokdemir, O. B. (2022). A decentralized structure to reduce and resolve construction disputes in a hybrid blockchain network. Automation in Construction, 134. doi:10.1016/j.autcon.2021.104056.

Sheng, D., Ding, L., Zhong, B., Love, P. E. D., Luo, H., & Chen, J. (2020). Construction quality information management with blockchains. Automation in Construction, 120, 103373. doi:https://doi.org/10.1016/j.autcon.2020.103373.

Suliyanti, W. N., & Sari, R. F. (2021). Blockchain-Based Implementation of Building Information Modeling Information Using Hyperledger Composer. Sustainability, 13(1), 321. Retrieved from https://www.mdpi.com/2071-1050/13/1/321.

Swan, M. (2015). Blockchain: Blueprint for a new economy: " O'Reilly Media, Inc.". ISBN: 9781491920497.

Tao, X., Das, M., Liu, Y., & Cheng, J. C. P. (2021). Distributed common data environment using blockchain and Interplanetary File System for secure BIM-based collaborative design. Automation in Construction, 130, 103851. doi:https://doi.org/10.1016/j.autcon.2021.103851.

Tao, X., Liu, Y., Wong, P. K. Y., Chen, K., Das, M., & Cheng, J. C. P. (2022). Confidentiality-minded framework for blockchain-based BIM design collaboration. Automation in Construction, 136. doi:10.1016/j.autcon.2022.104172.

Turk, Ž., & Klinc, R. (2017). Potentials of blockchain technology for construction management. Procedia engineering, 196, 638-645. https://doi.org/10.1016/j.proeng.2017.08.052.

Van Mölken, R. (2018). Blockchain across Oracle: Understand the details and implications of the Blockchain for Oracle developers and customers: Packt Publishing Ltd. ISBN: 9781788472166.

Vukolić, M. (2016). Hyperledger fabric: towards scalable blockchain for business. Retrieved from https://trustindigitallife.eu/wp-content/uploads/2016/07/marko_vukolic.pdf (Last accessed June 3, 2022).

Wang, Y., Han, J. H., & Beynon-Davies, P. (2018). Understanding blockchain technology for future supply chains: a systematic literature review and research agenda. Supply Chain Management: An International Journal, 24. doi:10.1108/SCM-03-2018-0148.

Webster, J., & Watson, R. T. (2002). Analyzing the Past to Prepare for the Future: Writing a Literature Review. MIS Quarterly, 26(2), xiii-xxiii.

Wu, L., Lu, W., Xue, F., Li, X., Zhao, R., & Tang, M. (2022). Linking permissioned blockchain to Internet of Things (IoT)-BIM platform for off-site production management in modular construction. Computers in Industry, 135. doi:10.1016/j.compind.2021.103573.

Xue, F., & Lu, W. (2020). A semantic differential transaction approach to minimizing information redundancy for BIM and blockchain integration. Automation in construction, 118, 103270. doi:https://doi.org/10.1016/j.autcon.2020.103270.

Zhang, Z., Yuan, Z., Ni, G., Lin, H., & Lu, Y. (2020). The quality traceability system for prefabricated buildings using blockchain: An integrated framework. Frontiers of Engineering Management, 7(4), 528-546. doi:10.1007/s42524-020-0127-z.

Zheng, R., Jiang, J., Hao, X., Ren, W., Xiong, F., & Ren, Y. (2019). bcBIM: A Blockchain-Based Big Data Model for BIM Modification Audit and Provenance in Mobile Cloud. Mathematical Problems in Engineering, 2019, 5349538. doi:10.1155/2019/5349538.

Zhong, B., Wu, H., Ding, L., Luo, H., Luo, Y., & Pan, X. (2020). Hyperledger fabric-based consortium blockchain for construction quality information management. Frontiers of Engineering Management, 7(4), 512-527. doi:10.1007/s42524-020-0128-y.

About EG-ICE and its Annual Workshop

The acronym EG-ICE (European Group for Intelligent Computing in Engineering) was established in 1993 to promote research on the interface between computing and engineering challenges across Europe by encouraging and improving contacts between researchers, fostering research collaboration and enhancing awareness of the latest developments. The group maintains active contact with similar groups in countries outside Europe and encourages participation by industry leaders who aim to increase application of advanced engineering informatics.

To achieve its aims, the group runs a yearly workshop and is active in the promotion, dissemination and exchange of ideas in order to provide effective links between research, industry and teaching. The EG-ICE 2022 workshop is not restricted to engineers. Thus, computer scientists, architects, psychologists and other interested people are encouraged to participate.

The EG-ICE International Workshop on Intelligent Computing in Engineering brings together international experts working on the interface between advanced computing and modern engineering challenges. Many engineering tasks require open-world resolution of challenges such as supporting multi-actor collaboration, coping with approximate models, providing effective engineer-computer interaction, search in multi-dimensional solution spaces, accommodating uncertainty, including specialist domain knowledge, performing sensor-data interpretation and dealing with incomplete knowledge. While results from computer science provide much initial support for resolution, adaptation is unavoidable and most importantly, feedback from addressing engineering challenges drives fundamental computer-science research. Competence and knowledge transfer goes both ways.

The workshop is intended to be a single-track event focusing on defining strategic aspects of the interaction of computing with engineering challenges. Also, current proposals for supporting engineering challenges according to these aspects will be evaluated and compared. As in previous workshops, the promotion, dissemination and exchange of knowledge and ideas will be supported through discussion periods within each session.

For more information, please visit https://www.eg-ice.org.

2022 EG-ICE Workshop Sponsors:

Host organizations: Aarhus University, Denmark

Technical University of Denmark, Denmark

Workshop sponsors: Aarhus University, Research Committee, International Collaboration & Networking

Technical University of Denmark, Department of Civil and Mechanical Engineering

Aarhus Kommune

Conrad GmbH

AARHUS UNIVERSITY DTU AARHUS KOMMUNE eg-ice conrad